GODS AND MORTALS IN EARLY GREEK AND NEAR EASTERN MYTHOLOGY

This volume centres on one of the most important questions in the study of antiquity – the interaction between Greece and the Ancient Near East, from the Mycenaean to the Hellenistic periods. Focusing on the stories that the peoples of the eastern Mediterranean told about the gods and their relationships with humankind, the individual treatments draw together specialists from both fields, creating for the first time a truly interdisciplinary synthesis. Old cases are re-examined, new examples discussed, and the whole range of scholarly opinions, past and present, are analysed, critiqued and contextualised. While direct textual comparisons still have something to show us, the methodologies advanced here turn their attention to deeper structures and wider dynamics of interaction and influence that respect the cultural autonomy and integrity of all the ancient participants.

ADRIAN KELLY is Tutorial Fellow in Ancient Greek Language and Literature at Balliol College, Oxford, and Associate Professor and Clarendon University Lecturer in Classics at the University of Oxford. He has recently co-edited (with P. J. Finglass) *Stesichorus in Context* (Cambridge, 2015) and *The Cambridge Companion to Sappho* (Cambridge, 2021), and is completing a *Cambridge Greek and Latin Classics* commentary on Homer, *Iliad* XXIII.

CHRISTOPHER METCALF is Official Fellow of The Queen's College, Oxford, and Associate Professor in Classical Languages and Literature at the University of Oxford. He is the author of *The Gods Rich in Praise: Early Greek and Mesopotamian Religious Poetry* (2015) and *Sumerian Literary Texts in the Schøyen Collection. Volume 1: Literary Sources on Old Babylonian Religion* (2019), and is pursuing research on early Greek poetry, and on ancient Mesopotamian (especially Sumerian) literature and religion.

GODS AND MORTALS IN EARLY GREEK AND NEAR EASTERN MYTHOLOGY

EDITED BY

ADRIAN KELLY
University of Oxford

CHRISTOPHER METCALF
University of Oxford

CAMBRIDGE
UNIVERSITY PRESS

University Printing House, Cambridge CB2 8BS, United Kingdom

One Liberty Plaza, 20th Floor, New York, NY 10006, USA

477 Williamstown Road, Port Melbourne, VIC 3207, Australia

314–321, 3rd Floor, Plot 3, Splendor Forum, Jasola District Centre, New Delhi – 110025, India

79 Anson Road, #06–04/06, Singapore 079906

Cambridge University Press is part of the University of Cambridge.

It furthers the University's mission by disseminating knowledge in the pursuit of education, learning, and research at the highest international levels of excellence.

www.cambridge.org
Information on this title: www.cambridge.org/9781108480246
DOI: 10.1017/9781108648028

© Cambridge University Press 2021

This publication is in copyright. Subject to statutory exception and to the provisions of relevant collective licensing agreements, no reproduction of any part may take place without the written permission of Cambridge University Press.

First published 2021

A catalogue record for this publication is available from the British Library.

Library of Congress Cataloging-in-Publication Data
NAMES: Kelly, Adrian, 1972– editor. | Metcalf, Christopher, 1986– editor.
TITLE: Gods and mortals in early Greek and Near Eastern mythology / edited by Adrian Kelly, Christopher Metcalf.
DESCRIPTION: New York : Cambridge University Press, 2021. | Includes bibliographical references and index.
IDENTIFIERS: LCCN 2020046741 (print) | LCCN 2020046742 (ebook) | ISBN 9781108480246 (hardback) | ISBN 9781108727174 (paperback) | ISBN 9781108648028 (epub)
SUBJECTS: LCSH: Mythology, Greek. | Mythology, Egyptian. | Mythology, Assyro-Babylonian.
CLASSIFICATION: LCC BL785 .G6325 2021 (print) | LCC BL785 (ebook) | DDC 202/.1109394–dc23
LC record available at https://lccn.loc.gov/2020046741
LC ebook record available at https://lccn.loc.gov/2020046742s

ISBN 978-1-108-48024-6 Hardback

Cambridge University Press has no responsibility for the persistence or accuracy of URLs for external or third-party internet websites referred to in this publication and does not guarantee that any content on such websites is, or will remain, accurate or appropriate.

Contents

List of Tables	*page* vii
List of Contributors	viii
Acknowledgements	x
List of Abbreviations	xi
Introduction Adrian Kelly and Christopher Metcalf	1

PART I CONTEXTS · 17

1 'Let Those Important Primeval Deities Listen': The Social Setting of the Hurro-Hittite *Song of Emergence* · 19
   Amir Gilan

2 Siting the Gods: Narrative, Cult, and Hybrid Communities in the Iron Age Mediterranean · 37
   Carolina López-Ruiz

3 Politics, Cult, and Scholarship: Aspects of the Transmission History of Marduk and Ti'amat's Battle · 58
   Frances Reynolds

4 The Scholar and the Poet: Standard Babylonian *Gilgameš* VI vs. *Iliad* 5 · 80
   Mark Weeden

PART II INFLUENCE · 107

5 Playing with Traditions: The Near Eastern Background to Hesiod's Story of the Five Human Races · 109
   André Lardinois

6	*Etana* in Greece Bruno Currie	126
7	Of Gods and Men: Animal and Plant Disputation Poems and Fables in Babylonia, Persia, and Greece Yoram Cohen	145
8	Tales of Kings and Cup-Bearers in History and Myth Christopher Metcalf	154
9	Heroes and Nephilim: Sex between Gods and Mortals Ruth Scodel	169
10	Berossus and Babylonian Cosmogony Andrew R. George	185

PART III DIFFERENCE — 199

11	Borrowing, Dialogue and Rejection: Intertextual Interfaces in the Late Bronze Age Ian Rutherford	201
12	Divine Labour Johannes Haubold	215
13	Influence and Inheritance: Linguistics and Formulae between Greece and the Ancient Near East Sylvie Vanséveren	229
14	Fate and Authority in Mesopotamian Literature and the *Iliad* Angus M. Bowie	243
15	Fashioning Pandora: Ancient Near Eastern Creation Scenes and Hesiod Bernardo Ballesteros Petrella	262
16	Sexing and Gendering the Succession Myth in Hesiod and the Ancient Near East Adrian Kelly	276

Bibliography	292
Index	340

Tables

1 SB *Gilgameš* VI, 1–10 and the evidence of the OB sign-lists *page* 91
2 The OB letter (*AbB* 3.2) and the OB sign-lists 93
3 The creation of Woman in *Genesis* and *Works and Days* 263
4 The Succession Myth in Hesiod's *Theogony* and Near Eastern texts 285

Contributors

ANGUS M. BOWIE, Lobel Fellow Emeritus in Classics, The Queen's College, University of Oxford

BRUNO CURRIE, Mason Monro Fellow and Tutor in Classics, Oriel College, University of Oxford

YORAM COHEN, Associate Professor of Assyriology, Tel Aviv University

AMIR GILAN, Professor in Hittitology, Tel Aviv University

ANDREW R. GEORGE, Emeritus Professor of Babylonian, School of Oriental and African Studies, University of London

JOHANNES HAUBOLD, Professor of Classics, Princeton University

ANDRÉ LARDINOIS, Professor in the Department of History, Art History, and Classics, and Chair of Greek Language and Culture, Radboud University

CAROLINA LÓPEZ-RUIZ, Professor, Department of Classics, Ohio State University

BERNARDO BALLESTEROS PETRELLA, Leverhulme Trust Early Career Fellow, Corpus Christi College, University of Oxford

FRANCES REYNOLDS, Shillito Fellow in Assyriology, Faculty of Oriental Studies, University of Oxford

IAN RUTHERFORD, Professor of Greek, University of Reading

RUTH SCODEL, D. R. Shackleton-Bailey Collegiate Professor of Greek and Latin, University of Michigan

SYLVIE VANSÉVEREN, Professor of ancient classical languages and Indo-European linguistics, Département d'enseignement de Langues et Lettres, Université libre de Bruxelles

MARK WEEDEN, Senior Lecturer in Near Eastern Studies, School of Oriental and African Studies, University of London

Acknowledgements

The editors would like to thank, firstly, all the participants and assistants at the conference *Divine Narratives in Greece and the Ancient Near East*, which was held in the Ioannou Centre for Classical and Byzantine Studies at the University of Oxford on the 3rd and 4th of July 2017. The conference was only possible because of generous funding received from the Craven Committee and the Board of the Faculty of Literae Humaniores at Oxford, the Interdisciplinary Institute of Balliol College, the Jowett Trust, and the London Centre for the Ancient Near East.

Thanks are also due to the contributors to this volume, with whom it was an unalloyed pleasure to work. Michael Sharp and his staff at Cambridge University Press showed their usual extraordinary levels of support, professionalism, and enthusiasm, as did the three anonymous readers for the press, whose keen eyes and sound judgements have no doubt improved the quality of this volume tremendously.

Abbreviations

Aside from those printed below, abbreviations in Near Eastern studies generally follow the *Reallexikon der Assyriologie*, while abbreviations of Greek and Roman authors and sources are the same as (or fuller than) those given in the *Greek–English Lexicon* of Liddell and Scott (9th edition, with a revised supplement, Oxford 1996) and the *Latin Dictionary* of Lewis and Short (Oxford 1879); journal titles follow the conventions set out in *L'Année Philologique*.

ATU	Aarne-Thompson-Uther: see Aarne and Thompson 1961 and Uther 2004.
CAD	Reiner, E., et al. 1973–2011 (eds.). *Chicago Assyrian Dictionary*. Chicago, IL.
DCCLT	Digital Corpus of Cuneiform Lexical Texts http://oracc.museum.upenn.edu/dcclt/index.html
ETCSL	Electronic Text Corpus of Sumerian Literature http://etcsl.orinst.ox.ac.uk/
HGL	Zimmermann, B., and Rengakos, A. 2011–14 (eds.). *Handbuch der griechischen Literatur der Antike*. Munich.
JPS	*Tanakh the Holy Scriptures: The New JPS Translation according to the Traditional Hebrew Text*. 1985. Philadelphia, PA.
KTU³	*Die keilalphabetischen Texte aus Ugarit* = Dietrich, Loretz and Sanmartín 2013
LfgrE	Snell, B., and Erbse, H. 1955–2010 (eds.). *Lexikon des frühgriechischen Epos*. 4 vols. Göttingen.
Perry	Perry, B. E. 1952. *Aesopica* I. Urbana, IL.
*OCD*⁴	Goldberg, S. M., and Whitmarsh, T. 2016 (eds.). *Oxford Classical Dictionary*. 4th ed. Oxford.
ORACC	Open Richly Annotated Cuneiform Corpus http://oracc.museum.upenn.edu/

RlA	Streck, M. P. et al. 1932–2018 (eds.). *Reallexikon der Assyriologie und Vorderasiatischen Archäologie.* 15 vols. Berlin and New York, NY.
SEAL	Sources of Early Akkadian Literature www.seal.uni-leipzig.de/

Introduction

Adrian Kelly and Christopher Metcalf

The aim of this volume, and of the conference in which it originated, is to encourage a more profound dialogue between scholars of early Greek and ancient Near Eastern literature, two areas of research that are usually separated by institutional boundaries in universities today but that nevertheless share a long history of fruitful interaction. It is well known, to take an early example relating to Homeric scholarship, that a foundational work of modern philology, the *Prolegomena ad Homerum* published in 1795 by the Hellenist Friedrich August Wolf, derived important inspiration from the text-critical approach to the Old Testament developed by the Orientalist Johann Gottfried Eichhorn.[1] In the case of Hesiod, it was to another follower of Eichhorn, the Biblical scholar Christian Schnurrer, that the young Friedrich Hölderlin dedicated his comparative study of the proverbs of Solomon and the *Works and Days*, submitted in 1790 as part of his MA examination at the Tübinger Stift.[2] The various degrees of previous and subsequent interaction between Hellenists and scholars of the ancient Near East, which naturally received a major impetus from the decipherment of the cuneiform script in the latter half of the nineteenth century, have been expertly documented and discussed, up to the late twentieth century, by Walter Burkert.[3] This was the time that saw the publication of the best-known and most influential works of current scholarship (at least in the field of Classics), Burkert's own studies of archaic Greece in the so-called Orientalising period, and Martin West's detailed comparative survey of archaic Greek poetry from Homer to Aeschylus.[4]

---

[1] Wolf 1795. On Eichhorn's influence, see Grafton, Most and Zetzel 1985: 18–26, 227–31.
[2] *Parallele zwischen Salomons Sprüchwörtern und Hesiods Werken und Tagen*, available, e.g., in the edition of Beissner 1961: 176–88. On Hölderlin, Schnurrer and the Stift, see Franz 2002.
[3] Burkert 1991a. Further important critical surveys are offered by Dowden 2001, Casadio 2009, Bremmer 2016, Yakubovich 2018 and Stevens 2019: 16–22.
[4] Burkert 1984, translated and revised as Burkert 1992; West 1997.

The efforts of these two scholars above all represented nothing less than a revolution: it is no longer possible nor desirable, in the twenty-first century CE, to write about the earliest period of Greek literary and cultural history without considering the contributions and impact of the civilisations we tend to subsume under the title of the 'ancient Near East'.[5] Whilst the study of Hesiod had long been inflected along these lines,[6] perhaps the biggest change wrought in the post-Burkert/West world is that no aspect of early Greek literature has remained unaffected, and that the change in our analytical habits has proven to be deep and lasting. Indeed, Robin Osborne astutely pointed out that the search for parallels between early Greek epic and the texts of the ancient Near East, and their deployment in an interpretative setting, had changed the game for good: 'What is really at stake is my ability to understand the *Iliad*.[7]

Inevitably this initial comparative drive was met with some caution, or even opposed by outright scepticism,[8] with scholars calling for a method that goes beyond juxtaposing literary works without considering their *Sitz im Leben*, and that addresses the difficult literary-historical questions raised by the complexities of cultural interaction and transmission. All the while, greater methodological sophistication was being brought to bear in several studies, as – amongst many others – Johannes Haubold wrote of the need to get away from drawing straight lines between far-flung texts,[9] Mary Bachvarova sought a common poetic language across the Mediterranean,[10] Christopher Metcalf stressed local sources and traditions as better explanations for apparent similarities,[11] and Carolina López-Ruiz addressed the manifold possibilities for exchange across a wide temporal and spatial range.[12] Scholarly interest in improving our understanding of the Near Eastern contribution to early Greek poetry and culture, particularly on the part of Hellenists, continues unabated,[13] and it is one purpose of this volume to offer a snapshot of this dynamic and thriving field as it stands.

---

[5] On the terminology, see van Dongen 2014.   [6] See, e.g., Walcot 1962, West 1966: 18–31.
[7] Osborne 1993: 232. For a comparative study of hymnic poetry, such as the *Homeric Hymns*, see Metcalf 2015a (with earlier literature). On the Greek lyric poets, see West 1997: 495–543.
[8] See, e.g., Mondi 1990, Most 1998, Koenen 1994, Haubold 2002, Kelly 2008, Kelly 2014.
[9] Haubold 2013a.
[10] Bachvarova 2005; more recent contributions (e.g., 2016) have tended towards seeing the relationship in a more genealogical manner.
[11] Metcalf 2015a.   [12] López-Ruiz 2010.
[13] To mention only some of the most recently published contributions on the relationship between the Homeric epics and the *Epic of Gilgameš*: West 2018, Meijer 2018, Matijević 2018, R. B. Rutherford 2019: 231–6 (the latter pair being more sceptical than the former); and now Clarke 2019. Rowe 2018 emphasises the general lack of interest that specialists of the Near East appear to have taken in the debate ('Assyriologists are true heirs to the Babylonian indifference towards

Indeed, the discussion has come to something of a watershed moment, as we move our attention generally from mapping similarities and differences to a more nuanced consideration of what each tradition can tell us in its own voice, reading through analogy rather than genealogy (alone). As with any change in scholarly direction, this is not universal, and interesting and fruitful work is still being done through more traditionally genealogical and source-critical means, as Classicists continue to map out a literary narrative history with one author consciously developing from and reacting to another, this time with the early Greek canvas massively expanded by the literature of the Sumerians, Hittites, Babylonians, Assyrians and Phoenicians.[14]

The papers gathered in the present volume are written by a collection of some of the most active contributors to the discussion, and they document a variety of new approaches and insights, as well as critical engagement with – and exemplifications of – the methods of previous scholarship. The chapters themselves have been drawn up into three parts, corresponding to the intellectual and methodological emphasis of each author, but these parts do not stand apart from one another in a mutually preclusive manner. The chapters of Part I ('Contexts') reflect a growing scholarly concern with elucidating the individual setting of each work of literature as a preliminary to any reliable comparative work. Those of Part II ('Influence') are not unaware of this precondition, but concern themselves more directly with the task of tracing the journey of narrative and literary features across several traditions, while the chapters in Part III ('Difference') – though, in their turn, not unconcerned with contexts or influence – place more critical emphasis on problematising that latter process, showing how common patterns, whatever the precise mechanics of their transmission, are declined in their individual settings and traditions.

Ideally, of course, all these lines of enquiry should be linked, and most of the papers could have been placed in more than one category. Thus, for example, Mark Weeden's discussion of the scribal context behind *Gilgameš* elucidates a particular setting for the production of Babylonian literature (and so is placed in Part 1), but it does so as part of a wider argument seeking to problematise the case which some have made for a connection

---

non-Babylonian traditions', Rowe 2018: 370), though his own contribution overlooks the substantial critical discussion by George 2003: 54–7.

[14] See, e.g., Currie 2016, though his contribution to this volume is closer in spirit to the new direction, and Lardinois 2018, and his contribution to this volume. Clarke 2019 represents a very sophisticated version of an intertextual reading between Greek and non-Greek traditions.

between that poem and an episode from the *Iliad* (and so could have been located in Part III). Similarly, Christopher Metcalf's contribution on the figure of the royal cup-bearer across several traditions traces the journey of these stories (hence its placement in Part II) but is also concerned not to opt for genealogy as the best explanation of their evolution (and so, once more, could have been placed in Part III).

Yet the conceptual integrity of the tripartition remains, since it was one of the main conclusions of the conference on which this book was based that much greater levels of dialogue are required on questions of context, influence and difference in future comparative study, and almost all of the chapters engage with this need more or less explicitly, and more or less positively.

Part I: Context

To begin in the Near East: an enviable feature of the literatures of its several cultures, from the perspective of the Hellenist, is that the abundant and diverse cuneiform textual record can at times provide contextual historical evidence for literary composition and performance – evidence of a kind that is generally unavailable to scholars of early Greek poetry. Knowledge of ancient performance contexts can, in turn, inform the question of historical transmission of Near Eastern material to Greece. The contribution by the Hittitologist Amir Gilan ('"Let Those Important Primeval Deities Listen": The Social Setting of the Hurro-Hittite *Song of Emergence*') thus revisits the case of the Hurro-Hittite poem formerly referred to (among other titles) as the *Song of Kumarbi*, now known under its recently recovered ancient title as the *Song of Emergence*, which narrates the early history of divine kingship and the birth of the Storm God. Since its decipherment, this Hittite adaptation of an earlier, now lost but probably Hurrian composition has been recognised as the clearest evidence for the Greek reception of Near Eastern mythology, as proven by numerous aspects, of both general structure and narrative detail, that the *Song of Emergence* shares with Hesiod's *Theogony*, especially the Succession Myth, which traces the sequence from the earliest divine kings to Zeus's birth and rise to power.[15] Yet the recent interest that Hittitology has taken in the rich corpus of Hittite ritual texts has yielded important information on the

---

[15] The parallels between the *Song of Emergence* and the *Theogony* (and related sources) have been enumerated and analysed many times: see most recently Rutherford 2018, and his contribution to this volume.

likely ritual contexts of the wider mythological cycle to which the *Song of Emergence* belongs, and possibly indeed of the *Song* itself: Gilan therefore assesses not only the Hittite cuneiform tablet on which the *Song* is preserved, as well as the family and scholarly background of the scribe responsible for copying it, but also discusses new progress made in more specialised studies, in particular by Carlo Corti, on the possible performance of the *Song* in festivals at Mount Hazzi (Jebel al-Aqra), the Greek Kasios, on the Mediterranean coast. As previous scholarship has seen, such performance offers what is currently the most attractive historical context for the transfer of the Storm God narrative to Greece, given the likely presence of Greek traders in the vicinity.[16]

This historical aspect is elaborated by Carolina López-Ruiz ('Siting the Gods: Narrative, Cult, and Hybrid Communities in the Iron Age Mediterranean'), who traces a path across the Mediterranean in locating the sites where Greek, Semitic (in particular Phoenician) and native populations interacted, her premise being that 'the literary and mythological entanglements, for the most part, followed the human entanglements'. Starting from the same Mount Hazzi or Jebel al-Aqra (here called Mount Saphon, its Semitic name) and crossing first to Crete and from there to Iberia, López-Ruiz draws attention to Near Eastern Storm God narratives that are less well known than the *Song of Emergence* but that similarly shaped Greek mythological and cultic conceptions of Zeus: these historically less successful narratives tend to furnish the Storm God with a fuller life cycle, including birth, journeys in maturity, and even death.

To turn to Mesopotamia, the contributions by Frances Reynolds and Mark Weeden further illustrate the recent preoccupations of specialised research on ancient Near Eastern literature with the ritual performances of mythological texts and the scholarly contexts of literary production. Reynolds' contribution ('Politics, Cult, and Scholarship: Aspects of the Transmission History of Marduk and Ti'amat's Battle') presents some results of her long-term research on an important source for several papers in this volume, the Babylonian Creation Epic *Enūma eliš*, with a focus on its complex relationship with Babylon's New Year festival as well as on its scholarly exegesis in Babylonian academic treatises. Both aspects, ritual and scholarly, provide important historical contextualisation for Hellenists interested in the affinities between the battle of Marduk and Ti'amat and Greek theomachies.

---

[16] See now Lane Fox 2018: xlii–iv, and Rutherford in this volume.

Weeden's chapter ('The Scholar and the Poet: Standard Babylonian *Gilgameš* VI vs. *Iliad* 5') directly addresses a popular literary-historical comparison between two well-known scenes, the encounter of Gilgameš and Ištar in the *Epic of Gilgameš* VI, and the encounter of Diomedes and Aphrodite in *Iliad* 5, but draws attention to possible links between the *Gilgameš*-episode and the Mesopotamian lexical tradition. These links lead Weeden to suggest that the episode may have emerged from a specifically Mesopotamian scholarly or didactic background, which, he argues, makes scenarios of oral transmission of *Gilgameš* to the Greek world seem questionable. As in the case of *Enūma eliš*, the immediate Mesopotamian context that Weeden provides to *Gilgameš* will have to be taken into account in any comparative effort to situate the literary texts in an even broader context.

Part II: Influence

Naturally, many contributions focus on particular literary comparisons in an attempt to trace historical influence from Near Eastern models on early Greek poets – and vice versa. Apart from identifying and assessing points of comparison that were previously overlooked or insufficiently appreciated, these contributions are united by their endeavour to reflect on the methods of cross-cultural comparison: by what means can historical influence be successfully demonstrated?

André Lardinois' contribution ('Playing with Traditions: Deliberate Allusions to Near Eastern Myth in Hesiod's Story of the Five Human Races') revisits the arguments for and against a Near Eastern inspiration of Hesiod's well-known Myth of the Ages (or Races), and takes this opportunity to reflect on the criteria that are available to us in assessing the plausibility of literary-historical influence. The degree of similarity between the literary comparanda will naturally remain the first and most obvious criterion, but Lardinois also postulates that 'the story or theme' should not also be 'part of an Indo-European or other tradition, or attributable to common human experience', and further, that the story or theme be 'quite unique and therefore unlikely to have been fashioned independently in Greece and the Near East'. Both considerations naturally oblige the scholar to cast the net more widely, beyond the two standard corpora of Greek and ancient Near Eastern literature, in order to gain an impression of how significant a given parallel is likely to be: to this end, Lardinois considers further evidence, ranging from Mesoamerica to the *Mahābhārata*. While the strength of the Near Eastern parallels nevertheless lead him to conclude that the Myth of the Ages is indeed likely to have been inspired by Near Eastern sources, Lardinois is also careful to explain how it came to be anchored in existing and more familiar Greek tales of gods and heroes.

Bruno Currie ('*Etana* in Greece') then investigates the links between the Akkadian poem *Etana*, the fragmentary Lykambes epode of the archaic Greek poet Archilochus, and the Aesopic fable of *The Eagle and the Fox*, carefully assessing both similarities and differences in these sources as well as in further, related Greek material, and also considering the possibility of further versions of *Etana* in India, Egypt and the folklore of the Baltic region. Taken together, these reflections lead Currie to distinguish, in particular, between a 'floating motif model' and a 'fixed text model' of transmission, both of which are, he concludes, discernible in the various manifestations of *Etana* in Greece and beyond.

A second important aspect of intercultural transmission is then emphasised by Yoram Cohen and Christopher Metcalf. Like Currie, Cohen is concerned with the fable ('The World of Gods and Men: Animal and Plant Disputation Poems and Fables in Babylonia, Persia, and Greece'), in this case the Akkadian fable of *The Date Palm and the Tamarisk*, which travelled eastward to Persia and westward to Greece: in both places, Cohen argues, the fable retained its 'deep structure' but underwent adaptations on the surface to suit the new localities. The fable posed a fundamental question to its audiences — is the cult of the gods more important than preservation of humans? — and provided, in Cohen's words, 'a platform on which views and beliefs of other cultures could be built, with the change of scene or characters as needed'.

Metcalf ('Tales of Kings and Cup-Bearers in History and Myth') presents a similarly flexible example that spans Mesopotamia, Anatolia and Greek sources on Persia. His argument is that a motif in the mythological prologue to the Hurro-Hittite *Song of Emergence*, according to which the early divine rulers Anu and Kumarbi are each said to have served as cup-bearer to the previous ruler before taking power, is likely to derive from older Mesopotamian legends revolving around the historical king Sargon of Akkad. While the *Song of Emergence* adapts the Sargonic motif to a narrative on the earliest divine kings, the same motif later emerges in connection with a human ruler, Cyrus the Great, in Persian legends that were known to the Greek writer Ctesias; Herodotus avoided the motif in his account of Cyrus, perhaps because he appears to have adopted it at an earlier point of the *Histories*, in the Lydian tale of Candaules and Gyges. In all instances the motif of the cup-bearer served to explain the emergence of a powerful human or divine dynasty seemingly from nowhere, but as in Cohen's case studies there was much scope for local adaptation.

Finally, the contributions of Ruth Scodel and Andrew George offer a reminder that just as Near Eastern sources can illuminate early Greek literature, so the latter can help us to interpret the former (this aspect is also discussed, more briefly, by Metcalf and Rutherford [below]). Scodel ('There Were Nephilim') examines *Genesis* 6:1–4, a difficult passage in which divine beings are said to have taken mortal wives, who bore them offspring described as 'the heroes of old, the men with a name'. Scodel supports the view that this reflects Greek influence on the Old Testament, and offers thoughts on the ways in which the Greek material was transmitted, and how the comparison can enhance our understanding of both the Greek and the Biblical narratives.[17]

George ('Mythical Time in Mesopotamia') offers some insights into a long-term research project that seeks to distinguish between myths and their various manifestations in literary sources, and thus approaches Mesopotamian mythology as a body of sacred, oral stories that lie in the background both of texts and of other forms of cultural expression. In this instance, George considers the work of the Babylonian priest and historian Berossus, in particular book I of his *Babyloniaca*, in which Berossus summarised Babylonian cosmogonic beliefs for a Greek readership.[18] While the links between this part of the *Babyloniaca* and the Akkadian poem *Enūma eliš* are well known, George shows that Berossus combined knowledge of that text with a Mesopotamian myth of origins on the primeval pair 'Father Sky and Mother Earth' that was never fixed in writing. Taken together with sporadic evidence from Sumero-Akkadian sources collected by George, the *Babyloniaca* of Berossus emerge as an important source on this influential but elusive myth, which, according to George, was overshadowed without being fully supplanted by the Marduk-centred theology of *Enūma eliš*.

Part III: Difference

The previous contributions have taken issues of historical context as the starting point from which to approach the interpretation of literary

---

[17] For a sustained (but problematic) argument for Greek influence on the Old and New Testaments, see now Louden 2018.

[18] See now Stevens 2019: 94–119 for a detailed critical analysis of Berossus as a 'scholar between two worlds'.

sources, and/or used literary comparisons as the basis on which to build arguments for (or against) historical influence. The chapters in this third part concentrate on differences between early Greek and Near Eastern literature, and the interpretative space this opens up to the scholar. Here the purpose of comparison is to reflect on the ways in which texts from different cultures engage with fundamental issues of common interest, while less attention is paid to the question of their historical relationships.[19]

Ian Rutherford ('Borrowing, Dialogue and Rejection: Intertextual Interfaces in the Late Bronze Age') engages explicitly with the challenges faced by any kind of comparative analysis: while the question of historical influence remains an attractive topic for discussion, Rutherford draws attention to the interpretative potential of differences, as opposed to the similarities on which comparative studies tend to focus. As he writes, an appreciation of differences may help us to see how one culture 'may be "receptive" to some aspects of other tradition, while blocking others, perhaps because they are not in line with its established norms'. Rutherford thus examines those aspects of Anatolian and Syrian Storm God mythology that, unlike the central elements of the *Song of Emergence*, seem not to have been adopted in early Greek sources, in particular the myth of the Storm God's conflict with the Sea, and reflects on the likely reasons that explain this apparent 'blocking'.

Building on his past research on early Greek and Mesopotamian epic poetry, Johannes Haubold's contribution ('Divine Labour') examines a peculiar theme in divine narratives, according to which human beings at one time replaced the gods as workers. Haubold considers the occurrence of this theme in the Akkadian poem *Atrahasīs*, the opening of the Biblical book of *Genesis* and early Greek epic, especially the *Iliad*. The comparison illustrates, in his words, that 'authors and audiences in the ancient world shared not just stories about the gods but also some of the larger questions that made them important. We cannot always tell how the stories travelled but we can certainly understand better how the texts work by considering the narrative resources they share.' In particular, the theme of divine labour allows us to appreciate how the Mesopotamian, Israelite and Greek traditions created important, and distinctively *different*, transitions in the shared history of gods and humans, and how the very concept of the gods at work gave rise, within each tradition, to implicit or explicit criticism and to

---

[19] See Haubold 2013: esp. 71–2 on this approach.

consequent attempts to rewrite the story, or at least to contain its supposedly undesirable theological implications.

Addressing the same literary-historical issue from a linguistic perspective, Sylvie Vanséveren ('Comparison: Relevance and Significance of Linguistic Features') takes a close look at the Homeric phrase 'hand of god', used in the *Iliad* in connection with a divinely ordained plague. While past scholarship has identified this phrase as a straightforwardly Near Eastern idiom, on the basis of analogies in several Semitic languages, Vanséveren broadens the horizon by juxtaposing Near Eastern and Indo-European perspectives, and, in a linguistic analogy to the literary studies of Lardinois and Ballesteros Petrella (see below), devotes special attention to the context of the phrase within the Greek epic-formulaic system. Her conclusion is sceptical of the explanatory value of the Near Eastern parallels in this particular instance.

Angus Bowie ('Fate and Authority in Mesopotamian Literature and the *Iliad*') considers another important topic in the rich body of early Greek and ancient Near Eastern divine narratives: the issue of fate and divine authority. In his analysis, Sumerian and Akkadian sources tend to describe fate as being under the control of the gods, who employ it as a tool in governing the universe; fate can be said to take physical shape, such as an inscribed tablet. In early Greek literature, on the other hand, fate is not a matter of divine decrees: here fate is mainly regarded as something assigned to individuals, and the Greek epic tradition is less explicit on the nature and physical shape of fate. Comparison of the theme of divine authority, which is a concern to both Mesopotamian and early Greek epic poetry, illustrates 'the wisdom of the use by the leading god or gods of consultation and tactical response to the demands of other deities': if autocracy leads to disaster, diplomacy is the tool by which the respective chief gods can preserve their authority.

The final two papers return to Hesiod, an author particularly familiar to Classicists seeking to deploy Near Eastern material. Firstly, Bernardo Ballesteros Petrella ('Fashioning Pandora: Ancient Near Eastern Creation Scenes and Hesiod') offers a detailed analysis of a(nother) famous Hesiodic narrative, the creation of Woman, that considers Mesopotamian, Egyptian and Biblical comparanda but also looks further, to Nordic mythology, ethnography and the study of folklore. Coupled with an understanding of the Pandora-scene's connections to episodes of adornment in other early Greek hexameter poetry, Ballesteros Petrella's analysis avoids simplistic notions of direct derivation from this or that Near Eastern source, and concludes that the tale of Pandora represents, instead, 'a Greek poet's declension of a common Eastern Mediterranean and Near Eastern mythological motif and compositional pattern'.

Finally, Adrian Kelly ('Sexing and Gendering the Succession Myth in Ancient Greece and the Near East') considers the case of the *Song of Emergence* that has proved central to several contributions collected here, but approaches the comparison, in a manner similar to Rutherford and Ballesteros Petrella, as an opportunity to appreciate the distinctive differences reflected in the various relevant sources. This chapter emphasises the role of female wife–mother figures as destabilising elements in Hesiod's *Theogony*, in contrast to the more limited roles of female characters particularly in the *Song of Emergence*, and locates that gendering theme within the wider context of early Greek mythology. For Kelly, comparison 'allows us to see the individual element working within its own context, to determine what is distinctive about each tradition and so, finally, to understand all of them better. Genealogy, at least in the way most Classicists would like to practise it, is neither possible nor profitable. But the analogy remains, and it can tell us a very great deal.'

Current and Future Perspectives

Amidst the diverse contributions collected here, some shared concerns and argumentative patterns can be discerned, and while none of these tendencies is radically new, as is usual in the study of antiquity, they nevertheless represent a shift in emphasis when compared to other recent research.

One such shared concern can be described as a heightened sense of self-awareness. Soon after the publication of Burkert's and West's major works, it was remarked that '[a]t present we are in a phase of expansion and we can determine from the excellence of our empirical data, to which West has now added colossally, that our views are better informed, more soundly based, than ever and that they will last – till the next downturn'.[20] So far as the study of historical literary relationships is concerned, the present collection of papers is not intended to mark the inception of such a downturn, but rather to document the attempts of current scholarship to reflect on its methods and to refine the means by which it arrives at conclusions. A recent review of the studies published in the wake of Burkert and West distinguishes between 'lumpers' and 'splitters', noting that '[t]he pursuits of the "splitters" (i.e., the minimalists) tend to be purely academic, while their opponents the "lumpers" frequently appear

[20] Dowden 2001: 167–8.

to be motivated by a desire to raise awareness of cross-cultural contacts among their colleagues or in the general public'.[21] If the editors of the present volume belong on the whole to the former category, their desire is not to downplay the significance of such contacts but rather to draw defensible conclusions from the available evidence. Any literary comparison that seeks to argue for historical influence must face the question: how meaningful are the parallels identified? Could alternative explanations be envisaged to account for the similarity? Comparison between any two (or more) literary corpora will inevitably reveal some commonalities, even when these corpora are historically unrelated, as illustrated, for instance, by recent comparative studies of the *Epic of Gilgameš*, *Beowulf* and medieval Japanese poetry.[22] A comparison that takes into account only those texts that are argued to be historically related is therefore problematic, as incidental similarities risk being mistaken for similarities based on genetic relationship.

One means to address this difficulty is to broaden the scope in order to get a better impression of the uniqueness of a given point of comparison: thus several contributors to the present volume consider not only the Greek and Near Eastern evidence, as is usual, but also look further, such as to Indian, Egyptian, other European and Mesoamerican mythology and folklore. Such approaches do seem to reflect a shift in emphasis. Burkert, who as a historian of Greek religion saw the value of viewing Greek practices 'against the background of more universal contexts',[23] frequently adduced the possibility of coincidental resemblance as a caveat, but tended not to elaborate its practical consequences, instead placing greater emphasis on the quantity and quality of the literary parallels, which seemed all the more meaningful in the light of the clear historical and archaeological evidence for Near Eastern influence on archaic Greece.[24] West followed

---

[21] Yakubovich 2018: 129.
[22] North and Worthington 2012, George 2012: 231–41. See further Metcalf 2017, and compare, e.g., the criticism of Louden 2011 by Budin 2012: 347: 'In sum, [Louden] does not provide sufficiently strong arguments for his parallels. They are not necessarily closer than parallels with fairy tales, Viking tales or Japanese mythology. To use [Near Eastern] myths to interpret the Greek or vice versa leaves one open to several methodological weaknesses'; or the remarks of Nagy 1982: 72 on Burkert 1977: 'And yet we must leave room for at least the possibility that, in any given instance where we find a Near Eastern analog, the analogy may be a matter of simple typological parallelism. From the standpoint of comparative religious studies, the same theme, detail, sequence – or all three – may theoretically be found even in radically different places at radically different times.'
[23] Burkert 1991b: 55, on society and religious ritual.
[24] For such caveats, see, e.g., Burkert 1991a: 163 n. 37 ('Es gibt bekanntlich auch Motivparallelen mit ganz entlegenen Traditionen'); Burkert 1992: 88, 106, 123–4; Burkert 2003: 48–69, 169; Burkert 2004: 29, 46–7; note the corresponding methodological critique of Casadio 2009: 139–43.

Introduction 13

his monograph on early Greek and ancient Near Eastern literature with a study of Indo-European poetry and myth, in which it became apparent that some of the Near Eastern elements in Greek poetry identified in the former book have Indo-European parallels as well: in his introduction to the latter work, West accordingly made some general allowance for the possibility of 'horizontal transmission', though the main discussion did not always clarify the extent to which this model was to be applied in each particular case.[25]

Once a wider view has been taken, the interpretation of the Greek, Near Eastern and other comparanda, and any argument for (or against) Near Eastern inspiration of the Greek sources, will still depend on the strength of the literary parallels. It is notable in this context that even the broadest conceivable comparative study by the Indologist Michael Witzel, which seeks to reconstruct a common and very remote origin of much of world mythology, acknowledges the *Song of Emergence* and the Hesiodic Succession Myth, in particular the shared motif of castration, as a 'useful, exemplary case' of 'secondary regionalism', i.e., of a local cross-cultural transfer of a myth that did not form part of any reconstructible shared inheritance.[26] But where the evidence is less clear, it may be necessary to adopt more flexible interpretations. In a recent study, Joshua Katz has discussed both the Near Eastern comparanda and the possible Indo-European prehistory to Hesiod's poetry, and has remarked in that connection that the Near Eastern and Indo-European (other than Indo-European Anatolian) dimensions do not have to be antithetical, as they are often conceived.[27] In practice, a feature that early Greek poetry shares with both Near Eastern and other Indo-European literatures could be attributed, in a form of literary-historical double motivation, both to a remote Indo-European inheritance and to more recent historical influence from Near Eastern models.[28] More generally, Greek literature may be thought to share certain broad, independently developed mythological conceptions with other ancient literatures, which, in the case of Near East literatures,

---

[25] West 2007: 19–25. See Metcalf 2015a: 223 n. 4, with further literature, and Katz 2018: 64 n. 13.
[26] Witzel 2012: 161, noted also by Rutherford 2018: 4.
[27] Katz 2018, citing Woodard 2007 as a partial exception with respect to Hesiod; add Briquel 1980.
[28] For some reflections along such lines, see, e.g., Mondi 1990: 156–7, Louden 2011: 5–6, Metcalf 2015a: 222–4. Compare also Yakubovich 2018: 130 on the methodological question, which would be complicated further if it were true that the genealogical view of Indo-European cultural inheritance is oversimplified: 'Il est donc probable que des modèles en réseaux seraient beaucoup plus pertinents qu'un simple arbre généalogique, ce dont certains indo-européanistes ne disconviennent pas' (Demoule 2018: 253).

may have facilitated the secondary transfer of more specific elements.[29] While these observations are not new in themselves, they can perhaps fairly be said to describe a task that remains to be accomplished by future research.

Second, the topic of 'blocking', explored in this volume in particular by Rutherford, is perhaps unusual (though not unprecedented) in a comparative endeavour, as it pays more attention to difference than to similarity.[30] West anticipated the criticism that 'I have ignored the great *differences* between Greek and Near Eastern literatures', adding that 'of course Greek literature has its own character, its own traditions and conventions, and the contrasts that might be drawn between it and any of the oriental literatures might far outnumber the common features. If anyone wants to write another book pointing them out, I should have no objection (though I do not promise to read it).'[31] While such a book is unlikely ever to be written, the contributions by Rutherford and Kelly do illustrate the potential of an approach along those lines, which helps to show, in the case of the myths of the Storm God and the transfer of power among the generations of the gods, that the Greek approach to non-Greek material was selective, adaptive and distinctive.

Finally, the comparative approach that largely eschews the literary-historical dimension has similarly been anticipated long ago, such as in Hölderlin's study of the proverbs of Solomon and Hesiod's *Works and Days*, mentioned at the start of this Introduction. More recently, it is notable that Kathryn Stevens' new cross-cultural intellectual history of the Hellenistic period – an age in which the potential for interaction between Greece and the non-Greek civilisations of Egypt and the Near East seems unlimited – seeks to move beyond the fraught question of Babylonian influence on various branches of Greek thought, and eventually adopts a more general comparative approach that shows how Greek and Babylonian scholarship of the period developed similar responses to their 'shared participation in the same imperial system'.[32] In the literary field, too, a broader knowledge of ancient sources can no doubt enrich the Classicist's appreciation of the familiar Greco-Roman material, beyond the difficult

---

[29] An analogous example is given by Witzel 2012: 93–4, 178 (the existence of aboriginal flood myths in Taiwan encouraged the adoption of the specifically Biblical tale of Noah), who also argues for a shared, very remote ('Laurasian') ancestor of Greek and Near Eastern mythology (Witzel 2012: 65–75). See further Burkert 2003: 57, Lane Fox 2008: 279–80, Meijer 2018: 19–20.

[30] Compare the exhortation of Raaflaub 2000: 56 that 'we should appreciate real analogies without overlooking obvious and important differences'.

[31] West 1997: viii.   [32] Stevens 2019: 277, see esp. 252–369.

search for sources and elusive origins. As an 'influence-free' comparative study of the similarities and differences between the *Epic of Gilgameš* and *Beowulf* remarks, 'things absent can be just as important as things present, and thematising them can add to our understanding and appreciation of the work. So, in the same way that hearing a C can cause us immediately to realise that another note is a D, so comparison can be very useful in reminding us of the possibilities of *Anderssein*, and concomitantly encouraging us to question why things are the way they are.'[33]

Four very recent examples suggest that such open-minded attitudes may be beginning to take hold in Hellenic scholarship: a work on the *Iliad* and the tradition of the Trojan War opens with a chapter comparing and contrasting the Homeric and Mesopotamian conceptions of poetry,[34] a detailed study of Solon fr. 13 draws lessons from Sumero-Akkadian wisdom poetry,[35] a monograph on Pindar supports an argument on his cultic poetry by an analogy with Sumerian liturgical texts,[36] and a new edition and commentary of Sophocles' *Oedipus Rex* places and interprets the foundling-narrative in a context that includes both Greek and non-Greek sources.[37] In Burkert's own words, 'there is an independent merit to the study of parallels, even where direct borrowing cannot be demonstrated, in that it can open up a fuller perspective on a *koinē*, within which the individual civilisation, for instance the Greek, manifests its specific characteristics ... The comparison allows us to overcome too narrow a perspective.'[38]

---

[33] North and Worthington 2012: 182. [34] Haywood and Mac Sweeney 2018: 7–39.
[35] Johnston 2019. [36] Spelman 2018: 135–6. [37] Finglass 2018: 49–50, 63–70.
[38] Burkert 2003: 43 (translated), noted also by Casadio 2009: 138–9, and elaborating the earlier formulation in Burkert 1992: 8.

PART I
Contexts

CHAPTER I

'Let Those Important Primeval Deities Listen'
The Social Setting of the Hurro-Hittite Song of Emergence

Amir Gilan

The mythological narratives of the so-called Kumarbi cycle, including the *Song of Emergence*, are often considered by Hittitologists among the very few compositions that came down to us from the Hittite world that deserve to be labelled *belles lettres*, written and copied for sheer aesthetic pleasure (van den Hout 2002: 867). In his important overview of Hittite mythology (1961), Hans Gustav Güterbock suggested that we should trace the ethnolinguistic origins of the Hittite mythological tales and their ways of transmission – since then a well-established venue of research in Hittite studies: 'In doing so,' he notes, 'we immediately make an observation concerning the literary form in which mythological tales have been handed down: only the myths of foreign origin were written as real literary compositions – we may call them epics – whereas those of local Anatolian origin were committed to writing only in connection with rituals' (Güterbock 1961: 146). In another classic article, an overview of Hittite literature, Güterbock observes that whereas local Anatolian myths were found in different tablet collections in the Hittite capital, on the citadel as well as in the great temple in the lower town, Mesopotamian and Hurro-Hittite mythological compositions in translation were solely found in the great temple.[1] More recently, Lorenz and Rieken (2010) again studied the find-spots of the 'foreign' Mesopotamian and Hurro-Hittite mythological compositions and located, based on the exclusive appearance of these compositions in tablet collections relating to the temple and to the neighbouring house of the slope, the social setting of Hurro-Hittite and Mesopotamian mythological compositions in translation at the scribal school. They concluded that such material 'played a prominent role in scribal training – and only in scribal training, while the myths of Asia Minor and Anatolia represent a practical literature, which was embedded

[1] Güterbock 1997 [1978]: 28. On the nature of the tablet collections in Ḫattuša, see van den Hout 2002.

in rituals and sacrificial acts'.[2] The excavations of the so-called temple precinct at the Upper City of Ḫattuša, conducted by Peter Neve in the years 1978–92, have unearthed the remains of further tablet collections in 'temple 15' and especially 'temple 16', consisting of, among others, the Middle Hittite *Song of Release* (SÌR *parā tarnumaš*) and a Middle Babylonian version of the *Epic of Gilgameš* (Wilhelm 2015: 307–8).

However, the appearance of 'foreign' Mesopotamian and Hurro-Hittite mythological compositions in tablet collections relating to the temple have led scholars to different assertions as well. Haas (2006: 128) and Archi (2007: 223) have proposed a performative, ritual setting for some of these compositions: in the words of the latter,

> The Hurrian epics, which the Hittites translated into their own language but never imitated, were held near the temple. Such lengthy and complex texts in a recitative style must have represented the indispensable basis of subsequent recitations. These performances undoubtedly took place in religious areas on the occasion of cultic celebrations and possibly also at the palace.

The case for a primarily cultic, performative setting of freely translated Hurro-Hittite and Mesopotamian compositions unearthed in Ḫattuša has been expanded by Bachvarova in her recent book (2016) as well as in earlier contributions. Continuing the work of Archi (2007, 2009) and others, Bachvarova suggests that these were oral-derived compositions, defined by metre, shared motifs and phraseology, and designated by the genre label SÌR (Bachvarova 2016: 13, 35–46; see already Bachvarova 2014). The first part of her book is devoted to the identification – often conjectural and speculative due to the fragmentary and circumstantial nature of the evidence – of the cultic contexts in which these compositions were performed. According to Bachvarova, establishing a performative setting for the Hurro-Hittite and Mesopotamian mythological compositions in Ḫattuša is essential not only for the understanding of the function of these compositions among the Hittites, but also for an understanding of the modes of transmission by which the Greeks came in contact with these Hurro-Hittite traditions. Bachvarova argues that the most important phase of transmission took place early, in the Late Bronze Age and in the Early Iron Age, and that it was indirect in nature, eventuating in religious

---

[2] Lorenz and Rieken 2010: 229: '[die mythologische Importliteratur] in der Schreiberausbildung – und zwar nur dort – eine prominente Rolle gespielt hat, während die kleinasiatischen-anatolischen Mythen Gebrauchsliteratur darstellen, die in Rituale und Opferhandlungen eingebettet waren'; see emphatically also Waal 2015: 271.

festivals, magical rituals and ancestor veneration rites, sponsored by royal patronage. At these ceremonies, she argues, practised throughout the Mediterranean, narrative songs were performed by bilingual poets, and these were the real agents of poetic transmission: 'transmission of Near Eastern epic to the Greeks was by means of oral poets, not scribes translating texts' (Bachvarova 2016: 53). The emphasis given to oral rather than written modes of transmission of ancient Near Eastern literature is one of the most central, and controversial, propositions of her book.

Chanting was an integral part of ritual action in Hittite Anatolia in all of its manifold cultic traditions.[3] Cohorts of male and female cult singers, often accompanied by musical instruments, are abundantly attested in Hittite festival literature, chanting in Hittite (Archi 2004a), Hattic (Rutherford 2008; Stivala 2016), Luwian (Mouton 2016b) and Hurrian. As keenly observed by Rutherford, cult singing in Hittite Anatolia usually accompanied and supported the ritual action, but was never the main focus of attention (Rutherford 2008: 77). The 'supporting' role of singing in Anatolian cultic action is often manifested in the titles of the 'Songs' (SÌR). These titles are frequently functional: they relate to the ritual context to which they belong or to the deity which received offerings during that rite, or denote the social identity of the performers. The following examples may suffice to illustrate this. The 'Songs' (SÌR$^{HI.A}$) of the men of (the town of) Ištanuwa (*KUB* 30.42 iv 14', Schuol 2004: 138) and the 'Song' of (the town of) Ti[ššaruliya] (*KBo* 14.117 iv 7', Waal 2015: 515) were performed by inhabitants of these towns, in the Ištanuwian dialect of Luwian and in Hattic respectively. The 'Songs of the Pigeons? of Šawoška of Ninive' (listed in the catalogue *KUB* 8.69 iii 1–2) were sung in a 'Hurrian' festival celebrated for that deity (Schuol 2004: 139–40). The 'Songs of the Prostitutes' ([... ŠA $^{MUNUS.MEŠ}$K]AR.KID SÌR$^{HI.A}$) relate to the cult of the local Anatolian goddess Titiwatti (*KBo* 23.97 rev. 9, *CTH* 639, Waal 2015: 458). Direct evidence for the existence of 'epic poets' is, in contrast, very sparse, consisting of two broken colophons of the *Song of Release* mentioning a male singer (^{LÚ}NAR, *KBo* 32.13 rev. iv–iii 18' and *KBo* 32.66 rev. 2', Waal 2015: 278, 279).[4]

---

[3] See especially the synthesis offered by Schuol 2004: 136–55. An updated, comprehensive state-of-the-art study of Hittite cultic singing is a desideratum.

[4] See also Bachvarova 2016: 36–7 with n. 60, mentioning also a reference to the poor pay of the singer in the *Song of Release* itself. On the phrase ŠA ^{LÚ}NAR *kuššani* 'for the (low) wages of a singer', see Neu 1996: 284.

The genre designation 'song' (SÌR), however, is also attested in the colophons of several lengthy literary compositions, often named after the main protagonist or subject of the song.[5] These include the *Song of Release* (*KBo* 32.11 iv 22'), the sixth tablet of the *Song of Kešše* (*KUB* 47.2 l. e. col. vi 1) and a Hittite adaptation of the *Epic of Gilgameš* (*KBo* 19.116 + *KBo* 6.31 rev. 1'–2').[6] Other compositions that are designated as 'songs' in their colophons belong to the Kumarbi cycle: the *Song of Emergence* (*KUB* 33.120 + *KUB* 48.97 + 1194/u iv 28', see below) and the *Song of Ullikummi* (*KUB* 33.95 + l. e. 1–2). As the proem of the composition about Silver contains the lines [*i*]*š-ḫa-mi-iḫ-ḫi-ia-an* KÙ.BABBAR-*an* ⌈*ša*⌉ -*né-ez-z*[*i-in* . . .] 'sing of him, the excellent Silver', Hoffner (2016: 39) suggests that the other compositions in the cycle, with the exception of the *Song of Emergence*, may have been also named after the main protagonist: *Song of Silver*, *Song of Hedammu* and *Song of LAMMA*.

Another nemesis of the Storm God was the Sea, who is featured in the Hittite mythological fragment *KBo* 26.105. There, the Sea is overflooding the earth and Kumarbi is ordering the gods to pay the Sea a tribute in order to prevent the catastrophe.[7] As noted by Houwink Ten Cate (1992: 119), the narrative, although fragmentary, is reminiscent of the Egyptian Astarte-Papyrus. The colophon of the Hurrian fragment *KUB* 45.63 rev. iv 7' identifies it as 'tablet one of (the Song) of Se[a]' (DUB.1^KAM ŠA A.A[B.BA), and probably as a Hurrian version of the same narrative.[8] A *Song of the Manly Deeds of Sea* was performed during a festival in honour of Mount Hazzi alias Mount Zaphon, the Jebel Aqra in the bay of Iskenderun – the abode of the Storm God.[9] It is often assumed that the *Song of the Manly Deeds of Sea*, sung at the festival in honour of Mount Hazzi, was identical with the Hurrian and Hittite mythological narrative fragments concerning the Sea mentioned above, but the evidence is by no means conclusive.

Nevertheless, the performance of the *Song of the Deeds of the Sea* during that festival in honour of Mount Hazzi remains the most compelling piece

---

[5] Waal 2015: 282. For different interpretations of the genre label SÌR, see Güterbock 1997 [1978]: 32, Wilhelm 1997a: 277–8 n. 1, Schuol 2004: 141–2, van Dongen 2010: 52–5, Waal 2015: 271 and Bachvarova 2016: 36–8.
[6] See now Waal 2015: 270–80 for a collection of these colophons.
[7] Edited by Schwemer 2001: 451–3 and Blam 2004. See also Rutherford 2001: 603–4, Haas 2006: 151–2 and Bachvarova 2016: 25–6 and n. 17.
[8] For the resemblance between the two fragments and the identification as 'song', see Haas 2006: 151–2. The same title also appears in two scholarly catalogue lists, cited by Rutherford 2001: 598.
[9] Houwink Ten Cate 1992: 116; Rutherford 2001: 598–9; Haas 2006: 152; Lane Fox 2008: 259–64; Lorenz and Rieken 2010: 229–30, Bachvarova 2016: 25–6, Corti 2017: 12. The relevant lines are cited below.

of evidence suggesting that narrative songs were indeed recited in ritual context. In a recent article, Carlo Corti (2017) identified further fragments that belong to the festival text outlining the *Festival for Mt. Ḫazzi* (*CTH* 785). This reconstruction not only considerably enhances our knowledge of the course of that festival, but also offers invaluable insights as to its historical and cultural context. Furthermore, the newly reconstructed *Festival for Mt. Ḫazzi* may also allude to the context of performance of another well-known narrative song of the Kumarbi cycle, the *Song of Emergence*, which I will now discuss in some detail.

The Hittite tablet, edited as *KUB* 33.120++ (*CTH* 344) is a badly preserved, often illegible text.[10] Nevertheless, the mythological composition inscribed on the tablet is one of the finest and most sophisticated works of literature to survive from the Hittite world. The composition is multilayered and represents a rich literary blend of Mesopotamian, Hurrian, Eastern Anatolian, Syrian and Hittite deities, locations and plotlines.[11]

The composition was designated until recently in the scholarly literature as 'The Kingship among the Gods' (Forrer 1936), 'Kingship in Heaven' (Güterbock 1946) or as the 'Song of Kumarbi' (Hoffner 1998). In 2007, however, Corti was able to join a new fragment to the main text, extending the end of the fourth column and completing the colophon at the end of the composition. The newly restored colophon reveals the original title of the composition as well as the name and genealogy of the scribe that copied it. It was shown by Corti to be *The Song of Emergence* or the *Song of Going Out*. It is instructive to take a closer look at the colophon:

KUB 33.120 + *KUB* 48.97 + 1194/u631 rev. iv 28'–35': (28') Tablet 1 of the Song of Emergence, not complete. (29') Hand of Ašḫapala, son of Tarḫuntaššu, (30') grandson of Kuruntapiya (31') and <great>grandson/ descendant of Waršiya, (32') apprentice of Ziti. This tablet was completely damaged, (33') I, Asḫapa<la> wrote it. (34') in front of Ziti.[12]

---

[10] Edited by Güterbock 1946. Very recent translations include Hoffner 2016 and Bauer et al. 2015. A recent online edition of the text is E. Rieken et al. (ed.), hethiter.net/: CTH 344 (INTR 2009-08-12). Older translations include Hoffner 1998: 42–5, Haas 2006: 133–43 and Pecchioli Daddi and Polvani 1990: 115–24. Recent studies include Corti 2007, van Dongen 2010, van Dongen 2012, Beckman 2011, Corti and Pecchioli Daddi 2012 and Strauss Clay and Gilan 2014.

[11] Haas 2006: 130–2; Archi 2007; Beckman 2011: 25; Bachvarova 2012: 112–14; Corti and Pecchioli Daddi 2012: 616.

[12] *KUB* 33.120 + *KUB* 48.97 + 1194/u631 rev. iv 28'–35': (28') DUB 1 KAM ŠÁ SÌR GÁxÈ.A ⌈NU.TIL⌉ (29') ŠU ᵐAŠ-ḪA-PA-LA DUMU ᵐᵈ10-TA-AŠ-ŠU (30') DUMU.DUMU-ŠU Š[Á] ⌈ᵐᵐᵈ⌉KAL.SUM (31') Ù DUMU.DUMU.<DUMU>-ŠU ŠÁ ᵐWA-AR-ŠI-IA (32') GÁB.ZU.ZU ŠÁ ᵐLÚ ki-i ṬUP-PU (33') ar-ḫa ḫar-ra-an ⌈e⌉-eš-ta (34') na-at am-mu-uk ᵐAš-ḫa-pa-<la>-aš (35')

The colophon reveals the long genealogy of the apprentice (GÁB.ZU.ZU) Ašḫapala, who copied the composition. A recent study by Shai Gordin (2015) on the scribal circles in Ḫattuša sheds more light on Ašḫapala, his supervisor Ziti, their respective families and careers. Ašḫapala was active in the thirteenth century BCE, during the reign of king Tudḫaliya IV. His genealogy goes back to his distant ancestor Waršiya, active at the very the end of the Old Hittite kingdom (Corti 2007: 115, Gordin 2015: 216). His grandfather, Kuruntapiya, is often identified with a high court official by that name during the reign of king Muwatalli II, acting as a witness to the Aleppo treaty as an *antuwašalli*-official and a scribe (*KBo* 1.6 rev. 21–2, Beckman 1999: 90; see, however, Devecchi 2010a: 20–1). He may have also copied a ᴹᵁᴺᵁˢŠU.GI magical ritual preserved in the small fragment *KBo* 13.240 (Torri 2008: 775–6; Gordin 2015: 216). His father Tarḫuntaššu was probably a high official as well, as his name may appear in a fragmentary letter (*KBo* 18.101 obv. 2, edited by Hagenbuchner 1989: 174–5) probably representing a correspondence between officials.

Ziti, the supervisor, belonged to one of the most illustrious scholarly families in Ḫattuša, descending from the fifteenth-century scribe Ḫanikkuili, who famously copied the Naram-Sin prism (*KBo* 19.99); Ḫanikkuili's father, Anu-šar-ilāni, was a Mesopotamian scribe active in Ḫattuša.[13] Ziti copied several tablets under the supervision of Anuwanza, one of the most influential and better documented scholar-scribes of the Late Empire Period. Among other things, Anuwanza had experience in copying partially or completely damaged tablets.[14] He continued to supervise other scribes and founded his own school (Gordin 2015: 179–85, 216–20). It seems that Ziti, his apprentice Ašḫapala, and their respective families belonged to the higher echelons of Hittite society. As recently argued by van den Hout, these were not merely professional scribes whose job it was to keep record, but scholar-scribes who 'increasingly, as their career advanced, were involved in scholarly endeavors rather than tablet production' (van den Hout 2015: 203).

The learned and erudite nature of the *Song of Emergence*, copied by Ašḫapala under the supervision of Ziti, perfectly illustrates van den Hout's thesis. So does the name of the composition. This is rendered in singular

---

PA-NI ᵐLÚ *IŠ-ṬUR*. On the colophon, see Gordin 2015: 127 and especially 152–3 and Waal 2015: 274–5.

[13] Gordin 2015: 179–84 offers a meticulous study of Ziti's (II) family, career, and the circle of scribes working with him. See also Torri 2011.

[14] On the career of Anuwanza, active during the reigns of Ḫattušili III and Tudḫaliya IV, see van den Hout 1998: 238–42; on his circle, see Gordin 2015: 166–98.

composite cuneiform sign, so far unattested elsewhere. The composite sign comprises the sign GÁ used as a container inside which the signs UD.DU.A, which form the compound sign read as È.A, are written. Corti draws attention to the trilingual lexical list *Erimhuš*, in which Sumerian PÀ.È.A is rendered as Akkadian *uṣ-ṣú-tù* and Hittite *pa-ra-a-kán pa-a-u-wa-ar*, to be translated as 'Emergence, Exit, Departure' (Corti 2007: 116–19 with references and previous literature; see also Weeden 2011: 102–3). Corti also convincingly restored the Hittite name of the 'song' in the colophon of *KUB* 47.56, a Hurrian fragment possibly representing a second tablet of the same composition.[15]

The title of the composition, unattested elsewhere in Hittite texts, is often translated 'mythologically' as the *Song of Genesis* or the *Song of Beginning* (Corti 2007: 120) but it probably refers, in a playful and ironic manner, to the main subject of the composition, recurring throughout it: the *Song of Emergence* or the *Song of Emerging* in the sense of unnatural births (Beckman 2011: 28, Strauss Clay and Gilan 2014). The notions of pregnancy and birth are also conveyed by the composite cuneiform sign itself, in which one sign contains others within it (Corti 2007: 116). More specifically, the *Song of Emergence* is concerned with births by a male parent. As noted by Beckman, the practical problems faced by a male in giving birth 'are a central concern of the text, which indeed takes its title from this comical yet serious situation as seen from the point of view of the divine children: Where should I emerge/come out (*parā uwa-*)?'[16] Admittedly, the verbal complex *parā uwa-* 'to emerge' is used to denote the unnatural birth in the composition (ii 32, 34, and it should most likely be restored at the broken end of ii 30; *šarā uwa-* 'to come up' denotes the appearance of KA.ZAL, the Heroic King, from Kumarbi's skull in ii 36-37). Its meaning, however, is very close to *parā pai-* 'to go out'. Perhaps *pa-ra-a-kán pa-a-u-wa-ar* was the closest term Ašhapala could find in the *Erimhuš* dictionary.

The events that led to these unnatural births by a male deity, narrated in the beginning of the *Song of Emergence*, are well known. After Alalu fled before the victorious Anu, the narrative continues to portray Kumarbi's overthrow of Anu in a more vivid and detailed manner,

---

[15] Corti 2007: 119, *KUB* 47.56 rev. 25': [DUB.]2?KAM NU.AL.TIL SÌ[R? *pa-ra-a-kán pa-*]⌈*a*⌉*-u-aš*, '[Tablet] 2 not complete, the S[ong of G]oing [Out]'. For the fragment, see Salvini and Wegner 2004: 38–9. For the colophon, see now Waal 2015: 280.

[16] Beckman 2011: 28, Hoffner 2016: 44 n. 64. For *parā uwa-* 'to come out/forward', see CHD P: 116.

culminating in Anu's castration (*KUB* i 18–27, recently translated by Hoffner 2016: 41):

> Kumarbi, Alalu's offspring, gave battle against Anu. No longer can he withstand Kumarbi's eyes, Anu. He wriggled loose from his hands and fled, Anu, and he set out for the sky. Kumarbi rushed after him, seized Anu by the feet, and dragged him down from the sky. (Kumarbi) bit off his genitals and his manhood united with Kumarbi's interior like Bronze. When Kumarbi had swallowed the manhood of Anu, he rejoiced and laughed out loud.

Anu, however, had the last laugh. He impregnated Kumarbi with several deities, among them the Storm God and his siblings, the vizier Tašmišu and the river Tigris (i 31–3). Thus, by usurping the heavenly throne by castrating Anu, Kumarbi tragically became a 'mother' to his own future usurper, his son the Storm God, setting up his own downfall. Kumarbi, called 'the father of all the gods' in the proem to the *Song of Ullikummi*,[17] is explicitly named the 'mother of Teššub' in a Hurrian prayer to Teššub of Aleppo.[18] As shown by Ayali-Darshan (2013), Kumarbi's 'preternatural' pregnancy is determined by a tradition according to which the Storm God had two fathers. According to this mythological constellation, also evident in Ugaritic mythological compositions, and later in the *Phoenician History* of Philon of Byblos, one of the fathers becomes an opponent of the Storm God whereas the other is his ally. As we have seen, Kumarbi's strange predicament becomes the central motor of the plot, probably also giving it its name.

To return to the colophon of *KUB*, the unique composite sign GÁxÈ.A denoting the title of the 'song' is not the only cuneiform sign found in the text connecting it to the lexical list *Erimhuš*.[19] Gordin, who meticulously studied the peculiarities of the handwriting of *KUB*, notes Ašḫapala's intriguing fondness of logograms consisting of the sign KA and containing an inscribed element inside it (Gordin 2015: 326). Several of these signs, not

---

[17] Hoffner 1998: 56.
[18] *KUB* 47.78 (= *ChS* I/8, 8) i 9'-14': 'You are the strong one, which I (praise), the bull calf of Anu! You are the strong one, which I (praise), your father Anu begot you, your mother Kumarbi brought you to life. For the city of Aleppo I summon him, Teššop, for the pure throne.' Edited by Thiel and Wegner 1984, 187–218. See Schwemer 2001: 454–5, Haas 2006: 251–2 and Campbell 2013: 32–6, whose translation is given here.
[19] On this text in Ḫattuša, see Weeden 2011: 99–103. See Metcalf 2015b: 46 on interactions between works of translated Hittite literature and lexical texts found in Ḫattuša. It remains an open question whether the 'author' of the *Song of Emergence* was drawing on the lexical list, or whether the lexical list was influenced by the literary text (for discussion of this problem in Sumero-Akkadian literature from Mesopotamia, see Weeden, Chapter 4 in this volume).

unique by themselves, also significantly appear in the *Erimhuš* dictionary, and may have inspired the creation of the *hapax* composite sign GÁxÈ.A (Weeden 2011: 102). Other unique and 'learned' logographic writings attested in include the mysterious theonyms ᵈA.GILIM and ᵈKA.ZAL. The latter logogram is likewise only attested so far in *KUB* and in the *Erimhuš* dictionary, equating KA.ZAL with Akkadian *mutellu* and Hittite *wa-al-li-u-ra-aš* 'proud, glorious' (*KBo* rev. 27', Weeden 2011: 135; Corti and Pecchioli Daddi 2012: 614, with references).[20] In their comprehensive discussion of the logogram ᵈKA.ZAL, Corti and Pecchioli Daddi (2012: 613–16) suggest that the otherwise unattested compound noun *walliura-* is in fact also found in the proem of the *Song of Emergence*, reviving an older reading by Forrer (1936: 693–4, and see below).

The colophon itself, the rare logographic writings attested in *KUB*, Ašḫapala's well-documented acquaintance with the *Erimhuš* dictionary and the considerable number of mistakes and malformed signs evident in the tablet are all clear indications of its scribal-scholarly setting (see already Corti 2007: 120). Gordin suggests that Ašḫapala, the apprentice of Ziti, copied the completely damaged tablet under the supervision of his master as a 'a scholastic or pedagogic exercise of sorts' (Gordin 2015: 326). Since Ašḫapala notes that he copied the 'original' tablet because it was completely damaged, it seems that the composition available to us represents a Late Empire Period copy of an Early Empire Period erudite, literary composition that was written in Hittite and that adapted, rather than translated, earlier mythological and literary materials, possibly in Hurrian, still unknown to us (Corti 2007: 120–1).

Another suggestive element, besides the genre label SÌR, that may indicate a performance setting is the self-referential proem of the *Song of Emergence* (Schuol 2004: 141; Bachvarova 2016: 36). Like other 'songs' of the Kumarbi cycle, the *Song of Emergence* begins with a proem. At the beginning of the *Song of Emergence*, it is the primeval deities who are invited to lend an ear:

> *KUB* 33.120++ obv. I 1–7 (§1): [...] the primeval deities who [are in the Dark Earth], [let those primeval]], important deities listen. Let Nara, [Napšara, Mink]i (and) Ammunki listen! Let Ammezzadu, [Tuḫuši, ...],

---

[20] Yet another parallel for this equation, found in a trilingual (Sumerian-Akkadian-Hittite) hymn to the Storm God (*CTH* 314), is demonstrated by Metcalf 2015a: 88 n. 26.

father and mother of [...] listen! (§2) Let [Enlil (and) Apand]u,[21] father and mother of Išḫara, listen! Enlil [and Ninlil,] who [below] and above are important and glorious[22] deities, [...] and radiance,[23] let them listen![24]

The primeval deities (Hittite *karuilieš šiuneš*), the intended audience of the *Song of Emergence*, belong to the first generation of gods.[25] These ancient, 'ancestor deities' (Hurrian *ammadena enna*, Wilhelm 2009: 66 with n. 26) reside in the netherworld and are sometimes designated in Hittite texts as 'lower deities' (Hittite *katereš šiuneš*), akkadographically as the ^{d}*A-NUN-NA-KE*$_4$, or as 'deities of the earth' (Hittite *taknaš šiuneš*).[26] In her recent study of the primeval deities in the Hittite sources, Lorenz-Link collected around thirty names of single deities that belong in that group (Lorenz-Link 2009: 210–16). The primeval deities regularly appear as witnesses, in different configurations, in Hittite state-treaties, beginning at the reign of Arnuwanda I.[27] Their appearance in the treaties is often attributed to the growing popularity of Hurrian-Kizzuwatnian religious elements in the Hittite royal family in that period (Archi 1990: 114–15, 120; Wilhelm 2009: 63). In the treaties, they often constitute a group of twelve deities. The primeval deities are also represented as a group of twelve, all nearly identical male deities holding scimitar-shaped swords, in chambers A and B in Yazılıkaya. However, the cohort of primeval deities attested in the texts includes goddesses as well. Among these deities are Ninlil, Antu and Apantu, the consorts of Enlil and Anu.[28] These Mesopotamian couples were also invoked to listen to the of the *Song of Emergence* (i 4–7). One core group of primeval deities, not including the

---

[21] For the reconstruction, see Archi 1990: 114, Haas 2006: 134 and Beckman 2011: 26, but see also Hoffner 2016: 40 with n. 14.

[22] For this reading, put forward by Forrer 1936: 693–4, see Corti and Pecchioli Daddi 2012: 614. The alternative reading, *wa-a[k-t]u-u-ri-iš* 'eternal', should be discarded. See now Hoffner 2016: 40 n. 15.

[23] Oettinger 2001: 458–9 and Haas 2006: 134, differently *HED* K: 303 and Beckman 2011: 26.

[24] *KUB* 33.120 + *KUB* 48.97 + 1194/u631 obv. i 1-7 (§1) [GE$_6$-*i* KI-*pí nu a-pé-e k*]*a-*⌈*ru-ú-i-li-ia*⌉ *-aš-kán* DINGIR^{MES}*-iš ku-i-e-eš* (2) [... *ka-ru-ú-i-l*]*i-iš* DINGIR^{MES}*-iš da-aš-ša-u-*⌈*e*⌉ *-eš iš-ta-*⌈*ma-aš-kán*⌉ *-du* ^{d}*Na-*[*ra-aš*] (3) [^{d}*Na-ap-ša-ra-aš* ^{d}*Mi-in-k*]*i-iš* ^{d}*Am-mu-un-*⌈*ki*⌉ *-iš iš-ta-ma-aš-*⌈*ki-ed*⌉ *-du* ^{d}⌈*Am-me-ez-za*⌉ *-du-u*[*š*] (4) [^{d}⌈*Tu-ḫu-ši-iš* ...]*x-aš at-ta-aš an-na-aš* ⌈*iš-ta*⌉ *-ma-aš-*⌈*kán-du*⌉ (§2) (5) [^{d}EN.LÍL ^{d}*A-pa-an-d*]*u-uš* ^{d}*Iš-ḫa-ra-aš at-ta-aš an-na-aš iš-ta-ma-aš-kán-du* ^{d}EN.LÍL-*aš* (6) [^{d}NIN.LÍ]L-[*aš kat-ta ša-r*]*a-a-ia ku-i-e-eš da-aš-ša-u-e-eš wa-*⌈*al-li*⌉ *-u-ri-iš* DINGIR^{MES}*-iš* (7) [...]x x[... *k*]*u-ul-ku-li-im-ma-aš-ša iš-ta-ma-aš-*⌈*kán*⌉ *-du*. See Haas 2006: 134, Beckman 2011: 26 and Hoffner 2016 for new transliterations and text reconstructions. A more comprehensive discussion is found in van Dongen 2010: 58–61, with previous literature.

[25] On the Hittite primeval deities, see the excellent overviews of Archi 1990, Haas 1994: 111–15, Wilhelm 2009 and especially the study of Lorenz-Link 2009: 165–222.

[26] See most recently Lorenz-Link 2009: 205–10.

[27] See Archi 1990 and Lorenz-Link 2009: 194–8 for attestations and discussion.

[28] Archi 1990: 116, Wilhelm 2009: 64. On the rock sanctuary in Yazılıkaya, see Seeher 2011.

more distant deities of Mesopotamian origin, consisted of seven deities, all male, of unknown origins: Nara, Namšara/Napšara, Minki, Tuḫuši, Ammunki, Ammizzadu and Alalu.[29] Even if mostly reconstructed, the first six deities seem to have constituted the audience invoked in the first section of *CTH* 344++ (i 1–4). Alalu was famously the first king in heaven according to the succession narrative opening the composition. He is explicitly described there as fleeing to the dark earth after his defeat by Anu.[30]

One question that is left unexplained in the preserved parts of the opening lines of the composition is why the primeval deities were addressed as the intended audience of the *Song of Emergence*, if not of the whole cycle of 'songs' (as suggested by Hoffner 2016: 40). Scholars suggested that primeval deities were invoked because of their longevity: as these deities belonged to the older generation of ancestor gods, they shared firsthand knowledge of the narrated events in time immemorial (Haas 1994: 113–14, Wilhelm 2009: 68–9, van Dongen 2010: 61–2 with further discussion). In fact, the primeval deities were not merely the intended audience of the composition. Several members of the group even took part in the plot. In a fragmentary and difficult dialogue (ii 4–15), A.GILIM, most likely the yet to be born Storm God, speaking from inside Kumarbi's belly, claims that he will be given positive properties, such as manliness, valour, wisdom and virility from various deities. These include Earth, Sky, Kumarbi, Enlil, Nara and other deities (Hoffner 1998: 43). In a badly preserved mythological fragment, *KUB* 33.105, the Storm God relates in retrospect how he was given Nara's wisdom and Anu's virility as well as other positive properties from several other deities (*KUB* 33.105 i 10'–14', *CHD* P: 328). The primeval deities appear in several other compositions belonging or relating to the Kumarbi cycle (all appearances are listed in Lorenz-Link 2009: 199–205).

Another question that is left unanswered in the preserved parts of the opening lines of the *Song of Emergence* concerns the question as to how the primeval deities, who habitually reside in the netherworld, were invoked by the 'performer' to hear his 'song'. As noted by Collins (2004: 56), communication with the primeval deities, invoking them from the netherworld, was a dangerous undertaking requiring ritual expertise. A broad

---

[29] Haas 1994: 114–15, Wilhelm 2009: 65–6. A comprehensive discussion of the origins of these deities is Lorenz-Link 2009: 216–19.
[30] *KUB* 33.120++ i 15: *pa-i-ta-aš-kán kat-ta-an-da da-an-ku-wa-i ták-ni-i* 'he (Alalu) went down to the dark earth' (see further Metcalf, Chapter 8 in this volume). On the 'Dark Earth' in Hittite religion, see Oettinger 1989–90 and Collins 2002.

overview of the Hittite religious literature reveals that the primeval deities were primarily invoked with a reason. In her study of these deities, Lorenz-Link lists only seven festivals in which miscellaneous primeval gods attended and received offerings, compared to sixty-eight magic rituals in which they took part (2009: 168–94). The primeval deities frequently, but not exclusively, appear in magic rituals of Hurrian-Luwian-Kizzuwatnian origins. They often take part, together with the Sun Goddess of the Earth, in purification rituals performed in order to dispose of impurities such as witchcraft, bloodshed, curse, perjury and various other contaminations. Most frequently, the primeval deities are requested to transport the contaminated vehicle, often a piglet, to the netherworld and to retain it there. As they reside in the netherworld, they seem to be immune to impurity or impure themselves.[31] They are also often invoked in 'taking from the earth rituals' (Hittite *taknaz dā-*)[32] as well as in substitution rituals, in which they are requested, sometimes in direct speech, to accept the substitution made by the practitioner, freeing the patient from a grim fate prefigured in an unfavourable omen.

Communication with the primeval deities was usually established by the digging of ritual pits, mostly outdoors.[33] The pits enabled the passage of the primeval deities between the worlds and the smooth dispatch of offerings and of vehicles accrued with impurity to the netherworld (Collins 2002: 226). In several rituals, figurines of the primeval deities were made by the practitioner, usually of clay. These figurines participate in the ritual and receive offerings and other forms of cultic care (Lorenz-Link 2009: 108–9 with references).

The invocation of the primeval deities for the purification ritual of a house (*CTH* 446), certainly one of the better-preserved and best-known rituals involving the deities of the netherworld, provides a good illustration to the ways the primeval deities were contacted in these rituals.[34] *CTH* 446 is a complex, elaborate and often inconsistent ritual. It was frequently copied in Ḫattusa: more than a dozen manuscripts have been identified so far, most of which date to the later phases of the Empire Period.[35] The composition itself, however, dates back to the first half of the fourteenth

---

[31] Wilhelm 2009: 93–5; Collins 2004: 56.
[32] See Görke 2010: 174–9 for a comprehensive discussion of the meaning of these rituals with previous literature.
[33] Haas 1994: 902–3, Collins 2002; Collins 2004; Lorenz-Link 1999: 189.
[34] Edited by Otten 1961. More recent translations are Collins 1997 and Miller 2008.
[35] See Miller 2008: 206 and n. 57. I would like to thank Andrea Trameri for sending me his new edition of the text in his unpublished MA thesis.

century BC, to the beginning of that period.[36] In the elaborate, two-day ritual, they were invoked and persuaded, even threatened, to rid a house of the impurity it had accrued by taking it to the netherworld with them. The ritual was performed by a male ritual practitioner (LÚAZU in several manuscripts, LÚḪAL in others). It took place in different locations, beginning at the contaminated house itself, where the practitioner employs several analogical magic similes in an attempt to separate the impurities from the house. The ritual activity continues at a river bank, where the practitioner invokes the infernal deities and creates figurines of them out of the clay of the river bank, sprinkled with oil and honey.[37] These include Aduntarri, Zulki, Irpitiga, Nara, Namšara, Minki, Amunki and Ābi (the deified pit), some of the deities that constituted the intended audience of the *Song of Emergence*.[38] After a long and fascinating excursus concerning the procurement of the water of purity required for the purification of the house, the practitioner returns to the contaminated house with the water. There, he performs a separate purification ritual for the blood contaminating the house. He creates a 'deity of blood' and entreats the infernal deities to give this blood, represented by the blood of a freshly slaughtered lamb, to the 'deity of blood' so that it will carry the fluid to the dark netherworld and secure it there. In order to enable the dispatch, the practitioner opens a pit as a 'gate to the netherworld'. The practitioner continues to persuade, even to threaten, the primeval deities, acting now as a tribunal, to correctly decide the case of the house's purification. At this point in the ritual, the practitioner prepares offerings to the primeval deities, making mention of their history in a short mythologem (*KBo* 10.45 + *ABoT* 2.30 iii 41–7):

> He (the exorcist) takes three birds. He offers two birds to the primeval deities and one bird to the pit. He says as follows: 'For you, ancients, neither cattle nor sheep will be laid out. When the Storm God drove you down to the dark earth, he established for you this offering.'[39]

---

[36] See Miller 2008: 207 for a collocation of the different manuscripts and their dating. Eighteen manuscripts are identified now according to the *CTH*.
[37] As noted by Miller 2008: 221 n. 110, the figurines were not made in the form of daggers, as previously assumed on the basis of a difficult reading.
[38] Archi 1990; Bachvarova 2016: 96–7.
[39] *KBo* 10.45 + *ABoT* 2.30 iii 41–7: (41) *nu-za* 3 MUŠEN *da-a-i* ⌜*nu-kán*⌝ 2 MUŠEN *A-NA* ᴰ*A.NUN.NA.KE₄* (42) BAL-*an-ti* 1 MUŠEN-*ma-kán A-NA* ᴰ*A-a-pí* BAL-*an-ti* (43) *nu ki-iš-ša-an te-ez-zi šu-ma-aš-kán ka-ru-ú-i-li-eš-ša-mi-i*[*t*] (44) *Ú-UL-aš-ša-ma-aš-kán* GU₄-*uš* UDU-*uš ki-it-ta-ri* (45) ᴰ10-*aš-ša-ma-aš-kán* [*ku*]-*wa-pí* GAM-*an-ta* GE₆-*i ták-ni-i* (46) *pé-en-ni-eš-ta nu-*[(*uš*)]-*ma-aš-kán ki ši-ip-pa-an-du-wa-ar* (47) *da-a-iš*.

The first day of the ritual ends with the offerings that follow this speech act. The mythologeme addressed to the primeval deities is often considered to refer to the beginning of the *Song of Emergence*, where Alalu is reported to have gone to the dark earth after his defeat to Anu (see most recently Bachvarova 2016: 97). At that time, however, the Storm God was not yet conceived, and the first tablet of the *Song of Emergence* is primarily concerned with the strange circumstances of his birth. The allusion to the banishment of the primeval deities by the Storm God in *CTH* 446 and their prescribed bird diet may therefore allude to another story.[40]

As the brief glimpse into the invocation of the primeval deities for the purification ritual of a house (*CTH* 446) has shown, and as the rich corpus of Hittite ritual literature confirms, communication with the primeval deities was not unmediated. Their invocation from the netherworld required mediation by magic practitioners. As far as we know, however, neither Ašḫapala, the apprentice (GÁB.ZU.ZU) who copied the tablet, nor Ziti, his mentor, were expert magic practitioners or professional exorcists. There is also no evidence in the preserved parts of the *Song of Emergence* that the 'original author' or the 'fictional narrator' of the 'song' was himself an expert magic practitioner or that he was assisted by one in order to invoke the primeval deities from the netherworld. There is also no evidence to suggest that Ašḫapala was a cult singer (^{LÚ}NAR) himself. Neither was Ziti, his supervisor. Neither Ašḫapala, the apprentice, nor Ziti had themselves invoked the primeval deities to listen while copying the tablet *KUB* 33.120++. All this suggests that the call on the primeval deities to listen is a poetic device, not a ritual conjuration. The intended audience of the *Song of Emergence*, the primeval deities residing in the netherworld, were 'merely' a fictional audience.[41] The genre label SÌR and the self-referential proems attested in several narrative songs may therefore denote highly literary compositions that only simulate an oral mode of performance, as contextually unbound works of literature often do.

---

[40] A banishment to the netherworld is also described in the mythological composition known as *Ea and the Beast* (*KBo* 31.95++, edited by Archi 2002: 4, 7 ii 10'–11'): [... -wa-r]a-aš-kán da-an-ku-⌜wa-i⌝ ták-ni-i ⌜kat-ta⌝-an-⌜ta⌝ ⁽¹¹'⁾ [... da-an-ku-wa-i ták-n]i-i kat-ta-an-⌜ta⌝ pé-en-na-i '[...] them down to the dark earth. He drives them ⁽¹¹'⁾ down t[o the dark earth]'. See also Bachvarova 2016: 97 n. 89 with earlier references; on the composition in general, see also Haas 2006: 143–4 and Rutherford 2011. According to Bachvarova 2016: 96, the allusion to the banishment of the primeval deities by the Storm God in the ritual *CTH* 446 'shows that the scribes who made the copies were sufficiently knowledgeable in the orally transmitted formulaic phraseology to unconsciously expand and contract the phrasing of the incantations', but the appearance of the same phrase in *Ea and the Beast* could equally be intertextual. On intertextuality in Hittite ritual and mythological texts, see Haas 2007.

[41] On fictional audiences, see, among others, Ong 1975.

There is, however, evidence that singers did sing a 'Song of Invocation' in a ritual setting, invoking the primeval deities from the netherworld. *KBo* 23.7, a ritual fragment, describes an invocation of the Primeval deities by a SANGA-priest at Mount Irrāna:[42]

> *KBo* 23.7 i 4–19:[43] [...] At Mount Irrāna [...] he goes to [in]voke[44] [...]. A singer/singers also [...]. As soon as the exorcist brea[ks] the thick- and the thin-breads, he places them (the breads) on wood. The wood is arranged [...]. The wood is placed close to a *ḫašikka*-tree; the SANGA-priest is expert in it. [...] by the deity. It is determined to open up the pits. [They] proceed and open up the pits for the primeval deities. Afterwards he pours a wine libation. The singer(s) sing(s) the 'Song of the Invocation of the Pr[imeval] Deities'. The gods [...]. As soon as it is finished, (§) they return and break [thick-breads] for the Storm Gods [...]. For that Storm God they break one thick-bread and also for that Storm God [...] likewise. He also pours a libation. As [soo]n as it is finished [...they] set [u]p [...].[45]

The ritual fragment *KBo* 23.7 was considered until recently to originate from Kizzuwatna. However, due to the distinctive offerings to two Storm Gods depicted in lines 15–17, Corti (2017) now argues that the fragment rather belongs to the *Festival for Mt. Hazzi* (CTH 785). The *Festival for Mt. Hazzi* was thus created in the town of Šapinuwa, the new capital of king Tudḫaliya III (Tašmišarri) and his wife Taduḫeba, the most 'Hurrian' of Hittite kings. The remarkable presence in the festival of two Storm Gods now reflects an Aleppine tradition emanating from Northwestern Syria, not far from Mount Hazzi, celebrating both the Storm Gods of Aleppo and of Mount Hazzi.[46] In Ugarit, the two deities were closely related to a concept of deified Kingship (Schwemer 2008: 11; Corti 2017: 11). The same concept is represented at the Šapinuwan *Festival for*

---

[42] On the fragment, see Haas 2003a: 273 and Lorenz-Link 2009: 180. A full edition is announced by Carlo Corti.
[43] The three first lines of the first column show only traces.   [44] Reconstruction after *HW²* Ḫ: 110.
[45] *KBo* 23.7 i 4–19: ⁽⁴⁾ [... A-N]A ḪUR.SAG*IR-RA-A-NA* x [...] ⁽⁵⁾ [*ḫal-z*]*i-ia-u-an-zi pa-iz-zi* ⌈LÚNAR⌉ *-ia-x*[...] ⁽⁶⁾ ⌈*nu*⌉ *ma-aḫ-ḫa-an* LÚAZU NINDA.GUR₄.RAḪI.A NINDA.SIGMEŠ *pár-š*[*i-a*] ⁽⁷⁾ ⌈*na*⌉ *-at-ša-an* GIŠ-*ru ša-ra-a da-a-i* GIŠ-*ru-ma* [...] ⁽⁸⁾ *i-ia-an* GIŠ-*ru-ma* GIŠ*ḫa-ši-ik-kán ma-an-ni-in-k*[*u-wa-an*] ⁽⁹⁾ *ar-ta-ri* LÚSANGA-*at-*⌈*za*⌉ I-DI IŠ-TU DINGIR-LIM x[...] ⁽¹⁰⁾ *nu a-a-pí ki-nu-ma-an-zi ḫa-an-da-a-it-ta nu ú-w*[*a-an-zi*] ⁽¹¹⁾ *ka-ru-ú-i-li-ia-*[*aš*] DINGIRMEŠ*-aš a-a-pí-ia ki-nu-w*[*a-an-zi*] ⁽¹²⁾ EGIR-ŠU-*ma* GEŠTIN *ši-pa-an-ti nu* LÚNAR *ka*[*-ru-ú-i-li-ia-aš*] ⁽¹³⁾ DINGIRMEŠ*-aš ḫal-zi-ia-u-wa-aš* SÌR SÌR-RU *nu* DINGIRMEŠ [...] ⁽¹⁴⁾ *nu ma-aḫ-ḫa-an zi-in-na-i* (§) ⁽¹⁵⁾ *na-at* EGIR-*pa ú-wa-an-zi nu A-NA* D10ḪI.A [NINDA.GUR₄.RA ḪI.A] ⁽¹⁶⁾ *pár-ši-ia-an-zi a-pé-e-da-ni* D10-*ni* 1 NINDA.GUR₄.RA [...] ⁽¹⁷⁾ *pár-ši-ia-an-zi a-pé-e-da-ni-ia* D10-*ni QA-TA*[*M-MA* ...] ⁽¹⁸⁾ ⌈*ši*⌉ *-pa-an-ti-ia nu ma-a*[*ḫ-ḫa-a*]*n zi-in-na-*[*i* ...] ⁽¹⁹⁾ [*ša-r*]*a-a ti-it-ta-*[*nu-u-wa-an-zi*...].
[46] Corti 2017: 11. See already Archi 2009: 219.

Mt. *Ḫazzi* by the *Song of Kingship* (*šarraššiyaš* SÌR), famously sung by a number of singers at the festival (*KBo* 8.86 i 6; see now Corti 2017: 4).[47]

The newly reconstructed *Festival for Mt. Ḫazzi* encompassed numerous offerings, processions as well as athletic games and competitions of a local Anatolian nature, such as cheese fighting.[48] A considerable section of the festival was devoted to the presentation and procession of the weapons of two dozen deities, a rather Syrian tradition (Corti 2017: 10). The preserved parts of the festival lists several other songs, each performed by a number of male singers during the ritual action, including the *Song of the Torch* and the *Song of the Road*, which were sung during the procession of the deities and their respective weapons. The *Song of Prosperity* and the *Song of the* apiri-*deities* were performed during offerings to entities bearing those names (Corti 2017: 8–9). The exact location of the above mentioned *Song of the Manly Deeds of Sea* within the festival is not certain as it is only preserved in two Late Empire Period duplicates of the festival. As these duplicates reveal, the *Song of the Manly Deeds of Sea* was performed, like the other songs that were sung in the *Festival for Mt. Ḫazzi*, by a number of male singers:

> *KBo* 42.2 i 15–18 (with duplicate *KUB* 44.7 i 11'–14', Archi 2009, 219): The singers sing the 'Song of the Manly Deeds of Sea': How the Storm God defeated Sea. While they are singing, the SANGA-priest goes ahead to Mount Arana.[49]

It is tempting to suggest that Mount Arana (ḪUR.SAG*AR-RA-NA*), mentioned as the destination of the SANGA-priest in *KBo* 42.2 i 18, is in fact identical with Mount Irrāna, (ḪUR.SAG*IR-RA-A-NA*), the location where a SANGA-priest invoked the primeval deities according to *KBo* 23.7.[50] Due to the accumulation of 'songs' in the *Festival for Mt. Ḫazzi*, among them the *Song of the Manly Deeds of Sea* with its clear Aleppine background, Corti intriguingly, if tentatively, identifies the *Song of the*

---

[47] It was previously suggested by Houwink Ten Cate (1992: 117) that this *Song of Kingship* (*šarraššiyaš* SÌR) was in fact the name of the composition now securely identified as the *Song of Emergence* by Corti (2007).

[48] Corti 2017: 8. On cheese fighting in Hittite Anatolia, see Cammarosano 2014.

[49] *KBo* 42.2 i 15–18 (with duplicate *KUB* 44.7 i 11'–14', Archi 2009, 219): (15) *nu* LÚNAR LÚ-*na-an-na-aš* Š[(*A* A.AB.BA SÌR SÌR-*RU*)] (16) *a'-ru-na-an-za ma-aḫ-ḫa-an* ᵈ10 [(*tar-aḫ-ta nu ku-it-ma-an* (17) *iš-ḫa-mi-iš-kán-zi* LÚSANGA-*m*[(*a pé-ra-an*)] (18) *I-NA* ḪUR.SAG*AR-RA-NA* [(*pa-iz-zi*)].

[50] Both mountains are, to my knowledge, not yet attested elsewhere. Archi 2009: 219 n. 25 connects Mount Arrana with the town of Arana, attested in *KUB* 23.68 rev. 19, the treaty between king Arnuwanda I and the men of Išmerika (*CTH* 133, Beckman 1999: 17). Interestingly, the men of Išmerika are connected to a LÚSANGA in several letters unearthed in Ortaköy/Šapinuwa (Corti 2017: 12 with references).

Invocation of the Primeval Deities sung in *KBo* 23.7 with the *Song of Emergence*, in whose proem, as we recall, the primeval deities were called upon to listen. He further suggests that 'it is highly probable that some songs of Tešub's Cycle have been created, in their Hittite adaptation, in this very period under Tuthaliya II/III, perhaps in the same Šapinuwa' (Corti 2017: 11–12). The damaged *Vorlage* that was copied by Ašḫapala, as stated in the colophon of, probably an older, Early Empire Period erudite composition (Corti 2007: 120–1), was perhaps also composed in this context.

One can also speculate whether the SANGA-priest (^{LÚ}SANGA), mentioned in the two ritual fragments, is no other than prince Kantuzili, the author of several letters unearthed in Šapinuwa/Ortaköy (see most recently Süel 2017). Prince Kantuzili, son of king Arnuwanda I and brother of Tuthaliya III, was appointed as 'Priest' of Teššub and Ḫebat in Kizzuwatna. The title 'Priest' enabled the Hittite Prince to fulfil the religious duties of the King of Kizzuwatna, whose office was apparently dissolved earlier (Wilhelm 2010a: 379). Kantuzili the 'Priest' is also identified as the 'Author' of several rituals,[51] a Hurrian invocation to Teššub and Ḫebat (*KUB* 27.42, edited by Haas 1984: 113–19) and the famous prayer to the Sun God (*CTH* 373, Singer 2002a: 33–6, Schwemer 2015). The elaborate *Festival for Mt. Hazzi*, as reconstructed, was conceived in Šapinuwa, perhaps in commemoration of Tudḫaliya's coronation or his Syrian campaigns, reaching, for the first time in many years, the North Syrian coast.[52] The festival, which combines local Anatolian and 'foreign' Aleppine traditions, is a perfect illustration of a royal-sponsored festival functioning as a motor of religious and cultural exchange, as envisaged by Bachvarova.

Was the *Song of the Invocation of the Primeval Deities*, sung at Mount Irrāna according to fragment *KBo* 23.7, none other than the famous *Song of Emergence*, as suggested by Corti (2017: 12), thus intriguingly establishing a ritual context of performance to one of the better-known mythological narrative 'songs'? The terse and fragmentary passage in *KBo* 23.7 does not, unfortunately, allow a definite answer. Like all other chants performed in Hittite rituals, including most of the 'songs' performed at the *Festival for Mt. Hazzi*, the *Song of the Invocation of the Primeval Deities* was only ancillary to the ritual action itself, the invocation of the primeval deities at Mount Irrāna by the SANGA-priest, even if, and this may be significant,

---

[51] *KUB* 17.22 iv 1' and *KUB* 30.56 iii 7'. See Singer 2002b: 310.
[52] As suggested by Corti 2017: 11 with references to earlier studies.

no reason is given in the fragment itself as to why the primeval deities were invoked there in the first place. It was also probably performed by a group of male singers, not by an expert singer-poet. Moreover, as I have suggested, the 'invocation' of the primeval deities in the *Song of Emergence* was probably 'merely' a poetic device, simulating an oral context of performance. However, due to the close proximity of the ritual action depicted in *KBo* 23.7 to the performance of the *Song of the Manly Deeds of Sea* in other late copies of the *Festival for Mt. Hazzi* (*KBo* 42.2 i 15–18 and duplicate *KUB* 44.7 i 11'–14', presented above), the *Song of the Invocation of the Primeval Deities* may have indeed incorporated motifs and mythologems that originated in Aleppo or in the vicinity of Mt. Hazzi, even relating to the *Song of Emergence*. The question as to how the highly literary composition *Song of Emergence* interrelates with the cultic chants it simulates must await further discoveries.

The *Festival for Mt. Hazzi*, as reconstructed by Corti, also bears upon the question of the transmission of the *Song of Emergence*, even if indirectly. As we have seen, the festival strongly reflects an Aleppine tradition, emanating from Northwestern Syria, where Mount Hazzi is located. As I have suggested elsewhere (Strauss Clay and Gilan 2014, and especially Gilan 2015b: 179–83), the *Song of Emergence* is intrinsically connected to the cult of the Storm God in Aleppo, as is especially evident in the singular portrayal of Kumarbi as his 'mother', as in a Hurrian prayer to Teššub of Aleppo (*KUB* 47.78, cited earlier). It was therefore argued that the kingdom of P/Walastin, which controlled both the temple of the Storm God of Aleppo and Mount Hazzi on the bay of Iskenderun, played a key role in the continuity of the cult of the Storm God of Aleppo into the first millennium BCE.[53] Therefore, it may have played an instrumental role in the passing on of the myth to the Greeks. Further support for the survival of the myth is now found in two recently published parallel inscriptions from Arsuz, located south of the bay of Iskenderun. The inscriptions are attributed to a certain Suppiluliuma, son of Manana, king of P/Walastin, dating, on palaeographic and stylistic grounds to the late tenth century (edited by Dinçol et al. 2015). As now shown by Weeden, the inscriptions contain yet another reference to Kumarbi (written Kumarma in the inscription) as a mother (*ARSUZ* §§ 4–5; Weeden 2018: 352–3).

---

[53] On the kingdom of P/Walastin, see Weeden 2013.

CHAPTER 2

Siting the Gods
Narrative, Cult, and Hybrid Communities in the Iron Age Mediterranean

Carolina López-Ruiz

Scholarly Narratives and Travelling Myths

When we study Greek and Near Eastern divine narratives, the investigation of their shared features often stops at the literary or mythological level.* Comparative studies of these literatures and mythologies, thus, can seem uncommitted to addressing questions of transmission and context.[1] The task is not easy, especially when dealing with the earlier Iron Age, when it is extremely difficult to pinpoint places where the transmissions or adaptations of specific narratives may have happened. Efforts to answer these questions, however, have grown exponentially in the last decade, with particular attention to specific regional contexts and literary corpora, as well as to the methodological challenges of comparativism.[2]

One such praiseworthy attempt to attach mythological narratives to material and geographical traces across the Mediterranean has been made by Robin Lane Fox in his monograph *Travelling Heroes: Greeks and their Myths in the Epic Age of Homer*.[3] Merging archaeological and literary sources, Lane Fox follows moving stories, adapted and transformed by Greeks from various Near Eastern traditions. His master narrative, however, is quite one-sided. He follows a trend that sees Euboeans 'everywhere', and postulates the travelling Euboean as the leading force behind the encounter between Greek and Near Eastern traditions in the early first millennium BCE. Accruing archaeological evidence and a careful

---

* This chapter has been written within the framework of the research project FFI2015–66484-P (co-ordinated by Marco Antonio Santamaría Álvarez) supported by the Spanish Ministry of Economy, Industry, and Competitiveness. I want to thank the volume editors for their careful review and helpful suggestions, as well as my colleagues Benjamin Acosta-Hughes, Fritz Graf, and Anthony Kaldellis for their assistance with particular points of this research.

[1] See the Introduction to this volume.
[2] See discussions in Nagy 2005 (on Greek epic), López-Ruiz 2010, 2014a (esp. on Northwest Semitic conduits), Doak 2012: 25–50 (Hebrew Bible), Moyer 2011 (Egypt), Bachvarova 2016: esp. 199–218 (Anatolia), and Currie 2016: esp. 200–22 (Homeric and Mesopotamian epics).
[3] Lane Fox 2008.

consideration of literary evidence, however, can be used to illustrate a more complex interaction between Levantines, Greeks of different origins, and other, almost-invisible native groups of the Iron Age. As I have argued elsewhere,[4] without excluding Euboeans and others, the group of Northwest Semites whom the Greeks (and we after them) called Phoenicians had a crucial role in the transfer of Near Eastern narratives. This is not a new idea, of course. The sheer proximity, westward enterprises of the Phoenicians, and frequency of interaction with Greeks in various scenarios (in Cyprus, Crete, the Aegean islands and mainland harbours and sanctuaries, and in Greek colonial realms such as Sicily and southern Italy) makes them the most familiar Near Eastern interlocutors for the Greeks. Simply put by James Whitley, 'Of all the peoples of the Levant, the Phoenicians were by far the most important, at least as far as Greeks were concerned.'[5] This view contrasts with recent works that downplay the Phoenician element in the so-called orientalising phenomenon from an art-historical perspective,[6] or that contest the validity of the Phoenicians as a historical entity at all.[7] It is not the goal of this essay to engage in this complex debate,[8] or to unnecessarily problematise a historical and ethnic-cultural category well established in antiquity.[9] Instead, I look at specific contexts where this contact with Northwest Semitic peoples, clearly including Phoenicians, is illuminating for particular sets of mythological narratives.

In terms of modes of contact, Lane Fox reads the Greek adaptations of Near Eastern characters, or epic-mythic motifs, in a rather rigid way, as the fruit of 'wishful interpretations', 'verbal coincidences', and other such types of creative misunderstandings.[10] The assumption is that variants in the motifs stem from an inherent misunderstanding of each other's religious narratives and languages, that is, that the borrowings happened *in spite of* the cultural divide, a view that largely leans on Momigliano's work on later periods, especially the Hellenistic milieu.[11] By contrast, I am not

---

[4] E.g., López-Ruiz 2010: esp. 23–47, 2014a.
[5] Whitley 2001: 110, cf. 105–6; cf. Burkert 1992: 21; Morris 1992; West 1997: 624–30.
[6] Feldman 2014; Martin 2017 [7] Quinn 2017.
[8] See López-Ruiz (forthcoming) and an impending monograph entitled *Phoenicians and the Making of the Mediterranean*.
[9] For a solid, source-based history of Phoenicia, see recently, Elayi 2018, Sader 2019; for their trading and colonial expansion, Aubet 2001, Lipinski 2004.
[10] Lane Fox 2008 *passim*, e.g., 221 about Mopsus. For a contrasting view of the same figure, see López-Ruiz 2009a.
[11] See, for instance, Lane Fox's statement that 'Greeks made little effort nonetheless and generally understood what they saw only in their own Greek terms. The underlying content was "lost in translation"' (Lane Fox 2008: 210); or that 'an informed contact with Near Eastern stories and

alone in seeing the transfer and adaptation of motifs as a by-product of a more profound process of hybridity caused by long-term coexistence. At times, we can even postulate an intentional adaptation of tropes and literary techniques by poets experimenting with new genres in archaic Greece (as I have argued for Greek cosmogonies).[12] In other words, the literary and mythological entanglements, for the most part, followed the human entanglements. Cultural complexity brought the expansion of the literary, religious, and symbolic repertoire, while in every instance the success of the adaptations depended on the success in making the new version locally meaningful.

This essay is not about presenting *new* archaeological or literary evidence of contact, even though some details may be new to some readers. As is the case for most works on this topic, my goal here is to contribute to the arduous scholarly reconstruction of how, where, and who transmitted divine narratives. By highlighting a slightly less familiar line-up of sources, I advance an alternative divine narrative focusing on Iron Age cultural interaction. At the first level, I follow a different trail than Lane Fox to trace shared Greek and Near Eastern myths to concrete places. Zooming in at Al Mina and Mount Saphon in North Syria, Eleutherna and Mt. Ida in Crete, and the archipelago of Gadir in south-western Iberia, archaeological data and cultic history can be married with ancient narratives about the Greek Storm God and his Semitic counterparts Baal, Melqart, and his incarnation as Heracles-Melqart. By moving our attention from the familiar Hesiodic Succession Myth (on which Lane Fox relies) to the Storm Gods' 'Life Cycle' narratives (birth-fight-death), what comes to the fore are not Euboean routes and Hesiodic narratives but Greek and Phoenician cultural and physical crossroads, in which the main god's 'biography' was tied to cultic activity. Secondly, at a 'meta' level, I offer my own

---

practice seems suggestively far from their reach' (227). Both statements evoke the attitudes of Momigliano 1975.

[12] See López-Ruiz 2010, and other references in note 2 above. Although Burkert, West, and others have also occasionally resorted to the idea of misunderstandings to explain the Greek side of the reception of literary/mythological motifs, their view of the relationship between these cultures was not built on an assumption of misunderstanding and intellectual or linguistic incompatibility. For instance, for Burkert (e.g., 1992, 2004) myths could travel and be adapted together with elements from a larger system of religious beliefs, wisdom, and ritual practices. Most recently, Bonnet and Bricault 2016 and Parker 2017 have expanded the study of 'moving gods' and (especially in Parker) their names and epithets, and show the mechanisms and the ease with which Greeks identified their and Near Eastern gods.

scholarly counternarrative, arguing that the map of the archaic Mediterranean often presented to us can be read in a Phoenician key (among others), moving the axis slightly away from the dominant Hellenocentric scholarly narratives, exemplified by Lane Fox and the work of others before him, especially John Boardman.[13]

At the end of my essay I offer some insights into the long trail of this particular tradition about Zeus and Melqart, which points to the tradition of euhemerism and the productive mutual identification of Greek and Phoenician gods prevalent in the Classical and Hellenistic period and onwards.[14]

But first, a general methodological disclaimer. I am not implying that we can read these sources as straightforward witnesses of Iron Age or archaic traditions. Selection, manipulation, distortion (= what Lane Fox characterises as 'misunderstandings'), and even invention are always part of the ongoing creation of these stories. Even so, we cannot discard the few precious sources that we have, chronologically scattered though they are. We are engaging in a task of 'archaeological' recovery and need to pay attention to the stratigraphy of the texts. But the prevailing Hellenocentric narratives, it should be noted, also resort to many of the same sources to reconstruct archaic mythical networks (e.g., Euboean), while not bothering to look into others and leaving aside more obscure threads of mythologies that do not conform either with Greek conceptions or with ours. Moreover, threads of information and tradition can be astonishingly long-lived within the written trail, and sometimes a late source (e.g., the scholia or the *Souda*) might be priceless sources for ancient traditions otherwise lost. In matters of cosmogony, for instance, ancient authors easily tend to reproduce earlier materials, and both old and new can coexist and be useful for the modern scholar: such is, for instance, the case with Philon of Byblos' Graeco-Phoenician euhemeristic cosmogony, where both Greek and demonstrably Canaanite mythical elements have merged, as indeed they had probably been already inseparable within Phoenician tradition for centuries.

---

[13] The Euboean dominance was already stressed in Boardman 1999, especially regarding Al Mina: cf. Boardman 2001, 2005, although he presents a more open view in his latest works (e.g., 2016). See also the Euboean emphasis in Popham and Lemos 1995 and Lemos 2002. For criticism, cf. Papadopoulos 1997 (and cf. 2011 for an update on the debate). Similarly, Malkin 2011 relegates the Phoenicians to the margins of Greek networks.

[14] On the range of the process of *interpretatio*, as well as the different mechanisms of additions of names or epithets to Greek gods, see Parker 2017: esp. 33–77.

Coming to Power in The Levant: Baal at Mount Saphon

The Late Bronze Age epics from Ugarit contain the essential elements of a long-lived narrative about the Storm God: divine kingship and a god who fights, dies, and comes back. At the centre of the *Baal Cycle*, the Storm God, who is the putative son of Ilu (or El) but the real son of Dagon, fights against the sea, 'Prince Yammu (Yam)'. This watery enemy is imagined as a serpentine monster, also called Litan (whence later Hebrew Leviathan), described as 'the Fleeing Serpent', 'the Twisty Serpent, the Potentate with Seven Heads', and 'the one who wields power with Seven Heads'; when Baal annihilated him, 'the heavens grew hot, they withered'.[15]

The fight between the thunder-bearer and a dragon or snake-like enemy is a most productive motif of divine epic, with a very long trajectory even into Medieval times through imagery of cavalry fights and Saints' battles.[16] Staying in our area and time, we can point to Leviathan's challenge against Yahweh in the Hebrew Bible,[17] and to the challenge to Zeus by Typhoeus/Typhon in Hesiod's *Theogony*, an epic battle revisited in the *Hymn to Apollo*, where it is re-enacted in the god's fight with Python, the serpent monster who had received and protected Typhon after his birth from Hera.[18] Already in the Bronze Age, the Hurrian and Anatolian traditions that poured into Hittite texts feature serpentine cosmic enemies, such as Illuyanka and Hedammu, while the mountain enemy Ullikummi also emerges from the water to defy the Storm God Teshub.[19] The motif's mobility across even Indo-European and Near Eastern mythologies has long been noted, embedded *within* the shared pattern of the succession of gods.

The Olympian version of the fight was situated on Mount Kassios, in the Greek tradition as transmitted by Apollodorus (1.39).[20] This is the first stop in our tour: today called Jebel al-Akra, this peak is no other than Ugaritic Saphon/Sapan (depending on hypothetical vocalisation). This is where Baal celebrated his triumph and Kothar-wa-Khasis built the palace for the Storm God. Saphon/Sapan is 'his royal throne', his 'resting place,

---

[15] As Mot ('Death') refers to him (*Baal Cycle*, CAT 1.5.I, transl. Smith 1997: 141).
[16] Rojas and Sergueenkova 2014.
[17] Is. 27:1, Ps. 74:14, Jb. 3:8, 4:25. A 'typhoon'-like Yam ('Sea') appears as Yahweh's enemy in the Hebrew Bible too: Ps. 74:13, Jb. 7:12, 26:12, 38:8; cf. Ps. 29; also Rutherford, Chapter 11 in this volume.
[18] Th. 820–80; h.Hom. 4.334–74. Demarous (a title of the Storm God Belos/Baal) fights Pontos (the Sea) in Philon's *Phoenician History* (Eus. PE 1.10.28).
[19] Güterbock 1948, Bachvarova 2017: 149–76 for a recent translation.
[20] Noted by Güterbock 1948: 131.

the seat of his dominion', which the god himself calls 'my mountain, Divine Sapan', 'the holy mountain of my heritage' (*Baal Cycle, CAT* 1.3. IV).[21] This mountain was also for the Hittites the scene of the Storm God's divine battles, called Mt. Hazzi. As has been noted, a transfer between the names of Baal's abode, Mount Saphon, and Zeus's own snaky enemy, Typhon, might be at play here.[22] We might be missing a Ugaritic narrative where Baal Saphon establishes his abode on the objectified defeated enemy, much as Mesopotamian Ea lives in the Apsu. The prevalence of 'mountain persons' (as Rojas calls them),[23] or monsters in mythological stories in Anatolia (where the Hurro-Hittite rock-monster Ullikummi confronts Kumarbi), might provide another clue in the incomplete chain of connections.[24]

At what point the Greek tradition transmitted in Roman times associated the Typhon myth with this Levantine mountain we cannot know, nor whether this landmark was consciously on Hesiod's radar. It is well known that this strip of coast in northern Syria saw an intense traffic between Greeks and Northwest Semitic groups starting in the Late Bronze Age. Commerce and personal relations between the Mycenaean and Canaanite realms were extensive and intensive, and left traces in exchanged artifacts, as perhaps best attested by the impressive shipwreck at Uluburun, whose unfortunate crew was formed mainly of Mycenaeans, Cypriots, and Canaanites.[25] This line of communication must have remained alive through the Iron Age, to some degree, perhaps through the role of Cyprus as cultural intermediary. At the end of the 'dark' centuries, this same area sees some of the earliest points of intensification of Greek and Levantine contact: the site of the ancient port of Ugarit, Rass al-Bassit (probably ancient Posideion), survived the catastrophic transition from the Late Bronze to the Iron Age, and was a port of call for Greek, Cypriot, and Phoenician merchants. Most famously, not far on the other (Turkish) side of the Orontes lies Al Mina. Both ports flanked the highest and most sacred peak by the coast. Pottery imports, not texts, are witness to the importance of these meeting points. But this is only a well-documented token of the much broader Greek interaction with the Northwest Semitic world, traces of which can be seen in our extant divine narratives. The area of North Syria and Cilicia, for instance, was one of the most continuous

---

[21] Translations by Smith 1997: 112–13.
[22] López-Ruiz 2010: 109–13 (Typhon–Saphon). For the range of ancient sources for Typhon, see also Ballabriga 1990 and Fowler 2001–13: I.27–30.
[23] Rojas 2019, chapter 3.   [24] Recent studies include Clay and Gilan 2014 and Corti 2017.
[25] Pulak 2008.

and resilient spaces for cultural contact between Aegean, Luwian, Phoenician, and Aramaic groups, as inscriptions in those regional languages and Greek names in them suggest (e.g., Ahhiyawa, Danuna, Mopsos, and Euarchos).[26]

Scattered pieces of the same puzzle are captured in archaic texts: Homer situates Typhon 'among the Arimoi' (*ein Arimois*, *Il.* 2.783), which probably points to the realm of the Aramaean states of the Syrian-Cilician area, and the B scholion on the same verse mentions that Typhon originated from an egg impregnated by Kronos in Cilicia;[27] Pindar places Typhon's birth in a Cilician cave, though he also imagines him dwelling by the volcanic areas of Cumae and the Aetna in Sicily (*P.* 1.16–20, 8.16); and it is also 'among the Arimoi' that Hesiod (*Th.* 304) places the hybrid creature Echidna (half nymph, half snake). Later historians such as Callisthenes, Strabo, and Pomponius Mela also point to the Cilician corner for a Greek tradition about Typhon, where mythical intersections with Anatolian and Semitic elements seem to map onto material, cultural, and perhaps ethnic entanglements.[28] In turn, as Lane Fox has emphasised, the fight between Zeus and Typhon was early on relocated from Syria and Cilicia to the central Mediterranean, resurfacing in areas where we also find hybrid communities, such as at Ischia/Pithekoussai.[29] This is a key link in his reconstruction of an Euboean trail. The emphasis is on the involvement of Euboeans in the colonisation of Pithekoussai,[30] their response to the volcanic emissions of the island, and their misinterpretation of the 'Arimoi' as a translation of *arima* ('monkey' in Etruscan), triggered in turn by the name of the island, 'Pithekoussai' (understood as containing the word *pithēkos*, 'monkey' in Greek).[31]

This is an example of a travelling iteration of one element present in the popular Greek Succession Myth. While the Euboean channel of transmission definitely has some traction, it is only part of the story. Different aspects of Greek cosmogony, including (but not exclusively) the *Theogony*, align with other cultural strands, inflected by Levantine motifs and not necessarily connected with Euboea. In the Canaanite tradition that was

---

[26] López-Ruiz 2009a and references there.   [27] Güterbock 1948: 131.
[28] E.g., Str. 13.4.6. See details and references in Lane Fox 2008: 292–301; West 1966: 250–1, on *Th.* 304; cf. West 1997: 303.
[29] Already in Pi. *P.* 1.18–20; cf. Str. 5.4.9, Hsch. s.v. 'Arimos'. See Lane Fox 2008: 407, n. 57. For this westernised Typhon, see Lane Fox 2008: 300–1.
[30] See Str. 5.4.9 for the Eretrians and Chalkidians as colonisers of the small island, who later abandoned it for Cumae in the mainland across.
[31] Lane Fox 2008: 132–5. The main source for this equivalence is Str. 13.4.6.

likely inherited by the Iron Age Phoenicians and other Levantines, for instance, the victory of the Storm God was not articulated as a Succession Myth. Instead, the narrative that has reached us focuses on the building of Baal's palace, his fights for power among peer, 'equal' authorities (Death and the Sea), and his death and eventual return to life and establishment in power. With Ilu/El (a 'Titanic' older god never banished) overseeing the new order, the Storm God's 'life-struggle-death' cycle (not the generational struggle) was at the centre. It may be that the Succession Myth, with the castration theme, is more tightly tied to Indo-European or Anatolian traditions (note, e.g., the Hurro-Hittite parallel for the castration), while the Titanomachy, with the figures of Kronos and Typhon, seems to belong to a Levantine, Northwest Semitic tradition, as I have argued elsewhere for these and other aspects of the Hesiodic cosmogony-theogony.[32] As pointed out above, the Typhon–Saphon connection might be tied to Phoenician presences and interactions with Greeks in both North Syria-Cilicia and the Bay of Naples, the latter attested epigraphically and materially, if not in Greek historiographical sources, which write them out of the colonial picture.[33] Curiously, we may find a lead for this connection in one of the fragments attributed to Epimenides, a key Cretan figure who is associated with cosmogonic and mythological traditions and with 'oriental' wisdom (and to whom I return below). In this mini-narrative, Typhon may have attacked Zeus's palace or abode directly, touching on the central theme of the Canaanite *Baal* epic, the building and establishment of the Storm God's palace. The tentative textual reconstruction would read:

> <ascended to the> royal palace while Zeus was <sleep>ing, won control <of the gates> and got <inside>. But Zeus came to the rescue, seeing that <even the royal palace had been taken>, and is said to have <kil>led (Typhon) <with a thunderbolt>.[34]

And indeed the trail of this narrative takes us to Crete and other places of interaction where Semitic presence is undeniable, and where non-mainstream Greek mythologies persisted for centuries.

---

[32] López-Ruiz 2010: esp. 84–129.
[33] For the Semitic presence in Pithekoussai, see, e.g., Docter 2000: 136–40, Docter and Niemeyer 1995, Ridgway 1994, and Kelley 2012.
[34] Phld. *De piet.* 61.1 (p. 46 Gompertz = *FGrH/BNJ* 457 F8, transl. David L. Toye; cf. alternative readings of the Greek text in Fowler 2001–13: I.97 (= F10).

Birth and Death in Crete: Zeus at Mount Ida

Our scavenger hunt leads us to Crete, another crossroads of Greek and Levantine interaction. That Zeus was born and raised on the island is a much better-known 'myth-fact' than the tradition that he also died and was buried there, probably because this non-Hesiodic tradition does not sound mainstream Greek, if Greek at all. The birth first: for Hesiod, the king of the gods came into the world on a cave at Lyktos, which he also calls 'the Aegean mountain' (*Th.* 477–91), although other mythical sources site his birth or raising in other mountains, and not only in Crete.[35] Some epic traditions report that he was entrusted to his aunt Themis, who gave him to the goddess or nymph Amalthea to be raised with the aid of a semi-divine goat.[36] He was also protected by the Couretes, male nymphs of sorts, who danced with clashing weapons to mute the cries of the infant, in some stories forming a whole army with other minor mountain deities known as the Corybantes.[37] So did Euripides' Maenads celebrate them (*Ba.* 120–3): 'O secret chamber of the Couretes and you holy Cretan caves, parents to Zeus, where the Corybantes with triple helmet,' as did also the *mystai* of Idean Zeus in Euripides' *Cretans* (fr. 472 Kannicht).[38]

And indeed, the episode is not firmly situated in myth on a single peak, or even a single region of the eastern Mediterranean, but the infancy of Zeus on Crete's mountains is a common trope, and it is on Mount Ida where the memory of the birth and hiding of Zeus left a most impressive material record. The unique deposits of orientalising and oriental materials in the Idean cave include bronze shields, bronze jugs, and ivories, among them one of the most representative orientalising *tympana* (although not really fitting the description of 'plates' or 'shields', as they are

---

[35] Hesiod's Lyktos (a town southeast of Knossos) cannot be reconciled with Dikte or Ida where Zeus is born in other traditions, and the epithet 'Aegean mountain' (*Th.* 484) need not be an allusion to the goat's role in nourishing Zeus, as the name was quite common (Aegean sea, etc.). There are Minoan sacred caves in the area, which may have been associated with Zeus's birth later on (West 1966 on *Th.* 484; Lane Fox 2008: 343). Other traditions situate his birth and raising in alternative mountains, e.g., Dikte, Trojan Ida, Messenian Ithome, Boeotian Thebes, Aegion in Achaea, and Olenos in Aetolia. On the myth's link to Ida, see also Lane Fox 2008: 344–5.

[36] Pseudo-Eratosthenes 2B8 D–K. The goat's protective skin was identified as the aegis by, e.g., Apollod. 2.7.5, and Hyg. *Astr.* 2.13.4; Callimachus is the first to name the goat itself Amalthea (*Hymn* 1.49); cf. Σ b *Il.* 15.229. The horn of Amalthea was already a source of wealth/plenty (e.g., Anacr. 361 *PMG*, Phoc. fr. 7 Gerber = Str. 4.15.6, Pherecyd. *FGrH* 3F42 = Apollod., *Epit.* 2.7.5). See Gantz 1993: 41–2 for more on the divine lineage of the goat and the story's other sources.

[37] E.g., in Call. *Hymn* 1.51–4.

[38] See Gantz 1993: 42, 147–8 for the many sources and variations on both groups.

often called).³⁹ These works of art contain narrative shortcuts themselves, the most famous one representing in Assyrianising fashion these protective *daimones* flanking a 'Master of Animals' who stands over a bull.⁴⁰

Coming down from the sacred mountain peak, we encounter the less well-known site of Eleutherna, where one of the richest collections of orientalising materials has been unearthed in recent decades, including evidence of Phoenician residence amidst the archaic Greek community. The settlement thrived in the middle of deep ridges on the way from the coast near Rhethymno to the peaks of Ida. The area was inhabited since prehistoric times, and Eleutherna's acropolis overflows with Greek and Roman remains dating all the way through the Byzantine period.⁴¹

Evidence of a thriving community from the ninth to the sixth centuries BCE comes from the necropolis known as Orthi Petra ('Upright Stone'). The site and its riches are now beautifully displayed in a new nearby museum. The Iron Age material from Orthi Petra shows a range of eastern Mediterranean parallels comparable to the assemblages from the most acclaimed cross-cultural centres of this period, be it Euboea, Olympia, Delphi, Samos, Perachora, or on Crete, Knossos, and Ida. The range of pottery types, gold jewellery, bronze and ivory work, lamps, and faience and glass objects point not only to the broader Aegean world and even southern Italy, but especially to the Levant and Egypt, with a strong presence of Cypriot, Phoenician, and 'Cypro-Phoenician' items, including orientalising shields of the sort attested in Mount Ida and elsewhere.⁴²

Among the various types of burials represented, the most surprising are four tombstones of a type attested only in Phoenician cemeteries, which are unequivocal proof of Phoenicians living and dying in Crete amidst Greeks.⁴³ A four-meter-tall obelisk also stood out in a regular archaic Greek necropolis, as did the strange cenotaph, which the excavator, Nikos Stampolidis, thinks was intended to commemorate the fallen warriors of the community. The archaic-style warriors sculpted at the top of the monument are particularly interesting, and he thinks they could represent Zeus's guardians, the Couretes. For Stampolidis, some other

---

[39] See Gunter 2009: 152, 100–1.
[40] Burkert 1985: 280, with general discussion of the Cretan Couretes and their mysteries in and 281–5 for the Kabeiroi and especially their cult in Samothrace. See also below. For orientalising Crete, the Idean cult (as well as the oriental traits of the cult of Apollo in Crete), and the *tympanon*'s origins, see also Burkert 1992: 63, 167 n. 42.
[41] See Stampolidis 2004. [42] For the necropolis, see Stampolidis 2002.
[43] Stampolidis 2016: 294; see also Stampolidis 1990 about the tombstones. For the implications of Phoenicians in Crete, see Stampolidis and Kotsonas 2006.

materials in the necropolis evoke the world of Homeric epic, such as a funeral pyre-burial that included banqueting skewers and the remains of a sacrificed man at the pyre's base (it is hard not to think of the funeral of Patroclus in the *Iliad* and the captives slain at his feet).[44]

To return to the Cretan myths about Zeus, apparently the not-so-mainstream versions included the idea of a death and rebirth cycle. At least this is implied by a Hellenistic writer known as Boeus, cited frequently by Antoninus Liberalis and Athenaeus. He is reported to say that at the Idean cave Zeus was born anew every year, in a ritual that included fire and blood.[45] The tradition must have had some traction, as it passed on to sources read much later by the Church father Eusebius of Caesarea (an avid, if disparaging, reader of ancient cosmogonic myths), who refers to the tomb of Zeus among the Cretans, following a version of this divine biography to which we shall return at the end of this chapter.[46] What in mainstream Greek culture might have seemed a hyper-anthropomorphic motif, that of a dead Zeus, found a natural home in the reinterpretation of Greek mythology by Euhemerus of Messene, who took on (and spread) the trend of historicising mythological traditions we call Euhemerism, in a work paraphrased by Diodorus of Sicily and Eusebius (via Diodorus). Indeed, from fragments of his work *The Sacred History* or *The Sacred Inscription* (c. 300 BCE), we see the articulation of the atheistic concept through inscriptions and monuments, which, the author fancied, demonstrated the historicity of the gods underlying local cults, with special attention to Zeus and his deeds as king and benefactor.[47] The work is presented as a bizarre journey to the fantastic island of Panchaea, somewhere beyond Arabia. At least to some degree, Euhemerus seems to be drawing on Cretan traditions, and he presents Zeus as a former Cretan ruler turned

---

[44] *Il.* 23.215. Stampolidis 2016: 285, fig. 4. (Pyre LL 90/91).
[45] Boeus *ap.* Ant. Lib. 19; cf. Pythagoras' initiation to the Idean Dactyls in Porph. *VP* 17. See Burkert 1985: 127, 280. It looks like Boeus wrote an *Ornithogony* ('Birth of the Birds'), maybe a parodic text (cf. Aristophanes' bird-centred parodic cosmogony, *Av.* 693–703).
[46] *PE* 3.10.20–2. See the partial quotation and comments below.
[47] For Euhemerus' fragments, see the edition of Winiarczyk 1991 and the study of Winiarczyk 2013. A treatise on the traditions about the 'earthly gods' was also attributed to him (Diodorus Siculus 4.1.3). For the burial of Zeus in Crete, Winiarczyk 2002: 40, ns. 51–3 (tombs of other gods listed in 197–8), also 2013: 33–41. For Winiarczyk 2013: 4–5, n. 23, 'Callimachus may equally well have been referring to the old Cretan tradition regarding Zeus' tomb, a theme also used by Euhemerus. Although Callimachus knew the Ἱερὰ Ἀναγραφή when writing *Iambus* 1, one cannot prove that he was alluding to this work in the *Hymn to Zeus*.'

euergetēs ('benefactor') for a fantastic island.[48] The island in fact may all but explicitly evoke Crete:

> There is on it [i.e., the island], on the summit of a towering mountain a sanctuary of Triphylian Zeus ... established there by Zeus himself at the time when he was king of the inhabited world and still dwelt among men. Within this sanctuary there is a gold stele on which are inscribed in the characters of Panchaea a summary account of the deeds of Ouranos, Kronos, and Zeus.[49]

The narrative of a 'dead Zeus' and mysteries associated with him is sited in Crete also through the figure of the Cretan sage Epimenides (mentioned above). The tradition of Zeus's Cretan tomb, in turn, was well known to Christian authors who engaged with the pagan idea of the dead gods, most famously Zeus, but also Dionysus and Asclepius (the latter, however, like Heracles, had human mothers in most accounts).[50]

Be that as it may, the otherwise universally 'un-Greek' idea of a dead god seems to have had a long life in Cretan folk traditions. One of these traditions moved away from Ida and placed the grave of Zeus specifically on Mount Juktas, south of Knossos, a mountain whose profile from afar was said to resemble that of the god. The deep fissure atop the important Minoan peak sanctuary on that mountain is today locally called 'the Tomb of Zeus', although the trail for this particular tradition is lost in the Middle Ages.[51]

---

[48] The name Panchaea seems to contain the Doric term *chaios* meaning 'good' (i.e., 'all good'). Doric dialect was used in Crete, which had three tribes (like the Doric states) and was considered the motherland of the Panchaeans (Zeus arrived from Crete, establishing his cult among the autochthonous inhabitants): see Clay and Purvis 1999: 101–2, nn. 12, 15. Crete is also perhaps the utopic island of Plato's *Republic*, and Atlantis is also called 'sacred' in *Critias* 115B (Clay and Purvis 1999: 101 n. 10).

[49] Euhemerus *FGrH/BNJ* 63, F2.5 = Eus. *PE* 2.2.57–9 = D.S. 6.1 and 5.46.1 (Cretan link) (transl. Clay and Purvis 1999: 99–100, 105); cf. Baumgarten 1981: 80–1. On the author, see Whitmarsh 2015: 152–5. The 'characters of Panchaea' are supposed to be hieroglyphs, cf. D.S. 5.46.7 further in the same text (Clay and Purvis 1999: 100 n. 7). Later in the same passage, Euhemerus has Zeus visit Kassios (who gives his name to the mountain) and then go to Cilicia and Syria, where he is entertained by Kilix and Belos, characters mapped onto the regions respectively (the latter as Semitic Baal).

[50] A poem on *The Birth of the Couretes and the Corybantes* was attributed to Epimenides, who was considered a Coures himself: Diogenes Laertius 1.109–15 (*FGrH* 457 T1). For the relevant fragments, see *FGrH* 457 F2 (= 41F Bernabé), F17 (= D.S. 5.79.4), and Callimachus' *Hymn to Zeus* 1.8 (II 42 Pfeiffer); see Winiarczyk 2013: 33–5 for more details and bibliography.

[51] Burkert 1985: 23, and 355 n. 21. The references go back to Evans 1921: 153–9. The sacred nature of Mount Juktas/Yuktas is marked by several sanctuaries, including the peak sanctuary at the top and the Anemospilia site lower down at the northern edge of the mountain, where there might be evidence of human sacrifice: Sakellarakis and Sarpouna-Sakellaraki 1997, cf. Hughes 1991: 13–17.

To close our brief Cretan stop, we know for sure that a very Canaanite-sounding narrative about Zeus as a rising and dying Storm God was sited in an area where a wealthy community including Levantine and other eastern Mediterranean merchants and artisans thrived. Iron Age Eleutherna, on the way to Mount Ida, marked physically the cultural crossroads at which our hybrid myths about Zeus were cultivated. Lane Fox does engage with the material evidence for Phoenician presence in Crete in the proximity to Mt. Ida, but chooses the model of imitation and adaptation for both orientalising materials and mythological motifs regarding the birth of Zeus: 'Myths about the god developed at the cave with the help of stories ultimately acquired by Greeks in the Levant, but its remarkable 'Oriental' range of offerings (i.e., at Mt. Ida) may be the exotic offerings of Cretan Greeks only.' Forced here to think beyond his Euboean framework, Lane Fox admits that 'the objects at the Ida cave may not point to Near Eastern worshippers, but they are a reminder that strong currents of eastern influence could run in the ninth and eighth centuries independently of Euboean carriers'. Still, he is explicit that such 'other' currents or influence in the Aegean (in his view still to be discovered) 'will not dislodge the scope of the Euboean trail which we have followed', insisting that 'this particular Euboean line and its consequences are singularly important and inter-linked'.[52] We now move to some of these other, non-Euboean links, which do not fit with Hesiod's Succession Myth (around which Lane Fox's route is largely constructed), or indeed with the familiar strands of Greek mythology and religion.

Rebirth in Tyre and Gadir: From Baal to Heracles-Melqart

Despite the fragmentary and chronologically dispersed nature of the evidence just discussed, something characteristically Phoenician is clear in the literary and archaeological material at the sites associated with Zeus's cult and birth-death narrative. And indeed the clearest version of the Storm God as a king deity who is born and dies comes from the Canaanite world, first in epic narratives about Baal, such as in the already-mentioned *Baal Cycle*.[53] Then, in the first millennium, the Phoenicians

---

For the Mt. Juktas tradition, see Winiarczyk 2013: 39–40 (with further references), and Karetsou 1981, who argues for an ancient origin. The area of Knossos (near Mt. Juktas) has also produced Phoenician and orientalising materials, including another tombstone (Kourou and Karetsou 1998), and the site of Kommos right across on the central-southern shores of Crete holds the key to a hub of mixed Greek-Phoenician commercial and cultic activity (Shaw 1989, 1998).

[52] Lane Fox 2008: 156–7 (quotations from 157).   [53] Smith 1997.

carrying the Canaanite torch had their own 'Baals', whose cults were surely accompanied by divine narratives that are now mostly lost.[54] But the Baal-equivalent at Tyre, Melqart, has left us more of a trail, in part thanks to the city's far-reaching colonial network. Specially relevant here is the annual death and resurrection ritual involving fire, the so-called *egersis* or 'awakening' of the god. We know little about it, but its connection with the dying and rising aspects of the Levantine Storm God are fairly obvious. The purifying and eternal-life-giving powers of fire, in turn, are not only attached to the 'Egyptian Heracles', as the Greeks called Melqart, but to the Greek Heracles himself, Zeus's son, through his death and apotheosis. The Phoenician trail will again take us, in the company of Herodotus, not to Euboea but to Tyre and Thasos in search for answers about which Heracles of the two was older and how there could be two of them, one an old god (Melqart) and one a divinised hero linked to a mortal mother and firmly situated within Greek collective memory in the distant heroic past, with other pre-Trojan War heroes.[55]

Skipping the chronological and mythographical discussion, I am interested in the trail of Greco-Phoenician interactions that the divine narrative of Heracles-Melqart leaves behind. The god's journey did not stop in the Aegean; his cult travelled from Tyre to the other end of the Mediterranean, to Gadir (Gr. Gadeira, modern Cádiz) on the Atlantic coast of Iberia, one of the oldest Phoenician metropoleis of the west, founded as early as the mid ninth century.[56] Not only do the topography and layout of the two island-cities mirror each other to an astonishing degree, but elements in their foundation stories and sacred landmarks also indicate a strong bond in their religious and symbolic landscape.[57] Melqart and Heracles fuse their stories there, in an interpretation that equates the Tyrian god-king not with the Storm God Zeus but with his son as a divinised, civilising hero and city-founder. At Gadir a most famous temple of the god marked the end of the known world and united the two axes of the Phoenician diaspora. In this Greco-Semitic tradition the temple was not only a house but also a grave of the god. As the native-Iberian geographer-ethnographer Pomponius Mela (writing in the mid first century CE) notes, the tradition

---

[54] On Phoenician literature, see López-Ruiz 2019.

[55] For Melqart, see Bonnet 1988, Bonnet and Bricault 2016: 21–44, and Parker 2017: 196–7 (on Thasos).

[56] See Aubet 2001, and 2019 for updated chronology and discussion of the westward expansion of Tyre colonisation, which recent excavations at the centre of Gadir (Teatro Cómico/Yacimiento Arqueológico Gadir) have proven to go back to the mid ninth century; see Gener et al. 2014.

[57] Álvarez Martí-Aguilar 2018, 2019.

that the temple guarded the actual bones of Heracles was a point of regional pride.[58] For centuries the temple and its incubation oracle was a landmark for the western Phoenicians, even into Roman times.[59] Most famously, at the outset of the Second Punic War, Hannibal visited the temple before departing on his epic crossing of Europe from Iberia to Italy. He thus created for himself a divine narrative of sorts as he followed the Heraclean route from west to east. As Richard Miles has argued, both Hannibal and his counterpart, the great Scipio Africanus, flirted with a euhemerised image of Heracles-Melqart, that is, of a god who could be conceived as both an historical figure and a precedent to their enterprises, a god who linked key points across a Mediterranean geography for which the two powers, Carthage and Rome, were competing.[60]

A Golden Age among the Atlantians

The far western Mediterranean and Atlantic shores beyond the Strait of Gibraltar were part of the Greek mythical imagination before we have any historical records about these regions. Stesichorus already situated here the fight between the three-headed monster Geryon and Heracles;[61] the western *eschaton*, where the sun dips into the Ocean, was also associated with the access to the Underworld,[62] and the ocean beyond the Straits was also the faraway home of Plato's imaginary Atlantids.[63] The proto-historic culture in southwest Iberia that the Greeks associated with these mythical episodes was known as Tartessos and emerged in the historical record towards the end of the archaic period. Tartessos' archaeological record marks it out as an orientalising culture thriving in the eighth to sixth centuries BCE, in unison with the arrival of Tyrian settlers

---

[58] Mela 3.46, cf. D.S. 5.20.1–3 for the temple.
[59] For the cultivation of Phoenician cultural and identity traits in Roman Turdetania (southwest of Iberia) with Gadir/Gades and the cult of Heracles-Melqart at its centre, see Machuca Prieto 2019.
[60] The Assyrian kings had already played this sort of king–god identification with respect to Marduk. For Euhemerism and culture heroes in the Near East, see López-Ruiz 2017c; for the Barcids, Miles 2010: 248, 314.
[61] Stesich. fr. 9 D–F (= Str. 3.2.11); cf. Anacr. 361 *PMG* (= fr. 4 Gentili-Prato = Str. 3.2.14).
[62] Strabo transmits traditions that Tartaros' name derived from 'Tartessos' (3.2.12), that Homer's Elysian Plains and Isles of the Blessed were there (3.2.13, referring to *Il.* 8.485–6), and that Erytheia (in Cádiz) was called the 'Blessed Isle' (3.2.11).
[63] Pl. *Ti.* 20d–25d, *Criti.* 108e–121c (esp. 114a–b, mentioning the region of Gadeira = Gadir). See the brief discussion in Celestino and López-Ruiz 2016: 103–4. For Iberia in the Greek imagination, see Gómez Espelosín 2009.

and their expansion in the coastal Peninsula from Almería to Cádiz to Lisbon and beyond.[64]

Phoenician colonisation of Iberia and North Africa, starting in the ninth century BCE, opened the far west to Greek explorers, Euboeans included. But direct knowledge of the world of the far western lands generally, and especially the peoples facing the Atlantic Ocean beyond the Straits, remained mainly within Phoenician and then Carthaginian circles until the Hellenistic period, with testimonies such as that of Pytheas of Massalia (fourth century BCE) as the exception.[65] Only then (after the second Punic War) did the entrance of Rome into Iberia allow for direct access to the west. Around the time of Hecataeus and Herodotus' enquiries, geographical and historical information about Tartessos (mainly mediated by Phocaeans) was slowly supplementing fantastic mythical allusions.[66] It is Herodotus who tells us about Arganthonius, a *basileus* of the Tartessians and benefactor of the Phocaeans in the sixth century.[67]

For the historian, the far west was hazy and its peoples included the 'Atlantes' living in the region of the Atlas mountains in North Africa.[68] The term, like Heracles' pillars chaining Africa and Europe, along with the Titan Atlas and the mysterious Hesperides (from Gr. *hespera* 'evening', also 'sunset', 'west'), evoked the circle beyond the straits between Iberia and North Africa, which was dominated by Phoenician-Carthaginian networks, including the Tartessic realm in Iberia. In this context we can place the only full mythical text stemming from Tartessos: the story of Gargoris and Habis, the first kings of the Tartessians, transmitted by the western Roman historian Pompeius Trogus (contemporary of Augustus) in his lost work the Philippic History, known from Justin's *Epitome* (of unknown date). The author was a Romano-Celtic who wrote about the West, and was, incidentally, our source for the foundation story of Carthage.[69]

---

[64] Celestino and López-Ruiz 2016: 125–72.
[65] For this travel account, see Cunliffe 2002. For the genre of *periploi*, see Celestino and López-Ruiz 2016: 47–9.
[66] See studies in Cruz Andreotti et al. 2006.
[67] Hdt. 1.163.1–4 (cf. Hdt. 1.165.1–2), and Hdt. 4.152.2–5 about an earlier encounter between the Greek Kolaios of Samos and the Tartessians. The Ionian connection is also clear in the allusion by Anacreon (see below).
[68] Hdt. 4.184.3–185.1. He professes ignorance of the lands further out in the Atlantic (3.115) but mentions the Atlas mountain, called 'pillar of heaven' by locals, and claims to know the names of all the 'Atlantes', the peoples living on the ridge of the mountain which 'extends as far as the Pillars of Heracles and beyond them' (4.185.1).
[69] *Epit.* 18.4–6; cf. Virgil's version in *Aen.* 1.418–57. For Carthage's foundation stories, see Lancel 1995: 20–2, Miles 2010: 58–62.

I will focus only on the opening lines of the legend, as they take us back in a circle to Crete and its mythical landscape (44.4.1–2):

> The forests of the Tartessians, in which it is said that the Titans waged war against the gods, were inhabited by the Curetes, whose most ancient king Gargoris was the first to collect honey. This prince, having a grandson born to him, the illegitimate offspring of his daughter, tried various means, through shame for her lack of chastity, to have the child put to death ...[70]

The story has obvious pan-Mediterranean elements, such as the heroic pattern of the child who is nearly killed by the king for fear of succession but ultimately survives and takes his rightful position (cf. Cyrus, Romulus and Remus, Oedipus, Moses). But it also feeds on Greek cosmogonic tradition, placing the Titans at the beginning of a Golden Age preceding civilisation. As a proper founder-hero, the child Habis will of course survive, miraculously protected by nature and fed by animals. He goes on to provide agriculture and civic order to his community, contrasting with the previous king Gargoris, whose link with the primitive world of hunting and gathering is represented by his introduction of honey. Some have seen here an indigenous story possibly about divine beings that was later historicised – i.e., euhemerised.[71] I have argued elsewhere that the civilising aspects fit within the 'first inventors' tradition, rooted most strongly in the Near East (Mesopotamia, Hebrew Bible), which by itself made it easier for eastern authors in Hellenistic and Roman times to historicise local myth, as we see in the fragmentary works of Berossus and Philon of Byblos.[72]

Most interesting is the presence of the Couretes as guardians of the forest of the Tartessians. This is not a simple Greek borrowing, I would argue, but a trope attached to myths of divine rearing and probably coming from a mythology of 'ages' in which they played a role. In other words, it is possible that this is a Tartessic version of a story of the rearing (and perhaps dying?) of Zeus, even part of a sort of Succession Myth, of the sort attested in Crete, which I argued was formed in a Greco-Phoenician context. This would have been a 'travelling myth' translocated to western shores (in Lane Fox's model), but in this case not carried by Euboeans either. Perhaps a key lies in Anacreon's verse, which brings together motifs mentioned above – the horn of Amalthea which nourished Zeus, and the wealth and longevity of the legendary king of the

---

[70] The translation is from Watson 1853 (modified); on Justin, see Yardley and Heckel 1997.
[71] de Hoz 2010: 484. See discussion in López-Ruiz 2017c.   [72] López-Ruiz 2017c.

Tartessians, all of which seem to have reached the sixth century Ionian poet's ears (fr. 361 *PMG*): 'I myself would not want the horn of Amalthea, nor for a hundred and fifty years to be king of Tartessos.'[73]

Trogus (or his source) was not the only one to place the rule of the Titans and hence Kronos in the far west. We find a strikingly close parallel to the Gargoris and Habis 'primitive' Golden Age setting in Virgil's *Aeneid* (8.319–31). Here Aeneas is received by Evander in the future territory of Rome, and he describes to the Trojan hero the land he sees and its mythical past: a land inhabited by Fauns (an allusion to Latinus' father, a kind of tree spirit called Faunus)[74] and by nymphs, and civilised by Saturn. According to the story, Saturn hid there (*latuit*, a pun with *Latium*), and during this Golden Age taught the natives the domestication of plants and animals and gave them laws.[75] Not only was Evander a culture hero himself, who introduced religion, writing, and laws,[76] but he was connected with the arrival of Heracles in Italic lands and the beginning of his cult (*Aen.* 8.184–275).

Some strand of this western cosmogony-theogony also made it to Philon of Byblos' *Phoenician History*. Following Greco-Phoenician trends of interpretation, this passage points to the Punic realm and the identification of Kronos with Baal Hammon (the main god of Carthage) and the broader western Punic realm (Libya, Sicily):

> The Phoenicians, whether by virtue of homonymy or in some allegorical way, have a different view of Kronos, as it is possible to see in the second book of Herennius Philon's *Phoenician History*. This history transmits that he was a king, as I said earlier, over Libya and Sicily and the western lands and that he founded a city, as Charax states, which was called Kronia at the time but now Sacred City, as Isigonus relates in his *On Palic Gods* and Polemon and Aeschylus in his *Aitna*, and as the whole of history has been interpreted according to Euhemerus ...[77]

The Biography of Zeus and Greco-Phoenician Euhemerism?

The resilience of this biographical trail of the Storm God is remarkable. It is not a coincidence that narratives about gods were transmitted through classical and Hellenistic into Roman times at precisely some of these

---

[73] (= fr. 4 Gentili-Prato) from Str. 3.2.14 (my translation).   [74] Ahl 2007 on *Aen.* 8.314.
[75] López-Ruiz 2017c: 282–3.   [76] E.g., Liv. 1.5.1; D.H. *Ant. Rom.* 1.31; Paus. 8.43.2.
[77] *FGrH/BNJ* 790 F5 (from John the Lydian, *On the Months* 4.154 [p. 170, 3–14 Wünsch], transl. Kaldellis and López-Ruiz 2009). The references we can trace correspond to Charax *FGrH* 103 F 32, Aeschylus fr. 11 Radt, and Euhemerus *FGrH* 63 T 4.

locales (Tyre, Gadir, Crete), or in association with them. These areas of contact are especially useful in helping us to retrieve Phoenician literature and mythology, which has been completely lost, but glimpses of which survive in Hellenistic and Roman historiography and antiquarianism, from Pompeius Trogus to Diodorus and Strabo, to Pausanias, Josephus, and Philon of Byblos. Sometimes it is only because of the attention paid to their 'pagan' content by early Christian authors that we can read about them. Thus in the last part of this essay I bring to attention these all-but-lost traditions via a passage by Eusebius of Caesarea, in which he traces ancient beliefs about gods who live and die inspired by the 'lives' of Zeus, from the Levant to Crete and the western Mediterranean. As pointed out above, Eusebius engages with a tradition of euhemerism. But Euhemerus, probably a Sicilian, was not the first or only one to rationalise religion and mythology. Others, from Xenophanes to Thales and Plato, had done it through allegory, natural philosophy, and plain expressions of atheism.[78] This tradition, however, was not alien to the Phoenician world (e.g., Philon of Byblos and Hannibal's use of the Heracles-Melqart figure), and I want to suggest that it became part of the construction of divine narratives attached to physical landmarks and sacred sites where Greek and Phoenician religions and folktales met. Again drawing on a long chain of previous sources, Eusebius states the following (*PE* 3.10.20–2):

> The first theologians among the Phoenicians, as we showed in the first Book,[79] had the recollection that Zeus – son of Kronos, born a mortal from a mortal – was a Phoenician by race (*genos*), while the Egyptians, appropriating the man, again recognised that he was a mortal, at least in this agreeing with the Phoenicians. And even the Cretans, who show the grave of Zeus in their territory, would be the third witnesses of the same thing. But also the Atlantians, and all those previously shown to have adopted Zeus according to their own local history, they all alike declared him a mortal, and recorded his mortal and human-like deeds – although they were not respectable or philosophical deeds, but rather absolutely full of complete indecency and lust.

Eusebius gives us, in a nutshell, the biography of a god, *the* main ancient god, who was born a mortal from Kronos, performed famous deeds (whether shameful or not), and died. Strangely, this odd passage traces for us a route from Phoenicia through Egypt to Crete and then on to the

---

[78] On pre-Hellenistic ideas of atheism, see Whitmarsh 2015: 75–124.
[79] This is a reference to Book 1 of Philon's *Phoenician History*, which fragments we have through Eusebius' quotations (from Porphyry) in his *Praeparatio Evangelica*; see Baumgarten 1981, with recent edition and commentary in *FGrH/BNJ* 790 (Kaldellis and López-Ruiz 2009).

far western Mediterranean. Although we cannot know for sure who Eusebius' source thought these 'Atlantians' were, this and other allusions by historians such as Herodotus and Diodorus of Sicily point to the far west.[80] It was in northwest Africa that the Titan Atlas gave his name to the famous mountain range and was imagined as holding the world while Heracles fetched the apples of the Hesperides. In Hesiod, Atlas holds up the heaven and is besides the Hesperides (*Th.* 517–20), and in an Homeric tradition he is the father of Calypso and 'knows the depths of the whole sea, and holds the tall pillars which hold earth and heaven apart' (*Od.* 1.52–4). Not coincidentally either, at Dido's Carthaginian court Virgil evokes the Titan Atlas as the mythological point of reference in relation to a cosmogony that happens to combine mythical and rationalising elements (perhaps following an euhemerised story?): the Tyrian cosmogony is sung by 'a student of Atlas, the maestro' (*Aen.* 1.740–7), who replaces the Muses as the source of poetic inspiration.[81]

Conclusions

In the route that I have followed, archaeological traces of cultural exchanges between Levantines, Greeks, and native groups can be connected at particular sites with ancient narratives about Zeus and his Semitic homologues Baal, Melqart, and his incarnation as Heracles-Melqart. At Al Mina and Mount Saphon in North Syria, Eleutherna and Mt. Ida in Crete, and the archipelago of Gadir in south-western Iberia, mixed communities are attested in tandem with a mythology about the life cycle of these gods. Their myths overlapped and underwent fusions and transformations when they were adapted, as Eusebius points out, to native histories.

Although this avenue of interpretation and the *longue durée* of these narratives deserves a separate, more in-depth treatment, this chapter has offered some clues and initial thoughts. Eusebius' work, for instance, is a fascinating source for pagan mythologies, given his polemic interest in refuting them, in this case for the euhemeristic narratives about the gods,

---

[80] *OCD*[4] s.v. 'Atlas'. Hdt. 4.184.3 is the first attested rationalising identification of the Titan with the mountains. Cf. D.S. 3.60 on the 'people of Atlas' (Atlas as bother of Kronos and father of the Atlantides) and 2.4.27 (Heracles restores the Atlantides to Atlas, here a brother of Hesperus). Besides knowing Euhemerus' work, Diodorus drew on lost ancient historians who wrote about the west, such as Timaeus of Tauromene (Sicily).

[81] In another post-Classical cosmogony, Apollonius of Rhodes evokes the 'age' of the Titans, ruled by Kronos and Rhea (1.493–515), while Zeus was raised in the Dictean cave on Crete.

attributed to ancient Phoenicians and Greeks. It is also interesting that the only substantial testimonies of Phoenician divine narratives we have, such as Philon's euhemeristic cosmogony and theogony, and a few other fragments of Phoenician cosmogonic thinking, engage with these rationalising trends, merging elements of natural philosophy and historicised mythology.[82] It is difficult for now to assess what this means in terms of the developments within Phoenician culture. As already noted, we are dealing with fragmented and almost totally vanished mythical-literary Phoenician traditions, where Philon (via Eusebius), Diodorus, and few others happen to be the main transmitters.

I cannot explore here the intersections between the narratives of divine and human kingship. That route would take us away from our topic and deep into Egyptian and Assyrian cultures and their influence on Phoenician religion and Hellenistic ideologies. The main point for our purposes is that euhemerism and traditional myth have one thing in common: unlike monotheistic religions, where the god becomes more of a philosophical abstraction, ancient Greek and Near Eastern gods have biographies – birth, journey, and sometimes even death. What Eusebius uses as proof of the aberrant pagan divine narratives, which transformed the gods into base humans, in fact preserves for us an important insight into one strand of Near Eastern mythical tradition. As in Euhemerus' 'fantastic journey', we have followed the trail of Zeus's lineage and his Canaanite-Phoenician doppelgänger who, as these late sources show, lived on even through fundamental philosophical transformations, from divine heroes of epic to quasi-historical, humanised figures.

Along the way, I have shown that the scholarly routes we can take to reveal the intersections between Near Eastern and Greek divine narratives are many, and not limited to Euboean ports of call, or to the Succession Myth pattern. There is a Phoenician trail that can be teased out despite the challenges posed by the sources. It is, historically, the 'losing' narrative, but one worth telling nonetheless.

---

[82] This type of trend is exemplified by the cosmogony attributed to Eudemus of Rhodes, and the one attributed to Mochus, both transmitted by Dam. *Pr.* 125 c (1 p. 323 Ruelle) (= *FGrH/BNJ* 784 F4, see López-Ruiz 2009b). On the Phoenician strand of this intellectual movement, see López-Ruiz 2017c and 2017b (on Philon of Byblos, not mentioned by Whitmarsh 2015).

CHAPTER 3

Politics, Cult, and Scholarship
Aspects of the Transmission History of Marduk and Ti'amat's Battle

Frances Reynolds

This chapter considers Mesopotamian expressions of the divine narrative of Marduk and Ti'amat's battle as scholarly productions situated in varying political and cultic contexts ranging from the late second to the late first millennium BCE.* The composition, transmission, and consumption of Marduk and Ti'amat battle mythology attested in Akkadian cuneiform texts is explored in relation to Mesopotamian, and particularly Babylonian, politics and cult. By assessing a range of compositions that have not previously been considered together, this chapter sheds new light on specific texts and on the creation and transmission of this combat narrative, especially in relation to Babylon's Esagil temple. These advances in knowledge contribute to our understanding of textual transmission and adaptation both within and between cultures.

Mesopotamian scholars deployed the combat myth of Marduk's victory over Ti'amat in different types of composition and in different contexts.[1] This battle was laden with political meaning, with the victorious god representing a human king, and was inextricably linked with ritual. This has fundamental implications for the myth's transmission. A key study by Frahm, published in two variant forms, investigated various responses to this narrative, especially with reference to Assyrian sources.[2] This chapter focuses on Babylonia and the role of Marduk's Esagil temple in Babylon. The corpus of sources includes a newly reconstructed calendar treatise, probably composed in the milieu of Hellenistic Esagil. Esagil's role and impact were responses to cultural change and interaction. Esagil with its associated cultic and scribal experts shaped expressions of this battle

---

* I would like to thank Adrian Kelly and Christopher Metcalf not only for their editorial support but also, together with Johannes Haubold, for their invitation to the *Divine Narratives in Early Greece and the Ancient Near East* conference, where I presented a preliminary version of this chapter.
[1] The absolutive form Ti'amat is established in modern scholarship, although a form with case vowel is probably correct (on *ti*-GEME₂, see, e.g., Borger 2008: 272–3).
[2] Frahm 2010b: 3–33 and 2011: 345–68.

myth. This demonstrates that interrelated political and cultic change can be fundamental to the composition, transmission, and consumption of mythological narrative.

A divine narrative dubbed *Enmešarra's Defeat*, followed by related material, occurs on a Late Babylonian tablet from Babylon, and Lambert considered this narrative to be a second-millennium forerunner to *Enūma eliš*, although a later date of composition is possible.[3] According to this narrative, Marduk defeated Enmešarra and sons in battle, decorating a wall and his seat with their commemorative representations, and thereby acquired the power of Enlil, the (at least initially) shared lordship of Anu, and the power of the Arrow star, as well as his city Babylon and temple Esagil.[4] A speech about city destruction also occurs in a recitation in Babylon's New Year festival in Nisannu, attested on another Late Babylonian tablet.[5] As an epilogue to *Enmešarra's Defeat*, the goat-fish praises Marduk, including references to his supremacy, Esagil, Babylon, and his unalterable words, both written down in the past and spoken.[6] The statements 'your cuneiform wedges were established in the past, / the utterance of your mouth cannot be changed' (column v 11–12 *santakkūku kunnū ina maḫar / ṣīt pîku ul uštepellu*) probably refer to the divine narrative itself, and this epilogue should be compared to the one in *Enūma eliš* (see below). Subsequent material on the tablet, possibly later in date, includes description of Babylon's New Year *akītu*-festival as attested in Nisannu: the gods assemble in Babylon and join Marduk in a martial procession to the *akītu*-house, accompanied by ritual performed by the Babylonian king.[7] It is possible that the speech about destruction only later became a component of the New Year festival and that the ritual material after the divine narrative is a Late Babylonian addition. If so, it could be argued that the latter at least indicates an increased focus on the relationship between a Marduk combat narrative and Babylon's New Year *akītu*-festival in Nisannu in the Esagil cult.

Marduk's defeat of Ti'amat is his best-attested battle victory. The fullest and most widely disseminated account occurs in the Akkadian narrative

---

[3] Lambert 2013: 281–9; see, e.g., Reynolds 2019: 1.8.2.2, cf. 1.7.3.2.1, commentary on § 4 i 28'–9' (Enmešarra–Qingu syncretism).
[4] Lambert 2013: 290–7, 493–4; Marduk is also allocated the Arrow star and the shared lordship of Anu in related material in column vi 18, 20–1.
[5] Lambert 2013: 283, 294–5, 494, column iv 18–27; Linssen 2004: 216–17, 225, lines 69–75.
[6] Lambert 2013: 283, 294–5, 494, column v 6–13; Lambert suggests that the goat-fish can be seen as the author.
[7] Lambert 2013: 296–7, column vi 1–17; on Babylon's New Year festival, see below.

poem *Enūma eliš*. There is a recent critical edition by Lambert and subsequent studies include Gabriel's detailed and insightful analysis of the poem.[8] The incipit *enūma eliš*, 'When on high', served as the ancient title and the epilogue describes the poem as *zamāru ša marduk*, 'song of Marduk'; however, the modern misnomer 'The Babylonian Epic of Creation' is sometimes still used.[9] This divine narrative validates and celebrates the rise of Marduk, the city god of Babylon, to supremacy over the Babylonian pantheon through his defeat and slaughter of the goddess Ti'amat, 'Sea', supported by her spouse Qingu.

In 2014 Gabriel surveyed the 184 primary sources for *Enūma eliš* known to him.[10] Drawing on his discussion, the following points are especially relevant here.[11] The standard format for *Enūma eliš* is seven two-column tablets, including a list of Marduk's names in Tablets VI–VII. The 184 sources in Babylonian and, slightly less commonly, Assyrian script include sixty-four tablets and one prism that are scribal training texts with extracts of *Enūma eliš* written by trainee scribes. This indicates the importance of *Enūma eliš* in scribal education, and the importance of pedagogy in the epic's transmission. In Assyria, sources come predominantly from Nineveh, some with seventh-century BCE Aššurbanipal library colophons, but also from the cities of Aššur, Kalḫu, and the outpost of Ḫuzirina in modern south-east Turkey; the great majority of sources from Babylonia are unprovenanced and were channelled through dealers in the late nineteenth century CE, but Babylon, Kiš, Mê-Turnat, Sippar, and Uruk are identifiable as find-spots. When precise find-spots are known, they can attest to cultic and royal connections: for example, tablets from Aššur and Ḫuzirina were found in the houses/schools of cultic experts; tablets from Kalḫu, Mê-Turnat, Sippar, and Uruk in temples; and a tablet from Kalḫu in a royal palace.[12] The oldest sources come from Aššur, dated to *c.* 1000 or 900 BCE, and all Assyrian sources predate the fall of the Assyrian Empire in the late seventh century BCE; Babylonian sources probably span the Neo-Babylonian to Parthian periods based on criteria including script and British Museum acquisition numbers. Gabriel analysed the twenty-one (mostly damaged) colophons on *Enūma eliš* source tablets from Aššur, Nineveh, Ḫuzirina, Mê-Turnat, and unspecified Babylonian sites, with identifiable dating in the period *c.* 700–500 BCE.[13] Colophons can include

---

[8] Lambert 2013; Gabriel 2014; see also Seri 2017.
[9] *Enūma eliš* I 1, VII 161; see, e.g., Gabriel 2014: 25–6, 108–11.
[10] Gabriel 2014: 29–70, 448–87.   [11] Gabriel 2014: 30–6.   [12] Gabriel 2014: 40–65, 77–81.
[13] Gabriel 2014: 36–40, 72–7.

information about the source material, tablet owner, and scribe; protective formulae invoking local deities; and the original setting of the tablet, including its location and date. For example, colophons on unprovenanced Babylonian tablets attest that one was copied from a wooden writing-board from Babylon; one was the tablet of a descendant of the *šangû*-priest of Ninurta; and one was dedicated to Nabû in his temple Ezida in Borsippa.[14] Studies of cuneiform scribal culture and textual transmission show that tablets and scholars could be mobile, so find-spots and colophons give limited information.[15]

As long argued by Lambert, *Enūma eliš* was probably composed in the milieu of Esagil under the Babylonian king Nebuchadnezzar I (1125–1104 BCE).[16] As Babylon's fortunes rose from a provincial backwater to the capital of an extensive territorial state, notably under Ḫammu-rāpi in the early second millennium BCE, the fortunes of Marduk as Babylon's city god also rose and in the course of that millennium he replaced Enlil as supreme god, becoming Babylonia's national god.[17] In the invasion of Babylonia by the Elamite king Kutir-Naḫḫunte in c. 1155 BCE, Marduk's principal cult statue was looted from Esagil, Babylonia's most important cult centre, and taken to Elam as booty. The Babylonian king Nebuchadnezzar I campaigned in Elam in c. 1105 BCE, retrieved Marduk's statue, and reinstalled it in Esagil amid great cultic celebration. With the correct ritual procedures, a god was believed to be immanent in his or her cult statue, so the looting and retrieval of Marduk's principal cult statue prompted a variety of historiographical narratives and theological explanations endowing the god with agency, rather than portraying his statue as the hapless pawn of warring armies.[18] The counterpoint of Nebuchadnezzar's victory over Elam and the restoration of Marduk and his Esagil cult probably triggered the composition of *Enūma eliš* as a celebration of Marduk's supremacy, including his victory over Ti'amat and foundation of this cult. Celebrating Marduk's supremacy inherently celebrated the supremacy of Babylonia and its king, Marduk's human counterpart. Ti'amat in *Enūma eliš* may have been analogous to Elam;[19] it is now known that this analogy occurs in a related calendar treatise of much later date (see below).

---

[14] Kämmerer and Metzler 2012: 151 Y+ (BM 45528+), 178–9 O (BM 40559), 227 B (BM 93016).
[15] See, e.g., Lenzi 2015: 170–1; on cuneiform myths and epics, including *Enūma eliš*, see Reynolds forthcoming.
[16] See, e.g., Lambert 2013: 3–4, 271–4, 439–44; Finn 2017: 44–7.
[17] For a nuanced study, see Tenney 2016. [18] See, e.g., Reynolds 2019: 2.2, 2.3.2.1.
[19] For a suggested development of this idea, see Yingling 2011: 37–8.

The narrative of *Enūma eliš* is briefly summarised here with a focus on the battle with Ti'amat and aspects relating to kingship and Esagil. It can be argued that material relating to Babylonian cult and specifically to Esagil is a major factor in the structure and content of this composition to an extent not previously realised. In Tablet I an initial theogony begins with male Apsû and female Ti'amat, deified fresh and salt water respectively, and culminates in male Anšar ('All Heaven') and female Kišar ('All Earth') having a son, Anu ('Heaven'), who begets his own son, Ea. Ea and the junior gods disturb Apsû and Ti'amat. Although Ti'amat defends them, Apsû plots their destruction but is killed by Ea in a pre-emptive strike. Ea and Damkina have a magnificent son, Marduk, in their new home, the cosmic realm Apsû formed from Apsû's corpse. Boisterous Marduk disturbs Ti'amat and, egged on by her supporters, she decides to annihilate him and his divine associates. Ti'amat musters a terrifying army, including eleven monsters, and appoints her spouse Qingu as commander-in-chief, awarding him the Tablet of Destinies. In Tablet II Ea reports on Ti'amat's murderous army to Anšar, leader of the junior gods. Anšar, Ea, and Anu in turn fail to face Ti'amat. At the instigation of his father Ea, Marduk offers himself to Anšar as the junior gods' champion against Ti'amat. Anšar accepts and Marduk demands that a joyous divine assembly in Ubšu-ukkinaki award him supreme power before he sets out to battle. In Tablets III–IV the assembled gods, convened by Anšar, feast and decree Marduk's destiny, and he is installed as supreme divine king. In Tablet IV Marduk keeps his side of the bargain and, armed with weapons including his bow, protected by magic, and supported by a divine army, he sets out to face Ti'amat and her army. After a battlefield exchange, the two protagonists meet. Ti'amat deploys aggressive magic against Marduk, but he traps her in his net and causes her to swallow the Evil Wind. This distends her belly as the perfect target for Marduk's arrow. After killing Ti'amat, he imprisons her allies, including the eleven monsters and Qingu, reckoning Qingu with the Dead Gods and commandeering the Tablet of Destinies. Marduk mutilates Ti'amat's corpse and her windborne blood signals his victory to the gods, who joyfully give him gifts on the battlefield.

In Tablets IV–V Marduk creates the earth and heavens by dividing Ti'amat's corpse and establishes shrines for Anu, Enlil, and Ea. Creation continues in Tablet V, as Marduk establishes the heavenly bodies to regulate the calendar, including his sovereign planet Nēberu, 'Crossing'. Marduk creates the heavens and earth, and gives the cosmic guide-ropes to Ea and the Tablet of Destinies to Anu. After reshaping Ti'amat's corpse,

Marduk installs commemorative images of the eleven monsters, his conquests, at the Gate of the Apsû. The joyful gods, after further gifts, do obeisance to Marduk. He cleans himself after the battle, arrays himself with royal insignia, and, enthroned in his cella, the assembled gods acknowledge him as Lugal-dimmer-ankia, 'King of the Gods of Heaven and Earth', and as the one who cares for their shrines. Marduk decrees that he will build his house, called Babylon, where the gods travelling from the Apsû and the heavens will stay overnight for a vigil before the decision-making assembly. Tablet VI opens with Ea creating man at Marduk's behest to free the gods from toil. Identified as the instigator of Ti'amat's attack, Qingu is killed to supply blood as man's animating principle. The grateful gods offer to make a shrine and a cella for Marduk, where they can stay overnight for a vigil. On Marduk's instructions, the gods build the first city, Babylon, and Marduk's temple Esagil, as well as their own shrines. After a joyful banquet in Esagil at Marduk's invitation, the assembled gods decree destinies for the proper running of the world. Anu names and catasterises Marduk's bow that launched the fatal arrow. Marduk is confirmed by the assembly as absolute king, and Anšar blesses him as the supreme god who will institute proper cult practices for mankind.

In Tablets VI–VII the gods award Marduk fifty names, with an assembly and ritual in Ubšu-ukkinaki. His names include allusions to him as the conqueror of Ti'amat and Qingu, the establisher of the cult of the gods, the recipient of gifts from the gods in the *akītu*-house, and the planet Nēberu. As in the explanatory works mentioned below, the list of Marduk's names makes elaborate use of wordplay and hermeneutics.

The epilogue in Tablet VII should be compared with the one in *Enmešarra's Defeat* (see above). The *Enūma eliš* epilogue prescribes that scholars (called *maḫrû*, 'eminent man'; *enqu*, 'wise man'; *mūdû*, 'expert') should study the poem, including transmitting it from father to son, and that they should open the ears of the king (called *rē'û*, 'shepherd'; *nāqidu*, 'herdsman'), so that, by not neglecting Marduk, the king and his land will flourish.[20] The didactic poem's transmission is probably attributed to an eminent/past man (*maḫrû*) speaking it in Marduk's presence, writing it down, and storing it for future listeners to hear.[21] The end of the poem is partially preserved on three tablets. A summarising couplet (*Enūma eliš* VII 161–2: *inannamma zamāru ša marduk / [ša] ti'amat ikmû(ma) ilqû šarrūti*,

---

[20] *Enūma eliš* VII 145–50; see Gabriel 2014: 84–92.
[21] *Enūma eliš* VII 157–8; see Gabriel 2014: 95–7.

'Here now is the song of Marduk, / [who] defeated Ti'amat (and) took kingship') concludes the epilogue on MS J from Ḫuzirina, followed by a double-ruling and a colophon; but on Neo- or Late Babylonian MS a, possibly from Sippar or Babylon, two broken lines follow this couplet before a double-ruling and probably continue the epilogue with material about a temple and Babylon (*Enūma eliš* VII 163–4; see further below).[22]

Enūma eliš had an intricate relationship with Babylon's New Year festival celebrated in the first month Nisannu and linked with the ideal spring equinox. Drawing on earlier tradition but chiefly attested in the first millennium BCE, this elaborate sequence of rituals, culminating in an *akītu*-festival when Marduk's statue processed to and from the *akītu*-house, could be seen as Babylonia's pre-eminent annual cultic event, and it confirmed the sovereignty of Marduk and his human counterpart the Babylonian king.[23] The main Marduk narrative in *Enūma Eliš* can be viewed as an origin myth and analogue for this *akītu*-festival.[24] Similarities between the Marduk narrative in *Enūma Eliš* and Babylon's spring New Year *akītu*-festival include the following: as Marduk's precondition for going to face Ti'amat, a divine assembly in Ubšu-ukkinaki decrees his destiny as supreme divine king (*Enūma eliš* II 153–IV 34); Marduk, supported by the gods his allies, advances to fight Ti'amat (*Enūma eliš* IV 59–70); he wins a battle victory over Ti'amat (*Enūma eliš* IV 71–106); he is showered with celebratory gifts by the gods, dons his royal insignia, and is enthroned in his cella (location unspecified) as supreme king by the assembled gods (*Enūma eliš* IV 133–4, V 77–116); after Babylon and Esagil have been built, Marduk enters his new temple, and the assembled gods decree destinies for the proper running of the world, confirm him as absolute king, and award him names with an assembly in Ubšu-ukkinaki (*Enūma eliš* VI 65–VII 144). These later assemblies frame a foundation myth: Babylon and Esagil are voluntarily built by the gods for Marduk in response to his decree, so they can assemble there to decree the world's

---

[22] In MS b, attributable to Late Babylonian Babylon, the final traces before a lacuna have been allocated to a colophon but could also be relevant. On MSS J, a, and b see Lambert 2013: 122–3, 132–3 VII 161–4; Gabriel 2014: 37, 73, 83, 97; Kämmerer and Metzler 2012: 314 (MS J = H; MS a = P; MS b = Q). On the provenance and dating of MS a (BM 91139 (82-9-18, 12220) + 93073 (82-9-18, 5647)+) and MS b (BM 35506 (Sp. III 12) + 99642 (83-1-21, 2004)) see Leichty 1986: xxxiii–iv; Clancier 2009: 192–3.

[23] See, e.g., Zgoll 2006; Ristvet 2015: 153–210; Deloucas 2016; Tenney 2016. Related ritual in Babylon in the seventh month, Tašrītu, affirmed kingship at the start of the year's second half (Ambos 2013). As attested, the Nisannu New Year festival had specific links with Marduk's victory over Ti'amat and is the focus here, but the less well-attested Tašrītu festival may also have been related to this ideology.

[24] See, e.g., George 1992: 286–91; Zgoll 2006: 43–4, 58.

destinies after an overnight vigil (*Enūma eliš* V 117–42, VI 47–100). Marduk was born in the Apsû, the domain of his father Ea, and when this narrative sequence begins, he does not yet have a domain or temple of his own (*Enūma eliš* I 79–82). Through a structured sequence of events (destiny-decreeing assembly – journey to battle – battle victory, celebration, and enthronement – journey to Esagil – destiny-decreeing assembly in Esagil), Marduk achieves supreme kingship and a permanent home of his own in the form of Esagil in Babylon, the gods' final assembly place.[25] It can be argued that the cella of post-battle celebration and enthronement is a mythological analogue to Babylon's *akītu*-house outside the inner city.

In Babylon's New Year *akītu*-festival, the start- and end-point for Marduk's statue in procession was his cella Eumuša in Esagil; on Nisannu days 8 and 11 in Esagil's Ubšu-ukkina courtyard there were assemblies of the gods before Marduk, when his statue was enthroned as the divine king on the Dais of Destinies; these assemblies framed the ritual processions on days 8 and 11 to and from Babylon's *akītu*-house, when Marduk's statue was accompanied by the Babylonian king and representations of gods, some brought to Babylon from other Babylonian cities for this festival; the two processions, representing Marduk's battle advance against Ti'amat on the way out and his original triumphant entry into his new temple Esagil on the way back, framed his victory and post-battle celebrations; the latter at least – in the form of Marduk's enthronement before the gods, gift-giving, and feasting – were set in Babylon's *akītu*-house in an uncertain location to the north of Babylon's inner city wall.[26] There is a ritual progression from and return to the principal seat of Marduk's authority, his cella Eumuša. A pair of destiny-decreeing assemblies in Ubšu-ukkina, where Marduk is declared king of the gods, frame the round trip to the *akītu*-house outside the inner city. Ritual tablets for events in the *akītu*-house are not extant, but it is attested in other sources as a structure where Marduk rested after the battle and celebrated his victory. The battle itself is linked with both the outward procession and the *akītu*-house.[27] In this ritual it can be argued that Eumuša in Esagil and the *akītu*-house are two seats of power of Marduk: the first is his long-term residence at the cultic heart of the inner city and the second is his short-

---

[25] On structure in *Enūma eliš*, see, e.g., Gabriel 2014: *passim*, including chapters 3–4; cf. Seri 2017: 835–6.
[26] See, e.g., George 1999: 70–7; Löhnert 2014: 268–9.
[27] Zgoll understood a ritual involving a *ḫarû*-vat performed before the procession moved away from Esagil as the key representation of Ti'amat's defeat followed by a victory procession to the *akītu*-house, but this is unlikely (Zgoll 2006: 34–40, 58–60). The link between a *ḫarû*-ritual and

term residence located outside it, a post-battle pavilion for a victorious warrior. The two cultic structures form the ritual's fixed spatial extremes, counterpoints balanced in a carefully constructed ritual framework.

Thus, Marduk's killing of Ti'amat and securing of kingship is pivotal both in the poetic narrative in *Enūma eliš* set in mythological/primeval time and in the ritual narrative in Babylon's New Year *akītu*-festival, designed for annual repetition each spring. In *Enūma eliš* VI the divine and human worlds intersect when man is created with the potential to relieve the gods from toil. However, to Marduk's greater glory, it is the grateful gods who voluntarily build for him Babylon and Esagil, as Babylonia's pre-eminent city and temple. There is probably an earlier aetiology for Ea's Ekarzaginna temple in the Esagil complex, when Marduk is said to install images of Ti'amat's eleven defeated monsters in the Gate of the Apsû to commemorate his victory (*Enūma eliš* V 73–6).[28] Marduk's victory and Babylon's New Year *akītu*-festival are linked in the list of Marduk's names, when he is called Dingir-Esiskur ('God of Esiskur'), with a prayer that he sit on high in the house of benediction (*bīt ikribī*, an Akkadian rendering of Sumerian e$_2$-siskur$_2$) and receive gifts brought in before him by the gods (*Enūma eliš* VII 109–11).[29] In the longest name entry and the last one before the Enlil and Ea names, the planet Nēberu controls the stars' crossing point, possibly at the turn of the year (the time of the spring New Year festival), and represents Marduk conquering Ti'amat (*Enūma eliš* VII 124–34).[30] At least two passages in the epilogue probably allude to the Esagil cult and possibly both to the New Year festival in Nisannu.[31] One passage probably prescribes priestly and royal participation in this festival, perhaps specifically the 'negative confession' ritual performed by Esagil's high priest and the Babylonian king in Eumuša, Marduk's cella in Esagil (*Enūma eliš* VII 147–50). The other passage may ascribe the origin of *Enūma eliš* to instruction that the high priest spoke before Marduk's statue and recorded in writing for future

---

Ti'amat's defeat is a comment in a ritual explanatory work relating to Babylon that is attested on a tablet belonging to a seventh-century BCE exorcist in Aššur and copied from a Nineveh source (Livingstone 1989: no. 37, 18'). Works of this nature interpreted a wide range of actions in different rituals in terms of various combat myths and probably added secondary mythological meaning to ritual specifics, rather than expressing embedded meaning (Frahm 2011: 339–44; see also below).

[28] See, e.g., Reynolds 2019: commentary on § 2 i 5'–6'.

[29] A Nabonidus stele from Babylon records that on Nisannu day 10, Marduk, as king of the gods, and the gods of heaven and underworld sit in Esiskur, the house of benediction (*bīt ikribī*), the *akītu*-house of Enlil's position, the latter signifying divine supremacy (Schaudig 2001: 3.3^a IX 3'–10').

[30] Gabriel 2014: 223–31. On Nēberu, originally signifying Mercury(?) but later Jupiter, and the turn of the year see Horowitz 2014: 6–8, 20–5; cf. Hunger and Steele 2018: 177.

[31] Gabriel 2014: 84–97.

kings to hear (*Enūma eliš* VII 157–8; on the epic's recitation see below). As outlined above, on Neo- or Late Babylonian MS a, possibly from Sippar or Babylon, the epilogue may end with two lines concerning a temple and Babylon, whereas the Neo-Assyrian MS J from Ḫuzirina lacks this material. Thus, in Babylonian MS a at least, it can be argued that the epilogue probably reached a final climax by emphasising the importance of Babylon's cult, perhaps specifically the New Year festival. This promotion of Babylon could be understood either as a Babylonian addition postdating the Ḫuzirina tablet or as earlier Babylonian material omitted in an Assyrian tradition that sought to play down this aspect. Like Babylon's New Year festival, *Enūma eliš* sought to affirm the sovereignty of Marduk, and correspondingly the Babylonian king, by means of the Esagil cult.

Sources for Babylon's New Year festival include a ritual series, partially preserved on Late Babylonian tablets, probably from Hellenistic Babylon, that gave instructions for the ritual performance, both speech and action. Tablet XXIII stipulates that on Nisannu day 4 the high priest of Eumuša (*šešgal* e₂-umuša) will recite the whole of *Enūma eliš* (written *e-nu-ma e-liš*; *enūma*(ud) *e-liš*) to Bēl after the second meal in the late afternoon, and this signifies a ritual recitation before Marduk's statue in Eumuša, his cella in Esagil.[32] During that night, the same tablet prescribes a Marduk prayer including two astral representations of his victory over Ti'amat: Marduk as the Arrow star (Sirius) measures out Ti'amat's water and Marduk as the Breast of the Scorpion star (Antares) tramples the breast of Ti'amat, represented by the Scorpion constellation overall.[33] A Late Babylonian tablet, probably from Hellenistic Babylon, partially preserves a copy of an Esagil ritual text for the ninth month Kislīmu. As part of a so-called palm festival, the text prescribes that on Kislīmu day 4 a singer <will recite> *Enūma eliš* (*e-nu-ma e-liš*) to Bēl at the time of the main morning meal and that in relation to *Enūma eliš* V 83, concerning gift-giving to Marduk after his victory, a cult practitioner will present a palm element to Bēl.[34] This shows that, at least on this Late Babylonian tablet, *Enūma eliš* played a role in the Esagil cult, including a ritualised narrative parallel, beyond the spring New Year festival and the month of Nisannu.

On current manuscript evidence, the recension of *Enūma eliš* with Marduk as protagonist was transmitted in Babylonia and Assyria in a

---

[32] Linssen 2004: 219–20, 228, lines 280–3; see, e.g., Gabriel 2014: 87–8.
[33] Linssen 2004: 220, 229, lines 309, 313; see, e.g., Reynolds 2019: commentary on § 13 iv 6, 19–20.
[34] Çağırgan and Lambert 1991–3: 96; see, e.g., Gabriel 2014: 88. Claims that *Enūma eliš* was recited in the seventh month, Tašrītu, arose from a misunderstanding of this Kislīmu ritual tablet (e.g., Zgoll 2006: 49).

generally stable form. However, this divine narrative and the battle with Ti'amat were also subject to reinterpretation. An elaborate scholarly discourse centred on this battle, sometimes in relation to the New Year *akītu*-festival in Nisannu. During the reign of Sennacherib after his destruction of Babylon in 689 BCE, the Marduk narrative in *Enūma eliš* was adapted for an Assyrian audience, both as a narrative poem and in the ritual context of an innovative form of the New Year *akītu*-festival.[35] Sources include a few manuscripts of the Assyrianised epic from Nineveh and Aššur;[36] a Sennacherib inscription describing an *akītu*-house outside Aššur's city walls, including ceremonial names and iconography on a bronze gate;[37] and *Marduk's Ordeal*, an Assyrian ritual explanatory work attested in Nineveh and Aššur versions, that reinterprets Babylon's New Year *akītu*-festival from a pro-Assyrian, anti-Babylonian standpoint.[38] Some brief remarks will suffice here. In Assyrianised *Enūma eliš* and Sennacherib's inscription, Assyria's national god Aššur replaces Babylonia's national god Marduk as the victorious warrior and supreme divine king. In Assyrianised *Enūma eliš* V, Aššur's decreeing the building of Baltil, a name of the city of Aššur, replaced Marduk's decreeing the building of Babylon. The reinterpretation in *Marduk's Ordeal* is more complex. Although Marduk can be replaced by Aššur and in part by Ninurta as a warrior god,[39] reference is also made to *Enūma eliš* and its recitation before Marduk in Nisannu; however, in an Assyrianising twist, Marduk's role in the *akītu*-house is reinterpreted as a junior god's imprisonment under Aššur's authority. In the Sennacherib inscription, the *akītu*-house and its cella have the Sumerian names [E-ab]ba-ugga and E-dubdub-ab[ba], glossed in Akkadian as *bīt kāmû tâmti* ('House that Defeats *Ti'amat*') and [*bīt mur*]*īb kiṣir tâmti* ('[House that Makes] the Host of Ti'amat [*Tremble*]'); the gate iconography depicted Sennacherib, Aššur advancing to fight Ti'amat with his army of gods, and Ti'amat with her creatures, but not the battle itself.

A narrative termed the *Exaltation of Nabû*, partially attested by two Neo-Assyrian tablets from Aššur, one a scribal training extract tablet,

---

[35] Frahm 2010b: 8–13 and 2011: 349–59; Pongratz-Leisten 2015: 416–26 and 2017: LVI–LXIV, LXXIII–LXXV (for a more cautious view of the role of ritual interpretation texts, see note 27 above); Parpola 2017: nos. 15, 52–4, including no. 52 rev. v 48': *qaqqad umāme ša tâmti*, 'the head of the beast of the Sea (Ti'amat)'.

[36] Lambert 2013: 4–5, Tablet I MS N, Tablet III MS D, Tablet V MS E, cf. 94 on Tablet IV 17; Lambert 1997a.

[37] Grayson and Novotny 2014: no. 160.   [38] Livingstone 1989: nos. 34–5.

[39] On the rise of Ninurta in Assyria in the late second and early first millennia, see, e.g., Annus 2002: 40–7.

describes Babylon's New Year *akītu*-festival with a focus on Marduk's son Nabû. Despite textual difficulties, it can be argued that Nabû probably went in martial mode to the *akītu*-house and, appeased, was temporarily installed there, later setting his feet on Ti'amat in his Esagil shrine, before his parents exalted his kingship.[40] This would accord with Nabû's increased prominence, including in the later Neo-Assyrian period,[41] and it can be posited that this narrative may be another Assyrianising reinterpretation, with a deity prominent in Assyria being promoted to Marduk's detriment.

It is likely that these Assyrianising innovations were essentially limited to Sennacherib's reign in response to his sack of Babylon in 689 BCE, when Marduk's principal cult statue was taken from Esagil to Assyria as booty.[42] After Babylon's sack, Sennacherib transferred the cultic topography of Babylon's New Year spring *akītu*-festival to the city of Aššur as part of a deliberate programme of cultural appropriation.[43] This should be compared to the retrieval of Marduk's statue by Nebuchadnezzar I probably triggering the original composition of *Enūma eliš*. Both scenarios involve royal campaigning and the forcible relocation of Marduk's principal statue into the king's own territory, although this was a return under Nebuchadnezzar and a removal to a derivative context under Sennacherib.

Thus, in response to political change, gods prominent in Assyria and the Assyrian king replaced Marduk and the Babylonian king, and the city of Aššur replaced Babylon, including key aspects of its cultic topography. As a displaced supreme deity, Marduk was either omitted or demoted. This should be compared to *Enūma eliš* where Marduk replaced Enlil as supreme god, also replacing Enlil's son Ninurta as the pre-eminent warrior god.[44] Similarly, in response to Marduk's progressive rise, Marduk, his son Nabû, his city Babylon, and his temple Esagil were endowed with aspects of Enlil, his son Ninurta, his city Nippur, and his temple Ekur, this process extending into the Late Babylonian period.[45]

---

[40] Lambert 2013: 346–9, 509–10; if reading 29: *maḫri*(igi)-*iš-šu₂*, 'in his presence', it is probable that the possessive suffix refers to Nabû and that he is the speaker in line 30. Cf. Livingstone 1989: no. 37: 24'–8'.
[41] On Ninurta–Nabû syncretism and the rise of Nabû, see, e.g., Pongratz-Leisten 1994: 96–105; Annus 2002: 44–7; Lambert 2013: 296–7 column vi 19, cf. 292–3 column iii 22.
[42] See, e.g., Frahm 2010b: 8–13 and 2011: 349–54.
[43] See, e.g., George 1999: 77–9; Frahm 2011: 352; Pongratz-Leisten 2015: 417–21 and 2017: LVI–LIX.
[44] See, e.g., Gabriel 2014: 397–401, 409–11.   [45] See, e.g., Tenney 2016; Reynolds 2019: 2.1.1.

Quotations from and allusions to *Enūma eliš* and Marduk's battle with Ti'amat and Qingu occur in an array of other Akkadian works, including royal inscriptions, literary compositions and commentaries, ritual texts and explanatory works, and treatises.[46] Akkadian expository compositions engage with Marduk's victory over Ti'amat as part of the process of interpretation; such scholarship may date back to the reign of Nebuchadnezzar I and intellectually innovative exposition continues into at least the Hellenistic period. A recently published Late Babylonian calendar treatise can now be added to this corpus.

Scholarly exegesis should be taken into account when considering the transmission of this battle myth. Scholars deployed sophisticated hermeneutics, including wordplay, as demonstrated by the list of Marduk's names in *Enūma eliš* VI–VII. Commentaries on *Enūma eliš* include one on lines from all seven tablets that is attested by Neo-Assyrian sources from Nineveh and Aššur and by Neo- or Late Babylonian sources possibly from Sippar or Babylon.[47] This commentary includes interpretation of lines in *Enūma eliš* VII in terms of Babylon's New Year *akītu*-festival in Nisannu.[48] Commentaries with quotations from *Enūma eliš* as the base text are a vector for the epic's transmission. Commentaries on other base texts and explanatory works can draw on Marduk's battle as part of the exposition. For example, a commentary on the so-called Marduk's Address to the Demons, attested by two Neo-Assyrian fragments from Aššur, interprets a line about Marduk not speaking in a blasphemous place by referring to Marduk sitting in the middle of the Sea (Ti'amat) in the *akītu*.[49] Ritual explanatory works linking Babylon's New Year *akītu*-festival in Nisannu with Marduk's victory over Ti'amat include an exposition of Marduk's names at seven stations of his journey to the *akītu*-house; as two Babylonian tablets attest, Marduk as Sirsir sitting in his processional boat Maumuša is interpreted as Marduk trampling Ti'amat, represented by the boat, and *Enūma eliš* VII 77 is quoted in support.[50] The treatise *Tintir = Babylon*, a celebration of Babylon's cultic topography, is attested by sources including Late Babylonian tablets attributable to Esagil and may have been

---

[46] For Akkadian examples, see Lambert 2013: 4–9, 221–4, 244–7, 326–9; Reynolds 2019: 1.6.3.5, 1.8.

[47] Frahm and Jiménez 2015: 295–333; Frahm et al. 2013–: 1.1.A, see also 1.1.B [accessed 22-04-2019].

[48] Frahm and Jiménez 2015: 309–13, 324, 326 lines 45', 49', 53'–4'.

[49] Geller 2016: 394–5, 7 (45); Frahm et al. 2013–: 2.2.1.A.a, 16 [accessed 22-04-2019].

[50] Cavigneaux 1981: 141, 175 79.B.1/30 6–8; George 1992: no. 59 6'–8' (dupl.); see Lambert 1997b: 78–80. For explanatory works linking various rituals with Marduk's victory over Ti'amat and Qingu, see, e.g., Reynolds 2019: 1.6.3.5.

composed under Nebuchadnezzar I.[51] A list of cultic seats, probably pedestals, includes one called Ti'amat, described as the seat of Bēl on which Bēl sits, in allusion to his battle victory, as well as a dais allocated to Sea (Ti'amat) and a seat allocated to Qingu, and it is probable that they were all in the Esagil complex and that at least the first pedestal was in Marduk's cella Eumuša.[52]

Thus, *Enūma eliš* and Marduk's battle were very potent expressions of kingship with strong political and ritual aspects, especially in relation to the New Year *akītu*-festival in Nisannu in Babylon and, derivatively, in Aššur. The divine king with his affirmed supremacy represented the human king: Marduk represented the king of Babylonia and, in variant Assyrianising traditions, the god Aššur represented the king of Assyria, whether directly replacing Marduk or occupying a position of authority over him. In relation to Babylon's New Year *akītu*-festival, Ninurta and Nabû could also partially replace Marduk, and both these replacements may have occurred in the context of Assyrianising works.

In contrast to these reinterpretations, Late Babylonian cuneiform scholars aimed to promote Marduk but their endeavours can be related to cultural interaction in the context of Babylonia and Babylon's reduced political power under externally imposed imperial rule. We know of accounts of Marduk's supremacy through victory in battle, including in a newly reconstructed calendar treatise. Although beyond the scope of this chapter on Akkadian sources, the *Babyloniaca* of Berossus contains related material that also originates from Esagil's elite.[53]

The divine narrative termed the *Defeat of Enutila, Enmešarra, and Qingu* was probably composed in Late Babylonian Babylon and is attested on three Late Babylonian fragments, probably from Sippar and Borsippa, and possibly all scribal training extract tablets.[54] Marduk achieves supremacy through Ninurta's conquests, and a Babylon setting is rich in gods and cultic topography. A complex relationship with *Enūma eliš* involves quotation of *Enūma eliš* I 22–6, as well as more loosely related material, and this should now be compared to the calendar treatise (see below). The warrior aspect of Marduk's role in *Enūma eliš* involved syncretism with Ninurta, the leading warrior god of the Nippur pantheon, but in this Enutila narrative it is striking that the most prominent warrior god is

---

[51] George 1992: 32–3; George 1997: 137–45; Clancier 2009: 449–50, 462–70.
[52] George 1992: *Tintir* II 1, 21, 31 (*ta!-ma-a-tu₂* is probably a singular form, 'Sea (Ti'amat)').
[53] See, e.g., Verbrugghe and Wickersham 2001: 13–91, F1; Haubold 2016.
[54] Lambert 2013: 326–9 (with related fragment DT 184), 497–8; see Reynolds 2019: 1.8.2.2

Ninurta under Marduk's authority. This narrative has the character of a late hybrid and Marduk as the supreme god outsourcing a warrior role to Ninurta would not conflict with this. Marduk probably commemorates Enmešarra's sons through cultic iconography at Ganzer, comparable to Ti'amat's monsters and the Gate of the Apsû.[55]

A newly reconstructed Late Babylonian calendar treatise deployed Marduk's battle with Ti'amat and Qingu in various ways as part of sophisticated exegesis centred on Esagil ritual.[56] This treatise is attested by three damaged Late Babylonian tablets, probably all from tablet collections associated with Esagil: it is likely that two are advanced pedagogical copies from c. 170 BCE and that one has an earlier Hellenistic date.[57] The treatise was probably composed in the Hellenistic period in the milieu of Esagil.[58]

This innovative exegetical treatise, melding traditional and Late Babylonian cuneiform scholarship, is set in Babylon, with a focus on Esagil rituals set in the past.[59] As preserved, the treatise has a calendrical structure and an overarching theme of the foreign invasion of Babylonia, especially Babylon, primarily by an enemy called Elam and secondarily by an enemy called Subartu. Past rituals at different times of year are interpreted as apotropaic against such invasion and astrological omens are interpreted as triggering these rituals. Warfare set in the more remote past provides historical precedents and a paradigm of three kings who relocated Marduk's statue through military incursions. Most important are the complementary pair of the Elamite king Kutir-Naḫḫunte, who invaded Babylonia and looted Marduk's statue from Esagil in c. 1155 BCE, and the Babylonian king Nebuchadnezzar I, who invaded Elam and reinstalled the statue in Esagil in c. 1105 BCE. The Assyrian king Tukultī-Ninurta I, who invaded Babylonia and looted Esagil and Marduk's statue in 1225 BCE, plays a secondary role. In accordance with the Babylonian perspective, the treatise culminates in an *ex eventu* prophecy that Babylonia and its king will triumph, and this should probably be understood as Marduk addressing Nebuchadnezzar I. Nebuchadnezzar I serves as a glorious historical analogue to the Late Babylonian king. The focus on securing Marduk's statue in Esagil and preventing Elamite invasion can be related to Late Babylonian anxieties about the kingdom usually called Elymais, from

---

[55] See, e.g., Reynolds 2019: commentary on § 2 i 5'–6'.
[56] For an edition and study of this treatise, see Reynolds 2019.   [57] Reynolds 2019: 3.1, 3.4, 4 E.
[58] Reynolds 2019: 1.5.   [59] The following draws on Reynolds 2019: chapters 1–2.

Greek Ἐλυμαΐς, but still denoted by the traditional terms (*māt*) *elamti*, '(land of) Elam', in Akkadian.[60]

In this treatise, warring human kings are represented by divine combatants, and the mythologising of war pervades the work and relates human warfare primarily to Marduk's Esagil cult.[61] Fundamental is the triad of Babylonia/Babylon, its primary enemy Elam, and its secondary enemy Subartu represented by Marduk, his primary enemy Ti'amat, and his secondary enemy Qingu as a mythological analogy. For example, through exegetic wordplay unattested elsewhere, Ti'amat as a female slave (geme$_2$; *amtu*) is linked with the city of the female slave (*āl amtu*) and Elam (*elamtu*); Qingu as a male slave (ir$_3$; *ardu*; subur) is linked with the land of the male slave (*māt ardu*) and (the land of) Subartu ((*māt*) *subartu*).[62]

Marduk's battle with Ti'amat and Qingu is incorporated into the treatise via a wealth of exegetical strategies, and *Enūma eliš* is the most closely related divine narrative. Exegesis in the context of astro-mythological battles includes unmarked quotation of *Enūma eliš* IV 49 // 75 about Marduk raising his flood weapon and unmarked near quotation of *Enūma eliš* IV 120 about Marduk counting Qingu with the Dead Gods.[63] As preserved, two otherwise unattested passages of narrative poetry about Marduk's conflict with Ti'amat and Qingu – in section 1 on [Nisannu] with a Du'ūzu setting and in section 2 on [Ayaru] – combine motifs and phrases found in various lines of *Enūma eliš* and these passages are influenced by earlier traditions, whether as quotation from unidentifiable source material or as original composition.[64] Section 1 recounts Ti'amat's preparations for battle, including her gift of the Tablet of Destinies and Anu's position to Qingu, and Marduk's confrontation with Ti'amat at the gods' request; section 2 recounts Marduk's killing of Ti'amat and Qingu, his assumption of sovereignty, retrieval of the Tablet of Destinies, and creation of commemorative images of Ti'amat's monsters in the Gate of the Apsû. These concise narrative passages focus on selected events in the battle, its build-up, and aftermath, as mythological representation of human warfare. The passage in section 1 occurs in the context of apotropaic ritual against invasion, while that in section 2 may be exegesis of the Bristle constellation as Marduk's arrow.

---

[60] See, e.g., Potts 2016: 348–406; Reynolds 2019: 2.3.3.2. [61] Reynolds 2019: 1.8, 2.2.
[62] Reynolds 2019: § 6 ii 8'–13'; see 1.9.4.1.2, 1.9.4.2.2.
[63] Reynolds 2019: § 13 iv 24–5, 32–3; see 1.8.1.1, 1.8.2.1.
[64] Reynolds 2019: § 1 i 4–12, § 2 i 1'–7'; see 1.8.1.1, 1.8.2.2.

Related references to Anu's position occur in the context of astrological omens of invasion linked with Marduk and Ti'amat's battle.[65]

Other omen-derived material in astro-mythological contexts is related to their battle, including the following. Through wordplay, the tenth month, Ṭebētu (ab; *tappattu*), is linked with Ti'amat as a twin (*tu'amtu*), melding Ti'amat and Qingu aspects, and section 13 on Ṭebētu contains elaborate astral representations of this battle, combining traditional and innovative syncretic material: Mars, the Goat-Fish constellation, and the She-Goat constellation represent Ti'amat; the Scorpion constellation, Corpse star/constellation, and Hyena star/constellation represent Qingu; Jupiter and probably the King star represent Marduk; and the Bow constellation and Arrow star represent his weapons.[66] Astro-mythology in the treatise is related to *Enūma eliš*, including Ti'amat's portrayal as she-goat and sea, and the catasterism of Marduk's bow.[67]

Apotropaic rituals in section 3 on Simānu, section 6 on [*Abu*], and section 13 on Ṭebētu are linked to Marduk, Ti'amat, and Qingu.[68] Babylon's spring New Year festival is the implicit background of section 1 on [Nisannu], and section 7 on [*Ulūlu*] refers to Nabû and Nergal not going in Nisannu, which probably concerns this festival's non-performance due to Elamite invasion.[69] Other points of connection with New Year rituals include the ritual series recitation on Nisannu day 5 with references to the Breast of the Scorpion and Arrow stars (see above). However, while the New Year festival with a focus on Marduk's victory over Ti'amat would have been a key element of the Esagil ritual context, the treatise's focus is mythologising human warfare, including the deployment of Marduk's battle with Ti'amat and Qingu, to support the interpretation of rituals at different times of year as apotropaic against Elamite and Subarian invasion. In the treatise, as preserved, the Babylonian king does not feature as a ritual participant. In the final narrative in section 14 a past king's neglect of Esagil probably angered Marduk into causing Elamite invaders to destroy the cult, in contrast to the pious king for whom Marduk prophesies victory and cultic renewal.[70] The treatise may have responded to the reality that imperial rulers did engage with Esagil but in a less intimate relationship than their Babylonian predecessors.[71]

---

[65] Reynolds 2019: § 3 i 17', § 4 i 34'; see 1.8.1.1, 1.8.2.2.
[66] Reynolds 2019: § 13 iv 1–20, 32–5, 39–40; see 1.7.3, 1.8.1.1.
[67] Reynolds 2019: 1.7.3.2.2, 1.7.3.2.3.
[68] Reynolds 2019: § 3 i 8', 16', § 6 ii 11'–12', § 13 iv 7–8, 14, 28–9; see 1.8.1.1, 1.8.2.2.
[69] Reynolds 2019: § 1, § 7 ii 26'–7'; see 1.2.   [70] Reynolds 2019: § 14.
[71] Reynolds 2019: 1.5, 1.6.2.2.

This unparalleled treatise exploited Babylonia's and especially Babylon's perceived vulnerability to war, and should be understood as an innovative response to changed political circumstances in the Late Babylonian period.[72] The threat was the disruption of Babylonian sovereignty, as held by Marduk and his human counterpart the Babylonian king. The treatise aimed to secure their sovereignty by preventing the externally imposed authority of a hostile foreign king, primarily the king of Elam (Late Babylonian Elymais) but also the king of Subartu. In a semantic exploration, omens and rituals were reinterpreted as portending but preventing such invasion, including the looting of Marduk's statue. While Marduk traditionally represented the Babylonian king, the treatise gave political relevance to Ti'amat and Qingu by interpreting them as representing the Elamite and Subarian kings respectively. The treatise builds the case that security depended on Esagil's scholars and cult practitioners correctly performing apotropaic rituals throughout the year. The treatise was composed from the perspective of a provincial Babylonia in the Late Babylonian period, when the traditional centrality and power of Babylon and Esagil had been lost under imperial rule and Marduk's statue was vulnerable to looting by invaders. Thus, Marduk's combat myth was deployed to map vulnerability onto victory.

This exegetic treatise developed the relationships of Marduk and Ti'amat's battle with Esagil rituals, astrological omens, astral representations, and human kings. In this way, their battle was given new political, cultic, and astronomical-astrological relevance, and was redeployed to support the aims of Esagil's Late Babylonian cuneiform scholars. The treatise quarried and reworked a wide range of traditional and later Mesopotamian cuneiform material, and exploited local traditions. This exploration aimed to secure renewed and contemporary relevance for Esagil's disempowered local elite, by situating them at the heart of kingship ideology as essential agents for Babylonia's security under its imperial rulers. The treatise should be seen as an expression of Late Babylonian clericalism and as an intellectual endeavour occupying the so-called middle ground or contact zone between a local elite and an externally imposed and more powerful hierarchy.[73] The treatise identifies the interests of these two groups in terms of the threat of the invading other. It can be viewed as a response to Hellenistic cultural contact primarily in the form of political change that had reduced Esagil's importance and increased its vulnerability.

---

[72] This discussion develops Reynolds 2019: 1.4, 1.5.   [73] See, e.g., Strootman 2013: 67–97.

The treatise was composed in the Late Babylonian, probably Hellenistic, period and written down in Akkadian cuneiform, very probably on a clay tablet or wooden writing-board that is no longer extant. The identities of the original composer, scribe, and manuscript owner are unknown. The treatise was transmitted and curated: it was copied onto clay tablets owned by senior scholars and these were stored. Tablet colophons enable us to identify some of the later copyists (probably advanced trainee scribes) and tablet owners as members of the prominent Mušēzib family, with a likely setting of *c.* 170 BCE.[74] All this activity took place in the context of Esagil's elite cuneiform scholars and cult practitioners and their associated library collections. Whether this intellectual endeavour in Akkadian cuneiform had any direct impact beyond this elite or beyond a wider but still very limited cadre of those able to understand Akkadian, even just by ear, is unknown. In the Hellenistic period local power in Babylon lay in the hands of Esagil's high priest (*šatammu*) and assembly (*kiništu*) until they were displaced in part by a governor of Babylon (*pāḫat bābili*) and the assembly of the politai (*puliṭū*) in the early second century BCE.[75] This treatise may not have reached, or influenced, the superimposed Hellenistic hierarchy, let alone the king, and may have found an audience only within the Esagil elite that created it in the hope of boosting their reduced prestige.

Some key themes recur in this study of Marduk and Ti'amat's battle across a range of Akkadian sources. As the city god of Babylon and supreme god of Babylonia, Marduk, including his manifestation in his principal cult statute, served as a divine analogue to the Babylonian king. The divine battle narratives in *Enmešarra's Defeat*, *Enūma eliš*, and the *Exaltation of Nabû* were all related to Babylon's spring New Year *akītu*-festival in Marduk's Esagil cult. This ritual traditionally confirmed the sovereignty of Marduk, immanent in his statue, and the Babylonian king as his human counterpart. In a range of Assyrianised sources, this nexus is transferred to Assyria's supreme god Aššur, the Assyrian king, and a derivative New Year *akītu*-festival of the city of Aššur. The complex relationships between *Enūma eliš* and Babylon's spring New Year *akītu*-festival include structural and narrative parallels. Aetiologies for Babylon, Esagil, the *akītu*-house, and the festival were integrated into the epic; and the epic's recitation in Esagil was integrated into the festival. The recitation of *Enūma eliš*, with associated ritual action, is also attested in Kislīmu on a Late Babylonian ritual tablet but the age of this practice is uncertain.

[74] Reynolds 2019: 3.4.   [75] Reynolds 2019: 2.1.2.

Politics, Cult, And Scholarship

Explanatory works explore relationships between Marduk, Ti'amat, and the Esagil cult. The *Defeat of Enutila, Enmešarra, and Qingu* and the newly reconstructed calendar treatise, both probably from Late Babylonian Babylon, each have a multilayered relationship with *Enūma eliš*, including quotation and more loosely related material about divine battles. It is significant that both works do not focus on Babylon's spring New Year festival but have a wider cultic scope. The Enutila narrative involves a plethora of Babylon temples and divine combatants. The treatise focuses on the Esagil cult, human kings, and Marduk's battle with Ti'amat and Qingu, but its overall aim is to validate Esagil rituals throughout the year as apotropaic against invading foreign kings and it incorporates a far wider range of material.

Politics, cult – primarily that of Esagil – and scribal education should be identified as key factors in shaping, reshaping, and expressing divine narratives of Ti'amat defeat.[76] Triggers for composition include the movement, actual or potential, of Marduk's principal cult statue beyond Babylonia.[77] This probably applies to both versions of *Enūma eliš*, reflecting Babylonian and Assyrian dominance, and also to the calendar treatise, reflecting Babylon's reduced power and increased vulnerability under imperial rule. On the basis of the treatise, it can be argued that Late Babylonian scholars wanted to boost Esagil and this may also be apparent in material after *Enmešarra's Defeat* and in one manuscript of the *Enūma eliš* epilogue. Scribal education as a transmission vector is attested by the extracts from *Enūma eliš*, the *Exaltation of Nabû*, and the Enutila narrative, as well as the advanced pedagogical copies of the treatise.[78]

Greater consideration should also be given to non-verbal transmission. This often involved divine combatants, sometimes as analogues to human protagonists. Channels included ritual action, cultic iconography, cultic artefacts, and cultic topography. All these apply to the New Year *akītu*-festival in Nisannu, primarily in Babylon but secondarily in Aššur, with journeys to and from the *akītu*-house through a ritual landscape involving cultic daises and processional boats. It can now be seen that cultic iconography commemorating divine conquests is specified in Enmešarra's Defeat, *Enūma eliš*, Sennacherib's description of his *akītu*-house gate, probably the Enutila narrative, the related fragment DT 184, and the calendar treatise.[79]

---

[76] For interactions between divine narrative and cult in scribal culture, see, e.g., Reynolds forthcoming.
[77] See, e.g., Finn 2017: 37–40.   [78] On scribal education, see, e.g., Lenzi 2015: 157–60, 170–1.
[79] See, e.g., Reynolds 2019: commentary on § 2 i 5'–6'.

As widely attested, the astral skyscape included heavenly bodies interpreted as representing divine combatants and weapons. Relevant sources considered in this study include *Enmešarra's Defeat*, *Enūma eliš*, a New Year festival recitation for Babylon, and the calendar treatise. However, questions of access to non-verbal representations are not easily answered and merit further study.

Scholarship, cult, and politics formed a powerful nexus.[80] It is important to stress that the key compositions in this chapter should be situated in the overarching context of cuneiform specialists whose expertise encompassed both scribal and cultic knowledge. Specialists associated with Esagil in Babylon, Marduk's principal temple, played a central role from the late second millennium BCE until the Hellenistic period. Relevant tablets stem from the family houses of cultic experts and from temple libraries, including library collections associated with Esagil. From *Enūma eliš* to the calendar treatise, the texts discussed here were written in scholarly Akkadian cuneiform with advanced scribal training as a prerequisite. The creation and transmission of textualised scholarship was an elite domain in Mesopotamia. Securing and sustaining good relations between humans and gods was a fundamental intellectual endeavour. Many works directly concerned the proper practice of divination and ritual, but divine narratives and associated explanatory texts should also be regarded as intrinsically didactic and cult related.

As well as defining channels of divine–human communication, divination and temple cult were adapted to contemporary political circumstances and played a key role in power negotiations between temples and the king. Scribes in temple milieux reflected those institutions' concerns in their composition, interpretation, and curation of textualised knowledge. Under Hellenistic rule, cuneiform scholarship was practiced by a cadre of elite families associated with temples in southern Mesopotamian cities. Late evidence from Babylon includes the calendar treatise and an astronomical diary recording that Antiochus III, triumphant after his anabasis, participated in Babylon's *akītu*-festival in Nisannu 205 BCE.[81]

As a powerful expression of divine and human kingship, the narrative of Marduk and Ti'amat's battle had long been intertwined with cultic and royal power and prestige. This study across a range of Akkadian sources demonstrates that it was deployed and redeployed in changing political and cultic realities, and that it retained its vitality and productivity from

---

[80] For broader studies, see, e.g., Lenzi 2015; Ristvet 2015: 153–228.
[81] Linssen 2004: 84; Ambos 2013: 121.

the late second millennium BCE until the final phases of cuneiform scholarship under imperial rule. An increased understanding of the changing impact of Esagil and its associated scholars on the transmission of this battle myth should inform approaches to the study of both intracultural and intercultural interactions.

CHAPTER 4

The Scholar and the Poet
Standard Babylonian Gilgameš VI vs. Iliad 5

Mark Weeden

Introduction

One major difference between the source material available for ancient Greek and Babylonian literature is the fact that cuneiform manuscripts survive in the form of clay tablets. Not only are these much closer in time to the period when the literature was a living art form than most manuscripts of ancient Greek literature (other than papyri), but being archaeological artefacts they can tell us something about their social use-context in antiquity, although all too rarely and imperfectly. There are downsides to this. The preservation of clay tablets in the ruins of cities that have been and continue to be destroyed repeatedly throughout history is usually much more fragmentary than for the Greek literary works, which have been copied and promulgated in unbroken tradition from the ancient world to the present day. However, the documentation is of a fundamentally different type: it belongs to contemporary society and culture and the circumstances of its production must be understood as participating in these contexts. This source-critical awareness – who was writing the texts down, and in what contexts – must play a role when initiating comparisons between literary works from Mesopotamia and ancient Greece.

The episodes involving the encounters between a hero and a love goddess in Standard Babylonian (SB) *Epic of Gilgameš* Tablet VI and *Iliad* 5 have recently been compared by B. Currie and M. R. Bachvarova, following the work of W. Burkert and M. L. West.[1] The relationship between the two is argued to have been a case of influence

---

[1] Burkert 1992: 96–9; West 1997: 360–3; Currie 2012a; 2016: 17–8; Bachvarova 2016: 325–6. The following contribution is essentially an expansion of a view expressed to Bruno Currie in an email exchange during 2011, which was kindly cited by him at Currie 2012a: 573 fn. 157. The text of my email later made the jump from footnote to main text at Jay 2016: 6. It is therefore high time for me to write something a little more formal about this, although research on some of the issues addressed here is still in its infancy and very little can be said beyond the level of supposition at this point. The completion of this chapter was enabled by a research semester at Kollegforschungsgruppe 2615,

depending on a transmission that may have come by way of Cyprus.² In Currie's analysis the encounter between Diomedes and Aphrodite in *Iliad* 5 is further to be thought of as a literary reception of and reaction to the *Gilgameš* passage.³ Both Bachvarova and Currie, to different degrees, posit bilingual poets as intermediaries.⁴

In this chapter, aspects of the *Gilgameš* episode will be reviewed which considerably complicate the question of transmission by poets (whether entirely oral or partially literate). These arise from the culturally specific context of the genesis of parts of the SB *Epic of Gilgameš* in the social environment of cuneiform writing and its concomitant education practices, about which we know a good deal. After initial consideration of modern scholarly traditions on the literary concept of 'intertextuality', the essay will present some preliminary evidence for a relationship between cuneiform literary texts (in this case passages from SB *Gilgameš* Tablet VI) and the cuneiform school environment. It is proposed that this is a fruitful line for further inquiry, with the potential to give considerable purchase in understanding SB *Gilgameš* as a historical literary artefact, one that was partially generated as written poetry. This analysis, if validated by further research, would make it more difficult to draw conclusions concerning historical processes of literary transmission based on comparisons between Homer and *Gilgameš*, without taking into account more closely the specific social and cultural circumstances in which the works were generated. For the moment, however, conclusions can only be applied to the minimal amount of text taken as a sample in this chapter. The following discussion therefore presents the germ of an idea for more extensive research.

In *Gilgameš* Tablet VI the hero returns from his expedition to the cedar forest, where he slaughtered its divine guardian, Humbaba.⁵ He is spied by Ištar, goddess of sex and war, who propositions him. Gilgameš rejects her advances by first comparing her to a series of useless and destructive objects or animals, and then listing the fates of the various lovers she had previously, who had all ended up being transformed in some negative

---

'Re-thinking Oriental Despotism', at the Freie Universität Berlin, January–April 2019. I am grateful to my hosts, Jörg Klinger and Eva Cancik-Kirschbaum, for allowing me latitude to pursue several different strands of research while in Berlin. Andrew George is to be thanked for making comments on a draft of the chapter. I am also grateful to the editors of this volume for their invitation to speak at the Divine Narratives conference, for their patience, and for bibliographical help.

² West 1997: 612–13.   ³ Currie 2016: 216.
⁴ Currie 2016: 219 comparing the effect the Greek-born Livius Andronicus had on Latin poetry; Bachvarova 2016: 326.
⁵ George 2003: 470–8.

fashion. Ištar then flies up to heaven and complains to her parents, Anu and Antu, and demands that they give her the Bull of Heaven in order to destroy Gilgameš, which they do. Gilgameš and his friend Enkidu kill the Bull of Heaven, and then Enkidu further insults Ištar by hurling one of its haunches at her.

In the *Iliad* the Achaean hero Diomedes is pursuing the Trojan Aeneas on the battlefield (5.297–310). The goddess Aphrodite, mother of Aeneas by the noble herdsman Anchises, intervenes by wrapping him in her protective garment (311–17). Diomedes sees that this is the 'feeble' Aphrodite, whom Athene has given him permission to engage, and he wounds her with his spear on the wrist so that she lets go of her son, who is scooped up in a cloud by Apollo (330–46). Diomedes warns her to leave the battlefield and she is led off in pain by dawn goddess Iris. She asks her brother Ares to lend her his chariot, so that she can go up to Olympus to complain to her father Zeus about the mortal Diomedes (347–62). There she is consoled by her mother Diōne (a divine name which is only mentioned once in Homer and is built from the same root as the name of Zeus – genitive *Dios*), who relates to her a catalogue of gods who have been hurt by mortals (Ares, Hera, Hades), and warns that Diomedes is a fool for thinking that he can attack the gods (381–415). Athene further insults Aphrodite, and Zeus echoes Diomedes' sentiments in order to warn her away from battle (416–30). Later in the narrative Diomedes also attacks and wounds the war god Ares with Athene's help (855–86).

The similarity between these episodes is supposed to involve both structural and etymological elements. Both narratives contain a conflict between a male hero and a female divinity. Ištar is the goddess of sexual love and war, while in the Homeric story Aphrodite is the goddess of love and Ares the god of war. In both stories the goddess has sky-deities as parents (Zeus and Diōne vs. Anu and Antu, literally Mr and Mrs Sky), and both involve a 'plaint in heaven' in front of these parents as well as a mythological catalogue, delivered in the one case by the hero (Gilgameš), and in the other by the divine mother (Diōne).[6] Currie discusses extensively and carefully whether this is a case of typological parallelism, in which a hostile (as opposed to an amatory) encounter between a love goddess and a male hero may be expected to include certain conceptual elements, or whether the Homeric text is in fact receiving and/or commenting on the Gilgameš text in some fashion as a form of intertextual allusion.[7] How the contact that would have enabled such a reception is

---

[6] Currie 2016: 173, 205.   [7] Currie 2016: 193–8.

supposed to have played out is problematic.[8] The following should give some idea of what would need to be accounted for if the hypothesis of a direct relationship between the two narratives is to be followed through in all implications. First we should clarify what we mean by intertextuality, and focus on a specific form of intertextual relationship that is meaningful for the ancient Near East, namely what some have called 'infrastructural' intertextuality.

Types of Literary Intertextuality

The notion of intertextuality as a literary phenomenon has different meanings in different fields and periods of modern academic discourse. During the 1960s, particularly in the exciting intellectual climate where concepts were developed that began to supersede the supremacy of structuralism in anthropological and cultural theory, intertextuality was seen as a relationship between texts of all kinds, whether spoken or written, a kind of global register for understanding text. In a critique of the formalist and structuralist tendency to reduce narrative to reproducible sequences of elements, Bakhtin had argued that texts existed in dialogue with each other and with different types of social language, rooted in everyday usage, with the novel being the verbal art form which exemplified the coexistence of different social languages or voices in one polyphonic discourse most vigorously.[9] Related to this approach there developed a questioning or redefinition of the idea of textual originality and of the critical dogma that the ultimate authority to determine the meaning of text resides with the author. Text was famously described by J. Kristeva as a 'mosaic of quotations'.[10] In the words of R. Barthes the text is a 'multi-dimensional space in which a variety of writings, none of them original, blend and clash'.[11] These and similar approaches to text and intertext formed part of an incremental assault on centre-focused, top-down approaches to understanding the relationship between text and meaning.

This wider notion of a basic depth to any text that makes it understandable, or changes its meaning via connection with other speech contexts and other texts, can be contrasted with the directed intertextuality, or allusion, that is used in certain other fields of academia. In Classical Studies

---

[8] Currie 2016: 199 explicitly leaves open the possibility that writing played a role in the transmission.
[9] Bakhtin 1981: 352–3 [originally published 1934–5].
[10] Kristeva 1986: 37 [originally published 1967].
[11] Barthes 1977: 146 [originally published 1967].

one thinks particularly of the way apparent citations of text A within text B can be said to change the meaning of text B, a practice of allusion that has been particularly popular in studies of Roman and Hellenistic poetry. One particularly egregious example of this scheme of interpretation comes with regard to Virgil *Aeneid* 6.460, spoken by Aeneas at his encounter with Dido in the underworld: *invitus regina tuo de litore cessi*, 'unwilling, queen, did I depart from your shore'. This line has been read as an echo of Catullus' translation of Callimachus' poem on the lock of hair from queen Berenike's head, which later turned up as a star (66.39): *invita regina tuo de vertice cessi*, 'unwilling, queen, did I depart from your crown'. For R. O. A. M. Lyne, this specific reference to Catullus' poem at the high point of pathos in the *Aeneid*, along with further echoes of the same poem contrasting Dido's fate with that of Berenike, added a disquieting voice that casts a shadow over the project that will end in the foundation of Rome.[12] Here the meaning of the surface text of the *Aeneid* of Virgil is supposed to be changed by direct reference to the text of a poem by Catullus.

This is not the only intertextual approach taken in Classical Studies with regard to this single line. More recently a different approach has been taken to the coincidence of these lines, one that explores a formulaic tradition of how to express leaving somewhere unwillingly, onto which a 'window' is opened through the Catullus reference, to use terminology developed by R. Thomas to describe the phenomenon more generally.[13] Precisely where the window is ultimately leading us as source-text for the tradition might be debated by different readers, whether Protesilaos and Laodamia (H. Pelliccia) or Theseus and Ariadne (G. Nagy), but this formulaic approach to the significance of the phrase as opposed to seeing a specific text as its terminal reference has something more in common with the broader culture-theoretical approach of Kristeva and Barthes to intertextual relationships than does the use of allusion, which presupposes a conscious manipulation of one text on the basis of the form of another text on the part of the author.[14]

The study of intertextuality in ancient Near Eastern texts has not been as popular as in Classical Studies, but one sees roughly similar parameters

---

[12] Lyne 1994: 168–74. Lyne is careful to use the term intertextuality while trying not to invoke authorial intention, but it seems difficult not to interpret this and other uses of the intertextual framework as a move towards reinstating the author's conscious manipulation of the text as a field of legitimate inquiry.

[13] Pelliccia 2010–11; Nagy 2013; for 'window reference', see Thomas 1986: 188–9.

[14] The intertextuality of Pelliccia and others has more in common with the notion of 'traditional referentiality' that has been developed for Homeric scholarship: see Foley 1999; Currie 2016: 4–9.

in approaches that have been taken thus far. B. Currie has argued for intertextual references between Standard Babylonian *Gilgameš* VI and the Inanna-Dumuzi songs of the Old Babylonian period on the one hand, as well as between Ištar and Išullanu from Gilgameš's mythological catalogue of Ištar's previous lovers and the Sumerian Inanna and Šukaletuda.[15] These are supposed to be particular references to specific texts that frame the reader's understanding of the narrative through echo and inversion. The Babylonian poem *Erra and Išum* has been read as an intertextual response to various poems, especially the Babylonian Creation Epic *Enūma eliš*.[16] By contrast, C. Metcalf has recently reviewed alleged cases of intertextual references in the composition known as the *Dialogue of Pessimism*, and concluded that these are varieties of proverbial expressions of Babylonian attitudes to the certainty of death and the limits of human life rather than references to specific texts.[17] This again sounds more like the type of expansive, formulaic view of intertextual reference as a dialogue between networks of texts and traditional phraseology rather than an intentional nod from one text to another that affects one's understanding of the text one is reading.

Beyond these, there is another type of intertextuality in Mesopotamian literature, namely that which J. C. Johnson has referred to as 'infrastructural'.[18] By this we mean reference to the large body of school-texts that were learned by Babylonian trainee scribes, consisting in large part of lexical lists.[19] These are not literary compositions which may provide a contrasting context for a verbal echo, but knowledge associated with the acquisition of cuneiform writing itself, that is organised according to clearly established principles, and which would be learned by apprentices according to curricula that are largely known and followed similar structures, even if they varied from place to place (and even within the same cities).[20] Johnson and M. J. Geller have suggested how this kind of 'infrastructural knowledge' might be called

---

[15] Currie 2016: 160–82.
[16] See Ponchia 2013–14: 63 n. 4 for a summary of recent attempts. For a strong approach to deliberate intertextual allusion in these texts, see Wisnom 2019.
[17] Metcalf 2013.
[18] Johnson 2015a: 4; Johnson and Geller 2015: 31: 'In light of the huge achievements in both mathematics and literary creativity in the Old Babylonian period, any reasonable account of Old Babylonian scholasticism must see the copying of lexical lists as an *infrastructural* practice rather than the pinnacle of scholastic achievement.'
[19] Veldhuis 2014.
[20] For example: Volk 1996; Veldhuis 1997; Tinney 1999; Veldhuis 2000; Volk 2000; Robson 2001, 2002; Tanret 2002, 2004; Veldhuis 2004, 2014.

upon in a Sumerian dialogue allegedly based around a school reunion, otherwise known as *Dialogue 1*.[21]

Such Sumerian dialogues are typically learned compositions, and it is not surprising that they should use references to scholastic texts as the sources of an intertextual subtext.[22] During the second millennium BCE, Sumerian died out as a living language and became a rarefied idiom, which was sometimes written in a very learned form that depended largely on the use of obscure forms known only from lexical lists, and was quite divorced from anything approaching a spoken language.[23] The school curriculum mainly consisted of learning Sumerian, at least throughout the second millennium in Babylonia and southern Mesopotamia, so it is unsurprising that Sumerian dialogue texts should use and contain references to this body of knowledge. The case with the Akkadian dialogue texts is less clear, and E. Jiménez has identified certain elements of them that appear to be based on oral poetic compositional techniques.[24] Almost certainly these dialogues had a performance context, although this does not have to exclude the possibility that they could also have had a learned infrastructure, whether conscious or not. In the following we shall try to demonstrate that the opening sections of the altercation between Gilgameš and Ištar have at least some of their roots in the world of school learning.

The Babylonian curriculum referred to above consisted of different types of lexical lists, arranged in order according to the level of difficulty.[25] Although there was nothing approaching a 'national' or standardised curriculum, and scribal education must have varied according to the specialisation that the apprentices were going to follow in life,[26] in general the students would proceed from basic wedge practice through to simple syllables (tu-ta-ti, mu-ma-mi, for example), then name-lists, which would introduce them to the use of logograms vs phonetic writings, and then on to thematically organised word-lists, which would introduce them to

---

[21] Johnson and Geller 2015. For a different assessment of the function and *mise en scène* of this dialogue, see Matuszak 2019, which I am grateful to have seen prior to publication. While interpreting many aspects of the dialogue differently on the basis of improved textual collation, Matuszak (2019: 2.2) does not dispute the general point that lexical lists (particularly the Lu-lists) have played a role in the construction of the text's argument, adding that proverbs, another element of the school curriculum, were also important.
[22] Crisostomo 2015.   [23] George 2009: 110; Bartelmus 2016.
[24] Jiménez 2017: 127, 133, 144   [25] Veldhuis 2014: 202–15.
[26] See also Crisostomo 2015: 126–31 for creative adaptation of sign-lists by students within certain parameters.

Sumerian vocabulary.[27] The main word-list was known as *Ura* (also referred to as HAR-*ra - hubullu*, abbreviated *Hh*), which was divided into sections broadly according to the semantic field of the words: wood, reed, metals, parts of the body, vessels, birds, toponyms.[28] These were learned in extracts. Another word-list was *Lú*, the list of professions, or perhaps more accurately a list of different types of human beings.

Although *Lú* is also found later in the curriculum, the word-lists are usually to be kept completely separate from the sign-lists, which form the next stages of cuneiform scribal education and are organised generally not according to the meanings of the signs, but according to different pedagogical approaches to classifying them. The sign-list *Ea* introduced the student to the principle of polyvalence, the fact that any one single cuneiform sign could have multiple phonetic values. At the other end of the spectrum, and the last lexical list in the first stage of the curriculum, was the difficult composition *Diri*, which introduced the student to complex logograms consisting of multiple Sumerian signs. In between come further sign-lists that are organised acrographically, i.e., according to whether they are written with the same sign at the front of any complex logogram: *Izi*, *Kagal* and *Nigga*. Thus the principles that guide the construction of these sign-lists are based around the cuneiform signs themselves, and the best way of teaching their use to the student and passing on the knowledge of writing to future generations.[29] Particularly if we discover systematic correspondences in the Akkadian text of the *Epic of Gilgameš* that reproduce patterns that are found in these sign-lists, then it may be an indication that whoever has composed or contributed to composing the poetic text has been through a scribal curriculum that involved learning these texts or texts like them.

This does not mean that connections between literary texts and lexical lists or other material of scribal learning have to be a matter of consciously learned use of language or even direct textual allusion. It may be that they are, but this is something that needs to be evaluated on a case-by-case basis. Such a relationship could also be an expression of no more than the fact that someone has learned to write, and that in doing so they have learned to associate words in certain ways. To investigate this properly would take a large project, well beyond the limits of this chapter. Here we can only sketch some possibilities for further research.

---

[27] Veldhuis 2014: 204–6. [28] Veldhuis 2014: 206. [29] Veldhuis 1997, 2004, 2014.

Numerous Caveats

The Standard Babylonian version of the *Epic of Gilgameš* in its eleven-tablet recension (with a twelfth tablet as a kind of appendix) is found on manuscripts at numerous sites in the first millennium BCE from a royal library in Nineveh to scholarly collections throughout Mesopotamia, but is commonly thought to have been compiled towards the end of the second millennium BCE, incorporating significant elements and much verbatim text from the Old Babylonian (OB) Akkadian versions: Tablet XI largely adapts the flood myth narrated in OB *Atrahasīs*, along with a prologue to Tablet I and an epilogue to Tablet XI.[30] Certainly the prologue to Tablet I, which has been associated with this version as opposed to the OB form of the epic, must have been added by the time of the tablet from Ugarit on which it is preserved, thus the late thirteenth or early twelfth centuries at the latest.[31] The selective Hittite translations of the epic may also be based on a version that may have had some resemblance to the SB version.[32] However, the manuscripts of that version all date to the first millennium BCE, and it is not clear that a uniform and stable text had been reached by the end of the second millennium BCE in all areas and contexts, however much we might like to think that it had.[33]

There are no OB sources which contain traces of Tablet VI. There was of course the Sumerian composition *Gilgameš and the Bull of Heaven*, of which one manuscript may even date to the Ur III period.[34] The earliest Akkadian versions that later became Tablet VI of the *Epic of Gilgameš* are Middle Babylonian (MB)/Late Bronze Age: a probably thirteenth-century tablet from Hattusa (MB Boğ₂) contains extracts from the story and notably omits the catalogue of insults directed by Gilgameš at Ištar.[35] Fragments of a tablet from Emar (presumably late thirteenth or early twelfth century BCE) do contain this, however, while also including significant elements which do not seem to have made it into the SB version.[36] The Emar version seems to have been written on a tablet that tells this story as a self-contained unit, and it is therefore difficult to tell to what extent the narrative was actually fitted into the longer *Epic of Gilgameš* at this stage. These earlier attestations of the textual tradition of

---

[30] Tigay 1982; George 2003: 32–3; Fleming and Milstein 2010 (developing a view that a core of the OB Gilgameš epic arose from direct engagement with written Sumerian forerunners); George 2018.
[31] Arnaud 2007: no. 42; George 2007: 253.
[32] Beckman 2003; Tigay 1982: 111–18; George 2007: 247–8. [33] George 2003: 31–2.
[34] Ni 13230 (Kramer, Çığ and Kızılyay 1969: 207, no. 149; Cavigneaux and Al-Rawi 1993: 101).
[35] George 2003: 320–5. [36] George 2003: 334–7.

this section of the *Epic* thus indicate that it was complicated. One cannot treat all narrations as if they belong to the same source, and one must be careful not to conflate different versions. Most importantly, it means that we cannot be sure at what point the text of the SB version of Tablet VI known from first-millennium manuscripts reached its classic form.

A further caveat to be observed here is that during the MB/LBA period a new generation of lexical material arises that is far more orientated towards scholarship and hermeneutics than the lexical lists of the OB period. Texts such as *Erimhuš* or *Nabnītu* are arranged in a very different fashion.[37] For a start, they tend to arrange words in groups that can be read in various different directions, both horizontally and vertically. The function of these texts remains to be investigated in greater detail, but it is clear that they use certainly Sumerian and (less obviously) Akkadian literature as one of the building blocks sustaining their arrangement.[38] These texts illustrate the close connection between literature and lexical material, and their investigation is bound to illuminate the use-context of literature in the cuneiform world. However, there is a problem in using this material for the question that this chapter has set itself, as it was likely to have been structured under the influence of literary texts. If one is investigating the relationship between verbal structure in literature and the structure of lexical material, which was developed according to different principles, then the risk is too great that the scholarly lists which had their genesis in the MB period are already too entangled with literature to give us any clarity. However, the nature of this entanglement is a fertile ground for further research, and encompasses a far more complex nexus of relationships between texts, whether they be literary, administrative or the stuff of school learning, than is posited by a theory of direct allusion from text A to text B.

Naturally this means that there is a disconnect between the literary material we are looking at, the manuscripts of which are firmly rooted in the first millennium BCE, and the lexical lists that we will be looking at, which are mainly rooted in the earlier second millennium BCE and also frequently monolingual Sumerian. We cannot even be completely sure that there was an Akkadian version of Tablet VI in the earlier second millennium, nor that the MB tablets we have were incorporated into the epic prior to the first millennium. Future research might like to look at possible relationships between the OB Gilgameš poetry and contemporary lexical material. This research, however, has been motivated by the allegations of transmission between *Gilgameš* and Homer, and therefore is

---

[37] Veldhuis 2014: 233–6; Boddy 2020.   [38] Michalowski 1998b; Boddy 2020.

limited by the material available. Due to the fact that the episode related in Tablet VI also seems to have a very different tone to the rest of the Standard Babylonian epic, the question is limited in this regard as well. Any conclusions regarding the small amount of text we will survey are further restricted in their applicability by the fact that this section of narrative seems to stand alone within the epic in the first place.

Standard Babylonian *Gilgameš* VI and the Sign-Lists

The Textual Register

For the purpose of experimentally testing a relationship between OB sign-lists and the text of SB *Gilgameš* VI, Table 1 presents the words, or their Sumerian equivalents, from the first ten lines that are found in sign-lists from the earlier part of the second millennium BCE. Excepted from the count are pronouns and prepositions. There are twenty-one cases where words found in SB *Gilgameš* VI, 1–10 can be paralleled in this group of sign-lists, in fact exclusively OB *Ea*, OB *Aa* (which is a bilingual and supposedly learned version of the former), and OB *Diri*, which is also bilingual. There are eleven cases where the words do not appear in these lists. In two of those eleven the words may occur in MB versions of the list (*apāru* and *dumqum*) which have been excluded from this data-collection on methodological grounds.

It is too early to say whether such a distribution is significant. One would need a much larger sample, which would also take a large amount of time to gather unless the collection was performed by machine-aided means. Conclusions, therefore, need to be extremely conditional and provisional. A brief diagnostic survey from an OB letter (Table 2) shows that a similar distribution can also be found here; there are in fact very few items – once personal names, pronouns and prepositions are factored out – that do not also occur in the early sign-lists. Letters, let us remember, were not considered to be a high level in scribal achievement.[39] Many show literary effects, and model letters were part of the educational environment, so it is not surprising that people who were educated to write use words that occur in the training materials for learning to write, but nevertheless we might under certain circumstances expect letters to display a different register to literary texts. Of course, we might expect the results to be very

---

[39] A Sumerian School Dialogue writes, 'You wrote a letter, but that is the limit for you' (Vanstiphout 1997: 589 line 20; Charpin 2010: 67).

Table 1 *SB* Gilgameš VI, 1–10 and the evidence of the OB sign-lists

SB Gilgameš VI English	SB Gilgameš VI	Monolingual OB texts	Bilingual OB texts
he washed	*imsi*	luḫ P-Ea 234	*mesûm* P-Aa, 234
his matted hair	*malêšu*	—	*malûm* Oxford P-Diri B, 456
he cleaned	*ubbib*	—	*ubbubu* Nippur P-Diri, 36a
			ebbum Oxford P-Diri A, 36
his equipment	*tillēšu*	—	—
he shook out	*unassis*	—	—
his locks	*qimmassu*	—	*qimmatum* P-Aa, 809: 1
over his back	*elu ṣērīšu*	—	*ṣērum* P-Aa, 41: 3
he threw down	*iddi*	—	*nadû* P-Aa, 10, 74:1
his dirty things	*maršâtīšu*	—	—
he put on	*ittalbiša*	—	*litbušum* P-Aa, 66:1
his clean ones	*zakâtīšu*	—	—
shirts	*aṣâti*	—	—
he slipped on	*ittaḫlipa*	—	*ḫalāpum* P-Aa, 102
it was bound	*rakis*	—	*rakā*[*sum*] OB secondary Nippur Aa, 1
a sash	*aguḫḫu*	—	—
Gilgameš	ᵈGIŠ-*gím-maš*	gím = TÚN P-Ea, 718	*pāšum* Nippur secondary P-Aa iii 7
his crown	*agâšu*	aga = TÚN P-Ea, 719	*agûm* Nippur secondary P-Aa iii 9
he put on (and?)	*ītepramma*	—	—
on the beauty	*ana dumqi*	—	—
of Gilgameš	*ša* ᵈGIŠ-*gím-maš*	see above	see above
eyes	*īnī*	igi P-Ea 399–402	

91

Table 1 (*cont.*)

SB Gilgameš vi English	SB Gilgameš vi	Monolingual OB texts	Bilingual OB texts
she raised	*ittaši*		*naštâm* Nippur secondary P-Aa iii 20
lady	*rubātu*		
Ištar	d15 (*Ištar*)	*nun* P-Ea 391-398	d*eš₄-tár* Oxford P-Diri B, 604-607
come to me	*alkamma*		d*ina*[*na*] Oxford P-Diri A, 344
Gilgameš	d GIŠ-*gím-maš*	see above	*alikum* Nippur P-Diri, 98
you (be my) spouse	*lū ḫā'ir atta*		see above
your fruits	*inbika*		*ḫāwi*[*rum*] Oxford P-Diri A, 365
(to me)	*yâši*		*inbu*[*m*] Nippur P-Diri X, 222b
make a gift to me (and?)	*qâšu qīšamma*	*ba* P-Ea, 146	—
you be my husband	*atta lū mutima*	—	—
let me be your wife	*anāku lū aššatka*	—	*aḫāzu ša aššatim* Nippur P-Diri, 49
let me yoke for you	*luṣamidka*	—	—
a chariot	gišgigir	gigir P-Ea, 56	—
lapis lazuli	na4za.gìn		*uqnûm* P-Aa, 167: 1
gold	kù-sig₁₇		—

Twenty-one lexemes are also found in these, whether in Akkadian or Sumerian; eleven are not. Pronouns and particles are not counted. P = Proto, a misleading designation for the older phases of the lexical lists, here kept for considerations of space; OB = Old Babylonian. (i) *apāru* (l. 5) is found in first-millennium Diri I 23 (diri SI.A = *a-pa-ru*). The lexeme may be attested in two of the Middle Babylonian Diri manuscripts from Ugarit with the spelling *a-pá-ru*. (ii) *dumqum* does not appear directly in OB Diri (contra *CAD* D 180), but is attested in Diri Ugarit A 389, corresponding to IGI.ÉRIN (i.e., Sumerian sig₅ = 'good', MSL 14: 74, constructed with the sign IGI = *īnum* 'eye'?).

Table 2 *OB letter (AbB 3.2) and the OB sign-lists*

English	*AbB* 3.2	Monolingual OB	Bilingual OB
because of my servant	*aššum ṣuḫāriya*		*ṣuḫārū* P-*Diri* 71a-c
of the hand of	*ša qāti*	*šu* … Nippur Nigga 156-192	Nippur Nigga Bil. r i 1-18[a]
started a law-suit	*igrê*		*gerû* OB Aa r. i 29[b]
female slave	*gēme (amtum)*	—	—[c]
quarrel	*ditbatum*		*dabābum* Nippur *Diri* A o iii 9
much	*mattum*		*mādum* OB Ea o i 19
rise up	*iliamma*		*elûm* Nippur *Diri* r. iv 11
at the side of her sons	*idi dumu.meš-ša*	du-mu = TUR OB Nippur Ea MSL 14,29 L.e. r. 1	
will litigate and	*idabbumma*		see above *dabābum*
my face	*pāniya*		SAG = *pānum* OB Aa r ii 5
I made grim and	*udanninma*		*dunnunum* P-Aa 163/3
her face (intentions)	*pāniša*		OB Nippur Ea o iii 19'
I did not carry	*ul ūbil*		—
according to my perspective	*kīma nitliya*		
I spoke to her	*ittīša adbub*		see above *dabābum*
thus I said to her	*kīam aqbīšim*		
so, I (said)	*umma anākuma*		
our brother	*aḫūni*		*qabû* OB Aa r ii 59, 62
little	*ṣeḫrum*		*ṣeḫrum* Oxford P-*Diri* a ii 7'
wife	*aššatum*	*šeš* OB Nippur Ea 623	*aḫāzu ša aššatim* Nippur P-Diri, 49
is not married …	*ul aḫizma*		

93

Table 2 (*cont.*)

English	AbB 3.2	Monolingual OB	Bilingual OB
our father	abūni		see above *aḫāzu ša aššatim*
a wife	aššatam		
has made him marry	ušāḫissu		
now his sons	inanna dumu.meš-*šu*		
have made claims against us	iptaqrūniāti	—	see above *dubbubum*
if this litigation	*šumma dabābum annûm*	—	
is not pleasing to you	lā ṭābakkimma		see above dumu.meš
your sons	dumu.meš-*ki*		
as a result of your ...	ina tabšītiki	—	see above *dabābum*
will not litigate	lā idabbubū		
but you should not litigate	attīma lā tadabbubima		
against you	ana pāniki		see above *pānum*
do not make us stand	lā tušazzeniāti		
we and your sons	nīnu u dumu.meš-*ki*	—	see above dumu
to the judges	ana di.ku₅.meš		
let us approach	i nisniq	—	
our affair	awātīni		*awātum* OB Aa r ii 67

[a] šu (hand) does not appear on its own in Nigga, but in compound forms.
[b] Karpeles 01; Civil 2010: 13 refers to this tablet as PAS 27 (Proto-Aa/Ea Secondary Sources). *gerū*, *pānum*, *qabû* and *awātum* are all found on this one tablet, which is edited by *DCCLT* (accessed 18 April 2019). They are found in different sections, apart from *qabû* and *awātum*.
[c] Middle Babylonian (according to *DCCLT* accessed 18 April 2019) Syllabary B has: [gémé] = ge-e = SAL×KUR = *amtum*, Civil 2010: 21, no. 1.2.1 r. ii 11′. According to Civil 2010: 19, however, the tablet is Neo-Babylonian.

different if we were looking at a letter about a different topic, with a different set of relevant lexemes.

One should also remember that not all professional scribes will have received the same education.[40] They may have been being educated to be certain kinds of scribes: administrators, legal secretaries, land surveyors and composers of royal inscriptions all require different faculties. Certain professionals (e.g., lamentation singers) were also educated in writing as part of their profession without being necessarily referred to as 'scribes'. It would be particularly inappropriate for us to reify the lexical lists as some kind of homogeneous block of knowledge to which all scribes or literate people will have had access. Even a quick look at Tables 1 and 2 shows that the data has been culled from a number of different manuscripts. In most cases a composite text has been used according to the presentation in the series *Materials for the Sumerian Lexicon*, which can be deployed for orientation, but which hides variations between manuscripts, which themselves hide variations in the kind of lexical data that students had access to and generated in different places, and sometimes even in the same place at the same time.[41] While this makes the task of systematically comparing the lexical contents of cuneiform texts with the evidence of lexical lists all the more daunting, it also should make clear to us what huge possibilities there are for research in this area, theoretically (in our wildest dreams) even giving us the possibility to localise the composition of literary texts.

Sign-Lists: Word and Phrase

The previous considerations concern only the preponderance of words found in the early sign-lists, which could be explained by the composers of SB *Gilgameš* VI, 1–10 having been through something like an education containing variations on these lists. There are, however, further observations that can be made on a possible intertextual relationship between the sign-lists and SB *Gilgameš* VI, 1–10 which may hint at a slightly higher level use of the sign-lists as intertextual source material. Here one needs to tread carefully, as the mechanics of textual reference come into play: authorial intention (if one can speak of such a thing sensibly), scribal whimsy (if one wishes to trivialise it) or, expressed in a less teleological

---

[40] Robson 2001.
[41] The individual manuscripts behind the composite texts are now easily available in the edition of the *DCCLT*, created and curated by N. Veldhuis. See further Crisostomo 2015: 126–31.

manner, the means by which the text signals meaning, above and beyond the immediate and primary meanings of the words chosen.

An OB four-sided prism of *Diri*, kept in Oxford, contains the word *malûm* 'dirty hair', and introduces us immediately to a pertinent world of association. The sign-list *Diri* is organised according to the structure of signs, but within the individual sections thematic complexes can be identified:[42]

b7	[[zaraḫₓ]]	(KI.KU.SAG)] [KI.KU].SAG	ni-is-sà-[tum]	wailing
b8	[[zaraḫ]]	[SAG.PA].LAGAB	ni-is-sà-[tum]	wailing
b9	[[sağ²-mudra₆]]	[SAG².MU].BU	ma-⌜a⌝-lu-[ú-um]	dirty hair
b10	[[udul]]	[ÁB].KU	⌜ú-tu⌝-ul-lu-[um]	chief herdsman
b11	[[udul]]	[ÁB].KU	⌜re⌝-[é]-⌜ú li-a⌝-[tim]	herdsman of cows
b12	[[lipiš]]	[ÁB].ŠÀ	⌜li⌝-ib-bu-[um]	inner body

Here it appears that the transition between a section of signs starting with the sign SAG and a section starting with the sign ÁB has been managed by the thematic association between wailing, dirty hair (as a symbol of grief) and the herdsman or shepherd, a group of contexts that one would expect to be found associated with the cult of the shepherd Dumuzi, suffering spouse of Inanna/Ištar whose periodic disappearance into the underworld is accompanied by wailing rites.[43] B. Currie has argued in some detail that the figure of Dumuzi forms a reverse foil for Gilgameš in this section of the epic.[44] The use of the term 'filthy hair' (*malûm*) brings us straight into that complex of associations with Dumuzi. The source for this does not have to have been the lexical list, of course, and it seems likely that there was a relationship of 'compositional interdependence' (to use J. Crisostomo's phrase) between the lexical lists and the Old Babylonian literary compositions.[45]

Currie argues that the toilette and seduction scene as we have it in *Gilgameš* VI is a reverse of those found in the OB Sumerian-language Inanna-Dumuzi songs. This asks us to countenance the transmission of these songs by unknown people in such a form that the *Gilgameš* sequence could be recognised as an inversion of them by the audience of Tablet VI around five centuries later.[46] This is of course not beyond belief, and it is

---

[42] *OECT* 4.153. The text here follows the edition of *DCCLT*.
[43] I am grateful to Fran Reynolds for pointing this out in the discussion following my paper at the conference. For Dumuzi as *uzullu* 'herdsman', see Farber 1977: 130 line 46.
[44] Currie 2016: 179.   [45] Crisostomo 2015: 131–8.
[46] Currie 2016: 183 evaluates the unknowns required to suppose a transmission of this scene to archaic Greece. The same unknowns need to be posited for a transmission within Mesopotamia. In the case of the Inanna-Dumuzi songs (Sefati 1998), Currie (2016: 165) mentions the Middle Babylonian Akkadian poem *erbamma rē'û* 'come in to me, shepherd' (Black 1983) as evidence that the Inanna-Dumuzi songs continued in Akkadian tradition. The poem undoubtedly has a very similar content to

certainly convincing that the figure of Dumuzi is being invoked in the manner he imagines, but it is also clear that Dumuzi existed as a figure outside of the specific literary texts which Currie uses as the targets of allusion. Indeed, we have concrete evidence for certain people using lexical lists such as *Diri*, and for those same kinds of people using in the broadest sense the *Epic of Gilgameš*. Those people are scholars and scribes, and it is among this group and their productive activity that we should look for contexts where a textual relationship might make sense.

On the level of writing, the name Gilgameš is spelled in most first-millennium SB manuscripts as ᵈGIŠ-*gím-maš*, but this spelling already appears in MB Ur during the second millennium BCE and presumably forms the basis for the phonetic variation ᵈGIŠ-*gim-maš* that is regular in manuscripts from Hattusa.[47] The sign value gím is given to the sign TÙN, which also has the value àga when it is *gunified* (i.e., has extra wedges added to it), as OB *Ea*, 718–19 explains to us.[48] As we learn from corresponding entries in a secondary version of OB *Aa* from Nippur, these two phonetic values of the same sign have the meanings *pāšum* 'axe' and *agûm* 'crown' respectively. The line (VI, 5) *Gilgameš agâšu itepramma* as written, therefore, contains a pun that is based on the name of Gilgameš as it is spelled: 'Mr "Axe/Crown" put on his crown'.[49] This play is only workable with this spelling of the name Gilgameš. In terms of intratextual significance this line is picked up in Enkidu's dream of the underworld, where his vision includes the observation 'the crowns were stowed away' (*kummusū agû*, SB *Gilgameš* VII, 194), i.e., the regalia of kingship were no longer relevant among the dead. The key line at SB *Gilgameš* (VI, 5), where the king is at the peak of his illustriousness such that he is propositioned by a goddess, is specially marked by the use of the double function of the sign TÙN (= axe, crown) directly followed by the word for crown.

---

the Sumerian ones, although it is quite different in tone and pace. The tablet's colophon tells us it was kept in a temple library or the library of a temple administrator of Ištar (Black 1983: 31). It is unclear to me to what extent this can be used as evidence of popular transmission.

[47] George 2003: 80–8; Rubio 2012: 4.

[48] *MSL* 14, 59. OB Nippur *Ea* PBS 5, 116 r ii' 1'–2'. The *DCCLT* edition makes clear that the sign has TÙNᵍ (i.e., one addition of extra wedges) corresponding to the phonetic value gi-ìm (*DCCLT* gi-iŋ₃) and TÙNᵍᵍ (i.e., twofold addition of extra wedges) corresponding to the value a-ga. These distinctions are elided towards the end of the Old Babylonian period and the single sign TÙN comes to have the values gím and àga (Rubio 2012: 4).

[49] George 2003: 88 makes the important qualification: 'the writing GIŠ-*gím-maš* has its origins in old traditions of spelling. If it was subject to speculative etymology and cryptography, that was a secondary development.' I would argue that it was precisely subject to a learned folk etymology of the type that Babylonian scholars engaged in especially during the second half of the second millennium BCE and the first millennium BCE.

Shortly after axe and crown in our secondary version of OB *Aa* from Nippur comes the entry iii 20: il = ÍL = *na-šu-ú-um*, which is the word that forms the verb in the next line of SB *Gilgameš* VI: *ana dumqi ša Gilgameš īnī ittaši rubūtu Ištar*, 'Lady Ištar looked covetously (lit. raised the eyes) on the beauty of Gilgameš'. This is possibly a coincidence (the entry is not preserved in standard OB *Ea*), but it leads us into a new complex of associations that also seem mediated by training in the art of writing. *īnī našûm* lit. 'to raise the eyes' is a well-known phrase with Biblical parallels that means to look upon covetously. Ištar looks on the 'beauty' of Gilgameš (*ana dumqi*). This of course seems perfectly logical, even if the only attestations of *dumqu* meaning physical beauty listed in the *Chicago Assyrian Dictionary* are from the *Epic of Gilgameš*.[50] The section on the sign NUN, which is the Sumerian writing inter alia for *rubûm* 'prince', comes directly after the section on IGI (= 'eye', Akkadian *īnum*) in OB *Ea* (see Table 1). We might also remember that the Sumerian word for *dumqu* is sig$_5$, which is composed of the signs IGI+ÉRIN. As noted in Table 1, sig$_5$ = *dumqum* does not appear in the sign-lists of the earlier second millennium BCE, although it makes an appearance in Middle Babylonian. If at all notable, these coincidences would appear to be semi-unconscious associations, which may be the result of having learned the text of OB *Ea*, and of thinking in writing or cuneiform signs as well as in language during the process of composition, rather than of any attempt to reinforce or redefine meaning through intertextually allusive reference. Whether observations such as these are viable can only be finally ascertained after a comprehensive overview of all of the language of the SB *Epic of Gilgameš* in comparison with that of the sign-lists, such as cannot be performed here. It seems quite possible that a Bakhtinian dialogue exists between this text and those ones. Currently one cannot prove it, but the existence of such a dialogue would beg the question with whom it was entertained. Here the point of reference is to the world of the schoolroom, rather than necessarily that of oral composition.

Standard Babylonian *Gilgameš* VI and the Word-Lists

Word and Phrase

The use of word-lists as comparators for language use has an entirely different value as evidence to that of the sign-lists. Instead of grouping entries according to the structure of the cuneiform signs they are composed

---

[50] *CAD* D 182, section 6.

of, the word-lists are organised according to semantic associations. It is perfectly possible that lexemes are listed together in the word-lists as well as occurring in phrases in poetic language simply because they belong to the same sphere of meaning and would be likely to occur together anyway, like 'knife and fork', for example. One can try to mitigate against this extra variable by seeing how often and in what other contexts the relevant concepts occur, but one can never be completely sure that association of words in a phrase is not simply due to the fact that they belong together anyway.

Ištar's speech to Gilgameš continues with mention of a number of wonderful things that will happen to him if he accepts her offer. The offer of the chariot she will yoke for him continues with descriptions of its wheels and 'horns':

11: *ša magarrūša ḫurāṣumma elmēšu qarnāša*
12: *lū ṣamdāta ūmī kūdanī rabbûti*

the wheels of which (are) gold and amber its horns
you shall have in harness 'storm-lions', huge mules

As pointed out by A. R. George, the horns of a chariot are dealt with in a section of the late version of the word-list *Ura* (Tablet 5, 25–7a).[51] However, an earlier monolingual version of the same lexical list, the OB 'Forerunner', brings the wheels and the horn into more direct contact with each other:

r i 12' ĝeš umbin-gigir	wooden chariot wheel
r i 13' ĝeš gag-umbin-gigir	wooden chariot wheel peg
r i 15' ĝeš si-gigir	wooden chariot horn

Whatever the horn of a chariot is, we here have it brought into close lexical contact with the wheel of the chariot. Possibly this was because 'wheel and horn' might have been a standard merism for 'chariot', and the proximity of the two in Old Babylonian *Ura* is a feature of the same associative processes that produce their juxtaposition here. However, it is not an association that occurs elsewhere, to my knowledge. The conclusion cannot be excluded that this is a coupling that has come about through association with the lexical lists.

The elements *ḫurāṣu* (kù-sig₁₇) 'gold' and *elmēšu* 'amber(?)' are also of interest. Even if we do not know precisely what element, stone or metal, is

---

[51] *MSL* 6, 6–7. George 2003: 830.

denoted by *elmešu*, we do know the Sumerian word for it: sù(-rá)-áĝ. This was used as a noun meaning 'brilliance' and as an adjective meaning 'brilliant' (lit. 'measured from afar') and is applied to and thus also comes to denote the object, whatever it is, as a transferred epithet.[52] sù-rá-áĝ is attested in OB *Ura* 2, 481–2 after tin, dark and light glass, and before kohl.[53] As an adjective, it is used in Sumerian literature as an epithet of Inanna/Ištar, of Su'en/Sîn the moon god and of gold and silver. One Sumerian literary attestation is of interest given the further context in SB *Gilgameš* VI, 7. The Sumerian poem *Enmerkar and the Lord of Aratta* involves a riddling contest between the kings of Uruk and Aratta, which results in the invention of writing and revolves around the acquisition of lapis lazuli from Aratta for the temple of Inanna in Uruk. Here we come across sù-rá-áĝ as an adjective describing silver and gold, to be heaped up in the courtyard of Aratta for Inanna.[54] Only a few lines later in SB *Gilgameš* VI, 15 Ištar wishes that *sippū arattû linaššiqū šēpīka* 'may the door-jambs and Aratta(-thrones) kiss your feet'. This line is of some narrative significance, as it is answered later during Gilgameš's insults (l. 41) where Gilgameš calls Ištar 'a shoe that bites the feet of its owner': *šēnu munaššikat šēpī bēlīša*. It is unlikely that the story of Enmerkar and the lord of Aratta was preserved beyond the OB period in written form, but the Aratta-throne and the notion of Aratta as the source of fine quality is attested in word-lists from that period on.[55] The density of interlinking echoes of Sumerian learned texts as well as Sumerian literature might suggest that these lines also were composed by people with knowledge of learned Sumerian, i.e., people who had learned how to write, and had been through a particular form of literate education.

Word-Lists and Narrative Structure

One further example will have to suffice to illustrate the possible relationship between the text we have been looking at and the word-lists of the OB school tradition, but also the difficulties of conducting such research.

---

[52] Mittermayer 2009: 142–3, 225–6.   [53] Edition *DCCLT*.   [54] Mittermayer 2009: 208.
[55] Mittermayer 2009: 33–6. C. Metcalf draws my attention to the unfortunately mutilated catalogue of past offenders against Inanna/Ištar in the Old Babylonian Sumerian poem *The Song of Inanna and Išme-Dagan* (Ludwig, Metcalf 2017), which appears to have points of overlap with the catalogue in SB *Gilgameš* VI (e.g., l. 22). Line 51 of the same composition has mention of 'Aratta, butted like a bull, [. . .] overturned,' which cannot prima facie be directly associated with the narrative in SB *Gilgameš* VI, but demonstrates the likelihood that there were multiple stories where Aratta, Inanna/Ištar and a bull appeared in some configuration.

The Scholar and the Poet

When Gilgameš begins his mythological catalogue of Ištar's former lovers, he begins with Dumuzi, the 'lover of your youth'.

46: *ana Dumūzi ḫāmiri ṣuḫrētīki*	to Dumuzi the lover of your youth
47: *šatta ana šatti bitakkâ taltīmeššu*	to him you allotted weeping year on year
48: *allalla bitruma tarāmēma*	you loved the speckled Allallu-bird
49: *tamḫaṣīšūma kappašu taltebrī*	you struck him and broke his wing
50: *izzaz ina qišāti išassi kappī*	he stands in the woods crying 'my wing'

We know a good deal about Ištar's relationship with Dumuzi the shepherd from other literary texts,[56] but we know nothing more than this mention about her relationship with the Allallu-bird. Andrew George pointed out that the Allallu-bird is the 'lesser shepherd-bird' in Sumerian, identified with the hoopoe, and that this is presumably what motivates the listing of this bird directly after Dumuzi the shepherd in the catalogue of Ištar's lovers.[57] Specifically he adduces the lexical text *Ura* 18 in its first-millennium version:[58]

239	sipa$^{\text{si-ba.mušen}}$	'shepherd-bird'	*re-é-a-um* 'shepherd'
240	sipa-tur^{mušen}	'lesser shepherd-bird'	*al-lal-lu*
241	sipa-tir-ra^{mušen}	'wood shepherd-bird'	*kub-ši bar-mat* 'speckle-cap'

Here the characteristic of the *allallu* as the junior partner of the 'shepherd-bird' is clearly established. The following entry, 'wood shepherd-bird', also gives us a further parallel with our literary context, given the *allallu*-bird now stands in the woods (*ina qišāti*). Can one say that it is not just the association of the particular bird (probably the hoopoe) with the shepherd in Sumerian that motivates the listing of *allallu* here, right after Dumuzi, but specifically its appearance in this word-list in this position? This might mean that the lexical list itself has formed a structural axis on which the catalogue in SB *Gilgameš* VI has been built at this point.

However, we would need to be able to follow this particular group of lines in *Ura* back into the OB period for this to be argued conclusively. Otherwise it is equally possible that the association of the *allallu*-bird with the woods has attracted the 'speckle-cap' into this position in the lexical list. The evidence does not suggest that the collocation as we have it in the first millennium BCE has great antiquity.[59] What evidence we do have

---

[56] *Descent of Inanna* (Sumerian): *ETCSL* t.1.4.1; *Descent of Ištar* (Akkadian): Lapinkivi 2010. Sumerian Love Songs: Alster 1993; Sefati 1998.
[57] George 2003: 834.   [58] *MSL* 8/2, 134.
[59] None of the monolingual Old Babylonian 'forerunners' to this part of *Ura* 4 (according to the OB tablet division) that are listed on the online resource for lexical lists (*DCCLT*) have appropriate

seems to indicate that during the thirteenth century not only the text of SB *Gilgameš* VI was in flux, as evidenced by the textual witnesses at Emar and Hattusa, but also the text that later became *Ura* 18.[60] At the very least we can confirm that it is the learned bilingual association of an Akkadian bird name with its Sumerian equivalent which has triggered the structure of the literary catalogue at this point in the epic. Further, we can observe the close thematic and chronological relationship between the development of the *Epic of Gilgameš* at this point and the development of the relevant thematic word-lists.

Orality and Literacy in Composition

What we have been looking at is thus a very different kind of intertextuality from the directed intertextuality or allusion that is commonly pursued in the field of Classical Studies, where meaning is supposed to be generated through reference to and inversion of or alignment with specific other texts. This is a kind of intertextuality that comes closer to the idea of a dialogue with multiple other texts that does not necessarily alter surface meaning through its terminal reference, but provides the background context for the lexical register of the text in the first place. Aside from providing reasons to be doubtful about some of the claims which have been made about direct textual relationships in the ancient Near East, my further claim would be that in some cases it may be possible to situate this background in the field of written literature.

The view that we are proposing is not a new kind of claim. Fleming and Milstein have for example proposed that what they see as the core of the OB *Epic of Gilgameš* was developed out of a written Sumerian model, an argument that would require an entirely separate discussion.[61] J. C. Johnson has also recently looked at the end of SB *Gilgameš* VI, 155, when

---

entries following OB Nippur *Ura* 4, 422 sipa^{mušen}, which is followed by the obscure entries LU$^?$ ^{mušen}, še$_{21}$^{mušen} and ĝi$_6$^{mušen} (Veldhuis 2004: 179). Only the variant prism from Sippar (*CT* 6, 14 ii 22–3) has kur-ma-di-lum^{mušen} and kur-⌈ma-dal⌉^{mušen} after the shepherd-bird, which are also not understood (Veldhuis 2004: 202, 265). For the earlier attestations of the sipa^{mušen} see Veldhuis 2004: 55, 103, 122, 164, 132.

[60] The sequence represented by first-millennium *Ura* 14, 239–40 (sipa^{mušen}, sipa-tur^{mušen}) does appear to be represented at Middle Babylonian Ugarit/Ras Shamra (*MSL* 8/2, 134). Also the version of the same text from Middle Babylonian Emar/Tell Meskene appears to have something similar to the first-millennium version, although it specifically omits the *allallu*-bird: (r i 14) sipa-lá^{mušen} x-' u-u (rē'û ?), (r i 15) sipa-tur-ra^{mušen} [ku-ub-ši] (r i 15) ⌈bar-ma⌉-at Msk 7498c+74171d (Arnaud 1985: 238, 434; Rutz 2013: 194). The same text also omitting the *allallu*-bird is also reproduced in a bilingual exercise tablet from Emar: Msk 7467 (Rutz 2013: 195).

[61] Fleming and Milstein 2010: 69–90; for a slightly different view, see Milstein 2016.

Enkidu throws the haunch (Akk. *imittu*) of the bull at Ištar, as an illustration of 'citationality' in Mesopotamian scribal practice, eventually leading back to a creative engagement with the sign-forms of the corresponding Sumerian words zag-udu 'haunch of a sheep' and zag-dib 'haunch of any other animal' (which only differ by one wedge) in lexical lists of the Old Babylonian period, which is also reflected in the Old Babylonian Sumerian version of *Gilgameš and the Bull of Heaven* (line 131: zag-dib-ba).[62] However, Johnson is careful to separate what he thinks are broadly oral from what he thinks are written forms of 'citationality'. The sequence of citational references from the SB *Gilgameš* VI, 155–9, where Enkidu throws the haunch and it is mourned by Ištar and her entourage, to the Sumerian *Gilgameš and the Bull of Heaven*, 130–9, where Gilgameš throws the haunch and distributes the meat to the townsfolk, and from there allegedly to the *Lugalbanda Epic*, where a bull is also slaughtered and a feast ensues (lines 365–85), is mediated for Johnson by 'the on-going function of banquets and feasts in Mesopotamian society as the primary instrument for the confirmation and calibration of social roles within Mesopotamian institutions'.[63] Johnson further talks of a 'zone of discursive interaction that normally existed in a purely oral medium', namely the relationship between the 'semantically over-determined' parallel feasting episodes in *Gilgameš and the Bull of Heaven* and SB *Gilgameš* VI, which he contrasts with the dialogue text he is discussing, where feasting also occurs, but where he is convinced that this belongs to the world of writing rather than that of orality. For me this is a false dichotomy. That Mesopotamians could recognise feasting and inversions of feasting hierarchies in literary texts is unproblematic. But one needs to be very careful if we understand this as saying that the process that led to the construction of the written texts as we have them was not inextricably bound up with interaction with multiple other texts that one came into contact with as part of scribal

---

[62] Johnson 2015b: 123–6. The notion of 'citationality' is derived from works by J. Derrida (1988) and C. V. Nakassis (2013), and explicitly allows for the creative re-making of traditional contexts through (truncated) citation: 'the recognition of a failure or neutralization within one domain, which serves as the springboard for a new type of citational domain' (Johnson 2015b: 126).

[63] Johnson 2015b: 128. It seems to be important for this account (Johnson 2015b: 126) that *imittu* (lit. 'right hand') can have the meaning 'penis', which puts a whole different perspective on the episode: 'Only in tandem with Gilgameš's rejection of the "the choicest cut" could {zag.dib} be reinvested with new meaning as a euphemism for the penis of the Bull of Heaven.' As Andrew George points out, this is unlikely to be the meaning of the word *imittu* in the SB epic at this juncture, however, as Enkidu says he wishes to do the same to her in the next line (SB *Gilgameš* VI, 156): 'However male she may have been elsewhere, the goddess of the Gilgameš epic is not likely to have had male genitals' (George 2003: 843).

education.[64] Whether *imittu* 'haunch' actually belongs in the category of words that can provide evidence for this entanglement would require a separate investigation.

The tentative hypothesis that could be drawn from the indications discussed above, from studying this tiny part of a large body of material, is that scholars and literati played a significant role in composing the SB *Gilgameš* VI as we have it. This also seems to correspond to the Babylonian memory of the authorial origin of the epic, namely that it was the work of Sîn-leqi-unninni, a Babylonian scholar most likely of the Kassite period. Modern scholars have also thought that this person was the one who was responsible for the reorganisation of the epic that resulted in the eleven-tablet version and for supplying the prologue and epilogue.[65] As we have seen, this must have happened at some point before the early twelfth century BCE at the latest. However, it seems that there was still a good amount of variation in the content of the text even at the time of the Emar and Boğazköy versions that contain content comparable to the later Tablet VI.

Just because we think it likely that literate scholars were involved in the composition of the epic as we have it does not mean that oral versions of the *Epic of Gilgameš* or of Gilgameš compositions did not exist. However, it may be that the written version of the poem was significantly different from any oral versions, unless the latter were in some sense dependent on the written tradition. The above considerations might indicate that the *Epic of Gilgameš* stems from a written version based on very different premises from those that might underlie an entirely oral composition, due to the fact that the use of cuneiform writing by scholars involved exposure to a complex and extensive training programme. The claim we are making is that our rich evidence for this scribal training may yet offer us glimpses into the workshop that created the epic's text, or at least parts of it. That oral methods of composition might also have played a role is not excluded by this account.

The main conclusion to be drawn from the above, albeit limited, research is that investigation of school-texts when dealing with

---

[64] It is possible that I have misunderstood Johnson here, as he does not explicitly say that the mutually commenting texts SB *Gilgameš* VI > *Gilgameš and the Bull of Heaven* > *Lugalbanda* arose in an oral environment, but he does contrast the relations seen between the feasting episodes contained in these texts (which may in the case of zag-dib = 'haunch' have had connections to a scholastic environment, but only [?] during the Old Babylonian period) and the so-called Class Reunion, which he sees as a product of a written environment (Johnson 2015b: 128).

[65] George 2003: 28–33.

Mesopotamian literature in Akkadian is something that can fruitfully be pursued, although with much difficulty and many caveats. A great deal more needs to be researched before we come to any firm conclusions about any of this: do other parts of the SB version have similar relations to the Sumerian of scribal instruction, or is it just this one, which also has a direct Sumerian predecessor in the form of the poem *Gilgameš and the Bull of Heaven* and which in any case seems to be a stand-alone composition in its own right? Do the OB Akkadian versions have similar relations with OB lexical lists as the SB version? If so, to what extent can they be said to have been formed by the lexical lists or, by contrast, to what extent have the lexical lists been formed by language that is used in *Gilgameš* or other literary texts? For these questions a thorough comparative lexeme inventory of literary texts and lexical lists would need to be created. It is possible that we can win ourselves a powerful tool for the understanding of Mesopotamian literature if we give credit to the scholars who wrote cuneiform for more than simple reproduction or copying of pre-existing texts.[66] At some stage and at some level they were also involved in developing and composing the texts themselves. The Mesopotamians certainly seem to have thought that was the case.

More broadly speaking, I would like add to those voices who encourage caution when considering parallels between one specific text and another, whether within Mesopotamia or between Mesopotamia and Greece.[67] There is so much missing evidence that comparing only texts and their relations with each other is bound to be an extremely truncated exercise in itself. The Mesopotamian source material transports a large amount of different types of data that, firstly, are not preserved at all in this form in the Greek world and, secondly, need to be taken into account when trying to understand Mesopotamian literature in the first place. These may place restrictions on the kind of scenarios we can reconstruct for any alleged transmission between Mesopotamia and Greece, especially regarding the relationship between a predominantly written and a predominantly oral type of transmission. Especially on the basis of the evidence we have for training in writing from Mesopotamia, there is a whole educational structure that goes along with it, and moreover one that changed and varied through time and from place to place. The cuneiform writing system itself was furthermore suited to interpretive interference in a way that alphabetic writing systems are not usually thought to have been. This too may have had an effect on the formation of the literary works in ways

[66] Crisostomo 2015; Johnson 2015b.   [67] Kelly 2014: 30–1.

that we are only beginning to understand. One can argue that the existence of parallels between Greek works and those of Mesopotamia is evidence for the existence of contacts in the first place.[68] That is as may be, but if one wishes to conduct such an inquiry into what those contacts might have been and how they may have been possible, I would move that it is necessary to include the culturally specific whole picture of the context in which the literary work is generated, in as far as this can be achieved, and where we happen to have far better chances of reconstructing this for Mesopotamia than we do for Greece. In this case, the literary work that is SB *Gilgameš* VI may not have been constructed in a context that was suited to moving around a great deal, at least not in oral transmission.

---

[68] '... literary evidence and its interpretation are part of the historical picture' (Currie 2016: 221).

PART II

Influence

CHAPTER 5

Playing with Traditions
The Near Eastern Background to Hesiod's Story
of the Five Human Races

André Lardinois

A frequently asked question about the Near Eastern background of early Greek stories is 'how, if at all, this material might affect our interpretation of Greek literature'.[1] This question entails another important one, namely whether or not the Greeks themselves were aware of the Near Eastern origin of any of these stories. Glenn Most has stated that 'the similarities between the *Iliad* and *Gilgameš* or the *Theogony* and *Enūma Eliš* are evident and fascinating for us, but they were quite unknown, and of no interest whatsoever, to the Greeks'.[2] In this chapter I will challenge this assumption. I will argue that Hesiod's audience was aware of the oriental or, at least, foreign origin of the story of the five human races,[3] and that Hesiod, or whoever composed the *Works and Days*,[4] did his best to make it acceptable to a Greek audience. This argument assumes that this story has a Near Eastern background and was recently imported into Greece when the poem in its current version was composed.[5]

In order to defend this thesis, I will discuss the criteria by which we can determine if a Greek story or theme was adopted from the Near East or not, including possible indications that it arrived relatively recently in

---

[1] López-Ruiz 2010: 34, quoting Haubold 2002: 2, quoting Halliwell 1998: 235. I would like to thank the two editors of this volume for their insightful and critical comments, which made me rethink and reformulate parts of my argument. I know they do not agree with all I say in this chapter, so they should not be held responsible for its failings.
[2] Most 2003: 385, quoted with approval by Haubold 2013a: 11.
[3] It is worth pointing out that Hesiod distinguishes between five (or four: see note 65 below) different human races (γένη), not ages, although the oriental story on which he based his account probably spoke of four metallic ages; cf. Currie 2012b: 39.
[4] By convention, I will refer to the poet of the *Works and Days* as Hesiod, although I am persuaded by the arguments of Nagy 1990 and others that Hesiod is a poetic persona who represents the internal narrator but not necessarily the actual poet-performer; see most recently Koning 2018. This question does not affect my argument in this chapter.
[5] I assume with most scholars that the version of the *Works and Days* we possess today dates back to the seventh century BCE, the same period that in the history of Greek art is referred to as the 'orientalising period'. On the dating of Hesiod's poems, see Koning 2018: 21–4.

Greece, and apply them to the story of the five human races in Hesiod. I will argue for a Near Eastern origin of this story against those who maintain that the story has a native Greek, a universal or Indo-European origin. The heart of the chapter is a demonstration that the way in which Hesiod introduces, adapts and integrates the story within the composition of the *Works and Days* as a whole strongly suggests that he expected his audience to be aware of its foreign origins. The paper ends with a discussion of what significance Hesiod or his audience would have attached to such recognisable foreign tales: would they have valued them more or less than their own native traditions?

The Near Eastern Origin of Hesiod's Story of the Five Human Races

I have identified the following six criteria that can help us to determine if we are dealing with an adaptation of a Near Eastern story or not.[6] They are for the most part based on earlier discussions about possible Near Eastern influences on Greek literature.[7] By an adaptation I mean a story or theme in Greek literature for which a Near Eastern story or theme is the most likely source, even if we have to postulate several intermediaries between the Greek and Near Eastern versions that have survived.[8] I have identified the following conditions for the identification of a possible Near Eastern parallel. They will be explained in further detail below:

(1) There is a reasonable correspondence between the Greek and the Near Eastern text(s).
(2) The story or theme is not also part of an Indo-European or other tradition or attributable to common human experience.
(3) It is quite unique and therefore unlikely to have been fashioned independently in Greece and the Near East.
(4) It occurs in isolation from other Greek traditions, which it contradicts.[9]

---

[6] For a more elaborate explanation of these criteria, see Lardinois 2018, where I also explain what I mean by 'Greece' and 'the Near East' in the Late Bronze/Early Iron Age and identify possible ways of transmission.
[7] E.g., Penglase 1994: 5–12; Bernabé 1995; van Dongen 2008; López-Ruiz 2014a: 159–65; Rollinger 2015 and Currie 2016: 1–38.
[8] Some have argued that only themes passed from one tradition to another (e.g., Mondi 1990), while others have emphasised the role whole narratives must have played in the transmission of stories and ideas from the Near East (e.g., Currie 2016: esp. 147–222). We don't have to choose between these two options.
[9] This criterion and the following one are applied in Burkert 1992: 88–127.

(5) It is found together with other adaptations from the Near East in the same Greek text or author.
(6) Its Near Eastern origin helps to clarify aspects of the Greek text.[10]

The first three of these criteria are essential for arguing that a story or theme in Greek literature originated in the Near East. The other three are optional, but when they are met, they are an indication that the adaptation probably happened relatively recently. I will now apply these six criteria to Hesiod's story of the five human races.

The first and most important criterion is that there should be a reasonable similarity between the Greek and the Near Eastern texts. In *Works and Days* 106–201, Hesiod accounts how first there was a human race of gold, which lived like gods, subsequently a silver and bronze race, which progressively got worse, then the race of heroes, who fought at Thebes and at Troy, and finally the present race of iron, in which there are diseases and humans have to work hard, and which, Hesiod predicts, could get even worse and then be destroyed by Zeus as well.

Many scholars have recognised a correspondence between this story and one Indian and two Near Eastern accounts, starting with Richard Reitzenstein.[11] The first one of these is the *Book of Daniel*, which is part of the Hebrew Bible. It dates to the second century BCE, although it draws on much older sources.[12] In the relevant sections (2:31–45), Daniel explains a dream to the Assyrian king Nebuchadnezzar, who had dreamt that he saw a great statue with a head made of gold, a chest and arms of silver, its middle and thighs made of bronze, its legs of iron and its feet partly of iron and partly of clay. Daniel explains that the different metals represent four successive kingdoms that progressively get worse. The last one of these is probably meant to refer to the contemporary kingdom of the Seleucids, which started as iron, but in the process got mixed with clay and has become brittle. The iron period in this story thus consists of two parts: a better and a worse half, just as in Hesiod. I will come back to this.

The other Near Eastern source is the *Avesta*, parts of which are preserved in the *Bahman Yast* and *Denkard*.[13] These texts are even younger, dating to the early Middle Ages, but they go back to much earlier material as well.[14] In them God presents to the great sage Zardust, known in the West as

---

[10] Cf. Currie 2016: 33–6, who uses the term 'meaningfulness' for this criterion.
[11] Reitzenstein 1924–5. See, more recently, West 1997: 312–19, Woodard 2007: 112–50, Rutherford 2009: 14–16 and Currie 2012b: 58–9.
[12] DiTommaso 2005: 49–50. These sources may include Hesiod's *Works and Days*, see below.
[13] West 1997: 313 n. 103.   [14] Boyce 1984.

Zarathustra, a vision in which he sees a tree with four branches: one gold, one silver, one steel, and one of adulterated iron. God explains that the branches represent four historical periods. It starts with Zardust's own time, in which God still speaks to him and the true faith was established. The times then progressively become worse until the devils, called Dews, take over in the age of adulterated iron.

A third text that is usually connected to these accounts is a passage from the Indian epic *Mahābhārata*, which attained its present form between the fourth century BCE and the fourth century CE.[15] In this passage four successive ages are described not in terms of metals but of throws of the dice. Just like the metals in the other versions of the story, these throws represent ages that progressively get worse.

Common to all these stories is the idea of four or five human ages that progressively get worse, resulting in the present age, and that are named after metals. This last feature is not found in the *Mahābhārata*, and it is therefore debatable if the Indian epic shows enough correspondence with the other texts to assume a connection. The resemblance between the other three stories is, however, close enough that it is reasonable to postulate a common source. The question then becomes what this source might have been and where we should locate it.

Michael Witzel has argued that the story of three or four ages is central to the mythologies of all peoples living in Eurasia and Northern and Middle America and goes back to a common tradition that formed itself in a period before the first passage of humans into the Americas (*c.* 20,000 BCE).[16] In that case it could have been part of a much older, Greek tradition as well. Witzel has to distinguish, however, between two versions of the tale: one dealing with different generations of gods and the other with different races of humans. In Mesoamerica, furthermore, the races of humans progressively get better, not worse.[17] The correspondence between these tales is therefore, in my view, not very close, and the common elements that remain (gods have ancestors, there were human races before the present one) could well have been arrived at by these peoples independently of one another. For the same reason, I am not convinced that we have to postulate a common origin for the Hesiodic story of the metal ages and the tale of the four human races in the

---

[15] van Buitenen 1973: xxiii–xxv.   [16] Witzel 2012: 86–90.
[17] Witzel 2012: 88–9. In ancient Greece both versions of the tale are attested: the divine succession myth and the story of the five human races. Both of these Greek stories, in their present form, seem to have been influenced by Near Eastern versions: for the divine succession myth, see note 40 below; I argue for the Near Eastern origin of Hesiod's story of the five human races in this chapter.

Mahābhārata. What makes the Hesiodic version of the story of the five human races, however, unique and closely corresponding to the versions of the story that are preserved in the *Book of Daniel* and the *Avesta*, is the identification of these races with metals. This detail shows that this particular conception of the different races of men must post-date the passage of humans into the Americas, because metallurgy was not discovered before the fourth millennium BCE.[18] The story probably originated in the Near East after 1200 BCE, when the melting down of iron ore was perfected and iron became more widely available, or earlier, but with a different kind of metal ranked as the least desirable one (see below).

Because all the corresponding texts are later than Hesiod's *Works and Days*, it has been argued that the line of transmission is from Hesiod to the *Avesta* and the *Book of Daniel*,[19] or that the story is derived from an older Indo-European tradition, linking up in this way with Hesiod.[20] I consider this very unlikely. For one thing the story in Hesiod sticks out from its immediate context, as we will see. It is chronologically incompatible with the story of Prometheus that Hesiod tells both in the *Theogony* and in the *Works and Days*, and it is also different from the ages of men as represented in the Homeric epics. Hesiod's insertion of the race of heroes, which is traditional but not associated with any type of metal, further indicates that he adapted an original story that spoke about four or five metal races. An Indo-European origin of this story is unlikely, if we exclude the story from the *Mahābhārata* as a parallel, as I have advocated. No trace of successive metal ages is found in the Vedas nor is it attested in the mythology of any other Indo-European people outside the Near East.[21]

The author of the *Book of Daniel* ascribes the dream that tells the story of the different metal ages to a Mesopotamian monarch, suggesting perhaps that he associated the story with this region.[22] It is therefore more likely that both the *Avesta* and the Hebrew Bible drew on an older,

---

[18] Witzel 2012: 88 does cite as a possible parallel to Hesiod's story a myth of the Navajo that distinguishes between a golden-coloured age, a silver- and copper-coloured one and a black age. Because metallurgy was invented only after humans crossed into the Americas, this myth must represent an independent tradition. Alternatively, the Navajo story was somehow influenced by the account in Hesiod or, more likely, by the *Book of Daniel* after the arrival of Europeans in the Americas.

[19] Boyce 1984: 70–2, Koenen 1994: 13. Koenen admits, however, that Hesiod 'grafted an heroic age onto a pre-existing narrative structure that catalogued the ages of mankind' and that 'the series of metallic ages is pre-Hesiodic' (24) and was influenced by oriental tales about cycles of ages, but he places this influence at an earlier period, in the second millennium BCE (25).

[20] Nelson 1998: 68, Woodard 2007: 112–50. [21] West 1997: 313 n. 104 and 2007: 23.

[22] For geographical references as possible indications of the origin of the story, see Currie 2016: 201–4.

Mesopotamian story, the more so since we find more examples of entities ranked by metals in Mesopotamian sources preceding Hesiod's account. Babylonian mystical and mythological explanatory works, dating to the second millennium BCE, identify gods in order of importance with precious metals: a Neo-Assyrian fragment of a god-list, for example, equates the chief god An with silver, while other gods are identified with gold (Enlil), copper (Ea) and tin (Ninazal).[23] Another set of tablets ranks a group of Babylonian gods as, respectively, silver (Angal), gold (Enmešarra), copper (Ea), tin (Ninmah) and lead (Ninurta).[24] In Hittite mythology the primordial god Kumarbi, who bears some resemblance to Kronos, the god who presides over the golden race in Hesiod's account, has a son named Silver, who briefly reigned in his stead.[25] The identification of gods and, possibly, their reigns with metals is therefore attested in the Near East before Hesiod's *Works and Days*. Akkadian sources further recognise multiple ages of men that are successively destroyed by the gods.[26] Finally, we find the equation of the moral impurities of Israël with base metals in the Hebrew Bible outside the *Book of Daniel* as well.[27]

I therefore consider it most likely that the story of the metal ages originated in Mesopotamia and spread from there to Greece, Iran and ancient Israel. It has been argued that this tale must have reached Greece in the Iron Age, because of the inclusion of iron as a metal of low value.[28] This is not necessarily the case: it is theoretically possible that the story reached Greece in an earlier period with a different list of metals, which Hesiod or one of his predecessors adapted to include iron.[29] There are other reasons, however, to assume that the story did reach Greece around the same time the *Works and Days* attained its present form, as we will see, making it likely that iron was already identified as the last metal in the Near Eastern story that Hesiod adapted.

The basic story of the metal ages has survived in two different versions. In the *Avesta* and in the *Book of Daniel* it is tied to a vision or dream that is given to a sage or king at the beginning of the cycle, in the golden age. The

---

[23] *CT* 24.49 (K.4349) E 3–6, quoted by Livingstone 1986: 182; cf. West 1997: 312.
[24] Livingstone 1986: 176–7.
[25] See Bachvarova 2016: 27–8 and 184–5 for the evidence; cf. Rutherford 2018: 9.
[26] For example, the Akkadian story of Atrahasīs, which distinguishes four ages of humans, the current one and three previous ages that were destroyed by the supreme god Enlil: López-Ruiz 2014b: 68–81; cf. Koenen 1994: 20–2.
[27] *Isa.* 1:22 and 25, *Jer.* 6:27–30, *Ezek.* 22:17–19 and *Mal.* 3:2–3, quoted by West 1997: 312.
[28] West 1997: 319; Rutherford 2009: 16.
[29] The Babylonian sources quoted above distinguish gold, silver, copper, tin and lead. They predate the widespread use of iron.

story in the *Works and Days*, on the other hand, is told by a poet towards the end of the cycle. This may of course be a coincidence, but it could also be an indication that these two versions represent two different stages in the telling of the story. In that case the Hesiodic version could have been the older one, from which the source of *Daniel* and the *Avesta* deviated by recasting the story as a vision set in the golden age. I consider it more likely, however, that Hesiod adapted the version of the story as preserved in the *Book of Daniel* and the *Avesta*, to cast himself as a (Near Eastern) prophet or seer, but now situated in the present, because there are other indications in the text that Hesiod is presenting himself as a prophet or holy man in this part of the *Works and Days*.[30]

The story in the *Book of Daniel* shares a unique feature with Hesiod's account in the *Works and Days*, which is the split of the current iron age into a bad and a potentially even worse period. This could have been part of the original story, but I would not exclude the possibility that the author of the *Book of Daniel* adopted this detail from Hesiod's poem, which in the Hellenistic period, when the author wrote, was a well-known Greek text. The Daniel story shares other similarities with the Avesta version, however, such as its setting in Mesopotamia and the presentation of the story as a dream or vision that is set in the Golden Age. The author of the *Book of Daniel* therefore must have drawn for his version of the story on an older Mesopotamian or Persian tale that inspired the Avesta story, as well.[31]

Of the three sources that preserve the tale no less than two are written in an Indo-European language: Greek and Persian. It is therefore understandable that some scholars have assumed that the story must have had an Indo-European origin and passed, either through Hesiod or a Persian source, to the one Semitic text that contains the story, the *Book of Daniel*.[32] I have argued above that I consider this unlikely. First one should recognise that, although the Persians, like the Hittites, spoke an Indo-European language, their culture, including their mythology, was heavily influenced by the Semitic cultures on which they bordered.[33] The story of the metal ages is not attested among any other Indo-European-

---

[30] Scodel 2014; cf. Currie 2007: 185–97, van Noorden 2015: 86.
[31] Boyce 1984: 71 argues that the mixture of iron and clay in *Daniel* is derived from the adulterated or intermixed iron found as the fourth type of metal in the Zoroastrian version of the story and that the Hebrew version of the story goes back to an Iranian tale. This explanation does not preclude influence from Hesiod's poem as well.
[32] Woodard 2007: 112–50. West 2007: 23 disagrees, and Calame 2009: 95–6 is sceptical.
[33] For the Hittites, e.g., Metcalf 2015a: esp. 79–103, Bachvarova 2016 and Rutherford 2018. The same has been argued, of course, for ancient Greece: e.g., Burkert 1992 and 2004, West 1997, López-Ruiz 2010 and 2014a.

speaking people nor in any archaic Greek source outside the *Works and Days*. It fits, on the other hand, the distinction of different human ages and the attachment of metals to different levels of gods in our Babylonian sources. A Semitic or Sumerian origin of the story, therefore, seems more likely than an Indo-European one. When the story passed from the Near East to Greece in the late eighth or seventh century BCE, it probably did so as an oral tale.[34]

Now that we have found a reasonable correspondence between the story of the five human races as narrated by Hesiod and Near Eastern sources and we have argued that it is unlikely that the Greeks inherited the story from an Indo-European tradition or derived it from common human experience, but probably adapted it from a Near Eastern tale, we still do not know if we are dealing with a recent adaptation or one that had been part of Greek culture for a long time. I have therefore identified three additional criteria that can help us to determine if an adaptation in Greek literature is relatively recent or not. The first one of these is the so-called argument of isolation, which applies when a story or theme stands out from its Greek context. If a parallel with a Near Eastern text contradicts better-attested Greek traditions, the story or theme is more likely to have been a recent adaptation. Adrian Kelly has objected to this criterion, arguing that the fact that a theme occurs only once or very sporadically in our Greek sources does not necessarily mean that it cannot be old and originally Greek.[35] He is, of course, right about this, but when we find, at the same time, a close parallel to this theme in a Near Eastern text, especially if it dates from more or less the same period as the Greek text,[36] it does make it more likely that it was recently adapted from the Near East than when the theme is repeated often and appears to be well integrated in other Greek texts. It does not prove it, but it does make it more plausible.

The story of the five human races is not found in archaic Greek poetry outside Hesiod's *Works and Days*. It is factually incompatible with the

---

[34] Oral transmission is now the consensus for the transmission of stories from the Near East to Greece in the Mycenean or archaic Greek period: see e.g., Henkelman 2006, López-Ruiz 2010: 5, Haubold 2013a: 24 n. 24, Bachvarova 2016: 5 and *passim*. Currie 2016: 198–9, 207, however, argues that (some) Greeks in the archaic period must have been acquainted with fixed texts, either in oral or written form, close to the texts we possess from the Near East, in order to explain some of the more comprehensive allusions. In later periods it is more likely that some Greeks learned to read cuneiform texts or texts written in Aramaic, Phoenician or Persian.

[35] Kelly 2008: esp. 260–73.

[36] Lardinois 2018: 901. If we include the Babylonian stories about the different ages of humans and the equation of gods with metals of different values, the period in which this theme is attested in the Near East extends from the middle of the second millennium through the middle of the first millennium BCE (*Daniel*) to the middle of the first millennium CE (*Avesta*).

story of Prometheus, which Hesiod narrates just before this story and which is also attested in the *Theogony*. It is also incompatible with the ages of men as represented in the Homeric epics. Homer only knows of two, or possibly three,[37] ages: the age of heroes, whom he characterises as demigods, and the current age of men. Hesiod obviously inserts the age of heroes, known from the Greek epic tradition, into the prototypical scheme of the four metal ages. Hesiod himself signals to his audience that this is a tale that is different from the Prometheus story by introducing it as 'another *logos* which I will summarise well and skillfully' (ἕτερόν τοι ἐγὼ λόγον ἐκκορυφώσω / εὖ καὶ ἐπισταμένως).[38] I will come back to this.

Hesiod's story of the metal races of men is surrounded by other possible adaptations of Near Eastern stories and themes. The whole genre of (extensive) wisdom literature, as exemplified by Hesiod's *Works and Days*, seems to have been influenced by Near Eastern and Egyptian precedents.[39] Hesiod's introduction of the story of the five races is different, however, from the way in which, for example, the story of the succession of divine kings, starting with Ouranos and ending with Zeus, is incorporated in the *Theogony*. This story has also been generally recognised as derived from Near Eastern sources, including the Hittite *Song of Emergence* and related compositions,[40] but it is fully integrated in the poem (not introduced as 'another story') and it does not contradict the dominant account of Zeus's descent in the Homeric epics.[41] This story therefore does not meet my fourth and sixth criteria: it does not occur in isolation from other, early Greek traditions, and the recognition of its Near Eastern origin, which I consider beyond doubt, is not necessary for understanding Hesiod's account. It therefore does not have to be a recent adaptation, but could have entered the Greek epic tradition already in the second millennium BCE.[42] The story of the different metal ages, on the other hand, is explicitly marked in the text as different from the preceding account of the conflict between Prometheus and Zeus.

---

[37] Most 1998: 121.
[38] *Op.* 106–7. For text and translation of the *Works and Days* I follow Most 2006–7.
[39] Walcot 1962, West 1997: 306–33, Rutherford 2009: 17–19 and Scodel 2014.
[40] Metcalf 2015a: 176 with extensive bibliography, adding Rutherford 2018 and Kelly, Chapter 16 in this volume.
[41] On alternative versions of the succession myth presented by divine characters in the epics, see Lardinois 2018. They should be distinguished from the version adopted by the narrator, which is very close to that of Hesiod.
[42] Rutherford 2018: 17–18.

Traditional Elements in Hesiod's Story of the Five Human Races

Hesiod's account of the metal races of men is laced with elements from traditional Greek mythology. Many of these elements have been identified by Glenn Most, who uses them to argue for the Greek origin of the story of the five human races.[43] A Greek origin of the story fails to explain, however, the incompatibility of the story with the preceding myth of Prometheus, which proclaims an immediate transition from a blissful period before Mekone, similar to the Golden Age, to the present age of men.

My contention is that Hesiod expected his audience to recognise the incompatibility of the two stories. As Richard Buxton remarks, 'To accuse Hesiod of inconsistency, of being unable to sustain a logical argument, would be wholly to misunderstand him. He *signals* the fact that the two stories are contradictory.'[44] What Hesiod subsequently does, however, is to insert elements from more traditional stories, such as the myth of Prometheus, into the 'foreign' and contradictory account of the successive metal ages. In this way he adapts the foreign story to its new Greek context without hiding what he is doing. This adaptation was made easier by the fact that the epic tradition already distinguished between different races of men (pre-flood or pre-Mekone, heroes, current generation), as we have seen, but the mapping of these races onto a series of metal races and expanding their number to five was something new.

Hesiod is here doing something that Dutch classicists have identified as 'anchoring innovation'.[45] He introduces a new story, borrowed from the Near East, into Greek mythology (an 'innovation'), but makes this story better understandable and more acceptable to his Greek audience by connecting it to ('anchoring it into') descriptions of gods, heroes and giants they know from their own tradition. Glenn Most remarks, at the end of the article in which he argues for the Greek origin of the story of the metal ages, 'I do not mean to suggest that Hesiod could not possibly have derived some degree of inspiration for his myth of the races from oriental

---

[43] Most 1998.
[44] Buxton 1994: 178. The attempt by Sourvinou-Inwood 1997 to reason away the differences in chronology between Hesiod's story of the five human races and the Prometheus story fails to convince. Her suggestion, for example, that the silver race lived just like the golden one under the reign of Kronos, and represents the paradisical state in which humans lived before Mekone, is not supported by Hesiod's text.
[45] Anchoring Innovation is the Gravitation Grant research agenda of OIKOS, the Dutch National Research School in Classical Studies. For more information see www.anchoringinnovation.nl. For a programmatic article, explaining the concept, see Sluiter 2017.

sources.'⁴⁶ My disagreement with him is therefore one of degree rather than principle. Most allows in this quotation for some elements of the story to be derived from the Near East (e.g., the list of metals), but he believes that most of the story is Greek. My contention is that most of the story is Near Eastern (e.g., the succession of four metal ages) and would have been recognised by his audience as such, but that Hesiod makes it Greek by adding known elements from earlier Greek traditions to it.

The first traditional elements that can be found in Hesiod's description of the golden race is its identification with the time of Kronos (*Op.* 111). Here he follows the chronology of the Succession Myth, which places the reign of Kronos before that of Zeus. In the *Theogony*, the reign of Kronos is depicted as cruel and tyrannical, but there was an equally old tradition that depicted the time of Kronos as happy and joyful.⁴⁷ This tradition is reflected not only in Hesiod's account of the golden race, but also in stories about Kronos' rule over the Islands of the Blessed, found in *Works and Days* 169 and, for example, in Pindar's *Olympian* 2.70–80.⁴⁸ The idea that before the current times there was a period when humans lived like gods is also presupposed by the Prometheus story.

In the *Works and Days*, the golden race is described in very similar terms to the Islands of the Blessed, which by the time of the composition of Hesiod's poem were already part of the Greek tradition:⁴⁹ those who dwell in them live 'with a spirit free of care' (ἀκηδέα θυμὸν ἔχοντες, *Op.* 170b = 112b) and the grain-giving field bears crops for them all year around (*Op.* 172–3 ≈ 117–18). After the golden race was ended, the people who were part of it are said to live on as 'spirits' (δαίμονες), whom Zeus appointed 'as guardians of mortal human beings: they watch over judgements and cruel deeds, clad in invisibility, walking everywhere upon the earth' (*Op.* 123b–5). The conception of such spirits seems to have been traditional too. We find the exact same description of *daimones* who assist Zeus as guardians of justice in the *Works and Days* (253b–5), and the recently discovered Brothers song of Sappho confirms the belief in such spirits in the archaic Greek period.⁵⁰ Finally, the golden race, like the other races of men (with

---

⁴⁶ Most 1998: 126.   ⁴⁷ Versnel 1993: 89–135, esp. 90–9 and 129–32.
⁴⁸ See West 1978: 194–5. The description of Kronus' rule over the Islands of the Blessed was elaborated upon in lines *Op.* 173a–e, which are found on two papyri.
⁴⁹ A reference to the Islands of the Blessed, as the Ἠλύσιον πεδίον, is found in *Od.* 4.561–9. See below.
⁵⁰ *Brothers Song* 14 and 18: Obbink 2016: 25 with Stehle 2016: 278–9.

the possible exception of the last race of iron),[51] is said to be created by the gods (*Op.* 109–10). This corresponds to stories about the creation of Pandora, as narrated both in the *Theogony* and in the *Works and Days* itself, or to tales about Prometheus' creation of humankind.[52] The references to races created out of gold and silver could also have reminded Hesiod's audience of Hephaestus' ability to create moving creatures out of silver and gold.[53]

The silver race is much inferior to the golden one. The people in it, after they grow up, 'suffer pains because of their acts of folly. For they could not restrain themselves from wicked outrage against each other nor were they willing to honour the immortals' (*Op.* 133b–5). One is reminded of stories such as those of Tantalus or Lycaon, who butchered their own sons and tried to feed them to the gods.[54] The fact that members of the silver race live on as 'blessed mortals under the earth', where they receive honours (*Op.* 141–2), could allude to existing cults of the dead or to the belief in evil spirits.[55]

Bruno Currie has well explained the skilful way in which Hesiod integrates the epic tradition that the heroes of old fought in armour of bronze (e.g., Ἀχαιῶν χαλκοχιτώνων, *Il.* 1.371) in his description of the race of bronze. Hesiod does not say that the members of this race were made of bronze, as the races of gold and silver were made from the metals after which they were named, but rather that they were named after their *use* of bronze, which makes them resemble the heroes who fought at Troy.[56] In this way Hesiod combines the *literal* use of bronze in previous generations, as proclaimed by the Greek epics, with the *metaphorical* quality of the metal in the sequence gold, silver, bronze and iron, suggested by the underlying Near Eastern tale.[57] Indeed, Hesiod suggests that the bronze race actually emerged from ash trees or ash tree nymphs (ἐκ μελιᾶν, *Op.* 145), an allusion to an older, Indo-European tradition that proclaimed

---

[51] Most 1998: 111–13. The golden and silver age are said to be created by the gods 'who have their mansions on Olympus' as a collective (*Op.* 110, 127), while the creation of the bronze age and the age of heroes is attributed to Zeus alone (*Op.* 143, 158). According to the alternative verses 173a–e, the age of iron was also created by Zeus.
[52] *Op.* 60–82; cf. *Th.* 570–84. On the sources for the story about Prometheus' creation of mankind, see Bremmer 2008: 33.
[53] Hom. *Il.* 18.417–21, *Od.* 7.91–4; cf. Most 1998: 110.   [54] Gantz 1993: 531–8 and 728–9.
[55] Cults of the dead: West 1978: 186. Evil spirits, who must be appeased: Clay 2003: 89–90.
[56] *Op.* 150–1: τῶν δ' ἦν χάλκεα μὲν τεύχεα, χάλκεοι δέ τε οἶκοι, / χαλκῷ δ' εἰργάζοντο· μέλας δ' οὐκ ἔσκε σίδηρος ('their weapons were of bronze, bronze were their houses, with bronze they worked; there was not any black iron').
[57] Currie 2012b: 45–7.

that humans were born from trees.⁵⁸ The way the supernatural strength of the bronze men is described is reminiscent of the description of the Hundred-Handers in the *Theogony*.⁵⁹ They are therefore described as a mix between primeval giants and the heroes who fought at Troy. Like most of these heroes, at least according to the Homeric epics, they go down to Hades after they die at each other's hands.

Hesiod's audience may well have thought that this was the extent to which he had integrated the heroic age into the succession of metal races and probably expected him to continue with a description of the iron age, but then Hesiod surprises them (and many later critics) by inserting a separate race of heroes. This race is furthermore introduced as 'more just and superior' (δικαιότερον καὶ ἄρειον, *Op.* 158) than the previous race of bronze, thus interrupting the progressive deterioration of the races found in all other versions of the tale. I will come back to this. The heroes are otherwise described as in the epics: they fight at Thebes and before the walls of Troy (*Op.* 161–5). The fact that these wars are explicitly said to have led to their destruction may be an allusion to Zeus's plan to stop the overpopulation of the earth by starting these two wars, as narrated in the *Cypria*.⁶⁰ Zeus awarded some of these heroes by settling them in the Islands of the Blessed after their death, as Menelaus and Helen are in the *Odyssey*.⁶¹

It is further worth mentioning that this race of heroes is referred to as demigods (ἡμίθεοι), a word attested only once in the Homeric epics (*Il.* 12.23), in a passage that explicitly looks back at the heroic age as a period distinct from the present one.⁶² It therefore may have been the common term for those semi-divine heroes who lived before the current generations of men.⁶³ Finally, there may be a humorous recognition of

---

⁵⁸ West 1978: 187 and 2007: 374–5. Clay 2003: 97 argues that this tradition is referred to in *Th.* 185–7 as well.
⁵⁹ *Op.* 148–9: 'Unapproachable they were, and upon their massive limbs grew great strength and untouchable hands out of their shoulders.' Cf. *Th.* 150–3 and 649. See Clay 2003: 91–7, who compares the bronze men to the armed warriors of Theban myth, the Spartoi, who sprang from the earth, and to the Giants. Most 1998: 122 points to Otus and Ephialtes, the two hubristic giants whom Odysseus sees in the underworld (*Od.* 11.305–20) as exhibiting some of the same features as the race of bronze. See also West 1978: 174 and van Noorden 2015: 77–8.
⁶⁰ Scholion D ad *Il.* 1.5, quoted by West 2003: 80–2.
⁶¹ *Od.* 4.561–9. For more heroes who in later sources were said to reside there, see West 1978: 192–3.
⁶² West 1978: 160, Martin 2018: 130. The term does appear more regularly in the Greek lyric poets.
⁶³ Most 1998: 111–13 may be right that Hesiod chooses the word γενεή (*Op.* 160) to designate the race of heroes instead of γένος, which he uses for the other races of men, in order to present them as an earlier *generation* of the present race of men rather than a whole new species. In so doing he would respect the fact that many aristocratic families traced their lineage back in an unbroken succession to the heroes. Cf. Koenen 1994: 11, Sourvinou-Inwood 1997: 11–12, and Clay 2003:

common tradition in that Hesiod makes Zeus alone responsible for creating this race of heroes and the previous race of bronze heroes, while the previous two races were the creations of all the gods together, since it was traditionally believed that 'father Zeus' (Ζεὺς δὲ πατήρ, *Op.* 143) was the begetter of many of these demigods.

The iron race is described in terms very similar to the conditions humans found themselves in after Mekone and after Pandora opened her jar. They are plagued day and night by toil and distress and worn down by suffering,[64] and, they receive from the gods a mixture of good and bad (*Op.* 179), just as Pandora was said to be 'a beautiful evil in exchange for good (i.e., fire)'.[65] One is also reminded of the two jars of Zeus in *Iliad* 24.527–33, from which Zeus gives to humans at best a mixture of good and evil. Yet, things could even get worse. Hesiod ends his description of the iron race with a prophecy about the possible further deterioration of this race.[66] Here, too, we find many echoes with themes that are picked up elsewhere in the *Works and Days*, such as a brother who is no longer a friend or men who speak crooked words and swear falsely.[67] I agree with those who argue that this deterioration of the present race of iron is not inevitable: it will only come about if people like Perses, or the 'gift-devouring' kings who support him, continue in their evil ways.[68] Hesiod presents them, and through them his audience, with a choice: preserve the present order, in which bad comes mixed with good things, or go down the path of injustice, at the end of which 'there will be no safeguard against evil' (*Op.* 201).

For Hesiod, humans have a choice between leading a relatively good or bad life. This is probably also the reason that he changes the original story of the metal ages, as it came to him from the Near East, and does not present the succession of human races as a progressive decline. Instead, he inserts the race of heroes as one that is in fact 'more just and superior' (*Op.* 158) than the previous race. Hesiod also never says that the bronze race is

---

93. Currie 2012b: 40–1 disagrees. Most 1998: 121 also recognises, however, that Homer makes a clear distinction between the heroes and 'such mortals who live now' (οἷοι νῦν βροτοί εἰσι, e.g., *Il.* 5.304).

[64] *Op.* 177–8. Cf. *Op.* 100–4.   [65] *Th.* 585, cf. *Op.* 57–8, *Th.* 602.

[66] On Near Eastern parallels for both the content and the form of this prophecy, see Scodel 2014.

[67] *Op.* 190–4, cf. 219–21. For more examples of themes that are echoed elsewhere in the *Works and Days*, see van Noorden 2015: 66–7.

[68] Most 1998: 117 n. 47: 'Interpreting the future tenses in the prophecy of lines 180–201 as predictions of an outcome from which there is no possible escape is not precluded by the rules of Greek grammar, but makes it impossible to understand why Hesiod should have bothered to compose this poem at all and stands in evident contradiction to the moderate optimism he expresses elsewhere.' Cf. Sourvinou-Inwood 1997: 4, Scodel 2014: 70.

worse than the silver one, as Jean-Pierre Vernant has pointed out.[69] One can of course deduce this from the metaphorical value of the two metals and the different fates of the two races after their death, but Hesiod introduces the bronze race as 'not similar to the silver one' (οὐκ ἀργυρέῳ οὐδὲν ὁμοῖον, *Op.* 144), while in the case of the silver race he says explicitly that it is 'much worse than the previous' golden race (πολὺ χειρότερον, *Op.* 127). Hesiod seems more interested in juxtaposing acts of reverence (golden race) and irreverence (silver race), bad warfare (bronze race) and heroic battles (race of heroes), or justice and injustice (iron race 1 and prophesied iron race 2) than in following the inevitable path of moral decline of the original story, as many critics have remarked.[70] My footnote to their work would be that Hesiod was doing this openly, in full view of his audience, which knew the oriental version of the story with its progressive decline of the different metal ages, and therefore was able to appreciate both Hesiod's deviations from this story and his insertions of allusions to common Greek traditions.

Early Greek Appreciation of Oriental Tales

It is impossible to know what Hesiod's original audience would have made of his adaptation of the story of the metal ages. All we can do is extract from Hesiod's wording how he presented it. For this I come back to the words with which he introduces the tale in lines 106–7: it is 'another story' (ἕτερον λόγον) that he will 'summarise' (if that is what ἐκκορυφώσω means)[71] both 'well and skilfully' (εὖ καὶ ἐπισταμένως), 'if you (i.e., Perses, but also his audience) want me to' (εἰ δ᾽ ἐθέλεις). The introduction of a story as a ἕτερος λόγος is unique in archaic Greek poetry. ἕτερος here could simply mean 'another, a second' story, but the *Lexikon des frühgriechischen Epos* may well be correct to list it under the meaning 'different, of another kind' of the adjective.[72] The word λόγος is ambiguous as well: it seems to be unmarked (any tale,[73] important or not) versus the marked

---

[69] Vernant 1965: 18 (1983: 7); cf. Most 1998: 108 and Clay 2003: 82.
[70] Vernant 1965 (1983), Koenen 1994: esp. 8–10, Most 1998: esp. 119–20, Clay 2003: 85 and Currie 2012b.
[71] See Wakker 1990 for this explanation with references to earlier discussions of the term.
[72] *LfgrE* 2.758, citing *Op.* 21 and *Od.* 9.302 as other examples of this use of the adjective; cf. van Noorden 2015: 70.
[73] Wakker 1990: 87–8 argues convincingly for the meaning tale ('Erzählung') rather than speech.

term *muthos*.⁷⁴ As West remarks concerning Hesiod's choice of the word *logos* here: 'Hesiod presents the story not as an absolute truth but as something that people tell, worth serious attention.'⁷⁵

Hesiod's specification that he tells the story 'well and skilfully' (εὖ καὶ ἐπισταμένως), emphasises the poetic skill with which he put the story together, which does not preclude, of course, that he also wanted his audience to learn from it: this is indicated by the phrase σὺ δ' ἐνὶ φρεσὶ βάλλεο σῇσιν ('you lay it up in your spirit') in the second half of line 107. The story helps to underwrite the central message of his poem, namely that people have a choice in leading a just life or not. My contention is that Hesiod felt the need to introduce the story nevertheless as an unmarked, alternative tale, because it was only recently introduced into Greece and therefore would still have been recognised by his audience as oriental or at least 'foreign'.⁷⁶

The ancient Greeks probably reacted differently to different oriental stories in different ways, as modern peoples do today to foreign stories. One may take as an example the very different, and often contradictory, reactions to American blockbuster movies in Europe: they are generally frowned upon by the cultural elites, but nevertheless very popular. I have argued elsewhere that some oriental tales are alluded to in the *Iliad* to underscore the lies told by, respectively, Hera and Poseidon.⁷⁷ Plato refers to his own version of the four metal races as a 'Phoenician lie' (Φοινικικόν τι [ψεῦδος]), a term that was apparently used for a story that people claim to be true, whereas in fact it is not.⁷⁸ It is, however, definitely not the case that the Greeks always considered tales that originated in the Near East as lies. The Succession Myth is a good counter example: despite its Hittite or Phoenician origin, it is at the heart of Hesiod's *Theogony* and presented there as absolutely truthful. It may even be that the oriental or foreign origin of the story, when it was first introduced, gave it more weight, just as the wisdom of Indian gurus today may find more resonance among

---

⁷⁴ Calame 2009: 64 with earlier bibliography. Contrast *Od.* 11.368 and *Op.* 10, where Hesiod describes his way of speaking in the poem as a whole as 'speaking a *muthos*' (μυθησαίμην) of 'truthful things' (ἐτήτυμα) to Perses.
⁷⁵ West 1978: 177.
⁷⁶ I believe the story was introduced into Hesiod's community in the late eighth or early seventh century BCE and had floated around long enough for him and his audience to know it, but short enough that it could still be recognised as foreign.
⁷⁷ Lardinois 2018. In the same article I argued that it is impossible to determine if Homer's or Hesiod's audiences would have recognised these tales as specifically 'oriental' (however they would have defined this term) or simply as 'foreign', i.e., not the type of story they were used to hearing.
⁷⁸ Pl. *Rep.* 414c, introducing the story in *Rep.* 415a–c; cf. Str. 3.5.5 (Vol. 1 440 Radt).

Western Europeans than their own Christian myths.[79] These Christian myths, of course, at one time had originated in the Near East as well. Hesiod's presentation of the story of the five human races, I would argue, falls somewhere in between these two extremes. It is not presented as a lie nor as a tale that his audience was necessarily expected to believe. It contradicts the canonical account of the Prometheus' myth, which Hesiod tells first, but it is still a serious story from which, if skilfully adapted and properly understood, one can learn about the human condition.

---

[79] I am thinking, for example, of the Bhagwan Shree Rajneesh, who was quite popular in Western Europe and the United States in the seventies and eighties of the last century; see Way and Way 2018.

CHAPTER 6

Etana *in* Greece

Bruno Currie

Introduction: The Question

The observable similarities between various extant Greek and Near Eastern poetic texts prompt one to ask whether there has been a transfer from one context to the other, which will typically mean, in the archaic period, from the Near East to Greece.* If one assumes such a transfer, one may ask what it is that gets transferred: mythology or poetry? Does the transferred entity have the status just of one or more free-floating motifs or of a more or less 'fixed text', not necessarily written?[1] And what levels of understanding and knowledge of the Near Eastern culture are we to imagine for early Greek receptions of Near Eastern mythology? One aspect of the last question pertains to poets, another to audiences. For the former, W. Burkert posited a rudimentary schooling in the Near East to account for the superficial-seeming acquaintance with certain canonical Mesopotamian texts, whose incipits were the object of allusions in early Greek epic; others have thought of bilingual poets, fully versed in each language and culture.[2] With respect to audiences, it is even less clear how much of this they could pick up on, and it has been doubted whether they would even have cared to make any connections with Near Eastern material, if they had been able to do so.[3]

These questions are usually pursued in connection with Near Eastern mythological poetry and early Greek hexameter poetry, for instance, *Gilgameš* and the *Iliad*, the Kumarbi cycle and Hesiod's *Theogony*.[4] But a significant contribution is also made by the Akkadian *Etana* 'epic' and

---

* I am grateful to the editors for various improvements.
[1] On 'fixed texts', not necessarily written, see Dowden 1996: 47–8; Fowler 2004: 230–1; Tsagalis 2011: 237–40; Montanari 2012: 2–3, 6–7; Currie 2016: 17–18 with n. 106, 21–2, 77, 102–3, 198–9 (specifically in the transfer of Near Eastern material to Greece).
[2] Burkert 1992: 95. See Currie 2016: 218–19.
[3] Most 2003: 385; Haubold 2013a: 11, 24, 29; Burgess 2015: 78–9.
[4] See, e.g., Burkert 1992: 96–9; West 1997: 276–86, 335–47; Currie 2016: 173–200, 208–10.

Archilochus' 'Lykambes epode', the latter a seventh-century composition close in date to the Homeric and Hesiodic epics.

Etana and Archilochus' Lykambes Epode

Both texts require introductions. *Etana* is known chiefly from three versions: an Old Babylonian version from the eighteenth to sixteenth centuries BCE, a Middle Assyrian version from the fourteenth to tenth centuries BCE, and a Standard Babylonian version from the tenth to seventh centuries BCE (abbreviated here respectively as OBV, MAV, and SBV). There are subtle differences between the three versions that need not detain us here.[5] It was evidently a well-known myth and poem in Mesopotamia.[6] It enjoyed a millennium of textual transmission in Akkadian cuneiform, and must also have enjoyed a parallel oral tradition.[7] A summary follows, based on the Standard Babylonian version:

> Etana is installed as king of Kiš. He builds a sanctuary to the god Adad in which a poplar grows, which becomes home to an eagle and a serpent. These swear an oath of friendship. After a while the eagle eats the serpent's young. The serpent complains to the sun god Šamaš, who instructs the serpent to lie in ambush in a dead ox's intestines. When the eagle comes to feed, the serpent seizes him, breaks his wing and throws him into a pit. In desperation the eagle prays to Šamaš; Šamaš undertakes to send a man to help him. In the meantime, Etana is praying in desperation to Šamaš because he has no heir. Šamaš tells him to help the eagle, who will help him in turn. Etana helps the eagle out of the pit and feeds him until he is returned to health. The eagle carries Etana on his back to heaven in quest of the plant of birth from Ištar. As they gain height, the eagle asks him three times how the land and sea look below. Etana answers with similes, until the land and sea are no longer visible. Etana is overcome with dizziness and asks to be taken back. The eagle drops him one league three times, catching him each time he falls. They fly subsequently to heaven and apparently[8] succeed in their quest (the end of the poem is not preserved).

---

[5] See Cooper 1977: 509–10; Röllig 1991: 283–4; Novotny 2001: x; Haul 2000: 6, etc.; Foster 2005: 534–5.
[6] Foster 2005: 533.
[7] On the oral tradition of *Etana*, several centuries either side of the cuneiform tradition, see Haul 2000: 39–44; Henkelman 2006: 813–14, 841–3, 847. Its two most distinctive episodes are illustrated on cylinder seals some 300 years earlier than the first extant textual witnesses. Aelian *NA* 12.21 (below, pp. 133–4) has plausibly been taken to indicate the continuing influence down to the third century CE of an oral Etana-tradition in some form. Winkelmann 2003 finds numerous elements of the Etana legend in Mesopotamian iconography reaching back into the fourth millennium BCE, reconstructing a myth and ritual complex from a prehistorical time before the legend was attached to Etana – putatively king of Kiš in the first half of the third millennium BCE.
[8] A son of Etana features in a Sumerian king list: Glassner 2004: 121.

Of Archilochus' poem we have ten fragments (frr. 172–81 Swift). The first two of these (on West's ordering) deal with Lykambes, who has apparently broken off Archilochus' bethrothal to his daughter (frr. 172–3 Swift).[9] The subsequent eight concern the fable of the Eagle and the Fox (frr. 174–81 Swift). The contours of this fabular narrative can be impressionistically supplemented by the Aesopic fable of *The Eagle and the Fox* (Fabula 1 Perry), which was evidently very substantially the same, though not identical in all respects.[10] The narrative, in a nutshell, is as follows:

> An eagle and a fox (or vixen) become friends, when one day the eagle decides to eat the fox's cubs. The fox prays to Zeus for revenge. The eagle subsequently takes smouldering meat from an altar and drops it in his nest. The nest catches fire and the chicks fall to the ground, whereupon the fox devours them.

Assessing the Similarities

The similarities between *Etana* and the Archilochean epode encompass genre, content, and form.[11] Both texts contain what we may recognise as a 'fabular' narrative, with speaking animals as the protagonists.[12] That is perhaps already suggestive, given that fable as a 'genre'[13] is often seen (by Babrius and by modern scholars) as a Mesopotamian import to Greece.[14] But more particularly, *Etana* and the Archilochean epode relay what is evidently the same fabular narrative: the friendship solemnly made between the two animals, eagle and serpent or eagle and fox, followed by the eagle's breaking of faith by eating the offspring of the serpent or fox; the aggrieved and impotent-seeming serpent or fox's imprecation of the eagle before a deity with the oversight of oaths; the eagle's incautious love of meat getting him into trouble; and, finally, the serpent or fox's revenge on the eagle.

---

[9] The traditional interpretation defended by Swift 2019: 329, is supported by D.Chr. 74.16 (cited by Bowie 2008: 138); cf. Gagné 2009: 265; Konstantinidou 2014: 305–7.
[10] On the date of the Aesopic fable, cf. da Cunha Corrêa 2007: 103 (first to third centuries CE).
[11] Cf. Adrados 1999–2003: i.349–50.
[12] The eagle-and-serpent narrative in *Etana* is not to be considered a 'fable' according to Haul 2000: 77 (not an 'allegorisches Spiel zur Ermahnung und Belehrung'), cf. 64–5. (For similar reasons, *Batrachomyomachia* is not a 'fable': van Dijk 1997: 126.)
[13] Problems with the term: Adrados 1999–2003: i.294–5.
[14] Babrius: (As)syrians (Prologue to Part ii 1–5); Callimachus: 'Lydians' (*Iamb*. 4, fr. 194.6ff. Pfeiffer). West 1997: 319–20 'there is no doubt that the Greek tradition derives from the Near East'; Kramer 1956: 124; Adrados 1999–2003: i.290–2.

Moreover, in both compositions, the fabular narrative contains extensive direct speech, which permits the animals developed, and contrastive, characterisation.[15] Specifically, *Etana*'s serpent and Archilochus' fox make speeches of virtually identical content in virtually identical narrative situations. The prayer to Šamaš from the serpent is as follows (*Etana* SBV II 59–71):[16]

> The serpent collapsed, weeping before Šamaš,
> [Before] Šamaš [the warrior his tears ran down],
> 'I trusted in you, [O warrior Šamaš],
> '(...)'
> 'Truly, O Šamaš, your net is the [wide] earth
> 'Your trap is the distant heaven.
> '[The eagle] must not es[cape] from your net,
> 'Th(at) malignant Anzu, who harboured evil [against his friend]!'

Part of the fox's prayer to Zeus in Archilochus' epode is preserved (fr. 177 Swift):

> 'O Zeus, o father Zeus, yours is the power in heaven,
> You oversee the deeds of men,
> Unlawful and lawful, and you are concerned
> With the transgression and justice of beasts.'

This is a particularly striking correspondence, about which more will be said later.[17]

In addition, both poems exploit connections between the framing biographical narrative and the embedded fabular narrative. Of Archilochus' epode, Gagné has spoken of a 'game of reflection that anchors the tale of the *ainos* in the framing of the biographical narrative'.[18] The description is equally applicable to *Etana*.[19] Etana's situation mirrors the eagle's: the eagle 'kept on beseeching Šamaš day after day, / "Am I to die in a pit? ... Save my life, me, the eagle!"' (II 121–2) and, ten lines later, Etana 'kept on beseeching Šamaš day after day, / "O Šamaš, you have dined from my fattest sheep! ... O lord, give the command, / Grant me the plant of birth ... Relieve me of my disgrace, grant me an heir!"' (II 131). The situation of the Archilochean speaker must also have mirrored that of the

---

[15] Cf. Trencsényi-Waldapfel 1959: 321.
[16] Translations throughout are from Foster 2005. Akkadian versions (OBV, MAV, SBV) can be found on *ORACC*.
[17] Trencsényi-Waldapfel 1959: 324. Burkert 1992: 122. Cf. *Myth of Sun's Eye*: Hoffmann and Quack 2007: 204; below, pp. 140–1.
[18] Gagné 2009: 255.   [19] Cf. Röllig 1991: 285–6.

fox in the fable. Although there are no clear verbal echoes, on the available textual evidence, it is likely that he represented himself as betrayed by Lykambes, much as the fox has been by the eagle.[20] Both poems are also permeated, in both the biographical framing narrative and the embedded fabular narrative, by the theme of childlessness. In the fabular narrative of *Etana*, the serpent loses its offspring, and in the framing narrative Etana is concerned about his childlessness. Both Archilochus' fox and eagle lose their offspring, and the speaker in the epode, having apparently been deprived of his promised bride through Lykambes' treachery, has lost a desired opportunity for procreation, an aspect of the epode emphasised in its reception by the Hellenistic epigrammatist Dioscorides.[21] These last kinds of correspondence are especially interesting because they concern both the fabular narratives and the framing narratives, and so suggest that Archilochus was somehow acquainted not just with the animal fable (which we could suppose enjoyed an existence independent of *Etana*),[22] but with a literary composition exhibiting the same complex narrative form as *Etana* itself.

Under further notable correspondences we may include a couple of details again from the fabular narrative. First, the oath of friendship sworn by the two animals.[23] The friendship in prospect is detailed in *Etana* SBV II 7–9:

> [The eagl]e made ready to speak, [saying to the serpent],
> '[Co]me, [let us make] friend[ship] (*rū'ūtu*),
> 'Let us be comrades, [you] and I.'

Compare Archilochus fr. 174 Swift: 'the fox and the eagle mingled partnership' (ξυν<εω>νίην / ἔμειξαν) or in Aesop's version, 'the eagle and the fox made (or pledged) friendship towards one another' (φιλίαν πρὸς ἀλλήλους σπεισάμενοι, *v.l.* ποιησάμενοι).

In both fabular narratives we find emphasis laid on the airborne eagle's apparent immunity from retaliation from the earthbound serpent or fox.[24] This is *Etana* SBV II 63–5:

---

[20] Cf. van Dijk 1997: 143 with n. 52; Carey 1986: 61.
[21] *AP* 7.352 'If we [the daughters of Lykambes] had been lewd and reckless, he would not have wanted to beget legitimate children from us': see Irwin 1998: 179; Brown 1997: 65–6, 69; cf. Gagné 2009: 254, 255, 261.
[22] Hengstl 2003: 207 and n. 18; West 1997: 503; da Cunha Corrêa 2007: 105.
[23] The oath is *Etana* SBV II 15–23 (similarly, the cat and the culture swear an oath in *Myth of the Sun's Eye*: Hoffmann and Quack 2007: 202). Compare the 'oath' (fr. 173.1 Swift) allegedly sworn between Archilochus and Lykambes in the biographical framing narrative.
[24] Haul 2000: 14 n. 44, 217.

Etana *in Greece*

'Now my nest is gone, [while his] ne[st is safe],
'My young are destroyed [while his young are] sa[fe].'[25]

Compare Archilochus fr. 176, where the eagle is evidently to be found 'sitting' on a steep and unapproachable 'lofty crag', 'scoffing at' or 'making light of' the fox's ability to do battle with him (σὴν ἐλαφρίζων μάχην: presumably an interior monologue of the fox).[26]

There are, of course, also differences between the two, some on the motival level:

(a) The eagle's antagonist is a snake in *Etana*, a fox in Archilochus, and the human protagonist of the framing narrative is linked to the wrong-doing animal, the eagle, in *Etana*, but to the wronged animal, the fox, in Archilochus.[27] It is hard to know how to evaluate this difference.[28] It may be relevant that the speaker identifies with a fox in another Archilochean fable, The Fox and the Monkey (frr. 185–7 Swift).[29]

(b) The eagle makes its nest on a 'lofty crag' (frr. 175.4, 176.1 Swift) in Archilochus, but in the crown of a poplar in *Etana*, at whose roots the serpent settles (II 5–6). (*Aesopica* 1 Perry has the eagle nesting on the top of a 'huge tree' and the vixen making her den in the undergrowth beneath the tree, as in *Etana*.)[30]

(c) To Šamaš, the sun god, in *Etana* corresponds not Helios in Archilochus (although Helios in Homer oversees oaths), but Zeus.[31]

(d) In *Etana*, Šamaš kills a wild ox for the serpent to ambush the eagle in; in Archilochus (and in Aesop), the eagle takes smouldering meat from an altar after a sacrifice (probably alluded to in Archil. fr. 180 Swift; cf. *Aesopica fab.* 1 Perry).[32]

---

[25] Cf. *Etana* OBV I/C 42–4 (Foster 2005: 537).
[26] Cf. *Aesopica* Fab. 1, οὐ μᾶλλον ἐπὶ τῷ τῶν νεοττῶν θανάτῳ ἐλυπήθη, ὅσον ἐπὶ τῆς ἀμύνης.
[27] Other animals in this role in the folktale (cf. ATU 222 'War between Birds (Insects) and Quadrupeds'): bear, mouse, jackal, cat, lion: Haul 2000: 82 (and 41–3); Winkelmann 2003: 604.
[28] da Cunha Corrêa 2007: 106–7. See further below, p. 142 n. 95.
[29] Compare the proverb of the Fox and Hedgehog, Archil. fr. 201 Swift; cf. Bodson 1987.
[30] In the Indian *Panchatantra*, a pair of crows live in a tree and a cobra lives in a hollow in the tree. In *Myth of Sun's Eye*, a vulture had offspring atop a mountain tree and a cat had offspring near a mountain. Below, pp. 138, 140.
[31] Adrados 1999–2003: i.322–3; Trencsényi-Waldapfel 1959: 324–6. Note the role of Re (= Helios) in *Myth of the Sun's Eye* (below, p. 140). Šamaš, Zeus, Helios, and Re as versions of 'the all-knowing god': Pettazzoni 1956: 49, 79, 145–51, 155–6.
[32] Cf. *Myth of the Sun's Eye* and *Panchatantra* (where the theft of the necklace also involves humans).

(e) The eagle's punishment in *Etana* is to get his wings broken and be left in a pit to starve, but his offspring are apparently left unharmed. In Archilochus and Aesop, the eagle himself is left unharmed, but his offspring are eaten by the fox.

Other notable differences are on the formal-narratival level:

(f) The framing narrative is a third-person narration in *Etana*, first-person in Archilochus.
(g) The fabular narrative and the framing narrative are on the same diegetic level in *Etana* (the 'Etana storyline' and 'eagle-and-serpent storyline' are co-ordinated storylines, with transitioning between the two).[33] In Archilochus, the fabular narrative and the framing narrative are on different diegetic levels, subordinate rather than co-ordinate (there is nesting, whereby the framing narrative embeds the fabular narrative).

However, the fact that it is possible to discuss differences in this way indicates how close these compositions are. Scholars speak quite confidently of 'influence' of *Etana* on Archilochus, or of 'dependence' of the latter on the former.[34] In so doing they are thinking of the fixed text model, not just floating motifs.

Floating Motifs and Oral Tradition

We have a good idea of what the floating motif model would look like here. Consider that most striking motif of *Etana* that is absent from Archilochus: a man's flight to heaven on an eagle. Four Greek myths or legends arguably exemplify the motif.[35]

First, Ganymedes being taken to Olympus in an eagle's talons.[36] This may not be very early; it is not attested before the fourth century BCE.[37] Besides, being involuntarily taken up in an eagle's talons is plainly not the same as riding on an eagle's back with a deliberate quest among the gods in view.[38] There *may* be some genetic relationship between the Ganymedes and Etana myths, but it is unclear, and polygenesis seems as plausible:

---

[33] Foster 2007: 63 'subplot'; cf. Hengstl 2003: 207 n. 18 'ungeschickt[e] Verflechtung der Handlungsstränge'; compare the *Odyssey*'s 'interlace technique' (de Jong 2001: xiv, 589–90).
[34] Haul 2000: 14 n. 44; Gagné 2009: 255 n. 12; Winitzer 2013: 458–9; cf. Trencsényi-Waldapfel 1959: 324, 326; Burkert 1992: 122–3.
[35] Cf. Daidalos and Ikaros: Duchemin 1995 (1957): 34; Haul 2000: 89.
[36] Ganymedes and Etana: Burkert 1992: 122; West 1997: 478, cf. 122; Dalley 1989: 189.
[37] Gantz 1993: 560.   [38] West 1997: 478.

'man carried by bird' is a recognised folktale motif (Thompson 1955–8: s.v. B552).[39] In short, any genetic connection seems weak at best, and is not to be conceived as a relationship between any specific 'texts'.

Second, Bellerophon attempting to ride Pegasos to Olympus in Greek myth would provide a closer comparandum, but for the fact that Pegasos is a winged horse, not an eagle.[40] Moreover, the motives for Bellerophon's ascent in the earlier mythological tradition (Homer, Pindar, and Euripides) are neither consistent nor clear,[41] which makes it hard to press further. Nevertheless, we will return to the relationship between Bellerophon and *Etana* later, in connection with Aristophanes' *Peace*, where, arguably, these two myths are conflated.[42]

Third, Alexander in the *Alexander Romance* (Pseudo-Callisthenes *Historia Alexandri Magni* 2.41, a work which may go back to the third century BCE) invents an ingenious mode of transportation to the sky. He has two large and strong birds starved, yoked together and enticed to fly by holding out horses' liver on a spear out of reach above their noses, while he himself was carried up in a bag of leather tied to the yoke. Again, a connection with *Etana* is not impossible, but seems distant at best.[43]

Fourth, Aelian tells a story to illustrate the love of humans that can be characteristic of animals, which runs as follows (*NA* 12.21):[44]

> The Chaldaeans[45] prophesied to Seuechoros, king of the Babylonians, that his grandson would deprive him of his rule, so he had his daughter locked away. Nevertheless she conceived a child, whom her custodians cast from the acropolis. The falling child was caught by an eagle and carried on its back to a garden. The gardener took a liking to the boy and brought him up. He was called 'Gilgamos', and became king of the Babylonians.

This miniature narrative is suggestive both because it inscribes the Babylonian provenance of the legend and because it associates what we recognise as an episode from the mythology of Etana with what we recognise clearly as the name of Gilgameš.[46] This confusion (conflation?)

---

[39] Cf. Haul 2000: 87–8.
[40] On Bellerophon and *Etana*, see Duchemin 1995 (1957): 34; Kirk 1970: 183, 226; Astour 1965: 266.
[41] Collard, Cropp and Lee 1995: 99. Seemingly a quest for immortality at Pind. *I.* 7.43–7; cf. *O.* 13.91–2.
[42] Below, pp. 136–7.
[43] Stoneman 1992: 106–10. Cf. Haul 2000: 89–90 (who also finds a version of the 'Hinabblick-Motiv' – below, p. 135 with n. 57, p. 139 with n. 75 – in the *Alexander Romance*).
[44] Henkelman 2006; West 1997: 478. Cf. Thompson 1955–8: B522.4 'Eagle carries off condemned child': Irish myth.
[45] 'Chaldaeans': Haubold 2013a: 145–6. [46] Currie 2016: 206.

of Etana with Gilgameš is less crass than it may seem: both are famous mythological Mesopotamian kings involved in a quest for a plant of immortality (Gilgameš) or birth (Etana), a quest that takes them on a prolonged journey well beyond normal human limits.[47]

The Aelian passage, post-dating Archilochus by some eight centuries, suggests some interesting perspectives on our question. First, Aelian's story bears the hallmarks of an oral tradition[48] that has seen a thorough refiguring of the original Babylonian myth, recombining the motif of the flight on the eagle's back with various other motifs familiar from Greek and/or Near Eastern myth and legend.[49] Second, for all that it is denatured, this story preserves, inscribes, consciousness of its Babylonian origins: a point to which we shall return.[50]

I take these cases to provide a telling contrast with what we can see with Archilochus' epode and *Etana*: a floating motif model, as opposed to a fixed text model. I postpone discussion of the implications (if any) for oral versus written transmission. Instead, I wish to consider two other arguable receptions of *Etana* in Greece where the fixed text model is conceivably in play.

The Fable of *The Eagle and the Dung-Beetle*

Another archaic and classical fable, of the Eagle and the Dung-Beetle, was known to Semonides (fr. 13 *IEG*) in the seventh century BCE. Aristophanes knew it in the late fifth century BCE as a '*logos* of Aesop'.[51] It has come down to us as '*Aesopica* 3 Perry'.[52]

Again, the reconstruction is not straightforward; the fable is attested in two divergent versions. In '*Aesopica* 3 Perry', an eagle kills the dung-beetle's suppliant, a hare. In a version preserved in the scholia to Aristophanes' *Peace*, the eagle has killed the dung-beetle's own young.[53] In both versions, the dung-beetle retaliates by rolling the eagle's eggs out of its nest until the eagle flies to Zeus and is granted a nesting-place on Zeus's lap. The odiferous dung-beetle, having followed the eagle to heaven, flies at Zeus and causes him to get to his feet and break the eagle's eggs again.

---

[47] Röllig 1984: 497; Haul 2000: 44–7; Henkelman 2006: 843; Winitzer 2013: 460–1.
[48] Henkelman 2006: 847–8.
[49] Princess vainly imprisoned to forestall conception of a mighty son: cf. Akrisios-Danaë-Perseus; Thompson 1955–8: T381. Hero exposed at birth: cf. Sargon (Foster 2005: 912), Moses, Kyros; Thompson 1955–8: R131. Henkelman 2006: 834–6.
[50] Below, pp. 141–3. [51] *Pax* 129–34. Cf. *Eq.* 1448, *Lys.* 695.
[52] Cf. *Life of Aesop*, 135–9; von Möllendorff 1994; cf. ATU 283H*. [53] ΣΣ Ar. *Pax* 129, 130.

This fable exhibits correspondences with *Etana* that the fable of the eagle and the fox lacks.[54] It combines the motif of a vendetta between an eagle and another animal (here, a dung-beetle) with the motif of the eagle flying to the gods in heaven. Admittedly, this is a flight to heaven without a passenger (and with a dung-beetle in pursuit). On the other hand, this flight to heaven is motivated by the eagle's concern for his progeny, as the eagle's flight to heaven in *Etana* is motivated by Etana's concern for his progeny.

In themselves these correspondences would not necessarily suggest dependence on *Etana*. But if we are to see the Archilochean and Aesopic fable of the eagle and the fox as influenced by Etana, then there is a parallel case for seeing the Semonidean and Aesopic fable of the eagle and the dung-beetle as influenced by Etana as well.

Aristophanes' *Peace*

Aristophanes' *Peace* explicitly draws on the fable of the eagle and the dung-beetle, but manifests several motifs that invite comparison with *Etana* itself. First, Trygaios' flight to the gods on the dung-beetle and his return to earth with Peace's attendants Opora and Theoria may be compared with Etana's flight to the gods and his (apparent) return to earth with the plant of birth.[55] Second, the feeding of the dung-beetle prior to the flight (*Pax* 1–37) resembles, with the comic addition of a scatological element, Etana's feeding of the wounded eagle.[56] Third, the descriptions of Trygaios' vertiginous ascent and the view of the earth below (*Pax* 154–78, 821–3) can be compared, again with scatological additions, to the 'looking-down motif' found in *Etana* (SBV III/A 31–42).[57] And fourth, whereas the Aesopic fable of *The Eagle and the Dung-Beetle* combined the characteristic themes of *Etana* – the feud between a bird and another animal and the flight to heaven, the latter without any human passenger – *Peace*, explicitly taking its cue from this Aesopic fable (*Pax* 129–34), presents a flight to heaven this time with a human passenger, but

---

[54] Duchemin 1995 (1957): 34 'offre précisément avec le mythe d'Étana une curieuse concordance'.
[55] Cf. *Etana* SBV III/C = Foster 2005: 553.
[56] Cf. the 'Etana-*Märchen*', ATU 537 (ii) (motif: 'The Grateful Eagle') 'the man nurses the bird for several years until it recovers, spending all his wealth'; cf. Haul 2000: 79, 82.
[57] On the 'Hinabblick-Motiv' motif in *Etana*, see Haul 2000: 23–7; 79–81, 90. In Ar. *Pax* and *Etana*: Duchemin 1995 (1957): 33–4. In the *Alexander Romance*: Haul 2000: 89, text to n. 321. In Etana-*Märchen* (ATU 537): Haul 2000: 82, cf. 79, 81.

borne by the dung-beetle, not the eagle.[58] Trygaios' comment that the dung-beetle was the 'only' 'winged'[59] creature discovered in the fables of Aesop to have gone to the gods (129–30) pointedly ignores the eagle: even in the fable of *The Eagle and Dung-Beetle* the dung-beetle followed the eagle to the gods' abode. A journey to heaven on the back of an eagle, therefore, appears to be a possibility studiedly overlooked in the comedy. It was a possibility, we know, that was realised in *Etana*. One may get the impression that the version of *Etana* is being deliberately bypassed in *Peace*: a way of 'making reference by refusing reference'.[60]

The sceptic will respond that this does not amount to a compelling case for *Etana*'s relevance to *Peace*.[61] It would be possible to dismiss some, at least, of these similarities as just coincidental and to see Aristophanes' comic manipulations of his explicit sources (Euripides' *Bellerophon* and Aesop's fable) as resulting in a constellation of motifs in the play that happens superficially to resemble *Etana* in certain respects. I admit that the case for dependence on or allusion to *Etana* is not compelling, but submit that it is suggestive, especially when we think about the interrelationship of the following motifs:

(1) (Euripides' *Bellerophon*) the winged horse Pegasos carries Bellerophon to heaven;
(2) (*Etana*) the eagle carries Etana to heaven;
(3) (Aesop's fable of *The Eagle and the Dung-Beetle*) the eagle and the dung-beetle both fly to heaven, without passengers;
(4) (Aristophanes' *Peace*) the dung-beetle carries Trygaios to heaven.

Aristophanes' conceit (4) is plainly and explicitly a comic pastiche of (1) and (3); this is paratragedy in the form of 'Aesopification' of a Euripidean model.[62] The presence of (2) in the comic mix is certainly not required; we can say simply that Aristophanes substitutes Aesop's dung-beetle for Euripides' Pegasos.[63] Yet the conceit is tighter, and perhaps funnier, with

---

[58] Cf. Duchemin 1995 (1957): 34, 35.
[59] The use of πετηνός (130), elsewhere of birds, is striking; Sem. fr. 13.1 *IEG* used ἑρπετόν of the dung-beetle.
[60] Cf. Dowden 1996: 53
[61] Cf. van Dijk 1997: 206 n. 133; Zogg 2014: 82 n. 436, critiquing Duchemin 1995 (1957).
[62] Hall 2013: 295 'what we are seeing here is the specific Aesopic parody of a tragic episode – its "Aesopification". For the winged horse of mythology is substituted the pathetic dung beetle of fable.'
[63] If Euripides' play emphasised the mythical variant in Σ *Il*. T 6.202a, '[*sc*. Bellerophon] pained at the destruction of his children', then his Bellerophon would have had a further point of resemblance to the dung-beetle. Cf. Collard, Cropp, and Lee 1995: 99.

it in the mix. The Aesopic fable (3) could be deemed to have established a kind of parity between dung-beetle and eagle in respect of flying to the gods; and if a comic poet is at liberty to interpret parity as intersubstitutability, then (3) seen against the background of (2) would by a kind of irresistible comic 'logic' generate (4).

Etana is not one of the explicit models of *Peace*, like Euripides' *Bellerophon* and Aesop's fable of *The Eagle and the Dung-Beetle*.[64] But Trygaios' journey to the gods in *Peace* may in principle have as many intertexts as Dionysos' opposite journey to the underworld in *Frogs*.[65] Nor does an ultimately Near Eastern 'source' for Aristophanes seem itself objectionable, if it is accepted for Archilochus, Semonides, and Aesop. A Near Eastern source has been posited for *Birds*, on the basis of the similarities of the city-building in the sky to an episode in the *Life of Ahiqar*.[66]

It should be emphasised that, on these readings, both the fable of the eagle and the dung-beetle, current in the seventh to fifth centuries BCE, and Aristophanes' *Peace* will imply knowledge of the whole *Etana* story, not just of the animal fable.

Etana inside and outside Greece

So far in considering '*Etana* in Greece' we have made a distinction between two models of transmission. On the one hand, a fixed text model, exemplified by Archilochus and, perhaps, Semonides, Aesop, and Aristophanes. On the other, a floating motif model found in Aelian's 'Gilgamos' story, the Ganymedes and Bellerophon myths, and the *Alexander Romance*. This picture may now be filled out by considering *Etana* outside of Greece.[67] I focus on three tales, or tale types, which have been connected with *Etana*. First, the Indian fable of *The Crows and the Cobra* contained within the *Panchatantra*, of perhaps *c.* 300 CE. Second, the Demotic Egyptian fable of *The Cat and the Vulture*, contained within the *Myth of the Sun's Eye*, of the second century CE.[68] And third, the

---

[64] The dung-beetle conflated with, and even addressed as, Pegasos: *Pax* 154, 723, cf. 135–9. Aristophanes does not mention Semonides: compare *Av.* 652–3, where only Aesop, not Archilochus, is mentioned apropos the fable of *The Eagle and the Fox*.
[65] Cf. Wright 2012: 95–6, 99–102.   [66] Ar. *Av.* 837–45, 1112–51. See Kurke 2011: 177–8 n. 46.
[67] *Etana*'s influence on *Genesis*: Winitzer 2013.
[68] For a German translation, see Hoffmann and Quack 2007: 195–229 (the whole embedding *Myth of the Sun's Eye*, here called not *Mythos vom Sonnenauge*, but *Die Heimkehr der Göttin*) esp. 202–4 (for the embedded fable of *The Cat and the Vulture*). For an overview, see Smith 1984.

so-called Etana-*Märchen*, collected mainly in Russia, Latvia, and Finland, in the nineteenth and early twentieth centuries.[69]

The fable of *The Crows and the Cobra* included in the *Panchatantra* runs as follows:

> A pair of crows live in a tree and a cobra lives in a hollow in the tree. The cobra repeatedly eats the crows' young. The crows consult their friend, a jackal, who lives at the bottom of another tree. On the jackal's advice, the female crow takes a necklace from some women of the king's harem as they bathe. Their attendants pursue the crow, who drops the necklace by the cobra's lair. The attendants find the cobra and club it to death.

This is probably still – just – recognisable as the 'same' fable as the eagle and serpent of *Etana*. It starts with an impressive correspondence of motif: the bird(s) are at the top of a tree, the snake at the bottom. There is also the shared pattern of unprovoked aggression followed by the aggressor's comeuppance, though the cobra is now the aggressor and the crows the avengers, and much else is changed. What correspondences there are exist purely on the level of motif, and those are very partial. Clearly this is not the fixed text model, though influence can still be posited.[70]

Things are different with the group of folktales known as 'Etana-*Märchen*' (the tale-type dubbed 'The Flight on the Grateful Eagle', numbered ATU 537) attested in the nineteenth and twentieth centuries in especially Eastern Europe and Scandinavia.[71] We find in this tale-type the following sequence of motifs:

> A man aims his gun three times at an eagle. When suddenly the bird speaks like a human being, the man spares it. The eagle has a broken wing and the man nurses the bird for several years until it recovers, spending all his wealth. The grateful bird carries the man on his back across the sea to his kingdom. On the way it frightens him three times by nearly dropping him into the sea (as the hunter had aimed three times at the bird).[72]

Although from this point the *Märchen* diverge considerably from *Etana*, this sequence of motifs tracks *Etana* closely. We find the motifs of the vulnerable eagle befriended by a man; the ability of man and bird to

---

[69] Geographical distribution: Röllig 1984: 496.
[70] Adrados 1999–2003: i.323: 'New elements have been introduced, therefore; topical elements, certainly, but the initial element corresponds: the bird and the serpent coexist together with a tree, there is betrayal and the death of the young, the punishment of the culprit. The point of departure is clearly Mesopotamia, as it is for the Greek fable.' Comparison of *Etana* with *Panchatantra* 1.4: Williams 1956: 75; Trencsényi-Waldapfel 1959: 318–19.
[71] Haavio 1955; Haul 2000: 79–81. Iraqi folktale of Shamshum al-Jabbar: Annus 2009: 90–1.
[72] Quoted from Uther 2004: 313–14.

Etana *in Greece* 139

understand each other's language (cf. *Etana* SBV III/A 1–8); the man feeding the bird; the man flying on bird's back; and the bird letting the man fall and catching him three times.[73] However, it is two additional correspondences that seem to put the link with *Etana* beyond reasonable doubt. First, the encounter of the man and the eagle is sometimes preceded by another tale-type, the 'War between Birds (Insects) and Quadrupeds' (ATU 222), which leaves the eagle wounded. In one case, moreover, the prelude to the man's discovery of the eagle is almost exactly as in *Etana*: a serpent and eagle feud because the eagle has eaten the serpent's young, whereupon the serpent breaks the eagle's wing.[74] The correspondences are not just with *Etana*'s framing narrative, but also with its fabular narrative. Secondly, when the eagle and man are airborne, the eagle asks the man three times, before dropping him, how the progressively receding land and sea appear to him, and the man each time answers in similes.[75] Again, this is almost exactly as in *Etana*.[76] The correspondences, accordingly, are not just on the motival level, but also on a narratival level, comprising direct speech and similes.

It seems next to impossible here to assume polygenesis. Extraordinary as the conclusion seems, these folktales and *Etana* must be genetically related.[77] Thus *Etana* becomes an intriguing test-case of the 'historic-geographic method' in folklore studies.[78] Some scholars assume that Mesopotamia is the origin of the myth and that it was diffused thence through South Arabia, the Balkans, Russia, and Scandinavia.[79] Others have emphasised that we cannot safely deduce that Mesopotamia was the origin of the folktale just because it provides (much) the earliest attestation of the folktale, and would see the origins and diffusion of the folktale as irretrievably in the dark.[80] These uncertainties aside, we can say that this is

---

[73] The differences are emphasised by Haul 2000: 85–6. The 'childbirth' theme is not a point in common: Haul 2000: 84; *pace* Henkelman 2006: 843.
[74] Haul 2000: 81, drawing on Levin 1994.
[75] *Etana* SBV III 31–41: after one league, the land has become one-fifth of its size, the sea has become like a paddock; after two leagues, the land has become a garden plot, the sea the size of a trough; after three leagues, Etana's eyes could not see the land or sea. Haavio 1955: 6 (folktale from Archangelsk): the first time, the sea looks like the bottom of a sieve; the second time, like a finger-ring; the third time, like the eye of a needle; cf. 7–8 (various similar Finnish folktales).
[76] Haul 2000: 81. Cf. Haavio 1955: 11.   [77] Haul 2000: 82, 87.
[78] Haul 2000: 85 critiques Levin's adoption of the historic-geographic method with the Etana myth. On the historic-geographic method in general: Röhrich 1987; Goldberg 1984, 2010.
[79] Röllig 1984: 496. According to Levin 1994, as summarised at Haul 2000: 85, the Etana myth originates in Mesopotamia and spreads in Eurasia in the Akkadian language via Assyrian traders who supposedly penetrate as far as the Volga region.
[80] Haul 2000: 87. Cf. Annus 2009: 89.

a fixed text model of transmission, presumably a (very largely) oral transmission, spanning astonishing stretches of time and place, language and culture.[81]

The Demotic Egyptian text *The Myth of the Sun's Eye* features a fable of *The Cat and the Vulture*, which goes thus:

> A vulture had offspring at the top of a mountain tree and a cat had offspring near a mountain. They swear an oath before the sun god Re not to feed each other's young to their own young when the other goes out to find food. The vulture then eats the cat's young. The cat complains to the sun god Re. The vulture subsequently sees a Syrian cooking wild donkey, takes a piece of meat in her beak, and brings it to her nest, not realising that there are glowing ashes on it. The fire burns the nest and the young, who fall to the ground at the bottom of the tree. The cat comes and reproaches the vulture for breaking their oath.

Again, this narrative is extremely close to *Etana*; or rather, to Archilochus-Aesop, as it has the vulture get its comeuppance by taking smouldering meat back to its nest.[82] Again, it is not just a matter of correspondence of motifs, but of elaborated narrative elements. In particular, the cat's complaint to Re closely resembles both the serpent's complaint to Šamaš in *Etana* and the fox's complaint to Zeus in Archilochus-Aesop.[83] Again, as with the 'Etana-*Märchen*', polygenesis seems to be excluded. But this time it is possible to feel more optimistic than with the 'Etana-*Märchen*' about a possible model of diffusion. Second-century CE Egypt was exposed to both Mesopotamian and Greek influence, and it is plausible that this particular Egyptian fable was imported from the Greek Aesopic tradition.[84] The telltale sign is that it is not the only embedded fable in the *Myth of the Sun's Eye* to correspond closely to a fable of Aesop: the fable of the Lion and

---

[81] Haul 2000: 82: 'Das Etana-Epos ist … ein schlagendes Beispiel für die große Stabilität, die Erzählstoffe in der mündlichen Volkserzählung durch Jahrtausende hindurch haben können.' Cf., on the reception of *Etana* in *Genesis*, Winitzer 2013: 459: 'the Genesis Eden tradition knew and made extensive use of the *Etana* legend as a whole'.
[82] Williams 1956: 72–3.
[83] 'Mögest Du mein Re[cht mit der Geie]rin kennen, die über meine Kinder hergefallen ist, nachdem sie die Eide gebrochen hat, die zwischen mir und ihr [festgesetzt waren]': Hoffmann and Quack 2007: 204.
[84] So, Adrados 1999–2003: i.330; Trencsényi-Waldapfel 1959: 322; West 1997: 404 n. 24; cf. S. R. West 2013: 84. Differently, Lazaridis 2016: 197 (on the fable of the Mouse and the Lion in Babr. [Perry 150] and *Myth of the Sun's Eye*): 'One cannot be sure whether these tales were originally composed in Greek, Aramaic, Akkadian, or Egyptian. Hence, in this case, although one can definitely sense a powerful interaction in this area of literary production, one cannot determine whether it only involved a Greek and an Egyptian side, or whether it was, what one would call nowadays, part of an international cultural heritage.'

Mouse (*Myth of the Sun's Eye* 18.11–35) also corresponds to Aesop's fable of the same name (150 Perry). In the third century CE, the *Myth of the Sun's Eye* was translated from Demotic into Greek.[85] But it would appear itself to have been significantly exposed to Greek influence before then; cultural interests and influences appear to have been mutual.[86] At any rate, in this case we appear to have both a fixed text model and a plausible model of diffusion.

Our discussion of *Etana* outside Greece again shows the value of having both a floating motif model and a fixed text model. This does not equate to models of oral transmission and of written transmission respectively. We may always, furthermore, be missing an indeterminate number of other fixed texts, which means we should not be too quick to point, among our extant texts, to a putative original or to a specific source and target pairing.

It is not even certain that reflections of the *Etana* complex in Greece must have an ultimately Mesopotamian origin. We have seen that there is room to doubt whether the Etana-*Märchen* have their origin in Mesopotamia. Yet the balance of probability must strongly favour Mesopotamia as being the hub from which this material radiated out to Hellenic (and likewise Hebrew?)[87] cultures, through whatever intermediaries. For one thing, Mesopotamia's influence, direct and indirect, on Greece is in general clear.[88] For another, the Mesopotamian *Etana* was a long-lived literary (and, seemingly, oral) classic, to which, like *Gilgameš*, it is relatively easy to impute an international reach.[89]

Consequences

This discussion of *Etana* has been useful, I hope, for helping us concretely to conceptualise what may be involved in fixed text and floating motif models of transfer. But I also believe that it illustrates the need to embrace both models, not just in general, but for the transfer even of the same mythical material.

We should note that Archilochus acknowledges the traditionality of his fable of The Eagle and the Fox: fr. 174.1 Swift: αἶνός τις ἀνθρώπων ὅδε,

---

[85] S. R. West 2013.
[86] Stoneman 1992: 112: 'what we do find in Egypt as nowhere else is a two-way traffic of Greek and native writing'.
[87] Winitzer 2013: esp. 443–4, 458–9.   [88] Dalley and Reyes 1998a, 1998b; Rollinger 2001.
[89] On the status of *Etana* (compared to *Gilgameš*), cf. Winitzer 2013: 457 and n. 92, 459–62.

'there is the following fable told by men'.[90] We have seen that this traditionality is not just feigned, but real.[91] Yet it remains a matter of surmise exactly what tradition Archilochus knew.[92] If he was thinking of Mesopotamian or more broadly Near Eastern tradition,[93] he does not oblige us as Callimachus does at the start of his fable of the Laurel and the Olive (*Iamb.* 4, fr. 194.6ff. Pfeiffer), advertising his *ainos* as one which 'the Lydians of old tell' (and in that case, too, we have an extant Babylonian analogue in the fable of *The Date Palm and the Tamarisk*).[94] It may be that this originally Mesopotamian/Near Eastern material became naturalised in Greek tradition at a very early date, and Archilochus and his contemporaries no longer had any awareness of it as being anything other than Greek tradition. Or it may be that awareness that this was a Near Eastern or Mesopotamian fable was just not relevant to Archilochus' poetic purpose in this epode. It is also hard to say how, if at all, Archilochus may have been exploiting knowledge in his (ideal) audience of the direction that the traditional fable took.[95] Be all this as it may, I would not want to discount, here or in general, the possibility of there being awareness of Near Eastern origins in early Greek poetic receptions of Near Eastern material.[96]

Babrius claimed the fable to be an ancient (As)syrian invention (μῦθος μέν ... Σύρων παλαιῶν ἐστιν εὕρεμ᾽ ἀνθρώπων, Prologue to

---

[90] The parallels (Pind. *N.* 9.6; Soph. *Tr.* 1) indicate that the genitive is subjective, not objective; compare and contrast Swift 2019: 31, 332–3.

[91] Compare Nic. *Th.* 343: ὠγύγιος δ᾽ ἄρα μῦθος ἐν αἰζηοῖσι φορεῖται, 'an ancient story is recorded among mortals', of the story of the snake's acquisition of the gift of rejuvenation, a story also attested in Mesopotamia (*Epic of Gilgameš* SBV XI 278–314). However, Nicander may have been thinking only of Greek tradition (Ibycus et al.: cf. Ael. *NA* 6.51); cf. Burkert 1992: 122–3.

[92] According to Rawles 2018: 57. Archilochus' use of this phrase 'marks the traditionality of the story in a general way', in contrast with Sim. fr. 579 *PMG* ἔστι τις λόγος, where one can see 'relatively sustained and detailed interaction with a specific earlier text', viz. Hes. *Op.* 287–92 (cf. Hunter 2014: 143). However, our investigation of the relationship of Archilochus' epode with *Etana* suggests that Archilochus' use of the phrase αἶνός τις ἀνθρώπων ὅδε resembles Simonides' usage rather than contrasting with it. With Archilochus, too, we should assume a 'relatively sustained and detailed interaction with a specific earlier text'. The difficulty lies in how to conceive of that 'specific earlier text': as a fixed text, certainly (though not necessarily fixed through writing); but as Greek or Near Eastern; and as attached to a specific author, or anonymous?

[93] West 1994 argues for a host of looser connections between Archilochus (and *iambos*) and Mesopotamia.

[94] Lambert 1960: 154; Adrados 1999–2003: i.361, cf. 303–5. The Akkadian poem in translation: Foster 2005: 927–9. See further Cohen, Chapter 7 in this volume.

[95] The Archilochean speaker is aligned with the fox, the wronged animal, in the fable, whereas Etana is aligned with the eagle, the wrong-doing animal. This kind difference could, in theory, be interpreted as a significant reversal. For the phenomenon of reversal in allusion, see Currie 2016: 27 and General Index *s.v.* 'opposition in imitation'. However, we have too little of Archilochus' poem for this kind of interpretation to be really viable.

[96] Currie 2016: 200–13.

Part ii 1–5),[97] and one fable of Babrius famously appears to offer an extremely close rendering of a Mesopotamian fable attested on a Babylonian tablet datable to 716 BCE. Here is the Babylonian version, in a normalization and a translation that gloss over some uncertainties:[98]

> *diqdiqqu ina muḫḫi pēri kī ušibu*
> *umma talīm idka anā-ma ina šiqi mê erâq-ma*
> *pēru ana diqdiqqi ippal*
> *kī tušibu ul īdē-ma kalaka mīnu*
> *kī tatbû ul īdē-ma*
>
> A wren, when it settled on an elephant,
> said: 'Dear brother, did I turn around your side?[99]
> At the watering place I will go far away.'
> The elephant made answer to the wren:
> 'When you settled, I was unaware: what do you amount to?
> When you get up, I will be unaware.'

And here is Babrius' (*Fab.* 84):

> κώνωψ ἐπιστὰς κέρατι καμπύλῳ ταύρου
> μικρόν τ' ἐπισχὼν εἶπε ταῦτα βομβήσας·
> 'εἴ σου βαρύνω τὸν τένοντα καὶ κλίνω,
> καθεδοῦμ' ἀπελθὼν ποταμίης ἐπ' αἰγείρου.'
> ὁ δ' 'οὐ μέλει μοι' φησίν 'οὔτ' ἐὰν μείνῃς
> οὔτ' ἢν ἀπέλθῃς, οὐδ' ὅτ' ἦλθες ἐγνώκειν.'
>
> A gnat, standing on the curved horn of a bull
> and pausing for a little, spoke thus, buzzing:
> 'If I weigh down your tendon and make it bend,
> I shall go away and sit down on the poplar by the river.'
> The other said, 'It's no concern to me, either if you stay
> or if you go away; nor did I notice when you came.'

Apart from the apparent naturalising and downsizing (Babylonian wren and elephant become gnat and bull in Greek),[100] this is an extremely close correspondence, once again, not just on the motival, but also on the lexical-stylistic and formal-narratival levels.[101] Erich Ebeling once wrote:

---

[97] 'Syrians' = Assyrians: Haubold 2013a: 25, 122.
[98] See Jiménez 2017: 327–8. Previous editions: Alster 2005: 367, cf. 343; Lambert 1960: 216–18, cf. 213–14 and 339.
[99] Jiménez 2017: 328: '"Brother, (if) I ... to your strength, I shall g[o off] at an irrigation (ditch).'"
[100] Elephants in Assyria and Mesopotamia: Trautmann 2015: 73–82.
[101] Lexical correspondence: *idka* – σου ... τὸν τένοντα, *anā-ma* – κλίνω, *erâq-ma* – ἀπελθών, *ul īdē-ma* – οὐδ'... ἐγνώκειν, *kī tušibu* – ὅτ' ἦλθες. Polyptoton: *ušibu* ... *tušibu* – ἀπελθών ... ἀπέλθῃς. Parallelism: *kī tušibu* ... *kī tatbû* – οὔτ' ἐὰν μείνῃς / οὔτ' ἢν ἀπέλθῃς.

Here for the first time we can make out for sure that not only the substance of a Greek fable corresponds with that of a Babylonian fable but even the wording down to matters of detail. In this case one may almost speak of the translation of a Babylonian original into Greek or at least of a paraphrase.[102]

Ebeling's comment seems to me important and essentially correct.[103] We have here a fixed text paradigm for the transfer from the Near East to Greece that may be as pertinent to the seventh century BCE (Archilochus) as it is to the second century CE (Babrius).

This model, involving the translation-cum-paraphrase of a fixed text (again, oral or written) implies a level of comfort with both source and target languages and cultures that most plausibly implicates a bilingual. In any event, the person responsible for the translation-cum-paraphrase could not fail to have been aware of what they were doing. Awareness of the non-Greek (whether specifically Mesopotamian or not) material is thus assured at least for the point at which it was first received into Greek tradition. But there can be no automatic presumption that that awareness was lost by the time the tradition reached Archilochus, and the closer Archilochus was to that putative person, the less likely that presumption becomes.

In their engagement with the literary traditions of the Near East, the Greeks have been said, in comparison with the Romans' engagement with the literary traditions of the Greeks, to be at the 'assimilative end' of the spectrum.[104] The early Greek poets, and certainly their public, were, on this view, at best dimly aware of any debts to Near Eastern literature. Instances of translation or paraphrase, however, suggest that assimilation was not the only possible mode,[105] and that we should not necessarily insist on the invisibility of Near Eastern sources to early Greek poets or their audiences.

---

[102] Ebeling 1927: 50, translated by Perry 1965: xxxiii. Cf. Williams 1956: 70; West 1969: 114–15; Burkert 1992: 214 n. 7; Adrados 1999–2003: i.324; Woodard 2007: 108.

[103] For Jiménez 2017: 328, this is an 'exceptional case of transmission between the Mesopotamian and the Greek fabulistic tradition'. For Haubold 2013a: 26, however, '[t]he fable ... offers us a useful lesson about how not to do comparative literature'; cf. 29: 'the fable cannot be read simply in terms of one literature borrowing from another'. Haubold (2013a: 27–8) is right that comparison between this Babylonian fable and Babrius led Ebeling, its first editor, to misinterpret *diqdiqqu* as 'gnat', and also that it is possible to see a lively dynamic in play in the different Greek versions of the fable (Babr. *Fab.* 84, Mesom. 11 Heitsch, Ach.Tat. 2.20–2). (Equally, one might also see a lively dynamic in play in the different Mesopotamian fables of *The Elephant and Wren*: cf. the Sumerian fable given at Jiménez 2017: 327.) But there is nothing here to detract from the fact that there is a staggeringly close relationship between the Mesopotamian and the Greek fable, whether a bull (Babrius) or an elephant (Mesomedes, Achilles Tatius) is involved, and that it is virtually impossible to interpret this relationship otherwise than as due to influence or borrowing.

[104] Feeney 1998: 65 (cf. Currie 2016: 208). [105] Currie 2016: 205–6.

CHAPTER 7

Of Gods and Men
Animal and Plant Disputation Poems and Fables in Babylonia, Persia, and Greece

Yoram Cohen

Introduction

Wisdom literature is one of the most diverse Mesopotamian genres. It is among the earliest, if not the earliest, literary creations on Mesopotamian soil.[1] And it survived till almost the last gasp of cuneiform culture at the close of the first millennium BCE.[2] It is also one of the most widely transmitted genres, spreading outside the borders of Mesopotamia and extending westwards all the way to Hittite Anatolia and to the east, to Susa. While most of Mesopotamian literature met its end with the demise of cuneiform culture, wisdom literature continued to live, albeit through many permutations, by virtue of its transmission to other cultures. The Mesopotamian wisdom corpus was carried beyond the cuneiform sphere through the medium of alphabetic Aramaic, Hebrew and Greek.[3] For a variety of reasons – the perishable media of transmission, the time span, and changing literary tastes – it is obvious that it survives in a fragmented state, hopelessly beyond repair.[4]

---

[1] For recent overviews of the definition of Mesopotamian Wisdom literature, see Cohen 2013: 7–19, and Cohen and Wasserman forthcoming. This study was written before the publication of Jiménez 2017, which brought to the discussion two newly recovered Mesopotamian compositions pertinent to my discussion. I have incorporated them into the chapter as far as the limits of this contribution permit.
[2] The wisdom composition *Ludlul Bēl Nēmeqi* was copied and studied by Neo-Babylonian students, as demonstrated by Gesche 2001. Proverbs also continued to be studied in the late first millennium; see Frahm 2010a and Alster 2007.
[3] While there is no doubt that Mesopotamian wisdom literature is not a hermetic corpus, there is a growing appreciation among scholars of the standardisation and organisation of wisdom works, either proverb collections or short compositions, into a fixed series. This series (designated as *iškaru*) was called *Sidu* and included thirty-five tablets of wisdom compositions (most of which are lost to us). The serialisation of wisdom literature is to be understood as part of a wider attempt in Mesopotamian intellectual circles to standardise a variety of works (mainly omens series): see Finkel 1986, Frahm 2010a, and Cohen 2018.
[4] There is as yet no study fully dedicated to the survival of Mesopotamian wisdom compositions beyond the world of cuneiform culture. Pertinent studies will be cited throughout this paper.

The purpose of this paper is to examine the transmission and reception of Mesopotamian wisdom literature in the ancient Near East and beyond by looking closely at one example. We will assess the relationship between the Mesopotamian wisdom composition *The Date Palm and the Tamarisk*, two newly recovered Mesopotamian works, and a few extra-Mesopotamian sources: these are a Persian disputation poem called *The Babylonian Tree*, a Greek Aesopic fable, a few proverbs belonging to the Ahiqar tradition, and *Iambus* IV of Callimachus.

The Date Palm and the Tamarisk, *The Date Palm and the Vine*, and *The Series of the Poplar*

The Date Palm and the Tamarisk is a debate poem between two trees, each seeking to outdo the other as to who is more useful for the world of gods and men.[5] Like other debate poems, it includes a mythological introduction, the setting in a royal banquet, the introduction of the contenders – the date palm and the tamarisk – and the debate itself. As has been suggested, the royal banquet setting hints at the original crowd for which the debate poems were intended: at first the poems were perhaps performed orally for the entertainment of the upper echelons of society before being committed to writing.[6]

The core of the debate poem is the debate itself. It consists of almost equal-length alternating perorations that create a balanced if somewhat monotonous composition, moving from one contestant to the other. Six exchanges between the date palm and the tamarisk (each of around ten verses) can be reconstructed. The outcome of the debate or the verdict (which in the Sumerian compositions is usually declared by a god) is missing from our composition. Whether *The Date Palm and the Tamarisk* included such a verdict at all is not known, because the end of the composition is lost from all sources.

The work boasts a long transmission history.[7] The poem, written in Akkadian, is known from several manuscripts from the second millennium and early first millennium. Although the composition was not retrieved from the Neo-Assyrian library of Assurbanipal (or any other Neo-Assyrian library), there is no doubt that the work was known, if not studied, during

---

[5] See Jiménez 2017: 28–39, Cohen 2013: 177–98, and Wilcke 1990. For a comprehensive study of the genre of Mesopotamian debate poems, see Jiménez 2017.
[6] Vanstiphout 1992; Jiménez 2017: 15–16.   [7] Cohen 2013: 178–9.

this later period, and was considered a 'series' (*iškaru*), according to a Nineveh library catalogue that mentions it (albeit in corrupt form) and provides the latest attestation of the work.[8]

The Date Palm and the Tamarisk was not the only Akkadian work of this genre to present a debate between two plants. A newly recovered composition, *The Date Palm and the Vine*, features a debate between the two eponymous plants.[9] Not much is preserved of this composition, which is known from first-millennium manuscripts, but it could have been composed earlier. Enough remains to see that this work shares with *The Date Palm and the Tamarisk* the overarching theme and some details, as we will see.

Another newly reconstructed work is *The Series of the Poplar*. It too presents a debate between the poplar tree and the ash, as well as, probably, additional trees.[10] It is even in a poorer state than *The Date Palm and the Vine*, but what remains there points to the same structure and main concerns.

We now turn to the transmission and reception of the Mesopotamian compositions in later alphabetic literatures. We will concentrate chiefly on *The Date Palm and the Tamarisk* because it is much better preserved and thus enables easier comparison than the two newly recovered works just discussed, though they will be invoked whenever appropriate.

The Babylonian Tree

The Date Palm and the Tamarisk has long been recognised as the source material of the Middle Persian tale, *The Babylonian Tree* (although its title is a mistranslation of *The Assyrian* [or the *Aramean*] *Tree*).[11] With the recovery of the two new works introduced above, there is no denying the possibility that they too may have served as source material for this Persian composition. Nevertheless, the transmission of these Mesopotamian

---

[8] Lambert 1960: 151, Jiménez 2017: 34.
[9] The work was only very poorly known but can now be more fully understood thanks to a new tablet, published and discussed by Jiménez 2017: 231–87.
[10] This composition was again previously known, but has benefited from the identification of a new manuscript. It is published and discussed by Jiménez 2017: 157–227.
[11] See Brunner 1980, West 2000: 96, and Tafażżolī 1995. The proximity of the Persian creation to its Mesopotamian antecedent could not have been fully appreciated at the time of Brunner's study (the most recent treatment of *The Babylonian Tree*), because the Emar source of *The Date Palm and the Tamarisk*, which has added a considerable wealth of details, had not yet been published: see Jiménez 2017: 133 and 282–7.

debate poems was not necessarily direct, but could have been mediated by Aramaic versions which are now lost (and see below). Because there are Parthian words interspersed in the text, *The Babylonian Tree* is considered to have been transmitted orally for a considerable period of time, before being committed to writing. The date of this Persian composition is not known, of course, but Strabo (16.1.14) mentions a Persian song that celebrates 360 uses of the date palm. This may provide us at least with a *terminus ante quem*, if the geographer refers to the same or a similar composition in one of its configurations.[12] The general rarity of dispute poems in Middle Persian literature may support the view that our tale was deliberately transmitted, that is, that the Mesopotamian debate poem – whichever it was, *The Date Palm and the Tamarisk* or *The Date Palm and the Vine* – was carefully and intentionally selected in order to convey a topic of concern for its author.

In the Persian *Babylonian Tree* the main contenders are the date palm and a goat, which replaces the tamarisk (or possibly the vine), although it occupies the same deep-structural meaning within the debate. The scene is set in Asur Province, where the two dispute; first to speak is the date palm (twenty-seven verses), to which the goat replies (ninety-four verses).

To begin with, the beginning of time is the chronological point of reference for both the Mesopotamian and the Middle Persian compositions.[13] In *The Date Palm and the Tamarisk*, the poem takes us back to the city of Kiš, where, according to the *Sumerian King List* (generally thought to have been written in its earliest form around the end of the third millennium, but known from manuscripts dating later), kingship was restored after the flood. It is in this city that the King of Kiš plants in his garden the trees that will star in the dispute.[14] *The Babylonian Tree* happens in the present but uses the past as a reference to the beginning of time. Because, as the goat says, things today are the same as in the distant past (l. 113), it follows that any present observation on the nature of things goes back to the beginning of time. Remarkably, there is also a reference to the reign of the mythical king Jamšed (l. 34), who, according to Persian traditions, bestowed upon mankind multiple useful inventions and technological innovations. In a sense, this echoes the role of the king in the Mesopotamian debate: he is the gardener who plants the first-ever species

---

[12] Brunner 1980: 196. In *The Babylonian Tree* there is an intertextual reference to the poem itself or one of its precursors ('a story of the Persian people'): see Brunner 1980: 298 l. 41.
[13] *The Babylonian Tree* and *The Date Palm and the Tamarisk* are cited from the editions of Brunner 1980 and Cohen 2013 respectively.
[14] Jiménez 2017: 36.

of the trees, and it is he who judges the outcome of the debate (although this part is missing from our manuscripts).

Secondly, both compositions place emphasis on the utility and benefit of the contenders for the upper echelons of society (king, nobles, governors), labourers of various kinds (farmer, craftsman), and common or poor folk (pauper, widow, orphan). In *The Date Palm and the Tamarisk*, the date palm asserts that 'our fruits are fit for the royal table, the king eats (them) and the crowd says "(the dates are) my gift" ... the orphan, the widow, the pauper ... they eat food (i.e., the dates) which never diminishes' (I 16–17, VI 20–1).[15] In *The Babylonian Tree*, the date palm 'bears sweet fruit for people' (4), as it says that 'the king eats of me when I newly bear fruit ... and those people who lack bread and wine eat fruit from me till they become filled' (8, 26–7).

Thirdly, characteristically for debate poems (unlike the short fable), both compositions display an encyclopedic knowledge of the uses of their contenders. The list-like enumeration of the utility and usefulness of the contenders is not supposed to impart knowledge, but rather to display control of extensive vocabulary, as well as the ability to employ imagery and metaphors.[16] In *The Babylonian Tree*, the various utensils made out of the date palm are listed: planks and masts (for ships), brooms (for cleaning), pestles (to pound rice and barley), fans (for fires), shoes and sandals (for the farmers and the shoeless), ropes, clubs, and pegs. They can be compared to the utensils of both trees in *The Date Palm and the Tamarisk*: wood (for manufacturing statues), a table (for the king), a cup (for the queen), a spoon (for the soldiers), a trough (for the baker), clothes (for the king), a sieve (for the brewer), a bed of palm fronds, a spade (for the farmer), tethering ropes, whips, ropes, and bolsters (for harnesses and wagon).[17] In its reply, the goat also provides a list of its contributions to mankind, but these are animal products and cannot compare with the products made of plants. However, the use of the goat in a ritual practice is the crux of understanding the relationship between the two debates, as we will see.

The similarities between the Persian composition and the Mesopotamian debate introduced above may either convince the believers or sow doubt in the hearts of the sceptics. The latter may say that, after all,

---

[15] The theme of providing both for the mighty and the feeble is also found throughout *The Date Palm and the Vine* and *The Series of the Poplar*.
[16] See Vanstiphout 1991.
[17] The usefulness of the date palm, vine, poplar, and ash is articulated in both works.

this comparison simply proves that all debates are similar, built on the same narrative outlines. Hence it does not necessarily follow that the Mesopotamian disputes were transmitted to the Persian literary sphere. However, there is a deeper structural level which seems to support the notion that the *The Babylonian Tree* relies on Mesopotamian precursors.

In *The Date Palm and the Tamarisk*, the tamarisk tree is chiefly celebrated for its use in the cult, specifically in purification rituals.[18] The tamarisk says it is the 'flesh to the gods', in other words, the wood out of which the god's statue was manufactured.[19] To this statue the dates of the date palm will be presented as an offering, like a present from a maid to her mistress (I 21–4). The tamarisk proudly proclaims that 'I am the exorcist priest (*mašmašākuma*), I renew the temple (II 36').' And further, it says, 'Behold: aren't my surroundings full of resin? Are they not full of incense? The priestess (*qadištu*) collects the "water" of the tamarisk, and then praise is given and a festival performed' (III 45'–7').[20] The tamarisk thus proudly proclaims its use in ritual. The date palm responds by saying that its fronds are also used in purification rites, but clearly its main contributions are the edibles it produces and its raw materials. The same reasoning is found in *The Date Palm and the Vine* debate poem, as both trees vie with each other, each boasting of its benefits to the cult.[21]

In the Persian *Babylonian Tree* the goat emphasises its cultic usage in the *yasna* sacrifice. It says '(f)or the almighty creator, radiant kind Ohrmazd for the pure religion of the Mazdeans, which kind Ohrmazd taught, one cannot do worship without me, who am the goat. For from me they make milk offerings … in the rites of the gods … the efficacy is from me' (47–52; cf. 100).

The axis of both debates is clear to see: it is set at the divide between the divine and human world. This is played out by two figures, each of whom is necessary to the maintenance of a separate domain: sacrifice, or the correct *ritus*, is essential for the well-being of the gods, while nourishment is essential for the survival of humans. It is this basic tension that was expressed in the Mesopotamian dispute between the tamarisk and the date

---

[18] See Streck 2004 for details.
[19] The tamarisk's wood as 'flesh of the gods' is mentioned also in *The Series of the Poplar*, II 16': see Jiménez 2017: 174–5. There is also external support from additional Mesopotamian sources of the tamarisk's use in the manufacture of divine statues: see Streck 2004: 277–8, Livingstone 1986: 92–112.
[20] For suggestions identifying the tamarisk's 'water' with Biblical manna, see Streck 2004: 279–82.
[21] Jiménez 2017: 248–9, 10'–12' (the date palm) and 250–3, 33'–9' (the vine).

palm, and also between the vine and the date palm.[22] And this theme was at the core of *The Babylonian Tree*, where the goat took over the role of the tamarisk (or the vine). As such, perhaps it is no surprise that, as a chief player in the Zoroastrian *yasna* rite, the goat won in *The Babylonian Tree* dispute. We do not know who won in *The Date Palm and the Tamarisk*, because all the sources – including the newly recovered debates – are missing their ends, but, following the Persian tale, perhaps the tamarisk tree was the victor.

Aesop and Callimachus

Turning westwards, we face two occasions where Mesopotamian sources can be suggested: in one of Aesop's fables and in Callimachus' *Iambus* IV.

When the story is retrieved in its Greek Aesopic version, like in *The Babylonian Tree*, we see that the tree versus tree debate is abandoned in favour of a tree versus animal exchange. In the Greek fable, the tree is the vine and, as in *The Babylonian Tree*, the animal is the goat which proceeds to consume the plant. Here is the fable: 'A goat ate the bud when the grape was sprouting. The vine said to him, "Why do you hurt me? Anyhow, I'll provide as much wine as they need when they sacrifice you."'[23] Despite the change of the chief actors, the structural axis of the Mesopotamian debate is retained: a goat, equalling sacrifice on the symbolic level, contends with a plant, which denotes consumables. And at the end the goat will be sacrificed and over its carcass a wine libation will be poured. This is parallel to what is found in the Mesopotamian debate: the tamarisk will be manufactured to produce a divine statue to which the dates of the date palm will be brought as offerings.

The source of the Greek Aesopic fable may have been *The Date Palm and the Tamarisk*, or perhaps *The Date Palm and the Vine*, but was possibly mediated by proverbs belonging to the Ahiqar story.[24] Although not preserved in the Aramaic remains of the Ahiqar story, other sources – Slavonic, Armenian, Syriac, and Arabic – tell of a dispute between the goat (or gazelle) and the madder plant (or sumac).[25] In all versions of the Ahiqar story, the plant serves as the ingredient for tanning the animal's skin once it is dead, hence the ritualistic context (wine over the goat's carcass) was

---

[22] This tension between the divine and humans is found already in the Sumerian debate poems, e.g., *The Debate between Grain and Sheep* 71–82 (grain) and 107–15 (sheep): *ETCSL* 5.3.2.
[23] Perry 1965: 487–8 no. 374.   [24] Adrados 1999–2003: 361.
[25] Conybeare et al. 1898: 21 (Old Church Slavonic), 52 (Armenian), 80 (Syriac), and 113 (Arabic); see also Brunner 1980: 199 n. 39.

removed from the story. It is not too difficult to understand why this was done, as such a sacrificial practice was foreign to the religious world at the receiving end of the fable after the Muslim conquest. However, the action (the animal eating the plant) and its consequence (the plant's eventual victory) were the same as in the Greek Aesopic version.[26]

The binary poles of divine and human domains we have been talking about have also been preserved in another of the transmissions of Mesopotamian debates into Greek – in Callimachus' *Iambus* IV.

It has been argued that the fable of the debate between two species of trees in *Iambus* IV was transmitted from an ancient Near Eastern source, and, even more specifically, that *The Date Palm and the Tamarisk* served as its model.[27] Let us look at this claim in more detail. The poem reports a tale from ancient Lydia. On Mount Tmolus, the laurel and the olive tree dispute who is of more worth. The olive tree naturally boasts of its productivity, giving oil cake (*stemphylon*) for the poor(?), oil, and pickled olive (75–7).[28] The laurel, Apollo's tree, responds by claiming for itself a cultic role by virtue of its association with diviners (*mantis*; and the diviner Branchus), sacrificers (*thytēs*), and the Pythia-priestess in the Delphic oracle (25–36).[29] The role of the laurel reminds one of the tamarisk's position in the Mesopotamian debate: it is the *mašmašu*-exorcist and the tree with whose resin and branches the *qadištu*-priestess fulfils purifying rites. The olive tree, selected by Athene as her representative tree, responds by detailing its own role in the cult (80–4).[30]

The result of the dispute in *Iambus* IV is not known to the reader, because the trees were interrupted by the bramble (which is an incorporation of another fable into the main story, whereby the lesser being, the bramble, interferes in the business of his superiors, the privileged laurel

---

[26] For further debates which may be indebted to the Mesopotamian sources, see Jiménez 2017: 35 n. 10, and 282–7.

[27] West 1969: 118–19; Adrados 1999–2003: 259–60, 320; Jiménez 2017: 132. For Callimachus and his use of the fable in *Iambus* IV, see Scodel 2011 (the edition is Trypanis 1958: 118–27).

[28] Kerkhecker 1999: 104–6.   [29] Kerkhecker 1999: 92–3.

[30] The olive as Athene's tree and the laurel as Apollo's refer back to another fable preserved in Phaedrus III 17 (= Perry 1965: 286–9). This is a fable where the gods choose trees as their symbols. They all choose either lofty trees or fragrant plants, but only Athene chooses the fruit-yielding, hence most beneficial tree – the olive. At the bottom of this story lies the dispute among the plant species, as in *The Date Palm and the Tamarisk* and *The Date Palm and the Vine*. The involvement of the gods reminds one of the introduction typical of Mesopotamian disputes, which starts at the time the gods created the world. It is also directly related to *The Date Palm and the Tamarisk*, where the association of the tamarisk with the divine is brought to the fore; see also below and the conclusion to this chapter. The dispute among the many species of the plant kingdom in Phaedrus is further reminiscent of the dispute among the plants in the Fable of Jotham (*Judges* 9); see Tatu 2006. Consider also the dispute between the thorn and the cedar tree in 2 *Kings* 14:9.

and olive).³¹ As in the Mesopotamian and Persian poems, the fable presents a debate among representatives of two domains: the laurel as the representative of the divine, and the multipurpose olive as that of humans. And, as in the Mesopotamian debates, each domain – whether divine or human – need not have remained exclusive to a single contender; as much as the date palm tries to outdo the tamarisk by retorting to claim its centrality to the cult, so the olive tree tries to prove its importance in select cultic practices.

Conclusion

We have traced the literary history of a Mesopotamian debate poem between two trees. But not much remained static: chief characters can be replaced and locations transposed. Consequently, arguments in support of the superiority of one over the other can change: the tamarisk became the goat or a laurel; the date palm changed into the olive tree; and the alluvial heartland of Mesopotamia was transposed to Mount Tmolus in Lydia. However, as we saw, the main deep structure was retained: the tamarisk or laurel (two non-fruit-bearing trees), and the goat represented the divine realm, while the date palm and olive tree (two fruit-bearing trees) stood on the side of the human world. This proves that in the transmission process it is not the details which have survived (although these were revealed on occasion to have been preserved), but rather the central question of the debate: which cultural value is of more importance? Is it the observation of the cult or the preservation of humans? It is this central concern at the heart of the Mesopotamian debate that was transmitted to Greek and Persian cultures and it is also the chief reason behind its transmission. Because the Mesopotamian poem asked this crucial question, it provided a platform on which views and beliefs of other cultures could be built, with the change of scene or characters as needed.³²

---

[31] Although it is possible that the olive had a vantage point at end of the poem; see Kerkhecker 1999: 108–15. A dispute between the bramble and the fir tree is found in the Aesopic tradition; see Babrius, no. 64 (Perry 1965: 80–1), Adrados 1999–2003: 295. The origin of the fable may lie in a short debate between the bramble and the pomegranate preserved in the Aramaic Ahiqar, which of course may go back to the Mesopotamian debate poems; see Lindenberger 1983: 167 no. 73 and Porten and Yardeni 1993: 38–9.

[32] There are other hints of the transmission of Mesopotamian disputes into Greek literature: see, e.g., Alster 1979, Moran 1978, and Bodi 2014. Most notable are the leftovers of what was probably a popular dispute between the eagle and the snake. It is recorded in abbreviated form in the Mesopotamian *Etana* poem; it may have served as the model for the meeting between the eagle and the fox in a fable repeated by Archilochus; see Adrados 1999–2003: 305 with previous literature, and Currie, Chapter 6 in this volume. For the episode of the eagle and the snake, see Winitzer 2013; for tales involving the fox, see Cohen 2017.

CHAPTER 8

Tales of Kings and Cup-Bearers in History and Myth

Christopher Metcalf

The starting point of this contribution is the mythological prologue that relates the early history of divine kingship at the beginning of the Hurro-Hittite *Song of Emergence* (*CTH* 344), a text familiar to Hellenists as the closest and most important Near Eastern comparandum to the Myth of Succession in Hesiod's *Theogony*. While the parallels between these two poems continue to offer scope for discussion (see, e.g., the contributions of Gilan, Kelly, and Rutherford, in this volume), I propose to concentrate on what appears to be a minor narrative detail in the *Song of Emergence* that does not usually attract comment but that, I will argue, allows us to study in some detail the transmission from Mesopotamia to Anatolia of a story-pattern that was ultimately connected to the twenty-third-century BCE king Sargon, and that was later transferred to the sixth century BCE Persian king Cyrus the Great, in legends recorded by Greek historians in the fifth century. The material to be considered here will also shed some indirect light on Hesiod's vision of divine kingship in the *Theogony*, as it will help to explain a discrepancy between his Myth of Succession and the *Song of Emergence*. From a methodological perspective, the present contribution will invite reflection on the criteria that allow us to construe relationships between texts from neighbouring cultures, both within the cuneiform world and in a Greek/Near Eastern perspective. As usual, the strength of the comparison will depend both on the quality of the literary parallels and on the historical plausibility of cross-cultural exchange.

I would like to begin by looking closely at the start of the theogonic narrative in the *Song of Emergence* (*KUB* 33.120+ i 7–22, *CTH* 344):

> Formerly, in ancient times, Alalu was King in Heaven. Alalu was seated upon the throne while mighty Anu, foremost of the gods, stood before him. He bowed down at his feet and placed the drinking cups in his hand. Alalu was King in Heaven for only nine years. In the ninth year Anu gave battle to Alalu. He defeated Alalu so that he fled before him. He went down to the Dark Earth. He went down to the Dark Earth and Anu took his seat upon

> the throne. Anu was seated upon the throne while mighty Kumarbi
> provided him with drink. He bowed down at his feet and placed the
> drinking cups in his hand. Anu was King in Heaven for only nine years.
> In the ninth year he gave battle to Kumarbi. Kumarbi, scion of Alalu, gave
> battle to Anu. Unable to withstand the gaze of Kumarbi any longer, Anu
> escaped from Kumarbi's grasp and fled, Anu, and he went to Heaven.[1]

Little is said of the first king, Alalu, except that he once ruled as king in heaven for nine years, until he was defeated by his cup-bearer Anu and fled into the 'dark earth', i.e., the underworld. Alalu plays no further role in the subsequent narrative, as far as it is preserved. Anu, his successor, likewise rules for nine years in heaven until he, too, is deposed by his cup-bearer Kumarbi, a descendant of Alalu; Anu then flees to heaven. This flight to heaven seems somewhat illogical, given that Anu was already enthroned there at the time when he was deposed, but the main aim of the prologue is to establish a polarising, heaven-and-earth aetiology, according to which the first divine king was deposed and became ruler of the underworld, while the second divine king was deposed and became the Sky God. This heaven-and-earth polarity is relevant to the main narrative of the *Song of Emergence*, since Alalu (representing the underworld) is described as the ancestor of Kumarbi, whereas Anu (representing the sky) is the father of Kumarbi's later antagonist, the Storm God.[2] But unlike his predecessor Alalu, who vanished to the underworld, Anu has a specific role that is important for the further development of the narrative: he is the Sky God whom Kumarbi castrates as he tries to escape, and this emasculation of Anu leads directly to Kumarbi's impregnation with the Storm God, whose birth and conflict with Kumarbi forms an important strand of the *Song of Emergence* and the larger cycle of poems to which it belongs.

Kumarbi, who rules after Anu and is a central figure in the *Song of Emergence*, is a Hurrian deity, but his predecessor Anu, and probably also Alalu, are gods of Mesopotamian origin. Anu is the ancient and famous Sky God whose name is derived from the Sumerian word 'an' ('sky'), while the lesser-known god Alalu is attested under the variant name Alala as an ancestor of An/Anu in Mesopotamian god-lists that date at least as far back as the Middle Assyrian period, and that were based on older texts: commenting on the *Song of Emergence*, W. G. Lambert thus thought it

---

[1] This is the translation of Beckman 2011: 27, modified in the final sentence according to the latest edition, by E. Rieken et al. (ed.), hethiter.net/: CTH 344 (TX 2012-06-08, TRde 2009-08-31), who read, upon collation, *na-aš*, '(and) he went to Heaven)', rather than MUŠEN-*aš* <*i-wa-ar*>, '<in the manner> of a bird'.
[2] See Hoffner 1975: 138–9, van Dongen 2012: 36, Corti and Pecchioli Daddi 2012: 617.

'quite possible that the earlier part involving Alala and Anu is derived ultimately from Mesopotamian sources'.[3] It is also conceivable that the damaged opening of the text, which calls on the former gods (who now dwell in the underworld) to listen to the poem, invokes Alalu as the ancestor of Anu, if one follows the reconstruction of Volkert Haas.[4] A mythological fragment from Hattusa that may represent an older, Hurrian version of the tale mentions Alalu, Anu and Kumarbi in close connection, and it in any case seems likely that the triad entered the *Song of Emergence* via Hurrian mediation.[5] According to Daniel Schwemer, the Mesopotamian elements in the *Song of Emergence*, including the sequence Alalu-Anu, could have entered Hurrian mythology as early as in the Old Akkadian period (twenty-third and twenty-second centuries BCE).[6]

But what is not attested outside the *Song of Emergence* (with one possibly significant exception to which I will return) is the notion that Anu and Kumarbi first served as cup-bearers to the divine kings whom they later deposed. This aspect has received rather less attention, although it is likely to be inspired ultimately by Mesopotamian models as well. As Beckman has noted, the poem does not explain how the first three divine kings came into being.[7] But the tale of the cup-bearer who deposes his king, takes power himself, and subsequently achieves far greater prominence than his predecessor, is plainly designed to explain how a line of rulers could emerge seemingly from nowhere: it is a narrative device that is intended to give a plausible account of the rise of a royal dynasty from obscure origins. As some commentators have pointed out, the same story-pattern is attested in Sumerian and Akkadian sources on the rise to power of one of the best-known historical figures of Mesopotamian history,

---

[3] Lambert 2013: 423 (see also 417–25). On this basis, the doubts expressed by Wilhelm 2009: 66–7 on the Mesopotamian origin of Alalu are probably unnecessary. On Mesopotamian elements in the *Song of Emergence*, see in general Güterbock 1946: 105–10; Pecchioli Daddi and Polvani 1990: 20, 127; Corti and Pecchioli Daddi 2012: 617.

[4] Haas 2006: 133–4.

[5] The passage in the Hurrian fragment is KUB 47.56 obv. 9'–12' (CTH 370.II), on which see especially Corti 2007: 111, 119–21 and Corti and Pecchioli Daddi 2012: 611, and further Salvini 1991: 129–30, van Dongen 2012: 25. The castration episode for which the *Song of Emergence* is best known (KUB 33.120+ i 23–36) is also alluded to in a Hurrian prayer (KUB 47.78 i 12'–14', CTH 791 = ChS I/8.8), see Haas 2006: 251–2.

[6] Schwemer 2001: 449–50. This conclusion was drawn by Speiser 1942: 101, very soon after the publication of the Hittite text. On the Hurrian pantheon and its connections to Mesopotamia, see recently Archi 2013.

[7] Beckman 2011: 260.

Sargon of Akkad, the founder of the Old Akkadian empire (2288–2235 BCE), and it is to these sources that I now turn.[8]

The earliest attestation of the Sargonic story-pattern occurs in an Old Babylonian Sumerian narrative known as the *Sumerian Sargon Legend* (or *Sargon and Ur-Zababa*). According to the extant text of this tale, Sargon was the cup-bearer of Ur-Zababa, king of Kiš. An ominous dream appeared to Sargon, who reported it to the king. Believing that the dream portended his death at the hands of Sargon, Ur-Zababa then devised a series of plots that were designed to kill his cup-bearer. While the conclusion of the tale is not preserved, the prologue states that the chief gods have decided to end the rule of Ur-Zababa, and Sargon is consistently described in the narrative as the protégé of the goddess Inana: it is therefore safe to assume that the lost continuation of the text narrated Sargon's displacement of Ur-Zababa and his eventual supremacy after his defeat of king Lugalzagesi of Uruk.[9] The tale of Sargon's rise from cup-bearer to king is also presupposed by the *Sumerian King List*, which describes Sargon as the son of a gardener and cup-bearer of Ur-Zababa, and by the later *Chronicle of the Esagila*, according to which Ur-Zababa anachronistically ordered his cup-bearer Sargon to alter the libations to the god Marduk in the Esagila-temple of Babylon: Sargon ignored his master, for which he was rewarded with the kingship by Marduk.[10]

The common story-pattern that underlies these versions is clearly designed to explain how an individual who was not of royal lineage was able to rise to his later position of dominance. Ur-Zababa, the king of Kiš whom Sargon first served and then displaced, is attested only in the literary-historical tradition, and only in connection with Sargon's rise to kingship. His name means simply 'He-of-Zababa', Zababa being the city god of Kiš, and there is no independent evidence, such as, e.g., in contemporaneous royal inscriptions or administrative records, to show that Ur-Zababa was a historical figure.[11] This analogy is in my view the

---

[8] The comparison has been made, e.g., by Cooper 1985: 37 n. 16, Pecchioli Daddi and Polvani 1990: 127, Bachvarova 2012: 113, López-Ruiz 2013: 141.
[9] *Sumerian Sargon Legend*, ed. Cooper and Heimpel 1984; see now also Foster 2016: 4–5, 348–50.
[10] *Sumerian King List* vi 31–6 and *Chronicle of the Esagila* 56–61, ed. Glassner 2004: 117–27, 263–9; see also Westenholz 1999: 35–6, Foster 2016: 262–4, Steinkeller 2017b: 181–6.
[11] *RlA* s.v. 'Ur-Zababa' (N. Rudik). On the meaning of 'Ur-' in Sumerian personal names, see Balke 2017: 405 n. 1353. On the early history of Kiš, up to and including the Sargonic period, see now Steinkeller 2013: 145–51 and 2017b: 181–92, who emphasises the absence of historical evidence for the existence of Ur-Zababa, and interprets the story of Sargon and Ur-Zababa as a probably fictional tale that was designed to explain the anomalous and disruptive emergence of Sargon and his empire: 'Since, from the perspective of Mythical History, Akkade was an anomaly, its origins had to be anomalous too. In this way, Sargon is consistently portrayed as an outsider and a *parvenu*'

simplest way to explain why the prologue to the *Song of Emergence* assigns the earliest kingship in heaven to Alalu, who was not a major god and plays no role in the rest of the poem: like Ur-Zababa, Alalu's sole function is to be superseded by the much more important Sky God Anu, who is described as 'foremost of the gods' even while he is still cup-bearer to Alalu, and whose significance to the later castration episode I have already mentioned. In an extension of the story-pattern, Anu is then deposed in turn by Kumarbi, who is a central figure in the subsequent narrative. While it has sometimes been seen as problematic that the *Song of Emergence* attributes the earliest divine rule to Alalu, as this seems inconsistent with his relatively obscure status in ancient Near Eastern religion,[12] I suggest that the aetiology of kingship that the *Song of Emergence* shares with the Sargonic tales in fact requires the first king to be a minor figure who serves merely as a stepping-stone for the greater ruler.

Given the similarity both in content and in narrative purpose, it seems plausible to regard the cup-bearer theme in the prologue to the *Song of Emergence* as a Mesopotamian element, and to connect it more particularly to the tale of Sargon. In historical terms this connection is supported by the fact that Sargon was demonstrably a figure of interest to the Hittites, since Hittite Sargon-narratives have been found at Hattusa, and the Old Hittite king Hattusili I (1650–1620 BCE) explicitly compared his royal exploits to those of Sargon, who also features in a Hurro-Hittite ritual that invokes deceased kings.[13] It is well known, furthermore, that the Sumero-Akkadian tales on the accession of Sargon provide early attestations of popular motifs that subsequently spread to other ancient and modern cultures: further examples include the motif of the 'Uriah letter', which probably forms the basis of one of Ur-Zababa's plots in the *Sumerian Sargon Legend*, and the motif of the infant that is abandoned and exposed at birth but later ascends to the exalted position to which it was always destined – this motif is attested in a later Akkadian narrative on the origins of Sargon.[14]

(Steinkeller 2017b: 189). The alternative view, which accepts that Ur-Zababa was a historical ruler of Kiš, has to rely on the dubious evidence of the *Sumerian King List* (Lafont, Tenu, Joannès and Clancier 2017: 173).

[12] van Dongen 2012: 36.

[13] As documented by Bachvarova 2016: 166–91; see also Gilan 2015a: 223–4, de Martino 2016: 26.

[14] On Sargon and the 'Uriah letter', see, e.g., Alster 1987, Afanas'eva 1987; on the *Birth Legend of Sargon* (ed. Goodnick Westenholz 1997: 36–49) and the motif of the exposed infant, see, e.g., Bauer 1882: 561–3, Lewis 1980: 149–267, West 1997: 439–40, Henkelman 2006: 832–7, Waters 2017: 48–59, Finglass 2018: 49–50, 63–70. For general discussion, see Haul 2009: 93.

It is of interest in this connection that Benjamin Foster has recently sought to identify the historical origin of the cup-bearer theme in a particular event in Sargon's reign. One of Sargon's early achievements was to defeat king Lugalzagesi of Uruk, the cultic seat of the Sky God An; probably as a consequence of this victory, Sargon adopted the title '*pašīšum*-priest of An'. Literary and administrative texts show that this type of priest was commonly responsible for the sustenance of the god, and Foster suggests that Sargon's adoption of this title in Uruk 'could be the origin of the story that he was once a cup-bearer'.[15] While it remains unclear when and how the Sargon legends were formed, Sargon's adoption of the *pašīšum*-priesthood may, if I understand Foster correctly, have been utilised as an ingredient in the story-pattern that was designed to explain the earliest part of his biography. While such attempts to identify historical kernels in Sargonic legend have inevitably been criticised,[16] Foster's suggestion nevertheless provides an attractive explanation that at least partly illuminates the origin of the cup-bearer theme, and connects it specifically to the deeds of Sargon of Akkad.[17]

Yet even if one prefers to consider any quest for the elusive historical origins of the cup-bearer theme to be futile, the content and function of the theme can in any case be said to agree with the historical reality of early Mesopotamia. In a recently published study, Walther Sallaberger has examined the historical attestations of cup-bearers in Mesopotamian sources of the third millennium BCE, and has noted that 'this job allowed

---

[15] Foster 2016: 161 n. 83. On the *pašīšum*-priesthood, see *RlA* s.v. Priester A.1 §5.3.1 (W. Sallaberger/F. Huber Vulliet); on historical information on the duties of the cup-bearer in the Old Akkadian period, see recently Maiocchi 2010. The intimate connection between king and cup-bearer is illustrated by a seal granted by king Ibbi-Sîn of Ur (2026–2003 BCE) to his cup-bearer Sîn-abūšu, who is described as the king's 'childhood friend': see Wilcke 1989, and further Frayne 1997: 389.

[16] Kuhrt 2003: 356–8.

[17] An alternative and even more speculative approach is to derive the Sargonic legend from early myths on the origins of Gilgameš: the latter's father is identified as a 'lil₂', i.e., a 'ghost' or possibly a 'nobody', by the *Sumerian King List*, iii 17–18, which may suggest a myth of Gilgameš's rise from humble origins, resembling the Sargonic biography, as noted, e.g., by George 2003: 106 with n. 64. It is also true that a very late Gilgameš-tale reported by Aelian (second–third centuries CE) describes him as the son of some undistinguished individual, and claims that he was later raised by a gardener (*NA* 12.21, see George 2003: 61; Henkelman 2006: 830–2), and Stephanie Dalley further draws attention (*per litteras*) to the well-known golden bowl from Hasanlu (north-west Iran, perhaps ninth century BCE), whose rich imagery may relate to Gilgameš at least in part, and which includes a scene depicting a man holding a beaker before an empty seat or throne, perhaps in the manner of a cup-bearer: on the bowl and its relationship to Gilgameš, see recently Ornan 2010: 235, 243–4, 248–9, with fig. 10, and Frayne 2010: 175, and, for other interpretations of the scene of the beaker, Winter 1989: 95–6. While thought-provoking, these possible analogies seem as yet insufficient to reconstruct a very early Gilgameš-narrative that served as a model to the legend of Sargon the cup-bearer: compare the general remarks of George 2003: 4–6.

a social advancement for "ordinary people" to enter the innermost circle of ruling families'.[18] Sallaberger makes this observation on the basis of the historical evidence, in particular administrative documents, and without reference to any literary material: yet the emphasis that he places on the social advancement that was made possible by the office of cup-bearer agrees very well, in my view, with the central function of the literary theme, which is to explain the rise of a new ruler who seemingly came from nowhere, entered a royal household and then – so the story goes – became king himself, accomplished great deeds and founded a new dynasty of his own.

In sum, both the similarity of the story-pattern and the historical evidence for the wide diffusion of Sargonic legends make it seem plausible to relate the opening of the Hurro-Hittite *Song of Emergence* to the story of Sargon the cup-bearer. The comparison is nevertheless complicated by the fact that possible parallels to the cup-bearer theme exist also in Hittite historiography: the Old Hittite king Mursili I (1620–1590 BCE), successor to Hattusili I, was said to have been murdered in a conspiracy involving his cup-bearer and brother-in-law Hantili, who then took the throne.[19] The main source for this story is a passage in the historical prologue to the so-called *Edict* of king Telipinu (1525–1500 BCE), where the episode occurs immediately after Mursili's return from his sacking of Babylon, generally dated to 1595 BCE.[20] While modern accounts of Hittite history generally accept the truthfulness of this account,[21] it is also evident that the historical prologue to the *Edict* serves as a deliberately crafted counterpart to the regulations on orderly royal succession that Telipinu later sets out: in Telipinu's vision of Hittite history the murder of Mursili constitutes, according to Amir Gilan, the end of a harmonious golden age and the beginning of murderous depravity within the royal family, which was to provoke the lasting anger of the gods.[22] Seen in this light, one might wonder whether the topos of the cup-bearer adds a literary-mythological facet to the sense of momentous transition from Mursili to Hantili. The accession of Sargon and the transitions from Alalu to Anu to Kumarbi are,

---

[18] Sallaberger 2019: 105.
[19] This further parallel has been noted in passing by *RlA* s.v. 'Mundschenk' B. §2 (G. Frantz-Szabó), Archi 1999: 147 n. 2, López-Ruiz 2013: 141.
[20] *Edict of Telipinu* §§10–11 (*CTH* 19), ed. Hoffmann 1984 and Gilan 2015a: 137–59. The same story was perhaps told in a fragmentary passage of a ritual text that may also have been composed in the time of Telipinu: see Beckman 2001 and Gilan 2015a: 171–2 on *CTH* 655, §11' (= *HFAC* 40+ rev.).
[21] Bryce 2005: 100, van de Mieroop 2016: 129–30, de Martino 2016: 30.
[22] Gilan 2015a: 158–77.

after all, important events that marked new beginnings in historical and mythological time. But it is also clear that the primary function of the cup-bearer motif, namely to explain how a major king was able to emerge from obscurity, does not apply to the murderer Hantili: the Sargonic story-pattern that tells how a great king came to power by deposing a minor one does not suit Hantili and Mursili, whose momentous achievements culminated in the aforementioned sack of Babylon. One may also note a later episode in the *Edict* (§ 25) in which an individual named Inara, who is described as 'chief of the cup-bearers', was involved in a large-scale conspiracy: here, too, the central narrative purpose of the Sargonic cup-bearer theme, to provide a background to a future great ruler, is absent, since Inara is not mentioned again subsequently, and in general it can be said that conspiracies and lethal intrigues were a well-documented feature of the Hittite court.[23]

There is no obvious reason, then, to view the plotting cup-bearers of the Old Hittite kingdom as further instances of the Sargonic story-pattern, as reflected also in the opening of the *Song of Emergence*. Rather, the events related in the *Edict of Telipinu* seem to be independent of the literary-mythological theme, and this may prove fatal to the conventional view that the cup-bearer theme in the *Song of Emergence* was inspired by Sargonic legends – would the murder of an Old Hittite king not provide a more immediate model, if it is even necessary to assume the existence of such a model? I maintain that both the similarity of the story-pattern and the historical evidence favour Sargonic inspiration in the *Song of Emergence*, and I would also suggest that while the events described in the *Edict* may be independent of the mythological material, they are perhaps not necessarily unconnected, in that the Old Hittite parallels may help to explain the presence of the Sargonic motif in the *Song of Emergence*.

To clarify this suggestion, I would offer the following reconstruction: since there are to my knowledge no parallels in Mesopotamian mythology of the cup-bearer theme in combination with the Alalu-Anu genealogy, it seems safe to assume that the Sargonic story-pattern was secondarily combined with the Alalu-Anu genealogy in Hurrian mythology, where it was further extended by the addition of Kumarbi according to the same story-pattern: together, these ingredients produced the prologue to the *Song of Emergence*, which is generally thought to have reached the Hittites in the Middle Hittite period, i.e., from the late fifteenth century BCE onwards.[24] It may be suggestive in this connection that the so-called

---

[23] Giorgieri 2008.   [24] See recently Corti and Pecchioli Daddi 2012: 617.

Theogony of Dunnu (ed. Lambert 2013: 387–95), a Babylonian narrative attested by a single Late Babylonian- or Persian-period copy that also revolves around successive generations of rulers, mentions, in a fragmentary episode, a 'servant of heaven' (*ṣeḫer* ᵈ*ḫamorni*, obv. 37) who takes over kingship: since *havorni* is the Hurrian word for 'heaven', occurring here in an Akkadian context, it seems possible to interpret this as a further reflection of the Hurrian story-pattern, transferred from Sargon to a theogony, as in the *Song of Emergence*.[25]

If we further accept, as modern historians do, that the Old Hittite king Mursili I really was murdered and replaced by his cup-bearer Hantili, and if this event was remembered by subsequent generations of Hittites, as the late Hittite copies of the *Edict of Telipinu* suggest, then the fact that the Sargonic story-pattern of the treacherous cup-bearer happened by chance to be paralleled in Old Hittite history may have encouraged the Hittite reception of the Hurrian myth in the Middle Hittite period.[26] The Sargonic story-pattern provided a convenient starting point from which to begin a narrative of kingship in general, but perhaps its resonance with earlier events in Hittite history made it seem particularly plausible to a Hittite audience. This might agree with the recent political interpretation of the wider theogonic cycle that has been put forward by Carlo Corti and Franca Pecchioli Daddi, according to which the fight for kingship and the eventual triumph of the Storm God might accord on a mythological level with the historical struggles for kingship that were resolved by Tudhaliya I/II at the start of what is now called the Middle Hittite or New Kingdom period.[27]

I would now like to turn to the first millennium, where the Sargonic story-pattern emerges again, this time in connection with the accession of Cyrus the Great (ruled *c.* 559–530 BCE). The Old Persian and Babylonian sources on the early life of Cyrus are sparse, identifying him only as a descendant of the royal dynasty of Anšan (an ancient Elamite city and region in the Iranian highland).[28] Greek writers such as Herodotus, Ctesias

---

[25] The comparison between this passage of the *Theogony of Dunnu* and the Hurro-Hittite story-pattern has been made by Lambert 2013: 389.

[26] This being the period in which Hurrian elements are thought to have become significant in Hittite culture, according to the available evidence (Klinger 2001: 202–8; Gilan 2015a: 12–13; Corti 2017: 15). It would thus seem less plausible to assume, conversely, that Hantili sought to model his treachery on the usurpation of Anu and Kumarbi in the Hurrian myth.

[27] Corti and Pecchioli Daddi 2012: 617. Fragmentary historical sources suggest that these struggles may have involved further instances of assassinations of kings by court officials: see Bryce 2005: 114–15, 122; de Martino 2016: 36–7.

[28] The main source being the *Cyrus Cylinder* 20–22 (ed. Schaudig 2001: 550–6, see also Curtis 2013); for historical discussion, see, e.g., Schaudig 2001: 24–7, Briant 2002: 13–28, Potts 2005, Kuhrt 2007, Waters 2017: 60–3.

and Xenophon, however, provide legendary accounts that show very clearly that the cup-bearer motif was at some point during or after the reign of Cyrus transferred from Sargon to this king, probably in a Persian or Mesopotamian context, from where it was adapted, in different ways, by Greek authors seeking to formulate a plausible narrative on the origins of this great empire-builder, who was, by one modern reckoning, 'responsible for about 90% of Persia's territorial conquests, achieved within the remarkably short time of 20 years'.[29]

The first source that I would like to consider in this connection are the *Persica* of Ctesias, who wrote in the second half of the fifth century BCE and the early fourth century BCE. In a section that is only indirectly transmitted via Nicolaus of Damascus (born *c.* 64 BCE) but is generally agreed to be derived from the *Persica*, Ctesias introduces the rise of Cyrus as a momentous event that led to the passing of power from the Medes to the Persians.[30] According to Ctesias, Cyrus' father was so poor that he had to resort to banditry for a living, while his mother herded goats: he was thus born in poverty and had no relation to the ruling Median kings. Following a custom that allowed poor people to become quasi-slaves of richer members of society in order to secure their sustenance, Cyrus approached a royal servant who was in charge of the decorators at the court of king Astyages. Cyrus thus began to work for this servant to make a living, and started to build a palace career like that of Joseph in Egypt, progressing from exterior decoration work to the inner part of the court and the entourage of the king. He did so well that he was eventually appointed cup-bearer (οἰνοχόος) by the king, whom he again served with distinction, to the point that he himself became powerful and was able to instal his father as satrap of the Persians. At this stage in the narrative Cyrus' mother relates to him a dream that she had while pregnant with him, which clearly portended Cyrus' future domination of all Asia. In the course of subsequent political troubles arising from a local revolt against the king, Cyrus does indeed take the opportunity to depose his lord Astyages after a lengthy military campaign, at the conclusion of which he takes the throne and the sceptre (*Persica* F8d* 1–46, ed. Lenfant 2004).

This narrative was once considered to have been freely invented by Ctesias on the basis of the very different Cyrus-narrative of Herodotus,[31]

---

[29] Kuhrt 2007: 170.
[30] On the inclusion of this section in the *Persica*, see Lenfant 2004: clxxvi, clxxix–xxx, with further references.
[31] *RE* s.v. 'Ktesias' col. 2058 (F. Jacoby): 'die ganze Jugendgeschichte des Kyros [ist] eine freie Schöpfung des K. auf herodoteischer Grundlage'. Cizek 1975: 544–7 described the version of

which I will discuss in a moment; others have postulated that it must reflect some older, native Iranian legend.[32] But as the Sumero-Akkadian evidence has become more widely available, most recent commentators have not failed to recognise the obvious similarities between Ctesias' account of Cyrus and the Sargonic story-pattern.[33] In both cases, the tale of the cup-bearer serves to explain the rise of a new royal dynasty seemingly from nowhere, the usurper achieving far greater distinction than the previous king. The emphasis on Cyrus' humble origins is also clearly reminiscent of the Sumero-Akkadian Sargon legends: Sargon's father was a gardener, according to the *Sumerian King List*, while Cyrus' father was a bandit, according to the *Persica*; in the later *Sargon Birth Legend*, Sargon himself worked as a gardener,[34] which resembles Cyrus' initial role as an outside decorator at the palace of Astyages. It therefore seems highly attractive to follow Dominique Lenfant in concluding that the Sargonic story-pattern has been applied to Cyrus in Persian legend, from where it entered the narrative of Ctesias, who claimed to have served as a doctor at the Persian court. Lenfant emphasises that Ctesias based his account not only on earlier Greek historians but also on Persian sources that he was able to access during his stay at the court, and which he employed to correct the versions of his predecessors (in particular Herodotus): according to Lenfant, Ctesias' version of the rise of Cyrus on the one hand constitutes evidence of his familiarity with Mesopotamian legends, but on the other also illustrates his lack of critical engagement with his sources, since he accepts the tale without question.[35] Amélie Kuhrt has argued that the transmission of the Sargonic story-pattern to Cyrus may have happened in Babylonia, where Cyrus ended the rule of king Nabonidus in October 539 BCE but continued the cult of a statue of Sargon that

---

Ctesias as a reworking of the Herodotean model in the inept and melodramatic manner that supposedly characterised early fourth-century BCE Greek literature.

[32] Nagel 1982: 118–20, Jacobs 1996: 87, Llewellyn-Jones and Robson 2010: 65.

[33] Momigliano 1969: 196–7, Drews 1974, Dalley and Reyes 1998b: 110, Briant 2002: 16, Kuhrt 2003, Lenfant 2004: lviii–lix, Haussker 2017: 108, Waters 2017: 54, 64.

[34] *Birth Legend of Sargon* 9–12; compare also the older Sumero-Akkadian bilingual extract in which Sargon appears in Ur-Zababa's garden (ed. Goodnick Westenholz 1997: 52–5).

[35] Lenfant 2004: xxxi, cxxiii–vii. A more sceptical view is maintained in the review of Bichler 2007 and in the fuller study of Rollinger 2011, who do not, however, engage with Lenfant's observations on the Sargonic parallel. Rollinger 2011: 338 compares the tale of Cyrus the cup-bearer to the earlier episode of Arbakes, the Median general who overthrew the Assyrian empire (F1b 24–8), but the similarities to the Sargonic story-pattern are far clearer (*pace* Rollinger, Ctesias does not present Arbakes as a cup-bearer or confidant of any sort to the Assyrian king; on Cyrus and Arbakes, see also Waters 2017: 69–70, 82). Madreiter 2012: 104 considers it more likely that the tale of Cyrus was a Greek invention by Ctesias than a retelling of a Near Eastern legend, but offers no evidence or arguments in support of this view.

Nabonidus had discovered in the course of his building-work at the temple of the Sun God (Ebabbar) in Sippar. Indeed Cyrus himself mentioned his religious works at Agade, the capital founded by Sargon, in the cylinder inscription that relates his capture of Babylon (*Cyrus Cylinder* 31), which has been taken as a sign of his interest in the Old Akkadian empire.[36]

An indirect trace of the Sargonic cup-bearer-theme is also found in Xenophon's *Cyropaedia*, a study of Cyrus as a paradigmatic great ruler generally thought to have been written in the 360s BCE. While this narrative of Cyrus' rise to power is on the whole very different from the version of Ctesias, a reference to the cup-bearer theme has nevertheless been detected. According to Xenophon, Cyrus was of noble birth, being a grandson of king Astyages, just as in the Herodotean account (Hdt. 1.107), and the first scene of the Cyrus-narrative in the *Cyropaedia* shows Cyrus, at the age of about twelve, dining with his mother and grandfather at court (1.3). In the course of this scene, Cyrus asks king Astyages to explain why he prizes his cup-bearer above all his other servants (1.3.8), to which the king replies that it is because the cup-bearer serves the wine so well. Wishing to win the king's esteem, Cyrus asks to be given the wine-cup, so that he may perform the duty of cup-bearer. His wish is fulfilled – Cyrus does the job with such earnestness that his mother and the king cannot help laughing, and the boy exclaims that he will depose the cup-bearer of his functions, since he is better at serving the wine (1.3.9). Deborah Gera comments that Xenophon, by narrating this harmless dinner party, may be trying to refute other versions of the story of Astyages and Cyrus, such as that of Ctesias: 'Xenophon is, perhaps, referring obliquely to the Ctesian tale, demonstrating how such a (false) story could have arisen: since Cyrus once jestingly poured wine for his grandfather Astyages, he was later thought to be the king's cup-bearer.'[37] While Xenophon does not draw directly on the Sargonic story-pattern to tell the story of Cyrus, he nevertheless uses it indirectly by referring to (but departing from) the version of Ctesias.

In the *Histories*, finally, Herodotus tells yet another version of the rise of Cyrus (1.95–130), based on the motif of the exposed child that we have encountered briefly in connection with Sargon. But Herodotus begins his narrative by stating that the version he will tell is the one related to him by Persians who are interested in the truth rather than in magnifying Cyrus,

---

[36] Kuhrt 2003: 354–6, Haubold 2013: 103–4, Foster 2016: 270–3, 278–9.
[37] Gera 1993: 156–7, see also Gray 2016: 314–16. On the differences between Ctesias' and Xenophon's portrayal of Cyrus, see Gera 1993: 210–11.

and that he would be able to give three other, different accounts of Cyrus' biography. According to Pierre Briant and Dominique Lenfant, one of these alternative versions that Herodotus chooses not to record may well have been the tale of the cup-bearer that was later adopted by Ctesias.[38] Parenthetically, I wonder whether Herodotus may have avoided that particular version in connection with Cyrus simply for the sake of *variatio*: for he had already used a very similar story-pattern at the start of the *Histories* in the tale of Gyges, who served not as a cup- but as a spear-bearer (αἰχμοφόρος) to the Lydian king Candaules before killing him, as a consequence of the well-known bedroom-scene with the king's wife, and finally taking the throne himself (1.6–12). This too is an episode that relates the beginnings of a royal dynasty: Candaules is the last ruler of the Heraclid line and Gyges the first of the Mermnads, according to Herodotus, just as Sargon moves the kingship from Lugalzagesi's Uruk to Akkade, according to the *Sumerian King List*, and as Cyrus overturns Median rule and inaugurates the Persian era. The story is thus designed to explain how a famous king (Gyges) was able to arise from nowhere, overtaking a previous, far less important and possibly non-historical ruler (Candaules), who, like Ur-Zababa in the *Sumerian Sargon Legend*, is not attested outside the literary tradition: just as Ur-Zababa's name means nothing more than 'He-of-Zababa (the city god of Kiš)', so the name Candaules is now thought to be based simply on a Luwian or Lydian word for 'ruler'.[39] A fuller analysis of this complex tale would require consideration of the variant versions that are attested in other Classical sources, but the Herodotean account, at least, could be interpreted as a further, much embellished instance of the familiar story-pattern that has been the topic of this contribution.[40]

To conclude. While many of the individual connections that I have discussed have been made before, there exists to my knowledge no previous survey of the cup-bearer theme that attempts to draw together the

---

[38] Briant 2002: 15–16, Lenfant 2004: lix.
[39] Hawkins 2013: 167–82, Högemann and Oettinger 2018: 70–1, 257–9.
[40] While the commentary of Asheri 2007: 81 on Hdt. 1.8–12 speaks merely of the 'oriental flavour of a court tale', Murray 2001: 430 seems to interpret the passage as an application of a specifically Persian royal narrative to a Lydian context. Neither the recent discussion of mythical elements in the first book of the *Histories* by Dewald 2012 nor the full study of Lydian history by Högemann and Oettinger 2018 mentions the possible Sargonic background. Högemann and Oettinger 2018: 34–5 instead adduce the rise of David (1 *Sam.* 16–2 *Sam.* 5), which indeed contains suggestive points of comparison (that cannot be elaborated here, for want of space) but lacks (or avoids) the central theme of usurpation (see McCarter 1984: 64–5). On other Greek versions of the tale of Gyges, see Pedley 1972: 15–18 and, on the dramatic fragment (*TrGF* adespota F 664), *HGL* 1 493–4. On Near Eastern elements in Herodotus in general, see recently Rollinger 2018.

Sumero-Akkadian, Hurro-Hittite and Greek evidence. There have no doubt been many occasions in history in which a king was deposed and replaced by a close confidant, and it would clearly be wrong to attempt to interconnect all descriptions of such events in historical or mythological texts – the murder of Mursili I by the usurper Hantili is an example from Old Hittite history that probably has nothing to do with the Sargonic story-pattern, and it is not difficult to find other, equally unrelated examples.[41] But the Sargonic story-pattern in its original context clearly served a specific function, namely to explain the sudden emergence on the historical stage of a great ruler who built a new dynasty and an empire seemingly from nothing. Whatever the origin of the story-pattern may have been, the central element of 'social advancement' that underlies it accords well with the historical reality of Mesopotamia in the third millennium BCE. If the same story-pattern with the same function occurs in later sources, and if it is historically conceivable that these later sources drew ultimately on older Sargonic legend, then I think that this constitutes good evidence for historical connections: this is what I have argued for the cup-bearer theme at the start of the Hurro-Hittite *Song of Emergence*, where the theme is transferred from human to divine kingship, and for the *Persica* of Ctesias, where it is transferred from Sargon to a new paradigmatic great king of the first millennium BCE, Cyrus. In the latter case Greek sources allow us to reconstruct a legend that happens not to be attested in contemporaneous Mesopotamian or Persian texts but that, if one follows Lenfant, indicates that Ctesias did have access to written or oral Near Eastern sources.[42]

Finally, the material considered in this chapter sheds some indirect light on the most famous comparandum to the *Song of Emergence*, the Myth of Succession in Hesiod's *Theogony*. While it is often noted that Alalu, the

---

[41] For a Mesopotamian example in a divinatory treatise, see *Manzāzu* Commentary 1 A iii 51 (ed. Koch-Westenholz 2000: 132–50): 'If (the liver displays certain features), the lord's cup-bearer will give him harmful potions to drink.' Perdiccas, a Macedonian noble who served under Alexander, was murdered by his own soldiers or bodyguards in 321 BCE (Diod. Sic. 18.36, Paus. 1.6.3). In the time of king Pyrrhus' campaign against Rome (early third century BCE), an offer was made to the Romans to assassinate the king by means of poison administered by his cup-bearer (Gell. 3.8, cf. Amm. 30.1.22 and Tubach 1969: 290 no. 3761). In modern times, the Congolese president Laurent-Désiré Kabila was murdered by one of his bodyguards in January 2001. See also the plots at court narrated by Ctesias F1b§20, F1δ*, F15§§48, 54; and further Thompson 1955–8 s.vv. K.2240 ('Treacherous officers and tradesmen'), K.2250 ('Treacherous servants and workmen').

[42] Lenfant 2004: lix n. 200 remarks that the Sargonic story-pattern was continued later still, in the legend of Ardashir, founder of the Sasanian empire, as noted by von Gutschmid 1892: 133–4. This parallel has sometimes been used to argue for an Iranian origin of the story-pattern: see, e.g., Bauer 1882: 560–1, Llewellyn-Jones and Robson 2010: 65.

first ruler in heaven in the Hurro-Hittite tale, has no counterpart in Hesiod's version, this minor discrepancy has tended to attract little further comment, as it is outweighed by the strong correspondences between the subsequent rulers (Anu/Ouranos, Kumarbi/Kronos and, very likely, the Storm God/Zeus). Yet, as I hope to have shown, the presence of Alalu is dependent on the cup-bearer theme: his sole function in the *Song of Emergence* is to play the role of the obscure early ruler who is deposed by an initially subordinate but eventually far more important figure, in this case the Sky God Anu. Since Hesiod's version makes no use of the cup-bearer theme, it is logical that it has no use for a ruler of Alalu's type.[43]

This may prompt the question: why did Hesiod not draw on this evidently productive story-pattern in composing his account of divine kingship in the Greek pantheon?[44] One possible explanation would be that the particular Near Eastern version of the myth that inspired Hesiod's *Theogony* simply did not contain this element. Another would be that the cup-bearer theme was known to Hesiod, but was felt to be either implausible, since cup-bearers in early Greek epic are generally depicted as firmly subordinate to their lords, or unnecessary, since the theme of generational conflict, coupled with the familiar epic motif of the female plotter (Gaia), provided an attractive and easily intelligible alternative means by which to advance the plot in the Myth of Succession.[45] Given our current ignorance of Hesiod's immediate sources, it is impossible to advance beyond such speculation, but I suggest that the above analysis of the cup-bearer theme provides a simple explanation, at least, for the absence of a direct Hesiodic counterpart to Alalu, the first divine king in the otherwise closely related Hurro-Hittite version.

---

[43] van Dongen 2011: 194–5 observes that Alalu seems a largely expendable figure in the Hurro-Hittite text, and suggests that he may not have featured in every version of the tale. I would add that Alalu could indeed be omitted in any version that did not draw on the cup-bearer theme, such as Hesiod's.

[44] López-Ruiz 2013: 144 points to *Orph.* fr. 154 Kern (= fr. 220 Bernabé), according to which Kronos was trapped (and castrated) by Zeus while drunk with honey (as a substitute for wine), as a Greek comparandum. While there are no concrete indications that this is a further instance of the cup-bearer motif (the clearer Near Eastern parallels to this episode occur in the Hittite *Song of Illuyanka*, CTH 321: West 1983: 135), the castration of Kronus can nevertheless be said to represent a secondary extension of the castration of Ouranos (Edmonds 2018: 233–4), and is thus comparable in formal terms to the secondary extension of the cup-bearer motif at the start of the *Song of Emergence* (from Alalu-Anu to Anu-Kumarbi).

[45] For the Homeric conception of the cup-bearer, see in particular the banqueting scene at *Od.* 9.1–10, a 'golden' passage famous in antiquity (Hunter 2018: 92–135), and for the tale of Ganymede, the cup-bearer to Zeus, see *Il.* 20.230–5, *h.Hom.* 5.202–6. On the theme of the female plotter, see Kelly, Chapter 16 in this volume.

CHAPTER 9

Heroes and Nephilim
Sex between Gods and Mortals

Ruth Scodel

1 וַיְהִי כִּי־הֵחֵל הָאָדָם לָרֹב עַל־פְּנֵי הָאֲדָמָה וּבָנוֹת יֻלְּדוּ לָהֶם:
2 וַיִּרְאוּ בְנֵי־הָאֱלֹהִים אֶת־בְּנוֹת הָאָדָם כִּי טֹבֹת הֵנָּה וַיִּקְחוּ לָהֶם נָשִׁים מִכֹּל אֲשֶׁר בָּחָרוּ
3 וַיֹּאמֶר יְהוָה לֹא־יָדוֹן רוּחִי בָאָדָם לְעֹלָם בְּשַׁגַּם הוּא בָשָׂר וְהָיוּ יָמָיו מֵאָה וְעֶשְׂרִים שָׁנָה
4 הַנְּפִלִים הָיוּ בָאָרֶץ בַּיָּמִים הָהֵם וְגַם אַחֲרֵי־כֵן אֲשֶׁר יָבֹאוּ בְּנֵי הָאֱלֹהִים אֶל־בְּנוֹת הָאָדָם וְיָלְדוּ לָהֶם הֵמָּה הַגִּבֹּרִים אֲשֶׁר מֵעוֹלָם אַנְשֵׁי הַשֵּׁם:

> [1] When men began to increase on earth and daughters were born to them, [2] the divine beings saw that the daughters of men were beautiful and took wives from among those that pleased them. [3] YHWH said, 'My breath will not abide in men forever, for he is flesh; let the days allowed him be a hundred and twenty years.' [4] The Nephilim were on the earth in those days, and later too, when the divine beings went to the daughters of men, who bore them offspring. They were the heroes of old, the men with a name.[1]
>
> (Gen. 6:1–4)

Scholars of both Greek and Biblical literature have argued that this famously difficult passage shows the influence of Greek thought about an age of heroes, although this interpretation is certainly not universally accepted.[2] Since scholarship has found so much influence on Greek mythology and culture from the Levant and the Near East, the proposal that the age of heroes was transmitted from Greece in the Early Iron Age may be surprising. Perhaps it should not be, since there is no reason to

---

[1] This translation is adapted from *JPS*.
[2] Bibliography in Darshan 2014a (text in Hebrew, with English summary and notes). On the Greek side, see Finkelberg 2004; on the Biblical, especially van Seters 1988 and Hendel 1987. Kraeling 1947 already compares Hesiod, though he does not postulate influence. Day 2012 argues against Greek influence, primarily because Hesiod is elsewhere influenced by Eastern myths rather than the reverse. Day also argues that, while the underlying myth identified the Nephilim with the children of the divine–mortal unions, the author of *Gen.* 6 rejects this.

expect that cultural influence will flow only in one direction.[3] This paper will not rehearse the arguments in detail, but will instead make suggestions both about how the Greek material was transmitted, and how a comparison of the Greek and Biblical narratives can contribute to a richer understanding of both. It does not, however, consider the varied and fascinating history of the interpretation of this passage in later antiquity through the modern period.[4] Inevitably, a truly monotheistic Judaism could not permit the *benê ha' elohîm*, the 'sons of god(s)', to be lesser divinities, the participants in the divine council of *Psalm* 82. Scholars, however, agree that these are divine beings.

The passage is extremely compressed, its relationship to its context (it immediately precedes the Flood narrative) is obscure, and it is hard to be certain exactly how the Nephilim are connected with the divine beings and with the heroes, or exactly what Nephilim are. In the most common and economical interpretation, Nephilim are the sons of the divine–mortal unions and are identified with the heroes of old. The Hebrew would also allow, however, that the Nephilim are the divine beings. They can hardly be independent of both divine beings and heroes, however, since they appear at two periods, both defined by sexual unions of gods and mortals and the birth of children of these unions.[5] At any rate, *gibborim*, the 'men with a name', cannot refer to anybody whose story has been narrated so far. Whether or not they are the same, neither Nephilim nor *gibborim* are part of the world of the author or his audience – these heroes are *ha'olam*, of old.

'And later too' needs to be taken seriously, as indicating two eras of divine–human relations. One feature of this doublet is particularly interesting. In the first verse about the *benê ha' elohîm*, they 'marry' the mortal women, while in the second, they simply go to them and have children by them. I would suggest that this is a significant distinction.

The Septuagint, of course, translated Nephilim as γίγαντες, but I see no reason to associate them with the Giants in the earlier Greek tradition. The Greek Giants are not the product of divine–human sex, and they fight with the Olympians. There is no indication in *Genesis* that Nephilim are antagonists of YHWH or other gods, and the passage seems to have

---

[3] See the discussion in the introduction to this volume, and also, e.g., Louden 2018, for sustained argument for Greek influence on the Jewish scriptural tradition.
[4] See Kugel 1997: 108–14.
[5] Soggin 1996 argues that the *gibborim* are not children of divine–mortal unions because elsewhere in the Hebrew Bible the word has no supernatural connotation – but this connection seems to be precisely the argument of the verse.

nothing to do with myths in which forces of chaos threaten divine order.[6] Indeed, the 'heroes of old, men of renown' sounds as if the writer admires them.[7] Still, since these verses immediately precede the flood narrative, it is reasonable to infer that those who located these verses at this point in the text associated Nephilim with the antediluvian period – which does not indicate that the original purpose of the Flood was to remove them.[8] That seems to be very unlikely, but the placement may reflect the Mesopotamian association of the Flood with overpopulation.[9] That is, both the Flood and the sexual relationships require that human population have increased, which could be a motive to locate this fragment at this point in the narrative. There are thus two problems for those who argue that the Flood must happen in order to destroy the Nephilim: first, that there seems to be nothing particularly wrong with such demigods, and second, that they still exist later.

The qualification that they also existed afterward, when the *benê ha'elohîm* again had sexual relationships with mortal women, surely refers to a time after the Flood, though still significantly before the time-perspective of the narrator. Here, too, the situation is not straightforward, for Nimrod is called the first *gibbor* at *Genesis* 10:8. Nimrod is there a city-founder (10:8–12), which is a characteristic of Greek heroes, but he has a purely mortal genealogy.

This complexity suggests not just varying traditions, but a common difficulty with boundaries in mythical history – in both Greek and Hebrew, we see a basic tension between rupture and continuity.[10] In the Mesopotamian context, there do not seem to be complexities surrounding the Flood. Humanity starts over, under different conditions. Hebrew integrates this idea, but it cannot entirely be reconciled with other traditional narratives that connect the earliest humanity with later people and even with the present. We might compare the problems with the genealogy of Cain, although that is surely priestly in origin. At *Genesis* 4:20–1, Jabal is called the 'father' (אֲבִי) of pastoralists, Jubal the father of musicians. If the Flood ends Cain's line and the continuity of history, what could this mean? Even if these are only metaphorical ancestors, the description implies a descent from an origin that the Flood would seem to cancel.

---

[6] Petersen 1979.
[7] Lemardelé 2010 argues that they represent traces of a rich tradition of West Semitic heroic stories.
[8] As argued by Hendel 1987.   [9] Kilmer 1972.
[10] Finkelberg 2004 argues that Homer makes his own world continuous with the Homeric past, while the Hesiodic texts present rupture, but Most 1998 argues that Hesiod does not mention a creation of the Iron Race because he saw his contemporaries as descendants of the heroes.

Darshan has argued for a close relationship between Greek genealogy and the Biblical post-flood narrative, since Mesopotamian versions do not narrate later descent-lines after the Flood or include culture-hero narratives (the origin of wine), as both Greek sources and the Hebrew Bible do.[11]

The decision of YHWH to limit the human life span (*Gen.* 6:3) is especially difficult.[12] Although the heroes before the flood live fabulously long lives that resemble and must ultimately be related to the long lives of antediluvians in Mesopotamian myth, while the postdiluvians gradually become more like ordinary humans, the Biblical narrative as we have it does not fulfil God's intention in this verse. The lifespans of Noah's descendants exceed 120 years. Even the three patriarchs live longer (Jacob dies at 147: *Gen.* 47:28). Either there were variant traditions in play about when mortal lifespans were fixed, or *Genesis* 6:3 refers to something else.

The only other passage in the Pentateuch that mentions Nephilim is the spies' report on the inhabitants of Canaan (*Num.* 13:33):

> And there we saw the Nephilim, the sons of Anak, who come of the Nephilim; and we were in our own sight as grasshoppers, and so we were in their sight.

This passage confirms one point about the Nephilim, that they were imagined as significantly larger than the people who formed the original audience of the text. In this passage, the spies do not see actual Nephilim but, apparently, their descendants, and the spies in any case are reporting their own, terrified perceptions.

Then there are the Repha'im, who sometimes seem to overlap with Nephilim. Here my concern is only with Repha'im who have descendants. However, they are also a special category of the dead, one that has parallels with Greek cult-heroes.[13] These Repha'im are earlier inhabitants of Canaan, and of exceptional stature. *Deuteronomy* 2:10–11 refers to a people called Emim by the Moabites, but they are said to be remnants of the Repha'im, 'like the Anaqim'. Repha'im are also past inhabitants of the region of Ammon. Og, the giant king of Bashan, is called a remnant of the Repha'im (*Deut.* 3:8–11; *Josh.* 12:1–4, 13:12). Joshua destroys all the Anaqim in Israelite territory (*Josh.* 11:22), but some survive in Gaza, Gad, and Ashdod. These are, of course, Philistine cities. These are presumably

---

[11] Darshan 2013, cf. Darshan 2014b. [12] Often treated as a late addition; see Perlitt 1990: 41–2.
[13] There are Ugaritic connections: Lewis 1989, Spronk 1986: 161–96. Doak 2012 argues that *Ezekiel* 32:17–32 attacks the belief in the power of ancient *gibborim*. Wyatt 2010 connects Repha'im with Titans; the names seem similar, but not the deeds.

ancestors of the Philistine descendants of the Rapha who fight against David's army at 2 *Samuel* 21:15–22, and also of Goliath, who comes from Gad but whose ancestry is not narrated. Repha'im and Nephilim have certain similarities, therefore: they are both very tall warrior-groups of the past. In different traditions, the people called Anaqim were said to be descended from both, and they survive in Philistine locations. And they are both associated not with the Israelites, but with their enemies.

It is indeed striking that the last survivors of the ancient giants, the ones who actually appear as *gibborim* and men of renown, are Philistines.[14]

There Were Heroes

There are obvious reasons to connect *Genesis* 6:1–4 with Greek rather than other traditions: only Greek defines a period of the past by the prevalence of divine–human sexual unions and the heroes who result. This is not a common theme to be attributed to an Eastern Mediterranean *koinē*, as far as the evidence shows. To be sure, sexual encounters between gods and mortals are not unusual in various mythologies, and are found in both Indo-European and Near Eastern texts. The five Pandavas had divine fathers because Kunti used a secret mantra to summon divinities to herself and her co-wife Madri (*Mahābhārata* 1.113–15).[15] Gilgameš has a goddess for a mother, and when Ištar propositions him he lists six of her unfortunate lovers (SB *Epic of Gilgameš* VI, 42–79).[16] The Hittite *Song of Illuyanka* (*CTH* 321) includes a divine–mortal sexual relationship in each of the two recorded versions. In the first, the goddess Inaras trades sex with the mortal Hupasiyas in return for his help against Illuyanka. When he disobeys her command not to look out of the window at his wife and children, she destroys him. In the second, the Storm God, whose eyes and heart have been taken by Illuyanka, begets a son with the 'daughter of a poor man'. This son marries Illuyanka's daughter and recovers the Storm God's eyes and heart, but when Illuyanka and the Storm God fight again, the son demands that his father kill him along with Illuyanka. Both encounters are disastrous for the mortals.[17]

In the opening of the Hesiodic *Catalogue of Women* – which is practically an encyclopedic narrative of the pre-Trojan War past – the poet announces the subject, women of the past who had sexual encounters with

---

[14] Finkelberg 2005: 158–60. [15] Translation van Buitenen 1973: 254–9.
[16] Abusch 1986 argues that Ištar is implicitly offering to make Gilgameš lord of the Underworld.
[17] See Mouton 2016a: 439–57; Beckman 1982.

gods, and then explains the conditions that made these possible (fr. 1.1–22 M-W = fr. 1.1–22 Most):

νῦν δὲ γυναικῶν ̣φῦλον ἀείσατε, ἡδυέπειαι
Μοῦσαι Ὀλυμπιάδες, κοῦραι Διὸς αἰγιόχοιο,
α̣ἳ τότ' ἄρισται ἔσαν̣ [καὶ κάλλισται κατὰ γαῖαν,
μίτρας τ' ἀλλύσαντο δ[ιὰ χρυσέην τ' Ἀφροδίτην,
μισγόμεν̣αι θεοῖς̣[ιν
ξυναὶ γὰρ τότε δα̣ῖτες ἔσαν, ξυνοὶ δὲ θόωκοι
ἀθανάτοις τε θε̣οῖσι καταθνητοῖς τ' ἀνθρώποις.
οὐδ' ἄρα ἰσαίωνες ομ[
ἀνέρες ἠδὲ γυναῖκες ε[
ὀϲϲόμεν[ο]ι̣ φɔ[εϲὶ] γῆρ[ας
οἳ μὲν δηρὸν ε.[..]κ.[
ἠϊ[θ]εοι, τοὺς δ' εἶθ[αρ].ε.[
ἀ[θ]άνατο̣ι [νε]ότητ[
τ̣ά̣ων ἔσπετέ μ[οι γενεήν τε καὶ ἀγλαὰ τέκνα,
ὅσσ[αι]ς δὴ παρέλ[εκτο πατὴρ ἀνδρῶν τε θεῶν τε
[σ]περμ[αί]νων τὰ [πρῶτα] γένος κυδρῶν βασιλήων
[ἧ]ς̣ τ̣ε Π[ο]σειδάω[ν
ὅσσαισί]ν τ' Ἄρης [
.....].η̣ι̣.ιντ[
ὅσσαις θ' Ἥφ]α̣[ι]στος π[
αἷσιν δ' αὖθ' Ε]ρμῆς .[
ἠδ' ὅσσαισι] βίη Ἡ[ρακλῆος

And now sing of the tribe of women, sweet-voiced / Olympian Muses, daughters of aegis-bearing Zeus, / those who were the best at that time [and most beautiful on the earth,] / and they loosed their girdles [and because of golden Aphrodite] / mingling with gods [...] / For at that time the feasts were in common and in common the councils / for the immortal gods and for mortal human beings; / and yet not equally long-lived [...] / men and women [...] / seeing in their spirit old age [...] / the ones for a long time [...] / youths, but the others at once [...] / immortals youthfulness [...] / Of these women tell m[e the race and the splendid children:] / all those with whom lay [the father of men and of gods,] / begetting at first the race of illustrious kings, / and with which ones Poseidon [...] / and [all those with whom] Ares [...] / [...] ... [...] / [and all those with whom Heph]aestus [...] / [and with which ones] Hermes [...] / [and all those with whom Heracles'] force ...[18]

---

[18] Text and translation based on Most 2006–7: II 43 (as throughout). Although it is not clear from the translation, there are letter traces for all the names of gods.

The proem then returns to the women, categorising them by the gods who were the fathers of their children: first, evidently, Zeus, then Poseidon, then Ares and probably Apollo in the gaps from verses 18–20, then Hermes and Heracles. This would lead an innocent hearer to expect that these gods will organise the narrative so that it offers the sexual relationships and children of each – but it was not organised that way at all.[19]

However, the proem demonstrates that this was a possible way to structure all this mythological material. Even though the *Catalogue* actually operates very differently, the sexual relations between divinities and mortal women could serve as an organising principle for narrating history from a time when men and gods feasted together to the end of that special time before the world that we know. The catalogue of gods, moreover, apparently reflects both power and the number of sexual encounters. Ares, for example, is more prominent in this context than in the Homeric epics, where he is marginalised – wounded by the mortal Diomedes (with Athene's aid) and rebuked by Zeus (*Il.* 5.846–98), restrained by Athene from avenging the death of his son Ascalaphus (*Il.* 15.113–42) and incapacitated by the same goddess in the *theomachia* (*Il.* 21.391–414), a comic figure when Hephaestus makes a public spectacle of his adultery with Aphrodite (*Od.* 8.296–361). However, he has a significant place in heroic genealogies: in the *Iliad* he is named as the father of Ialmenus and Ascalaphus (2.511–16); in the Hesiodic *Shield* of Cycnus (57); in Euripides' *Alcestis* of Thracian Diomedes (498); in Hesiod's *Theogony* of Harmonia the wife of Cadmus (937; it does not matter that the verses are probably not Hesiod's).[20]

The Catalogue does not list all divine fathers of heroic progeny – the river gods, for instance, are absent – while Heracles in the tradition produces his heroic sons while still mortal. Presumably he receives a place in the *Catalogue* because his descendants were important. To be sure, not all heroes of epic have divine ancestry, let alone a divine parent, while stories of divine–mortal sexual interactions are not entirely absent from later periods. Nonetheless, sexual unions between mortals and gods are a defining aspect of the time of the heroes, and that time is distinct from everything later.

In Greek, sometimes goddesses initiate liaisons with mortal men or are forced into sexual encounters with them. The Dawn goddess abducts young men, and one hero, Memnon, is born of such a union (Hes. *Th.*

---

[19] West 2007: 425–7.
[20] A recent treatment of Ares' simultaneous importance and marginalisation is Millington 2013.

984–5).[21] Harmonia is married to Cadmus (Pindar *P.* 3.86–95), and Thetis to Peleus (*Il.* 24. 59–63). Aphrodite is the mother of Aeneas (*Il.* 2.820). Calypso claims that the male gods resent the goddesses who have relations with mortal men, and lists some mortal lovers of goddesses who have been killed by the gods (*Od.* 5.118–28). Such relationships often end badly. Anchises, when he learns that he has had sexual relations with a goddess, says 'a man who sleeps with immortal goddesses comes to be without vitality' (*h.Hom.* 5.188–90).[22]

Far more often, however, male gods initiate relationships with (or simply rape) mortal women. The women frequently suffer as a result of the encounter, but the stories typically have a happy ending for them. Divine–mortal sex in archaic Greek poetry is rarely transactional: its cause is sexual desire from the side of the divinity, not a wish to generate particular progeny. Some versions of the birth of Helen are an exception, although her mother may then be the goddess Nemesis rather than the mortal Leda (*Cypria* fr. 9 Bernabé = fr. 7 Davies = fr. 10 West). Similarly, although the reasons for the marriage of Peleus and Thetis vary, Thetis' desire plays no part in any version before Apollonius of Rhodes (Hera at *Argonautica* 4.806 calls it γάμου θυμηδέος, 'a pleasing marriage'). Yet, although the gods' desire seems random, the result could be considered systematic.

Families claiming descent from these unions were prominent throughout the Greek world. Herodotus (2.43) reports the discomfiture of his predecessor Hecataeus of Miletus when priests in Egyptian Thebes showed him statues of 343 generations of high priests, although Hecataeus claimed a divine ancestor sixteen generations earlier. In the Greek context, the process must have been circular: narratives of divine–human sex made claims of divine ancestry possible, while elite families had every reason to make such claims, which meant that more such narratives had to be generated, prompting even more claims. The only limits were that the children of divine–mortal unions had to be special in some way, so that those without wealth or power could not sustain them.

The past in which gods and mortals produced heroic children constituted the era immediately preceding historical time for the earliest Greek poets, and its conclusion is marked and brought about by the Trojan War,

---

[21] Boedeker 1974: 67–84.
[22] While scholars have debated exactly what Anchises fears and whether this passage shows Near Eastern influence, there is no question that sex with goddesses is dangerous: Giacomelli 1980: 16–18; Crane 1988: 66–7; Tsomis 2004; Faulkner 2008: 248–51 (on 188–90); Richardson 2010: 242–3 (on 187–90); Olson 2012: 229–30 (on 187–9).

or by the Theban and Trojan Wars together. It is striking, however, how unmotivated its end is. This firmly delineated heroic time is clearest in Hesiod's *Works and Days*, where the heroes constitute the fourth of the Five Races (*Op.* 157–72):

> αὖτις ἔτ' ἄλλο τέταρτον ἐπὶ χθονὶ πουλυβοτείρηι
> Ζεὺς Κρονίδης ποίησε, δικαιότερον καὶ ἄρειον,
> ἀνδρῶν ἡρώων θεῖον γένος, οἳ καλέονται
> ἡμίθεοι, προτέρη γενεὴ κατ' ἀπείρονα γαῖαν.
> καὶ τοὺς μὲν πόλεμός τε κακὸς καὶ φύλοπις αἰνὴ
> τοὺς μὲν ὑφ' ἑπταπύλωι Θήβηι, Καδμηίδι γαίηι,
> ὤλεσε μαρναμένους μήλων ἕνεκ' Οἰδιπόδαο,
> τοὺς δὲ καὶ ἐν νήεσσιν ὑπὲρ μέγα λαῖτμα θαλάσσης
> ἐς Τροίην ἀγαγὼν Ἑλένης ἕνεκ' ἠυκόμοιο.
> ἔνθ' ἦ τοι τοὺς μὲν θανάτου τέλος ἀμφεκάλυψε[23]
> τοῖς δὲ δίχ' ἀνθρώπων βίοτον καὶ ἤθε' ὀπάσσας
> Ζεὺς Κρονίδης κατένασσε πατὴρ ἐς πείρατα γαίης.
> καὶ τοὶ μὲν ναίουσιν ἀκηδέα θυμὸν ἔχοντες
> ἐν μακάρων νήσοισι παρ' Ὠκεανὸν βαθυδίνην,
> ὄλβιοι ἥρωες.

> Zeus, Kronos' son, made another (race) in turn upon the bounteous earth, a fourth one, more just and superior, the godly race of men-heroes, who are called demigods, the generation before our own upon the boundless earth. And war and dread battle destroyed these, some under seven-gated Thebes in the land of Cadmus while they fought for the sake of Oedipus' sheep, others brought in boats over the great gulf of the sea to Troy for the sake of fair-haired Helen. There the end of death shrouded some of them, but upon others[24] Zeus the father, Kronos' son, bestowed life and habitations far from human beings and settled them at the limits of the earth; and these dwell with a spirit free of care on the Islands of the Blessed beside deep-eddying Ocean – happy heroes.

For Hesiod, 'heroes' is the 'standard' term, while 'half-gods' (ἡμίθεοι) is another name 'they are called' (καλέονται), but the role of divine parentage in producing this race goes unmentioned. Hesiod offers no cause why this race, more just and better than those before them, had to perish.[25] The wars have immediate causes – the inheritance of Oedipus, the theft of

---

[23] This much-disputed line is missing in a papyrus (though found in two others) and is ignored in the commentary of Proclus, so it is likely to be an early rhapsodic interpolation; see West 1978 *ad loc.*: 193–4. If retained, it means that some of the heroes died, while others were transported; if removed, it probably means that all the heroes were transported.
[24] Again following Most 2006–7: 1.101, I here accept the authenticity of a disputed verse (see previous note).
[25] I disagree with Rosen 1997: 486–7, who sees implicit disapproval of the heroes.

Helen – and the removal of some or all heroes to the islands of the blessed maintains theodicy, but the poet does not point to any Plan of Zeus. However, the poet's failure to assign any cause to the wars is not especially salient, since he has also not explained the end of the Golden Race.[26] The Silver Race is destroyed by Zeus, and the Bronze Race self-destructs, but the good Races must vanish because the Iron Race is the present. In the *Works and Days*, the heroic race appears to be the human population of its age.

Other texts offer reasons for the heroes' disappearance. The Trojan War or the two epic wars, as I argued more than thirty years ago, replace the Flood, which serves as the main division in Mesopotamian myth.[27] In the epic *Cypria*, Zeus initiates the Trojan War in order to reduce human population, a theme that echoes the flood in. Our information about this part of the *Cypria* comes from a mythographic D-scholium on *Iliad* 1.5 (fr. 1 Bernabé = fr. 1 Davies = fr. 1 West, here cited after West):

> ἄλλοι δὲ ἀπὸ ἱστορίας τινὸς εἶπον εἰρηκέναι τὸν Ὅμηρον. φασὶ γὰρ τὴν Γῆν βαρουμένην ὑπὸ ἀνθρώπων πολυπληθίας, μηδεμιᾶς ἀνθρώπων οὔσης εὐσεβείας, αἰτῆσαι τὸν Δία κουφισθῆναι τοῦ ἄχθους· τὸν δὲ Δία πρῶτον μὲν εὐθὺς ποιῆσαι τὸν Θηβαϊκὸν πόλεμον, δι' οὗ πολλοὺς πάνυ ἀπώλεσεν, ὕστερον δὲ πάλιν τὸν Ἰλιακόν, συμβούλωι τῶι Μώμωι χρησάμενος, ἣν Διὸς βουλὴν Ὅμηρός φησιν, ἐπειδὴ οἷός τε ἦν κεραυνοῖς ἢ κατακλυσμοῖς ἅπαντας διαφθείρειν· ὅπερ τοῦ Μώμου κωλύσαντος, ὑποθεμένου δὲ αὐτῶι γνώμας δύς, τὴν Θέτιδος θνητογαμίαν καὶ θυγατρὸς καλῆς γένναν, ἐξ ὧν ἀμφοτέρων πόλεμος Ἕλλησί τε καὶ βαρβάροις ἐγένετο, ἀφ' οὗ συνέβη κουφισθῆναι τὴν γῆν πολλῶν ἀναιρεθέντων. ἡ δὲ ἱστορία παρὰ Στασίνωι τῶι τὰ Κύπρια πεποιηκότι.

> Others said that Homer spoke on the basis of a tale. For they say that the Earth, weighed down by the overpopulation of humans, while there was no human piety, asked Zeus to be lightened of the burden. And Zeus first caused the Theban war, through which he destroyed very many, and afterwards the Trojan one, with Momus as an adviser, which is what Homer calls '(the) Plan of Zeus', since he could destroy them all with thunderbolts or floods. Momus prevented this, and suggested two strategies to him, the mortal marriage of Thetis and the birth of a beautiful daughter, from both of which a war took place between Greeks and non-Greeks, and so it was the result that the earth was lightened when many were killed. The tale is found in Stasinus, who composed the *Cypria*.

This summary is very problematic – certainly not all this material goes back to the archaic epic, but it is impossible to determine exactly how

[26] Clay 2003: 87 suggests that the race, all male, could not reproduce.   [27] Scodel 1982.

much.[28] The role given Momus, who is Blame personified, is especially uncertain.[29] However, the crucial information is confirmed by the quotation from the poem that follows (fr. 1 Bernabé = fr. 1 Davies = fr. 1 West):

> ἦν ὅτε μυρία φῦλα κατὰ χθόνα πλαζόμεν' αἰεὶ
> <ἀνθρώπων ἐπίεζε> βαρυστέρνου πλάτος αἴης,[30]
> Ζεὺς δὲ ἰδὼν ἐλέησε καὶ ἐν πυκιναῖς πραπίδεσσι
> κουφίσαι ἀνθρώπων παμβώτορα σύνθετο γαῖαν,
> ῥιπίσσας πολέμου μεγάλην ἔριν Ἰλιακοῖο,
> ὄφρα κενώσειεν θανάτωι βάρος. οἱ δ' ἐνὶ Τροίηι
> ἥρωες κτείνοντο, Διὸς δ' ἐτελείετο βουλή.

There was a time when innumerable tribes [of humans], constantly wandering across the earth, [pushed down on] the surface of the heavy-bosomed earth. Zeus, seeing, took pity, and in his thoughtful mind agreed to lighten the all-feeding earth of humanity, blowing up the great strife of the Trojan War, so as to lighten the weight by death. And the heroes were killed at Troy, and the will of Zeus was fulfilled.

Here there is a motive for the Trojan War, to reduce the human population, but it does not explain why the reduced population could not include heroes or the children of future divine–mortal sexual relations.

The Hesiodic Catalogue apparently did explicitly present a Plan of Zeus to end the heroic period. Exactly what happens is uncertain because the papyrus is lacunose, but it appears that a purpose of the war is precisely to remove the demigods (fr. 204.95–104 M-W = 155.95–104 Most):

> πάντες δὲ θεοὶ δίχα θυμὸν ἔθεντο
> ἐξ ἔριδος· δὴ γὰρ τότε μήδετο θέσκελα ἔργα
> Ζεὺς ὑψιβρεμέτης, μεῖξαι κατ' ἀπείρονα γαῖαν
> τυρβάξας, ἤδη δὲ γένος μερόπων ἀνθρώπων
> πολλὸν ἀϊστῶσαι σπεῦδε πρ[ό]φασιν μὲν ὀλέσθαι
> ψυχὰς ἡμιθέω[ν . . . .].οισι βροτοῖσι
> τέκνα θεῶν μι[...].[..].ο.[ὀφ]θαλμοῖσιν ὁρῶντα,
> ἀλλ' οἳ μ[ὲ]ν μάκ[α]ρες κ[. . . . . .]ν ὡς τὸ πάρος περ
> χωρὶς ἀπ' ἀν[θ]ρώπων [βίοτον κα]ὶ ἤθε' ἔχωσιν
> ...

---

[28] On the 'Mythographus Homericus', see van Rossum-Steenbeek 1998: 85–116; on this scholium and the *Cypria*, see West 2013: 25–6; Burkert 1992: 102–3; Currie 2015: 285.
[29] Mayer 1996.
[30] West 2013: 82–3 follows a supplement of Peppmüller, ἐβάρυνε βαθυστέρνου, where Bernabé and Davies have ἐπίεζε βαρυστέρνου. The sense is very similar.

> All the gods were divided in spirit in strife. For high-thundering Zeus was devising wondrous deeds then, to stir up trouble on the boundless earth; for he was already eager to annihilate most of the race of speech-endowed human beings, a pretext to destroy the lives of the semi-gods [...] to mortals children of the gods [...] seeing with eyes, but that the ones blessed [...] as before apart from human beings should have [life an]d habitations.

Again, something seems missing. Zeus wants to separate the demigods from mortals, but there is no explanation of why he has this plan, or how he intends to keep the gods from continuing to produce demigods.[31] No Greek text explicitly addresses the reason why the gods stopped having relations with mortal women. The beginning of the *Catalogue* links the earlier practice with a more general closeness between gods and mortals at an earlier time, but no extant part of the poem explains why Zeus chose to change.

What finally happens to the demigods? In the Homeric epics, they generally die just like other mortals. In the *Iliad*, even Heracles is said to have died (*Il.* 18.117–19).[32] In *Works and Days* 167–72, some or all of the heroes (the sense of the Greek is disputed) go to the Islands of the Blessed. In fr. 204 of the *Catalogue* (cited above), it is uncertain whether those who are to have 'life and habitations' far from mortals are the demigods or the gods.[33] Just as different texts stress continuity or rupture between heroes and later humanity, different texts provide differing afterlives for the heroes.

In the *Homeric Hymn to Aphrodite*, Zeus, exasperated at Aphrodite's boasting about the gods' affairs with mortals (48–52), makes Aphrodite conceive intense desire for Anchises, so that she will no longer be able to mock the other gods. In one interpretation, the *Hymn* thereby explains the end of the heroic age.[34] While this may be right, there is no sign that gods are embarrassed about sex with mortal women in other early Greek texts, so that the *Hymn* is not a representation of common Greek thought about the end of the heroic age, but a witty invention. In any case, the *Hymn* itself makes no reference to the end of the heroic age, and Zeus seeks only to end Aphrodite's gloating, not sexual relations with mortals. The audience would have to infer that if Aphrodite can no longer boast of her

---

[31] For the problems of this passage, see Ormand 2014: 202–16 and below, note 34.
[32] So Griffin 1977.
[33] Gods: Thalmann 1984: 105–7; Cerutti 1998: 166–7; demigods, West 1985: 120; Koenen 1994: 40. See Hirschberger 2004: 418–19.
[34] van der Ben 1986: 31–2; Clay 1989: 192–3, followed by Olson 2012: 28–9; Faulkner 2008: 14–18 is more doubtful. Richardson 2010 does not address the issue.

power over the other gods, she will no longer exert that power. If this interpretation is right and the audience should draw that inference, the poem has trivialised a significant change in the human condition.

Heroes and Nephilim

The Greek Age of Heroes is the only real parallel for the Nephilim. There are, however, some clear distinctions between the Hebrew and Greek versions of this past time of mighty men born of divine–mortal sexual unions. First, in Greek the most powerful of the gods are most frequently the progenitors of heroes, while the Nephilim are the progeny of unnamed divinities who are evidently inferior to YHWH. Second, while even in Greek it is mostly male gods who beget children on mortal women, goddesses sometimes enter sexual relationships with mortals. The Biblical text assumes only male divinities. But third, and for my purposes most important, the Greek demigods are most often ancestors of Greeks themselves. This, again, is not a universal rule, for the Greek genealogies also define relationships between Greeks and others. The end of Hesiod's *Theogony*, for example, sends children of Odysseus by Circe to Etruria (*Th.* 1011–16), and Medeius, son of Medea (who is descended from Helios the sun god), is ancestor of the Medes (1000–3).[35] Nonetheless, in general when Greeks told stories about the children of mortals and gods, their alleged descendants were mostly the elite of Greek communities. Praising the ancestors of the contemporary elite is a core purpose of genealogical poetry.[36] The heroes could also be recipients of cult in Greek city-states. Nobody within the 'us' of the Hebrew Bible claims any relationship with any of these gods or their children. These are the gods of others.

The antediluvian Nephilim are the product of actual marriages between gods and women. The only Greek god who really marries a mortal is Dionysus, but several divine–human relationships produce children who are divinised – Apollo and Coronis, Zeus and Leda, Zeus and Alcmene. It seems at least possible that the antediluvian Nephilim are in this ambiguous category, and that YHWH's complaint that his spirit will not contend with humanity forever, because he is flesh (בָּשָׂר), reflects this possibility of apotheosis, whether for the women or for their children. YHWH wants a clear division between divine and mortal. *Genesis 6:3*, in this reading, is specifically about the mothers of Nephilim and the

---

[35] West 1966 *ad loc.*: 429–30.   [36] Fowler 1998.

Nephilim themselves. Because marriages disrupt the divine/mortal boundary, YHWH declares a limit on lifespans.

Yet there were descendants of Nephilim or other semi-divine humans later. After the Flood, however, the *b'nai elohim* do not 'take as wives' mortal women, but 'go to' them, and while their offspring are still Nephilim, they belong to a recognisably mortal category. Indeed, they are 'men with a name', which in Greek terms means that they have the fame that is precisely the hero's consolation for mortality.

Other commonalities between Greek and Hebrew legend probably represent an Eastern Mediterranean *koinē* with Phoenicians as important participants and transmitters.[37] However, this theme appears only in Greek and Hebrew, which suggests a narrower channel. If the Nephilim are the heroic ancestors of others, they are so particularly of the Philistines. Here I enter yet another swamp of controversy. Many scholars see the Phoenicians as the obvious link between Greeks and Hebrews.[38] The association between Philistines and these ancient, powerful beings of partly divine ancestry suggests that they were the transmitters.

The Philistines appear to come from the Aegean (or from Cyprus, or from Anatolia) after the collapse of Mycenaean palace culture, and to have close links with Aegean culture through Iron Age I (twelfth–tenth centuries BCE).[39] Skeletal remains from Ashkelon indicate that new, southern European people arrived during the transition from the Bronze to the Iron Age, but that by the later Iron Age the European markers have become very weak.[40] There is a Mycenaean strain in Philistine material culture of this period. The people we call Philistines arrive from either the Aegean or from zones of contact with the Aegean. Their arrival is not marked by destruction, and from the start their material culture incorporates local elements.[41] Aegean-style pottery is not always used for the same functions it had in Aegean culture.[42] Nonetheless, their material culture is distinct, with connections to the Aegean and Cyprus. In Iron Age II (tenth–sixth centuries BCE), distinctly non-Canaanite styles and practices become less salient.[43]

---

[37] See Darshan 2014a on migration and colonisation stories.   [38] See van Seters 1988.
[39] Janeway 2015: 119, summarising the ceramic evidence from Tell Tayinat (in the Amuq Valley in Southern Anatolia), says that it supports 'the traditional immigration model'. At this site, as elsewhere, there are no signs of destruction associated with the new arrivals, and the resulting culture is mixed (Janeway 2015: 122–3). See also Millek 2017.
[40] Feldman et al. 2019.   [41] Maeir and Hitchcock 2017: 151–2.   [42] Stockhammer 2017.
[43] See Shai 2011 and Faust 2015.

There was clearly a complex process of 'transculturalism' or 'entanglement'.[44] In this context, it seems a reasonable speculation that *Genesis* 6:1–4 represents a fragment of Philistine mythology, and that some Iron Age Philistine elites claimed divine ancestry, as elite Greeks often did. Several passages in the Hebrew Bible that refer to Nephilim or Repha'im mark them as enemies. In the mythic narrative that goes back before the flood, they are not the ancestors of any identified group. Just as the traditions seem uncertain about whether the Nephilim belonged only to the very remote, prediluvian past, or they had at least descendants in the time of the early monarchy, so the Philistines themselves, anachronistically, make fleeting appearances in *Genesis*.

To conclude: the depiction of various peoples as giants in the Hebrew Bible is based on Philistine, or originally Greek, mythology (which does not imply that Philistines were Greek, but only that the Aegean strain in their culture included the heroic past). Philistines themselves have both giant and Aegean associations. Scholars have suspected a Greek background for Goliath, whose elaborate bronze panoply seems more Greek than Canaanite: he wears bronze greaves into battle (1 *Sam.* 17:5–6).[45] Single combats are not completely unparalleled in the Hebrew Bible; they are implied in 2 *Samuel* 2:19–23, again between Philistines and David's elite warriors. There is a striking episode of single combat in the much earlier Egyptian *Story of Sinuhe* (*Sinuhe* B 111).[46] Nonetheless, the motif is very prominent in Greek narrative, but very muted in Hebrew.[47] Scholars have compared to David and Goliath the account in the *Iliad* given by Nestor of his defeat of Ereuthalion (7.136–56), a young and inexperienced warrior against a mighty giant or, in its structure of challenge and response, the single combat between Hector and Ajax (*Il.* 7.54–91).[48]

Hebrews adapted this Philistine mythology and then extended it to others as the Hebrews mythologised their conquest of the land. Their achievement is greater because the enemies are almost superhuman. In Greek, different texts stress continuity or discontinuity between the heroic time and the present, but texts also differ in the extent to which heroes

---

[44] Maeir and Hitchcock 2017.
[45] Yadin 2004; Zorn 2010 argues that the panoply makes sense if Goliath is imagined as a chariot warrior of a bygone era.
[46] De Vaux 1959.
[47] For the same theme in early Aegean/Minoan art, see the Pylos combat agate: Stocker and Davis 2017. For the history of the stone itself, which originated in India and travelled to the Aegean via Mesopotamia: Caubet and Yon 2019.
[48] West 1997: 214; Finkelstein and Silberman 2006: 198–9 (they think of direct influence of the *Iliad* in the seventh century).

become immortal or have a privileged afterlife. The Homeric epics are outliers in both respects, stressing continuity and allowing only Menelaus to escape mortality (*Od.* 4.561–9).[49] The Hebrew text reflects a different negotiation of the problem, putting marriages and the supreme god's intervention against them at an earlier stage, while allowing further divine–mortal sex and heroic children into a later, indefinite past. Neither Greek nor Hebrew can satisfactorily explain why the heroic age ended.

The transmission of such narratives, like any cultural exchange, is complex. Because Greek art and literature borrowed so much, we may slip into assuming that all parallels should be interpreted the same way, but there is no reason for all borrowing to go in the same direction. Narratives move across linguistic and cultural boundaries, and their contexts and meanings change as their new tellers use them.

---

[49] Griffin 1980: 90–6; Schein 1984: 69; Graziosi and Haubold 2005: 124–5.

CHAPTER 10

Berossus and Babylonian Cosmogony
Andrew R. George

The transmission of Mesopotamian mythological ideas to the Greek world was not confined to a short period. Much has been written on the presence of ancient Near Eastern myth in Hesiod's *Theogony*, and its transmission to archaic Greece through Hurrian and Hittite sources in Anatolia and Phoenician intermediaries in the Mediterranean.[1] This has led to a special focus on the archaic period as a time of transmission. In fact, Greek writers continued to be interested in Near Eastern myth throughout antiquity. From the sixth century CE comes another very striking manifestation of this interest: the account of oriental cosmogonies in the Neoplatonist Damascius' *De primis principiis*. His citation of a Babylonian theogony is clearly dependent on knowledge, at some remove, of the Babylonian Creation Epic, *Enūma eliš*.[2] Damascius names his source as Eudemus of Rhodes, a pupil of Aristotle who flourished in the late fourth century BCE.[3]

Situated between the twin peaks of Hesiod and Damascius is another writer of Greek, the Babylonian historian Berossus. He flourished in the early third century BCE, a generation after Eudemus of Rhodes, and wrote a historical ethnography of ancient Mesopotamia, the *Babyloniaca*.[4] In Book 1 he summarised for a Greek readership Babylonian beliefs about the beginning of the universe, in which the influence of *Enūma eliš* is less striking than in Damascius' and Eudemus' theogony but also clearly recognisable.

---

[1] See, e.g., West 1997: 276–333, López-Ruiz 2010; also Kelly, Chapter 16 in this volume.
[2] See Heidel 1963: 75–6, Talon 2001.
[3] See Dalley and Reyes 1998b: 110–11, Betegh 2002, Haubold 2013b: 36, Lambert 2013: 422, Dillery 2015: 235–6. For the Orphic cosmogonies, see now Meisner 2018, esp. ch. 3 (on Eudemus).
[4] On Berossus and ancient Mesopotamia, see, e.g., Komoróczy 1973b, Kuhrt 1987, Gesche 2001: 34–5, Beaulieu 2006, De Breucker 2003, 2012. A comprehensive bibliography of Berossus is printed in Haubold *et al.* 2013: 309–23; add Dillery 2015.

About 250 years later, the Roman Vitruvius Pollio reported in his treatise on architecture that Berossus was a 'Chaldean' who was educated in Babylon but moved to Asia (Minor) and the island of Cos (*De architectura* 9.7). In the second century CE a Christian apologist, Tatian the Syrian, wrote that Berossus was a 'priest of the god Bel' (*Oratio ad Graecos* 36). In classical antiquity the term 'Chaldean' referred to those Babylonians who were experts in astrology and other Babylonian scholarly lore (e.g., Strabo 16.1.6). These were not 'priests' exactly, but many of them were closely associated with the great temple of Marduk (Bel) at Babylon. As a 'Chaldean', Berossus would have had access to the ancient written traditions of Babylonia, most of which were still extant in his lifetime.

Berossus' work is known only from later writers. The passages on the origins of the universe are handed down in an Armenian translation of Eusebius' universal history, the *Chronicon*, and in excerpts of the original Greek quoted by the Byzantine monk Georgius Syncellus in his *Ecloga chronographica*. Eusebius wrote the *Chronicon* early in the fourth century CE, the Armenian translation of it was made at least 150 years later, and Syncellus was active in the early ninth century. Eusebius himself did not know the *Babyloniaca* directly, but only through the works of intermediaries, such as the lost epitome of Alexander Polyhistor (d. 40 BCE) and probably also the work of Juba of Mauretania (d. *c.* 23 CE).[5] While it is not possible to be sure about how closely Eusebius' work matched Berossus', being at several removes from it, the Armenian translation and Syncellus' Greek are sufficiently in harmony to allow confidence in them as faithful at least to Eusebius.

The passage of the *Babyloniaca* that bears on Babylonian cosmogony occurs in the two versions of Eusebius' *Chronicon* preserved by Syncellus and in the Armenian translation, conventionally known as Fragment One (F1a–b). Syncellus' Greek was edited by Felix Jacoby and the Armenian version by Josef Karst.[6] The two versions of the passage are presented synoptically in Dutch by Geert De Breucker in his monograph on the *Babyloniaca* and again online, with English translations, at *Brill's New Jacoby*.[7] I give his English translation of the version handed down by Syncellus:[8]

---

[5] For these dates, see Madreiter 2013: 259–60, Schironi 2013: 235 n. 1.
[6] Jacoby 1958: *FGrH* III C 367–73, Karst 1911: 7–9.
[7] De Breucker 2012: 222–30, De Breucker 2010.
[8] Other modern English translations can be found in Burstein 1978, Verbrugghe and Wickersham 2001, and Dillery 2015: 227–8, which all combine both versions of the passage.

> There was a time, he says, when everything was [darkness and] water and that in it fabulous beings with peculiar forms came to life. For men with two wings were born and some with four wings and two faces, having one body and two heads, male and female, and double genitalia, male and female ... [a list of monstrous beings follows]. Over all these a woman ruled named Omorka.[9] This means in Chaldaean Thalatth, in Greek it is translated as 'Sea' (Thalassa) ... When everything was arranged in this way, Belos rose up and split the woman in two. Of one half of her he made earth, of the other half sky; and he destroyed all creatures in her ... For when everything was moist, and creatures had come into being in it, this god took off his own head and the other gods mixed the blood that flowed out with earth and formed men. For this reason they are intelligent and share in divine wisdom. Belos, whom they translate as Zeus,[10] cut the darkness in half and separated earth and sky from each other and ordered the universe. The creatures could not endure the power of the light and were destroyed. When Belos saw the land empty and barren,[11] he ordered one of the gods to cut off his own head and to mix the blood that flowed out with earth and to form men and wild animals that were capable of enduring the air. Belos also completed the stars and the sun and the moon and the five planets. Alexander Polyhistor says that Berossus asserts these things in his first book.

Another pair of fragments recapitulates these events:[12]

> Syncellus: They say that in the beginning all was water, which was called Sea (Thalassa). Bel made this one by assigning a place to each, and he surrounded Babylon with a wall.
> Armenian: All, he said, was from the start water, which was called Sea. And Bel placed limits on them (the waters) and assigned a place to each, allocated their lands, and fortified Babylon with an enclosing wall.

To those who know the Babylonian Creation Epic, *Enūma eliš*, the parallels between these passages and the Babylonian poem will be obvious. Berossus' statements that 'Belos rose up and split the woman in two. Of one half of her he made earth, of the other half sky' form a two-sentence epitome of *Enūma eliš* Tablets I–V, in which Marduk (at Babylon commonly known as Bel) triumphed over the ancestral female Tiamat 'Sea' in

---

[9] Variant in Greek Omoroka, in Armenian Markaye; on this, see Komoróczy 1973b: 132–3, Oshima 2011: 171–2, Lambert 2013: 473, De Breucker 2012: 327–8.
[10] The Armenian version glosses: 'and into Armenian as Aramazd' (Karst 1911: 8 n. 7). Bel is Akkadian for 'Lord'.
[11] 'Barren' is a much deployed emendation of the opposite: the original text reads καρποφόρον 'fertile'. Haubold translates 'an empty and fruit-bearing tract of land' (2013b: 41). In this unamended reading, the potential productivity of the land was the motivation for Bel's creation of humans to cultivate it – a better fit with Babylonian traditions.
[12] De Breucker 2012: 230–1 F1c–d, my translation.

single combat, then turned her upper half into the sky and her lower half into the earth.

The narrative poem *Enūma eliš* was the classic statement of Babylonian imperial theology, asserting the primacy of Babylon and its god, Marduk.[13] It was recited in the cult of Marduk and copied out in school by boys learning to write. It is thus no surprise that Berossus' account of cosmogony in the *Babyloniaca* shares common ground with the Babylonian Creation Epic, for *Enūma eliš* was an essential text in scribal education at Babylon, even in the late first millennium.[14] Any Babylonian scholar of traditional education, and especially a scholar associated with the temple of Marduk, would have known it better than perhaps any other ancient Mesopotamian composition.[15]

But, while *Enūma eliš* was in the first millennium BCE the most prominent statement of cosmogonic mythology at Babylon, it was itself a reworking of much older mythology. Careful reading has long suggested that *Enūma eliš* was not Berossus' only informant in the matter of cosmogony. A study of the material by a mid-twentieth-century Assyriologist, Alexander Heidel, elicited the comment, 'There can be no doubt not only that Berossus based his account on *Enūma elish* but that he utilized a number of different creation stories.'[16] Unfortunately, he did not elaborate.

The latest editor of *Enūma eliš*, W. G. Lambert, came to a different conclusion. He noted that 'Berossus had been a priest of Marduk at his major shrine', and that 'his account presumably reflects current traditions of the Marduk priesthood' and 'bears a general similarity to the Epic', but found it 'doubtful that he had ever read *Enūma eliš*'.[17] This last view is hard to accept, in light of new evidence for the prominence of *Enūma eliš* in scribal education at Babylon before, during and after Berossus'

---

[13] The most recent edition and translation is to be found in Lambert 2013: 1–144.
[14] A recent assertion that 'extracts from the Babylonian Epic of Creation have not been found in scribal school exercises' (Dalley 2013: 170) needs adjusting in the light of Petra Gesche's study of the school curriculum of the Neo- and Late Babylonian periods. Noting twenty-three examples of excerpts on school exercise tablets, she wrote 'sehr häufig schrieben die Schüler Exzerpte aus dem Weltschöpfungsepos *Enūma eliš*' (Gesche 2001: 177 with n. 683). Lambert's critical edition (2013) took the total number of such excerpts to fifty-seven.
[15] At least thirty-one of the Late Babylonian manuscripts in Lambert's edition of *Enūma eliš* (2013) come from collections of tablets which Clancier's study of the British Museum's inventory shows very likely to derive from the Marduk temple at Babylon (2009: 192–3). The apparent paucity of manuscripts of *Enūma eliš* from that location observed by Clancier himself (2009: 208) is thus radically corrected by Lambert's subsequent publication.
[16] Heidel 1963: 81.   [17] Lambert 2013: 464.

lifetime.[18] Berossus does not adhere slavishly to the text of *Enūma eliš*, it is true, but that is no reason to suppose he had not learned it at school and that his work was not informed by it.

Not long after Heidel, Komoróczy linked some of the features in Berossus' *Babyloniaca* to mythology found in other Sumerian and Akkadian narrative poetry, particularly as regards the tradition that early men grazed on grass like sheep, the story of the sage Oannes, the sparing of the town of Sippar from the Flood, and the name of the Flood hero, Xisuthros.[19] In doing so Komoróczy attributed to Berossus direct knowledge of ancient Sumerian narrative poems, which he maintained must accordingly have survived from the Old Babylonian period into the first millennium BCE. This position remains problematic because very few Sumerian mythological narratives are known to have survived to the first millennium.

In the matter of the Flood hero's name, there is no need to posit the survival of such ancient texts, for Berossus was almost certainly informed by the Babylonian *Dynastic Chronicle*.[20] This rather fragmentary composition reports the early history of mankind, including an extended passage with a literary account of the Flood that names the Flood hero as Ziusudra (~ Berossus' Xisuthros).[21] Berossus would certainly have known the *Dynastic Chronicle* as the canonical account of Babylonian history, from the antediluvian kings to the first millennium, but its fragmentary state and comparative neglect by scholarship means that it has sometimes been overlooked as a source of his knowledge.[22]

It emerges from the preceding paragraphs that, in considering Babylonian cosmogony and mythology, we can expect some of Berossus' sources to be well known to us, like *Enūma eliš*; others little known, like the *Dynastic Chronicle*; and, we can be sure, still others completely unknown. In what follows sources of the second category are proposed.

---

[18] See note 14. Clancier's study of the British Museum's inventory has shed new light on date as well as provenance. The date range of the museum's 80-6-17 collection (accessioned on 17 June 1880) is determined by the presence in it of large numbers of Late Babylonian astronomical tablets, including many diaries of the fourth and third centuries BCE (Clancier 2009: 433–5). Lambert's edition of *Enūma eliš* (2013) utilises twenty-four manuscripts from this very collection, including twenty-one excerpts on school tablets.

[19] Komoróczy 1973b.

[20] See Finkel 1980: 71–2, Davila 1995: 206–7 and, more positively, De Breucker 2013: 22.

[21] Finkel 1980: 68–9; Glassner 2004: 126–35.

[22] The most prominent example is Dalley 2013, where various well-known Babylonian narrative poems are considered as sources of Berossus' account of the Flood, but the *Dynastic Chronicle* is not mentioned, even though manuscripts roughly contemporaneous with Berossus are extant (De Breucker 2013: 22).

Burstein's commentary on Berossus' cosmogony called attention to what appeared to him to be a doublet: two broadly matching statements about the separation of sky and earth by Bel, the destruction of the primeval beings, and the creation of mankind.[23] In the translation quoted above (p. 187), the first statement occupies the text from 'Over all these a woman ruled' to 'and share in divine wisdom'. The second runs from 'Belos, whom they translate as Zeus' to 'capable of enduring air'. Burstein attributed the repetition to Polyhistor. The position taken here is that the double account of the separation of sky and earth can be understood to present variant Babylonian traditions and would then be original to Berossus.

The two cosmogonic statements identified by Burstein both begin with the sundering of earth and sky, and both end with the creation of human beings from divine blood and clay. However, there are telling differences at the outset. In the first, Bel attacks the female Omorka, splits her in two and makes heaven and earth from the two halves of her corpse. As already noted, this is clearly derived from *Enūma eliš*. Berossus goes on to relate that Bel then destroyed the creatures living inside her, which reflects Marduk's destruction of Tiamat's army in *Enūma eliš* (IV 111–18). In the second statement Bel makes earth and sky by dividing the darkness that existed in the beginning with water. The creatures are unable to bear the light thus created, and die of their own accord. The salient variant attends the separation of sky and earth, in the one account achieved by splitting the primeval water in two and in the other by the division of darkness.

It has been suggested that the division of darkness as a creative act is the result of Christian influence, an intrusion into an epitome of Berossus' text of ideas from *Genesis* (1.4), where light intervenes in darkness.[24] There is, however, no call to look so far, for the account of cosmogony handed down in *Enūma eliš* was not the only such account known to Babylonian scholars of the late period. They also knew a separate mythology of Father Sky and Mother Earth, of which the story in *Enūma eliš* is a tendentious adaptation introduced toward the end of the second millennium BCE to promote the cult and theology of Marduk and Babylon. Sky and Earth mythology already occurs in the oldest intelligible cuneiform literature, and is probably very much older than that, for it has been identified in other Asian cultures, and seems to be widespread.[25] Its presence in ancient

---

[23] Burstein 1978: 15; see also Dillery 2015: 238.
[24] See, e.g., Horowitz 1998: 133, Dillery 2015: 229.   [25] Witzel 2012: 128–37.

Mesopotamia has been studied sporadically,[26] but because of the prominence of *Enūma eliš* in the Babylonian canon and the absence from that canon of a literary elaboration of Sky and Earth mythology in narrative form, its prevalence and influence remain underestimated.

The Mesopotamian mythology of Father Sky and Mother Earth can be reconstructed from short statements and allusions in many and various ancient cuneiform texts, Sumerian and Akkadian. The following is a recapitulation of the writer's fuller presentation of these sources.[27]

The early mythological narratives from Mesopotamia present An 'Sky' and Ki 'Earth' as a primeval male–female pair containing the potential for procreation. This cosmogonic pair occurs in many mythologies but, in the view of the comparative mythologist Michael Witzel, it is not indigenous to sub-Saharan Africa. He accordingly identifies the cosmogonic pair 'Father Heaven, Mother Earth' as characteristic of what he calls 'Laurasian', out-of-Africa mythology.[28] Like many others, Witzel points out that much mythology about the beginning of the world speaks more of emergence than creation – the first things are not made by some superhuman agent, but just are, and so it would seem with Sky and Earth. That is not to deny them a parent, however. In Mesopotamian theogony the precursor of all was water.[29] In *Enūma eliš* the primeval water is called Tiamat 'Sea', but the theogonic traditions of the Babylonian god-lists know it as the ancestral ocean Namma. Namma's epithet *Ama-tud-anki* 'Birth-Giving Mother of Sky and Earth' makes clear her role as the parent of Father Sky and Mother Earth.[30]

The continuity and evolution of Sky–Earth mythology in ancient Mesopotamia are best observed by placing the evidence diachronically, starting with the third millennium BCE.

Early Dynastic Period

Literary compositions from the mid-third millennium represent the oldest surviving literature. Mostly written in Sumerian, these archaic

---

[26] See, e.g., van Dijk 1964, Komoróczy 1973a, Westenholz 2010, Lisman 2013.
[27] Repeated from the German in George 2016a: 13–16.
[28] Witzel 2012: 128–32. For a non-partisan reaction to Witzel's Laurasia v. Gondwana theory, see Allen 2014. Witzel's knowledge of Mesopotamian cosmogonic mythology was confined to *Enūma eliš*, which he found roughly to fall in with the 'Laurasian' narrative pattern. The Mesopotamian Sky–Earth mythology, which was unknown to him, adheres to it even more closely (George 2016a).
[29] The precedence of water finds formal expression in a late bilingual incantation which asserts that before anything was created, 'all the lands were sea' (Lambert 2013: 370 l. 10).
[30] Lambert 2013: 418–19.

compositions are not fully intelligible, but the following references to Sky–Earth mythology are clear:

(1) Barton cylinder:[31] 'In those days', i.e., in primeval mythical time, a violent cosmic storm in Nippur led to a 'conversation' (inim dab$_6$) between An 'Sky' and Ki 'Earth'. The result of this intercourse is lost in a short lacuna, but seems to be the birth of the two sibling deities Enlil and Ninhursanga, for they are present when the text resumes. They copulate, expressed in human terms (ĝiš mu-ni-dug$_4$), and the mother goddess Ninhursanga conceives.

(2) Ukg. 15:[32] An 'Sky' and Ki 'Earth' emerged, then 'Earth was making (her) vulva manifest in her left (hand), ... Lord Sky was there, standing ready in the manner of a young male. Sky and Earth made noise together.'[33] The text goes on to observe that this was before the Enki–Ninki gods were born, and before sun and moon gave light.

(3) *OIP* 99 113 ii and 136 iii:[34] The god Enlil separated Sky from Earth and Earth from Sky.

Sky and Earth were not static, for these texts report two myths at the start of creation: the intercourse of Sky and Earth, and their separation.[35] The intercourse of Father Heaven and Mother Earth is a story element that Witzel finds characteristic of 'Laurasian' mythology: still unseparated, they are in 'permanent sexual union, so that their children were kept in permanent darkness between them'.[36] In the oldest Mesopotamian texts their intercourse is described in terms of conversation (1) and noise (2). The explicit references to Earth's genitals and Sky's virility in (2) indicate that the intercourse is sexual, as it clearly is later (11–14). The separation of Sky and Earth occurs through the agency of a third party, Enlil (3), and takes place in Nippur (1), later Enlil's cult-centre and traditionally the centre of the world. The attribution of this development to an agent indicates that a crucial question which much occupies modern physicists seems already to have arisen. Where now we ask, 'If there was a Big Bang, what caused it?', the Babylonians speculated on how primeval matter came to be flung apart and, already in the third millennium, identified the agent as the god Enlil. His name, whatever it originally signified, came to be

---

[31] Alster and Westenholz 1994. [32] Sollberger 1956: 57, transl. by J. Bauer in Volk 2015: 3–4.
[33] i 2–ii 2: ki-e gal$_4$ gáb-na dalla ha-mu-ak-e, ... an en-nam šul-le-éš al-gub, an ki téš-ba šeg$_{12}$ an-gi$_4$-gi$_4$. My interpretation draws on (but also departs from) Wiggermann 1992: 282, Sjöberg 2002: 230–1, Rubio 2013: 5.
[34] Lambert 1981: 90, following J. Krecher; with further parallels: Ceccarelli 2015: 201.
[35] Lambert 2013: 169–71. [36] Witzel 2012: 128.

understood in cosmic terms as 'Lord Air', identifying him as the matter that filled the void between Sky and Earth.[37] Thereafter sexual relations between gods became anthropomorphic, and the mother goddess immediately became pregnant (1).

Ur III Period

Little survives of the Sumerian literature of the late third millennium, but one composition bears on our topic:

(4) NBC 11108:[38] Sky and Earth both existed. It seems that light was imprisoned inside them: 'Day was not bright, Night lay round about.'[39] As a result, vegetation did not grow.

This composition seems to speculate on conditions at the beginning of things. The idea of primeval darkness is common and has already been met in Mesopotamia (2). At an early stage in the evolution of the cosmos, the sun was confined in the solid Sky and its rays did not penetrate through to Earth. Comparative mythology offers many examples of the captivity of the sun, and they are widespread in Witzel's 'Laurasian' mythology.[40]

Old Babylonian Period

Literature from the early second millennium abounds, in Sumerian especially, but also in Akkadian. The following is a selection of the material that bears witness to Sky–Earth mythology, in Sumerian unless otherwise identified:

---

[37] For discussions of the etymology of Enlil's name, in Akkadian Illilu, see, e.g., Michalowski 1998a, Edzard 2003, Feliu 2006. It was at first written EN-é, of uncertain meaning, only later EN-LÍL (Steinkeller 2010). The translation 'Lord Air' (e.g., Bottéro 1992: 233), var. 'Lord Ether' (Wiggermann 1992: 282), is thus probably not valid for the earliest times but a secondary interpretation. Michalowski rejects it entirely, maintaining that Sum. líl does not mean 'air'. However, he did not take into account the many contexts outside lamentation texts where a translation 'open air, empty space' recommends itself (George 2010: 114–15). In the Nippur Compendium, Enlil's female counterpart Ninlil is translated bēl zaqīqi 'lord of air' (George 1992: 152–3 iii 4'). The masculine gender of 'lord' obviously projects the translation on to Enlil himself, and thus shows that some Babylonian scholars shared with modern commentators the idea that this name gained meaning in mythology through an interpretation of the later spelling, EN-LÍL, as en 'lord' and líl 'space, air'.
[38] van Dijk 1976.   [39] Obv. 8: u₄ nu-zalag gi₆ àm-mu-lá: see Sjöberg 2002: 242–3, Rubio 2013: 7.
[40] Witzel 2012; 139–48; note also the mytheme of the sun's disappearance in ancient Anatolia, e.g., Hoffner 1990: 26–9.

(5) *Ewe and Grain* 1:[41] Sky and Earth exist together as a 'mountain massif' (hur-sag), i.e., in a state of unity, and beget the Anunna gods.

(6) *Enkig and Ninmaḫ* 1–2:[42] Sky and Earth were separated at the beginning, before the Anunna gods were born and goddesses married and gave birth.

(7) *In Praise of the Mattock* 1–7:[43] Enlil separates Sky and Earth at Nippur-Duranki, in order to let 'seed come forth from Earth'.

(8) *Gilgameš and the Netherworld* 8–9:[44] Sky separates from Earth and vice versa.

(9) *School Account of Creation.* (one Old Babylonian ms.) 1:[45] 'When Sky and Earth, faithful twins, became separated', goddesses came into existence.

(10) *Dispute between Tree and Reed* 5–6:[46] 'In a holy place, a pure place, she made herself lovely for holy Sky, and Sky, lofty An, mated there with broad Earth', and they produced the dispute's antagonists.

(11) *Inanna and the* numun-*grass* 10:[47] 'Sky impregnated Earth, Earth gave birth' to the eponymous plant.

(12) *Lugale* 26:[48] 'Sky copulated with lovely Earth', and she bore the monstrous Azag.

(13) Akkadian incantation against stomach-ache:[49] 'the sky inseminated the earth'.

(14) Reinterpreted in other Akkadian incantations, e.g., *YOS* XI 5: 1:[50] 'Anu impregnated the sky, the sky bore the earth.'

The idea that Sky and Earth were once one but then parted company is prominent in these second-millennium passages too. While some ancient Mesopotamian sources attribute the separation to Enlil (3, 7), another tradition is apparent, that it occurred spontaneously, without the intervention of a third party (6, 8, 9). The emergence of goddesses and their marriages (6, 9) specifically emphasise the new potential for procreation and allude to the initial pregnancy of the mother goddess (1). The idea that new generations of gods were born to Sky and Earth, already met in (1) and (2), is strongly present (5, 6, 9). The separation of Sky and Earth was necessary for plants to grow (7), evincing a belief that when they were joined together as one, it was too dark for growth (4); only when light was

---

[41] Alster and Vanstiphout 1987.   [42] Lambert 2013: 330–45; Ceccarelli 2016.
[43] *ETCSL* 5.5.4 *The Song of the Hoe* (visited August 2015); transl. by G. Farber in Volk 2015: 69–76.
[44] Gadotti 2014a.   [45] Lambert 2013: 350–60.   [46] Wilcke 2007: 46.
[47] Kramer 1980; Wagensonner 2009.   [48] van Dijk 1983.
[49] George 2016b: 128–9 II.E.7 no. 7 v 39 // no. 8 ii 22'.   [50] Wasserman 2008: 73–4.

introduced could the seed sprout.[51] Earth grows beautiful, and she provokes desire in Sky (10). The result is procreation, which is sexual (10–14). Their union is not limited to a single momentous event (1–2) but recurs, producing beneficial things, such as plant life (10–11), but also malign entities that the younger gods will later have to subdue (12). Passage (7) is followed by an episode relating how Enlil himself cultivated the spot in Nippur where Sky and Earth were finally sundered so that mankind could grow like plants from the wound. The place of sundering was named Duranki 'Bond of Sky and Earth', and the ground where mankind sprouted under Enlil's husbandry was Uzu-mua 'Flesh-Grower'.[52]

The last two passages are in Akkadian. This language has the vocabulary to differentiate the cosmic entity of Sky (*šamû* 'the sky, heaven') from the sky god (Anu), a subtlety not possible in Sumerian, in which both ideas are expressed by the same word, An. The old idea of the intercourse of An and Ki can now be expressed in more impersonal terms (13). More importantly, Akkadian permits an evolution in cosmogonic thought: in (14) Anu impregnates not Earth but Heaven, and between them they produce Earth anthropomorphically. In this view Sky has become a male–female pair, able to procreate without Earth. In later Akkadian texts Anu's wife is Antu, a female version of himself. Theologians untangled the matter by equating Antu with Sky, to match the derivation of her name, but also with Earth, in accordance with the old mythology.[53]

Akkadian Texts in First-Millennium Copies

By the first millennium BCE an established corpus of literature had emerged, comprising both revised Old Babylonian compositions and more modern texts, like *Enūma eliš*. Intellectual life was bilingual, but most compositions handed down in the scribal tradition were Akkadian, including three incantations which begin with these cosmogonic statements:

(15) *First Brick* obv. 24:[54] 'When Anu created the sky', the god Ea (Enkig) created his cosmic domain (cf. *Enūma eliš*).

---

[51] A variant of this idea occurs in later Anatolian mythology, according to which Sky and Earth are separated not by Air but cut 'with a copper cutting tool', probably the sun god's saw (*The Song of Ullikummi*, CTH 345, Hoffner 1990: 59). In this way the sun itself brought light into the space between them and things could grow.
[52] Jacobsen 1970: 112–14, George 1992: 259.
[53] *An = Anu* and another god-list begin their statements of the Babylonian pantheon with three fundamental cosmic equations: An 'Sky' = Anu (m.), An 'Sky' = Antu (f.), An-Ki 'Sky–Earth' = Anu and Antu (m.+f.); quoted by Lambert 2013: 418–19.
[54] Lambert 2013: 376–83.

(16) *Worm and Toothache* 1–2:[55] 'After Anu created the sky', the sky created the earth.
(17) *AMT* 42 4 rev. etc.:[56] 'When Anu impregnated the sky,' Ea established plant life on earth.

The distinction between matter and agency is by this time orthodox. The sky is a cosmic entity, but also a divine personality who created it (15, 16), and fertilised it to set in motion a chain reaction that created new life on earth (16, 17, already in 14).

The ancient Mesopotamian mythology of Father Sky and Mother Earth was never written out in a narrative poem and evidently belonged to oral tradition. Nevertheless, thanks to the allusions to it collected above, this mythology remains visible across more than 2,000 years. To summarise it: Father Sky and Mother Earth are in union inside their parent Namma, the primeval Ocean. Being male and female, they cannot help but reproduce, and within them grow successive generations of gods, the ancestral Enki–Ninki deities, who dwell in darkness. After an unstable number of pairs, two other gods are born who, unlike the Enki–Ninki gods, are important in mythology: Enlil and his big sister Ninhursanga. Ninhursanga's name means 'Lady of the Mountain Massif', which suggests that she represents the potential for evolution in the fabric of Earth that will later determine how its surface is modelled into its familiar shape and contours. Enlil is 'Lord Air', perhaps not originally, but so understood in the historical periods. The act of his birth has the unavoidable consequence of pushing Sky and Earth apart and separating the primeval Ocean into the waters above and the waters below.

The evolution of the cosmos after the sundering of Father Sky and Mother Earth is recorded by the kinship terms used of the gods in Sumerian literary and religious texts. Sky, now Anu, is free from the embrace of Earth and so able to mate with another partner, his mother Namma. From their union is born Enkig, who takes control of the waters below the earth. Enlil mates with his sister Ninhursanga (also with Ninlil = female Enlil), and they beget (among others) Nanna the moon god and Ninurta the warrior god. The moon, ancient and pale, fathers Utu the sun god and a third celestial light, Inanna (Venus). All the main elements of the current cosmos are now in place: there is remote sky ('heaven'), earth shaped in its contours, between them air to breathe, water in the necessary

---

[55] Lambert 2013: 400.   [56] Lambert 2013: 401.

places to feed rain and springs, light to bring forth food from the soil, and a lunar cycle to measure time.

This story is the basic mythology that was adapted by the poet of *Enūma eliš* in composing a poem that attributed all creative initiative and power to Marduk.[57] The mythology of Sky and Earth was not fully supplanted by the new Marduk orthodoxy, however. Because it pervaded the traditional literature of Babylonia, and that literature remained accessible while cuneiform continued to be a technology of writing, Berossus would undoubtedly have known it. And so it seems possible that in his *Babyloniaca* he gave a synthesis of both the stories he knew of the sundering of heaven and earth.

The distinction between the two accounts is partly obscured by the use in both of the name Bel 'Lord', which referred in Babylonia mostly to Marduk, but sometimes to Enlil, according to context. As already observed, the story of Marduk's triumph in battle and dismembering of Tiamat 'Sea' from *Enūma eliš* is easily recognisable in this passage:[58]

> Over all these a woman ruled named Omorka. This means in Chaldaean Thalatth, in Greek it is translated as 'Sea' (Thalassa) ... When everything was arranged in this way, Belos rose up and split the woman in two. Of one half of her he made earth, of the other half sky; and he destroyed all creatures in her ... Belos also completed the stars and the sun and the moon and the five planets.

But, alongside Marduk's triumph (and partly enclosing it, as transmitted by Eusebius), it would appear that Berossus placed the myth of the separation of Father Sky and Mother Earth by Enlil, in which the cosmos evolves without a battle and the key act of creation is the banishment of darkness and the creation of light. Echoing some of the texts quoted above in the exposition of Sky–Earth mythology (2, 4), the passage displays a strong interest in the theme of darkness and light:[59]

> There was a time, he says, when everything was [darkness and] water and that in it fabulous beings with peculiar forms came to life ... Belos, whom they translate as Zeus, cut the darkness in half and separated earth and sky from each other and ordered the universe. The creatures could not endure the power of the light and were destroyed.

Berossus' text inevitably suffered misinterpretation and corruption during its multifarious and centuries-long transmission down to Eusebius. The history of its transmission is even such that it is often not possible to

[57] George 2016a: 24–5.   [58] De Breucker 2010.   [59] De Breucker 2010.

be fully certain of the book's original contents. Accordingly discussion of those contents, and conclusions developed in consequence – including those offered here – should always be qualified by a measure of reservation. What can be said is that it looks to be the case that the *Babyloniaca* combines two different accounts of cosmogony, stemming from separate but co-existing traditions: on the one hand the ancient Sky–Earth mythology, on the other the reworked mythology of *Enūma eliš*. If that is indeed so, Berossus was indulging an eclecticism that is not unknown in ancient Near Eastern literary composition. A more prominent example is the dual account of the creation of Adam in *Genesis*.

PART III
Difference

CHAPTER 11

Borrowing, Dialogue and Rejection
Intertextual Interfaces in the Late Bronze Age
Ian Rutherford

Introduction

What's the point of comparing ancient literary traditions?* There are two main answers to that.[1] The first is that it can be used to prove origins, whether recent cultural contact and influence, or alternatively residues of fairly recent migrations (such as those of speakers of Indo-European languages). Much recent work on the subject by scholars such as Martin West and Walter Burkert comes down to using comparison in this 'historical' way. The second answer, argued for eloquently by Marcel Detienne,[2] is that comparison can give us an idea of what's distinctive about different cultural traditions. In principle, if we're using comparison in this 'comparative' or 'typological' way, it doesn't matter whether or not there is an historical relationship between the cultures or literatures considered; one could compare ancient Greek myths with those of Japan, for example – although even there one could probably assume an historical connection in respect of some hypothetical Paleolithic migration.[3]

Each of these approaches is fraught with problems. The first, which comes down to looking for similarities, runs the risk of attaching significance to patterns which could be coincidental, universal, or the result of convergent development. It is with some justification that J. Z. Smith in a famous paper warned that deducing influence (i.e., causation) from similarity is a form of magical thinking of the sort identified by nineteenth-century anthropologists.[4] The second approach, which bases itself on differences, faces the problem that the choice of which differences to focus on seems culturally determined, subjective and possibly arbitrary. How can

---

* Thanks to the editors, and audiences in Oxford and Warsaw, where I gave an early version in 2016, and to Barbara Kowalzig for encouraging me to think seriously about the sea.
[1] Malul 1990's study of the relation between Mesopotamian culture and the Hebrew Bible is an excellent guide, though he doesn't discuss Greece.
[2] Detienne 2008.   [3] See Witzel 2012.   [4] Smith 1990.

this be scientific? Is the solution just to accept that, as Marcel Detienne argues, successful comparison is a process of probing from various directions the thought mechanisms of different cultures, a process which requires creativity and imagination on the part of the *comparateur*?

In practice, it is often possible to apply both approaches to the same data set, if we're dealing with traditions that may well have been in indirect contact over centuries or even millennia, but which may nevertheless have developed in different directions. It is, however, vital to keep the approaches distinct, and to be vigilant about whether we're making an historical claim (a feature in tradition A led to a similar feature in tradition B) or a typological one (similarities in traditions A and B are to be explained by the fact that they belong to the same macro-tradition, with differences reflecting different choices made by the traditions).

One example of this composite approach is the theoretical model sketched by Johannes Haubold (2002), who sees the mytho-historical poetry of Western Asia and the Western Mediterranean belonging to the same 'generic' tradition (perhaps the result of long-term diffusion in multiple directions), in which various sub-traditions have developed in different ways; as he shows, in some cases we can think of them as having developed different answers to the same thematic question, such as the origins of mankind. In this model, then, historical connections, resulting in broadly similar culture, are ancient, indeterminate and taken for granted, and the challenge lies in comparing the differences in the traditions.

Things may not be as neat as this, however, and the possibility of recent historical influence tends to reassert itself, however much we try to exclude it. This does not just concern similarities, which could be the result of ancient or less-ancient contact. Differences, too, can be explained in two ways: not only as traces of independent development over the *longue durée*, but also as signs of comparatively recent rejection or of resilience. One culture may be 'receptive' to some aspects of other tradition, while blocking others, perhaps because they are not in line with its established norms.[5] That general point has been made by art historians who have observed that Late Bronze Age Aegean art imitated some Eastern artistic motifs but seemed to reject others.[6] In this chapter I propose to test this model of differing degrees of receptiveness on some aspects of the *Kingship in Heaven Cycle*.

---

[5] See Ulf 2009.
[6] For example Crowley 1989: 218 argued that the Myceneans accepted one motif from the iconography of Mitanni in N. Syria, the 'Mitannian Griffin', but did not accept a related one, the 'Griffin Demon'; so 281: 'Aegean art accepts fully only those motifs whose symbolism strikes a chord in the Mycenaean consciousness or the Minoan before it, and neither the striking nature of

KIHC: Dissemination and Origins

The term *Kingship in Heaven Cycle* (*KIHC*) is generally applied to a set of Hurro-Hittite narratives surviving in the Hittite archives at Boğaz-Köy, but known to have been translated or adapted from Hurrian versions which were current in Northern Syria in the first part of the second millennium BCE.[7] Carlo Corti has recently argued persuasively that this process of translation happened in the early fourteenth century BCE as the result of incursions in the region made by the Hittite king Tudhaliya III/Tasmisarri, whose close links to Hurrian culture have been illuminated by recent finds of texts in the Hittite city of Sapinuwa.[8]

KIHC includes two elements. The *Song of Emergence* narrates the conflicts between the early gods and the origin of the current generation,[9] led by the Storm God Tessub who is born from the head of Kumarbi. It probably also told of Tessub's early struggles to confirm his position. This myth was apparently also told in the form of a prophecy in the fragmentary narrative *Ea and the Beast*.[10] Other songs narrate later episodes in which the current order is challenged by the underworld gods, led by Kumarbi: the song about the sea monster Hedammu and that of the rocky monster Ullikummi. Hedammu succumbs to being seduced by the sonic and visual charms of Sauska (the Hurrian version of Ištar, now known to have been called Anzili by the Hittites).[11] Mighty Ullikummi, whose deafness and blindness make him immune to seduction, almost overwhelms the cosmos as he rises from the Mediterranean, viewed by the gods from Mt. Hazzi/Mons Kasios (Jebel el Aqra) near Ugarit. But eventually they overcome him by separating him from the earth, using the same tool that was used in primordial time to separate earth and sky (perhaps a hint that this episode closes the sequence?).

Also probably to be grouped here is the *Song of Kurunta*, concerned with Kurunta (written with the sumerogram LAMMA) of Karkemish, a stag god, who was set on the divine throne by Ea and the primeval gods. Kurunta's rule is a sort of Golden Age; the spontaneous appearance of food discourages men from working and making sacrifices, and the end comes

---

the design, nor the popularity of the motif in its own tradition, can force on the Aegean a motif which is symbolically incompatible.'

[7] On *KIHC*, see Hoffner 1990; Haas 2006; Rutherford 2009.
[8] Corti 2017. For the issue of Hittite translation or adaptation of Hurrian themes and motifs, see Archi 2009.
[9] Title from Corti 2007; but Corti 2017: 12 refers to it as the song of the 'Going out', 'Beginning' or 'Birth'. For the poem, see now Beckman 2011.
[10] See Archi 2002, Rutherford 2011.   [11] Wilhelm 2010b.

when Ea and the other primeval gods themselves depose him.[12] The gradual shift of Ea's allegiance from Kumarbi's side to that of the new generation seems to have been a fundamental theme of the whole cycle (see Hoffner 1990: 41–2). The *Song of Kurunta* thus deals with an earlier period than those of Hedammu and Ullikummi, when Tessub's control of the cosmos is still not fully established (see Haas 2006: 144–7).

Another poem that must either belong to the *KIHC* or be closely related to it is the fragmentary *Song of the Sea*. The main evidence is a Hurrian text with the colophon '1st tablet of the [song of/song of the deeds of] the sea'; its content is unfortunately uncertain: Haas took it as describing a flood, while Dijkstra has seen it as a description of primordial chaos.[13] There are also relevant Hittite fragments; one of them (*KBo* 26.105) seems to refer to a flood, and a demand for tribute, which Kumarbi and the gods ask Sauska to deliver.[14] In what follows, we shall be most concerned with the *Song of the Sea*.

Even in the Late Bronze Age the *KIHC* was manifestly intercultural, like the *Epic of Gilgameš* and some other narratives. We have already seen that Hurrian versions were translated into Hittite. There may be traces of it also in the local traditions of Ugarit: Carolina López-Ruiz has shown that the sequence of deities found in sacrificial lists there is compatible with the generations of gods in the *Song of Emergence*.[15] Ugarit is also right next to Mt. Hazzi/Mons Kasios (known at Ugarit as Mt. Ṣapanu), which plays a role in the *Song of Ullikummi* and probably also in the *Song of the Sea*, which has a striking parallel in the Ugaritic narrative of the conflict between Baal (whose palace was on the same mountain) and Yamm (the Sea). Hittite texts attest a festival for Mt. Hazzi, perhaps established in Sapinuwa in the early fourteenth century, and the running order for the festival included performances of the *Song of the Deeds of the Sea* (*KUB* 44.7) of the cult of Mt. Hazzi, and of the *Song of the Invocation of the Primeval Gods*, which Corti has recently suggested could be the *Song of Emergence* itself.[16]

---

[12] For the *Song of LAMMA*, see Haas 2003b. Hoffner grouped with these the *Song of Silver*, which is questionable.

[13] Haas 2006: 151; Dijkstra 2011: 67.

[14] Hurrian: *KUB* 45.63; Hittite: *KBo* 26.105 (see E. Rieken et al. (ed.), hethiter.net/: CTH 346.9 (INTR 2009-08-24); Haas 2006: 151–2; Schwemer 2001: 451–3. The thesis that the *Song of the Sea* belongs to *KIHC* was suggested first by Houwink ten Cate 1992: 117. On the text, see Rutherford 2001. Dijkstra 2011: 68–70 wonders whether the Hurrian text was in fact related to the Hedammu myth, which also involves the sea.

[15] López-Ruiz 2010: 101–4.

[16] Corti 2017: 12; for a different view see Gilan, Chapter 1 in this volume.

There was even a mid-second-millennium Egyptian version of the *Storm God and the Sea*, *Astarte and the Sea*,[17] where the role of the Storm God is taken by the Egyptian deity Seth, who, besides being the opponent of Osiris, was himself a sort of Storm God who fought off the chaotic Apophis. Mt. Hazzi is not mentioned in that text, although other Egyptian texts mention 'Baal of Mt. Ṣapanu'. The cult and myths of Baal may have been brought to Egypt by the Hyksos invaders in the eighteenth century BCE.[18]

A case has been made for the *Song of the Sea* having originated in N. Syria in the early eighteenth century BCE. The earliest evidence is a text surviving from Mari on the Euphrates, which purports to be a letter from the god Adad of Aleppo to king Zimri-Lim, announcing that he has put him back on the throne and sent him the weapons with which he defeated the sea; another text from Mari announced that the weapons, having arrived, were now at Terqa, a religious centre to the north of Mari dedicated to the Syrian deity Dagan.[19] The weapons must have been symbolic objects of some sort, presumably used in rituals with songs.[20] The broader historical context for this may be the military confrontation between Aleppo/Yamhad and Assyria at this time, the intention being that Adad of Aleppo would protect Mari against Assyrian invasion.[21]

---

[17] See now Ayali-Darshan 2017: 196–9, who puts this in the context of various magical spells that feature Levantine deities. For the text, see Collombert and Coulon 2000; Schneider 2011–12. We have fragments of an Egyptian narrative in which the Sea floods the earth, demands tribute from the gods, which is brought by Astarte, and is eventually defeated by Seth (i.e., Baal). The text claims to have been composed in the reign of Amenhotep II (?) (late fifteenth century BCE), before Egypt is known to have been in contact with Ugarit, and it has recently been argued to be more likely to date a century later, and to have been composed to celebrate the foundation by Ramesses II of a new capital at Qantir/Pi-Ramesses, close to the former Hyksos capital at Avaris.

[18] Direct Egyptian contact with Ugarit cannot be traced any further back than Amenophis III (fourteenth century BCE), although Egypt campaigned in Northern Syria in the preceding century: see Singer 1999: 621–2. The cult of Baal in general in Egypt is known from even earlier, first established apparently at Avaris in the North Eastern Delta by the Hyksos (who may themselves have had Amorite origins), perhaps in the eighteenth century BCE. It seems possible that that this Baal of Avaris was already Baal Ṣapuna or at least related to him. The first Egyptian evidence may be a seal from Tell Dab'a from the eighteenth century BCE: Porada 1984. See Morris 2015: 329–32 on the '400 year stele', which commemorates the cult in Avaris; the iconography on it seems identical to that of Baal Ṣapuna. Another site in the North Eastern Delta that may be linked to the deity is Baal Ṣephon, a station on the itinerary followed by Moses according to the Hebrew Bible (*Exod.* 14:2–4). Mamy stele: Stadelmann 1967: 37–9; Morris 2015: 330, Levy 2014.

[19] *FM* 7.38 – Mari A 1968; Durand 1993; *FM* 7.5 = Mari A 1858; Durand 1993: 53; Schwemer 2001: 226–7; Schwemer 2016: 81–2.

[20] There was a singer (nargallum) present in the negotiations for the wedding between the royal houses: see Pruzsinszky 2011: 32.

[21] Durand 1993; Tugendhaft 2017: 47–61.

While it is possible that this Syrian myth reflects an earlier Hurrian version – it is worth noticing that a document from Mari talks of women being taught Subarian music, which may be Hurrian[22] – a Syrian origin is likelier because the myth suits the area of Yamhad/Aleppo: the sea that Adad defeated was probably the Eastern Mediterranean, since Ugarit was within the political sphere of Yamhad at this time (cf. Singer 1999: 617). Ayali-Darshan also thinks that this Syrian version has influenced the Ullikummi story, where the gods view the towering monster from the vantage point of Mt. Hazzi next to Ugarit.[23]

If the earliest tradition of the Storm God and the Sea was Syrian, there must be a good chance that all of these poems were known in Syria in this period, and the question then becomes whether the earliest versions of the story were in fact Amorite-Syrian. One clue in that direction is that the two main deities in the succession myth, the Storm God and Kumarbi, can plausibly be identified with major gods of the region; the Storm God is obviously Adad of Aleppo, and Kumarbi was sometimes identified with Dagan, the main god of the Mari region of Syria.[24] Dagan was in fact probably regarded as father of the local Storm God, Addu.[25] Another clue might be that the *Song of Hedammu* and *Song of LAMMA* both associate Kumarbi with the town of Tuttul in North Syria, about 100 miles North of Mari on the confluence of the Euphrates and the Balih rivers. This was a second major centre for the worship of Dagan in the eighteenth century BCE besides Terqa mentioned above, and like it within Mari's sphere of influence.[26] So the possibility arises that other songs in the *KIHC* should be seen as Hurro-Hittite versions of Syrian myths, starting with the *Song of Emergence*, in which Adad of Aleppo would originally have succeeded Dagan. This could reflect the religious politics of the region, symbolising the supremacy of Adad of Aleppo while incorporating Dagan into his story.

Greece and *KIHC*

The earliest evidence for a Greek reception of *KIHC* is of course Hesiod's *Theogony*, normally thought to have been composed about 700 BCE. There

---

[22] See Pruzsinszky 2011.
[23] Ayali-Darshan 2015. Another branch of this myth may surface in the Babylonian myth of Marduk and Tiamat: see Jacobsen 1968; Day 1985: 11, n. 26. For traces of other Babylonian myths about divine conflict with the sea, see Lambert 2013: 205–7, 236–47.
[24] Archi 2004b.   [25] See Feliu 2003: 294.
[26] *Song of Hedammu*: Siegelova 1971: 70–1; *Song of LAMMA* §7 in Hoffner. See Feliu 2003: 299; Bachvarova 2016: 51 n. 131.

are lots of similarities, particularly between the *Song of Emergence* and the Succession Myth in the *Theogony*. Kronos and Kumarbi both emasculate the Sky God, and both give birth to a new generation of gods, so that their generation becomes that of the older gods. Tessub is born through Kumarbi's head, as Athene is born from that of Zeus. Zeus and Tessub both fight monsters with the help of their siblings. There are also differences. For instance, in laying out the genealogies Hesiod works with a single family tree, while in *KIHC* Kumarbi's family is independent of Anu. And in respect of chronological sequence, the *KIHC* seems to work on the principle of regular periods of alternation between the rightful rulers of the cosmos and imposters or *tarpanallis*, some of whom may rule for nine years, while the *Theogony* structures time as a progression from chaos to the present cosmic order.

Despite the differences, the core of similarities surely indicates that these myths belong to the same general cultural milieu; but there is also a second factor, namely that Pindar and Aeschylus situated Typhon in Cilicia, presumably thinking of the so-called Cave of Typhon (*Cennet ve Cehennem*) at Corycus where, in the Roman period, there seems to have been a thriving tradition about Typhon, apparently preserved in the Luwian cultural stratum.[27] This is quite near Mt. Kasios, which takes us back to the figure of Baal Ṣapanu. In Apollodorus and Strabo the battle between Zeus and Typhon is partly fought at Mt. Kasios,[28] perhaps reflecting the state of affairs in the Seleucid period, when 'Zeus Kasios' becomes a major deity known right across the Mediterranean, presumably promoted by the Seleucids.[29] The absence of references to Zeus Kasios and Mt. Kasios before the Hellenistic period is striking. However, Herodotus (3.5) already links Typhon with another 'Mt. Kasios' in north-west Egypt

---

[27] See Houwink ten Cate 1961: 206–15; Lytle 2011.

[28] Str. 16.2.7, Apollod. 1.6.3. On the geography, Gatier 2016: 261. It has recently been suggested there might be a reference to this battle(?) in a fragment of the late sixth-century historian Acusilaos, preserved in a papyrus roll from Herculaneum, but this is very speculative: Fowler 2000–13: II.28 on Acus. fr. 8 = Epimenid. fr. 10.24. Bonnet 1987: 134 thought that Aeschylus' description of Typhon breathing 'smoke, the brother (κάσιν) of gleaming fire' may be an echo of Kasios.

[29] The Byzantine historian Malalas (8.11 Thurn = 8.12 Jeffreys, 105; = Pausanias of Antioch *BNJ* 854 F 10) tells us that the site for the major Seleucid city of Seleucia Pieria (Samandağ) was chosen after an eagle flew there when a sacrifice was being conducted on Mt. Kasios just to the south; translation in Ogden 2017: 100; Cohen 2006: 126. According to Malalas 2.6 (2.7 Jeffreys 13–14) and Malalas 8.14 (8.15 Jeffreys, 106), Kasos was the name of one of the brothers of Io who was sent in search of her, married a Cypriot princess Amyke, and founded Antigoneia; Amyke is clearly the eponym of the Amuq Valley, and Kasos could be linked to Mt. Kasios: see Ogden 2017: 148–9. A dedication from 187 BCE has been discovered at Aigeai in the Bay of Iskenderun to Zeus Kasios made on behalf of Antiochus III (*SEG* 51–1846).

near Lake Serbonis, which presumably has something to do with the impact of Baal Ṣapanu on Egypt mentioned in the previous section.[30]

Some aspects of this nexus have been overstated. For example, I'm not convinced that Typhon is Near Eastern in origin. He's nothing like any of the opponents of Tessub. His multi-headedness recalls the *musmahhu* whom Ninurta fights (and who is also taken as the model for the Hydra), but surely multi-headedness in monsters must have occurred to people all over the world.[31] His name is sometimes linked to Mt. Ṣapuna, or Baal of Ṣapuna (in the same way that Greek Turos ['Tyre'] corresponds to Phoenician Ṣur),[32] but the resemblance is not exact. The semantics are also tricky: a shift from a warrior deity to a monster.[33] On balance it seems likelier that the idea of the monster, along with the name ('smoker'), is Greek.[34]

The most plausible hypothesis is the area of the Levant, Cilicia and Cyprus, where Luwians, Phoenicians and Greeks co-existed in what must have been a sort of transcultural network. Merchants worked this route over decades, which inevitably produces a gradual assimilation of myth and ritual practice. The Greeks are usually supposed to have been in this area in the eighth century BCE, but there was Greek presence on Cyprus long before then.

A few years ago Jenny Strauss Clay and Amir Gilan (2014) argued that the context for contact could have been the Iron Age Luwian kingdom of Tell Tayinat, very close to Al Mina and Ugarit. Thus intercultural connections in the area of Al Mina are now being interpreted as Greek-Luwian whereas until quite recently they used to be thought of as Greek-Phoenician.[35] This area had been intermittently under the control of Aleppo, which, as we have seen, probably had an interest in the *Kingship in Heaven* songs from early on.

I wonder, however, if this is early enough. The Succession Myth seems very well integrated into Greek religion by the time we encounter it in

---

[30] See above, pp. 203–6. Carrez-Maratray 2001 doubts this, unjustly. See Verreth 2006, Chuvin and Yoyotte 1986.
[31] Haider 2005 on the monster seems too optimistic.
[32] See Gruppe 1889. Lipinski 1995: 249–50 tends to believe it.
[33] Maybe it can be explained by the hypothesis that the Greeks identified Baal Ṣapuna as the god of their enemies (rather as Baal Ṣapuna-Seth becomes the enemy of the gods in Greco-Roman Egypt). It is even possible that this change happened in Egypt (Ṣapuna > Seth > Typhon).
[34] Watkins 1995: 460–3 in fact suggests that Typhon is an Indo-European term, and a doublet of Python, which is also Indo-European. Incidentally, it has also been suggested that Sappho's name might be a hypocoristic theophoric name based on Ṣapuna: Zuntz 1951.
[35] On the background of this fast developing area, see Weeden 2013.

Homer and Hesiod. This is part of a more general problem with hypotheses about East–West diffusion. Contact could easily have happened much earlier than current thinking allows, and much earlier than our first evidence for it; some of it could have been up to a millennium earlier. In the case of the Succession Myth, the Late Bronze Age has much to be said for it; we know from the treaty between Sausgamuwa of Amurru and the Hittite Tudhaliya IV that Greeks were in the area of the Levant in the thirteen century BCE.[36]

An important role could have been played by Ugarit, which was at a major intersection, in geographical terms between Syria and the Mediterranean (Cyprus and Crete), and in geopolitical terms between Anatolia to the North and Egypt to the South. Baal Ṣapuna functioned as the international face of Ugaritic religion (contrasting to the local Baal of Ugarit).[37] Ugarit must have been a centre for merchants, e.g., from Hittite Ura on the South coast of Turkey near Cilicia,[38] and from Crete, such as Sinaranu who in a surviving document was granted exemption all duties (Baal Ṣapuna was invoked to guarantee the arrangement).[39] Merchants could well have disseminated the myths: they may for all we know have witnessed performances or dramatisations of them at festivals in the city.[40] The story of Baal's conflict with Yamm may reflect the need for traders to be safe from storms; the dedication of stone anchors in the temple at Ugarit could be part of the same pattern.[41]

But this moment of interaction could have occurred earlier still. I mentioned above that the *Song of the Sea* seems to have been known in Aleppo and Mari in the eighteenth century BCE, and I raised the possibility that other poems in the cycle may have been known in Syria as well at this time. This hypothesis would be compatible with a different model for borrowing. The cuneiform texts from Mari mention Cretan (or Cretan-style) goods, which is *prima facie* evidence for contact of some sort.[42] It also seems that during the reign of Zimri-Lim of Mari (eighteenth century

---

[36] See Beckman et al. 2011: no. 2, 63; Devecchi 2010b.
[37] For the international dimension, see Smith 2016: 85. The bibliography is huge: Fauth 1990, Koch 1993, Healey 2007, Bonnet 1987, Lane Fox 2008; on rituals, see Smith 2016: 81–4, and Corti 2017, who has reconstructed the festival of Mt. Hazzi as performed in the Hittite city of Sapinuwa in the first half of the fourteenth century BCE.
[38] On the Merchants of Ura, see Beckman 1999: no. 32. The ship discovered at Uluburun off the coast of Lycia may have called at Ugarit: see Pulak 1997: 252, Bachhuber 2006: 356. We should also think of the 'international style' or 'international koine' which tends to be found in coastal regions: cf. Feldman 2006: 144.
[39] See Heltzer 1989 and 1996: 439–48.   [40] See Rutherford 2019a.
[41] Frost 1991; Wachsmann 1998: 292–3. Anchors were also dedicated at Byblos and Kition.
[42] Alberti 2012.

BCE) a Cretan boat was manufactured, possibly for ritual use by the king on the Euphrates.[43] So it is not impossible that knowledge of Syrian myth became known in the Aegean around this time.[44]

Again, we could think of merchants from these areas attending festivals in places like Aleppo and Terqa, witnessing the performances of ritual and hearing the myths. Aleppo's geopolitical location may help to explain why Hadad of Aleppo was of interest to so many different groups in the ancient Near East at different periods: in the late third millennium it was controlled by Ebla, and records from there document visitors from a number of places;[45] in the early second millennium BCE it was of interest to Mari and in the later second millennium to Hatti, Nuzi, Ugarit, Emar, Tunip and Alalah.[46] Equally, the sanctuary of Dagan at Terqa, like that at Tuttul, while not a major centre of political power, was a shared source of religious prestige, where leaders from a wide area of Syria and Mesopotamia made pilgrimages.[47] So prima facie this would give us a model for the dissemination of these narratives from Syria in the eighteenth century BCE, a full millennium before Burkert's Orientalising Period, and long before these narratives were even translated into Hittite. But it is not just a matter of crude dissemination from East to West; rather, shared knowledge of these myths is something that allows for the formation of shared traditions.

It is also possible that some artistic influence goes from West to East. There is reason to think that Minoan artists produced frescos at sites in the Levant and Syria.[48] The Ugaritic idea that the craftsman deity Kothar-wa-Hasis was resident in Crete perhaps reflects knowledge of Crete as a centre of craft and manufacture.[49] Presumably, 'Aegeanness' had a certain cultural prestige at this time.[50] If art could travel from Crete to Syria and the Levant, it seems possible that myths could travel as well and, if we allow that Minoan Crete might have already had theogonic myths, then it is not out of the question that these influenced Syrian mythology as early as the eighteenth century BCE. It must be admitted that language would have been an

---

[43] See Guichard 1993 and 2005: 162–3. Guichard 1993 compares the model boat on the Haghia Triadha sarcophagus, which has been thought to symbolise the journey of the soul after death. See Gallou 2005: 45; on the Ayia Triadha Sacrophagus, see Long 1974: 46, 48–9; Laffineur 1991.
[44] I don't consider here the evidence of seals, for which see Aruz 2008: 61–7, 137–43.
[45] Archi 2010: 9.   [46] Schwemer 2001: 490.   [47] See Feliu 2003: 102, 303.
[48] See Niemeier and Niemeier 1998; on Qatna, see von Rüden 2011: 99–114; Pfälzner in collaboration with von Rüden 2008; on Alalah, von Rüden 2017 and Koehl 2013. For the possibility of borrowing from Mycenaean Greece to the Near East in the Late Bronze Age, see López-Ruiz 2010: 38–43.
[49] Aruz 2008: 139–43 discusses hints of seal technique moving from the Aegean to the Levant.
[50] See von Rüden 2011: 113.

additional obstacle in the case of myth; and although the Mari texts mention foreign musicians, they do not mention musicians from Crete.[51]

Differences

So far I have been mostly concerned with the first of the two approaches I distinguished in the introduction, namely using similarities to make a case for borrowing. In this section, I want to turn to the second approach, namely using differences to understand what is distinctive about each cultural tradition, looking at the Greek response to the *Song of the Sea*.

In contrast to most peoples of the ancient Near East, the Greeks don't have a major myth with the theme 'the gods versus the sea'. Greek religion has various maritime gods, most prominent among them Poseidon, whose sphere of activity combines the sea, earthquakes and horses;[52] and perhaps, following Robert Parker, we should see his mode of action as 'turbulence and the power to overcome it'.[53] Poseidon resembles the Ugaritic Yamm in being one of three brothers presiding over sky, sea and underworld.[54] However, he never starts a cosmic war against Zeus, although the possibility of conflict between them seems to be implied in the fifteenth book of the *Iliad* where Zeus threatens open conflict against Poseidon unless he stops supporting the Greek army (*Il.* 15.165: 'since I say I am better far than he in might, and the elder by birth').[55] Besides Poseidon, there was Okeanos/the Ocean stream, and various minor deities such as Nereus, father of the Nereids or sea-nymphs. One of the most memorable marine episodes in Hesiod's *Theogony* is the birth of Aphrodite (188–200), created from the genitals of Ouranos which fall into the sea (*pontos*), which explains the goddesses' epithets Ourania and Pontia.[56] Thus in a sense, the Greek counterpoint to Hedammu and Ullikummi, two monsters associated with the sea in *KIHC*, is the cosmic goddess of love.

---

[51] Ziegler 2007.
[52] It is in the latter function that Poseidon was identified with Elqonera ('El the creator of the earth') in early Roman Palmyra. In the Hellenistic period the chief god of Berytus (a local Baal?) had the Greek translation Poseidon, as in dedications at Delos. See Teixidor 1977: 42–3. Töyräänvuori 2016: 379–81 (= 2018: 331–3) suggests that Poseidon's association with horses could be anticipated at Ugarit as well.
[53] Parker 2011: 90.
[54] One might expect the fathers El and Kronos to correspond as well, but in fact they are different, since El remains the head of the pantheon: see Smith 2001: 136.
[55] López-Ruiz 2014c: 4. Yasumura 2013 speculates that the *Iliad* shows traces of conflict between the gods.
[56] Both epithets with a Near Eastern background: for Ourania, see Metcalf 2015a: 182–90; for Pontia, Ayali-Darshan 2010.

The usual myth was that Zeus was allied with the sea. In the *Iliad* (1.399–406), Achilles, whose mother is the sea nymph Thetis, persuades her to intercede with Zeus on his behalf by reminding her of how she boasts that she once helped Zeus when the other gods wanted to 'bind' him. She got a hundred-handed giant to support him, a creature 'whom the gods call Briareus, but all men Aegaeon' (403–4). Aegaeon may well be intended to be understood as the eponymous deity of the Aegean Sea,[57] and this was how the Homeric passage seems to have been understood by the fifth-century poet Ion of Chios, who claimed in one of his dithyrambs (*PMG* 741) that Aegaeon was summoned from the ocean by Thetis and taken up to protect Zeus, and that he was the son of Thalassa (Sea). The hundred-handers also support Zeus in his fight against the Titans in Hesiod's *Theogony*; there's no trace of a marine dimension, except that one of them, Briareus, married a daughter of Poseidon, Kymopoleia (*Th.* 817–19).

The only exception to this, at least among early sources, is the fragmentary early Greek epic, the *Titanomachia*, ascribed to Eumelus of Corinth, where Aegaeon is the son of Ge and Pontos, and it is said that 'that living in the sea he fought together with the Titans', i.e., *against* Zeus.[58] How to explain this is not certain: it could be a conscious reaction against the panhellenic version of the *Iliad*, but it's perhaps more likely to be a trace of a tradition inspired by Oriental sources, either one that had reached Greece before Homer (and to which the Homeric version would have been a reaction), or one that came to Greece more recently;[59] it should be borne in mind that Corinth had good connections with the Near East.[60]

How should we explain the absence of a myth of conflict between Zeus and Sea in the mainstream Greek tradition? Perhaps it could be seen as a matter of theology, that is to say that in Greek religious imagination the sea had always been an integral part of the dominant cosmic order and not

---

[57] See Fowler 1988.
[58] *Titanomachia* fr. 3 Bernabé = Σ A.R. 1.1165c. That scholion also preserves the information that Kinaithon in his *Heraklea* (fr. 7 Bernabe) said that Aegaeon was defeated by Poseidon and thrown into what is now called by Apollonius the 'Cairn of Aegaeon' (ἡρίον Αἰγαίωνος) off the coast of Mysia: Fowler 2000–13: II.69. Later sources: Antimachus of Colophon fr. 14 Matthews (= Σ Veron. Verg. *Aen.* 10.565): *Homerus amicum Aegeona d<icit> Iovis, sed Antimachus in tertio Thebaidos d<icit> adversum eum armatum*; Virgil, *Aen.* 10.565 has Aegaeon the hundred-hander fighting against Zeus. See West 2002: 111–12; Tsagalis 2017: 53–6; Radermacher 1938: 267–8. Pherecydes fr. 43 Fowler says that the Aegean sea is called after Poseidon because he is called Aigaios.
[59] West 2002: 111; Tsagalis 2017: 54. Bremmer 2008: 76 and 87–8 argued for more extensive oriental influence on the *Titanomachia*.
[60] Morris and Papadopoulos 1998, Ziskowski 2016.

opposed to it. But I want to argue that the difference could in part be the result of an ideological choice: to make that case, I have to make two assumptions.

First, the Greeks would tend to have been associated by Near Eastern peoples, e.g., the Neo-Assyrians, with the sea.[61] At the end of the eighth century BCE, Sargon says of his attack on the Greeks that 'like a fisherman he caught the Yaunaya in the mist of the sea like fish'. The Yaunaya are presumably the Ionians or something like them.[62] The Hittites already defined the sea as the border of their empire in the second millennium,[63] so that Mycenaeans may have been associated with the sea and indeed associated themselves with it.[64]

My second assumption is that myths of this sort can be read politically.[65] In the study of Greek myth and religion it is acknowledged that some sorts of myth have some sort of political or social significance – local aetiologies, myths of migration or autochthony, or myths embodying collective ideology.[66] Classicists are less used to the idea that cosmogonic myths, like those of Hesiod's *Theogony*, could have political significance. However, cosmogonic poetry in the ancient Near East often seems to have a political function; one purpose of *Enūma Eliš* is manifestly to promote Marduk the god of Babylon, for example (Lambert 2013: 248–75; Reynolds, Chapter 3 in this volume). We have already seen a clear use of the myth of the Storm God and the Sea at Aleppo. The Baal Cycle from Ugaritic may also have a political function, primarily that of promoting local royal authority.[67] Mark Smith suggested in 1997 that 'the Baal Cycle's presentation of a relative weak Baal aided by other deities against the threatening cosmic powers of Yamm and Mot may have reflected the

---

[61] Haubold 2013a: 100–1.
[62] Casabonne 2004: 1 suggests that this ethnonym might derived from 'Yam'; NB: the Neo-Babylonian form of the word is Yamnaya, though Brinkman 1989: 54 cautions that this is a writing convention. For Egyptian evidence that term 'Ionian' was already around in the Bronze Age, see Gander 2015: 476–83.
[63] As three times in the *Edict of Telipinu*: CTH 19, §3, §6, §8.
[64] Notice that in Beckman's reconstruction of the Milawata Letter (*KUB* 19.55 + *KUB* 48.90, line 13 = *AhT*5 in Beckman, Bryce and Cline 2011: 124–5), Tudhaliya IV boasts that he has recently established 'again' a sea border for the Hittite kingdom in the West. In another text (*KUB* 56.15 ii 15–25 = *AhT*26) the Hittite queen Puduhepa made a vow to the Sea God (written A.AB.BA), asking that Piyamaradu, a Western Anatolian warlord known to have taken refuge in Ahhiyawa, be sent to her. On this text, see Rutherford 2019b.
[65] See Corti and Pecchioli Daddi 2012: 617.   [66] Kowalzig 2007.
[67] See Töyräänvuori 2016: 65–74 (= 2018: 51–9). Tugendhaft 2017 has a more sophisticated view, seeing the Baal narratives as a response to increasingly divinised kingship in Hatti.

status of Ugarit and its ruling dynasty in a world dominated by the great Egyptian and Hittite empires'.[68]

If we combine Smith's analysis with the first point, we can see that it would have been possible to interpret the narrative of the Storm God and the Sea as a conflict between Ugarit or some other state that claimed to be protected by the Storm God and one of the peoples associated with the sea, which in the Bronze Age could have included Minoans and Greeks. This association could have been made by either side. From the Greek point of view, the possibility of this interpretation might have made them deeply uncomfortable with narrative, at least with the version (the only one attested) where the Sea loses the battle. For Greeks, the sea, loosely associated with Poseidon, was generally a positive force which worked with rather than against the cosmic order. This more positive valorisation of the sea, I would suggest, would have tended to block the successful translation of the narrative to the Aegean. This explains why although the Storm God and Sea is one of the most mobile of ancient narratives, finding a home even in Egypt, which was usually unaccommodating of foreign religion, it is absent from mainstream Greek poetry, with the exception of the epichoric *Titanomachia* (as a result of political or conceptual hostility).

To conclude, the divine narratives associated with Anatolian and Syrian Storm Gods and their adversaries circulated widely in the Western Mediterranean in the Middle Bronze, Late Bronze and Early Iron Ages, and it seems likely that there was some interaction with early Greek narrative traditions over this period. A plausible hypothesis is that this happened in the contact zone of the north-east corner of the Mediterranean, where Minoans, Mycenaeans and, later, Greeks encountered West Asiatic and Anatolian traditions in areas of Ugarit/Tell Tayinat and Cilicia. While it remains likely that most of the borrowing went from East to West, we should not rule out the possibility that Minoans also exported mythological narratives, as they exported visual art. Finally, rather than being focused solely on finding evidence for borrowing in the form of parallels between different traditions, we should also find time to consider differences between traditions, bearing in mind that an idea is more readily borrowed when it is already more or less consonant with the borrower's pattern of thinking, and that some West Asiatic myths matched Greek patterns of thinking better than others.

---

[68] Smith and Parker 1997: 84–5 (thanks to Töyräänvuori 2016: 66 = 2018: 53 for this reference). See also Smith 1994: 105. This idea is developed by Tugendhaft 2012 and 2017, arguing that the tributary relationship of Baal and Yamm reflect actual interstate politics of the period.

CHAPTER 12

Divine Labour

Johannes Haubold

There were many interlocking narratives about the gods in the ancient Mediterranean and the Near East. Some involve fighting, some involve sex. Many focus on how the gods relate to humans – in cult as well as in daily life. All these stories enabled people from across the ancient world to imagine, celebrate and sometimes criticise the beings that they worshipped. And it is in a way no surprise that such stories were exchanged in an attempt better to understand how all human beings, whatever languages and traditions they knew best and could bring to the discussion, related to the gods. In this chapter, I want to single out a group of divine narratives that seem to me of particular interest and which have received relatively little attention: narratives in which human beings come to replace the gods specifically as workers. The gods of ancient Greece, the Levant and Mesopotamia lead a life of privilege and leisure, in contrast with human beings. This easy life defines their existence, but it turns out that divine existence, in the past, used to involve hard work. It is this period of divine labour, and the story-telling that attaches to it, which is the focus of this chapter.

Babylon

One important formulation of divine labour can be found in the opening lines of the Babylonian *Poem of the Flood*, or *Atraḥasīs*, which reads very much like a workers' revolt. The passage is best preserved in the Old Babylonian version (Tablet 1 1–6 Lambert/Millard):

> When the gods in the way of man
>   carried out the work (*dullu*) and bore the toil
> the toil of the gods was great,
>   the load was heavy, the difficulty was much.
> The seven great Anunnaki   5
>   made the Igigi bear the toil.

Once upon a time the gods had to work the land on behalf of Enlil. The work was so hard and the drudgery so unbearable that they turned on their master: they burned their tools, descended on Enlil's palace and demanded redress. Initially, Enlil was perplexed, but then he called a council and a solution was found: henceforth human beings would do the work of the gods. I quote from the Standard Babylonian version of the text discovered in Sippar (SB *Atrahasīs* II 61–74 Al-Rawi/George):

> Anu opened his mouth
> and said to the god his brother:
> 'Why do we blame them?
> Too hard was their labour (*dullu*), their suffering too much.
> 65 Every day the earth ...,
> the labour was too hard, we could hear the tumult.
> But there is a task to do.
> Bēlet-ilī, the mother goddesses, is present.
> Let the mother goddess create human-kind,
> 70 so man can bear the burden of the gods.
> Let her create human-kind,
> so it can carry the yoke, the task imposed by rulership.
> Let it carry the yoke, the task imposed by Enlil.
> Let man take over the burden of the god.'

Three points seem worth noting about this story. First, the poet assumes that there is work to be done in the early universe and that someone has to do it. As long as there are only gods, it follows that the gods must work. But, and that is my second point, this state of affairs cannot last. Quite apart from the fact that it leads to a divine rebellion, it also results in a confusion of crucial categories: the toiling gods, the poet tells us in the opening line of the poem, were like man (Akk. *awīlum*).[1] This in turn leads to my third point: human beings have to bear what the gods will not. In other words, the story recognises the theological significance of human labour.

So, what does the work amount to that so riles the gods? The poet uses several different terms to describe it, but the very first, *dullu*, is arguably the most significant: it covers a range of meanings from general drudgery to forced labour and even ritual activity (*CAD* s.v.). In all these cases, *dullu* refers to a task that cannot be avoided. Its opposite is *andurāru*, 'freedom', conceived as an exemption from such tasks (*CAD* s.v.). In *Atrahasīs*, the

---

[1] OB *Atrahasīs* I 1, quoted above. The precise meaning of the line was debated already in antiquity and continues to be debated in modern scholarship; see Lambert/Millard 1969: 146, Shehata 2001: 23–4, Kvanvig 2011: 39–43, Ziegler 2016, Wöhrle 2018.

creation of mankind establishes *andurāru* for the gods (OB *Atrahasīs* I 235–43 Lambert/Millard, modified):

> Mami made ready to speak 235
> and said to the great gods:
> 'I have completed the work that you asked of me. 237/8
> You have slaughtered a god with his intelligence.
> I have removed your heavy burden 240
> and have imposed your toil on man.
> You ... a cry for mankind:
> I have loosened the yoke and established release (*andurāra aškun*).'

In a sense, this is a political solution to the problem of divine labour: the gods become effectively a leisured class. *Atrahasīs* has little positive to say about what that means in terms of their lifestyle, but other texts address the question.

Enūma eliš, for example, accepts that human beings were created to relieve the gods of their work obligations. Again the word is *dullu* (*Enūma eliš* VI 7–8 Lambert, modified):

> 'Let me create mankind,
> they shall bear the gods' burden (*dullu*) so that the gods may rest.'

The central idea behind this passage is clearly taken from *Atrahasīs*: humankind is created in order to do the gods' work (*dullu*) for them.[2] However, the poet of *Enūma eliš* suppresses any reference to forced labour and, instead, presents the gods as grateful for the creation of humankind and only *then* setting to work, as volunteers, to build a temple for Marduk, which would also function as a place where they could rest (*Enūma eliš* VI 47–64).[3] So here the gods willingly put in two years of work towards their own retirement, as it were.[4]

A crucial word in this connection is *pašāḫu*, which is prominent in *Enūma eliš* but absent from *Atrahasīs*.[5] Akkadian *pašāḫu* means something like 'be at rest', or 'be relaxed' (*CAD* s.v.) – and in *Enūma eliš* it describes

---

[2] For the intertextual allusion to *Atrahasīs* see Wisnom 2014: 173–5.
[3] Noted by Katz 2011: 131 and others since. A broken passage in *Enūma eliš* V 139–42 may refer to the work of provisioning the gods (Wisnom 2014: 174), but the emphasis, in this case, appears to be on the future rather than any work that the gods have already done on Marduk's behalf.
[4] In *Enūma eliš* VI 60 the Anunnaki make bricks 'for one year' (*šattu ištât*). In the second year (*šanītu šattu ina kašādi*, VI 61) they build Esagila, the main temple of Marduk in Babylon. These are the only precise measures of time in the poem, and they come just after Marduk has created the astronomical year (Tablet V 40–2).
[5] The relevant passages in *Enūma eliš* are listed in the index to Talon 2005: 120. Particularly relevant to the present argument is *Enūma eliš* VI 8, quoted above.

in positive terms what the gods are, or rather, what they become after their retirement.[6] At one level, we might see this merely as one attempt among many to sanitise an inherited myth: Marduk, the *Enūma eliš* poet insists, was not the kind of monarch who would make other gods toil for him. But the poet also hints at a more fundamental reinterpretation of the inherited story. The gods in *Atraḫasīs* operate within a strict historical framework: there was once a time when they were like human beings, but that time has now passed. In *Enūma eliš*, this historical narrative is overlaid with a potentially ahistorical set of theological and moral concerns: should gods *ever* behave like human beings? Does it not compromise their divinity if they once laboured for their ruler and, more importantly, does it not damage the ruler's authority if he first subjected them and then had a revolt on his hands? *Enūma eliš* was embedded in Babylonian state religion in a way that *Atraḫasīs* was not, which may explain why it encouraged revisionist thinking along these lines.[7] At a more general level, what we see here is an innate instability in stories of divine labour, which makes them an easy target for theological critique. I discuss more examples of such critique in the course of this chapter.

Israel

The motif of divine labour was also known in the Levant. The opening chapter of *Genesis* describe how God created the world in six days and how he ceased from his work on the seventh. At this point his activity is described as מְלָאכָה, an 'occupation' or 'business' (*Gen.* 2: 1–3):

> And the heaven and the earth were completed, and all their host. And God completed his work (מְלָאכָה) which he had carried out on the seventh day; and he rested on the seventh day from all his work (מְלָאכָה) which he had done. And God blessed the seventh day, and made it holy; because on it he rested from all his work which he had done in creation.

Hebrew מְלָאכָה is not a negative term, and certainly does not mean 'drudgery' (Brown-Driver-Briggs *s.v.* לְאָךְ). Nor does שָׁבַת, the verb used to describe what happens on the seventh day, necessarily imply that God was resting from toil.[8] There is a debate about the meaning of שָׁבַת, which

---

[6] Cf. *Enūma eliš* VI 8 *šunu lū pašḫu*.
[7] For the *Sitz im Leben* of *Enūma eliš* in Babylonian state religion, see Pongratz-Leisten 1994, Zgoll 2006: 48–51, Gabriel 2014: 70–106, Reynolds, Chapter 3 in this volume.
[8] Westermann 1974: 237–8.

goes back to antiquity.[9] What matters here is that God's initial bout of activity was in no sense an imposition.

Work as labour and toil emerges later in the text, when man and woman eat from the forbidden fruit and are evicted from the Garden of Eden (*Gen.* 3: 17–19):

> And to Adam he said: 'Because you have listened to the voice of your wife, and have eaten of the tree of which I commanded you not to eat; the earth is cursed for you. With toil (עִצָּבוֹן) you shall eat of it all the days of your life. It shall bring forth thorns and thistles for you and you shall eat the herb of the field. In the sweat of your face you shall eat bread until you return to the earth; since you were taken from it; for you are dust and shall return to dust.'

The language here (עִצָּבוֹן, 'labour, toil, pain'; זֵעַת, 'sweat') suggests the hard graft that in *Atrahasīs* upsets the gods and is eventually passed on to human beings. In the Bible, the work of God and the work of humans have nothing in common. God worked on a specific project for a specific amount of time. Human beings then brought an entirely new, open-ended, form of drudgery upon themselves.[10]

It is difficult to establish what connections there might be between this picture of divine and human labour and what we find in Babylonian texts such as *Atrahasīs* or *Enūma eliš*. Scholars since Hermann Gunkel have argued that the early chapters of *Genesis* owe much to Babylonian models,[11] though the lines of transmission remain uncertain. Speculation about transmission should in any case not distract us from the task of interpreting the texts, as I have argued extensively elsewhere.[12] The Bible, too, is interested in the history of labour. There was work to do in the early universe, and God did it. This period of divine activity culminates in the creation of man, who henceforth takes charge of matters on earth. In the Bible, as already in *Atrahasīs*, there is thus a sense that man is created in order to carry on what God has started. However, the Bible configures the transfer differently. Toil and sweat become a necessity only *after* God creates man – and they arise as the result of man defying God's command.

---

[9] Jenni-Westermann *s.v.* שָׁבַת. For ancient interpretations see, for example, the translations of שָׁבַת in the Septuagint (2× καταπαύω, 'cease') and Jerome's Vulgate (*cesso*, 'cease', in *Gen.* 2:2 but *requiesco*, 'rest', in *Gen.* 2:3).

[10] At *Gen.* 2:5 and 2:15 man is needed to 'till' (Hebr. עָבַד) the garden of Eden and 'guard' it (Hebr. מָרַשׁ), but this is not a matter of God passing on work that he initially had to do himself, nor is it described as especially arduous.

[11] Gunkel 1895. For a recent attempt to pinpoint influence from *Enūma eliš*, see Frahm 2013.

[12] Haubold 2013a.

Now, this seemingly unified picture of divine and human work is in fact the result of a complex process of redaction. Mark Smith has recently argued that the 'Priestly' narrative of *Genesis* 1–2:4a can be read as a commentary on the older 'Jahwist' creation story of *Genesis* 2:4b–3.[13] According to him, the author(s) of *Genesis* 1 reframed the Jahwist story of how God created life on earth by prefacing it with an account of how he created the wider universe, and especially the heavens.[14] The effect, Smith argues, is a new interpretation of God's work, one that emphasises his sacred, and sanctifying, presence in the world since time immemorial.

Of particular interest in this context is the fact that, as part of the process of reframing which Smith detects in the Priestly redaction of the Biblical creation account, the line between divine and human activity becomes more clearly articulated. Already the Jahwist appears to have avoided any suggestion that God had to work in the way that human beings do. However, Smith points out that he still uses the humdrum verb עָשָׂה, 'make', to describe God's creation of the world in *Genesis* 2:4b, the same word that also describes human work. The Priestly narrator, by contrast, uses בָּרָא, 'create', when introducing his account at *Genesis* 1:1, a word that refers specifically to divine activity.[15] The effect is, yet again, to emphasise the timeless sanctity of God's work.[16] We detect here a process of refinement that seems driven by theological qualms not dissimilar to those that motivated the rewriting of *Atrahasīs* in *Enūma eliš*.

Greece

The question arises of whether a concern with divine labour, which I have argued is present in Mesopotamia and the Levant, can also be detected in the ancient Aegean. In Greek epic, as in other ancient traditions, gods and humans share a history.[17] In the course of that history, they emerge as beings who mutually define each other. The endpoint of that development is captured in a famous passage in the *Iliad*, where Achilles describes the

---

[13] Smith 2010: 129–38. The two creation narratives of *Genesis* 1–2:4a and 2:4a–3 have long been traced to two distinct source traditions, the 'Priestly Source' (P) and the 'Jahwist' (J) respectively; see Wellhausen 1899 and, for a recent overview, Baden 2009.
[14] Smith points out that the priestly redactor(s) invert the Jahwist formula 'earth and heavens' to indicate a shift in priorities ('heavens and earth'); see Smith 2010: 130–1.
[15] Smith 2010: 132–3. Smith acknowledges that the Priestly author(s) use(s) עָשָׂה as well as בָּרָא but insists, rightly in my view, that בָּרָא carries thematic significance.
[16] In a similar vein, we may contrast the spoken commandments of *Gen.* 1:1–2:4a with the hands-on approach of *Genesis* 2:7–8, 13–19 and 21–2.
[17] Graziosi and Haubold 2005: 35–62.

gods as ἀκηδέες, 'untroubled', in contrast with suffering humankind (Hom. *Il.* 24.525–6):

> 'In this way have the gods spun life for wretched mortals,
> that they live in unhappiness while the gods have no sorrows.'

Achilles describes human beings as 'wretched' (δειλοί) and glosses this by adding that they live 'with grief' (ἀχνύμενοι) while the gods 'have no sorrows' (ἀκηδέες εἰσί). Elsewhere Homer adds that the gods are ἀθάνατοι 'un-dying' and ἀγήραοι 'un-ageing'.[18] Human beings, of course, are mortal, and are subject to ageing. In other words, Greek epic focuses on suffering and death, where the emphasis in *Atrahasīs* is on suffering and labour.

One reason why Achilles does not mention manual labour among the suffering that separates mortals from gods is that he himself does not engage in it: in the heroic age, the emphasis is on heroic deeds rather than labour. Of course, because there are houses and there is bread, work must happen in the background, and occasionally we do hear about it, but such allusions tend to be fleeting.[19] Manual work becomes a thematic concern only in the post-heroic age Hesiod describes in the *Works and Days*. Human life, Hesiod says, was once without evils and harsh 'drudgery', Greek πόνος (Hes. *Op.* 90–3):

> For before this the tribes of men lived on earth
> apart and free from ills and hard toil (πόνος)
> and dreadful sicknesses which bring the Fates upon men;
> for in misery men grow old quickly.

It was as a punishment for the theft of fire that Zeus created the need for work among the many other evils (κακά) which beset human life.[20] There are remarkable parallels here with the Biblical story of the fall: both texts explain the less pleasant aspects of agricultural labour as a curse that human

---

[18] Passages and discussion in *LfgrE* s.vv.
[19] Animal husbandry, for example, is not uncommon in the *Iliad*, but the poet hardly ever goes into detail. Thus, Aeneas implies (*Il.* 20.90–1) that he personally looks after his flocks, but the emphasis is entirely on his encounter with Achilles, rather than the hard work actually demanded of shepherds. Manual labour plays a more prominent role in the Iliadic similes, which portray a post-heroic world, and in the Shield of Achilles (*Il.* 18.441–9), which adopts a related outlook. For similar reasons, the *Odyssey* with its setting closer to post-heroic life has more to say about work than the *Iliad* (see, for example, *Od.* 18.357–75), though it never truly emphasises how hard manual labour actually is.
[20] Hesiod can see work in a more positive light, as timely ἔργα ('deeds') that ward off 'wretched poverty' (Hes. *Op.* 638). However, that does not give it a positive value in and of itself. As he makes clear in his portrayal of the Golden Race (Hes. *Op.* 109–20), work is a necessary evil that we would much rather do without.

beings brought upon themselves. In the Bible, God plants the garden of Eden, but there is no suggestion that he needs to work the land in order to eat. Zeus, likewise, was never a farmer. In fact, he and the other gods do not even eat bread.[21] There are, however, some aspects of divine history as Hesiod knew it which recall the gods of *Atrahasīs* too, and their decision to hand over their drudgery to human beings. The story of the gods' toil is told in Hesiod's *Theogony*, and it is linked there to their struggle with the Titans. In lines 629–38 we hear:

> For with soul-destroying toil (πόνος) they fought for a long time,
> 630 the Titan gods and the offspring of Kronos
> against one another in mighty battles,
> the brilliant Titans from high Othrys,
> the gods from Olympus, givers of good things,
> whom lovely-haired Rhea bore in union with Kronos.
> 635 So they, with bitter ... were then fighting each other
> continually for ten full years,
> and there was no resolution to the hard strife, nor an end,
> for either side, and the issue of the war hung evenly balanced.

The Greek noun that Hesiod uses to describe the fight between gods and Titans is πόνος, 'toil', the same term that he employs in *Works and Days* to describe the human condition. It reappears when the war between Olympians and Titans finally comes to an end (*Th.* 881–5):

> But when the blessed gods had completed their toil (πόνος),
> and settled by force the matter of status with the Titans,
> they asked far-seeing Olympian Zeus to reign and rule over
> the immortals, by Earth's prompting.
> 885 And he divided the honours well amongst them.

'Toil', it would seem, is a feature of divine history in Greek epic too – though it is not understood in quite the same way as in the Babylonian narrative tradition. Already Aristarchus pointed out that Homer used πόνος primarily of fighting,[22] and that is certainly how it is used in the *Theogony* passage quoted above: the gods have been fighting the Titans 'by force' (βίηφι). After their victory they assume their divine prerogatives (τιμαί) and hence the roles in which we know them today.[23] Implied in this process is a definition of what it means to be a god in early Greek epic:[24] the gods are 'blessed' (μάκαρες at *Th.* 881), in contrast with

---

[21] Hom. *Il.* 5.441, with Haubold 2013c: 32. [22] Lehrs 1882: 73–5.
[23] For ancient readers this was a crucial aspect of divine history: see Hdt. 2.53.2–3, with Clay 1989: 8.
[24] Haubold 2017: 30–2.

'wretched' humankind; and they are blessed because they have completed their 'toil' (πόνος), conceived as a ten-year battle which recalls the ten-year-long struggle of the Trojan War.[25]

Neither Homer nor Hesiod ever explicitly states that the gods passed their πόνος on to the heroes (from the Titan War to the Trojan War, as it were) – but that, I suggest, is precisely what the texts assume. Here I take inspiration from Jenny Strauss Clay, who argues that, 'by deflecting the erotic interest of the gods onto mortals, Zeus brings stability to Olympus'.[26] A similar process of deflection, I argue, can be detected when it comes to the toil of battle. The *Iliad* is full of references to the πόνος of heroic fighting.[27] Indeed, this was felt to be such a characteristic feature of Homeric narrative that the *Contest of Homer and Hesiod* quotes, as Homer's most representative passage of poetry, some lines which describe precisely the dreadful πόνος of the heroic battlefield (*Certamen Homeri et Hesiodi* 12 Bassino):

> But King Panoides asked each of them (i.e., Homer and Hesiod) to recite the finest passage from his own poetry. So Hesiod went first (there follows an extract from the so-called farmer's calendar in the *Works and Days*):
> . . .
> Then it was Homer's turn (*Il.* 13.339–44):
> . . .
> The deadly battle bristled with the long spears
> that they held to slice the skin; eyes were dazzled
> by the brightness of the bronze in the shining helmets,
> the fresh-polished corselets, and the gleaming shields
> as the armies clashed. It would have been a bold-hearted man
> who felt joy at seeing that toil (πόνος), and not dismay.

Homer's selection of lines is telling, not least because it fails to conform to modern expectation. Nobody today would choose these lines from Book 13 as the best passage in the *Iliad*: the conversation between Achilles and Priam, from which I quoted above, would be a likelier candidate. Still, the ancient selection deserves attention, not least because it is crucially concerned with the heroes and their 'toil'.[28]

The gods, by contrast, are characterised by their leisure. We are all familiar with the Olympian scenes of the *Iliad* which show feasting and

---

[25] West 1966: 341 *ad Th.* 636 points out the parallel with the Trojan War but puts it down to 'use of the formulaic progression "for nine years ... and in the tenth ...".
[26] Clay 2003: 171.   [27] *LfgrE* s.v. πόνος I 2 discusses the relevant passages.
[28] Graziosi 2002: 175–80 discusses other reasons why 'Homer' selects this particular passage.

bantering gods, and the gods of epic are of course called ῥεῖα ζώοντες, 'living with ease'.[29] Yet, the Iliadic gods do still take an interest in the πόνος ἀνδρῶν, the 'toil of men', as it is often called – be it as spectators or indeed as participants in the action.[30] The following is a characteristic example of the gods watching the heroes toil on earth (*Il.* 7.442–4):

> Thus the long-haired Achaeans were toiling (πονέοντο);
> and the gods were sitting by the side of Zeus, the lord of lightning,
> and marvelled at the great work of the bronze-clad Achaeans.

The context here is a detailed description of how the Achaeans built a great tomb for their dead, and, as an extension of the tomb, a defensive wall around their camp (*Il.* 7.433–41). The Achaean wall has long been seen as a symbol of the monumental text of the *Iliad*,[31] but it is symbolic also in the sense that it draws a distinction between the toiling heroes and the leisured gods. Its construction is the result of much effort. Yet when Apollo destroys it later in the text, he does so 'very easily' (*Il.* 15.360–6):

> 360 There they poured forth in battle lines, but Apollo led the charge
> holding the mighty aegis. And he kicked down the wall of the Achaeans
> very easily, as a child kicks down sand by the seashore,
> who has made a castle for his own harmless pleasure
> and then wipes it off with his hands and feet for entertainment.
> 365 Just so, Phoebus, you wiped off the great labour and toil of the Achaeans,
> and put panic into their hearts.

Apollo kicks down the great wall on which the Achaeans expended 'much labour and toil' (πολὺν κάματον καὶ ὀϊζύν at *Il.* 15.365) 'very easily' (ῥεῖα μάλ', at 15.362), like a child kicks down a sandcastle on the beach. The contrast between human hard work and divine ease is perhaps most obvious in the case of the Achaean wall, but many other passages in the *Iliad* underline how easily the gods accomplish what they want. Aphrodite ends the mortal struggle between Paris and Menelaos 'with ease, as a god does' (ῥεῖα μάλ' ὥς τε θεός, *Il.* 3.381). The same formulation describes Apollo frustrating Achilles just when he is about to kill Hector (20.444). Homer not only contrasts human effort with divine ease but makes divine privilege a matter of human frustration: the gods keep humans in check by devolving their toil to them and then nullifying their exertions.

---

[29] For discussion of Homer's feasting gods, see Graziosi and Haubold 2005: 65–75; for the gods having an 'easy life' (ῥεῖα ζώοντες), see Hom. *Il.* 6.138, *Od.* 4.805, 5.122.
[30] For the Homeric gods as spectators of human action, see Griffin 1978 and 1980: 179–204.
[31] Ford 1992: 147–57.

Generally speaking, the Homeric gods stay clear of any sustained effort, or involvement in human toil. Zeus never descends to earth and on one famous occasion gets bored even just watching the 'toil of men'.[32] Other gods, who do enter the battlefield, do not usually stay for long.[33] There is a formulaic line in Homer which describes a god leaving a mortal after a battlefield conversation, departing 'through the toil of men'.[34] Such formulations suggest that the gods are only temporary visitors to a realm of toil which belongs properly to (mortal) men on earth.[35]

Occasionally, however, the gods do get embroiled, as for example when Hera labours to gather an army against Troy (Hom. *Il.* 4.24–8):

> But Hera could not contain the anger in her chest and said to him:
> 'Most dreadful son of Kronos, what word have you spoken?   25
> How can you frustrate my toil (πόνος) and make it come to nothing,
> and the sweat I have sweated from my exertion? My horses got tired
> while I gathered the people against Priam and his children.'

Hera's 'toil' (πόνος) in helping to gather the Achaean army risks being frustrated by Zeus's actions. This is not a position in which a goddess should find herself, as Hera points out later in the text (*Il.* 4.57–8):

> But it is necessary not to frustrate my toil (πόνος),
> for I too am a god and from the same family as you.

The possibility that Hera's 'toil' might have been in vain bears very directly on her status as a goddess: καὶ γὰρ ἐγὼ θεός εἰμι, she says, 'for I too am a god'. Zeus understands the seriousness of her complaint (*Il.* 4.68), but there is a sense, beyond the specifics of this particular situation, that a god in the *Iliad* should not sweat human matters in the way that Hera does. Indeed, the gods repeatedly tell each other that they should not. In the 'Theomachy' of Book 21, Poseidon sees it as his duty to fight with Apollo, only to be told by the younger god that there is no point fighting over

---

[32] *Il.* 13.2–6, discussed in Haubold 2013c.
[33] Ares, unavoidably, does get involved in the fighting, and indeed can be understood as a personification of 'everything that is hateful in war' (Burkert 1985: 169). It must be said, though, that his interventions are also fitful and sometimes prevented altogether (*Il.* 15.113–42).
[34] Hom. *Il.* 13.239 = 16.726 = 17.82 (ὣς εἰπὼν ὃ μὲν αὖτις ἔβη θεὸς ἂμ πόνον ἀνδρῶν).
[35] Stories about Heracles tend to confirm this point: exceptionally hard labour wins him immortality, after which he does not have to work anymore. In Homer and, especially, Hesiod, the transition is made clear: while still a human being, Heracles is beset with toil (e.g., *Il.* 15.30 πολλὰ περ ἀθλήσαντα), but his troubles are over once he becomes a god; cf. Hes. *Th.* 950–5 (τελέσας στονόεντας ἀέθλους), *Catalogue of Women* fr. 22.25–33 (Most). Labour can also be used to indicate potential loss of status for a god. A clear example of this is given in *Catalogue of Women* fr. 59 (Most): Zeus, instead of punishing Apollo by throwing him into Tartarus, makes him work for the mortal Admetos instead. The story seems to be presupposed in *Il.* 2.763–7.

mortals.[36] The exchange deserves attention here, because it revolves around a past episode of divine labour: Poseidon reminds Apollo how they once worked together under Laomedon but were denied the payment that had been agreed. Poseidon demands revenge on the Trojans (21.435–60), but Apollo answers with the thought that such issues should not trouble the gods at all and certainly not lead them to new wars (21.461–7). There is a tension here between a historical perspective (the gods used to engage in πόνος but should now stick to their leisure and truly live up to their epithet ῥεῖα ζώοντες) and a different, more theological conception which denies the possibility of history, and historical development, for the gods. It is never dignified for them to engage in the πόνος of war. I already pointed out that the poet of *Enūma eliš* reinterprets what in *Atrahasīs* was a matter of historical development out of concern for what a Greek reader might call τὸ πρέπον, 'propriety'.[37] A similar phenomenon can be observed in the *Iliad*, where the behaviour of the gods may be considered not historically but in abstract theological terms: should a god *ever* behave like Poseidon or Hera? Is it ever right that a god – any god, at any time – should toil in the way that they do? Homer acknowledges that some gods specialise in manual labour, notably the divine craftsman Hephaestus, who is said to 'sweat' (ἱδρόω at *Il.* 18.372) and 'toil' (πονεῖσθαι at *Il.* 18.380) in his workshop. However, Hephaestus is clearly the exception that proves the rule (and even he needs a very good reason to toil on behalf of a human being). For most Homeric gods, 'toil' of any sort, and especially the toil and suffering of war, is inappropriate. This kind of thought leads the way for the philosophically inflected critique put forward by Xenophanes (frr. 23–5 DK):

One god, the greatest among gods and men,
comparable to mortals neither in appearance nor in thought.
He is all eyes and mind and ears.
But without any toil (πόνος) he moves everything with the thinking of his mind.

These lines have been much discussed.[38] I cannot explore their full philosophical implications here, nor is it necessary to do so. What matters in the present context is that Xenophanes articulates a theological critique not unlike those we have already seen in *Enūma eliš*, *Genesis*, and indeed

---

[36] For the tone of the passage, and its wider significance, see Kelly 2007a: 333–4, Graziosi 2016.
[37] On 'appropriateness' (τὸ πρέπον) in ancient Greek literary scholarship see Nünlist 2009: 250; Schironi 2018: 427–33.
[38] For a recent example, see Warren 2013, who argues that keeping the divine and human realms clearly separate is, for Xenophanes, a matter of piety.

Homer. According to Xenophanes, divinity, at least in its highest form, is incompatible with toil. His god controls everything ἀπάνευθε πόνοιο, without breaking into sweat. As Xenophanes acknowledges elsewhere (fr. 11 DK), the target of his polemic is the depiction of the gods in Homer and Hesiod. So what he does here, yet again, is collapse the history of gods and men into abstract questions of a theological nature: Should gods ever behave like men? Should there be any circumstance in which they have to labour? In Homer and Hesiod, the answer is a qualified 'yes', and it is based on an understanding that the gods have a history, like the rest of the world. But already in Homer there is a sense that the toiling Hera is an anachronism even in the heroic age, and Xenophanes exploits this issue to challenge the very possibility of divine labour and, indeed, divine history.

Conclusion

I have argued three main points. First, authors and audiences in the ancient world shared not just stories about the gods but also some of the larger questions that made them important. We cannot always tell how the stories travelled, but we can certainly understand better how the texts work by considering the narrative resources they share.

My second point is more specific, and it concerns stories about the gods that involve historical change. Some texts ask how the gods acquired a ruler. Others concentrate on the transition from divine to human history, and imagine this as a process whereby divine labour comes to an end and human toil begins. Different texts have different ways of connecting these two developments. In *Atrahasīs*, the gods pass their own work directly on to humans. Other texts are less direct but still mark that transition. I have broadly outlined the possibilities moving from the oldest text, *Atrahasīs*, and Mesopotamia, to the Levant and to Greece.

My third point is that divine labour, as an idea, was open to challenge even within those traditions where it was most clearly articulated. The toiling gods of *Atrahasīs* became an embarrassment to the poet of *Enūma eliš* and those of Homer and Hesiod scandalised Xenophanes, who after all was also composing hexameters and therefore placed his work in the same tradition – later recategorisations as 'philosophy' notwithstanding. The priestly redactors of *Genesis* adopted a more oblique approach, reframing traditional material rather than rewriting or rejecting it wholesale. However, they too sought to contain the potentially damaging implications of divine labour.

The critiques of divine labour presented in this chapter were articulated in different ways, at different times (late second millennium in Mesopotamia, mid-first millennium in Israel and Greece), and in different cultural settings. Clearly, they cannot be shoehorned into a single cultural 'movement', let alone a historical 'moment'. Still, they do arise from a broadly shared repertoire of ideas and concerns – about religious propriety. How this repertoire was shared is a question that has been asked repeatedly but that cannot be answered beyond speculation, given the scarcity of relevant evidence.[39] The main point here is that we are faced with a problem concerning both story-telling and ritual propriety. It is a problem that will have interested the priests of Jahweh and Marduk, but also, say, the Greek thinker Xenophanes, given his deep concern with proper ritual behaviour as well as decorous narrative. What we can see, then, is a widespread preoccupation with a simple question: How could humans possibly want to worship toiling gods? Deities surely should have it better than that.

---

[39] López-Ruiz 2010: 23–47 discusses several different models for the spread of cosmogonic narrative in the Iron Age Mediterranean, including international commerce and life in bilingual families. She argues that shared ideas and stories passed to Greece from the Northern Levant, but while this is attractive in principle, we cannot exclude other pathways of transmission.

CHAPTER 13

Influence and Inheritance
Linguistics and Formulae between Greece
and the Ancient Near East

Sylvie Vanséveren

Scholars have long sought to illuminate the background to Greek literature and myth by two types of comparison, one based on the notion of genetic kinship and its Indo-European heritage, the other on derivation or diffusion from Near Eastern cultures.[1] This field of research is concerned with matters both small and large, from single words and expressions to parts of stories, even entire narratives and their underlying concepts. These approaches, when pursued in isolation, lead to apparently irreducible results and present quite contrasting points of view.[2] From a methodological perspective, there are many questions about the criteria we can use to identify the interplay of contacts and influences between the Greek and Eastern worlds.

In this chapter, I will focus on the role of comparison in evaluating the probative significance of linguistic features shared between traditions, in terms both of their form and their meaning. In the first section, I will examine the basic principles of comparison, discussing some phrases which are often taken as key examples in discussions weighing the value of the Indo-European and the Near Eastern material. In the second, I will concentrate on one specific example in Homeric Greek (λοιμοῖο βαρείας χεῖρας *Il.* 1.97). This expression has been defined by M. L. West as a 'semiticism' and compared to the expression 'hand of god' found in several Near Eastern sources, in relation to ideas of heaviness and illness. As I will show, the Greek expression must be studied for itself as an integral part of the narrative, i.e., as an element involved in the construction of the narrative. Similarly, the Oriental data must be considered in detail.

---

[1] See, for example, Burkert 1992, West 1997 and the references given below (note 7). For the sake of simplicity, I retain the standard terms 'Near East', 'Near Eastern', 'Oriental' etc., although they are quite artificial: cf., for example, van Dongen 2008, van Dongen 2014.
[2] See Metcalf 2015a: 223 n. 4 for an example, and the Introduction to this volume.

This kind of linguistic/thematic parallel must therefore be thoroughly contextualised in order for us properly to evaluate West's claim.

Linguistic features are indeed at the core of the matter in several previous studies, pertaining to the question of borrowing and diffusion from some Indo-European and non-Indo-European languages into Greek. According to Watkins, 'it is linguistic comparison – comparative linguistics – which is the source of the distinction, the discrimination between areal similarities and genetic similarities'.[3] The comparative method relies on the principle of correspondences in form and meaning, and it is based on singular details: etymology, morphological characteristics, choice of meaningful words, specific narrative devices, and expression of particular concepts or ideas.[4]

This method can lead to positive demonstrations of direct influence, as Watkins showed with regard to the Greek word δέπας, which refers to a cup but also to the vessel used by the Sun in its night journey eastward.[5] The comparison is first between Greek and Anatolian, which show parallel formulae (Hitt. *šarā uwa- arunaz . . . nepiši*, Gr. εἰσανιέναι, εἰσαναβαίνειν ἐξ Ὠκεανοῖο . . . οὐρανόν 'to come up to the sky from Ocean'), related to the Sun or the Dawn rising from the sea and going up into heaven. Besides the expression οὐρανὸν εἰσαναβαίνειν, Greek poets also have δέπας εἰσαναβαίνω 'to come up to a bowl', which Watkins explained as a loan from Luw. **dapi*, CAELUM. The Luwian sign has the shape of a bowl and the image of the sky is then that of an inverted bowl. Thus, he concluded, the image can explain how the Greek word for 'bowl' comes from the Luwian word for 'sky, heaven'.

Inversely, negative results are also possible, as with the case of the alleged parallels between the Homeric expression ἦρα (φέρειν) 'to bring satisfaction' and Hittite *warri eš-* 'to help': the latter phrase is part of a productive system (cf. the derivatives *warrišša-* 'to help, to come to help', *warrae-* 'to come to help') and is especially used in contexts with a military semantic specificity. On the other hand, this connotation is absent in Greek, where the archaic ἦρα can be replaced by the more recent χάριν.[6] This parallel was not the result of derivation or, if it was, the derivation was so ancient as to lie beyond the cultural memory of the Greeks.

---

[3] Watkins 2001: 59 ('the power of the comparative method lies in its sensitivity to similarity due both to genetic filiation and areal diffusion alike') and 63 ('it is linguistic comparison – comparative linguistics – which is the source of the distinction, the discrimination between areal similarities and genetic similarities').

[4] Cf. Katz 2005: esp. 26–7.   [5] Watkins 2007.

[6] García-Ramón 2006, García-Ramón 2011: 89–90.

Taking this as our methodological principle, a study of individual details should allow us to identify genetic inheritance or diffusion (or at least to distinguish between the two), though sometimes other possibilities – independent developments, and universals – may remain. Nonetheless, conclusions will often depend on the methodological perspective that is adopted through (or before) the analysis – as illustrated below by short examples.[7]

One example where diffusion of morphological features has been suggested relates to the use of particular suffixes, such as the imperfective *-sk-* suffix in the Ionic dialect in Homer and East Ionic, or *-yo-* for the patronymic adjective in Aeolic. These suffixes are also found in Anatolian languages (imperfectives in *-ske-* in Hittite, *-za-* in Luwian; patronymic adjectives in *-ya-* in Luwian). Scholars have argued that these elements were transferred from Anatolian into Greek, through East Ionic and Aeolic respectively,[8] but this case is now widely rejected, because these linguistic features can be understood as archaisms developed within the Greek language itself, which would make the hypothesis of an external source unnecessary.[9] The same issue arises when phrases in Greek find parallels in both other Indo-European and also Near Eastern languages. Emblematic expressions such as 'broad sky', 'broad earth', and 'broad sea', are regularly taken as examples of borrowing from Akkadian into Greek:

- 'broad earth': Akk. *erṣetu šuddultu, erṣetu rapaštu*; Gr. εὐρεῖα χθών
  (Ved. *kṣā́m ... pr̥thvī́m*, Av. *zą̇m pərəθβīm*)
- 'broad heaven': Akk. *šamû rapšūtu*, Gr. οὐρανὸν εὐρύν; Hitt. AN-*iš palḫa-*
  (Ved. *urú ... antarikṣa-*)
- 'broad sea': Akk. *tâmtu rapaštu*, Gr. εὐρέα πόντον
  (Ved. *ápaḥ ... pr̥thvī́ḥ*, Av. *āpō ... pərəθβīš*)

Here, the existence of analogous expressions in other Indo-European languages has the consequence that the Near Eastern parallels can be seen as unnecessary or superfluous.[10] From the point of view of the Indo-

---

[7] Literature about the methodological issues is abundant. For some recent works, among others (with references to previous studies), see Noegel 2007, Kelly 2008, Rutherford 2009, Haubold 2013a, López-Ruiz 2014a, Metcalf 2015a, Rollinger 2015, Currie 2016. See also the Introduction to this volume.
[8] Watkins 2001: 58.
[9] Hajnal 2018: 2046: 'the assumption of an Anatolian interference is not necessary, because there is a plausible explanation for the East Ionic epic *sk*-iteratives within the Greek language itself'. For detailed studies on the Greek and Hittite data, see Daues 2009, who concludes, on the basis of the value of the forms and their uses, that independent developments are possible.
[10] Cf. García-Ramón 2011: 91–5, for whom comparisons with Akkadian are unfounded ('grundlos', 91) and unnecessary ('unnötig', 95).

European comparative method, phrases can be etymologically connected or not, since form can evolve while preserving meaning. For example, in the case of Gr. εὐρέα πόντον and Ved. *ápaḥ ... pṛthvîḥ*, the words are not etymologically related, but the whole expression refers to the same image of the sea seen as broad.[11] One may of course ask what particular conception is relevant here, since the 'broadness' of the earth, the sky or the sea can be a quite general and common idea, but the existence of an Indo-European parallel considerably weakens the case that this expression was derived from Akkadian. Caution of this sort must be exercised in the other direction as well: the traditional Indo-European identity of a well-established and -evidenced formula such as 'swift horse(s)' (Ved. *āśúm áśvam*, Av. *āsu.aspa-*, Gr. ὠκέες ἵπποι, and also OEng. *swifta mearth*, OI. *eich lúaith*) has been doubted despite the etymological connection between the Greek, Vedic and Avestan formulae, since being swift is a general characteristic of horses.[12] Though it is tempting to suggest a link, there is nothing in this phrase that must be defined as an 'Indo-European touch' rather than an independently occurring feature. The comparative method should allow us, therefore, when looking at the Near Eastern material, to judge where the parallels are indeed cases of borrowing, and not simply independent developments or universals.

Specific concepts and metaphorical expressions could be better candidates to define the 'touch', but, here too, the question of origin can often be a difficult one. The image of the night wearing a spangled veil, studied at length by J. Katz,[13] is an illustrative case. This concept is found widely distributed in Greek, behind or informing images where the night 'hides' the world and its people, as in νυκτὶ καλύψας 'having shrouded with darkness' (*Il.* 5.23); ἀμφὶ δὲ ὄσσε κελαινὴ νὺξ ἐκάλυψεν 'the dark night shrouded his eyes' (*Il.* 5.310, for a dying hero); ἡ ποικιλείμων νὺξ ἀποκρύψει φάος 'the night in a starry robe will conceal his brightness' (Aesch. *Prom.* 24); μελάμπεπλος δὲ Νὺξ ἀσείρωτον ζυγοῖς / ὄχημ' ἔπαλλεν 'black-robed Night drove furiously the chariot / drawn by a yoked pair' (Eur. *Ion* 1150–1). The concept has been compared to Near Eastern data (the star-spangled garment of Babylonian deities and the representation of the starry sky),[14] but is also found in other Indo-European traditions (Latin *nox quando mediis signis praecincta uolabit* (Ennius 414 Skutsch),

---

[11] Watkins 1995: 43.
[12] Cf. Matasović 1996: 72–4. See also Katz 2000: 360–2, Platte 2017: 7–10 for *$h_1ōkewes\ h_1ekwōs$ as a figura etymologica 'the swift swifties'. If the name of the 'horse' itself is the 'swift one', the speed can indeed be seen as an inherent characteristic of the horse.
[13] Katz 2000.   [14] West 1997: 579–80.

'when the night surrounded by constellations will fly'; Iranian *vaŋhana-stəhrpaēsah-* 'star-spangled garment'), and even elsewhere, far beyond Indo-European and Near Eastern cultures. The image is impressive and clearly metaphorical but, again, nothing can be concluded about a possible Oriental 'origin' of this Greek conception of the night.

We come now to the central topic of this chapter, the Greek phrase λοιμοῖο βαρείας χεῖρας (*Il.* 1.97), which has been compared by Martin West to the expression 'hand of god' in several Near Eastern sources.[15] It finds no correspondence in other Indo-European languages. The question is thus slightly different from that posed by the previous examples, where we had to weigh evidence in both directions, and can thus be seen as a particular test case. Even without considering a possible Near Eastern origin, the reading of *Iliad* 1.97 has long been a source of controversy. While modern editions generally adopt the reading of the third-century BCE critic Aristarchus (a), the 'vulgate' tradition has another text (b):

(a) οὐδ' ὅ γε πρὶν Δαναοῖσιν ἀεικέα λοιγὸν ἀπώσει
πρίν γ' ἀπὸ πατρὶ φίλῳ δόμεναι ἑλικώπιδα κούρην

'he will not remove the unseemly devastation from the Danaans
until they give back the bright-eyed girl to her father'

(b) οὐδ' ὅ γε πρὶν λοιμοῖο βαρείας χεῖρας ἀφέξει
πρίν γ' ἀπὸ πατρὶ φίλῳ δόμεναι ἑλικώπιδα κούρην

'he will not withhold his heavy hands from the pestilence
until they give back the bright-eyed girl to her father'

The reading of Aristarchus – which is not found in the MSS, but which the scholia tell us was in the 'city' edition of Massilia and the edition of the scholar Rhianus – is generally preferred by modern scholars from the syntactic point of view, making Δαναοῖσιν the implicit subject of δόμεναι in the following verse (which would otherwise need to be supplied from the context).[16] Another argument in favour of this reading is that (b) as translated above would make no sense,[17] while understanding the expression differently, viz. with λοιμοῖο as a possessive genitive ('he will not withdraw the heavy hands of the plague'), involves a kind of

---

[15] West 1997: 223.
[16] Cf. Leaf 1900: 11, followed for example by Latacz *et al.* 2000: 63. Anyway, line 98 (πρίν γ' ἀπὸ πατρὶ φίλῳ δόμεναι ἑλικώπιδα κούρην) remains ambiguous, since Agamemnon is the only figure responsible for the situation and he alone has to give back the girl, not all the Greeks.
[17] Leaf 1900: 11 *ad* 1.97.

personification which is both very un-Homeric[18] and inelegant.[19] Moreover, the usual Homeric formula is λοιγὸν ἀμύνω, which refers to the desperate military situation of the Greeks as a consequence of Achilles' anger,[20] so Aristarchus' reading is also consistent with the fact that the wrath of Apollo and the anger of Achilles are parallel causes of the Greek army's destruction. Finally, this more traditional phrasing at *Il.* 1.456 (ἤδη νῦν Δαναοῖσιν ἀεικέα λοιγὸν ἄμυνον 'now remove the unseemly devastation from the Danaans') would echo Aristarchus' version at the end of the episode, when Chryses asks the god to stop the plague.

This does not leave much in favour of the vulgate reading, which nonetheless has some proponents. For instance, Chantraine adduces in its support the expression θανάτοιο βαρείας χεῖρας 'the heavy hands of death' (*Il.* 21.548),[21] with a personification of death attested elsewhere in the *Iliad* (14.231). A different argument, and the one with which we are mostly concerned here, is put forward by West, who uses Near Eastern comparanda to identify a 'Semitic idiom by which a pestilence (or other affliction) is described as the hand of a god, which lies upon the sufferer or sufferers and may be perceived as heavy'.[22] The reading λοιμοῖο βαρείας χεῖρας would thus be a 'striking Semiticism' and the reading to be retained against Aristarchus' more banal variant. But to see if West is right, we have to examine, firstly, the Oriental material at greater length and in its own context.

The expression 'hand of god(s)' is indeed frequent and typical in Akkadian sources, as well as in the Old Testament, at El Amarna, and Ugarit. Several examples have been collected by West. In the Neo-Assyrian diĝir-šà-dab₍₅₎-ba prayers, the hand of the god is said to be powerful (*dannu, kabtu*): l. 33 *dan-na-at* ŠU-*ka a-ta-mar še-ret-ka* 'your hand is terrible, I have experienced your punishment' (transl. Lambert).[23] In *Ludlul bēl nēmeqi* III 1, the supplicant complains *kab-ta-at* ŠU-*su ul a-le-'i-i na-šá-šá* 'his hand was so heavy I could not bear it' (transl. Annus and

---

[18] Leaf 1900: 11 *ad* 1.97; cf. also Pulleyn 2000: 151–2 ('will not keep his heavy hands from [inflicting] plague').
[19] Kirk 1985: 63.
[20] Nagy 1979: 74–6. Achilles is usually linked with the idea of removing the λοιγός (*Il.* 1.341, 16.32, 16.75, 16.80, 18.450).
[21] Chantraine 1956: 103–5. Incidentally, Chantraine reminds us that this precise personification of λοιμός is put forward by Leaf in Soph. *OT* 27 in order to explain *Il.* 21.548. Cf. also de Lamberterie 1990: 528.
[22] West 1997: 223; West 2011: 85, 383.
[23] Lambert 1974: 274. See now the comprehensive edition of Jaques 2015: 64–108.

Lenzi).[24] In *Atrahasīs*,[25] the god Enlil sends a disease (*murṣu*) against humanity, then drought and famine, and finally the flood. The disease, drought and famine will end if the humans honour the god Namtar who 'will lift his hand' (I 384 = 399, II ii 15 *li-ša-aq-qí-il qá-as-sú* '(Namtar) will lift his hand'; I 410, II ii 28 *ú-ša-aq-qí-il qá-as-su* 'he lifted his hand'). In texts from the Mari archive (*ARM* 26),[26] the expression is used about a plague: the 'hand of god' no longer strikes the land, (*ú-ul* [*ú-la-ap-p*]*í-it* 260, 7), or has become calm (*qa-at* [DI[ĜIR]-*li*]*m*...[*i*]*t-tu-uḫ* 260, 5–6; same phrase at 265, 30]). It is also used to describe the illness of individuals,[27] including in oracular contexts.[28] Moreover, the expression 'hand of Nergal' is found once in the Amarna Letters in reference to a plague that afflicts the land:[29] *EA* 35, 10–15 'Behold, the hand of Nergal is now on my country; he has slain all the men of my country, and there is not a (single) copper-worker. So, my brother, do not be concerned'; 35–9 'My brother, do not be concerned that your message has stayed three years in my country, for the hand of Nergal is in my country and in my house. There was a young wife of mine that now, my brother, is dead' (transl. Moran). In the Old Testament, the hand of Yahweh is said to be heavy[30] and to send tumours: 1 *Samuel* 5:6 'And the hand of Yahweh was heavy upon the people of Ashdod, and he terrified them and afflicted them with piles' (transl. West); *Exodus* 9:3 'now the hand of Yahweh is about to be upon your livestock which is in your fields, upon the horses, the asses, the camels, the cattle, and the sheep, a very grievous plague' (transl. Roberts); *Exodus* 9:15 'for now I should have put forth my hand and smitten you and your people with the plague' (transl. Roberts). In these last two passages, the hand of God is closely associated with the concept of plague, disease (*deber*), and they are sometimes interpreted almost as equivalents, since the 'hand of god' is connected with the power of God, manifested

---

[24] Annus and Lenzi 2010: 23, 38. See now also Oshima 2014: 3–14.
[25] Lambert and Millard 1969: 68–9, 70–1, 76–7.
[26] Durand 1988: 562. French translations from Durand.
[27] Durand 1988: 222, 299–300 (letter 83, 9–10 *te-re-tum ša e-pu-šu qa-at iš₈-tár-ra-da-an* 'Les présages que j'ai faits (veulent dire) "Main d'Ištar de Radan"'; letter 136, 8 *ú-ul qa-at* [ᵈX-*ma*] 'Il ne s'agit point de la "main" du dieu').
[28] Durand 1988: 223 (letter 84, 8–10 1-*šu a-na šu-*[*lum be-lí-ia*] *e-pu-úš-ma te-re*[-*tim*] *ù a-na qa-at i-lu-tim e-pu-úš-ma* 'une première fois, relativement au salut [en général] de mon Seigneur, j'avais pris les présages. Je [les] ai faits (aussi) relativement à la "Main de la Divinité"').
[29] Moran 1992: 107–9. Moran translates ᴰMAŠ.MAŠ with Nergal; another possibility is the West-Semitic reading Rašpu/Rešep, god of pestilence and fertility, cf. Hellbing 1979: 22.
[30] Hebr. כבד 'to be heavy', cf. Akk. *kabtu*, Ug. *kbd*.

through plague and disease.[31] The connection between the hand of god and disease is particularly clear in the Assyrian and Babylonian omens, where the expression directly refers to the illness ('hand of x', where x is a god or a demon). Examples are numerous.[32] As in Mari, the phrase is also regularly used in omen contexts in Akkadian.[33]

To these data, we may add another letter from Mari,[34] where the 'hand of Ištar-radana' as a sickness is said to be heavy: *ARM* 10, 87 16–19: [*ù*] *qa-at iš₈-tár-ra-da-na ù be-lí i-de ki-ma qa-at iš₈-tár-ra-da-na e-li-ia da-an-na-at* 'C'est bien la main d'Ištar-radana. Or, mon seigneur sait que la main d'Ištar-radana est plus forte que moi/est lourde sur moi' (transl. Dossin). Finally, a letter from Ugarit tells about a plague that is devastating the land, *RS* 4.475: 'also the "hand of a god" is here, for death (here) is very strong' (transl. Pardee).[35] The 'hand of god' is also attested in Hittite, in the dream of Muršili II, where the king explains that he lost his ability to speak because he has been terrified by a violent storm. Later then, he had bad dreams: *KBo* 4.2 iii 46–7 (*CTH* 486)[36] *nu-mu-kán za-az-ḫi-⸢i⸣ an-da* ŠU DINGIR-*LIM a-ar-aš* KAxU-*iš-ša-mu-kán ta-pu-ú-ša pa-it* 'in a dream, the hand of the god touched me and my mouth went sideways (i.e. ceased to function)'.[37]

To sum up, the elements are quite precise and specific in the Near Eastern texts: the expression 'hand of god' has a fundamentally negative

---

[31] Roberts 1971: 249–50, Blair 2009: 155. As shown by Roberts, non-prophetic contexts are to be distinguished from prophetic contexts (with expressions like 'the hand of god came upon me/him', 'the hand of god was strong upon me/him' [with חזק 'to be strong'], e.g., *Ezek.* 1:3, 3:14, 33:22; *Jer.* 15:17; *Isa.* 8:11): the last appears to be a secondary development of the general use attested in relation to illness and plague. Cf. also Malamat 1998: 142–6. *Deber* (and *rešep*) is in some passages interpreted as the personification of demons, although this remains debated: cf. Caquot 1956, Schretter 1974: 131–41, Blair 2009, Münnich 2013: 215–37.

[32] For examples, see *CAD* s. v. *qātu* 1e; Scurlock and Andersen 2005. Cf. also Labat 1951, van der Toorn 1985: 77–80, Heeßel 2007, Steinert 2012: 219–22, Steinert 2014: 88–90.

[33] Labat 1951: xxiii, Freedman 1998: 30–1 (tablet 1, 79 DIŠ URU GURUŠ.MEŠ-*šú* ḪUL URU BI ŠU DINGIR-*šú* 'If a city's young men are evil, that city [will suffer from] the hand of its god', transl. Freedman.

[34] Cited by Roberts 1971: 246–7. See also Dossin 1967: 132–3. Another example given by Roberts is to be ruled out: *ARM* 3, 61, 10–12 DINGIR-*lum a-na a-ka-al* GU₄.ḪI.A *u₃ a-wi-lu-tim qa-ta-am iš-ku-un* has rather the turn of phrase *qāta šakānu* 'to start, to take up', cf. *CAD*, s.v. *šakānu* 5a and Kupper 1950: 82–3: 'le dieu s'est mis à dévorer boeufs et gens'.

[35] Pardee 1987: 68–9 for the text; cf. Dhorme 1933: 235–7, Dhorme 1934: 395–6 for the text and a new translation 'la main des dieux est ici, car la peste est très forte', Albright 1941: 43–6 ('and the hand of the god is here, for the pestilence is exceeding sore'). The letter is cited by Roberts 1971: 247–8, 'and the hand of the god(s) is very strong here like death'. In this last translation, the adjective (*'azzu* 'strong') is connected with *yadu* ('hand') rather than with *môtu* ('death'), and so the connection he makes is unjustified.

[36] See Görke 2015, and also Lebrun 1985, Mouton 2007: 161–4 (text n. 41).

[37] See Beckman 1983: 185.

connotation, and is typically used without an adjective in relation to illness and plague perceived as a divine punishment (Mari, Ugarit, Amarna, *Atraḫasīs*, Old Testament). The 'heavy hand of god' is closely connected with the power of the deity in its negative manifestations (and, more rarely, positive ones, but in those cases with another adjective, as in the prophetic passages of the Bible). In prayers and *Ludlul bēl nēmeqi*, the hand of the god is said to be heavy upon an individual. It is not specifically associated with illness, but with a general state of physical and mental suffering, social adversity and divine hostility.[38] Furthermore, the use of body parts in a figurative way is a case of linguistic universals, the hand being commonly associated with the idea of acting and power, while the conceptualisations and expressions may be culturally specific.[39] From a comparative perspective, we may here pinpoint as a singular detail the fact that a precise concept (illness, plague) is connected to a particular expression ('hand of god', without adjective) in the Near Eastern material.

The connection between the Near Eastern 'hand of god' and the Homeric λοιμοῖο βαρείας χεῖρας seems at first sight fairly striking. Several facts seem to support it: firstly, the Homeric expression is isolated within early Greek epic; secondly, the image is impressive; thirdly, the god is Apollo, closely related to Near Eastern plague gods like Rešep, Nergal or Yarri,[40] all gods associated with bows and arrows, and they send disease and epidemics. The parallels may be tabulated thus:

God	Rešep	Apollo
plague	plague	λοιμός
'hand of god'	'hand of Rešep'	λοιμοῖο βαρείας χεῖρας

The analogy is not precise across all these figures, of course, and the case is complicated by the fact that Apollo also recalls the Vedic archer god Rudra. This figure is accompanied by a mole or a rat; his arrows cause fever, cough and poisoning; he is also a healer. These characteristics are expressed in the Vedic hymns focusing on the benevolent side of Rudra and on his healing hand.[41] This clouds the issue and raises in another way

---

[38] van der Toorn 1985: 58–67, 122–4.
[39] Studies for Akkadian (U. Steinert), Hittite (S. Görke), Ugaritic (E. Martin), Hebrew (A. Wagner), Greek (J. Stenger) have been the subject of the collected volume edited by Müller and Wagner 2014. Cf. also for 'hand' Steinert 2012: 219–222, De Martino and Imparati 1998, Gross 1970, Norin 1997.
[40] Schretter 1974, Faraone 1992: 125–7, Münnich 2013.
[41] *RV* 2.33.7 'Where, o Rudra, is that merciful hand of yours, which is healing remedy, the bearer away of malady that comes from the gods? You should now be indulgent toward me, o bull'; 10a 'Worthily you bear the arrows and the bow and worthily the sacrificial neck ornament of all forms';

the question of the *origins* of a Greek or Indo-European divine figure connected to disease and healing.[42]

However, if λοιμοῖο βαρείας χεῖρας is to be understood as a semiticism, the comparison involves form *and* meaning. These are equally important, for the concept and the way it is expressed will be as relevant as singular details. Only this can allow us to distinguish between independent parallels, diffusional phenomena, or a common origin. Possibilities of adaptations and transformations still exist, of course, but the parallel should reflect some trace of its source. Another key point is to determine whether the parallel is significant for the Homeric text, whether it leads to the most persuasive interpretation of the passage, and whether the passage can be understood without reference to the parallel, i.e., by appealing to the structure and semantic potential of Homeric epic alone.

Finally, then, we return to the Homeric material. West translates *Iliad* 1.97 thus: 'nor will Apollo sooner withdraw the heavy hands of plague, than . . .' On the parallel with the 'hand of god', he comments, 'this is the equivalent of Apollo's removing his heavy hands in the *Iliad* passage'. We see here a slight slippage from Apollo to λοιμός, as if λοιμοῖο βαρείας χεῖρας were the god himself. This may seem pedantic, but this imprecision in West's summary, probably induced by the comparison itself, has important implications for the interpretation of the phrase: if the 'heavy hands' are Apollo's, then Chantraine's comparison with θανάτοιο βαρείας χεῖρας is weakened, since the deity is not actually denoted within the expression λοιμοῖο βαρείας χεῖρας – instead, the 'hands' belong to the 'plague'.

The Greek syntagm βαρείας χεῖρας is quite common in Homeric epic, and belongs to an extended formulaic system comprising the different adjectives for the hand. But, as a matter of fact, the specific expression 'hand of god' is not attested in Homeric Greek, and the hands of the gods are never said to be heavy, while those of heroes are.[43] The hands of the gods are associated with protection (*Il.* 4.249 ὄφρα ἴδητ' αἴ κ' ὕμμιν ὑπέρσχῃ χεῖρα Κρονίων 'so you may know if Kronos' son will hold his hand over you'; *Il.* 24.374 ἀλλ' ἔτι τις καὶ ἐμεῖο θεῶν ὑπερέσχεθε χεῖρα 'yet still there is some god who has held his hand above me'), or with threats and violent acts (*Il.* 1.567 ὅτε κέν τοι ἀάπτους χεῖρας ἐφείω 'if I lay my unconquerable hands

---

14ab 'Might Rudra's lance avoid us. The hostile thought of the turbulent one, though great, shall go around us. Slacken the taut (bows) for our bounteous (patrons). Be merciful to our progeny and posterity, o munificent' (transl. Jamison and Brereton).

[42] Puhvel 1970: 372–3, Puhvel 1987: 58, 138, West 2007: 148.

[43] About the use and value of χείρ of gods and heroes in the Homeric epic, see Gross 1970 (with Near Eastern parallels), Stenger 2014: 169–73 for 'hand'.

upon you'; *Il.* 16.703–4 ἀπεστυφέλιξεν Ἀπόλλων / χείρεσσ' ἀθανάτῃσι 'Apollo battered him backward with his immortal hands'; 791–2 πλῆξεν δὲ μετάφρενον εὐρέε τ' ὤμω / χειρὶ καταπρηνεῖ 'he struck his back and his broad shoulders with a flat [stroke of the] hand').

The heroic hand is par excellence the instrument of holding an object (bow, spear) and refers to action (e.g., *Il.* 1.76–7 τοὶ γὰρ ἐγὼν ἐρέω· σὺ δὲ σύνθεο καί μοι ὄμοσσον / ἦ μέν μοι πρόφρων ἔπεσιν καὶ χερσὶν ἀρήξειν 'I will speak. But you, pay attention and swear to me that you will be willing to help me with words and hands'), essentially in military contexts (e.g., *Il.* 13.814 ἄφαρ δέ τε χεῖρες ἀμύνειν εἰσὶ καὶ ἡμῖν 'we too have hands to ward them off', *Il.* 15.741 τῷ ἐν χερσὶ φόως, οὐ μειλιχίη πολέμοιο 'the victory is in our hands, and not in softness in battle'; *Il.* 21.294 μὴ πρὶν παύειν χεῖρας ὁμοιίου πολέμοιο 'do not stop your hands from the battle'). Mortals lift their hands in prayers (e.g., *Il.* 1.351 χεῖρας ὀρεγνύς, *Il.* 7.130 χεῖρας ἀεῖραι, *Il.* 1.450 χεῖρας ἀνασχών) and take someone by the hand to be listened to (e.g., *Il.* 6.253 ἔν τ' ἄρα οἱ φῦ χειρὶ ἔπος τ' ἔφατ' ἔκ τ' ὀνόμαζε 'she clung to his hand and called him by name and spoke to him'; cf. 406, 485). Above all, the hand of heroes is related to the notion of physical power, notably in battles (μένος καὶ χεῖρες ἄαπτοι, μένος χειρῶν, βίη καὶ χεῖρες, κρατερός καὶ χερσὶ πεποιθώς).

Among the several epithets used of the hand, βαρύς refers to the notion of strength and power and also relates to the idea of heaviness and oppression.[44] The adjective refers to the hand as an agent, a potential danger in hostile or threatening actions[45] (*Il.* 1.219 ἦ καὶ ἐπ' ἀργυρέῃ κώπῃ σχέθε χεῖρα βαρεῖαν 'he spoke and laid his heavy hand on the silver sword hilt'; *Il.* 1.88–9 οὔ τις ἐμεῦ ζῶντος καὶ ἐπὶ χθονὶ δερκομένοιο / σοὶ κοίλῃς παρὰ νηυσὶ βαρείας χεῖρας ἐποίσει 'so long as I am alive and see the daylight on earth, no one shall lay his heavy hands on you beside the hollow ships'). The adjective is therefore associated with the idea of activity, violence and the consequences that follow. These characteristics constitute singular details specific to the Homeric expression and its usage, something which deserves to be taken into consideration alongside the Semitic material.

Bringing together the different elements involved here, we can now attempt to judge the relevance of the comparison between the Semitic

---

[44] de Lamberterie 1990: 525–38, especially 328 for an example where βαρεῖαι χεῖρες is parallel to χερσὶ στιβαρῇσι 'strong hands' and has a positive connotation (*Il.* 23.686–7). The negative idea of oppression is found, for example with ἄτη (dreadful error), ἔρις (terrible quarrel), κακότης (burden of evil), ὀδύνη (unbearable pain), and φθόγγος (sad, frightening sound/voice).

[45] Eide 1986: 7–10.

'hand of god' expressions and the Homeric λοιμοῖο βαρείας χεῖρας. On the one hand, the singular detail in the Semitic expressions is the association of the god's (heavy) hand with disease. This constitutes the 'Oriental touch', where the way of saying (the expression 'hand of god') and the meaning (disease, epidemic) are of equal importance. However, neither of these features is reflected on the Greek side: the heavy hands are those of heroes, not gods, and we do not find the expression 'hand of god' related elsewhere to the idea of disease. These differences considerably weaken the comparison between the Semitic and the Greek expressions. There may certainly be links between Apollo and the Oriental gods connected to pestilence, but this does not in itself illuminate the origin or meaning of the Greek expression. As a result, reading the Homeric verse in the light of the Near Eastern phrase is not persuasive or compelling, as no salient elements can be highlighted to support the connection.

On the other hand, the peculiarity in Homeric Greek is the use of a typical heroic formula about the plague sent by Apollo, and this requires explanation. The application of the 'heavy hand' expression to λοιμός is certainly meaningful and consistent with the epic narrative and context, in which context we should look for its origin. After all, the plague episode begins with a νοῦσον κακήν (*Il.* 1.10) sent by the god. A few lines later, Achilles uses πόλεμος and λοιμός together to speak about the two causes of death in the Greek army (*Il.* 1.60–1 εἴ κεν θάνατόν γε φύγοιμεν / εἰ δὴ ὁμοῦ πόλεμός τε δαμᾷ καὶ λοιμὸς Ἀχαιούς 'if we can escape death, if truly war and plague together shall bring low Achaeans', transl. Pulleyn). Apollo is acting in a hostile way towards the Greeks, bringing destruction in the army like an enemy. The Homeric λοιμός is thus a νοῦσος and at the same time shares some characteristics with the λοιγός, which is typically a military destruction. This kind of mixture seems consistent with the combination proposed above for the formula βαρείας χεῖρας.

At this stage, we still have to choose between the readings of Aristarchus and the vulgate tradition. To help us, the table below summarises the evidence concerning the god Apollo and the hero Achilles, in relation to the λοιγός and λοιμός arising as consequences of their respective anger:

Apollo	Achilles
μῆνις	μῆνις
plague	withdrawal
λοιγός, λοιμός	λοιγός
(Ar. ἀεικέα λοιγὸν ἀπώσει)	
vulg. λοιμοῖο βαρείας χεῖρας	βαρεῖα χείρ of heroes

As we can see, Achilles' anger is parallel to Apollo's and, like the god's, is called μῆνις.[46] This anger is manifested on the divine side by the sending of pestilence and on the mortal by the withdrawal of the hero. The consequences are similar and lead to a λοιγός – or a λοιμός that is at the same time a λοιγός in the case of Apollo, as it destroys the Greek army. From there, the Aristarchean reading ἀεικέα λοιγὸν ἀπώσει keeps the idea of λοιγός, while using a verb with a warlike connotation.[47] In the vulgate reading, the phrase βαρείας χεῖρας is taken from the mortal sphere and applied to λοιμός, which is therefore also embedded in the context of war. We can also recall the expression θανάτοιο βαρείας χεῖρας, which is perhaps modelled on λοιμοῖο βαρείας χεῖρας, and which appears, indeed, in a context involving λοιγός: the devastation that falls on the Trojans once Achilles has returned to combat (*Il.* 21.138, 250 Τρώεσσι δὲ λοιγὸν ἀλάλκοι, about Scamandros wanting to protect the Trojans from the massacre). A moment later, Achilles is in front of Troy and causes panic. Apollo wants to preserve the Trojans (21.538–9 . . . ἵνα λοιγὸν ἀμύναι (*v.l.* ἀλάλκοι) '. . . to repel [*v.l.* ward off] destruction from the Trojans') and just after he sends the hero Agenor and guards him ὅπως θανάτοιο βαρείας χεῖρας ἀλάλκοι 'to ward off the heavy hands of death' (548). The acts of Apollo thus establish here a link between λοιγός and θανάτοιο βαρείας χεῖρας. So, although Aristarchus' reading is consistent with the language of Homeric epic, the unique expression found in the vulgate responds to the primacy, and then the extension, of Achilles' anger in the *Iliad* as it is deployed to describe Apollo's opening intervention in the poem.

We have tried in this chapter to examine the question of the Near Eastern influence on archaic Greece by taking a narrow path, that is, by focusing on some single expressions and formulae. The comparative method attempts to identify singular details and characteristic elements, which should make it possible to identify inheritance and influence. The way things are said (the form) and the values associated with them (the meaning) are crucial and interdependent elements for analysis. Several examples were discussed to show the importance and interdependence of these two elements for this kind of study. The second part of the chapter examined the Greek expression λοιμοῖο βαρείας χεῖρας to see if the touted relationship with Near Eastern 'hand of god' phraseology was

---

[46] See Nagy 1979: 73–7, 142–4, Muellner 1996: 96–102, Scodel 2007.
[47] The use of the verb ἀπωθέω at *Il.* 1.97 is quite significant, since it generally appears in passages referring to battles, and has a violent connotation (cf. for example, *Il.* 8.96; 533, 13.367, 15.503, 18.13 and the notable counterexample of *Il.* 24.508).

actually useful in explaining the origin and meaning of the Homeric text. But in terms of both form and meaning, the link is missing. The broad context that implicates Apollo does not seem sufficient to go beyond a surface convergence that remains vague and imprecise. Since the Semitic data does not ultimately shed light on the Greek expression, we turned, finally, to epic diction to try to understand it. This made it possible for us to highlight an internal cohesion linking λοιμοῖο βαρείας χεῖρας (and θανάτοιο βαρείας χεῖρας) to the concept of λοιγός, and thus to account for the transferral of the image of the heroes' 'heavy hands', natural in that context, to the hostile actions of Apollo in Book 1. Ultimately, then, a singular detail can also be used to clarify an expression in the context of epic diction. We therefore have good reason not to leap to external parallels as the best explanation for Homeric textual phenomena without examining the totality of the evidence, on both sides of the equation, in their own contexts first.

CHAPTER 14

Fate and Authority in Mesopotamian Literature and the Iliad

Angus M. Bowie

In *Iliad* 16, when Zeus suggests that he might save his son Sarpedon, Hera replies (16.440–3):[1]

> Dread son of Kronos, what a thing that is to say! Do you intend to rescue from woeful death a mortal man long ago destined to his fate? Do it, but not all of us other gods will be pleased with you.

When Zeus orders the gods to keep out of the battle in *Iliad* 8, he threatens any who disobey with dread punishment and boasts of his power over them (8.19–27):

> If all of you, gods and goddesses, were to hang a golden chain from heaven and take hold of it, you would not drag from heaven to earth Zeus the highest counsellor, not even if you were to make a great effort. But whenever I really wanted to pull on it myself, I would draw you up along with the earth and sea; then I would tie the chain about the pinnacle of Olympus and everything would be left in mid-air. So far am I above gods and men.

In these two passages the relationship between Zeus and fate, and the question of Zeus's authority amongst the gods, are brought starkly to the fore. Both topics have been much discussed, and it is the purpose of this chapter to conduct a cross-cultural comparison of the *Iliad*'s ideas on them with what is to be found in Mesopotamian literature, in order to gain some new perspectives on how the two traditions treat these questions.[2] This is, then, a simple exercise in 'comparative religion' with a relatively narrow scope. No claims are made therefore about the genealogical or historical relationships between the two, and there is no intention to attempt to give a full account of the problems of the concept of 'fate' or of its operation in

---

[1] Quotations are according to the *Oxford Classical Texts*; translations are my own.
[2] For a book-length application of this method, see Haubold 2013a. A small number of comparative remarks will also be made about Hittite ideas of fate.

the two cultures. Something similar could have been achieved by comparing Homer with other Greek writers, but a specific cross-cultural approach, whilst being more manageable, offers a greater disparity of material and may therefore illuminate in unexpected ways, giving a clearer sense of what is distinctive in the Homeric treatment.[3] There is of course an artificiality in comparing a poem which, while it has a long tradition behind it, dates from a particular time and context, with evidence from a highly disparate set of periods, places and genres, but the nature of the material available to us makes it hard to avoid this if one wishes to pursue a comparison of this kind.

We shall discuss fate first and then authority.

Fate

Mesopotamia

In discussing the Mesopotamian material, I shall for convenience concentrate largely on Sumerian literature,[4] noting some Akkadian equivalences since, apart from some significant differences to be noted below, there is a close correspondence between Sumerian and Akkadian texts, which share, for instance, a common eulogistic phraseology.[5]

The Sumerian word for 'fate' is 'nam-tar', literally 'a destiny decided'; the Akkadian *šīmtu* is a feminine noun from the verb *šiāmu*, 'to determine'.[6] This idea of determination is central to the operation of fate. The notion that gods, either individually or in groups, determine fates is a regular refrain throughout Sumerian literature.[7] This power lies

---

[3] In making this comparison between 'Greece' and 'the Near East' I am not implying that these are entirely separate entities, nor that either of them forms a block with unchanging geopolitical and chronological boundaries: against such ideas and the casual (or indeed any) use of the term 'Near East', see van Dongen 2014. For convenience too I use 'epic' very loosely.

[4] Unless indicated, Mesopotamian texts are Sumerian. Texts and translations are conveniently available in the *ETCSL*, whence the numerical references are taken. A selection of the texts is also available in Black et al. 2004. Translations of Akkadian texts (which are identified as such) are from Foster 2005, except where otherwise indicated. I am very grateful indeed to Christopher Metcalf for help with bibliography on Near Eastern matters.

[5] The relationships between Sumerian and Akkadian literature are highly complex; for a brief exposition, see Foster 2005: 78–84. On the rhetoric of the eulogies, see Metcalf 2015a.

[6] See, e.g., Lämmerhirt and Zgoll 2009: 146–7. Hittite NAM-*aš* and GUL/*gul-šu-u-wa-ar* similarly indicate the 'determining' of fate, see Schwemer 2009: 156, Waal 2019 (on the reading of the Hittite word and signs). Latin *fatum*, from *fari* 'say', is thus closer to this concept in origin than it is to Greek *moira* (see below), though in use it is similar to that of *moira*.

[7] See Lambert 1972, Oppenheim 1977, Rochberg-Halton 1982, Drewnowska and Sandowicz 2005, Lämmerhirt and Zgoll 2009 (with further bibliography in 153–5), Steinkeller 2017a.

particularly in the hands of the main gods, such as An and Enlil, but other gods have it in hymns in their honour, especially Inana, who 'rivals great An ... He dare not proceed against her command. Without Inana great An makes no decisions, and Enlil determines no destinies.'[8]

Fates are naturally decreed at the start of events or lives: before the gods were created, there were no fates decreed (*Enūma eliš* I 7–8, ed. Lambert 2013), sunrise is 'where the fates are decided' (*Gudea Cyl. A* xxvi 3). The idea of building a temple for Ningirsu is conceived 'on the day when in heaven and earth the fates had been decided',[9] and a 'fated brick' is moulded for the purpose.[10] When great gods or kings are born, a fate is decreed for them: Ninurta's mother tells Enlil to 'decide a great fate for the son who is your avenger!' (*Lipit-Eštar D*, 5–15), and King Sin-iqišam is an 'exalted lord, for whom a favourable destiny was determined while he was still in the good womb!'[11] Other entities, too, have their fates given them: Enki determines those of the cities of Sumer, Urim and Meluḫa (*Enki and the World Order*, 192–237). After a crucial battle, Ninurta determines the future fates for mountains and stones (*Lugale*, 411–18).[12] A fly helps Inana, and 'young lady Inana decreed the destiny of the fly: "in the beer-house, may ...... bronze vessels ...... for you"' (*Inana's Descent to the Netherworld*, 399–403). Plants (*Enki and Ninhursaga*, 198–219) and rivers (*Lugalbanda and the Anzud-bird*, 90–110) too receive their fates. The decreeing of fate is thus a way in which gods maintain orderly control of the universe.

A fate can be created for specific circumstances, as Marduk demands before fighting Tiamat and Qingu: 'convene an assembly, and proclaim for me an exalted destiny' (*Enūma eliš* II 158). Conversely, a good fate can be a reward for exceptional service. Nam-zid-tara, a *gudu*-priest, is rewarded by Enlil for a clever response (*Enlil and Nam-zid-tara*, 25–7), and king Šulgi as one who 'fitted out the holy barge' (*Šulgi R*, 64–70); in myth the Anzud

---

[8] *Inana C*, 1–17; cf. 109–14, 203–8, 264–71. So Nergal is told in *Šu-ilišu A*, 18–23 'you are the junior Enlil! It is in your power to determine destinies.' Cf. also Ištar, Inana's Akkadian equivalent, in *Hymn to Ištar*, 14 (Foster 2005: 86): 'she grasps in her hand the destinies of all that exists'; see vii–x for her importance; *Great Prayer to Ištar*, 18–24 (Foster 2005: 596). See also Metcalf 2015a: 33–49 (esp. 46f.).
[9] *Gudea Cyl. A* i 1–4; cf. *Enki and the World Order*, 89–99.
[10] *Gudea Cyl. A* i 10–16, v 2–10, vi 6–8, etc.; cf. *The Lament for Nibru*, 1–11, *Enki and Ninmah*, 1–11.
[11] *Sîn-iqišam A* 1–11. A more disabused view is taken in *The Instructions of Šuruppag*, 254: 'The wet-nurses in the women's quarters determine the fate of their lord.'
[12] See also the recently published Old Babylonian Sumerian version of *Adapa*, where Enki decrees the destiny of the South Wind (Cavigneaux 2014: 28, line 180; the text actually attributes the decreeing to the wind, which must be a small slip), and Cavigneaux's note *ad loc.* (33).

bird offers Lugalbanda the choice of a fate for his generous treatment of his nest (*Lugalbanda and the Anzud bird*, 90–100). A bad fate may be a punishment, as the male prostitute finds in the Akkadian *Descent of Ištar to the Netherworld* (103–8). In one case, a fate accompanies death: 'May Nanna decree your fate on the day of sleep' (*An Elegy on the Death of Nannaya*, 88–98). In hymns and prayers, the emphasis naturally tends to be on good fates, but in the Akkadian *Epic of Gilgameš*, a gloomier view of human fate is found,[13] in the idea that 'the doom of mortals' is death at a time the gods will not disclose.[14]

It is regularly stated that fate is unchangeable. When the flood is decreed, 'a decision that the seed of mankind is to be destroyed has been made. The verdict, the word of the divine assembly, cannot be revoked. The order announced by An and Enlil cannot be overturned' (*The Flood Story*, C18–28). Ninurta's orders are 'unalterable, his allotted fates are faithfully executed' (*Lugale*, 24–47), his 'fixing of destinies cannot be upset' (*Ur-Ninurta C*, 50–3), and Enlil is one 'whose utterances cannot be overturned! Nunamnir, whose decisions cannot be altered' (*Būr-Suen B*, 1–13). Mortals also fail to have fate changed, as in the case of King Naram-Suen who, when faced with the destruction of Agade, 'in order to change what had been inflicted (?) on him, tried to alter Enlil's pronouncement' (*Cursing of Agade*, 94–9): he failed.

However, there are cases where fate is changed, notably in the cases of the destruction of cities. The most striking example is the *Lament for Sumer and Urim*. This begins with the lines (1–3, 55):

> To overturn the appointed times, to obliterate the divine plans, the storms gather to strike like a flood. An, Enlil, Enki and Ninḫursaĝa have decided its fate – to overturn the divine powers of Sumer, to lock up the favourable reign in its home, to destroy the city.

The new fates replace the earlier, and the new fate is unchangeable: 'its fate cannot be changed. Who can overturn it? It is the command of An and Enlil. Who can oppose it?' (56–7). This change is explained later (366–9):

> Urim was indeed given kingship but it was not given an eternal reign. From time immemorial, since the Land was founded, until people multiplied, who has ever seen a reign of kingship that would take precedence for ever? The reign of its kingship had been long indeed but had to exhaust itself.

---

[13] Such speculation on fate is not in fact a regular feature of Mesopotamian epic.
[14] Cf. SBV x 59, 234, 320–2.

Similarly, but more pointedly, the chaos that ensued after the death of Ur-Nammu is explained as follows: 'because An had altered his holy words completely, ... and because, deceitfully, Enlil had completely changed the fate he decreed' (*Ur-Namma A*, 8–14). Inana's complaints are to no avail: '"if there are divine ordinances imposed on the Land, but they are not observed, there will be no abundance at the gods' place of sunrise"' (203–15); she can only compensate him with fame in future.[15] In some cases, after the destruction, fate can again be changed to a better future, as in the case of *The Lament for Nibru* (193–200):[16]

> Enlil who has decreed your fate has said, 'My city, you have placated my sacred heart towards you.' He has returned to you! ... True city, he has decreed your great fate and made your reign long!

What is noticeable here is that fate is a rather abstract entity. It has no corporeal existence.[17] In part, this is to do with the nature of much of the evidence: in works whose purpose is to praise gods, it is natural that they should be represented as in control, rather than relying on, say, old ladies with spindles. More popular literature presents a slightly different picture, as in the proverb, 'Fate is a dog – well able to bite. Like dirty rags, it clings, saying: "Who is my man? Let him know it."'[18]

Fate does have a physical, though not anthropomorphised,[19] existence in the few references to it as inscribed on tablets.[20] An writes a tablet for king Šulgi (*Šulgi D*, 53–60), and such references occur particularly (and naturally) in connection with Nisaba, goddess of accounting and scribal education,[21] and with her husband Haia, 'who holds the great tablets ...

---

[15] For fame as part of fate after death, cf. also *Ur-Namma A*, 217–33, *Inana and Šu-kale-tuda*, 290–310, and the Akkadian *Adapa and the South Wind* fr. D 12 (Foster 2005: 530).

[16] That the idea of changing fate was not necessarily viewed as problematic can be seen from the remark made by a scribe to a pupil in *E-dub-ba-a C*: 'Nisaba has placed in your hand the honour of being a teacher. For her, the fate determined for you will be changed and so you will be generously blessed' (60–72).

[17] The Fates are, however, personified in an Akkadian hymn marking the restoration of Ištar's cult-objects, in a list of gods who rejoice: 'May the Fates, goddesses of the land, be glad' (Foster 2005: 332, line 49).

[18] *Proverbs: Collection 2 + 6*: 11; cf. 'Fate is a cloth stretched out in the desert for a man. Fate is a raging storm blowing over the Land' (12–13).

[19] Though note the 'fate demon' in *A Man and his God* 120–9 'he eradicated the fate demon which had been lodged in his body'; cf. 10–17, 69–74.

[20] Though the Hittite root *gulš-* means literally 'inscribe', there are no certain instances of written tablets of fate in Hittite sources, though there is one reference in a Hurrian text to the 'tablet of life'; see Schwemer 2009: 157.

[21] E.g., *Enlil-bāni A*, 37–48 'Nisaba ... has placed his (?) name on the tablet of life.' Cf. also *Gudea Cyl. A* iv 23–v 1; *Nisaba A*, 1–9; *The Keš temple hymn*, 10–20. In the account of Sargon II's eighth campaign, the month of July 'determines the plans of the human denizens of this world' and these

palace archivist of heaven and earth, who keeps count of every single assignment, who holds a holy reed-stylus and covers the great tablets of destiny with writing!' (*Rīm-Sîn B*, 1–8).

In three cases, narratives rather than hymns or eulogies, the physicality of the tablet takes on a major importance, in the form of the 'tablet of destiny'.[22] There is only one actual description of this artefact, on an inscription of Sennacherib:[23]

> The Tablet of Destinies, the bond of supreme power, dominion over the gods and underworld ... the link of the Canopy of Anu and Gansir which Aššur, king of the gods, took in his hand and held at his breast – a representation of his form, the replica of his proper appearance, is depicted on it: he grasps in his hand the leashes of the great heavens.

The tablet thus symbolises the holding together of the universe and gives the supreme deity the means to exercise his power.

In the Sumerian *Ninurta and the Turtle* and the Akkadian *Enūma eliš* and *Anzu*, possession of this tablet is crucial to that exercise of power.[24] It seems that it is important for the good order of the universe that the tablet is in the correct hands; when it is usurped, it offers great power to its possessor, but that is overcome by the decreeing of a special fate in the second text and a stratagem in the third.

In the humorous Sumerian poem *Ninurta and the Turtle*, the fragmentary text begins with the Anzud chick explaining to Ninurta that 'I let the divine powers go out of my hand ... This tablet of destinies returned to the *abzu*. I was stripped of the divine powers' (B 1–4). The beneficiary is Enki, ensconced in the *abzu*, who is unwilling to lose the tablet, and so pays Ninurta great honours. Ninurta is not satisfied and 'sets his sights on the whole world'; Enki fathoms Ninurta's plan and sets about foiling it, which is where the turtle comes in, though the ending is lost (B 29–30).

Possession of the tablet of destiny plays an important role in *Enūma eliš*, in that Marduk's triumph is crowned by taking it from Tiamat's champion Qingu: 'the tablet of destinies which Qingu had taken and carried, / He

---

are inscribed by Ninšiku 'on a hoary tablet' (Foster 2005: 791, line 6). See also Focke 1998: 205–6 on this topos.

[22] On this tablet and its relationship to power, see esp. Lawson 1994: 19–48. Comparable perhaps is Inana's collection and transporting in the Boat of Heaven of the 'divine powers' (the 'me') given her by Enki (*Inana and Enki*, F1–13).

[23] See George 1986; the translation is his.

[24] For other references to this tablet, cf., e.g., the Babylonian myth of the *Twenty-one 'Poultices'* (*LKA* 146 obv. 6–10, quoted by Lawson 1994: 47), *Erra* IV 44 (Foster 2005: 903), and in the human sphere, Marduk's prophecy concerning Nebuchadnezzar I: 'I delivered all lands (into his power) ... I gave him the [tablet?] of destinies' (Foster 2005: 389).

took charge of it as a trophy(?) and presented it to Anu' (v 69–70). It is in *Anzu* however that its powers are most strikingly seen. When the Igigi bring news of the birth of the spectacular bird Anzu, Enlil appoints him guardian of the entrance to his chamber (Late Version I 63). However, Anzu is fascinated by Enlil's 'lordly crown, his divine apparel, / ... the tablet of destinies in his hands', which Enlil puts aside as he bathes (I 66–7). Anzu then decides (I 72–5):

> I myself will take the gods' tablet of destinies,
> Then I will gather to myself the responsibilities of all the gods,
> I shall have the throne for myself,
> I will take power over authority.
> I will be commander of each and every Igigi-god.

The power of the tablet is then displayed by the result of the theft (I 83–5):

> Awful silence spread, deathly stillness spread.
> Their father and counsellor Enlil was speechless.
> The cella was stripped of its divine splendour.

When attempts to find a champion to tackle Anzu fail, the great mother goddess Bēlet-ilī agrees to send her husband Ninurta, son of Enlil. It is her fundamental structure of authority, underpinned by the tablet, that is threatened (I 204–8):

> I made all the Anunna gods,
> To my brother I [...] supremacy,
> I assigned kingship of heaven to Anu.
> Anzu has thrown into confusion the kingship I appointed,
> The tablet of destinies, ... Anzu ... has taken control.

In the ensuing battle, the power of the tablet is further made manifest. Ninurta shoots an arrow, but it returns (II 66–9):

> Because he held the tablet of destinies of the gods in his hand,
> The bowstring brought forth arrows,
>   but they did not approach his body.
> Battle dies down, attack was held back,
> The fighting stopped,
>   within the mountain they did not conquer Anzu.

Encouraged by advice from Ea however, Ninurta is finally victorious, and the return of the tablet is the key feature, as Ea says to Dagan (III 37–9):[25]

---

[25] Whether Ea speaks or Enlil is uncertain.

'The warrior Ninurta took control
of the tablet of the gods' destinies for his own hands.
Send to him, let him come to you.
Let him place the tablet of destinies in your lap.'

In Sumerian and Akkadian literature, therefore, fate is something which the gods control by decree and through which they maintain order in the universe. It can be awarded for merit and, though often said for eulogistic reasons to be unchangeable, can be altered to maintain that order.[26] In a few cases it is represented by a tablet, possession of which is crucial to power. It is mentioned much more often in prayers and hymns than in epic.

Iliad

The Sumerian and Akkadian words for 'fate' pointed up a central feature of fate's role in the world, and the Greek terminology highlights a major difference between the two systems.[27] Mesopotamian 'fate' was essentially a matter of 'decree'. In Greek, the main words, *moira*, *moros*, are from *(s)meiromai* 'to receive as one's share (*meros*)'; *aisa*, essentially a synonym for *moira*, is from a root * h_2ei- 'give, take' (cf. *ainumai, aiteo*) and so again comes to mean 'part';[28] the less common *potmos* 'that which falls out' is from *pipto* 'fall'.[29] The idea of fate being determined by someone is not absent in the *Iliad*, but it is much more attenuated; fate is something which people have as their lot, but where it comes from is far from clear.[30]

---

[26] The idea that fate can be changed by appropriate actions by mortals is central to Mesopotamian divination.
[27] On fate in Homer, see, e.g., Nägelsbach 1884: 116–41 (useful collection of relevant passages), Bianchi 1953, Pötscher 1960, Ramat 1960, Dietrich 1965, Nilsson 1967: 361–8; Allan 2006 (esp. on the relationships with Near Eastern literature), Scodel 2017 (on the metapoetics of fate); *LfgrE* s. vv. μοῖρα, μόρος, αἶσα and πότμος.
[28] See Chantraine 1999: s.v. II.33–9.
[29] See Dietrich 1965: 270–1, and West 2007: 383 on IE words for fate meaning 'turn out, happen'. A further term, κήρ, plays less of a role. It comes closest to 'fate' in 23.78–9 'since hateful *ker* has engulfed me, which took possession of me at birth', but more usually it refers to death or the agents of death (e.g., *Il.* 2.302); it is personified on Achilles' shield (18.535–7); see generally Dietrich 1965: 240–8, who overstates its impersonality. Homer's picture of the *keres* is very different from the extravagant description in [Hes.] *Sc.* 248–57.
[30] The idea of fate as a portion appears in various Indo-European traditions: as well as Lachesis, related to λάχος 'portion', cf. the Latin *Morta*, one of the *Parcae*, and the Gaulish goddesses of abundance *Canti-smerta* and *Ro-smerta* both from **smer-*, and Old English *meotod*, Old Saxon *metud*, Norse *miǫtuðr* all from **med-* in the sense 'measure'; see West 2007: 381–2, and Chantraine 1999: s.v. II.675.

Since the world of the *Iliad* is not a literate one,[31] the absence of reference to physical tablets of fate is not surprising.[32] There are however more significant differences between the traditions. In Homer, gods, individually or together, do not create fates in the apparently free way that Mesopotamian gods regularly do, especially in hymns.[33] There are only two examples where they might seem to create fates: the words of Menelaus about his duel with Paris, 'let him die, for whichever of us fate and death have been prepared (τέτυκται)' (3.101), and the similar ones of Achilles comparing his fate with Heracles', 'if a similar fate really has been prepared for me' (18.120). Here, however, the verb is in the impersonal passive, and 'fate has been prepared' effectively means little more than 'it is fate that he die' (μοῖρα [ἐστί] θανεῖν, e.g., 7.52, 16.434).

The idea of a fate being given at birth, which is a notable feature of the Mesopotamian evidence, is also very rare.[34] There are again but two cases. Hera says that she and other gods have come down to protect Achilles, but that (20.127–8):

> later he will undergo what Aisa spun with her thread for him at his birth, when his mother bore him ...

Hecuba uses very similar language of Hector (24.209–10).[35] No-one says, as for instance does Pindar to Zeus about the newly-founded city of Aetna, 'I ask you to grant to the children of the Aetnaeans a fate of good governance (μοῖραν εὔνομον) for a long time' (*N.* 9.29–30).

If the Homeric gods do not control fates as do the Mesopotamian gods,[36] Homeric fate itself appears to be more active – 'appears' because, though 'fate' is often the subject of a verb, we are almost never dealing with

---

[31] Though NB the 'baleful signs' (σήματα λυγρά) carried by Bellerophon (6.168, 176, 178) and perhaps the marks made on the lots drawn for the duel with Hector: 'each marked his lot with a sign' (ἐσημήναντο, 7.175).

[32] The contrast between literate recording of fate and its retention in the minds of the gods mirrors a fundamental difference between Mesopotamian and Greek concepts of literature, which in the former is something that is composed and recorded in writing in order to be performed, whereas the Greeks depended on memory and the Muses: see Metcalf 2015a: 141–50.

[33] It is to some extent a matter of genre, but in general the Mesopotamian fates tend to be good, whereas those in Homer tend to be uncertain or presumed to be bad, being regularly called, e.g., κραταιή ('powerful'), ὀλοή ('destructive'), κακή ('evil'), or δυσώνυμος ('ill-named', so 'hateful'; see Dietrich 1965: 194–5); in thirty of forty-seven instances in the *Iliad*, *moira* is associated with death (Dietrich 1965: 212).

[34] This is, however, also a feature of Hittite theology, where the GUL-š-/Gulša- 'fate goddesses' number a man's days; Išduštaja and Papaja do the spinning; see Gurney 1977: 18, Schwemer 2009: 156–7, Waal 2019.

[35] For fate and spinning in Indo-European tradition, see West 2007: 379–85.

[36] This is not explicitly stated in the *Iliad*, but see *Od.* 3.236–8 'nor can the gods ward off death from a man, dear to them though he is, when the dread fate (*moira*) of woeful death seizes him'.

living beings.[37] The Fates never actually appear in the narrative (with spindles or otherwise), as opposed to in the mouths of characters. The situation is very different from that obtaining in Hesiod (*Th.* 904–6):

> the *Moirai*, to whom Zeus has given most honour, Clotho, Lachesis and Atropos, who grant to mortal men the possession of good or evil.

Nor does any god have any direct dealings with them, in the way, say, that Apollo goes to negotiate with them over the fate of Croesus (Hdt. 1.91.3–4). Gods sometimes know what is fated, but we are never told how.[38]

The *Moirai* occur in the plural only once,[39] in a rather general remark by Apollo that 'the *Moirai* have given mankind a heart that can bear trouble' (24.49), which does not really touch on their powers over events. When 'fate' occurs with other similar abstractions, an element of personification could be involved, as in Agamemnon's putting the blame on 'Zeus, *Moira* and the Fury that walks in darkness' (19.87), and Xanthus' putting it on 'the great god and mighty *Moira*' (19.410). Here it is notable that fate is just one actant among a number and not necessarily the main one. In, e.g., 17.478 'death and *moira* overtook him', or 24.132 'near him stood death and mighty *moira*', it would be harder to claim personification rather than a *façon de parler*.[40] Even in dramatic phrases like 'mighty *moira* drove him to face god-like Sarpedon' (5.629.) or 'destructive *moira* bound Hector to stay there' (22.5), it is not certain whether this is a colloquialism or a theological statement.[41]

Aisa cuts even less of an actual figure than *Moira*.[42] It is three times the subject of the phrase '(it is) fate' (1.416, 16.707, 24.224), and its spinning is referred to once (20.127–8; quoted above). Characters may be assured (16.707) or assure themselves (6.487) that things that are not *aisa* will not happen, but it is a less concrete concept than *moira*. *Moros* is very like *aisa*, and *potmos* (×12) is entirely an abstract idea, which one 'meets' (2.359) or 'laments' (16.857).

---

[37] Cf. Nilsson 1967: 362, discussing the Greek words for 'fate': 'es kann keine persönliche, konkrete Göttin sein, die mit solchen Wörtern bezeichnet wird'.
[38] See further note 44 below.
[39] On *Moira* in Homer, see Dietrich 1965: 194–231; on *moros*, 260–70.
[40] Cf. Ares' almost casual reference to fate, when insisting on avenging the death of his son: 'though it be my *moira* to lie struck by Zeus's thunderbolt' (15.117–18).
[41] Cf. also 13.602, 16.849 and 18.119.
[42] On *Aisa* in Homer, see Bianchi 1953, Dietrich 1965: 249–60.

So, generally, gods (×5), Homer (×9) and characters (×18) attribute actions to fate, but it is rare that they attribute *great* importance to it,[43] as opposed to blaming it for their misfortunes. It is here that Homer differs considerably from Mesopotamian literature.

This brings us to the question of the changing of fate, which occurred in special circumstances in Mesopotamia. In Greece, things are more complicated. There are a number of places where the gods are keen to keep fated events on track. For instance, three times Apollo acts to prevent Aeneas (17.319–23) and Troy (16.707, 780, 21.515–7) from suffering 'beyond what was *moros* / *aisa*' (ὑπὲρ μόρον / αἶσαν), i.e., before their allotted time, and Poseidon stops Aeneas risking his life 'beyond fate' (ὑπὲρ μόρον).[44] Here there is no sense that the gods could actually change fate, simply that they are required to preserve what is destined.

The possibility of changing fate is, however, raised on three occasions which each have the same structure and nearly the same wording. We started this chapter with Hera's complaint about Zeus's suggestion that Sarpedon be saved, and when Zeus later suggests saving Hector, Athene replies with almost exactly the same words, that a man πάλαι πεπρωμένον αἴσῃ ('long ago destined to his fate') must die (22.178–81). When in Book 4 Zeus suggests saving Troy, Hera reacts in the same way, though this time fate is not specifically mentioned (4.5–29).

It is clear from Hera's and Athene's words that Zeus could change fate at these moments: note especially the curt imperative 'do it' (ἔρδε). However, he does not. There has been much discussion of why precisely he does not, but the preservation of fate does not seem to be the only or even the most important consideration. Though in two cases fate is mentioned in the emphatically pleonastic phrase 'long ago destined to his fate',[45] other considerations are given at least as much prominence. If, in the case of Hector, Athene mentions only the fact that his death is fated, in the other

---

[43] Contrast, for instance, the fragment attributed to Archilochus (fr. 16 *IEG*), 'Chance and *Moira* grant everything to a man, Pericles.'

[44] Cf. also 2.155 (Athene at the Greek flight to the ships), 20.28–30 (Zeus starting the Theomachia for fear Achilles may sack Troy). These passages raise the broader question of whether the other gods have a similar knowledge of fate to Zeus. The number of cases where they evince such knowledge is limited, which may be significant, and no other god makes the kind of authoritative statement about the future that Zeus does at 8.470–83. Apollo and Poseidon clearly know something of what is planned, but how much more they know is not clear. It is notable too that humans also claim such knowledge, as Agamemnon (4.163–8), Hector (6.447–9) and Helenus (7.52–3).

[45] For πεπρωμένος elsewhere, cf. only ὁμῇ πεπρωμένον αἴσῃ ('who was allotted a similar portion', 15.209) of Poseidon, and Achilles on himself and Patroclus, ἄμφω γὰρ πέπρωται ὁμοίην γαῖαν ἐρεῦσαι ('for it is fated that we both redden the same earth', 18.329).

two episodes other considerations have a major role. In the case of Sarpedon, the reference to fate is followed by an understated threat of the gods' displeasure and, by implication, the possible implications for Zeus's authority (16.446–9):[46]

> Take care that some other god too may wish to send his beloved son from the mighty battle, because many sons of the immortals are fighting around the great city of Priam, whom you will annoy greatly.

When Zeus suggests that Troy itself be saved, Hera responds (4.25–9):

> Dread son of Kronos, what a thing to say! How can you want to make my labours in vain and fruitless, and the sweat I sweated in my efforts? My pair of horses were worn out as I gathered my people.

Here, at what is a much more crucial moment involving the whole city rather than a single man, it is notable that she makes no reference to fate, but again brings up considerations concerned with the relationships between Zeus and the other gods, especially herself, and about her own status and importance. Ever in Zeus's mind must be the time that the main anti-Trojan trio wanted to tie him up and salvation came only through Thetis' bringing of Briareus (1.396–406). This is not to deny that the fact that the deaths of Sarpedon and Hector are fated was a determinant in Zeus's decision-making, but it is notable that neither he nor Hera nor Athene (nor indeed Homer) places the main emphasis on it.

From these three episodes, it is clear that Zeus has the possibility of changing fate, but the text avoids strong suggestions that he does not change it *simply* because the deaths are fated: displeasure amongst the gods is what the text foregrounds. Zeus appears to be ambivalent about the changing of fate. In each case, there are reasons for doing so: Troy surpasses all cities in its generosity to the gods (4.44–9), Hector was a diligent sacrificer (22.170–2) and Sarpedon is his son and 'dearest of men' (16.433). These considerations must weigh heavily: what more can men do to please the gods than sacrifice generously? However, considerations of the reactions of other gods ultimately weigh more heavily. His ambivalence is best summed up by his own paradoxical remark to Hera when acquiescing in her desire for the destruction of Troy: 'I have granted you this willingly with a heart that is unwilling' (ἑκὼν ἀέκοντί γε θυμῷ, 4.43). This is very different from the power the Mesopotamian gods exercise in

---

[46] A similar argument is used by Athene to Ares, when he wants to re-enter the battlefield despite Zeus's forbidding it (15.133–41).

deciding or changing fates or the great powers given by possession of the tablet of destinies.[47]

Fate is important in the *Iliad*, therefore, but the facts that its efficacy is not foregrounded in the way that it can be in Mesopotamian texts, and that Zeus seems moved more by considerations of maintaining his power, suggest that divine authority is more of a concern to him. To this we now turn.

Authority

Mesopotamia

The question of Zeus's relationship with fate is part of the wider question of the nature and extent of his power as chief of the gods. For insights into this, we can turn to the Akkadian flood story, *Atrahasīs*.[48] This poem provides us with two depictions of Enlil's use of his divine authority when challenged, which take rather different courses. In the conflict with the Igigi, he seems, if not always strong and stable, to operate a relatively collegial system, and the problem reaches a relatively speedy resolution. In dealing with noisy humanity, however, he is much more autocratic, causes dissatisfaction amongst the gods and eventually is outwitted by Enki. The tone of the two parts is also very different; the first has elements of humour, the second is more full of sound and fury signifying death and destruction.

In the first part, we find the Igigi hard at work (OBV 1 23–6):

> The Igigi-gods were digging watercourses,
> The waterways of the gods, the life of the land,
> The Igigi-gods dug the Tigris river,
> And the Euphrates thereafter.

After 3,600 years, they are naturally somewhat fed up with this, and 'were complaining, denouncing, / Muttering down in the ditch' (1 39–40). Deciding to depose Enlil, they burn their tools and surround his house. Enlil is rather unprepared for this, does not realise he is surrounded and has to be roused from bed by Nusku. To confront the Igigi, he cautiously positions the armed Nusku in front of himself, who expresses surprise at his master's fear: 'My lord, your face is gone as pale as sallow as tamarisk! /

---

[47] It is different too from the idea found in the *Mahābhārata* that fate and the will of the gods are one and the same thing, which is also not the case in Mesopotamia. See, e.g., Johnson 1998: xix–xxiii.
[48] See Lambert and Millard 1969.

Your own offspring! Why did you fear?' (I 93–4). Nusku suggests seeking the help of Anu and Enki, but Enlil is uncertain what to do until Anu suggests they find out who is responsible for the revolt. When he learns that absolutely all the Igigi have joined in the revolt, Enlil weeps, but immediately, and for the first time, takes the initiative, instructing Anu to have the Anunnaki choose a god for destruction. This is done, but Anu expresses sympathy for the Igigi and the neglect of them by the gods (I 175–8):

> What do we denounce them for?
> Their forced labour was heavy, their misery too much.
> Every day the Earth was . . .
> The outcry was loud, we could hear their clamour.

The womb goddess is then charged with creating mankind, in which she is helped by Enki, with rules set down covering the future birth of children.

Throughout this episode, then, we have a sense of Enlil not really being in charge of or on top of things and rather dependent on the advice of Nusku, Anu and Enki. On the other hand, there is a sense not only of unity of purpose amongst the Anunnaki in the face of the Igigi's revolt, but also of the justness of the latter's complaint and the need to address it. The creation of mankind then seems to bring the problem to a satisfactory close, at the cost of one god, of whom a ghost is made: 'lest he be forgotten, let the spirit remain' (I 218).

The second episode begins and ends in a similar fashion to the first, and contains episodes of a similar structure, suggesting the two are complementary. It begins with problems with the humans, not revolting this time like the Igigi but merely being vexatious, and there is again a slight element of comedy about it (I 333–60):

> Twelve hundred years had not gone by,
> The land had grown numerous, the peoples had increased,
> The land was bellowing like a bull.
> The gods became disturbed by their uproar,
> Enlil heard their clamour.
> He said to the great gods,
> 'The clamour of humankind has become burdensome to me,
> I am losing sleep to their uproar.
> [ ] let there be ague . . .'

Desiring to protect the humans, Enki advises the mortal Atrahasis that they should honour only Namtar, the god responsible for the disease (I 374–9). Namtar is eventually shamed into stopping it: 'he was shamed

Fate and Authority 257

by the gift and withdrew his hand. The ague left them' (I 410–11). The solution is eventually found in a set of rules, again created by Enki with the help of the womb goddess, which will lay down laws not about birth rites but restrictions at birth on the size of the human population. A difference from the first part is immediately noticeable, however, in that this time Enlil is in no doubt about whether he is to resort to violence; he needs no help or advice but immediately condemns the humans to destruction.

This pattern is repeated 600 years later, when Enlil again immediately demands a famine, and Enki advises the same trick, this time involving the god Adad. Gaps in the text obscure what happens next, but things have clearly escalated. Dissent amongst the gods becomes clear, with Enki and Enlil falling out. The gods demand that Enki create a flood, but he refuses. Tablet II ends with someone saying explicitly 'The gods commanded annihilation, Enlil committed the evil deed against the peoples' (II viii 34–5).

The difficulties of this 'evil deed' become clear in the flood. Humans are destroyed but the gods suffer too. Mami apportions blame (III 51–4):

> Where has Anu gone to, the chief decision-maker,
> Whose sons, the gods, heeded his command?
> He who irrationally brought about the flood,
> And relegated the peoples to catastrophe?

The other gods join in her misery. The unwisdom of killing the humans has become clear: no sacrificial food. After another long gap, the gods have been given food, but even here there is dissention, as Enlil and Anu, showing no remorse, avail themselves of the offerings (III v 39–45):

> Nintu arose to rail against all of them,
> 'Where has Anu come to, the chief-decision-maker?
> Has Enlil drawn nigh the incense?
> They who irrationally brought about the flood,
> And relegated the people to catastrophe?'

Furthermore (III vi 6–8):

> (Enlil) was filled with anger at the Igigi-gods.
> 'All we great Anunna gods
> Resolved together on an oath.'

Anu divines that Enki was to blame, but he is unrepentant: 'I did it indeed for your sakes! I am responsible for safeguarding life' (III vi 18–19).

There are gaps in the text, but some idea of what happened may be given by the fact that two lines preserved of Enki's speech are very close to a line in what he says in the Akkadian *Epic of Gilgameš* after its account of the Flood (SBV XI 183–91):[49]

> 'You, the sage of the gods, the hero,
> how could you lack counsel and bring on the Deluge?
> On him who transgresses, inflict his crime! ...
> Instead of your causing the Deluge,
> a wolf could have risen, and diminished the people.'

This advice is taken, which suggests that harmony was finally restored by a compromise, and Enlil, no doubt accepting Enki's criticisms and his justifications of his opposition to him, has Enki and Nintu/Mami in the assembly of gods reach an agreement on controlling the human population.

The effect of Enlil's (and Anu's) autocratic response to the problem of human noise was thus turmoil in heaven and earth, and recriminations in heaven. Autocratic responses, without the sanction of the other gods leads to chaos, both amongst the gods, who suffer greatly in the flood, and the humans, who are nearly annihilated. It is striking that neither Enlil nor Anu seems to have any shame. Notable too is the complaint, twice made by Mami/Nintu, that Enlil did not deliberate, an especial flaw in the 'counsellor of the gods'.[50] The contrast with the first episode involving the Igigi underscores the message, as does the parallelism between the two episodes. The poem is a remarkable demonstration of the importance of a harmony in the universe, in which the importance of the role and rights, not just of more minor deities but also of the human race, is acknowledged. Unwisdom in the deployment of authority by the most powerful gods, without consultation of or agreement with their fellow-deities, leads to general distress and destruction, which only the intelligence and cunning of a god like Enki prevents from being terminal for all.

Iliad

Atrahasīs thus allows us to reflect on Zeus's apparently surprising willingness not to exercise his authority on a number of occasions. We have discussed above the three cases where Zeus suggests that a fated outcome should be put off. In the case of Sarpedon, he merely indicates his uncertainty: 'my heart tends in two directions as I ponder this' (16.436). However, with Troy he is careful to involve the other gods in the decision-

---

[49] The translation is from George 2000: 95.   [50] Moran 1971: 60.

making, 'let us consider how these matters shall be' (4.14), and with Hector he goes one step further and hands the decision to them, 'but come, gods, consider and deliberate' (22.174). In each case, Zeus gets a very negative answer and he backs away from his original suggestion.

In the second passage with which this chapter began, we have the most strident instance of Zeus's attempt to impose his authority, but it is striking how this attempt falls flat at the first sign of opposition. Athene acknowledges his power and promises they will not join the battle, but (8.36–40):

> 'We will give useful suggestions to the Argives so that they do not all perish because of your anger.' Cloud-gathering Zeus, smiling at her, answered, 'Take heart, my child, Trito-born; I am not speaking seriously, and I want to be nice to you.'

Zeus has in the past used physical strength to impose his authority, as Hephaestus (1.590–3) and Sleep (14.242–62) recount and Zeus reminds Hera (15.18–24), but at this crucial moment such tactics seem to offer no advantage in the politics of Olympus, and it is not many lines before Hera and Athene are in their chariot on the way to the battlefield in despite of Zeus's warnings, and it is only the threat of a thunderbolt and maiming that brings them grudgingly back into line (8.350–432). But even here Zeus shows a clear understanding of the situation he is in. At the end of his speech, he explains the aim of his threats (8.406–8):

> So that grey-eyed Athene may know when it is her father she is fighting. But I am not so angry or indignant with Hera, because it is always her way to frustrate my commands.

His resignation before and acquiescence in Hera's relentless opposition to Troy stands out.

It may be in the same spirit that, after he has awoken from the sleep after his tricking by Hera, he speaks threateningly to her of how he dealt with her the last time she crossed him, and then, after Hera has rather unconvincingly sworn she has done nothing wrong, sets out the events that will occur 'until the Achaeans capture steep Troy through the designs of Athene' (15.70–1). At the same time, he recalls another determinant of his actions, his promise to Thetis, and forcefully restates his position on fulfilling that promise (15.72–7; cf. 1.396–406). Once again, he is having to negotiate between what the three most powerful gods want and what he has committed himself to. In this he is successful, in that Hera goes back to Olympus to warn the other gods (albeit grudgingly) against transgressing Zeus's commands (15.78–112), a message which is reinforced when

Athene has to persuade Ares not to re-enter the battle because of the death of his son – even this is not reason enough to go against Zeus (15.113–42). Hera and Athene may here act grudgingly, but Zeus has given them what they want. Iris is sent to bring Poseidon back from the battle whither he went when Zeus's attention was elsewhere (13.1–16), and Apollo is told to go and revive the wounded Hector (15.143–8). Everyone on Olympus now has what they want (though there are elements in the form of the deaths of children which Zeus and Thetis could wish away), and from now on divine intervention in the battle is restricted to events which do not threaten either the giving of honour to Achilles or the fall of Troy. Apollo prepares the death of Patroclus (16.788–806), and Poseidon saves Aeneas (20.330–52) and Apollo Hector (20.438–54). Even Zeus's suggestions about saving Sarpedon and Hector involve individuals not, as in Book 4, the whole city of Troy. Having tried to keep the gods out of the battle for so long, Zeus finally encourages them to fight amongst themselves in the *Theomachia* (21.383–513), but the ensuing combats, with their strong burlesque elements, seen for instance in Athene's treatment of Ares (21.391–414) or Poseidon's almost weary suggestion to Apollo that they should fight for form's sake (21.435–40), seem to reinforce the idea that matters are now settled as far as the gods are concerned.

The contrast between Zeus's threatening outbursts in *Iliad* 8 and 15 points to a development in his strategy. It has become clear that Hera and Athene, and indeed Poseidon, are not going to back down from their insistence on a Greek victory. He must balance his desire to give honour to Achilles, as he is bound to do by Thetis' preservation of his power in the past, with the need to acquiesce in what the most powerful among the other gods wish, whatever his doubts about it. Zeus's wisdom here is also visible when one compares it to the disastrous consequences of the insistence on getting their own way of the key human actors, Agamemnon, Achilles and Hector.

All in all, therefore, comparison with the many Mesopotamian hymns and prayers and stories like *Anzu* shows how fate is less central to power in the *Iliad* than in the Mesopotamian epic. There are no tablets or other tokens possession of which gives Zeus power in the world; there is no sense that Zeus controls things because he is in control of fate;[51] fates are not decreed in special circumstances, such as in return for good deeds for the

---

[51] There is not the same closeness which is expressed in Hes. *Th.* 904–6, where Thetis bears the Moirai to Zeus, 'to whom he granted the greatest honour (*timē*)': Zeus here takes over the parentage of the Moirai, though earlier they were the daughters of Night (217).

gods. That Zeus could change major aspects of fate is clear from the exchanges with Hera and Athene,[52] but circumstances are always such that he does not.

Comparison with *Atrahasīs* reinforces the wisdom of the use by the leading god or gods of consultation and a tactical response to the demands of other deities: the autocratic behaviour of Enlil leads to disaster for the universe as a whole, and only Enki's interventions bring about resolution. No such mediator is required by Zeus, who is on his own as far as tactics are concerned: unlike Hera and Athene, the pro-Trojan gods make little or no attempt to sway him to their aim of saving Troy. Ultimately, of all the main leaders in the *Iliad* it is the diplomatic Zeus who comes through with his authority intact, even if what happens causes him great pain.[53]

---

[52] Cf. also his intervention to make Patroclus forget Achilles' words of warning, which brings about Patroclus' end before his time (16.685–90).

[53] For a more detailed analysis of Zeus's navigation of the politics of Olympus, see Elmer 2013: 146–74.

CHAPTER 15

Fashioning Pandora
Ancient Near Eastern Creation Scenes and Hesiod

Bernardo Ballesteros Petrella

Hesiod's narratives of the creation of the Woman in the *Theogony* and *Works and Days* – where she is called Pandora – have been considered a goldmine of orientalia (*Th.* 562–93, *Op.* 42–105).* Yet the critical excavation of this goldmine, while fruitful, has typically been disorderly. The present contribution will discuss some of the results of this research, and bring in a number of Near Eastern creation scenes that have not been discussed in this connection.[1] Ultimately, I hope to make a methodological point by distinguishing, as an archaeologist would, the significance of each layer. But the comparativist who seeks to read Hesiod in a Near Eastern context faces a different challenge to the archaeologist dealing with stratigraphy. Rather than distinguishing layers by diachrony, this chapter attempts to assess the qualitatively different contribution that each comparandum offers to our understanding. This will entail differentiating and mediating between two poles: on the one hand, the myths in their aetiological dimension, and on the other, their concrete narrative instantiations in the extant literary texts.[2]

The strongest parallel to Hesiod's scenes on the level of myth comes from the 'Yahwistic' account of the creation of Woman in *Genesis* 2–3, which has been compared to the *Works and Days* passage since Christian

---

* I wish to thank Adrian Kelly, Christopher Metcalf and Frances Reynolds for their comments on earlier drafts of this chapter, and the first two (along with Johannes Haubold) for their invitation to contribute to the conference; and Angelo Colonna and Adriano Orsingher for their help with the Egyptian evidence and the Greek archaeological material respectively.

[1] The label '(ancient) Near East' is here used conventionally, without implying a reified or indistinct concept, nor a mutually exclusive definition in opposition to Greece (or 'the West'). For a recent critique of the uses of the term, see van Dongen 2014. This chapter will deal with Levantine, Egyptian, Mesopotamian and Anatolian contexts.

[2] For the purpose of the present argument, a satisfactory definition of 'myth' can be that given by Burkert 1979: 23: 'a traditional tale with secondary, partial reference to something of collective importance', where the complex intertwining of different types of semantic structures does not overshadow the sequence of actions (in the broadest sense) which makes a myth a tale in the first place, cf. Burkert 1979: 1–34.

Table 3 *The creation of Woman in* Genesis *and* Works and Days

		Genesis (Jones 1966)	Hesiod (Most 2006)
(a)	easy livelihood	2:15–16: *Yahweh God took the man and settled him in the garden of Eden to cultivate and take care of it. Then Yahweh God gave the man this admonition: 'You may eat indeed of all the trees in the garden.'*	*Op.* 42–7: *For the gods keep the means of life concealed from human beings. Otherwise you would easily be able to work for just one day only to have enough for a whole year even without working... But Zeus concealed it, enraged in his heart.*
(b)	woman created	2:18–24	*Op.* 60–82 (cf. *Th.* 570–84)
(c)	woman's act	3:1–7 (eats forbidden fruit, offers it to the man)	*Op.* 94–5 (removes lid from jar)
(d)	loss of easy livelihood	3:17: (Yahweh God to man) *'Accursed the soil because of you. With suffering shall you get your food from it every day of your life.'*	*Op.* 90–2, 94: *For previously the tribes of men used to live upon the earth entirely apart from evils, and without grievous toil, and distressful diseases, which give death to men... but the Woman...*

antiquity.[3] An outline of structural correspondences is easily drawn, following a recent assessment (Table 3; cf. Musäeus 2004: 63–4).

Beyond the sequence highlighted in the left-hand column, one should note that in both myths the divine punishment is ultimately caused by a *trickster* – the Serpent/Prometheus – who leads mankind to overcome a divine prohibition. In the 1930s, Franz Dornseiff concluded that a common ancient Near Eastern traditional background should be reckoned with, and this position has recently been advocated by Immanuel Musäus.[4]

One could object that an important peculiarity of the Greek myth, which decidedly separates it from the Biblical one, lies in Pandora's opening of the jar from which evils are released. Ethnographic research

---

[3] Tert. *De Corona* 7.3; Orig. *Contra Celsum* 4.37–8; see further Musäus 2004: 136–42.
[4] Cf. Dornseiff 1934: 61 (1955: 218): 'Wenn zwei größere literarische Werke in der östlichen Mittelmeerwelt, die beide am Rand der alten vorderasiatischen Kulturwelt entstanden sind, höchstens durch 250 Jahre voneinander getrennt, wahrscheinlich durch beträchtlich geringere Zeit, so im Bau und Inhalt ihrer Einleitungsstücke übereinstimmen, so kann man nicht an Zufall glauben ... Wir haben also hier altvorderasiatische überkommene Erzählungsform zu erkennen.' Musäus 2004: 64: 'die Kombination der Hauptmotive ... rückt die beiden Geschichten in eine so große gegenseitige Nähe, daß die Annahme eines gemeinsamen Hintergrundes einiges für sich hat'.

offers several parallels for the motif of evils enclosed in a container (which is sometimes opened or broken), including Hittite ritual texts.[5] The creation of mankind from earth or clay is equally widespread in folklore.[6] Nevertheless, the correspondence between the sequence of events set out above appears to remain unparalleled, and the ethnographic comparanda do not necessarily militate against Dornseiff's interpretation.

However, beyond what we may call a common mythical syntax (in terms of a sequence of similar events directed toward the same aetiology), the two narratives hold little in common on the level of detail and literary realisation. This is especially true of the creation scene, on which this chapter concentrates. In *Genesis*, the woman is not created from earth, as man and Hesiod's woman, but from man's rib; nor is the creation process described at particular length. The most obvious difference, however, is that the Greek creation scene is a collective enterprise: in the *Theogony*, at Zeus's command Hephaistos fashions the maiden from earth and water and Athene adorns her; in the *Works and Days*, the divine participation is expanded as a function of the name-aetiology (Pan-dora = all gifts), which is absent from the *Theogony*, and of a more detailed characterisation of the creature.

Such details of the Greek texts bring us away from the Holy Land, and down to Deir el-Bahari on the west bank of the Nile, close to Luxor, where Queen Hatshepsut built her magnificent mortuary temple in the first half of the fifteenth century BCE. On the walls of the middle-level northern colonnade, fragmentary reliefs and explanatory texts preserve a narrative of the queen's divinely ordained birth and coronation. Hatshepsut is daughter of the god Amun, who asks Khnum, the god of craft, to accomplish the creation. Thus, Khnum is portrayed moulding figurines on a potter's wheel (one being Hatshepsut, the other her *ka*), while the fertility goddess Heket extends the symbols of life to the figurines.[7] After the queen is born, the child is presented to the divine assembly, who pay homage to her.[8] Once grown up, Hatshepsut receives her crown from Atum, then from Amun, and is attributed various names from several gods.

Peter Walcot presented these scenes as 'the closest parallel to the description of the preparation of Pandora in the *Theogony*'.[9] He concentrated on

---

[5] Evils enclosed in a vessel: Frazer 1912: II.320, Bonner 1937, Trencsényi-Waldapfel 1966: 65–75, Snider 1973, Haas 1976: 199–200 (Hittite), Bremmer 2008: 29 n. 50; cf. *Od.* 10.19–27 (Aeolus' bag), and Horálek 1987 on this as a folk tale motif.
[6] God(s) create man from earth/clay: Frazer 1918: I.3–29, Thompson 1955–8: I.67 (s.v. A.15.4).
[7] Naville 1896: plate XLVIII, text translated by Breasted 1906: 82.
[8] Naville 1898: plate LVI, text translated by Breasted 1906: 89.   [9] Walcot 1966: 62–79, here 68.

the golden headband made by Hephaistos and put on the Woman's head by Athene, and on the Woman's presentation to the assembly of gods and men (Hes. *Th.* 578–84):

> And around her head she placed a golden headband (στεφάνην χρυσέην), which the much-renowned Lame One made himself, (580) working it with his skilled hands, to do a favor for Zeus the father. On this were contrived many designs, highly wrought, a wonder to see (θαῦμα ἰδέσθαι), all the terrible monsters the land and the sea nourish; he put many of these into it, wondrous (θαυμάσια), similar to living animals endowed with speech, and gracefulness breathed upon them all. (585) Then, when he had contrived this beautiful evil in exchange for a good, he led her out to where the other gods and the human beings were, exulting in the adornment of the mighty father's bright-eyed daughter; and wonder (θαῦμα) gripped the immortal gods and the mortal human beings when they saw the steep deception, intractable for human beings. (transl. Most 2006)

Pointing to well-attested contacts between Egypt and Mycenaean Greece, and to supposed Egyptian influences on Mycenaean conceptions of kingship, Walcot saw Bronze Age relics in Hesiod's account, ultimately to be connected to Egypt. There are several problems with this reconstruction, but two aspects are of interest for the present discussion. First, the indigenous context of Hesiod's passage is completely overlooked. In the *Theogony*, the poet depicts the adornment of the Woman with the traditional instruments of the so-called seduction scene: the object of the adornment is to elicit wonder (θαῦμα) and/or desire (ἔρος) from the one who is to be seduced.[10] This is the case of Hera and Zeus in the *Iliad*, Penelope and the suitors in the *Odyssey*, and Aphrodite and Anchises in the *Homeric Hymn to Aphrodite*.[11] But the best parallel comes from the sixth *Homeric Hymn*, again devoted to Aphrodite (*h.Hom.* 6.5b–13):

> (5) and the Horai with headbands of gold received her gladly, and clothed her in divine clothing. On her immortal head they put a finely wrought diadem, a beautiful gold one [cf. Hes. *Th.* 578], and in her pierced ear lobes flowers of orichalc and precious gold. (10) About her tender throat and her white breast they decked her in golden necklaces, the ones that the gold-crowned Horai themselves would be decked with whenever they went to the gods' lovely dance at their father's house. When they had put all the

---

[10] On 'adorning (for seduction)' scenes in early Greek hexameter poetry, cf. esp. Forsyth 1979, Janko 1992: 173–9, Edwards 1992: 312–13, Brown 1997, Currie 2016: 147–60.

[11] Hera → Zeus (Hera adorns herself: *Il.* 14.166–88), cf. 14.293b–6; Penelope → the suitors (Athene adorns Penelope: *Od.* 18.190b–7), cf. 18.208–13; Aphrodite adorned by the Charites (*Od.* 8.364–6); Aphrodite → Anchises (Aphrodite is adorned by the Charites: *h.Hom.* 5.58–66), cf. 84–91; cf. *Cyp.* frr. 4–5 Bernabé, Aphrodite adorned before the Judgement of Paris.

finery about her body, (15) they led her to the immortals [cf. Hes. *Th.* 585–9], who welcomed her on sight and took her hand in greeting; and each of them prayed to take her home as his wedded wife, as they admired the appearance (εἶδος θαυμάζοντες) of violet-crowned Cytherea. (transl. West 2003)

Aphrodite is born, adorned with a headband (στεφάνη) by the Horai, and then presented to the divine assembly; all the gods desire her.[12] Now the Woman fashioned by Hephaistos is to cause amazement and *eros* in Prometheus' brother Epimetheus, as is most clearly visible in the *Works and Days*. In the *Theogony*, however, Hephaistos presents her first to gods and men, with a striking recasting of the hymnic topos whereby the deity, after birth, is presented to the assembly of the gods.[13]

The narrative urgency to bring about punishment is possibly one reason why in the *Works and Days* Pandora is immediately sent to Epimetheus, and no presentation to the gods takes place. Nevertheless, the divine community comes into sharp focus through the elaborate collective fashioning of the bride (Hes. *Op.* 69–82). Unlike the recently born gods, the Woman of the *Theogony* is introduced to a mixed group including men; the sacrificial banquet at Mekone (Hes. *Th.* 535–61) is likely still present in the audience's mind, though, considering the events that have intervened, hardly as the same gathering. The *Theogony* scene, as part of the narrative on Zeus's ultimate triumph in the divine world and coming at a time where gods and men still shared meals and seats ([Hes.] fr. 1.7 M-W), displays the Woman as a universally impressive sign of Zeus's power. The more sustained divine participation in the *Works and Days* is played up by Pandora's name-aetiology, and stresses her being a collectively divine product in the context of a stronger contrast between the human and divine realms. The agency with which the gods endow her (rather absent from the *Theogony*) is a prelude to her irremediable act. Despite these differences, the extensive deployment of conventional features found elsewhere in early hexameter poetry clarifies that neither scene represents a

---

[12] Luginbühl 1992: 215–16 does not consider the traditional character of the topos, and unconvincingly concludes that Aphrodite's adornment in *h.Hom.* 6 is a 'Vorbild' for Hesiod's depiction. Graziosi 2017 offers a theological reading of this Hymn in the light of Homer and Hesiod's images of Aphrodite.
[13] Newborn Greek deities joining/presented to the divine assembly: Hes. *Th.* 53–79 (Muses), 201–2 (Aphrodite); *h.Hom.* 19.35–47 (Pan), 28.4–16 (Athene, already in Olympus); cf. *h.Hom.* 3.2–13, 186–206; *h.Hom.* 4.322–8a. See West 1966: 224, and more recently Chappell 2012: 179 and 182, Graziosi 2017: 47–8. The 'hymnic' character of the *Theogony* when it comes to defining a deity's prerogatives is discussed by Metcalf 2015a: 123; for a recent treatment of the poem as a hymn to Zeus, see Scully 2015: 30–49.

crowning ritual. Indeed, the Woman's headband (worn by Aphrodite in *h.Hom.* 6.7) is no crown, but a golden diadem for which archaeological examples are preserved from Iron Age Greece.[14] A closer 'Oriental' context (most recently assessed by Currie 2016) lies in Babylonian, Hurro-Hittite and Ugaritic adornment-and-seduction scenes, not in the Egyptian crowning ritual.

Equally important, and this is our second point against an Egyptian direct line to Hesiod, is that the mythical divine creation and collective crowning of the king also occurs in Mesopotamian texts. One early first-millennium composition, first adduced by Walter Burkert in connection to Pandora, is relevant here.[15] After the gods create mankind, the god of wisdom Ea asks the Lady of the Gods Bēlet-ilī to fashion the king, and several deities provide the newborn with attributes; the supreme sky god Anu produces the crown (*Creation of the King*, VS 24.92, 30'–41'; ed. Mayer 1987: 56):

> Ea made ready to speak, said to Bēlet-ilī:　　　　　　　　　　　　30'
> 'You are Bēlet-ilī, mistress of the great gods,
> you are the one who gave shape to the human-man.
> Make a king, a counsellor-man,
> adorn his whole body with excellence,
> see to his features, make fair his body.'　　　　　　　　　　　　　35'
> Bēlet-ilī fashioned the king, the counsellor-man,
> they gave the king warfare on behalf of the [great] gods.
> Anu gave his crown, Enlil gave [his throne],
> Nergal gave his weapon, Ninurta gave [his splendour],
> Bēlet-ilī gave [his features].　　　　　　　　　　　　　　　　　　40'
> Nusku entrusted him *with advice*(!), and [*stood before him*].
> 　　　　　　　　　　　　　　　(transl. after Foster 2005: 497).[16]

The final lines of the preserved text overlap with the end of an Assyrian hymn exalting King Assurbanipal's coronation (but not his birth or creation).

---

[14] Cf. Blümer 2001 II: 112–13. The standard work remains Ohly 1953 (on eighth-century golden headbands), but cf. Higgins 1980: 96–7, Hiller 1991: 80, Brown 1997: 39 n. 66, Treister 2001: 9–15, Crielaard 2007: 172–5, Panagiotopoulos 2012: 140–3. According to Steiner 2001: 116, Pandora's adornment resembles that of Greek cultic statues, cf. Francis 2009: 13 nn. 33, 35. Luginbühl 1992: 218–19 mentions headbands and garlands worn by brides in sixth-century BCE Athenian black-figure pottery, and Pandora's crown in the Ashmolean Museum krater (Oxford V525) depicting Zeus, Hermes and Epimetheus.

[15] Burkert 1991a: 173, cf. West 1997: 310–11; Luginbühl 1992: 217–18 and Bremmer 2008: 26 would not exclude a direct connection between this coronation scene and Hesiod.

[16] For 41' *ú-ma-'i-ir* ᵈ*Nusku ú-ma-lik-⌈ma iz⌉-z[iz ma-ḫar-šú]* cf. *Assurbanipal's Coronation Hymn*, LKA 31 rev. 8: *um-ta-'i-ir-ma* ᵈ*Nusku ma-li-ki ma-ḫar-šú ul-ziz*, where VS 24.92, 38'–43' ≈ LKA 31 rev. 5–10.

Here, after the collective attribution, the gods are invited to assemble and to bless the king (*Assurbanipal's Coronation Hymn*, LKA 31 rev. 15–16; ed. Livingstone 1989: 27):

> Gather, all the gods of heaven and earth!
> Bless King Assurbanipal, the counsellor-man!
> (author's transl.)

It is a matter of debate whether and how these Akkadian compositions are related to actual coronation rituals.[17] From a literary perspective, it is to be noted that the praised king typically partakes of qualities bestowed or appreciated by several gods according to their prerogatives, in keeping with a topos of Mesopotamian royal self-representation and hymnology that can be traced as far back as the late third millennium BCE at least. Suffice it here to recall a famous passage from a hymn of Šulgi, king of Ur in the twenty-first century BCE (*Šulgi A*, 7–15, transl. after *ETCSL* 2.4.2.1):

> I am a child born of Ninsun.
> I am the choice of holy An's heart.
> I am the man whose fate was decided by Enlil.
10 I am Šulgi, the beloved of Ninlil.
> I am he who is cherished by Nintu.
> I am he who was endowed with wisdom by Enki.
> I am the powerful king of Nanna.
> I am the growling lion of Utu.
15 I am Šulgi, who has been chosen by Inana for his attractiveness.

Thus, the Egyptian and Mesopotamian narratives present close parallels to Hesiod's compositional sequences, including (a) creation operated by the crafty god and goddess, (b) collective attributions, and (c) presentation to the divine assembly. From a Greek perspective, however, Hesiod construes moments (b) and (c) by connecting two Greek typical scenes: the adornment for seduction, and the presentation of the newborn deity to the divine assembly, whereas the central elements in the Egyptian and Babylonian texts (that is, kingship and crowning) are utterly absent. This difference, and the Greek compositional background, allow us decisively to conclude that a direct historical connection between these scenes and Hesiod's depiction becomes an unnecessary hypothesis; and this remains true in spite of the fact that they provide the most detailed parallels on the level of poetic realisation.

---

[17] Cf. Dietrich 2003. Müller 1989 and, more recently, Jiménez 2013 investigate the literary-traditional background to these works.

Fashioning Pandora

But if we return to the mythic-aetiological level from which we began, in the *Genesis* episode, Mesopotamian literature has more to say. The relevant texts, however, do not relate to the creation of kings but to that of mankind. As discussed by Johannes Haubold (Chapter 12 in this volume), the classic Mesopotamian aetiology is that man was moulded from clay to labour in the gods' stead. In a sense, this agrees with *Genesis* and Hesiod, except that in Mesopotamia mankind was designed for that task *ab initio*, and labour and toil did not result from a 'fall' or a decline in status; in addition, a differentiated creation of woman plays no part in Mesopotamia. This confirms our conclusion that the *Genesis* aetiological myth is the closest to Hesiod.

What *Genesis* cannot provide, however, if not minimally in the figure of the Serpent, is the literary elaboration deriving from a polytheistic cast of divine characters. We have seen that the Serpent plays the part of the *trickster*, but it is undeniable that whilst *Genesis* highlights the guilt of Adam and Eve, mankind stands rather in the background in Hesiod's story, in *Enki and Ninmah*, and (to a lesser degree) in *Atraḫasīs*. The focus here lies decidedly on the internecine conflicts within the divine world, even though, of course, mankind's condition remains the ultimate aetiological goal.

Thus, *Atraḫasīs*, the Old Babylonian mythical history of mankind from its creation until after the Flood, has naturally become a central focus of comparison with the Prometheus myth. Again, however, we need to distinguish between myth and poetic realisation. The similarities between Prometheus and Enki/Ea, both helpers of mankind against an angry chief god, are well known, but they are quite superficial in Hesiod, and become prominent only in much later sources.[18] As late as the fourth century, for instance, Prometheus is not unmistakably attested as the creator of mankind.[19] It is generally accepted that the Flood story was not presupposed by the Hesiodic *Catalogue*, although it is not impossible that the myth was already current in Greece by Hesiod's time.[20] Considering Enki/Ea's closeness to the Mesopotamian Flood hero, it is surely intriguing that

---

[18] On Prometheus and Enki/Ea, cf. Duchemin 1974: 33–67, 1995: 151–86, S. R. West 1994, Penglase 1994: 197–229.

[19] *Aesop*. 430 Perry might constitute the oldest evidence, along with Heraclid. Pont. 38B Schütrumpf (a corrupted passage) and Philemon fr. 93 K-A: cf. Perry 1962: 304–6, 336. Prometheus is not the creator of mankind in Pl. *Prt.* 320d–21.

[20] For the Flood (not) in the *Catalogue of Women* see still M. L. West 1985: 55–6; cf. Fowler 2000–13: II.113–21. On Homeric cosmic watery destructions, possibly working against a Near Eastern background, cf. Scodel 1982 and, recently, Haubold 2014. For a thought-provoking reading of Hesiod's cosmic history as presupposing the Flood story, cf. Rudhardt 1970 and 1981.

the *Catalogue*, in agreement with the later tradition, presents Prometheus as the father of the Greek Flood hero Deucalion (frr. 2, 4 M-W). However, we may be certain that Prometheus was not the creator of mankind in Hesiod, nor is the Flood story ever mentioned in the *Theogony* or the *Works and Days*.

Therefore, as far as Hesiod is concerned, juxtaposing Prometheus and Enki/Ea is of limited value. Perhaps, rather than trying to force the Babylonian evidence onto the Greek, we should think in structural terms, by looking at how the characters' roles contribute to the shaping of the narrative on the one hand, and to its mythic-aetiological purpose on the other.

Charles Penglase offers a detailed comparison between *Atrahasīs* and the Prometheus story in Hesiod, and seeks to clarify the parallels by considering Prometheus as blending aspects of the leader of the rebellious gods of the Babylonian poem (both oppose the chief god) and aspects of Ea (both help mankind against the chief god). In turn, the role of Ea would be perceptible in Hesiod through a dichotomy between Prometheus and Hephaistos, who fashions the creation.[21] Yet if one concentrates on the creation scenes and their context, it is easy to see that the role of Ea is not matched by Prometheus, but by Zeus. Both give instructions for the creation, both find a solution to achieve a new balance in cosmic order after a crisis. In *Atrahasīs*, as in *Enki and Ninmah*, the crisis stems from a revolt of the working gods, while in Hesiod, it comes from Prometheus' tricks; in both cases, the resolution defines a clear-cut separation between toiling mankind and the gods.[22]

Seeing creation as a means to resolution permits us to set this parallel in a broader context of several ancient Near Eastern creation scenes. One obvious mismatch with the Mesopotamian creation of mankind is that in Hesiod mankind was already there to play a crucial part in Zeus's cosmic trouble. The fundamental analogy, instead, lies in the narrative pattern whereby a cosmic crisis is resolved through an act of creation. In fact, the instances of this topos beyond creation-of-mankind situations come closer to Hesiod's use of Pandora.

In the Sumerian poem *Inana's Descent to the Netherworld* (*ID*), and the Akkadian version *Ištar's Descent* (*IšD*), the crisis concerns the infertility of the land, caused by the goddess' disappearance. But Enki/Ea creates two

---

[21] Penglase 1994: 216–26.
[22] *Atr.* OB Tablet 1. For the text of *Atrahasīs*, see Lambert and Millard 1969 (here 53–65), with Shehata 2001. A translation of the surviving evidence is Foster 2005: 227–80.

figures (or a single figure, in the Akkadian poem) who will trick the Queen of the Netherworld Ereškigal into permitting Inana/Ištar's return.[23] This comes closer to Hesiod, even if Enki performs the creation alone, and not by moulding clay, but the dirt of his fingernails (the Akkadian is hardly specific on the process). It comes closer because the created figures are sent over to another domain which is causing trouble, and because these creatures are liminal, ambiguous figures capable of overcoming cosmic limits to foster the divine master plan (Enki/Ea's creatures will not be kept in the Netherworld – they become officiants of the goddess).

Another relevant case is the Akkadian *Agušaya* poem, from the time of Hammurabi (eighteenth century). Here, Ištar's customary impetuousness threatens cosmic order, to the point of menacing Ea's abode (*Agušaya* A, col. iv 10–21).[24] To set things right, Ea creates a virtual duplicate of Ištar among the assembled gods (v 1–33). Her name is Ṣāltum 'Strife': by facing one like herself, Ištar will come to her senses. Though the text is severely fragmentary, it appears that Ea agrees to get rid of Ṣāltum after achieving his aim.

It is also worth considering the Standard Babylonian *Epic of Gilgameš*. In Tablet I, as Gilgameš behaves recklessly, the poem's action is triggered when the mother goddess, prompted by the gods, creates Enkidu from clay, as a match for the main hero (SBV *Gilgameš* I 94–100; ed. George 2003: 542–5):

> They summoned Aruru, the great one:
> 'You, o Aruru, gave shape to [man:] (cf. *Creation of the King* 32') 95
> now give shape to what he suggests [lit. his idea]!
> Let him be *equal to the storm* of his heart
> let them rival each other and so let Uruk be rested.'
> When Aruru heard this,
> she gave shape to Anu's [var. Enlil's] idea in her heart. (cf. *IšD* 91) 100
> Aruru washed her hands,
> she took a pinch of clay, she threw it down in the wild.
> In the wild she gave shape to Enkidu, the hero,
> an offspring of silence, knit strong of Ninurta.
> (transl. after George 2003)

Ea is absent from this version, which presents some textual and exegetical problems. But Andrew George may well be correct in positing, as a likely background, a longer version where Ea gave instructions.[25]

---

[23] *IšD* 222–3 *ETCSL* 1.4.1, *IšD* K 162, 91–2 (ed. Lapinkivi 2010: 19).
[24] *VS* 10.214 (ed. Streck: *SEAL* 2.1.5.1).   [25] Cf. Tigay 1982: 192–7, George 2003: 788.

Like Inana/Ištar's officiants, and Ṣāltum, so is Enkidu sent over to re-establish a balance. And Enkidu, like Ṣāltum, will eventually be taken away by the gods.[26]

Hesiod's sequence displays strong structural similarities here: Prometheus, helping mankind, defies the chief god and endangers cosmic order by giving fire to men; Zeus replies by ordering the creation of the Woman, to be sent over to Epimetheus and become the progenitor of womankind. What should make us quite positive about a Near Eastern background to Hesiod's scene is the pivotal centrality of the creation scene.

It is worth recalling that this is the only creation scene attested in the early Greek hexameter corpus, and, of course, the creation from earth by a crafty god with the help of a goddess is as widespread as it could be in the Near East; elsewhere in Greek epos, although the Greeks did have a concept that mankind came from earth and water (*Il.* 7.99, with Kirk 1990: 247), humans are assumed to come to light either through generation or to come forth through permutation – from stones, dragon teeth, or even ants.[27] In the words of Jean Rudhardt,[28]

> In Greek myths, with the exception of Orphic myths, the birth of man is not a unique, clearly identifiable event. Men appear here and there, in different ways, and, in the history of the world, this issue does not seem to be essential. Hesiod therefore is at liberty not to speak of it.

The possibility remains that Hesiod conceived of the human race as having come forth from (ash-)trees, visualised as ash-tree Nymphs, the Meliai (Hes. *Th.* 563–4, cf. *Od.* 19.162–3). At *Th.* 50 the race of men is connected to the race of Giants, and at *Th.* 185–7 the birth of the Giants is connected to that of the Melian Nymphs (both from Gaia as a result of contact with the blood of Ouranos' severed genitals). At *Op.* 144–6 Zeus makes the human Bronze Race 'from the Meliai', and this race shares characteristics with the Giants (hybris, warlike character).[29] Marianne Luginbühl concludes that Greek concepts of human origin by *formatio*

---

[26] See Hawthorn 2015 for a comparison and psychoanalytical interpretation of Ištar/Agušaya and Gilgameš/Enkidu in these texts as 'doubles'.
[27] Permutation from ants: cf. [Hes.] fr. 205 M-W (Myrmidons), stones cf. [Hes.] fr. 234 M-W (Flood myth), from a dragon's teeth cf. Stes. fr. 96 D-F (Theban myth).
[28] Rudhardt 1986: 232 n. 4: 'dans les mythes grecs, à l'exception des mythes orphiques, la naissance de l'homme ne constitue pas un événement unique, clairement identifiable. Des hommes apparaissent ici et là, de différentes façons et, dans l'histoire du monde, la chose ne semble pas essentielle. Hésiode peut donc n'en pas parler.'
[29] Cf. West 1966: 221, 1978: 187, Clay 2003: 104–5; and West 2007: 375–6 for the role of trees in mankind's origins in Indo-European traditions.

developed later, and possibly through contact with the Near East, than those based on *emersio*, of Indo-European ascendance.[30] Though it should be noted that *emersiones* are by no means exclusively Indo-European,[31] the picture fits well with a scenario which is increasingly credited among scholars, one where Near Eastern elements enter pre-existing Greek or Indo-European frameworks.[32]

To remain in the Indo-European realm, it may be useful to compare a fascinating old-Norse myth best known from the poem *Þrymskviða*.[33] The Asgardian gods are at a loss, as the giant Thrymr has seized Thorr's hammer Mjǫllnir; in exchange for the hammer, Thrymr desires the goddess Freyja. The Æsir in their assembly persuade Thorr to adorn himself as a bride and to wear Freyja's necklace. The trick succeeds, and Thorr recovers Mjǫllnir. Here we find an important parallel, for Thorr 'the adorned bride' can be seen as another liminal figure sent over to the enemy side to restore cosmic order. But we do not find a creation scene as in the ancient Near Eastern sources, and in Hesiod. While this comparandum is not necessarily to be taken as evidence of an Indo-European background to Hesiod's divine narrative, it does highlight the Near Eastern connection in respect to the creation scene's syntactical function.

Still, this Near Eastern nexus should not impede us from appreciating that, as we saw, Hesiod's shaping is entirely Greek in terms of poetic craft: the creation is given very little space, and the central concern is the adornment. The fact that there seems to be no obvious traditional background for such moulding creations (they are not implied by *Il.* 7.99, and Hephaistos' tripod robots and golden maidservants at *Il.* 18.374–9, 417–20 are pure metalwork), might point to a relatively recent date for the cross-over, during the Early Iron Age. Hints from the Levant come from the *Genesis* narrative, and from the Late Bronze Age Ugaritic *Keret* epic, where the chief god El creates from clay a female 'Dispeller of Disease', whom he sends to cure the ill king, and restore the Land's fertility (*KTU*³ 16.v.23–41, transl. Greenstein 1997: 38–9):

---

[30] Luginbühl 1992: 263–5.
[31] See Frazer 1918: I.29–42 *passim* ('evolution'), and Lisman 2013 for *emersio* in Sumerian anthropogenies.
[32] Mondi 1990: 147–57, 187–9; López-Ruiz 2014a: 163–4; Metcalf 2015a: 222–4; Katz 2018; Kelly (Chapter 16 in this volume) and Rutherford (Chapter 12 in this volume).
[33] The poem stands in the Codex Regius (thirteenth century CE), but some of its traits may well be pre-Carolingian; it is edited by Neckel and Kuhn 1983; English translation in Larrington 2014: 93–7. See the introductory essay by Ross 2002.

So answers Kind El the Compassionate:
'Stay seated, my sons, on your seats,
on your elevated thrones.
As for me, I'll use skills and create!
I'll create a Remover of Illness,
a Dispeller of Disease!'
He fills his hand [with soil].
With good soil he fills his [fingers].
He pinches off some clay
[*In the nine lines 31–8, either broken or missing, El completes his creation.*]
A cup [he takes in his hand]
A cha[lice he holds in his right]
You are Sh[ataqat . . .]

Concerning Anatolia, aside from the Hittite version of the *Gilgameš* episode (again from the Late Bronze Age), it is worth recalling Volkert Haas' hypothesis of a connection between Pandora's jar and Hittite containers of evils.[34] More recently, Norbert Oettinger has drawn connections between the Pandora episode and Hittite scapegoat rituals where the dispelled beings are adorned as brides. The scapegoat is meant to bring the contamination away from the community toward the *other*.[35] But a cross-cultural discourse on the varying connections between ritual and myth is well beyond the scope of the present contribution. A ritual dimension, for example, is hardly perceptible in the case of *Þrymskviða*, where the disguise is above all a function of the trick, and in Hesiod, where the adornment enchants Epimetheus; in both cases, the harm is just conveyed, not expelled (that is to say, Pandora and Thorr/the bride were not a harm for the gods).

It is now appropriate to draw some conclusions on Hesiod's Woman and the Near Eastern literary sources. We have seen that *Genesis* 2–3 represents the strongest structural parallel to the *Works and Days* episode on the mythic-aetiological level: the creation of Woman, and her untimely action, explain human labour. But there is little here on the level of poetic realisation. Much closer in this sense are the Egyptian and Babylonian Creation narratives culminating in the crowning of the human ruler and collective divine attributions. But it is precisely the crowning that shows these scenes to be of limited diagnostic value, for Pandora is no queen, nor is she to be praised (though she *is* admired). This has enabled us to describe

---

[34] See above, note 5.
[35] Oettinger 2010, cf. Hoffner 1973. The mythical paradigm here is, of course, the story of the Trojan horse. See further Burkert 1979: 59–77, Faraone 1992: 100–2.

Hesiod's craft within a Greek poetic context, in that the *Theogony* scene combines, very much as the sixth *Homeric Hymn* to Aphrodite, an adorning-for-seduction scene with the typical presentation of the newborn deity to the divine assembly. Between these two poles (that of the aetiological myth, and the mismatched detailed parallel) other Mesopotamian creation scenes appear to constitute the most important structural comparanda. In these narratives, as in Hesiod, the fashioning of a liminal creature is the nodal point in the divine master plan to fix a cosmic imbalance.

It is true that the virtual 'isolation' of Hesiod's creation scenes within Greek *epos* directs us to the Near East.[36] But it is no less true that this common Near Eastern pattern has been fully adapted to serve Hesiod's aim (in both his poems) to glorify Zeus, and to do so in terms which would hardly have struck his audiences as somehow strange or foreign. His scenes are profoundly ingrained within, and expressed through, the poetic and theological system of early Greek epic – to the point that one should not see here an 'Oriental' scene in Hesiod, but a traditional Greek poet's declension of a common Eastern Mediterranean and Near Eastern mythological motif and compositional pattern.

---

[36] On the dangers of a comparative approach 'by isolation' which seeks to detach features in Greek texts from their context, see Kelly 2008. Haubold 2013a and Metcalf 2015a show how to engage in comparative study while avoiding this.

CHAPTER 16

*Sexing and Gendering the Succession Myth in Hesiod and the Ancient Near East**

Adrian Kelly

Introduction

This chapter begins with two apologies, the first to scholars of Near Eastern literature for once again using their texts basically to elucidate something about an early Greek author, and the second to the reader for taking yet another look at such a well-known issue – the relationship between Hesiod's so-called Succession Myth and its various comparanda in the traditions of the Ancient Near East.[1] Both, perhaps, can be justified by the context and purposes of this book. Elsewhere I have argued that there is room for considerable scepticism about the enthusiasm with which Classicists have subscribed to one, rather simplistic, version of *ex Oriente lux*.[2] This conclusion is not driven by a desire to stop Near Eastern literatures from making a 'claim on the Homeric reader' or to avoid a 'committed reading' of those literatures;[3] indeed, this chapter will try to offer such a reading of the Succession Myth in a number of ancient cultures. Instead, my objections are methodological: though it is growing more marginal, the still tenacious Classical approach to this material remains in the grip of a 'parallelomania' which overplays similarities and downplays differences between these traditions, and tries to make individual Greek authors the conduits, if not the actual translators, of Near Eastern material.

It is perhaps no surprise that this should have happened, when we remember that the intellectual parameters of Classics, just like any other

---

* I would like to thank my former student Laura Wills, from whom I learned much when I first explored this area whilst supervising her undergraduate thesis on Greek and Near Eastern goddesses. I would also like to thank several colleagues – specifically Bernardo Ballesteros Petrella, Renaud Gagné, Johannes Haubold, Ian Rutherford, Selena Wisnom, and especially Christopher Metcalf – for helping me try to overcome the fact that I am only a scholar of early Greek literature.
[1] The term is retained here, despite the just criticisms of van Dongen 2014; its use does not imply any kind of cultural uniformity, but it remains a convenient shorthand.
[2] See Kelly 2008, Kelly 2014.   [3] Haubold 2013a: 32.

discipline, are shaped by its heritage. Two strands in particular have played important roles here: firstly the much later relationship between Greek and Roman literature, and secondly the authority of 'textual criticism' – the process by which the authentic, original version of a text is established by sorting out and weighing its visible, individual manuscript sources. It was almost inevitable that the certainties predicating these relationships and processes should be transposed, with varying levels of self-awareness, back onto the study of early Greek literature.[4] But, aside from being powerfully redolent of Whig history with its parade of epoch-altering heroes, this approach oversimplifies the means, complexities and the length of cultural contacts between Greece and its neighbours, which must stretch all the way back at least into the middle Bronze Age. Instead, we should prefer a 'longue durée' to some of my colleagues' 'big bang' approach.[5]

Traditions in Dialogue

Given these methodological predilections, Classicists have long been drawn to the Succession Myth in Hesiod's *Theogony*, and modern scholarship holds with almost one voice that its similarities with a Hurro-Hittite text of the thirteenth century BCE, known now as the *Song of Emergence* (*CTH* 344), are so thorough and pervasive that they can only be explained in terms of the Greeks borrowing the story from the Hurro-Hittite tradition.[6] Indeed, the most pressing question has for long been not if but when and where this 'event' took place. Moreover, do we opt for a personalised approach, in which Hesiod himself did it, or a more tradition-centred one, where these features were part of Greek epos for many generations before Hesiod himself?[7] Sceptical voices have been

---

[4] See Currie 2016, which avowedly uses the (much later) Augustan poets and their dynamics as a model for early Greek literary history, and even tries to transpose such a dynamic onto Sumerian and Babylonian poetry.

[5] For examples of this approach, see recently Lardinois 2018 and his Chapter 5 in this volume. For criticism, see Metcalf 2017 (review of Bachvarova 2016). I note, however, that this book and the conference on which it is based reveal the extent to which this kind of enquiry no longer represents the direction of study in the comparative project. See the Introduction, above 1–3.

[6] For recent discussions with (voluminous) earlier bibliography, see West 1997: 103–5, 278–92; Rutherford 2009: 9–36; López-Ruiz 2010: 87–94; Rutherford 2018: esp. 4–6, 12–13. The title has only recently been recovered (Corti 2007; van Dongen 2011: 182 n. 3 terms it the *Song of Going Forth*), and the text is generally linked with other tablets to make what is known as the *Kingship in Heaven Cycle* (a.k.a. the *Kumarbi Cycle*), though even the term 'cycle' is now not uncontroversial: Archi 2009: 211.

[7] The otherwise excellent study of van Dongen 2011: 190, 194f. tries to sketch out Hesiod's own role in the process, but he does not deny the story's currency in Greek contexts at the time, and he

raised,[8] but there does seem to be a good prima facie case for positing some kind of direct interaction between traditions here.

Before examining the similarities which have given rise to this conclusion, we should take a step back, methodologically and diachronically. When arguments are made about the Greeks 'borrowing' or 'inheriting' elements from Near Eastern cultures, there is usually little or no consideration of what existed before the putative moment of derivation. When, on the other hand, scholars do invoke the Indo-European background in this connection, they are usually trying to deny or qualify that derivation, and so they use that background in an either/or way: if an apparently 'Near Eastern' element in a Greek text can be paralleled in an Indo-European setting, then it is no longer evidence for the influence of the Near East. This is an important argument to invoke against those scholars who are too quick to suggest derivation, especially when they seek to isolate a particular moment or person responsible, but its strength must depend upon the individual example, and preclusive purposes are in any case hardly the limit of the utility or interest to be found in the Indo-European background.

This is especially so in the case of the Succession Myth, which several scholars have studied in a range of Indo-European contexts. Parallels for the 'kingship in heaven' have been found to varying levels of specificity in Iranian, Indian and Norse mythologies: Stig Wikander saw a close parallel with the late tenth-century CE Iranian *Shāhnāmeh* or 'Epic of Kings' (though he too swiftly discounted the effect of earlier Mesopotamian tradition), Dominique Briquel contrasted the hatred and violence in the Greek tradition with the relative peaceability of roughly parallel patterns and motifs in the *Mahābhārata*, and C. Scott Littleton traced the 'same broad framework' in Norse stories of creation.[9] More recently, Nick Allen compared Hesiod's picture with the five generations of god-heroes in the *Mahābhārata* to reconstruct an Indo-European 'protonarrative', with several, though more diffuse, points of contact.[10] But, even leaving aside the question of their relative temporal and historical positioning, none of

---

proceeds largely on the somewhat subjective basis of 'how ingeniously the tripartite scheme of the theme works in the *Theogony*' (190). Strauss Clay and Gilan 2014 suggest a direct link based on a very small and precise verbal inconcinnity in both Hesiod and the *Song of Emergence*. For a similar range of traditional versus personalised arguments about Homer's relationship to Near Eastern texts and traditions, see Kelly 2008.

[8] See esp. Mondi 1990. [9] Wikander 1952; Briquel 1980, Littleton 1970a (~ 1970b).
[10] Allen 2004; see also Sergent 1997: 333–5.

these traditions shows the systemic resemblance to the Greek story we see in the *Song of Emergence*, and some details are at best very partial parallels. We should not, however, therefore simply discount the importance of this material, since

> the Greeks, at the same time as they assimilated oriental contributions, were able to interpret them according to Indo-European conceptions. What matters in the end is not the ultimate provenance of any element of the myth – such as the name of Zeus or the idea of the struggle between the divine generations – but the way in which these features are arranged and presented by the Greeks in a coherent system: ... at this level the persistence of Indo-European patterns is sometimes felt, integrating Mediterranean or Eastern material if applicable.[11]

That is, their Indo-European background probably furnished the Greeks with a series of roughly comparable stories about the generational transfer of power in royal and divine contexts which opened the way, as it were, for processes of later interaction.[12] It may be doubted whether there was a consistent Indo-European tradition containing all or most of the elements as known in Hesiod and the *Song of Emergence*,[13] viz. conflict between three generations of gods, mutilation of the first generation, redefinition of the victorious gods, and a final battle between the new regime and the older gods. But we may be sure that without at least some of these similarities, however distantly framed, the interaction between Greeks and Hurro-Hittite culture might well have been 'blocked'.[14]

---

[11] Briquel 1980: 247: '[l]es Hellènes, en même temps qu'ils ont assimilé des apports orientaux, ont pu les interpréter en fonction de conceptions indo-européennes. Finalement ce qui importe, c'est non la provenance ultime de tel élément du mythe – nom de Zeus ou idée de la lutte entre des générations divines – mais la manière dont ces traits s'ordonnent dans la représentation des Grecs en un système cohérent: ... à ce niveau la persistance de schémas indo-européens [se fait parfois] sentir, intégrant le cas échéant des données méditerranéennes ou orientales'; see also Katz 2018: 63: 'an obvious desideratum for the modern study of Hesiod is, therefore, a holistic understanding of how Indo-European prehistory and Near Eastern analogues contribute together to the formation of Hesiodic language and thought'.

[12] Witzel 2012: 65–75 (esp. element 7 on table 2.7), 161 for 'Laurasian' systems and their interaction. For a recent demonstration of the importance of the Indo-European heritage in Greek cosmogonical thinking, see now Mitchell 2018.

[13] Cf. Littleton 1970a: 396–400. Even if we were to decide that 'kingship in heaven' was an Indo-European pattern, or at least a possibility within that tradition, it would not materially change the argument of this chapter, since the Greek myth's similarities with the Hurro-Hittite tradition are much closer and more numerous than with any other known form of this story. For the required caution in these matters, see the comments of Puhvel 1987: 22–3.

[14] See Rutherford, Chapter 11 in this volume, for analysis of why the story of Baal's fight with the Sea does not cross into the Greek world; also below, note 48, on Greek and Indian cosmogonic traditions.

That the Greek tradition did not suffer this fate is certain. The parallels between the eighth- or seventh-century BCE *Theogony* and the thirteenth-century BCE *Song of Emergence* are well known, and so they are recalled here only briefly. They begin with the sequence Ouranos–Kronos–Zeus on the Greek side closely matched in Anu–Kumarbi–Teššub/Tarhunta on the Hurro-Hittite, showing the threefold transfer of power from the sky god to the cunning god, and then to the Storm God. The particular shared details are also very similar: (i) Kumarbi bites off the genitals of Anu as Kronos lops off the genitals of Ouranos with a sickle, and (ii) both Kumarbi and Kronos swallow a stone, instead of a child, which later becomes a cult object; (iii) the gods of the third generation emerge from the body of the overthrown god (Kronos vomits, Kumarbi gives birth); and (iv) finally, Kumarbi's birthing of Teššub seems also to find some kind of parallel in Zeus's swallowing of Metis and the birth of Athene later in the *Theogony* (886–900, 924–9).[15]

Yet the Hurro-Hittite tradition is not the only one to show some kind of parallel to the *Theogony*'s Succession Myth. The late second-millennium BCE Babylonian Creation Epic, *Enūma eliš*, shares (i) the idea that the father's dislike for his children is the cause of the trouble (Ouranos and Kronos/Apsu), and (ii) the somewhat destabilising role of the primordial female god (Gaia/Tiamat) – an important principle in the Greek, as we shall see, but not quite in the same way for the Hurro-Hittite tradition. Another Babylonian work, the *Theogony of Dunnu* – whose text is dated to the first millennium BCE but whose story is as early as the start of the second millennium – shares with Hesiod a focus on incest and intergenerational violence, but details are sparse.[16]

Though it is clear that some of Hesiod's story is closer to the *Song of Emergence* than the other texts listed here, the evidence does not allow us to reach a firm conclusion on the questions of when and where any interaction took place: some scholars argue for an early cross-over directly through an Anatolian interface in the Late Bronze Age, while others have suggested a more direct route, closer in time to Hesiod in the Early Iron Age, through Neo-Hittite Kingdoms in Northern Syria and/or

---

[15] For other parallels, esp. those involving Typhaon, and the seminal scattering which gives birth to Aphrodite, see the works listed above, note 6.

[16] For excellent summaries of all this material, see the works listed above, note 6; for English translations, Lambert 2013, López-Ruiz 2014b. For more on the relationship between *Dunnu* and the *Song of Emergence*, see Metcalf, Chapter 8 in this volume.

Phoenicians in the Levant.[17] This chapter does not seek to lump for one or other route, though a lot of our evidence for the Succession Myth in the Phoenician case comes in the work of Philon of Byblos, a Greek of the first/second century CE, who claims to have access to an old Phoenician cosmogony of 'Sanchuniathon'. Preserved by Eusebius, the bishop of Caesarea in the fourth century CE (*PE* 1.10.1–53), this story seems in many ways to resonate with the Hesiodic tale, and contains several of the same details, such as the castration of Ouranos, who is hostile towards his children, by his son El/Kronos.[18] When read in conjunction with Late Bronze Age Ugaritic texts, such as the fourteenth- or thirteenth-century BCE *Baal Cycle*, this narrative may provide another hint of the traditions from which Hesiod or his forebears could have drawn, but Erik van Dongen was surely right to doubt its independent probative worth: Philon was writing with a good knowledge of Hesiod, and so his evidentiary value is a little questionable.[19] In any case, neither Philon nor the early Ugaritic material shows the crucial feature of the Succession Myth with which we are concerned in this chapter, and so will play no further part in the discussion.

My own view of the interactive dynamic is that it was a process, with several points of contact, beginning in the Late Bronze Age but continuing down into the Early Iron Age, through several conduits. But is that it? Is this all we can say – that on current evidence we cannot be more precise than this? That may well be correct and cautious in genealogical terms, but it's surely not the only way Classicists can seek illumination in the Near East, particularly with this exciting nexus of texts. In an earlier article which no-one has read and even fewer people agree with, I suggested that the distinctive qualities of Homeric battle narrative, when viewed next to the Near Eastern literary representations of combat, show just how different from its neighbours – in fact, how odd – was the early Greek epic tradition in its 'aestheticisation' and 'narrativisation' of battle;[20] these terms simply mean that battle becomes the context and topic for

---

[17] For a recent, excellent overview of the options, see Rutherford 2018: 17–19, who sensibly refuses to narrow it down in this way.

[18] See Littleton 1970a: 385, Cors i Meya 1999–2000, López-Ruiz 2010: 94–101.

[19] van Dongen 2011: esp. 183–4.

[20] Kelly 2014. For a different view, which gathers details and motifs in the usual manner, see Rollinger 2015. For criticism of this method, see Kelly 2008. Rollinger 2015 faults the latter article for failing to recognise that the process of adaptation changes the material, but we must try to distinguish between similarities that are fortuitous or the result of native developments and those that are actually parallels derived from external sources. Otherwise we have no scholarly method at our disposal – just a cataloguing exercise masquerading as one.

interesting narrative, rather than simply a usually non-episodic confirmation of the overpowering might of, or divine support behind, the victor, as we find it generally in Near Eastern and Egyptian sources. The question of genealogy – though it tends to point one in the Indo-European direction – seemed less interesting than analogy, viz. what the comparison with other traditions could show us. In this case, it revealed that the Greeks liked long, detailed, dramatic and sinuous descriptions of battle, and were pretty much alone of the Late Bronze Age civilisations in the Aegean basin and Mesopotamia in doing so.

As scholars are increasingly recognising, and as the Oxford conference from which this volume originated made clear, we have to move beyond cataloguing similarities and constructing genealogies, and start thinking about what Near Eastern material tells us in analogical terms – i.e., what each culture or text is doing with shared or common elements. When we turn to the comparative material in this spirit, we notice immediately a big difference between (and within) the Near Eastern and early Greek traditions of the Succession Myth, i.e., the pattern as we find it narrated in Hesiod (but assumed in Homer and worked out in different ways in the *Homeric Hymns*). This difference, in short, is sex and gender, or the role played by these phenomena within the logic of the myth.[21]

Let us look first at the Greek side, both within and beyond Hesiod: here it is always the chief consort working through the children who undermines the father, in a variety of ways.[22] In the *Theogony*, Gaia becomes irritated by her husband's treatment of her and her children. First of all she invites volunteers from among her children to overthrow Ouranos, and then arms Kronos with an adamantine sickle and 'instructs him in the whole deception' (δόλον δ' ὑπεθήκατο πάντα 170; cf. 159–75). Similarly annoyed by Kronos' practice of swallowing her children as soon as they are born, Rheia consults Gaia and Ouranos about the means to prevent the same thing happening to Zeus. On their advice, she goes to Lyktos (where she is received by Gaia) to give birth to Zeus and then hands Kronos a stone in his place (459–91). Hera, the final consort, is shown in Hesiod and beyond as constantly trying to overcome or thwart Zeus's or his sons'

---

[21] I recognise the differentiation of 'sex' as a biological function from 'gender' as a social construct, in the standard manner, but their close interrelationship in the material makes more focus on this unnecessary in the current chapter. For recent discussions of these issues in the Near Eastern context, see, e.g., Asher-Greve 2001, Parpola and Whiting 2002, Bolger 2008, Asher-Greve and Westenholz 2013: 15–28, Budin 2014, Peled 2016, Cooper 2017; also below, note 28.

[22] See the foundational work of Bonnafé 1985: esp. ch. 5, and now Lye 2018.

desires, but having very little luck in the process (*Th.* 314–15, 328–9, 927–9).²³ In effect, she is the frustrated 'maternal plotter' in the pattern of the Succession Myth.

Interestingly, Gaia and Ouranos are constantly involved in the subsequent stages of the Succession Myth, often in what have seemed to scholars to be contradictory ways: they advise both Kronos about what could happen to him at the hands of his son (463–5) and Rheia about how to go about making it happen (474–6); they warn Zeus about what could happen to him at the hands of his son (888–900), and Gaia is also on several other occasions said to have guaranteed or aided his succession 'by her plans' (ἐννεσίηισι πολυφραδέεσσι 494, φραδμοσύνηισιν 626), whilst she produces Typhaon as the apparently final challenge to Zeus's reign (820–2). Gaia is clearly the dominant figure in this picture of alternating allegiances, and her ambiguity is similarly to be explained by the focus on sex and gender in Hesiod or the Greek tradition more generally,²⁴ a function of the ambivalence within which female participation and power is framed therein.

Hera's frustration is important, since the repetition of the Succession Myth is prevented in the Greek setting largely by the sexual politics of Zeus, manifest in many separate ways throughout early *epos*. Firstly, he swallows the pregnant Metis and thus himself produces Athene (*Th.* 888–900), whose birth represents the diverted threat to his reign: she shows, by her eternal virginity, that she will not destabilise Zeus by bringing forth a rival to challenge him. Immediately after Athene's birth in the *Theogony* (924–6), Hera produces Hephaistos out of anger with her husband and therefore without his help, and the link between Zeus's parthenogenesis – and Hera's less successful attempt to rival it – is made even clearer in the *Homeric Hymn to Apollo* (307–30f.).

Secondly, this behaviour is entwined with another aspect of Olympian sexual politics, in that Zeus has powerful offspring with several female gods who are not his chief consort – Apollo from Leto, Hermes from Maia, Dionysos from Semele, Heracles from Alcmene, etc. (*Th.* 918–20, 938–9, 940–2, 943–4 etc.). These figures will help to establish his rule by ridding the earth of primeval monsters and creatures whose subversive actions are frequently engendered or encouraged by the Succession Myth female deities: Typhoeus, for instance, is the child of Gaia in Hesiod (and of

---

[23] See esp. Pirenne-Delforge and Pironti 2016: 23–103; on Hera's conflict with Zeus's children, see Pirenne-Delforge and Pironti 2015.
[24] See below, pp. 290–1, for brief discussion of other, later Greek receptions.

Hera in the *Homeric Hymn to Apollo*, *h.Hom.* 3.307–9), whilst Hera nurses the Lernaian Hydra (314–15) and the Nemean Lion (328–9). These 'monster challengers' of course have a long and varied tradition – Anatolian, Mesopotamian and Ugaritic – but that is not my concern here.[25] But it is neither coincidental nor an empty metaphor that the birth of Typhoeus in Hesiod is achieved by Gaia but explicitly 'through (the plan of) golden Aphrodite' (διὰ χρυσῆν Ἀφροδίτην *Th.* 822). Sex and gender, everywhere.[26]

Thirdly, as the flipside of this coin, Zeus's genealogical self-control is extended to his control over the sexual freedom of others, something made clear by the very structure of the *Theogony* itself, which closes with marriages of decreasing cosmological significance, finally ending with the children of goddesses and their lovers.[27] But it is also a fundamental concept throughout early Greek *epos*, with, e.g., Calypso complaining of the gods' double standards in matters of sexual freedom (*Od.* 5.116–29), Zeus's plan to marry off his daughter Persephone in the *Homeric Hymn to Demeter*, and Aphrodite finding her powers curtailed and turned on her by Zeus in the *Homeric Hymn to Aphrodite*.

In other words, the sexing and gendering of the Succession Myth in Hesiod resonates with a process which is foundational, in several different ways, to the whole *Götterapparat* of early Greek *epos*. But when we turn to the Near Eastern material, we do not see this anywhere in any version of the Succession Myth.[28] That is not to say that sexual politics are unimportant in these traditions, as we will see, but the Greeks seem to entwine sex and gender into the very DNA of the myth in a very different, much more obvious, and much more thorough way.

This can be demonstrated by reference to Table 4, where the texts are tabulated by reference to a pattern made up of four elements – marriage, treatment of/attitude to children, maternal plotting, and overthrow. Not all of the texts feature such an arrangement, of course, and one might charge with some justice that the whole concept is too influenced by the conceptual primacy of the Hesiodic story. Nonetheless, tabulation does

---

[25] For recent re-evaluations of this theme in ancient Near Eastern culture, see the essays in Scurlock and Beal 2013; on the Indo-European tradition, see Watkins 1995, West 2007: 255–9; for the widest possible view, see Witzel 2012: 148–54.
[26] For a different view, see Metcalf 2015a: 183 n. 36.
[27] See Kelly 2007b: 389–94. Whether these closing catalogues are authentically Hesiod's work is not settled, but irrelevant for my point: they were early a part of this poem's tradition.
[28] Studies of gender and divinity in Near Eastern literature are a relatively recent phenomenon: see Lambert 1987, Frymer-Kensky 1992, Harris 2000, Sonik 2009, Asher-Greve and Westenholz 2013, Budin 2014; see also above, note 21.

Table 4 *The Succession Myth in Hesiod's Theogony and Near Eastern texts*

	Hesiod, *Theogony*	Hittite *Kingship in Heaven*	*Enūma eliš*	*Theogony of Dunnu*
A		**Alalu**		**Ha'in**
marriage		–		Earth (s.?)
children		–		?
maternal plot		–		Earth with Shakkan
overthrow	Alalu by Anu			Ha'in [killed] by Shakkan
1	**Ouranos**	**Anu**	**Apsu**	**Shakkan (s.)**
marriage	Gaia (m.)	–	Tiamat	Earth (m.)/Sea (s.)
children	Ouranos prevents	–	Apsu hates, Tiamat vexed	?
maternal plot	Gaia with her children	–	Tiamat refuses	?
overthrow	Ouranos [castrated] by Kronos	Anu [castrated] by Kumarbi	Apsu [killed] by Ea (ggs.)	Shakkan [killed] by Laḫar, Earth by Sea
2	**Kronos (s.)**	**Kumarbi**	**(Anšar) Ea/Tiamat/Qingu**	**Laḫar (s.)**
marriage	Rheia (s.)	–	Damkina (m.)	Sea (mother)
children	Kronos eats	Kumarbi gestates	Tiamat et al. hate	
maternal plot	Rheia with children, Gaia/Ouranos		Tiamat with children, older gods	?
overthrow	Kronos by Zeus	Kumarbi by Teššub	Tiamat [killed] by Marduk	Laḫar & Sea [killed] by [x]
3	**Zeus (s.)**	**Teššub (s.)**	**Marduk (s.)**	**[x] (s.)**
marriage	Hera (s.) etc.	–	–	River (s.)
children	Zeus honours Gaia/Hera	–	–	?
maternal plot		–	Marduk creates	?
overthrow	Zeus kills Typhaon	Teššub defeats Lamma, Silver, Hedammu, Ullikummi	–	[x] & River killed by [y] (below)
4				**[y] (s.)** **[z] (s.)**
marriage				Ga'u (s.) Ningestinna
children				? ?
maternal plot				? ?
overthrow				[y] & Ga'u killed by [z]

allow us to see the texts side by side, and it also shows how individual is the treatment found in the *Theogony*. One of the things which should be immediately clear is the universality in Hesiod of maternal plotting – where the wife/mother plots against the consort/chief god through, or because of, her children's interests.

Now compare this with the Hurro-Hittite *Song of Emergence* (*CTH* 344) where Kumarbi takes over almost all generative functions, both literally in the gods he engenders after swallowing Anu's genitals, and in the four later challengers he produces to overthrow Teššub – Lamma, Silver, Ullikummi and Hedammu (*CTH* 343, 345–6, 348). Though some of these figures are indeed the result of heterosexual intercourse, the agency or attitude of the mother towards the process of succession is entirely undervalued.[29] What matters here is Kumarbi's repeated plans to overthrow Teššub, and throughout the story there is no room for the maternal plotter so prominent in Hesiod. Indeed, as Campbell has most recently argued,[30] the birthing powers of Kumarbi are designed to unify the lines of Anu and Kumarbi in the person of Teššub, and should be considered an innovation on a 'more natural' pattern in which a female deity would be involved, since the story 'transgresses the laws of sexuality and gender in order to underline the power of the male god and his creative role'.[31] For all the similarites with which we began, the difference between the Greek and Hurro-Hittite traditions on this point is striking.

The figure of the maternal plotter is, however, clearly evident in the two Babylonian texts. The first and most obvious is Tiamat in *Enūma eliš*, and her role in plots is shown twice, first *e contrario* where she refuses to join Apsu in his quest to destroy their children, effectively resigning herself 'to her spouse's death for the sake of her children'[32] (I 29–46). It seems to be assumed here that she is naturally considered an essential figure in any such move, since Apsu bothers to try persuading her to join his project, and her failure to assent to the proposal is later brought back on her as a rebuke by the other gods (I 113–20). As they make clear, Tiamat's refusal to plot actually helps to bring about the succession. The second occasion is the more obvious one (I 110–62 and ff.), where Tiamat swiftly moves from being an outraged parent persuaded by her children to attempt the destruction of the new god Marduk (and so glut her anger against Anšar

---

[29] There is reference to a pregnancy and birth for Earth in this process, but the tablet at this point is severely damaged, and more we cannot say: see Beckman 2011: 31–2. The marginalisation of the female deity has been noted as typical of second-millennium Babylonian texts as a whole: Frymer-Kensky 1992: 70–80, Asher-Greve and Westenholz 2013: 22–8; also below, notes 36 and 38.
[30] Campbell 2013.   [31] López-Ruiz 2010: 143.   [32] Harris 2000: 84.

for the overthrow of Apsu) to a monster configured along the lines of the typical challenger to the deity's rule, such as in the Sumerian *Lugale* (*ETCSL* 1.6.2) or the Akkadian *Epic of Anzu*.[33] Though maternity is an important part of Tiamat's initial motivation, her transformation into a terrifying beast at the very least de-emphasises the sexed and gendered elements in her character.[34]

That is not to deny a patriarchal motive or function to the text,[35] not least since Marduk's creation of man (Tablet VI) surely makes a point about the relative importance of the male/female role in his universe, especially next to analogous scenes of human creation elsewhere in Mesopotamia (e.g., *Enki and Ninmah* 1–43 [*ETCSL* 1.1.2]; *Atrahasīs* OB I 189ff., LB II 67ff.; *Epic of Gilgameš* SBV I 94–104).[36] In *Enūma eliš*, Tiamat's twin roles – mother and monster – are mirrored in the duality, almost indeterminacy, of her aims vis-à-vis the Succession Myth: as she is attempting to prevent the succession of Marduk, so she promotes at the same time the succession of her son, and then spouse, Qingu. On both occasions, however, she fails to foster her favoured regime through to the desired end. So here we have a maternal plotter of the general sort we encounter in the Greek tradition, but a thoroughly reconfigured one, where the poet de-emphasises her sexed and gendered maternity in favour of monstrosity, and pointedly makes her fail in the context of intergenerational strife and its transfer of power.

Similarly sexed and gendered, but in a very different way, is the *Theogony of Dunnu*, in which Earth suggests a sexual liaison to her son Shakkan, a coupling which precedes his killing of his father.[37] This sets up the pattern to be repeated over several generations, of a son marrying his mother and/or sister, and killing his father and, sometimes, mother as well – truly a myth to make Oedipus feel a bit of an amateur. Whether intentional or not, the first incest does have a political ramification in the death of Ha'in, and one may suspect (despite the text's laconic nature) that Sea's murder of her mother Earth had something to do with some kind of

---

[33] See above, note 25.
[34] Harris 2000: 87: 'The very one-sided, misogynistic depiction of the old goddess Tiamat relates to her "masculine" behaviour, which threatened patriarchal norms.'
[35] Cf. Sonik 2009.
[36] See Frymer-Kensky 1992: 70–80; Budin 2014. Selena Wisnom reminds me that only males (Ea, Marduk) are involved in the creation of man in *Enūma eliš*, a strikingly gendered aspect to that poem which is also matched in the way that elsewhere (e.g., *Anzu*) it is the mother who encourages the god to fight the challenger, whilst in *Enūma eliš* that role is played by Marduk's father, Ea. For other mothers, see below, p. 288.
[37] See Lambert 2013: 387–92.

power conflict arising from their relative status as the wives of Shakkan, and the need to eliminate a rival in the marriage to Laḫar. Fortunately this kind of thing gets resolved in the next three generations, when both father and mother are killed immediately by the new ruler.

So the nexus of sex and gender does play a role in the versions of the Succession Myth we find in the Mesopotamian traditions, though with nothing like the almost formulaic regularity we find in Hesiod: whereas Gaia and Rheia succeed in their efforts to bring about succession (and Hera necessarily fails, repeatedly), Tiamat in *Enūma eliš* unwittingly brings about succession first through non-participation and then through failure; while Earth in *Dunnu* apparently succeeds in her aim of having the husband replaced by her son, but she is then killed by her daughter (who also happens to be her love-rival), thus setting up a pattern in which the mother is invariably murdered at the moment of succession or shortly thereafter. Incidentally, the negative depiction of the maternal figure in these texts is the exception rather than the rule in Mesopotamian literature. For instance, in *Enki and Ninhursag* (*ETCSL* 1.1.1) the latter, despite her anger at Enki, still assists him in his birthing crisis, while in *Enlil and Ninlil* (*ETCSL* 1.2.1), Ninlil perseveres against her ill treatment at the hands of Enlil to bear him children. The mother goddess is more usually supportive in stories of monster challengers, as in the *Epic of Anzu*, where Mami suggests and then advises Ningirsu (OB) or Ninurta (SB) on his quest; or in Ninlil's cautioning of Ninurta after his defeat of Asag in *Lugale*.[38]

In itself, the comparison with the Near Eastern texts helps a Classicist better to understand a distinctive quality about the way in which Greeks shaped this kind of story for their requirements. It is certainly beyond my competence to use this material to make a generalisation about sexual politics in several different Near Eastern civilisations over an enormous time span,[39] but it is striking how the same concern about specifically female usurpation of male power is only *sometimes* found, in a variety of forms, in the Near Eastern traditions, but has been woven deeply into the very fabric of Greek theological narrative. Only the Greek tradition makes

---

[38] See generally Frymer-Kensky 1992: 14–31, 70–80; Asher-Greve and Westenholz 2013; Gadotti 2014b; also above, note 36, for the ways *Enūma eliš* self-consciously downplays this maternal positivity.

[39] For recent discussions of the status and roles of women in the ancient Near East, see Bolger 2008, Gadotti 2011, Lion and Michel 2016, Stol 2016. For more reasons not to indulge in this kind of generalisation, see van Dongen 2014.

the goddess a source of constant danger to the upholding of divine order. Sex and gender have become, indeed, almost the foundational concepts of that order.

One should probably pursue the comparison only this far, with the individual traits of these several traditions made clearer by analogy, but the temptation to speculate about genealogy is irresistible. As we have seen, the Greek and Mesopotamian traditions both reflect the destabilising potential of the female in the Succession Myth, though the Mesopotamian goes out of its way to reduce that potential or redirect it through non- or de-sexed and -gendered channels. The Hurro-Hittite tradition is the outlier here, in the way it has Kumarbi take over all generative functionality, but in another sense it shows the same tendency as the Mesopotamian texts in erasing or marginalising the maternal plotter. That is, both of these traditions could be seen as secondary reflections or refractions of an 'original', much simpler pattern of succession, where a (naturally) female figure gives birth to the god who will usurp her husband — the pattern that the Hesiodic version reflects more directly, and uses repeatedly. One shudders to make these sorts of absolutist judgements across cultural and temporal boundaries, but such a reconstruction would imply that the Near Eastern traditions on this point were more complex, developed and sophisticated than the Greek.[40] It would also suggest that there were at least two nodes of interaction, one Anatolian and one Mesopotamian, feeding into the long prehistory of this theme in Greek literature.[41] It is very hard to believe that Hesiod himself was so multicultural or multilingual as personally to combine these two rather different approaches to the Succession Myth for the first time in an Hellenic context.[42]

---

[40] See Kelly 2014: 53 for a similar suggestion about Greek and Near Eastern attitudes to narrative violence.
[41] See especially Rutherford, Chapter 11 in this volume. He suggests several routes and times of transfer, including the possibility of Minoan intermediaries through Aleppo and Mari in the eighteenth century BCE – even before the Hittite translations of Hurrian material! – which might support my suggestion that the Greek tradition, in its simplicity, preserves a very old version of this tale. A further, fascinating ramification is that 'shared traditions' could then travel back into the Near East on the back of 'Aegean' cultural prestige (as evidenced in Cretan artistic motifs in the Levant). Rutherford's chapter is yet another blow to the simplistic, stemmatological methods typical of Classicists in this area.
[42] As Christopher Metcalf suggests to me, this also sits ill with Hesiod's self-presentation as someone with limited experience of travel (*Op.* 618–94). Though this may well be a conventional element of the persona, it obviously speaks to the kinds of stances which his first audience(s) would have found congenial, meaningful and authoritative.

Nonetheless, however much fun this kind of speculation may be, even this is a case of *obscura per obscuriora*. Such a conclusion may also be too influenced by the primacy of the Hesiodic model in my conception of the phenomenon, and so – as Pindar (*O.* 1.52) – I stand back. At the least, the comparative evidence shows us how long, how varied, and above all how syncretistic, was the early Greek tradition of the myth. As López-Ruiz has put it,

> [t]he extant versions of these stories ... bear witness to a rich and complex Eastern Mediterranean pool of mythic traditions in which the Greeks were also diving for many centuries.[43]

The process denoted by this aquatic metaphor, by the way, did not start – and it definitely did not stop – with Hesiod. Though this chapter has focused on his *Theogony* as our primary evidence for the earliest period, there were other early Greek versions of cosmic history, and the process of interaction with the Near East around this story continued long after Hesiod's text had become a classic. We have already mentioned one such figure, Philon of Byblos, but there were several others: in his *On Principles* (125c), the fifth-century CE Neoplatonist Damascius cites Eudemos of Rhodes (fourth century BCE) and an undated Phoenician sage, Mochus, for a Phoenician cosmogony which has no trace of intergenerational conflict, but which contains familiar details like the cosmic egg found in the Orphic tradition.[44] Moreover, it is clear that Berossus (third century BCE), a Babylonian writing in Greek under the Seleucids, clearly knew *Enūma eliš* or something very much like it, summarising its narrative in the first book of his *Babyloniaca*.[45] However it was transmitted into the later Greek world, the continuing influence of the *Song of Emergence* may also be seen in the cosmogony partially preserved in the fourth-century Derveni Papyrus, where Zeus apparently swallows the phallus of Ouranos (frr. 8, 12 Bernabé), becomes pregnant (fr. 12.2–4) and then proceeds to create the world (frr. 15–18).[46] In fact, these later texts are much closer in their details to the Near Eastern traditions,[47] and they have a much better claim than Hesiod's *Theogony* to have been produced by direct and

---

[43] López-Ruiz 2010: 127.
[44] See López-Ruiz 2010: 130–70; Meisner 2018: 88–118; also Mitchell 2018 for Indian parallels.
[45] See Frahm 2010b, Haubold 2013b and George, Chapter 10 in this volume.
[46] See López-Ruiz 2010: 137–44, 167–9; Meisner 2018: 51–86. For a different view, see Kotwick and Janko 2017: 207–12.
[47] See Burkert 2004: 92; Meisner 2018: 21–44.

identifiably personalised interaction between specific texts and authors.[48] If anything, Hesiod shows us that the Greeks had been long prepared for these later experiments, providing the broad structural similarities in the narrative which could allow even further and closer cross-pollination. His *Theogony* thus performs the very same role which the Indo-European background played for him and his tradition, forming the landscape from which Near Eastern territory appeared not only recognisable, but attractive. That, however, is a discussion for another day.

Conclusion

As the mother of the main character in *Monty Python's Life of Brian* (1979), the late, great Terry Jones manages to encapsulate – unintentionally, of course, since 'she' is talking about her son's attitude to his uncertain parentage – the Greeks' view of divine power: 'Sex, sex, sex, that's all they think about, eh?' For the early Greeks, the story of Zeus's accession to power and the establishment of his rule was profoundly sexed and gendered in its nature and logic. Not only does Zeus possess and contain the frustrated maternal plotter, not only does he control the sexual behaviour and parturitive potential of the other female gods, not only does he fail to make the same sexual errors as his predecessors in having all his children with one wife – in fact, Hesiod's *Theogony* serves as a charter text for nothing less than eternal male domination. This is the distinctively Greek take on this widespread ancient motif of the Succession Myth: its nexus of sex and gender is more pronounced than in the Hurro-Hittite tradition, which patriarchalises by denying roles and agency to female deities in a context where they might be expected; and it is even more pronounced than in the Mesopotamian tradition, whose texts explicitly show the temporary success, but ultimate defeat, of any such female attempt to undermine the male deity's dominance. Comparative study allows us to see the individual element working within its own context, to determine what is distinctive about each tradition and so, finally, to understand all of them better. Genealogy, at least in the way most Classicists would like to practise it, is neither possible nor particularly profitable. But the analogy remains, and it can tell us a very great deal.

---

[48] For precisely this development in Greek contact with Indian cosmogonical traditions, see Mitchell 2018. She well shows how inherited similarities allowed greater specific interactions (and prevented 'blocking': see above, note 14), whereby the convergences become much clearer after the increase in direct contact following Alexander's invasion.

Bibliography

Aarne, A., and Thompson, S. 1961. *The Types of the Folktale. A Classification and Bibliography*. 3rd ed. Helsinki.

Abusch, T. 1986. 'Ishtar's Proposal and Gilgamesh's Refusal. An Interpretation of "The Gilgamesh Epic", Tablet 6, Lines 1–79', *History of Religions* 26.2: 143–87.

Acosta-Hughes, B., Lehnus, L., and Stephens S. A. 2011 (eds.), *Brill's Companion to Callimachus*. Leiden.

Adrados, F. R. 1999–2003. *The History of the Graeco-Latin Fable (translated by Leslie A. Ray and F. Rojas del Canto)*. Leiden.

Afanas'eva, V. K. 1987. 'Das sumerische Sargon-Epos. Versuch einer Interpretation', *Altorientalische Forschungen* 14: 237–46.

Agostaniani, L., Arcamone, M. G., Carruba, O., Imparati, F., and Rizza, R. 1998 (eds.). *Do-ra-qe pe-re. Studi in memoria di A. Quattordio Moreschini*. Pisa and Rome.

Ahl, F. 2007. *Virgil, Aeneid*. Oxford and New York, NY.

Aikhenvald, A., and Dixon, R. M. W. 2001 (eds.), *Areal Diffusion and Genetic Inheritance. Problems in Comparative Linguistics*. Oxford.

Alberti, L. 2012. 'Making Visible the Invisible: Cretan Objects Mentioned in the Cuneiform Texts of Mari and Archaeological Discoveries in Crete in the II Millennium BC', *SMEA* 54: 7–32.

Albright, W. F. 1941. 'Two Letters from Ugarit (Ras Shamrah)', *BASOR* 82: 43–9.

Allan, W. A. 2006. 'Divine Justice and Cosmic Order in Early Greek Epic', *JHS* 126: 1–35.

Allen, N. J. 2004. 'Bhīṣma and Hesiod's Succession Myth', *International Journal of Hindu Studies* 8: 57–79.

2014. 'Comparing Mythologies on a Global Scale. A Review Article (of Witzel 2012)', *Journal of the Anthropological Society of Oxford* 6: 99–103.

Alster, B. 1979. 'An Akkadian and a Greek Proverb', *WO* 10: 1–5.

1987. 'A Note on the Uriah Letter in the Sumerian Sargon Legend', *Zeitschrift für Assyriologie* 77: 169–73.

1993. 'Marriage and Love in the Sumerian Love Songs', in Cohen, M. E., et al. (eds.), *The Tablet and the Scroll: Near Eastern Studies in Honor of William W. Hallo*. Bethesda, MD: 15–27.

2005. *Wisdom of Ancient Sumer*. Bethesda, MD.
2007. *Sumerian Proverbs in the Schøyen Collection*. Bethesda, MD.
Alster, B., and Vanstiphout, H. 1987. 'Lahar and Ashnan. Presentation and Analysis of a Sumerian Disputation', *Acta Sumerologica* 9: 1–43.
Alster, B., and Westenholz, A. 1994. 'The Barton Cylinder', *Acta Sumerologica* 16: 15–46.
Álvarez Martí-Aguilar, M. 2018. 'The Network of Melqart: Tyre, Gadir, Carthage, and the Founding God', in Naco, T., and López-Sánchez, F. (eds.), *Warlords, War, and Interstate Relations in the Ancient Mediterranean, 404 BC–AD 14*. Leiden: 113–50.
2019. 'The Tyre–Gadir Axis', in López-Ruiz and Doak 2019 (eds.), 617–26.
Ambos, C. 2013. *Der König im Gefängnis und das Neujahrsfest im Herbst: Mechanismen der Legitimation des babylonischen Herrschers im 1. Jahrtausend v. Chr. und ihre Geschichte*. Dresden.
Annus, A. 2002. *The God Ninurta in the Mythology and Royal Ideology of Ancient Mesopotamia*. State Archives of Assyria Studies XIV. Helsinki.
2009. 'Review Article. The Folk-Tales of Iraq and the Literary Traditions of Ancient Mesopotamia', *Journal of Ancient Near Eastern Religions* 9: 87–91.
Annus, A., and Lenzi, A. 2010. *Ludlul bēl nemēqi. The Standard Babylonian Poem of the Righteous Sufferer*, SAAC 7. Helsinki.
Archi, A. 1990. 'The Names of the Primeval Gods', *Orientalia* 59.2: 114–29.
1999. 'The Steward and His Jar', *Iraq* 61: 147–58.
2002. 'Ea and the Beast: A Song Related to the Kumarpi Cycle', in Taracha 2002 (ed.), 1–10.
2004a. 'The Singer of Kaneš and His Gods', in Hutter, M., and Hutter-Braunsar, S. (eds.), *Offizielle Religion, lokale Kulte und individuelle Religiosität, Akten des religionsgeschichtlichen Symposiums 'Kleinasien und angrenzende Gebiete vom Beginn des 2. bis zur Mitte des 1. Jahrtausends v. Christus', Bonn, 20.–22. Februar 2003*. Alter Orient und Altes Testament 318. Münster: 11–26.
2004b. 'Translation of Gods: Kumarpi, Enlil, Dagan/NISABA, Halki', *Orientalia* ns 73: 319–36.
2007. 'Transmission of Recitative Literature by the Hittites', *Altorientalische Forschungen* 34.2: 185–203.
2009. 'Orality, Direct Speech and the Kumarbi Cycle', *Altorientalische Forschungen* 36: 209–29.
2010. 'Hadda of Halab and His Temple in the Ebla Period', *Iraq* 72: 3–17.
2013. 'The West Hurrian Pantheon and Its Background', in Collins and Michalowski 2013 (eds.), 1–21.
Arnaud, D. 1985. *Recherches au pays d' Aštata, Emar VI.1, Textes sumériens et accadiens*. Synthèse no 18. Paris.
2007. *Corpus des textes de bibliothèque de Ras Shamra-Ougarit (1936–2000) en sumérien, babylonien et assyrien*. Sabadell.
Aro, S., and Whiting, R. M. 2000 (eds.). *The Heirs of Assyria. Proceedings of the Opening Symposium of the Assyrian and Babylonian Intellectual Heritage Project*. Helsinki.

Aruz, J. 2008. *Marks of Distinction: Seals and Cultural Exchange between the Aegean and the Orient (ca. 2600–1360 BC)*. Mainz.
Aruz, J., Benzel, K., and Evans, J. M. 2008 (eds.). *Beyond Babylon: Art, Trade, and Diplomacy in the Second Millennium BC*. Exhibition catalogue, The Metropolitan Museum of Art. New York, NY.
Aruz, J., and Seymour, M. 2016 (eds.). *From Assyria to Iberia: Art and Culture in the Iron Age*. New York, NY.
Asher-Greve, J. 2001. 'Stepping into the Maelstrom: Women, Gender and Ancient Near Eastern Scholarship', *NIN – Journal of Gender Studies in Antiquity* 1: 1–22.
Asher-Greve, J., and Westenholz, J. 2013. *Goddesses in Context: On Divine Powers, Roles, Relationships and Gender in Mesopotamian Textual and Visual Sources*. Göttingen.
Asheri, D. 2007. 'Book I', in Asheri, Lloyd and Corcella 2007, 57–218.
Asheri, D., Lloyd, A., and Corcella, A. 2007. *A Commentary on Herodotus: Books I–IV*. Oxford.
Astour, M. C. 1965. *Hellenosemitica: An Ethnic and Cultural Study in West Semitic Impact on Mycenaean Greece*. Leiden.
Aubet, M. E. 2001. *The Phoenicians and the West: Politics, Colonies, and Trade*. 2nd ed. Cambridge.
  2019. 'Tyre and Its Colonial Expansion', in López-Ruiz and Doak 2019 (eds.), 75–87.
Audley-Miller, L., and Dignas, B. 2018 (eds.). *Wandering Myths: Transcultural Uses of Myth in the Ancient World*. Berlin and Boston, MA.
Ayali-Darshan, N. 2010. '"The Bride of the Sea"': The Traditions about Astarte and Yamm in the Ancient Near East', in Horowitz, E., Gabbay, U., and Vukosavovic, F. (eds.), *A Woman of Valor: Jerusalem Ancient Near Eastern Studies in Honor of Joan Goodnik Westenholz*. Madrid: 19–33.
  2013. 'Baal, Son of Dagan: In Search of Baal's Double Paternity', *JAOS* 133: 651–7.
  2015. 'The Other Version of the Story of the Storm-God's Combat with the Sea in the Light of Egyptian, Ugaritic, and Hurro-Hittite Texts', *Journal of Ancient Near Eastern Religions* 15: 20–51.
  2017. 'The Death of Mot and His Resurrection (KTU3 1.6 II, V) in the Light of Egyptian Sources' *UF* 48: 1–20.
Bachhuber, C. 2006. 'Aegean Interest on the Uluburun Ship', *AJA* 110: 345–63.
Bachvarova, M. 2005. 'The Eastern Mediterranean Epic Tradition from *Bilgames and Akka* to the *Song of Release* to Homer's *Iliad*', *GRBS* 45: 131–54.
  2012. 'From "Kingship in Heaven" to King Lists: Syro-Anatolian Courts and the History of the World', *Journal of Ancient Near Eastern Religions* 12: 97–118.
  2014. 'Hurro-Hittite Narrative Song as a Bilingual Oral-Derived Genre', in Kapelus and Taracha 2014 (eds.), 77–110.

2016. *From Hittite to Homer: The Anatolian Background of Ancient Greek Epic*. Cambridge.
  2017. 'Hittite Myths', in López-Ruiz 2017a (ed.), 149–76.
Baden, J. S. 2009. *J, E, and the Redaction of the Pentateuch*. Tübingen.
Bakhtin, M. 1981. *The Dialogic Imagination. Four Essays by M. M. Bakhtin* (ed. M. Holquist, M., trans. Emerson, C. and Holquist, M.). Austin, TX.
Balke, T. E. 2017. *Das altsumerische Onomastikon: Namengebung und Prosopografie nach den Quellen aus Lagas*. Münster.
Ballabriga, A. 1990. 'Le dernier adversaire de Zeus: le mythe de Typhon dans l'épopée grecque archaïque', *RHR* 207.1: 3–30.
Baragwanath, E., and de Bakker, M. 2012 (eds.). *Myth, Truth, and Narrative in Herodotus*. Oxford.
Bartelmus, A. 2016. *Fragmente einer grossen Sprache. Sumerisch im Kontext des kassitenzeitlichen Babylonien*. Berlin.
Barthes, R. 1977. 'The Death of the Author', in *Image, Music, Text* (trans. Heath, S.). London: 142–9.
Bartoloni, P., and Campanella, L. 2000 (eds.). *La ceramica Fenicia di Sardegna, dati, problematiche, confronti. Atti del Primo Congresso Internazionale Sulcitano*. Rome.
Baruchi-Unna, A., Forti, T., Aḥituv, S., Eph'al, I., and Tigay, J. H. 2017 (eds.). *'Now It Happened in Those Days': Studies in Biblical, Assyrian, and Other Ancient Near Eastern Historiography Presented to Mordechai Cogan on His 75th Birthday*. Winona Lake, IN.
Bassino, P. 2019. *The Certamen Homeri et Hesiodi: A Commentary*. Berlin and Boston, MA.
Bassino, P., Canevaro, L., and Graziosi, B. 2017 (eds.). *Conflict and Consensus in Early Greek Hexameter Poetry*. Cambridge.
Bauer, A. 1882. 'Die Kyrossage und Verwandtes', *Sitzungsberichte der philosophisch-historischen Classe der kaiserlichen Akademie der Wissenschaften* 100: 495–578.
Bauer, A., Görke, S., Lorenz, J., and Rieken, E. 2015. 'Mythologische Texte in Hethitischer Sprache', in Janowski, B., and Schwemer, D. 2015 (eds.), *Weisheitstexte, Mythen und Epen*. Texte aus der Umwelt des Alten Testaments. Neue Folge 8. Gütersloh: 145–76.
Baumgarten, A. I. 1981. *The Phoenician History of Philo of Byblos: A Commentary*. Leiden.
Beaulieu, P.-A. 2006. 'Berossus on Late Babylonian History', in *Oriental Studies 2006: Special Issue of Oriental Studies*. Beijing: 116–49.
Beckman, G. M. 1982. 'The Anatolian Myth of Illuyanka', *JNES* 14: 11–25.
  1983. *Hittite Birth Rituals*. Studien zu den Boğazköy-Texten 29. Wiesbaden.
  1999. *Hittite Diplomatic Texts. Second Edition*. Society of Biblical Literature: Writings from the Ancient World 7. Atlanta, GA.
  2001. 'Ḫantili I', in Richter, Prechel and Klinger 2001 (eds.), 51–8.

2003. 'Gilgamesh in Hatti', in Beckman, G. M., Beal, R. H., and MacMahon, G. (eds.), *Hittite Studies in Honor of Harry A. Hoffner Jr. on the Occasion of His 65th Birthday*. Winona Lake, IN: 37–57.

2011. 'Primordial Obstetrics: "The Song of Emergence" (CTH 344)', in Hutter and Hutter-Braunsar 2011 (eds.), 25–33.

Beckman, G. M., Bryce, T., and Cline, E. H. 2011. *The Ahhiyawa Texts*. Atlanta, GA.

Beissner, F. 1961 (ed.). *Hölderlin: Sämtliche Werke. Vierter Band*. Stuttgart.

van der Ben, N. 1986. '*Hymn to Aphrodite* 36–291: Notes on the Pars Epica of the Homeric Hymn to Aphrodite', *Mnemosyne* 4.39: 1–41.

Bernabé, A. 1995. 'Influences orientales dans la littérature grecque: quelques réflexions de méthode', *Kernos* 8: 9–22.

Betegh, G. 2002. 'On Eudemus Fr. 150 (Wehrli)', in Bodnár, I., and Fortenbaugh, W. M. (eds.), *Eudemus of Rhodes*. New Brunswick, NJ: 337–57.

Bianchi, U. 1953. Διὸς αἶσα: *destino, uomini e divinità nell' epos nelle teogonie e nel culto dei Greci*. Rome.

Bichler, R. 2007. Review of Lenfant 2004, *Gnomon* 79: 396–400.

Bierl, A., and Lardinois, A. 2016 (eds.). *The Newest Sappho: P. Sapph. Obbink and P. GC inv. 105, frs. 1–4*. Leiden.

Black, J. A. 1983. 'Babylonian Ballads: A New Genre', *JAOS* 103.1: 25–34.

Black, J. A., Cunningham, G., Robson, E., and Zólyomi, G. 2004. *The Literature of Ancient Sumer*. Oxford.

Blair, J. M. 2009. *De-Demonising the Old Testament*. Tübingen.

Blam, J.-F. 2004. 'Le chant de l'Océan: Fragment KBo XXVI 105', in Mazoyer, M. and Casabonne, O. 2004 (eds.), *Antiquus Oriens: Mélanges offerts au Professeur René Lebrun Vol. 1*. Collection KUBABA, Série Antiquité, 5. Paris: 69–81.

Blümer, W. 2001. *Interpretation archaischer Dichtung. Die mythologische Partien der Erga Hesiods*. 2 vols. Münster.

Blum, E., and Lux, R. 2006 (eds.). *Festtraditionen in Israel und im Alten Orient*. Gütersloh.

Boardman, J. 1999. *The Greeks Overseas: Their Early Colonies and Trade*. 4th ed. London.

2001. 'Aspects of "Colonization"', *BASOR* 322: 33–42.

2005. 'Al Mina: Notes and Queries', *Ancient West and East* 4: 278–91.

2016. 'The Ages of Heroes: Greeks and Phoenicians on the Wine-Dark Sea', in Aruz and Seymour 2016 (eds.), 206–15.

Boddy, K. 2020. *The Composition and Tradition of Erimḫuš*. Cuneiform Monographs 52. Leiden.

Bodi, D. 2014. 'Cross-Cultural Transformation of Animal Proverbs (Sumer, Mari, Hebrew Bible, Aramaic, Aḥiqar and Aesop's Fables)', *Aliento* 5: 1–30.

Bodson, L. 1987. 'Le renard et le hérisson (Archiloque, fr. 201 West)', in Servais, J., Hackens, T., and Servais-Soyez, B. 1987 (eds.), *Stemmata. Mélanges de philologie, d'histoire et d'archéologie grecques offerts à Jules Labarbe*. Liège: 55–9.

Boedeker, D. 1974. *Aphrodite's Entry into Greek Epic*. Mnemosyne Suppl. 32. Leiden.
Bolger, D. 2008 (ed.). *Gender through Time in the Ancient Near East*. Lanham, MD.
Bombi, R., Cifoletti, G., Fusco, F., Innocente, L., and Orioles, V. 2006 (eds.). *Studi linguistici in onore Roberto Gusmani*. Alessandria.
Bonnafé, A. (1985), *Eros et Eris: Mariages divins et mythe de succession chez Hesiode*, Lyon.
Bonner, C. 1937. 'The Sybil and the Bottle Imps', in Casey, R. P., Lake, S., and Lake, A. K. 1937 (eds.), *Quantulacumque. Studies Presented to K. Lake*. London: 1–8.
Bonnet, C. 1987. 'Typhon et Baal Saphon', in Lipinski, E. 1987 (ed.). *Studia Phoenicea V. Phoenicia and the East Mediterranean in the First Millennium BC*. Leuven: 101–43.
   1988. *Melqart: Cultes et mythes de l'Héraclès tyrien en Méditerranée (Studia Phoenicia 8)*. Leuven.
Bonnet, C., and Bricault, L. 2016. *Quand les dieux voyagent: cultes et mythes en mouvement dans l'espace méditerranéen antique. Histoire des religions*. Geneva.
Borger, R. 2008. 'Zur neuen Schulausgabe des babylonischen Weltschöpfungsepos', *Orientalia* 77: 271–85.
Bottéro, J. 1992. *Mesopotamia: Writing, Reasoning and the Gods*, transl. Z. Bahrani and M. van De Mieroop. Chicago, IL.
Bowie, E. L. 2008. 'Sex and Politics in Archilochus' Poetry', in Katsonopoulou, D., Petropoulos, I., and Katsarou, S. 2008 (eds.), *Archilochos and His Age*. Paros II. Athens: 133–43.
Boyce, M. 1984. 'On the Antiquity of Zoroastrian Apocalyptic', *Bulletin of the School of Oriental and African Studies* 47: 57–75.
Breasted, J. H. 1906. *Ancient Records of Egypt. Historical Documents. Vol. II: The Eighteenth Dynasty*. Chicago, IL.
Bremmer, J. N. 2008. *Greek Religion and Culture, the Bible, and the Ancient Near East*. Leiden.
   2016. 'The Ancient Near East', in Eidinow and Kindt 2016 (eds.), 605–15.
Briant, P. 2002. *From Cyrus to Alexander: A History of the Persian Empire*. Winona Lake, IN.
Brinkman, J. A. 1989. 'The Akkadian Words for "Ionia" and "Ionian"', in Sutton, R. F. 1989 (ed.), *Daidalikon: Studies in Memory of Raymond V. Schoder, S. J.* Wauconda, IL: 53–71.
Briquel, D. 1980. 'La "Théogonie" d'Hésiode. Essai de comparaison indo-européenne', *RHR* 197: 243–76.
Brown, A. S. 1997. 'Aphrodite and the Pandora Complex', *CQ* 47: 26–47.
Brown, C. G. 1997. 'Iambos', in Gerber, D. E. (ed.), *A Companion to the Greek Lyric Poets*. Leiden: 11–88.
Brunner, C. J. 1980. 'The Fable of the Babylonian Tree', *JNES* 39: 191–202 and 291–302.
Bryce, T. 2005. *The Kingdom of the Hittites*. Oxford.

Budin, S. L. 2012. Review of Louden 2011, *CR* 62: 345–7.
  2014. 'Fertility and Gender in the Ancient Near East', in Masterson, M., Sorkin Rabinowitz, N., and Robson, J. 2014 (eds.), *Sex in Antiquity. Exploring Gender and Sexuality in the Ancient World*. London: 30–49.
van Buitenen, J. A. B. 1973. *The Mahābhārata. Vol. 1. The Book of the Beginning*. Chicago, IL.
Burgess, J. S. 2015. *Homer*. London and New York, NY.
Burkert, W. 1977. *Griechische Religion der archaischen und klassischen Epoche*. Stuttgart.
  1979. *Structure and History in Greek Mythology and Ritual*. Berkeley, CA.
  1984. *Die orientalisierende Epoche in der griechischen Religion und Literatur*. Heidelberg.
  1985. *Greek Religion*. Cambridge, MA.
  1991a. 'Homerstudien und Orient', in Latacz 1991 (ed.), 155–81.
  1991b. *Greek Religion: Archaic and Classical*. Oxford.
  1992. *The Orientalizing Revolution: Near Eastern Influence on Greek Culture in the Early Archaic Age*. Cambridge, MA.
  2003. *Kleine Schriften II: Orientalia*. Göttingen.
  2004. *Babylon, Memphis, Persepolis: Eastern Contexts of Greek Culture*. Cambridge, MA and London.
Burstein, S. M. 1978. *The Babyloniaca of Berossus*. Malibu, CA.
Buxton, R. 1994. *Imaginary Greece: The Contexts of Mythology*. Cambridge.
Çağirgan, G., and Lambert, W. G. 1991–93. 'The Late Babylonian Kislīmu Ritual for Esagil', *Journal of Cuneiform Studies* 43.45: 89–106.
Calame, C. 2009. 'The Succession of Ages and Poetic Pragmatics of Justice: Hesiod's Narrative of the Five Human Species', in *Poetic and Performative Memory in Ancient Greece*. Cambridge, MA and London: 59–103.
Cammarosano, M. 2014. 'Rejoicing in the Gods: The Verb *Dusk-* and Hittite Cheese Fighting', in Kapelus and Taracha 2014 (eds.), 138–70.
Campbell, D. 2013. 'On the Theogonies of Hesiod and the Hurrians: An Exploration of the Dual Natures of Teššub and Kumarbi', in Scurlock and Beal 2013 (eds.), 26–43.
Cancik-Kirschbaum, E., van Ess, M., and Marzahn, J. 2013 (eds.). *Babylon. Wissenskultur in Orient und Okzident*. Berlin and Boston, MA.
Caquot, A. 1956. 'Sur quelques démons de l'Ancien Testament (reshep, qeteb, deber)', *Semitica* 6: 53–68.
Cardona, G., Hoenigswald, H., and Senn, A. 1970 (eds.). *Indo-European and Indo-Europeans*. Philadelphia, PA.
Carey, C. 1986. 'Archilochus and Lycambes', *CQ* 36: 60–7.
Carrez-Maratray, J.-Y. 2001. 'De l'Oronte au Nil: Typhon et Saphon', *Transeuphratène* 21: 87–100.
Casabonne, O. 2004. 'Rhodes, Cyprus and Southern Anatolia during the Archaic and Achaemenid Periods: The Ionian Question', *Colloquium Anatolicum* 3: 1–14.
Casadio, G. 2009. 'Ex oriente lux?', in Riedweg (ed.) 2009, 123–61.

Caubet, A., and Yon, M. 2019. 'Importation asiatique en Grèce mycénienne. La "Combat Agate" de Pylos', in Chambon, Guichard and Langlois 2019 (eds.), 189–201.
Cavigneaux, A. 1981. *Textes scolaires du temple de Nabû ša ḫarê 1*. Baghdad.
  2014. 'Une version sumérienne de la légende d'Adapa (Textes de Tell Haddad x)', *Zeitschrift für Assyriologie* 104: 1–41.
Cavigneaux, A., and Al-Rawi, F. 1993. 'Gilgameš et taureau de ciel (šul-mè-kam). (Textes de Tell Haddad IV). *Revue d'Assyriologie et d'Archéologie Orientale* 87.2: 97–129.
Ceccarelli, M. 2015. 'Bemerkungen zur Entwicklung der Beschwörungen des Marduk-Ea-Typs: Die Rolle Enlils', in Archi, A. (ed.), *Tradition and Innovation in the Ancient Near East*. Winona Lake, IN: 193–204.
  2016. *Enki und Ninmaḫ*. Tübingen.
Celestino Pérez, S., and Blánquez Perez, J. 2013 (eds.). *Patrimonio cultural de la vid y el vino*. Badajoz and Madrid.
Celestino Pérez, S., and López-Ruiz, C. 2016. *Tartessos and the Phoenicians in Iberia*. Oxford.
Cerutti, M. V. 1998. 'Mito di distruzione, mito di fondazione: Hes. fr. 204, 95–103 M-W', *Aevum Antiquum* 11: 127–78.
Chambon, G., Guichard, M., and Langlois, A.-I. 2019 (eds.). *De l'Argile au numérique: Mélanges assyriologiques en l'honneur de Dominique Charpin*. Leuven.
Chantraine, P. 1956. 'Le problème du choix en philologie', *Studi italiani di filologia classica* 27–8: 103–5.
  1999. *Dictionnaire étymologique de la langue grecque*. 2 vols. Paris.
Chappell, M. 2012. 'The Opening of the Homeric Hymn to Apollo', in Bouchon, R., Brillet-Dubois, P., and Le Meur-Weissman, N. 2012 (eds.), *Hymnes de la Grèce antique. Approches littéraires et historiques*. Lyon: 177–82.
Charpin, D. 2010. *Reading and Writing in Babylon*. Cambridge, MA and London.
Chuvin, P., and Yoyotte, J. 1986. 'Documents relatifs au culte pélusien de Zeus Casios', *RA* ns 1: 41–63.
Cizek, A. 1975. 'From the Historical Truth to the Literary Convention: The Life of Cyrus the Great Viewed by Herodotus, Ctesias and Xenophon', *AC* 44: 531–52.
Clancier, P. 2009. *Les bibliothèques en Babylonie dans la deuxième moitié du 1er millénaire av. J-C*. Münster.
Clarke, M. 2019. *Achilles beside Gilgamesh. Mortality and Wisdom in Early Epic Poetry*. Cambridge.
Clay, D., and Purvis, A. 1999. *Four Island Utopias: Plato's Atlantis, Euhemeros of Messene's Panchaia, Iamboulos' Island of the Sun, Sir Francis Bacon's New Atlantis*. Newburyport, MA.
Clay, J. S. 1989. *The Politics of Olympus. Form and Meaning in the Major Homeric Hymns*. Princeton, NJ.
  2003. *Hesiod's Cosmos*. Cambridge.
Clay, J. S., and Gilan, A. 2014. 'The Hittite "Song of Emergence" and the Theogony', *Philologus* 58: 1–9.

Cohen, G. M. 2006. *The Hellenistic Settlements in Syria, the Red Sea Basin, and North Africa.* Berkeley, CA.
Cohen, Y. 2013. *Wisdom from the Late Bronze Age.* Atlanta, GA.
  2017. 'Heads or Tails? The Transmutations and Peregrinations of a Sapiential Theme', in Baruchi-Unna et al. 2017 (eds.), 539–52.
  2018. 'Why "Wisdom"? Copying, Studying, and Collecting Wisdom Literature in the Cuneiform World', in Oshima 2018 (ed.), 41–59.
Cohen, Y., and Wasserman, N. 2021. 'Mesopotamian Wisdom Literature', in Kynes 2021 (ed.).
Collard C., Cropp M. J., and Lee K. H. (eds.) 1995. *Euripides: Selected Fragmentary Plays I.* Warminster.
Collins, B. J. 1997. 'Purifying a House: A Ritual for the Infernal Deities (1.68)', in Hallo, W. W. 1997 (ed.). *The Context of Scripture Volume 1, Canonical Compositions from the Biblical World.* Leiden, New York, NY and Cologne: 168–71.
  2002. 'Necromancy, Fertility and the Dark Earth: The Use of Ritual Pits in Hittite Cult', in Mirecki, P., and Meyer, M. 2002 (eds.). *Magic and Ritual in the Ancient World.* Leiden, Boston, MA and Cologne: 224–41.
  2004. 'A Channel to the Underworld in Syria', *Near Eastern Archaeology* 67.1: 54–6.
Collins, B. J., Bachvarova M. R., and Rutherford, I. 2008 (eds.). *Anatolian Interfaces: Hittites, Greeks and Their Neighbors. Proceedings of an International Conference on Cross-Cultural Interaction, September 17–19, 2004, Emory University, Atlanta.* Oxford.
Collins, B. J., and Michalowski, P. 2013 (eds.), *Beyond Hatti: A Tribute to Gary Beckman.* Atlanta, GA.
Collombert, P., and Coulon, L. 2000. 'Les dieux contre la mer', *BIAO* 100: 193–242.
Conybeare, F. C., Rendel Harris, J., and Smith Lewis, A. 1898. *The Story of Ahikar from the Syriac, Arabic, Armenian, Ethiopic, Greek and Slavonic Versions.* London.
Cooper, J. S. 1977. 'Symmetry and Repetition in Akkadian Narrative', *JAOS* 97: 508–12.
  1985. 'Sargon and Joseph: Dreams Come True', in Kort and Morschauser 1985 (eds.), 33–9.
  2017. 'Female Trouble and Troubled Males: Roiled Seas, Decadent Royals, and Mesopotamian Masculinities in Myth and Practice', in Zsolnay, I. 2017 (ed.), *Being a Man ... Negotiating Ancient Constructs of Masculinity.* London and New York, NY: 112–24.
Cooper, J. S., and Heimpel W. 1984. 'The Sumerian Sargon Legend', in Sasson 1984 (ed.), 67–82.
Cors i Meya, J. 1999–2000. 'Traces of the Ancient Origin of Some Mythic Components in Philon of Byblos' Phoenician History', in Molina, M., Márquez Rowe, I., and Sanmartín, J. (eds.), *Arbor Scientia: estudios del Próximo Oriente Antiguo dedicados a Gregorio del Olmo Lete con ocasión de su 65 aniversario.* Sabadell: 341–8.

Corti, C. 2007. 'The So-Called 'Theogony' or 'Kingship in Heaven': The Name of the Song', *SMEA* 49: 109–21.

   2017. 'From Mt. Hazzi to Šapinuwa. Cultural Traditions in Motion in the First Half of the 14th Century BC', *Mesopotamia* 52: 3–20.

Corti, C., and Pecchioli Daddi, F. 2012. 'The Power in Heaven: Remarks on the So-Called Kumarbi Cycle', in Wilhelm 2012 (ed.), 611–18.

Crane, G. 1988. *Calypso: Backgrounds and Conventions of the* Odyssey. Beiträge zur antiken Philologie 131. Frankfurt am Main.

Crielaard, J. P. 2007. 'Eretria's West Cemetery Revisited: Burial Plots, Social Structure and Settlement Organization during the 8th and 7th Centuries BC', in Mazarakis Ainan, A. 2007 (ed.). *Oropos and Euboea in the Early Iron Age*. Volos: 169–94.

Crisostomo, J. 2015. 'Writing Sumerian, Creating Texts: Reflections on Text-Building Practices in Old Babylonian Schools', *Journal of Ancient Near Eastern Religions* 15: 121–42.

Crowley, J. 1989. *The Aegean and the East: An Investigation into the Transference of Artistic Motifs between the Aegean, Egypt, and the Near East in the Bronze Age*. Jonsered.

Cruz Andreotti, G., Le Roux, P., and Moret, P. 2006 (eds.). *La invención de una geografía de la Península Ibérica I. La época republican*. Madrid.

da Cunha Corrêa, P. 2007. 'A Human Fable and the Justice of Beasts in Archilochus', in Finglass, P. J., Collard, C., and Richardson, N. J. 2007 (eds.), *Hesperos: Studies Presented to M. L. West on His Seventieth Birthday*. Oxford: 101–17.

Cunliffe, B. 2002. *The Extraordinary Voyage of Pytheas the Greek*. New York, NY.

Currie, B. G. F. 2007. 'Heroes and Holy Men in Early Greece. Hesiod's *Theios Aner*', in Coppola, A. 2007 (ed.). *Eroi, eroismi, eroizzazioni della Grecia antica a Padova e Venezia*. Padua: 163–203.

   2012a. 'The *Iliad*, Gilgamesh and Neoanalysis', in Montanari, F., Rengakos, A., and Tsagalis, C. (eds.), *Homeric Contexts: Neoanalysis and the Interpretation of Oral Poetry*. Berlin and Boston, MA: 543–623.

   2012b. 'Hesiod on Human History', in Marincola, J., Llewellyn-Jones, L., and Maciver, C. 2012 (eds.), *Greek Notions of the Past in the Archaic and Classical Eras: History without Historians*. Edinburgh: 37–64.

   2015. 'Cypria', in Fantuzzi and Tsagalis 2015 (eds.), 281–305.

   2016. *Homer's Allusive Art*. Oxford.

Curtis, J. 2013. *The Cyrus Cylinder and Ancient Persia*. London.

Dalley, S. 1989. *Myths from Mesopotamia*. Oxford.

   1998 (ed.). *The Legacy of Mesopotamia*. Oxford.

   2013. 'First Millennium BC Variation in Gilgamesh, Atrahasis, the Flood Story and the Epic of Creation. What Was Available to Berossos?', in Haubold et al. 2013 (eds.), 165–76.

Dalley, S., and Reyes, A. T. 1998a. 'Mesopotamian Contact and Influence in the Greek World: 1. To the Persian Conquest', in Dalley 1998 (ed.), 85–106.

   1998b. 'Mesopotamian Contact and Influence in the Greek World 2. Persia, Alexander, and Rome', in Dalley 1998 (ed.), 107–24.

Darshan, G. 2013. 'The Biblical Account of the Post-Diluvian Generation (*Gen.* 9: 20–10: 32) in the Light of Greek Genealogical Literature', *VT* 63: 515–35.
　2014a. 'The Story of the Sons of God and the Daughters of Men (*Gen.* 6:1–4) and the Hesiodic Catalogue of Women', *Shnaton, an Annual for Biblical and Ancient Near Eastern Studies* 23: 155–78.
　2014b. 'The Origins of the Foundation Stories Genre in the Hebrew Bible and Ancient Eastern Mediterranean', *JBL* 133.4: 689–709.
Daues, A. 2009. 'Zum Funktionsbereich des Suffixes *-skelo- im Junghethitischen und Homerischen', in Lühr and Ziegler 2009 (eds.), 82–99.
Davila, J. R. 1995. 'The Flood Hero as King and Priest', *JNES* 54: 199–214.
Day, J. 1985. *God's Conflict with the Dragon and the Sea: Echoes of a Canaanite Myth in the Old Testament.* Cambridge.
　2012. 'The Sons of Gods and Daughters of Men and the Giants: Disputed Points in the Interpretation of *Genesis* 6: 1–4', *Hebrew Bible and Ancient Israel* 1.4: 427–47.
De Breucker, G. E. E. 2003. 'Berossos and the Mesopotamian Temple as Centre of Knowledge during the Hellenistic Period', in MacDonald, A. A., Twomey, M. W., and Reinink, G. R. (eds.), *Learned Antiquity: Scholarship and Society in the Near East, the Greco-Roman World, and the Early Medieval West.* Leuven: 14–23.
　2010. '*BNJ* 680: Berossus', *Brill's New Jacoby*, general editor Ian Worthington, online edition.
　2012. *De Babyloniaca van Berossos van Babylon. Inleidung, editie en commentar.* Doctoral Dissertation, University of Groningen.
　2013. 'Berossos: His Life and His Work', in Haubold et al. 2013 (eds.), 15–28.
Deger-Jalkotzy, S., and Lemos, I. 2006 (eds.). *Ancient Greece from the Mycenaean Palaces to the Age of Homer.* Edinburgh.
Dell, K. Forthcoming (ed.). *The Biblical World.* 2nd ed. London and New York, NY.
Deloucas, A. A. N. 2016. *Balancing Power and Space: A Spatial Analysis of the Akitu Festival in Babylon after 626 BCE.* Research Master's Thesis, Leiden University.
Demoule, J.-P. 2018. 'Le Problème archéologique indo-européen', in Demoule, Garcia and Schnapp 2018 (eds.), 249–53.
Demoule, J.-P., Garcia, D., and Schnapp, A. 2018 (eds.). *Une histoire des civilisations.* Paris.
Derrida, J. 1988. *Limited Inc.* (translated S. Weber and J. Mehlman). Evanston, IL.
Detienne, M. 2008. *Comparing the Incomparable.* Stanford, CA.
Devecchi, E. 2010a. '"We Are All Descendants of Šuppiluliuma, Great King": The Aleppo Treaty Reconsidered', *WO* 40: 1–27.
　2010b. 'Amurru between Hatti, Assyria, and Ahhiyawa. Discussing a Recent Hypothesis', *Zeitschrift für Assyriologie* 100: 242–56.

Dewald, C. 2012. 'Myth and Legend in Herodotus' First Book', in Baragwanath and de Bakker 2012 (eds.), 59–85.
Dhorme, E. 1933. 'Deux tablettes de Ras-Shamra de la campagne de 1932', *Syria* 14: 229–52.
  1934. 'Nouvelles archéologiques', *Syria* 15: 393–6.
Dietler, M., and López-Ruiz, C. 2009 (eds.). *Colonial Encounters in Ancient Iberia: Phoenician, Greek, and Indigenous Relations*. Chicago, IL.
Dietrich, B. C. 1965. *Death, Fate, and the Gods. The Development of a Religious Idea in Greek Popular Belief and in Homer*. London.
Dietrich, M. 2003. 'Das Ritual für die Krönung des Assurbanipal', in Kiesow, K., and Meurer, T. 2003 (eds.). *Textarbeit. Studien zu Texten und ihrer Rezeption aus dem Alten Testament und der Umwelt Israels*. Münster: 127–56.
Dietrich, M., Loretz, O., and Sanmartín, J. 2013 (eds.). *Die keilalphabetischen Texte aus Ugarit, Ras Ibn Hani und anderen Orten. Dritte, erweiterte Auflage*. Münster.
van Dijk, J. 1964. 'Le motif cosmique dans la pensée sumérienne', *Acta Orientalia* 28: 1–59.
  1976. 'Existe-t-il un "Poème de la Création" sumérien?', in Eichler, B. L. (ed.), *Kramer Anniversary Volume: Cuneiform Studies in Honor of Samuel Noah Kramer*. Kevelaer and Neukirchen-Vluyn: 125–33 and pl. 8.
  1983. *lugal ud me-lam-bi nir-ğál: Le récit épique et didactique des Travaux de Ninurta, du Déluge et de la Nouvelle Création*. 2 vols. Leiden.
  1997. *Ainoi, Logoi, Mythoi: Fables in Archaic, Classical, and Hellenistic Greek Literature*. Leiden.
Dijkstra, M. 2011. 'Ishtar Seduces the Sea-Serpent. A New Join in the Epic of Ḥedammu (KUB 36, 56 + 95) and Its Meaning for the Battle between Baal and Yam in Ugaritic Tradition' *UF* 43: 53–83.
Dill, U., and Walde, Ch. 2006 (eds.). *Antike Mythen. Medien, Transformationen, Konstruktionen (Fritz Graf Festschrift)*. Berlin and New York, NY.
Dillery, J. 2015. *Clio's Other Sons: Berossus and Manetho*. Ann Arbor, MI.
Dinçol, B., Dinçol, A., Hawkins, J. D., Peker, H., Öztan, A., and Çelik, Ö. 2015. 'Two New Inscribed Storm-God Stelae from Arsuz (İskenderun): ARSUZ 1 and 2', *AS* 65: 59–77.
DiTommaso, L. 2005. *The Book of Daniel and the Apocryphal Daniel Literature*. Leiden.
Doak, B. 2012. *The Last of the Rephaiim. Conquest and Cataclysm in the Heroic Ages of Ancient Israel*. Boston, MA and Washington, DC.
Docter, R. F. 2000. 'Pottery, Graves and Ritual 1: Phoenicians of the First Generation in Pithekoussai', in Bartoloni and Campanella 2000 (eds.), 135–49.
Docter, R. F., and Niemeyer, H. G. 1995. 'Pithekoussai: The Carthaginian Connection. On the Archaeological Evidence of Euboeo-Phoenician Partnership in the 8th and 7th Centuries BC', *ASNP* n.s. 1: 101–15.

van Dongen, E. 2008. 'The Study of Near Eastern Influences on Greece: Towards the Point', *Kaskal: Rivista di storia, ambienti e culture del Vicino Oriente antico* 5: 233–50.
  2010. *Studying External Stimuli to the Development of the Ancient Aegean. The 'Kingship in Heaven'-Theme from Kumarbi to Kronos via Anatolia*. Doctoral Thesis, University College, London.
  2011. 'The 'Kingship in Heaven' Theme of the Hesiodic *Theogony*: Origin, Function, Composition', *GRBS* 51: 180–201.
  2012. 'The Hittite *Song of Going Forth* (CTH 344): A Reconsideration of the Narrative', *WO* 42: 23–84.
  2014. 'The Concept of 'the Near East': A Reconsideration', in Rollinger and Schnegg 2014 (eds.), 253–67.
Dornseiff, F. 1934. 'Antikes zum Alten Testament. 1. Genesis', *ZATW* 52: 57–75 [repr. in Dornseiff, F. 1955. *Antike und Alte Orient. Interpretationen*. Leipzig: 72–94].
Dossin, G. 1967. *Correspondance féminine, ARM 10*. Paris.
Dowden, K. 1996. 'Homer's Sense of Text', *JHS* 116: 47–61.
  2001. 'West on the East: Martin West's *East Face of Helicon* and Its Forerunners', *JHS* 121: 167–75.
Drewnowska, O., and Sandowicz, M. 2005 (eds.). *Fortune and Misfortune in the Ancient Near East: Proceedings of the 60th Rencontre Assyriologique Internationale at Warsaw 21–25 July 2014*. Winona Lake, IN.
Drews, R. 1974. 'Sargon, Cyrus and Mesopotamian Folk History', *JNES* 33: 387–93.
Duchemin, J. 1957. 'Recherche sur un theme aristophanien et ses sources religieuses: les voyages dans l'autre monde', *Études classiques* 25: 273–95 [reprinted in Duchemin 1995, 26–47].
  1974. *Prométhée. Histoire du mythe, de ses origines orientales à ses incarnations modernes*. Paris.
  1995. *Mythes grecs et sources orientales*. Paris.
Durand, J.-M. 1988. *Archives épistolaires de Mari*. ARM 26. Paris.
  1993. 'Le Mythologème du combat entre le Dieu de l'orage et la Mer en Mésopotamie', *Mari* 7: 41–61.
Ebeling, E. 1927. *Die babylonische Fabel und ihre Bedeutung für die Literaturgeschichte*. Leipzig.
Edmonds III, R. G. 2018. 'Deviant Origins: Hesiod's Theogony and the Orphica', in Loney, A. C., and Scully, S. (eds.), *The Oxford Handbook of Hesiod*. Oxford: 225–42.
Edmunds, L. 2014 (ed.). *Approaches to Greek Myth*. 2nd ed. Baltimore, MD.
Edwards, M. W. 1992. 'Homer and Oral Tradition: The Type-Scene', *Oral Tradition* 7: 284–330.
Edzard, D. O. 2003. 'Enlil, Vater der Götter', in Marrassini, P. (ed.), *Semitic and Assyriological Studies Presented to Pelio Fronzaroli*. Wiesbaden: 173–84.
Eide, T. 1986. 'Poetical and Metrical Value of Homeric Epithets: A Study of the Epithets Applied to χείρ', *SO* 61: 5–17.

Eidinow, E., and Kindt, J. 2016 (eds.). *The Oxford Handbook of Ancient Greek Religion*. Oxford.
Eidinow, E., Kindt, J., and Osborne, R. 2016 (eds.). *Theologies of Ancient Greek Religion*. Cambridge.
Elayi, J. 2018. *The History of Phoenicia*. Atlanta, GA.
Elmer, D. F. 2013. *The Poetics of Consent. Collective Decision Making and the Iliad*. Baltimore, MA.
Evans, A. 1921. *The Palace of Minos: A Comparative Account of the Successive Stages of the Early Cretan Civilization as Illustrated by the Discoveries at Knossos. Volume 1: The Neolithic and Early and Middle Minoan Ages*. London.
Fantuzzi, M., and Tsagalis, C. 2015 (eds.). *The Greek Epic Cycle and Its Ancient Reception. A Companion*. Cambridge.
Faraone, C. 1992. *Talismans and Trojan Horses. Guardian Statues in Ancient Greek Myth and Rituals*. New York, NY and Oxford.
Farber, W. 1977. *Beschwörungsrituale an Ištar und Dumuzi. Attī Ištar ša ḫarmaša Dumuzi*. Akademie der Wissenschaften und der Literatur Veröffentlichungen der Orientalischen Kommission Band xxx. Wiesbaden.
Faulkner, A. 2008. *The Homeric Hymn to Aphrodite: Introduction, Text, and Commentary*. Oxford.
Faust, A. 2015. 'Pottery and Society in Iron Age Philistia: Feasting, Identity, Economy, and Gender', *BASOR* 373: 167–98.
Fauth, W. 1990. 'Das Kasion-Gebirge und Zeus Kasios. Die antike Tradition und ihre vorderorientalischen Grundlagen', *UF* 22: 105–18.
Feeney, D. 1998. *Literature and Religion at Rome: Cultures, Contexts, and Beliefs*. Cambridge.
Feldman, M., Master, D. M., Bianco, R., Burri, M., Stockhammer, P. W., Mittnik, A., Aja, A., Jeong, C., and Krause. J. 2019. 'Ancient DNA Sheds Light on the Genetic Origins of Early Iron Age Philistines', *Science Advances* 5.7 (3 July 2019).
Feldman, M. H. 2006. *Diplomacy by Design: Luxury Arts and an 'International Style' in the Ancient Near East, 1400–1200 BCE*. Chicago, IL.
    2014. *Communities of Style: Portable Luxury Arts, Identity, and Collective Memory in the Iron Age Levant*. Chicago, IL.
Feliu, L. 2003. *The God Dagan in Bronze Age Syria*. Leiden.
    2006. 'Concerning the Etymology of Enlil: The An = Anum Approach', in del Olmo Lete, G., Feliu, L., and Millet Albà, A. (eds.), *Šapal tibnim mû illakū. Studies Presented to Joaquín Sanmartín*. Barcelona: 229–46.
Finglass, P. J. 2018. *Sophocles: Oedipus the King*. Cambridge.
Finkel, I. L. 1980. 'Bilingual Chronicle Fragments', *Journal of Cuneiform Studies* 32: 65–80.
    1986. 'On the Series of Sidu', *Zeitschrift für Assyriologie und Vorderasiatische Archäologie* 76: 250–53.
Finkel, I. L., and Geller, M. J. 2007 (eds.). *Disease in Babylonia*. Leiden and Boston, MA.

Finkelberg, M. 2004. 'The End of the Heroic Age in Homer, Hesiod, and the Cycle', *Ordia Prima* 3: 11–24.
  2005. *Greeks and Pre-Greeks. Aegean Prehistory and Greek Heroic Tradition.* Cambridge.
Finkelstein, I., and Silberman, N. A. 2006. *David and Solomon: In Search of the Bible's Sacred Kings and the Roots of the Western Tradition.* New York, NY.
Finn, J. 2017. *Much Ado about Marduk: Questioning Discourses of Royalty in First Millennium Mesopotamian Literature.* Boston, MA and Berlin.
Fischer, P. M., and Bürge, T. 2017 (eds.). *'Sea Peoples' up to Date. New Research on Transformations in the Eastern Mediterranean in the 13th–11th Centuries BCE. Proceedings of the ESF-Workshop held at the Austrian Academy of Sciences, Vienna, 3–4 November 2014.* Vienna.
Fleming, D. E., and Milstein, S. J. 2010. *The Buried Foundation of the Gilgamesh Epic: The Akkadian Huwawa Narrative.* Leiden.
Focke, K. 1998. 'Die Göttin Nin-imma', *Zeitschrift für Assyriologie* 88: 196–224.
Foley, J. M. 1999. *Homer's Traditional Art.* University Park, PA.
  2005 (ed.). *A Companion to Ancient Epic.* Oxford and Malden, MA.
Ford, A. 1992. *Homer: The Poetry of the Past.* Ithaca, NY.
Forrer, E. 1936. 'Eine Geschichte des Götterkönigtums aus dem Hatti-Reiche', *AIPhO* 4: 687–713.
Forsyth, N. 1979. 'The Allurement Scene: A Typical Pattern in Greek Oral Epic', *California Studies in Classical Antiquity* 12: 107–20.
Foster, B. R. 2005. *Before the Muses. An Anthology of Akkadian Literature.* 3rd ed. Bethesda, MD.
  2007. *Akkadian Literature of the Late Period.* Münster.
  2016. *The Age of Agade: Inventing Empire in Ancient Mesopotamia.* Abingdon and New York, NY.
Fowler, R. L. 1988. 'AIΓ- in Early Greek Language and Myth', *Phoenix* 42: 95–113.
  1998. 'Genealogical Thinking, Hesiod's Catalogue, and the Creation of the Hellenes', *PCPhS* 44: 1–19.
  2000–13. *Early Greek Mythography.* 2 vols. Oxford.
  2004. 'The Homeric Question', in Fowler, R. L. (ed.). *The Cambridge Companion to Homer.* Cambridge: 220–32.
Fox, M. V., Hurowitz, V. A., Hurvitz, A., Klein, M. L., Schwartz, B. J., and Shupak, N. 1996 (eds.). *Texts, Temples, and Traditions: A Tribute to Menachem Haran.* Winona Lake, IN.
Frahm, E. 2010a. 'The Latest Sumerian Proverbs', in Melville and Slotsky 2010 (eds.), 155–84.
  2010b. 'Counter-Texts, Commentaries, and Adaptations: Politically Motivated Responses to the Babylonian *Epic of Creation* in Mesopotamia, the Biblical World, and Elsewhere', *Orient* 45: 3–33.
  2011. *Babylonian and Assyrian Text Commentaries: Origins of Interpretation.* Münster.

2013. 'Creation and the Divine Spirit in Babel and Bible: Reflections on Mummu in *Enūma eliš* I 4 and Rûaḫ in *Genesis* 1:2', in Vanderhooft and Winitzer 2013 (eds.), 97–116.

Frahm, E., Frazer, M., Jiménez, E., and Wagensonner, K. 2013–. *Cuneiform Commentaries Project*, http://ccp.yale.edu/.

Frahm, E., and Jiménez, E. 2015. 'Myth, Ritual, and Interpretation: The Commentary on *Enūma eliš* I–VII and a Commentary on Elamite Month Names', *Hebrew Bible and Ancient Israel* 4: 293–343.

Francis, J. A. 2009. 'Metal Maidens, Achilles' Shield, and Pandora: The Beginnings of "Ekphrasis"', *AJPh* 130: 1–23.

Franz, M. 2002. 'Schule und Universität', in Kreuzer 2002 (ed.), 62–71.

Frayne, D. R. 1997. *The Royal Inscriptions of Mesopotamia. Early Periods, Volume 3/2: Ur III Period (2112–2004 BC)*. Toronto.

  2010. 'Gilgameš in Old Akkadian Glyptic', in Steymans 2010 (ed.), 165–208.

Frazer, J. G. 1912. *Pausanias's Description of Greece*. 6 vols. London.

  1918. *Folklore in the Old Testament. Studies in Comparative Religion, Legend, and Law*. 3 vols. London.

Freedman, S. M. 1998. *If a City Is Set on a Height. The Akkadian Omen Series Šumma alu in mēlê šakin, Vol. 1*. Philadelphia, PA.

Frost, H. 1991. 'Anchors Sacred and Profane: Ugarit-Ras Shamra, 1986: The Stone Anchors Revised and Compared', in Yon, M. 1991 (ed.), *Ras Shamra-Ougarit VI: Arts et Industries de la pierre*. Paris: 355–410.

Frymer-Kensky, T. S. 1992. *In the Wake of Goddesses: Women, Culture, and the Biblical Transformation of Pagan Myths*. New York, NY.

Gabriel, G. 2014. *Enūma eliš – Weg zu einer globalen Weltordnung*. Tübingen.

Gadotti, A. 2011. 'Presence in Absentia: Portraits of the Feminine in Sumerian Literature', *JAOS* 131: 195–206.

  2014a. '*Gilgamesh, Enkidu and the Netherworld*' and the Sumerian Gilgamesh Cycle. Berlin.

  2014b. 'The Feminine in Myth and Epic', in Chavalas, M. W. 2014 (ed.), *Women in the Ancient Near East*, London and New York, NY: 28–58.

Gagné, R. 2009. 'A Wolf at the Table: Sympotic Perjury in Archilochus', *TAPhA* 139: 251–74.

Gallou, C. 2005. *The Mycenaean Cult of the Dead*. Oxford.

Gander, M. 2015. 'Asia, Ionia, Maeonia und Luwiya? Bemerkungen zu den neuen Toponymen aus Kom el-Hettan (Theben-West) mit Exkursen zu Westkleinasien in der Spätbronzezeit', *Klio* 97: 443–502.

Gantz, T. 1993. *Early Greek Myth. A Guide to Literary and Artistic Sources*. Baltimore, MD and London.

García-Ramón, J. L. 2006. 'Hitita *u̯arr-* "ayudar" y *karia-^{mi/tta}* "mostrar benevolencia", hom. ἦρα φέρειν (y χάριν φέρειν) 'dar satisfacción', IE **u̯erH-* "favorecer" y **ĝʰer(H)-* "estar a gusto, desear"', in Bombi et al. 2006 (eds.), 825–46.

2011. 'Idiome in hethitischer Literatur und in griechischer Dichtung. Anatolische bzw. akkadische Lehnübersetzungen oder indogermanische Phraseologie?', in Hutter and Hutter-Braunsar 2011 (eds.), 83–97.

Gatier, P.-L. 2016. 'Géographe mythologique de l'Oronte dans l' Antiquité', in Parayre, D. 2016 (ed.), *Le fleuve rebelle. Géographie historique du moyen Oronte d' Ebla à l'époque medieval.* Beirut: 249–70.

Geller, M. J. 2016. *Healing Magic and Evil Demons: Canonical Udug-hul Incantations*. Berlin.

Gener, J. M., Navarro, M. A., Pajuelo, J. M., Torres, M., and López, E. 2014. 'Arquitectura y urbanismo de la Gadir fenicia: El yacimiento del Teatro Cómico de Cádiz', in Botto, M. (ed.), *Los fenicios en la Bahía de Cádiz: Nuevas investigaciones*, Collezione di Studi Fenici 46. Rome: 14–50.

George, A. R. 1986. 'Sennacherib and the Tablet of Destinies', *Iraq* 48: 133–46.

1992. *Babylonian Topographical Texts.* Leuven.

1997. '"Bond of the Lands": Babylon, the Cosmic Capital', in Wilhelm 1997b (ed.), 125–45.

1999. 'E-sangil and E-temen-anki, the Archetypal Cult-Centre', in Renger 1999 (ed.), 67–86.

2000. *The Epic of Gilgamesh. The Babylonian Epic Poem and Other Texts in Akkadian and Sumerian.* London.

2003. *The Babylonian Gilgamesh Epic: Introduction, Critical Edition and Cuneiform Texts.* 2 vols. Oxford.

2007. 'The Gilgamesh Epic at Ugarit' *Aula Orientalis* 25.2: 237–54.

2009. *Babylonian Literary Texts in the Schøyen Collection.* Cornell University Studies in Assyriology and Sumerology 10. Bethesda, MD.

2010. '*Bilgames and the Bull of Heaven*: Cuneiform Texts, Collations and Textual Reconstruction', in Baker, H. D., Robson, E., and Zólyomi, G. (eds.), *Your Praise Is Sweet. A Memorial Volume for Jeremy Black*. London: 101–15.

2012. 'The Mayfly on the River: Individual and Collective Destiny in the Epic of Gilgamesh', *Kaskal: Rivista di storia, ambienti e culture del Vicino Oriente antico* 9: 227–42.

2016a. 'Die Kosmogonie des alten Mesopotamien', in Gindhart, M., and Pommerening, T. (eds.), *Anfang und Ende. Vormoderne Szenarien von Weltentstehung und Weltuntergang.* Darmstadt: 7–25.

2016b. *Mesopotamian Incantations and Related Texts in the Schøyen Collection.* Bethesda, MD.

2018. 'Enkidu and the Harlot: Another Fragment of Old Babylonian Gilgamesh', *Zeitschrift für Assyriologie* 108.1: 10–21.

Gera, D. 1993. *Xenophon's Cyropaedia: Style, Genre, and Literary Technique.* Oxford.

Gesche, P. D. 2001. *Schulunterricht in Babylonien im ersten Jahrtausend v. Chr.* Münster.

Giacomelli, A. 1980. 'Aphrodite and After', *Phoenix* 34: 1–19.

Gilan, A. 2015a. *Formen und Inhalte althethitischer historischer Literatur.* Heidelberg.
  2015b. 'A Bridge or a Blind Alley? Hittites and Neo Hittites as Cultural Mediators' in Faber, R., and Lichtenberger, A. 2015 (eds.), *Ein pluriverses Universum: Zivilisationen und Religonen im antiken Mittelmeerraum.* Mittelmeerstudien 7. Paderborn: 167–190.
Giorgieri, M. 2008. 'Verschwörungen und Intrigen am hethitischen Hof', in Wilhelm 2008 (ed.), 351–75.
Glassner, J.-J. 2004. *Mesopotamian Chronicles.* Atlanta, GA [translation of Glassner, J.-J. 1993. *Chroniques mésopotamiennes.* Paris].
Goedicke, H., and Roberts, J. J. M. 1975 (eds.). *Unity and Diversity: Essays in the History, Literature, and Religion of the Ancient Near East.* Baltimore, MD and London.
Görke, S. 2010. *Das Ritual der Aštu (CTH 490) – Rekonstruktion und Tradition eines hurritisch-hethitischen Rituals aus Boğazköy/Ḫattuša.* Culture and History of the Ancient Near East 40. Leiden and Boston, MA.
  2015 (ed.). *Muršilis Sprachlähmung (CTH 486)*, hethiter.net/: CTH 486 (INTR 2015-10-21).
Goldberg, C. 1984. 'The Historic-Geographic Method: Past and Future', *Journal of Folklore Research* 21: 1–18.
  2010. 'Strength in Numbers: The Uses of Comparative Folktale Research', *Western Folklore* 69: 19–34.
Gómez Espelosín, J. 2009. 'Iberia in the Greek Geographical Imagination', in Dietler and López-Ruiz 2009 (eds.), 281–97.
Goodnick Westenholz, J. 1997. *Legends of the Kings of Agade.* Winona Lake, IN.
Gordin, S. 2015. *Hittite Scribal Circles: Scholarly Tradition and Writing Habits.* Studien zu den Boğazköy-Texten 59. Wiesbaden.
Grafton, A., Most, G. W, and Zetzel, J. E. G. 1985. *F. A. Wolf: Prolegomena to Homer 1795. Translated with Introduction and Notes.* Princeton, NJ.
Gray, V. 2016. 'Herodotus (and Ctesias) Re-enacted: Leadership in Xenophon's *Cyropaedia*', in Priestley and Zali 2016 (eds.), 310–21.
Grayson, A. K., and J. Novotny 2014. *The Royal Inscriptions of Sennacherib, King of Assyria (704–681 BC), Part 2.* The Royal Inscriptions of the Neo-Assyrian Period 3/2. Winona Lake, IN.
Graziosi, B. 2002. *Inventing Homer: The Early Reception of Epic.* Cambridge.
  2016. 'Theologies of the Family in Homer and Hesiod', in Eidinow, Kindt and Osborne 2016 (eds.), 35–61.
  2017. 'Divine Conflict and the Problem of Aphrodite', in Bassino, Canevaro and Graziosi 2017 (eds.), 39–61.
Graziosi, B., and Haubold, J. 2005. *Homer: The Resonance of Epic.* London.
Greenstein, E. L. 1997. 'Kirta', in Parker, S. B. 1997 (ed.), *Ugaritic Narrative Poetry.* Atlanta, GA: 9–48.
Griffin, J. 1977. 'The Epic Cycle and the Uniqueness of Homer', *JHS* 97: 39–53.
  1978. 'The Divine Audience and the Religion of the *Iliad*', *CQ* 28: 1–22.
  1980. *Homer on Life and Death.* Oxford.

Gross, A. K. 1970. 'Götterhand und Menschenhand im homerischen Epos', *Gymnasium* 77: 365–75.
Gruppe, O. 1889. 'Typhon-Zephon', *Philologus* 48: 487–97.
Guichard, M. 1993. 'Flotille crétoise sur l'Euphrate?', *Nouvelles assyriologiques brèves et utilitaires* 1993.2: 44–5.
  2005. *La vaisselle de luxe des rois de Mari*. Paris.
Gunkel, H. 1895. *Schöpfung und Chaos in Urzeit und Endzeit: Eine religionsgeschichtliche Untersuchung über Gen. 1 und Ap. Jon 12*. Göttingen.
Gunter, A. C. 2009. *Greek Art and the Orient*. Cambridge.
Gurney, O. R. 1977. *Some Aspects of Hittite Religion*. Oxford.
Güterbock, H. G. 1946. *Kumarbi: Mythen vom churritischen Kronos aus den hethitischen Fragmenten zusammengestellt, übersetzt und erklärt*. Zurich and New York, NY.
  1948. 'The Hittite Version of the Hurrian Kumarbi Myths: Oriental Forerunners of Hesiod', *AJA* 52: 123–34 + plate III.
  1961. 'Hittite Mythology', in Kramer, S. N. 1961 (ed.), *Mythologies of the Ancient World*. New York, NY: 139–79.
  1997. 'Hethitische Literatur', in Hoffner, H. A., and Diamond, I. 1997 (eds.), *Perspectives on Hittite Civilization: Selected Writings of Hans Gustav Güterbock*. Assyriological Studies 26. Chicago, IL: 15–38.
von Gutschmid, A. 1892. *Kleine Schriften. Dritter Band: Schriften zur Geschichte und Literatur der nicht-semitischen Völker von Asien*. Leipzig.
Gyselen, R. 1992 (ed.). *Banquets d'Orient*. Louvain.
Haas, V. 1976. 'Die Unterwelts- und Jenseitsvorstellungen im hethitischen Kleinasien', *Orientalia* 45: 197–212.
  1984. *Die Serien itkaḫi und itkalzi des AZU-Priesters, Rituale für Tašmišarri und Tatuḫepa sowie weitere Texte mit Bezug auf Tašmišarri*. Corpus der hurritischen Sprachdenkmäler I/1. Rome.
  1994. *Geschichte der hethitischen Religion*. Handbuch der Orientalistik 1.15. Leiden and New York, NY.
  2003a. *Materia Magica et Medica Hethitica. Ein Beitrag zur Heilkunde im Alten Orient. Unter Mitwirkung von Daliah Bawanypeck*. Berlin and New York, NY.
  2003b. 'Betrachtungen zu CTH 343, eine Mythos des Hirschgottes' *AOF* 30: 296–303.
  2006. *Die hethitische Literatur: Texte, Stilistik, Motive*. Berlin and New York, NY.
  2007. 'Beispiele für Intertextualität im hethitischen rituellen Schriftum', in Groddek, D., and Zorman, M. 2007 (eds.), *Tabularia Hethaeorum. Hethitologische Beiträge. Silvin Košak zum 65. Geburtstag*. Wiesbaden: 341–51.
Haavio, M. 1955. *Der Etanamythos in Finnland*. Helsinki.
Hägg, R., and Marinatos, N. 1981 (eds.). *Sanctuaries and Cults in the Aegean Bronze Age. Proceedings of the First International Symposium at the Swedish Institute in Athens, 12–13 May 1980*. Stockholm.

Hagenbuchner, A. 1989. *Die Korrespondenz der Hethiter: Die Briefe mit Transkription, Übersetzung und Kommentar.* Texte der Hethiter 15–16. Heidelberg.
Haider, P. 2005. 'Von Baal Zaphon zu Zeus und Typhon', in Rollinger, R. 2005 (ed.), *Von Sumer bis Homer*. Münster: 303–37.
Hajnal, I., and Posch, C. Forthcoming. 'Graeco-Anatolian Contacts in the Mycenaean Period', www.academia.edu/1822403/Graeco-Anatolian_Contacts_in_the_Mycenaean_Period.
Hall, E. 2013. 'The Aesopic in Aristophanes', in Bakola, E., Prauscello, E. L., and Telò, M. 2013 (eds.), *Greek Comedy and the Discourse of Genres*. Cambridge: 277–97.
Halliwell, S. 1998. 'Subject Reviews (Greek Literature)', *G&R* 45: 235–9.
Harris, R. 2000. *Gender and Aging in Mesopotamia*. Oklahoma, OK.
Harrison, T., and Irwin, E. 2018 (eds.). *Interpreting Herodotus*. Oxford.
Harte, V., and Lane, M. 2013 (eds.). *Politeia in Greek and Roman Philosophy*. Cambridge.
Hartenstein, F., and Rösel, M. 2009 (eds.). *JHWH und die Götter der Völker: Symposium zum 80. Geburtstag von Klaus Koch*. Neukirchen-Vluyn.
Haubold, J. 2002. 'Greek Epic: A Near Eastern Genre?', *PCPhS* 48: 1–19.
  2013a. *Greece and Mesopotamia: Dialogues in Literature*. New York, NY.
  2013b. '"The Wisdom of the Chaldaeans": Reading Berossos, *Babyloniaca* Book 1', in Haubold et al. 2013 (eds.), 32–45.
  2013c. 'Ethnography in the *Iliad*', in Skempis and Ziogas 2013 (eds.), 19–36.
  2014. 'Kulturkontakt aus der Sicht des Homerslesers', in Rollinger and Schnegg 2014 (eds.), 325–42.
  2016. 'Hellenism, Cosmopolitanism, and the Role of Babylonian Elites in the Seleucid Empire', in Lavan, Payne and Weisweiler 2016 (eds.), 89–102.
  2017. 'Conflict, Consensus and Closure in Hesiod's *Theogony* and *Enūma eliš*', in Bassino, Canevaro and Graziosi 2017 (eds.), 17–38.
Haubold, J., Lanfranchi, G. B., Rollinger, R., and Steele, J. 2013 (eds.), *The World of Berossos*. Wiesbaden.
Haul, M. 2000. *Das Etana-Epos. Ein Mythos von der Himmelfahrt des Königs von Kiš*. Göttingen.
  2009. *Stele und Legende: Untersuchungen zu den keilschriftlichen Erzählwerken über die Könige von Akkade*. Göttingen.
Haussker, F. 2017. 'The *Ekthesis* of Cyrus the Great: A Case Study of Heroicity versus Bastardy in Classical Athens', *Cambridge Classical Journal* 63: 103–17.
Hawkins, S. 2013. *Studies in the Language of Hipponax*. Bremen.
Hawthorn, A. 2015. '"You Are Just Like Me": The Motif of the Double in the Epic of Gilgamesh and the Agushaya Poem'. *Kaskal: Rivista di storia, ambienti e culture del Vicino Oriente antico* 12: 451–66.
Haywood, J., and Mac Sweeney, N. 2018. *Homer's Iliad and the Trojan War: Dialogues on Tradition*. London.
Healey, J. F. 2007. 'From Sapanu/Sapunu to Kasion: The Sacred History of a Mountain', in Watson, W. G. E. (ed.), 'He Unfurrowed His Brow and

Laughed'. *Essays in Honour of Professor Nicolas Wyatt (Alter Orient und Altes Testament* 299*)*. Münster: 141–51.

Heeßel, N. P. 2007. 'The Hands of the Gods: Disease Names, and Divine Anger', in Finkel and Geller 2007 (eds.), 120–30.

Heidel, A. 1963. *The Babylonian Genesis*. Chicago, IL.

Heinz, M., and Feldman, M. H. 2007 (eds.). *Representations of Political Power: Case Histories from Times of Change and Dissolving Order in the Ancient Near East*. Winona Lake, IN.

Hellbing, L. 1979. *Alasia Problems*. Göteborg.

Heltzer, M. 1989. 'Sinaranu, Son of Siginu and Trade Relations between Ugarit and Crete', *Minos* 23: 7–13.

  1996. 'The Economy of Ugarit', in Watson and Wyatt 1996 (eds.), 423–54.

Hendel, R. 1987. 'Of Demigods and the Deluge. Toward an Interpretation of Genesis 6: 1–4', *JBL* 106.1: 13–26.

Hengstl, J. 2003. 'Rechtliche Aspekte der Adler-Schlangen-Fabel im Etana-Epos', in Selz, G. J. 2003 (ed.), *Festschrift für Burkhart Kienast zu seinem 70. Geburtstag dargebracht von Freunden, Schülern und Kollegen*. Münster: 201–23.

Henkelman, W. F. M. 2006. 'The Birth of Gilgameš (Ael. *NA* xii.21). A Case-Study in Literary Receptivity', in Rollinger and Truschnegg 2006 (eds.), 807–56.

Henkelman, W. F. M., and Kuhrt, A. 2003 (eds.). *A Persian Perspective: Essays in Memory of Heleen Sancisi-Weerdenburg*. Leiden.

Higgins, R. 1980. *Greek and Roman Jewellery*. 2nd ed. London.

Hiller, S. 1991. 'Die archäologische Erforschung des griechischen Siedlungsbereiches im 8. Jh. V. Chr.', in Latacz 1991 (ed.), 61–88.

Hirsch, H., and Hunger, H. 1982 (eds.). *Vorträge gehalten auf der 28. Rencontre Assyriologique Internationale in Wien, 6–10 Juli 1981*. Horn.

Hirschberger, M. 2004. *Gynaikon Katalogos und Megalai Ehoiai. Ein Kommentar zu den Fragmenten zweier Hesiodeischer Epen*. Munich.

Högemann, P., and Oettinger, N. 2018. *Lydien: Ein altanatolischer Staat zwischen Griechenland und dem Vorderen Orient*. Berlin and Boston, MA.

Hoffmann, I. 1984. *Der Erlaß Telipinus*. Heidelberg.

Hoffmann, F., and Quack, J. F. 2007. *Anthologie der demotischen Literatur*. Berlin.

Hoffner, H. A. 1973. 'Incest, Sodomy and Bestiality in the Ancient Near East', in Hoffner, H. A. 1973 (ed.). *Orient and Occident*. Neukirchen–Vluyn: 81–90.

  1975. 'Hittite Mythological Texts: A Survey', in Goedicke and Roberts 1975 (eds.), 136–45.

  1990. *Hittite Myths*. Atlanta, GA.

  2016. 'The Kumarbi Series of Myths (4.6)', in Lawson Younger, K. 2016 (ed.), *The Context of Scripture, Volume 4: Supplement*. Leiden: 39–44.

Hoffner, H. A. with Beckman, G. 1998. *Hittite Myths*. 2nd ed. Atlanta, GA.

Horálek, K. 1987. 'Geist in Glas', in Ranke, K., and Bausinger, H. 1975–2015 (eds.), Vol. 5, 922–8.

Horowitz, W. 1998. *Mesopotamian Cosmic Geography*. Winona Lake, IN.
　2014. *The Three Stars Each: The Astrolabes and Related Texts*. Vienna.
Houwink ten Cate, P. H. J. 1961. *The Luwian Population Groups of Lycia and Cilicia Aspera during the Hellenistic Period*. Leiden.
　1992. 'The Hittite Storm God: His Role and His Rule according to Hittite Cuneiform Sources', in Meijer, D. J. W. 1992 (ed.), *Natural Phenomena: Their Meaning, Depiction and Description in the Ancient Near East*. Amsterdam: 83–148.
van den Hout, Th. 1998. *The Purity of Kingship. An Edition of CTH 569 and Related Hittite Oracle Inquiries of Tuthaliya IV*. Documenta et Monumenta Orientis Antiqui 25. Leiden, Boston, MA and Cologne.
　2002. 'Another View of Hittite Literature', in de Martino, S. und Pecchioli Daddi, F. 2002 (eds.), *Anatolia Antica. Studi in Memoria di Fiorella Imparati*. Eothen 11. Florence: 857–78.
　2015. 'In Royal Circles: The Nature of Hittite Scholarship', *Journal of Ancient Near Eastern History* 2: 203–27.
Hoz, J. de. 2010. *Historia lingüística de la Península Ibérica en la Antigüedad I. Preliminares y mundo meridional prerromano*. Madrid.
Hughes, D. D. 1991. *Human Sacrifice in Ancient Greece*. New York, NY and London.
Hunger, H., and Steele, J. 2018. *The Babylonian Astronomical Compendium MUL.APIN*. London and New York, NY.
Hunter, R. L. 2014. *Hesiodic Voices: Studies in the Ancient Reception of Hesiod's Works and Days*. Cambridge.
　2018. *The Measure of Homer: The Ancient Reception of the Iliad and the Odyssey*. Cambridge.
Hutter, M., and Hutter-Braunsar, S. 2011 (eds). *Hethitische Literatur: Überlieferungsprozesse, Textstrukturen, Ausdrucksformen und Nachwirken. Akten des Symposiums vom 18. bis 20. Februar 2010 in Bonn*. Alter Orient und Altes Testament 391. Münster.
Irwin, E. 1998. 'Biography, Fiction, and the Archilochean *Ainos*', *JHS* 118: 177–83.
Jacobs, B. 1996. 'Kyros der Grosse als Geisel am medischen Königshof', *Iranica Antiqua* 31: 83–100.
Jacobsen, Th. 1968. 'The Battle between Marduk and Tiamat', *JAOS* 88: 104–8.
　1970. 'Sumerian Mythology: A Review Article', in Moran, W. L. (ed.), *Toward the Image of Tammuz and Other Essays on Mesopotamian History and Culture*. Cambridge, MA: 104–31.
Jacoby, F. 1958. *Die Fragmente der griechischen Historiker (FGrH), III Geschichte von Staedten und Voelkern, C Autoren über einzelne Laender, 1 Aegypten–Geten*. Leiden.
Jamison, S., and Brereton, J. P. 2014. *The Rigveda. The Earliest Religious Poetry of India*. Oxford.
Janeway, B. 2015. *Sea Peoples of the Northern Levant? Aegean-Style Pottery from Early Iron Age Tell Tayinat*. Winona Lake, IN.

Janko, R. 1992. *The Iliad, A Commentary. Volume IV: Books 13–16*. Cambridge.
Jaques, M. 2015. *Mon dieu qu'ai-je fait? Les diĝir-šà-dab(5)-ba et la piété privée en Mésopotamie*. Orbis Biblicus et Orientalis 273. Fribourg and Göttingen.
Jay, J. E. 2016. *Orality and Literacy in the Demotic Tales*. Leiden and Boston, MA.
Jiménez, E. 2013. '"The Creation of the King": A Reappraisal', *Kaskal: Rivista di storia, ambienti e culture del Vicino Oriente antico* 10: 235–54.
  2017. *The Babylonian Disputation Poems with Editions of the Series of the Poplar, Palm and Vine, the Series of the Spider, and the Story of the Poor, Forlorn Wren*. Leiden and Boston, MA.
Johnson, J. C. 2015a. 'Introduction. "Infrastructural Compendia" and the Licensing of Empiricism in Mesopotamian Technical Literature', in Johnson, J. C. 2015 (ed.), *In the Wake of Compendia. Infrastructural Contexts and the Licensing of Empiricism in Ancient and Medieval Mesopotamia*. Berlin: 1–28.
  2015b. 'Iteration, Citation and Citationality in the Mesopotamian Scholastic Dialogue *The Class Reunion*', in Cancik-Kirschbaum, E. and Traninger, A. (eds.), *Wissen in Bewegung. Institution – Iteration – Transfer*. Wiesbaden: 105–32.
Johnson, J. C., and Geller, M. J. 2015. *The Class Reunion: A Critical Edition and Annotated Translation of the Sumerian Literary Dialogue 'Two Scribes'*. Leiden and Boston, MA.
Johnson, W. J. 1998. *The Sauptikaparvan of the Mahābhārata. The Massacre at Night*. Oxford.
Johnston, A. 2019. 'Knowledge, Suffering and the Performance of Wisdom in Solon's *Elegy to the Muses* and the Babylonian *Poem of the Righteous Sufferer*', *Cambridge Classical Journal* 65: 1–21.
Jones, A. 1966. *The Jerusalem Bible*. London.
Jones-Bley, K., Huld, M. E., and Della Volpe, A. 2000 (eds.). *Proceedings of the Eleventh Annual UCLA Indo-European Conference, Los Angeles, June 4–5, 1999*. Washington, DC.
de Jong, I. J. F. 2001. *A Narratological Commentary on the Odyssey*. Cambridge.
Kämmerer, T. R., and K. A. Metzler 2012. *Das babylonische Weltschöpfungsepos Enūma elîš*. Münster.
Kaldellis, A., and López-Ruiz, C. 2009. '*BNJ* 790: Philon of Byblos', *Brill's New Jacoby*, general editor Ian Worthington, online edition.
Kapelus, M., and Taracha, P. 2014 (eds.). *Proceedings of the Eighth International Conference of Hittitology in Warsaw, Poland, Sept. 5–9, 2011*. Warsaw.
Karageorghis, V., and Stampolidis, N. C. 1998 (eds.). *Eastern Mediterranean Networks: Cyprus-Dodecanese-Crete, 16th–6th Century BC*. Athens: 243–54.
Karetsou, A. 1981. 'The Peak Sanctuary of Mt. Juktas', in Hägg and Marinatos 1981 (eds.), 137–53.
Karst, J. 1911. *Eusebius Werke, fünfter Band. Die Chronik aus dem Armenischen übersetzt*. Leipzig.
Katz, D. 2011. 'Reconstructing Babylon: Recycling Mythological Traditions towards a New Theology', in Cancik-Kirschbaum, van Ess and Marzahn 2011 (eds.), 123–34.

Katz, J. T. 2000. 'Evening Dress: The Metaphorical Background of Latin *uesper* and Greek ἕσπερος', in Jones-Bley, Huld and Della Volpe 2000 (eds.), 69–93.
 2005. 'The Indo-European Context', in Foley 2005 (ed.), 20–30.
 2018. 'The Prehistory and Analogues of Hesiod's Poetry', in Loney and Scully 2018 (eds.), 61–77.
Kelley, O. 2012. 'Beyond Intermarriage: The Role of the Indigenous Italic Population at Pithekoussai', *OJA* 31.3: 245–60.
Kelly, A. 2007a. *A Referential Commentary and Lexicon to Homer, Iliad VIII*. Oxford.
 2007b. 'How to End an Orally-Derived Epic Poem', *TAPhA* 137: 371–402.
 2008. 'The Babylonian Captivity of Homer: The Case of the Διὸς Ἀπάτη', *RhM* 151: 259–304.
 2014. 'Homeric Battle Narrative and the Ancient Near East', in Cairns, D., and Scodel, R. 2014 (eds.), *Defining Greek Narrative*. Edinburgh: 29–54.
Kerkhecker, A. 1999. *Callimachus' Book of Iambi*. Oxford.
Kieffer, R., and Bergman, J. 1997. *La main de Dieu. Die Hand Gottes*. Tübingen.
Kilmer, A. D. 1972. 'The Mesopotamian Concept of Overpopulation and Its Solution as Reflected in the Mythology', *Orientalia* 41: 160–77.
Kirk, G. S. 1970. *Myth: Its Meaning and Function in Ancient and Other Cultures*. Berkeley and Los Angeles, CA.
 1985. *The Iliad, A Commentary. Volume I: Books 1–4*. Cambridge.
 1990. *The Iliad, A Commentary. Volume II: Books 5–8*. Cambridge.
Kleber, K., Neumann, G., and Paulus, S. 2018 (eds.). *Grenzüberschreitungen: Studien zur Kulturgeschichte des Alten Orients*. Münster.
Klinger, J. 2001. 'Die hurritische Tradition in Ḫattuša und das Corpus hurritischer Texte', in Richter, Prechel and Klinger 2001 (eds.), 197–208.
Koch, K. 1993. 'Hazzi-Safon-Kasion. Die Geschichte eines Berges und seiner Gottheiten' in Janowski, B. K., Koch, G., and Wilhelm, G. 1993 (eds.), *Religionsgeschichtliche Beziehungen zwischen Kleinasien, Nordsyrien und dem Alten Testament. Internationales Symposion Hamburg 17.–21. März 1990, Orbis Biblicus et Orientalis* 129. Göttingen: 171–223.
Koch-Westenholz, U. 2000. *Babylonian Liver Omens*. Copenhagen.
Koehl, R. B. 2013. 'The Near Eastern Contribution to Aegean Wall Painting and Vice Versa', in Aruz, J., Graff, S., and Rakic, Y. 2013 (eds.), *Cultures in Contact: From Mesopotamia to the Mediterranean in the Second Millennium BC*. New York, NY: 170–9.
Koenen, L. 1994. 'Greece, the Near East, and Egypt: Cyclic Destruction in Hesiod and the Catalogue of Women', *TAPhA* 124: 1–34.
Kogan, L. E., et al. 2010 (eds.). *City Administration in the Ancient Near East: Proceedings of the 53^e Rencontre Assyriologique Internationale Volume 2*. Winona Lake, IN.
Komoróczy, G. 1973a. '"The Separation of Sky and Earth". The Cycle of Kumarbi and the Myths of Cosmogony in Mesopotamia', *Acta Antiqua Academiae Scientiarum Hungaricae* 21: 21–45.
 1973b. 'Berosos and the Mesopotamian Literature', *Acta Antiqua Academiae Scientiarum Hungaricae* 21: 125–52.

Koning, H. H. 2018. 'The Hesiod Question', in Loney and Scully 2018 (eds.), 17–29.
Konstantinidou, K. 2014. 'Responses to Perjury: Human Responses', in Sommerstein, A. H., and Torrance, I. C. (eds.), *Oaths and Swearing in Ancient Greece*. Berlin and Boston, MA: 303–14.
Kort, A., and Morschauser, S. 1985 (eds.). *Biblical and Related Studies Presented to Samuel Iwry*. Winona Lake, IN.
Kotwick, M., and Janko, R. 2017. *Der Papyrus von Derveni*. Berlin and Boston, MA.
Kourou, N., and Karetsou, A. 1998. 'An Enigmatic Stone from Knossos: A Reused Cippus?', in Karageorghis and Stampolidis 1998 (eds.), 243–54.
Kowalzig, B. 2007. *Singing for the Gods. Performances of Myth and Ritual in Archaic and Classical Greece*. Oxford.
Kraeling, E. G. 1947. 'The Origin and Significance of *Gen.* 6:1–4', *JNES* 6: 193–208.
Kramer, S. N. 1956. *History Begins at Sumer: Thirty-Nine Firsts in Recorded History*. Philadelphia, PA.
  1980. 'Inanna and the *Numun*-Plant: A New Sumerian Myth', in Rendsburg, G., Radler, A., and Winter, A. M. (eds.), *The Bible World: Essays in Honor of C. H. Gordon*. New York, NY: 87–97.
Kramer, S. N., Çig, M., and Kizilyay, H. 1969. *Istanbul Arkeoloji Müzelerinde bulunan Sumer edebîtablet ve parcaları (Sumerian Literary Tablets and Fragments in the Archaeological Museum of Istanbul), I*. Ankara.
Kreuzer, J. 2002 (ed.). *Hölderlin-Handbuch: Leben – Werk – Wirkung*. Weimar.
Kristeva, J. 1986. 'Word, Dialogue and Novel', in Moi, T. 1986 (ed.), *The Kristeva Reader*. New York, NY: 34–61.
Kugel, J. 1997. *The Bible as It Was*. Cambridge, MA.
Kuhrt, A. 1987. 'Berossus' *Babyloniaka* and Seleucid Rule in Babylonia', in Kuhrt, A., and Sherwin-White, S. (eds.), *Hellenism in the East*. London: 32–56.
  2003. 'Making History: Sargon of Agade and Cyrus the Great of Persia', in Henkelman and Kuhrt 2003 (eds.), 347–61.
  2007. 'Cyrus the Great of Persia: Images and Realities', in Heinz and Feldman 2007 (eds.), 169–91.
Kupper, J. R. 1950. *Correspondance de Kebri-Dagan*. ARM 3. Paris.
Kurke, L. 2011. *Aesopic Conversations: Popular Tradition, Cultural Dialogue, and the Invention of Greek Prose*. Princeton, NJ.
Kvanvig, H. S. 2011. *Primeval History: Babylonian, Biblical and Enochic. An Intertextual Reading*. Leiden.
Kynes, W. 2021 (ed.). *The Oxford Handbook of Wisdom and Wisdom Literature*. Oxford.
Labat, R. 1951. *Traité akkadien de diagnostics et pronostics médicaux*. Paris and Leiden.
Laffineur, R. 1991. 'La mer at l'au delà dans l'Egée préhistorique', in Laffineur, R. 1991 (ed.), *Thalassa. L'Egée préhistorique et la mer*. Liège: 231–7.

Lafont, B., Tenu, A., Joannès, F., and Clancier, P. 2017. *La Mésopotamie: de Gilgamesh à Artaban, 3300–120 av. J. C.* Paris.
Lämmerhirt, K., and Zgoll, A. 2009. 'Schicksal: A (in Mesopotamien)', in *RlA* 12: 145–55.
Lambert, W. G. 1960. *Babylonian Wisdom Literature*. Oxford.
　　1972. 'Destiny and Divine Intervention in Babylon and Israel', *Oudtestamentische Studiën* 17: 65–72.
　　1974. 'Dingir. šà. dib. ba Incantations', *JNES* 33: 267–322.
　　1981. 'Studies in UD.GAL.NUN', *Oriens Antiquus* 20: 81–97.
　　1987. 'Goddesses in the Pantheon: A Reflection of Women in Society', in Durand, J.-M. 1987 (ed.), *La femme dans le proche-orient antique*. Paris: 125–30.
　　1997a. 'The Assyrian Recension of *Enūma Eliš*', in Waetzoldt and Hauptmann 1997 (eds.), 77–9.
　　1997b. 'Processions to the Akītu House', *Revue d'Assyriologie et d'archéologie orientale* 91: 49–80.
　　2013. *Babylonian Creation Myths*. Winona Lake, IN.
Lambert, W. G., and Millard, A. R. 1969. *Atra-ḫasīs. The Babylonian Story of the Flood*. Oxford.
de Lamberterie, C. 1990. *Les adjectifs grecs en -υς. Sémantique et comparaison*. Louvain-la-Neuve.
Lancel, S. 1995. *Carthage: A History*. Oxford and Cambridge, MA.
Lane Fox, R. 2008. *Travelling Heroes: Greeks and Their Myths in the Epic Age of Homer*. London.
　　2018. 'Introduction: Travelling Myths, Travelling Heroes', in Audley-Miller and Dignas 2018 (eds.), xxxiii–liv.
Lapinkivi, P. 2010. *The Neo-Assyrian Myth of Ištar's Descent and Resurrection*. Helsinki.
Lardinois, A. 2018. 'Eastern Myths for Western Lies: Allusions to Near Eastern Mythology in Homer's *Iliad*', *Mnemosyne* 71: 895–919.
Larrington, C. 2014. *The Poetic Edda*. Oxford.
Latacz, J. 1991 (ed.). *Zweihundert Jahre Homer-Forschung. Rückblick und Ausblick*. Stuttgart.
Latacz, J., Nünlist, R., and Stoevesandt, M. 2000. *Homers Ilias. Gesamtkommentar, Band 1. Erster Gesang*. Munich and Leipzig.
Lavan, M., Payne, R. E., and Weisweiler, J. 2016 (eds.). *Cosmopolitanism and Empire: Universal Rulers, Local Elites, and Cultural Integration in the Ancient Near East and Mediterranean*. Oxford.
Lawson, J. N. 1994. *The Concept of Fate in Ancient Mesopotamia of the First Millennium. Toward an Understanding of Šimtu*. Wiesbaden.
Lazaridis, N. 2016. 'Different Parallels, Different Interpretations: Reading Parallels between Ancient Egyptian and Greek Works of Literature', in Rutherford, I. 2016 (ed.). *Greco-Egyptian Interactions: Literature, Translation, and Culture, 500 BC–AD 300*. Oxford: 187–207.

Leaf, W. 1900–1. *The Iliad. Edited, with Apparatus Criticus, Prolegomena, Notes, and Appendices*. 2 vols. 2nd ed. London.
Lebrun, R. 1985. 'L'aphasie de Mursili II = CTH 486', *Hethitica* 6: 103–37.
Lehrs, K. 1882. *De Aristarchi Studiis Homericis*. 3rd ed. Leipzig.
Leichty, E. 1986. *Catalogue of the Babylonian Tablets in the British Museum VI: Tablets from Sippar 1*. London.
Lemardelé, C. 2010. 'Une gigantomachie dans la Genèse? Géants et heroes dans les texts bibliques compiles' *RHR* 227.2: 155–74.
Lemos, I. S. 2002. *The Protogeometric Aegean: The Archaeology of the Late Eleventh and Tenth Centuries BC*. Oxford.
Lenfant, D. 2004. *Ctésias de Cnide: La Perse, L'Inde, autres fragments*. Paris.
Lenzi, A. 2015. 'Mesopotamian Scholarship: Kassite to Late Babylonian Periods', *Journal of Ancient Near Eastern History* 2: 145–201.
Levin, I. 1994. 'Über eines der ältesten Märchen der Welt', *Märchenspiegel* 4: 2–6.
Levy, E. 2014. 'A Fresh Look at the Baal-Zaphon Stele', *JEA* 100: 293–309.
Lewis, B. 1980. *The Sargon Legend: A Study of the Akkadian Text and the Tale of the Hero Who Was Exposed at Birth*. Cambridge, MA.
Lewis, T. 1989. *Cults of the Dead in Ancient Israel And Ugarit*. Atlanta, GA.
Lindenberger, J. M. 1983. *The Aramaic Proverbs of Ahiqar*. Baltimore, MD.
Lion, B., and Michel, C. 2016 (eds.). *The Role of Women in Work and Society in the Ancient Near East*. Leiden.
Linssen, M. J. H. 2004. *The Cults of Uruk and Babylon: The Temple Ritual Texts as Evidence for Hellenistic Cult Practice*. Leiden and Boston, MA.
Lipinski, E. 1995. *Dieux et déesses de l'univers phénicien et punique*. Leuven.
  2004. *Itineraria Phoenicia*. Studia Phoenicia 18 (Orientalia Lovaniensia Analecta 127). Leuven.
Lisman, J. J. W. 2013. *Cosmogony, Theogony and Anthropogeny in Sumerian Texts*. Münster.
Littleton, C. Scott. 1970a. 'Is the 'Kingship in Heaven' Theme Indo-European?', in Cardona, G., Hoenigswald, H. M., and Senn, A. (eds.), *Indo-European and the Indo-Europeans: Papers Presented at the Third Indo-European Conference at the University of Pennsylvania*. Philadelphia, PA: 383–404.
  1970b. 'The 'Kingship in Heaven' Theme', in Puhvel, J. 1970 (ed.), *Myth and Law Among the Indo-Europeans*. Berkeley, CA: 83–121.
Livingstone, A. 1986. *Mystical and Mythological Explanatory Works of Assyrian and Babylonian Scholars*. Oxford.
  1989. *Court Poetry and Literary Miscellanea*. Helsinki.
Llewellyn-Jones, Ll., and Robson, J. 2010. *Ctesias' History of Persia: Tales of the Orient*. Abingdon.
Löhnert, A. 2014. 'Ubšu'ukkina', in *Reallexikon der Assyriologie und Vorderasiatischen Archäologie* 14: 268–9.
Loney, A. C., and Scully, S. 2018 (eds.). *The Oxford Handbook of Hesiod*. Oxford.
Long, C. R. 1974. *The Ayia Triadha Sarcophagus: A Study of Late Minoan and Mycenean Funerary Practices and Beliefs*. Göteborg.

López-Ruiz, C. 2009a. 'Mopsos and Cultural Exchange between Greeks and Locals in Cilicia', in Dill and Walde 2009 (eds.), 382–96.
  2009b. '*BNJ* 784: Laitos (-Mochos)', *Brill's New Jacoby*, general editor Ian Worthington, online edition.
  2010. *When the Gods Were Born. Greek Cosmogonies and the Near East.* Cambridge, MA.
  2013. 'The King and the Cupbearer: Feasting and Power in Eastern Mediterranean Myth', in Celestino Pérez and Blánquez Pérez 2013 (eds.), 133–51.
  2014a. 'Greek and Near Eastern Mythologies. A Story of Mediterranean Encounters', in Edmunds 2014 (ed.), 154–99.
  2014b. *Gods, Heroes, and Monsters. A Sourcebook of Greek, Roman, and Near Eastern Myths in Translation.* 1st ed. Oxford.
  2014c. 'Greek and Canaanite Mythologies: Zeus, Baal, and their Rivals', *The Religion Compass* 8/1: 1–10 (online).
  2017a. *Gods, Heroes, and Monsters: A Sourcebook of Greek, Roman, and Near Eastern Myths in Translation.* 2nd ed. Oxford.
  2017b. '"Not That Which Can Be Found among the Greeks": Philo of Byblos' and Phoenician Cultural Identity in the Roman East', *Religions of the Roman Empire* 3.3: 366–92.
  2017c. 'Gargoris and Habis: A Tartessic Myth of Ancient Iberia and the Traces of Phoenician Euhemerism', *Phoenix* 71.3–4: 265–87.
  2019. 'Phoenician-Punic Literature', in López-Ruiz and Doak (eds.), 258–68.
  Forthcoming. 'Phoenicians and the Iron Age Mediterranean: a Response to Phoenicoskepticism', in Hall, J., and Osborne, J. eds. *The Connected Iron Age: Interregional Networks in the Eastern Mediterranean, 900-600 BCE.* Chicago, IL.
López-Ruiz, C., and Doak, B. 2019 (eds.). *Oxford Handbook of the Phoenician and Punic Mediterranean.* New York, NY and Oxford.
Lorenz, J., and Rieken, E. 2010. 'Überlegungen zur Verwendung mythologischer Texte bei den Hethitern', in Fincke, J. C. 2010 (ed.), *Festschrift für Gernot Wilhelm anlässlich seines 65. Geburtstages am 28. Januar 2010.* Dresden: 217–34.
Lorenz-Link, U. 2009. *Uralte Götter und Unterweltsgötter. Religionsgeschichtliche Betrachtungen zur 'Sonnengöttin der Erde' und den 'Uralten Göttern' bei den Hethitern.* Doctoral Thesis, University of Mainz.
Louden, B. 2011. *Homer's Odyssey and the Near East.* Cambridge.
  2018. *Greek Myth and the Bible.* London.
Ludwig, M.-C., and Metcalf, C. 2017. 'The Song of Innana and Išme-Dagan: An Edition of BM 23820+23831', *Zeitschrift für Assyriologie und Vorderasiatische Archäologie* 107.1: 1–21.
Luginbühl, M. 1992. *Menschenschöpfungsmythen. Ein Vergleich zwischen Griechenland und dem Alten Orient.* Bern.
Lühr, R., and Ziegler, S. 2009 (eds.). *Protolanguage and Prehistory. Akten der XII. Fachtagung der Indogermanischen Gesellschaft, Krakau, 11.–16.10.2004.* Wiesbaden.
Luraghi, N. 2001 (ed.). *The Historian's Craft in the Age of Herodotus.* Oxford.
Lye, J. 2018. 'Gender in Hesiod', in Loney and Scully 2018 (eds.), 175–90.

Lyne, R. O. A. M. 1994. 'Vergil's *Aeneid*: Subversion by Intertextuality. Catullus 66.39–40 and Other Examples' *G&R* 41/1: 187–204.
Lytle, E. 2011. 'The Strange Love of the Fish and the Goat: Regional Contexts and Rough Cilician Religion in Oppian's *Halieutica* 4.308–73', *TAPhA* 141: 333–86.
Machinist, P. 2000. 'The Sea Peoples and Their World', in Oren 2000 (ed.), 53–83.
Machuca Prieto, F. 2019. 'Unravelling the Western Phoenicians under Roman Rule: Identity, Heterogeneity and Dynamic Boundaries' in Cruz Andreotti, G. (ed.), *Roman Turdetania: Romanization, Identity and Socio-cultural Interaction in the South of the Iberian Peninsula between the 4th and 1st Centuries* BCE. Leiden and Boston, MA: 130–47.
Madreiter, I. 2012. *Stereotypisierung – Idealisierung – Indifferenz. Formen der Auseinandersetzung mit dem Achaimeniden-Reich in der griechischen Persika-Literatur*. Wiesbaden.
  2013. 'From Berossos to Eusebius – A Christian Apologist's Shaping of "Pagan" Literature', in Haubold et al. 2013 (eds.), 255–75.
Maeir, A., and Hitchock, L. 2017. 'The Appearance, Formation, and Transformation of Philistine Culture: New Perspectives and New Finds', in Fischer and Bürge 2017 (eds.), 149–62.
Maiocchi, M. 2010. 'The Sargonic "Archive" of Me-^{sá}sag$_7$, Cup-Bearer of Adab', in Kogan et al. 2010 (eds.), 141–52.
Malamat, A. 1998. *Mari and the Bible*. Leiden and Boston, MA.
Malkin, I. 2011. *A Small Greek World: Networks in the Ancient Mediterranean*. Oxford.
Malul, M. 1990. *The Comparative Method in Ancient Near Eastern and Biblical Legal Studies*. Neukirchen-Vluyn.
Marks, J. H., and Good, R. M. 1987 (eds.). *Love and Death in the Ancient Near East. Essays in Honor of Marvin H. Pope*. Guilford.
Martin, R. P. 1989. *The Language of Heroes: Speech and Performance in the Iliad*. Ithaca, NY.
  2018. 'Hesiodic Theology', in Loney and Scully 2018 (eds.), 125–41.
Martin, S. R. 2017. *The Art of Contact: Comparative Approaches to Greek and Phoenician Art*. Philadelphia, PA.
de Martino, S. 2016. *Da Kussara a Karkemish: Storia del regno ittita*. Turin.
de Martino, S., and Imparati, F. 1998. 'La "mano" nelle più significative espressioni idiomatiche ittite', in Agostaniani, Arcamone, Carruba, Imparati and Rizza 1998 (eds.), 175–85.
Matasović, R. 1996. *A Theory of Textual Reconstruction in Indo-European Linguistics*. Frankfurt am Main.
Matijević, K. 2018. 'Zur Beeinflussung der homerischen Epen durch das Gilgamesch-Epos. Mit einem Exkurs zu einer neuen Datierungsthese der Ilias', *Klio* 100: 599–625.
Matuszak, J. 2019. 'Es streite, wer kann! Ein neuer Rekonstruktions- und Interpretationsversuch für das sumerische Schulstreitsgespräch, Dialog 1', *Zeitschrift für Assyriologie und Vorderasiatische Archäologie* 109.1: 1–47.

Mayer, K. 1996. 'Helen and the ΔΙΟΣ ΒΟΥΛΗ', *AJPh* 117: 1–15.
Mayer, W. R. 1987. 'Ein Mythos von der Erschaffung des Menschcs und des Königs', *Orientalia* 56: 55–68.
McCarter, P. K. Jr. 1984. *II Samuel: A New Translation with Introduction, Notes and Commentary*. New York, NY.
Meijer, M. 2018. 'Parallelen tussen de *Ilias* en het *Gilgameš*-epos', *Phoenix* 64.2: 8–23.
Meisner, D. A. 2018. *Orphic Tradition and the Birth of the Gods*. Oxford.
Melville, S. C., and Slotsky, A. L. 2010 (eds.). *Opening the Tablet Box: Near Eastern Studies in Honor of Benjamin R. Foster*. Leiden.
Metcalf, C. 2013. 'Babylonian Perspectives on the Certainty of Death'. *Kaskal: Rivista di storia, ambienti e culture del Vicino Oriente antico* 10: 255–67.
 2015a. *The Gods Rich in Praise. Early Greek and Mesopotamian Religious Poetry*. Oxford.
 2015b. 'Old Babylonian Religious Poetry in Anatolia: From Solar Hymn to Plague Prayer', *Zeitschrift für Assyriologie und Vorderasiatische Archaeologie* 105: 42–53.
 2017. Review of Bachvarova 2016. *CR* 67: 3–5.
Michalowski, P. 1998a. 'The Unbearable Lightness of Enlil', in Prosecký, J. (ed.), *Intellectual Life of the Ancient Near East*. Prague: 237–47.
 1998b. 'Literature as a Source of Lexical Inspiration' in Braun, J., Lyczkowska, K., Popka, M., and Steinkeller, P. (eds). *Written on Clay and Stone. Ancient Near Eastern Studies Presented to Krystyna Szarzynska on the Occasion of Her 80th Birthday*. Warsaw: 65–73.
van de Mieroop, M. 2016. *A History of the Ancient Near East ca. 3000–323 BC*. Chichester.
Miles, R. 2010. *Carthage Must Be Destroyed: the Rise and Fall of an Ancient Civilization*. London.
Millek, J. 2017. 'Sea Peoples, Philistines, and the Destruction of Cities: A Critical Examination of Destruction Layers "Caused" by the "Sea Peoples"', in Fischer and Bürge 2017 (eds.), 11–140.
Miller, J. L. 2008. 'Ein Ritual für die Reinigung eines Hauswesens durch eine Beschwörung der Unterirdischen (CTH 446)', in Janowski, B., and Wilhelm, G. 2008 (eds.), *Texte aus der Umwelt des Alten Testaments, Neue Folge, Band 4: Omina, Orakel, Rituale und Beschwörungen*. Gütersloh: 206–17.
Millington, A. 2013. *War and the Warrior: Functions of Ares in Literature and Cult*. PhD Dissertation, University College London.
Milstein, S. 2016. 'Outsourcing Gilgamesh', in Person, R., and Rezetko, R. (eds.), *Empirical Models Challenging Biblical Criticism*. Atlanta, GA: 37–62.
Mitchell, F. 2018. 'The Universe from an Egg: Creation Narratives in the Ancient Indian and Greek Texts', in Cobb, M. A. (ed.), *The Indian Ocean Trade in Antiquity: Political, Cultural, and Economic Impacts*. London: 171–90.
Mittermayer, C. 2009. *Enmerkar und der Herr von Aratta. Ein ungleicher Wettstreit*. Fribourg.

von Möllendorff, P. 1994. 'Die Fabel von Adler und Mistkäfer im Aesoproman', *RhM* 137: 141–61.
Momigliano, A. 1969. *Quarto contributo alla storia degli studi classici e del mondo antico*. Rome.
  1975. *Alien Wisdom. The Limits of Hellenization*. Cambridge.
Mondi, R. 1990. 'Greek Mythic Thought in the Light of the Near East', in Edmunds, L. 1990 (ed.), *Approaches to Greek Myth*. Baltimore, MD: 142–98.
Montanari, F. 2012. 'Introduction: The Homeric Question Today', in Montanari, F., Rengakos, A., and Tsagalis, C. (eds.), *Homeric Contexts: Neoanalysis and the Interpretation of Oral Poetry*. Trends in Classics Supplementary Volumes 12. Berlin and Boston, MA: 1–10.
Montanari, F., Rengakos, A., and Tsagalis, C. 2009 (eds.). *Brill's Companion to Hesiod*. Leiden and Boston, MA.
Moran, W. L. 1971. 'Atraḫasis: The Babylonian Story of the Flood', *Biblica* 52: 51–61.
  1978. 'Puppies in Proverbs – From Šamši-Adad to Archilochus?', *Eretz Israel* 14 (H. L. Ginsberg Volume): 32–7.
  1992. *The Amarna Letters*. Baltimore, MD and London.
Morris, E. F. 2015. 'Egypt, Ugarit, the God Ba'al, and the Puzzle of a Royal Rebuff', in Mynářová et al. 2015 (eds.), 315–31.
Morris, I., and Powell, B. B. 1997 (eds.). *A New Companion to Homer*, Leiden and New York, NY.
Morris, S. 1992. *Daidalos and the Origin of Greek Art*. Princeton, NJ.
Morris, S., and Papadopoulos, J. 1998. 'Phoenicians and the Corinthian Pottery Industry', in Rolle, R., Schmidt, K., and Docter, R. F. 1998 (eds.), *Archäologische Studien in Kontaktzonen der antiken Welt*. Göttingen: 251–63.
Most, G. 1998. 'Hesiod's Myth of the Five (or Three or Four) Races', *PCPhS* 43: 104–27.
  2003. 'Violets in Crucibles: Translating, Traducing, Transmuting', *TAPhA* 133: 381–90.
  2006–7. *Hesiod* (2 vols.). Cambridge, MA and London.
Mouton, A. 2007. *Rêves hittites. Contribution à une histoire et une anthropologie du rêve en Anatolie ancienne*. Culture and History of the Ancient Near East 28. Leiden and Boston, MA.
  2016a. *Rites, mythes et prières Hittites*. Paris.
  2016b. 'The Festivals of Lallupiya-Ištanuwa: Local Traditions or Part of the Religion of the Hittite State?' in Müller 2016 (ed.), 119–32.
Moyer, I. 2011. *Egypt and the Limits of Hellenism*. Cambridge.
Müller, G. G. W. 2016 (ed.). *Liturgie oder Literatur? Die Kultrituale der Hethiter im transkulturellen Vergleich. Akten eines Werkstattgesprächs an der Akademie der Wissenschaften und der Literatur. Mainz, 2.–3. Dezember 2010*. Studien zu den Bogazköy-Texten 60. Wiesbaden.
Müller, H.-P. 1989. 'Eine neue babylonische Menschenschöpfungserzählung im Licht keilschriftlicher und biblischer Parallelen. Zur Wirklichkeitsauffassung im Mythos', *Orientalia* 58: 61–85.

Müller, K., and Wagner, A. 2014 (eds.). *Synthetische Körperauffassung im Hebräischen und den Sprachen der Nachbarkulturen*. Münster.
Muellner, L. 1996. *The Anger of Achilles*. Ithaca, NY.
Münnich, M. M. 2013. *The God Reshep in the Ancient Near East*. Tübingen.
Murray, O. 2001. 'Herodotus and Oral History', in Luraghi 2001 (ed.), 16–44.
Musäus, I. 2004. *Der Pandoramythos bei Hesiod und seine Rezeption bis Erasmus von Rotterdam*. Göttingen.
Mynářová, J., Onderka, P., and Pavúk, P. 2015 (eds.). *There and Back Again – the Crossroads II. Proceedings of an International Conference Held in Prague, September 15–18, 2014*. Prague.
Nägelsbach, C. F. 1884. *Homerische Theologie*. 3rd ed. Nuremberg.
Nagel, W. 1982. *Ninus und Semiramis in Sage und Geschichte: Iranische Staaten und Reiternomaden vor Darius*. Berlin.
Nagy, G. 1979. *The Best of Achaeans. Concepts of the Hero in Archaic Greek Poetry*. Baltimore, MD and London [1999 revised edition, Center of Hellenic Studies: https://chs.harvard.edu/CHS/article/display/5576].
    1982. Review of Burkert 1977, *CPh* 77: 70–3.
    1990. 'Hesiod and the Poetics of Panhellenism', in *Greek Mythology and Poetics*. Ithaca, NY: 36–82 [~ Luce, T. J. 1982 (ed.), *Ancient Writers*, Vol. 1. New York, NY: 43–73].
    2005. 'The Epic Hero', in Foley 2005 (ed.), 71–89.
    2009. 'Hesiod and the Ancient Biographical Tradition', in Montanari, Rengakos and Tsagalis 2009 (eds.), 271–311.
    2013. 'Virgil's Verse *Invitus, Regina* ... and Its Poetic Antecedents', in Fodor, P. Mayer, Gy., Monostori, M., Szovák, K., and Takács, L. (eds.), *More modoque: Die Wurzeln der europäischen Kultur und deren Rezeption im Orient und Okzident. Festschrift für Miklós Maróth zum siebzigsten Geburtstag*. Budapest: 155–65.
Nakassis, C. V. 2013. 'Citation and Citationality', *Signs and Society* 1.1: 51–78.
Naville, E. 1896. *The Temple of Deir el Bahari (Vol. 2): The Ebony Shrine, Northern Half of the Middle Platform*. London.
    1898. *The Temple of Deir el Bahari (Vol. 3): End of Northern Half and Southern Half of the Middle Platform*. London.
Neckel, G., and Kuhn, H. 1983. *Edda: Die Lieder des Codex Regius nebst verwandten Denkmälern. I: Text*. 5th ed. rev. Heidelberg.
Nelson, S. 1998. *God and the Land: The Metaphysics of Farming in Hesiod and Vergil*. Oxford.
Neu, E. 1996. *Das hurritische Epos der Freilassung Bd. 1: Untersuchungen zu einem hurritisch-hethitischen Textensemble aus Ḫattuša*. Studien zu den Bogazköy-Texten 32. Wiesbaden.
Niemeier, W.-D., and Niemeier, B. 1998. 'Minoan Frescos in the Eastern Mediterranean', in Harris-Cline, D., and Cline, E. H. 1998 (eds.), *The Aegean and the Orient in the Second Millennium: Proceedings of the 50th Anniversary Symposium in Cincinnati, 18–20 April 1997*. Liège: 69–98.

Nilsson, M. P. 1967. *Geschichte der griechischen Religion. Vol. 1.* Munich.
Noegel, S. B. 2007. 'Greek Religion and the Ancient Near East', in Ogden 2007 (ed.), 21–37.
van Noorden, H. 2015. *Playing Hesiod: The 'Myth of the Races' in Classical Antiquity.* Cambridge.
Norin, S. 1997. 'Die Hand Gottes im Alten Testament', in Kieffer and Bergman 1997 (eds.), 49–63.
North, R., and Worthington, M. 2012. '*Gilgamesh* and *Beowulf*: Foundations of a Comparison', *Kaskal: Rivista di storia, ambienti e culture del Vicino Oriente antico* 9: 177–217.
Novotny, J. R. 2001. *The Standard Babylonian Etana Epic = State Archives of Assyria Cuneiform Texts ii.* Helsinki.
Nünlist, R. 2009. *The Ancient Critic at Work: Terms and Concepts of Literary Criticism in Greek Scholia.* Cambridge.
Obbink, D. 2016. 'The Newest Sappho: Text, Apparatus Criticus, and Translation', in Bierl and Lardinois 2016 (eds.), 13–33.
Oettinger, N. 1989–90. 'Die 'dunkle Erde' im Hethitischen und Griechischen', *WO* 20.21: 83–98.
  2001. 'Hethitisch -ima- oder: Wie ein Suffix affektiv werden kann', in Wilhelm 2001 (ed.), 456–77.
  2010. 'Sündenbock, Pandora und hethitisch *dammili pedi*', *Hethitica* 16: 111–20.
Ogden, D. 2007 (ed.). *A Companion to Greek Religion.* Oxford.
  2017. *The Legend of Seleucus: Kingship, Narrative and Mythmaking in the Ancient World.* Cambridge.
Ohly, D. 1953. *Griechische Goldbleche des 8. Jahrhunderts v. Chr.* Berlin.
Olson, S. D. 2012. *The Homeric Hymn to Aphrodite And Related Texts: Text, Translation and Commentary.* Berlin.
Ong, Walter J. 1975. 'The Writer's Audience Is Always a Fiction', *Publications of the Modern Language Association* 90: 9–21.
Oppenheim, A. L. 1977. *Ancient Mesopotamia. Portrait of a Dead Civilization*, rev. ed. by E. Reiner. Chicago, IL.
Oren, E. D. 2000 (ed.). *The Sea Peoples and Their World: A Reassessment.* Philadelphia, PA.
Ormand, K. 2014. *The Hesiodic Catalogue of Woman and Archaic Greece.* Cambridge.
Ornan, T. (2010). 'Humbaba, the Bull of Heaven and the Contribution of Images to the Reconstruction of the Gilgameš Epic', in Steymans 2010 (ed.), 229–60.
Osborne, R. 1993. 'À la grecque', *Journal of Mediterranean Studies* 6: 231–7.
Oshima, T. 2011. *Babylonian Prayers to Marduk.* Tübingen.
  2014. *Babylonian Poems of Pious Sufferers.* Tübingen.
  2018 (ed.). *Teaching Morality in Antiquity.* Leipzig.
Otten, H. 1961. 'Eine Beschwörung der Unterirdischen aus Bogazköy', *Zeitschrift für Assyriologie und Vorderasiatische Archäologie* 54: 114–57.

Papadopoulos, J. K. 1997. 'Phantom Euboians', *JMA* 10: 191–219.
  2011. '"Phantom Euboians": A Decade On', in Rupp and Tomlinson 2011 (eds.), 113–33.
Panagiotopoulos, D. 2012. 'Würdezeichen auf dem Haupt', in Buchholz, H.-G. 2012 (ed.), *Archaeologia Homerica. Die Denkmäler des frühgriechischen Epos. Kapitel D, Erkennungs-, Rang- und Würdezeichen*. Göttingen: 109–58.
Pardee, D. 1987. 'As Strong as Death', in Marks and Good 1987 (eds.), 65–9.
Parker, R. 2011. *On Greek Religion*. Ithaca, NY.
  2017. *Greek Gods Abroad: Names, Natures, and Transformations*. Oakland, CA.
  1997 (ed.), *Ugaritic Narrative Poetry*. Atlanta, GA.
Parpola, S. 2017. *Assyrian Royal Rituals and Cultic Texts*. State Archives of Assyria xx. Helsinki.
Parpola, S., and Whiting, R. M. 2002 (eds.). *Sex and Gender in the Ancient Near East: Proceedings of the 47th Rencontre Assyriologique Internationale, Helsinki, July 2–6 2001*. 2 vols. Helsinki.
Pecchioli Daddi, F., and Polvani, A. M. 1990. *La mitologia ittita*. Brescia.
Pedley, J. G. 1972. *Ancient Literary Sources on Sardis*. Cambridge, MA.
Peled, I. 2016. *Masculinities and Third Gender: The Origins and Nature of an Institutionalized Genderotherness in the Ancient Near East*. Münster.
Pelliccia, H. 2010–11. 'Unlocking *Aeneid* 6.460: Plautus' *Amphitryon*, Euripides' *Protesilaus* and the referents of Callimachus' *Coma*', *CJ* 106: 149–221.
Penglase, C. 1994. *Greek Myths and Mesopotamia. Parallels and Influence in the Homeric Hymns and Hesiod*. London.
Perlitt, L. 1990. *Riesen im alten Testament*. Göttingen.
Perry, B. E. 1962. 'Demetrius of Phalerum and the Aesopic Fables', *TAPhA* 93: 287–346.
  1965. *Babrius and Phaedrus*. London and Cambridge, MA.
Pettazzoni, R. 1956. *The All-Knowing God: Researches in Early Religion and Culture* (trans. H. J. Rose). London.
Petersen, D. L. 1979. 'Genesis 6: 1–4, Yahweh and the Organization of the Cosmos', *JSOT* 13: 47–64.
Pfälzner, P. 2008 (in collaboration with von Rüden, C.). 'Between the Aegean and Syria: The Wall Paintings from the Royal Palace of Qatna', in Bonatz, D., Czichon, R. M., and Kreppner, F. J. (eds.), *Fundstellen: Gesammelte Schriften zur Archäologie und Geschichte Altvorderasiens ad honorem Hartmut Kühne*. Wiesbaden: 95–118.
Pirenne-Delforge, V., and Pironti, G. 2015. 'Héra et les enfants de Zeus: la 'fabrique' de l'Olympe entre textes et images', in Belayche, N., and Pirenne-Delforge, V. (eds.), *Fabriquer du divin: Constructions et ajustements de la représentation des dieux dans l'Antiquité*. Liège: 41–58.
  2016. *L'Hera de Zeus: ennemie intime, épouse définitive*. Paris.
Platte, R. 2017. *Equine Poetics*. Washington, DC.
Ponchia, S. 2013–14. 'Hermeneutical Strategies and Innovative Interpretation in Assyro-Babylonian Texts: The Case of *Erra and Išum*', *State Archives of Assyria Bulletin* 20: 61–72.

Pongratz-Leisten, B. 1994. *Ina šulmi īrub: Die kulttopographische und ideologische Programmatik der akītu-Prozession in Babylonien und Assyrien im I. Jahrtausend v. Chr.* Mainz.
   2015. *Religion and Ideology in Assyria.* Boston, MA and Berlin.
   2017. 'The Assyrian State Rituals: Re-invention of Tradition', in Parpola 2017, xxxi–lxxv.
Popham, M. R., and Lemos, I. S. 1995. 'A Euboean Warrior Trader', *OJA* 14: 151–7.
Porada, E. 1984. 'The Cylinder Seal from Tell el-Dab'a', *AJA* 88: 485–8.
Porten, B., and Yardeni, A. 1993. *Textbook of Aramaic Documents from Ancient Egypt 3: Literature, Accounts, Lists.* Jerusalem.
Pötscher W. 1960. 'Moira, Themis und τιμή im homerischen Denken', *WS* 73: 5–39.
Potts, D. T. 2005. 'Cyrus the Great and the Kingdom of Anshan', in Sarkosh Curtis and Stewart 2005 (eds.), 7–28.
   2016. *The Archaeology of Elam: Formation and Transformation of an Ancient Iranian State.* 2nd ed. Cambridge.
Priestley, J., and Zali, V. 2016 (eds.). *Brill's Companion to the Reception of Herodotus in Antiquity and Beyond.* Leiden.
Pruzsinszky, R. 2011. 'Singers, Musicians and Their Mobility in Ur III Period Cuneiform Text', in Dumbrill, R. (ed.), *Proceedings of the International Conference of Near Eastern Archaeomusicology (ICONEA) 2009–2010.* London: 31–9.
Puhvel, J. 1970. 'Mythological Reflections of Indo-European Medicine', in Cardona, Hoenigswald and Senn 1970 (eds.), 369–82.
   1987. *Comparative Mythology.* Baltimore, MD and London.
Pulak, C. 1997. 'The Uluburun Shipwreck', in Swiny, S., Hohlfelder, R., and Swiny, H. W. 1997 (eds.), *Res Maritimae: Cyprus and the Eastern Mediterranean from Prehistory to Late Antiquity: Proceedings of the Second International Symposium 'Cities on the Sea', Nicosia, Cyprus, October 18–22, 1994.* Atlanta, GA: 233–62.
   2008. 'The Uluburun Shipwreck and Late Bronze Age Trade', in Aruz, Benzel and Evans 2008 (eds.), 288–310.
Pulleyn, S. 2000. *Homer, Iliad 1, edited with an Introduction, Translation and Commentary.* Oxford.
Quinn, J. C. 2017. *In Search of the Phoenicians.* Princeton, NJ.
Raaflaub, K. A. 2000. 'Influence, Adaptation, and Interaction: Near Eastern and Early Greek Political Thought', in Aro and Whiting 2000 (eds.), 51–64.
Radermacher, L. 1938. *Mythos und Sage bei den Griechen.* 2nd ed. Brünn.
Ramat, P. 1960. 'La figura di Moira in Omero alla luce dell'analisi linguistica', *SIFC* 32: 215–48.
Ranke, K., and Bausinger, H. 1975–2015 (eds.). *Enzyklopädie des Märchens: Handwörterbuch zur historischen und vergleichenden Erzählforschung, 5.* Berlin and New York, NY.
Rawles, R. 2018. *Simonides the Poet: Intertextuality and Reception.* Cambridge.

Renger, J. 1999 (ed.). *Babylon: Focus Mesopotamischer Geschichte, Wiege Früher Gelehrsamkeit, Mythos in der Moderne*. Saarbrücken.
Reinink, G. J., and Vanstiphout, H. L. J. 1991 (eds.). *Dispute Poems and Dialogues in the Ancient and Mediaeval Near East: Forms and Types of Literary Debates in Semitic and Related Literatures*. Leuven.
Reitzenstein, R. 1924–5. 'Altgriechische Theologie und ihre Quellen', *Vorträge der Bibliothek Warburg* 4: 1–19 [reprinted in Heitsch, E. 1966 (ed.). *Hesiod. Wege der Forschung* 44. Darmstadt: 439–49].
Reynolds, F. 2019. *A Babylon Calendar Treatise: Scholars and Invaders in the Late First Millennium BC*. Oxford.
  2021. 'Cuneiform Myths and Epics in the Ancient Near East', in Dell 2021 (ed.).
Richardson, N. 2010. *Three Homeric Hymns*. Cambridge.
Richter, T., Prechel, D., and Klinger, J. 2001 (eds.). *Kulturgeschichten: Altorientalische Studien für Volkert Haas zum 65. Geburtstag*. Saarbrücken.
Ridgway, D. 1994. 'Phoenicians and Greeks in the West: A View from Pithekoussai', in Tsetskhladze and de Angelis 1994 (eds.), 35–46.
Riedweg, C. 2009 (ed.). *Grecia Maggiore: Intrecci culturali con l'Asia nel periodo antico*. Basel.
Ristvet, L. 2015. *Ritual, Performance, and Politics in the Ancient Near East*. Cambridge.
Roberts, J. J. M. 1971. 'The Hand of Yahweh', *VT* 21: 244–51.
Robson, E. 2001. 'The Tablet House: A Scribal School in Old Babylonian Nippur', *Revue d'Assyriologie et d'Archéologie Orientale* 95: 39–66.
  2002. 'More Than Metrology: Mathematics Education in an Old Babylonian Scribal School', in Steele, J. M., and Imhausen, A. (eds.), *Under One Sky: Mathematics and Astronomy in the Ancient Near East*. Alter Orient und Altes Testament, 297. Münster: 325–65.
Rochberg-Halton, F. 1982. 'Fate and Divination in Mesopotamia', in Hirsch and Hunger (eds.) 1982, 363–71.
Röhrich, L. 1987. 'Geographisch-historische Methode', in Ranke, K., and Bausinger, H. 1975–2015 (eds.), Vol. 5, 1011–30.
Röllig, W. 1984. 'Etana', in Ranke, K., and Bausinger, H. 1975–2015 (eds.), Vol. 4, 493–99.
  1991. 'Überlegungen zum Etana-Mythos', in Gamer-Wallert, I., and Helck, W. 1991 (eds.), *Gegengabe: Festschrift für Emma Brunner-Traut*. Tübingen: 283–8.
Rojas, F. 2019. *The Pasts of Roman Anatolia: Interpreters, Traces, Horizons*. Cambridge.
Rojas, F., and Sergueenkova, V. 2014. 'Traces of Tarhuntas: Greek, Roman, and Byzantine Interaction with Hittite Monuments', *JMA* 26.2: 135–60.
Rollinger, R. 2001. 'The Ancient Greeks and the Impact of the Ancient Near East: Textual Evidence and Historical Perspective', in Whiting, R. M. (ed.), *Mythology and Mythologies: Methodological Approaches to Intercultural Influences*. Helsinki: 233–64.

2011. 'Ktesias' Medischer Logos', in Wiesehöfer, Rollinger and Lanfranchi 2011 (eds.), 313–50.

2015. 'Old Battles, New Horizons. The Ancient Near East and the Homeric Epics', in Rollinger and van Dongen 2015 (eds.), 5–32.

2018. 'Herodotus and the Transformation of Ancient Near Eastern Motifs', in Harrison and Irwin 2018 (eds.), 125–48.

2018 (ed.). *Conceptualizing Past, Present and Future: Proceedings of the Ninth Symposium of the Melammu Project.* Münster.

Rollinger, R., and van Dongen E. 2015 (eds.). *Proceedings of the Seventh Symposium of the Melammu Project Held in Obergurgl, Austria, November 4–8.* Münster.

Rollinger, R., and Schnegg, K. 2014 (eds.). *Kulturkontakte in antiken Welten: vom Denkmodell zum Fallbeispiel. Proceedings des internationalen Kolloquiums aus Anlass des 60. Geburtstages von Christoph Ulf, Innsbruck, 26. bis 30. Januar 2009.* Leuven, Paris and Walpole, MA.

Rollinger, R., and Truschnegg, B. 2006 (eds.) *Altertum und Mittelmeerraum: Die antike Welt diesseits und jenseits der Levante. Festschrift für Peter W. Haider zum 60. Geburtstag.* Stuttgart.

Rosen, R. 1997. 'Homer and Hesiod', in Morris and Powell 1997 (eds.), 463–88.

Ross, M. C. 2002. 'Reading Þrymskviða', in Acker, P., and Larrington, C. 2002 (eds.), *The Poetic Edda: Essays on Old Norse Mythology.* London: 177–94.

van Rossum-Steenbeek, M. 1998. *Greek Readers' Digests? Studies on a Selection of Greek Literary Papyri.* Mnemosyne Supplements 175. Leiden.

Rowe, I. M. 2018. 'Homer's Origin of All Things and Babylonian Cosmogony: Revisiting Burkert's Thesis', in Rollinger 2018 (ed.), 369–80.

Rubio, G. 2012. 'Reading Sumerian Names, II: Gilgameš', *Journal of Cuneiform Studies* 64: 3–16.

2013. 'Time before Time: Primeval Narratives in Early Mesopotamian Literature', in Feliu, L., et al. (eds.), *Time and History in the Ancient Near East.* Winona Lake, IN: 3–17.

von Rüden, C. 2011. *Die Wandmalereien aus Tall Mišrife/Qaṭna im Kontext überregionaler Kommunikation.* Wiesbaden.

2017. 'Producing Aegeanness – An Innovation and Its Impact in Middle and Late Bronze Age Syria/Northern Levant', in Burmeister, S., and Bernbeck, R. 2017 (eds.), *The Interplay of People and Technologies. Archaeological Case Studies on Innovation.* Berlin: 225–49.

Rudhardt, J. 1970. 'Les mythes grecs relatifs à l'instauration du sacrifice. Les rôles corrélatifs de Prométhée et de son fils Deucalion', *MH* 27: 1–15.

1981. 'Le mythe hésiodique des races et celui de Prométhée: recherche des structures et des significations', in *Du mythe, de la religion grecque et de la compréhension d'autrui.* Geneva: 246–81.

1986. 'Pandora. Hésiode et les femmes', *MH* 43: 231–46.

Rupp, D. W., and Tomlinson, J. E. 2011 (eds.). *Euboia and Athens: Proceedings of a Colloquium in Memory of Malcolm B. Wallace, Athens 26–27 June 2009. Publications of the Canadian Institute in Greece 6.* Athens.

Rutherford, I. 2001. 'The Song of the Sea (ŠA A.AB.BA SÌR): Thoughts on KUB 45.63', in Wilhelm 2001 (ed.), 598–609.
  2008. 'The Songs of the Zintuḫis: Chorus and Ritual in Anatolia and Greece', in Collins et al. 2008 (eds.), 73–83.
  2009. 'Hesiod and the Literary Traditions of the Near East', in Montanari, Rengakos and Tsagalis 2009 (eds.), 9–35.
  2011. 'Ea and the Beast: The Hittite Text and Its Relation to the Greek Poetry', in Hutter and Hutter-Braunsar 2011 (eds.), 217–26.
  2018. 'Kingship in Heaven in Anatolia, Syria and Greece: Patterns of Convergence and Divergence', in Audley-Miller and Dignas 2018 (eds.), 3–22.
  2019a. 'Religious Networks and Cultural Exchange: Some Possible Cases from the Eastern Mediterranean', in Da Riva, R., Lang, M., and Fink, S. 2019 (eds.), *Literary Change in Mesopotamia and Beyond and Routes and Travellers between East and West. Proceedings of the 2nd and 3rd Melammu Workshops.* Münster: 227–38.
  2019b. 'Puduhepa, Piyamaradu and the Sea: KUB 56.15ii15–24 (AhT26) and Its Background', in Süel, A. (ed.). *Proceedings of 2014 Hittite Congress.* Ankara: 869–79.
Rutherford, R. B. 2019 (eds.). *Homer: Iliad Book XVIII.* Cambridge.
Rutz, M. J. 2013. *Bodies of Knowledge in Ancient Mesopotamia. The Diviners of Late Bronze Age Emar and Their Tablet Collection.* Leiden and Boston, MA.
Sader, H. 2019. *The History and Archaeology of Phoenicia.* Atlanta.
Sakellarakis, Y., and Sarpouna-Sakellaraki, E. 1997. *Archanes: Minoan Crete in a New Light, Vol. 1.* Athens.
Sallaberger, W. 2019. 'The Cupbearer and the Cult-Priest in the Temple: External and Internal Cultic Practitioners in Early Bronze Age Mesopotamia', *Journal of Ancient Near Eastern Religions* 19: 90–111.
Sallaberger, W., and Westenholz, A. 1999. *Mesopotamien: Akkade-Zeit und Ur III-Zeit.* Freiburg and Göttingen.
Salvini, M. 1991. 'Betrachtungen zum hurritisch-urartäischen Verbum', *Zeitschrift für Assyriologie* 81: 120–32.
Salvini, M., and Wegner, I. 2004. *Die mythologischen Texte. Corpus der hurritischen Sprachdenkmäler I/6.* Rome.
Sarkosh Curtis, V., and Stewart, S. 2005 (eds.). *Birth of the Persian Empire.* London.
Sasson J. M. 1984 (ed.). *Studies in Literature from the Ancient Near East by Members of the Amerian Oriental Society Dedicated to Samuel Noah Kramer.* New Haven, CT.
Schaudig, H. 2001. *Die Inschriften Nabonids von Babylon und Kyros' des Großen samt den in ihrem Umfeld entstandenen Tendenzschriften.* Münster.
Schein, S. 1984. *The Mortal Hero.* Berkeley, CA.
Schironi, F. 2013. 'The Early Reception of Berossos', in Haubold et al. 2013 (eds.), 235–54.
  2018. *The Best of the Grammarians: Aristarchus of Samothrace on the Iliad.* Ann Arbor, MI.

Schneider, T. 2011–12. 'Wie der Wettergott Ägypten aus der großen Flut errettete: Ein 'inkulturierter' ägyptischer Sintflut-Mythos und die Gründung der Ramsesstadt', *Journal of the Society for the Study of Egyptian Antiquities* 38: 173–93.

Schretter, M. K. 1974. *Alter Orient und Hellas. Fragen der Beeinflussung griechischen Gedankengutes aus altorientalischen Quellen, dargestellt an den Göttern Nergal, Rescheph, Apollon.* Innsbruck.

Schuol, M. 2004. *Hethitische Kultmusik: Eine Untersuchung der Instrumental- und Vokalmusik anhand hethitischer Ritualtexte und von archäologischen Zeugnissen.* Orient-Archäologie 14. Rahden.

Schwemer, D. 2001. *Die Wettergottgestalten Mesopotamiens und Nordsyriens im Zeitalter der Keilschriftkulturen.* Wiesbaden.

— 2008. 'The Storm-Gods of the Ancient Near East: Summary, Synthesis, Recent Studies. Part II', *Journal of Ancient Near Eastern Religions* 8: 1–44.

— 2009. 'Schicksal: B bei der Hethitern', in *Reallexikon der Assyriologie und Vorderasiatischen Archäologie* 12: 155–7.

— 2015. 'Hittite Prayers to the Sun-god for Appeasing an Angry Personal God. A Critical Edition of CTH 372–74' (with a glossary by Ch. Steitler)' in Jaques 2015, 349–93, 421–57.

— 2016. 'Wettergottheiten. A. Philologisch', *RlA* 15.1–2: 69–91.

Scodel, R. 1982. 'The Achaean Wall and the Myth of Destruction', *HSPh* 86: 33–50.

— 2007. 'The God's Visit to the Ethiopians in Iliad 1', *HSPh* 103: 83–98.

— 2011. 'Callimachus and Fable', in Acosta-Hughes, Lehnus and Stephens 2011 (eds.), 368–83.

— 2014. 'Prophetic Hesiod', in Scodel, R. 2014 (ed.), *Between Orality and Literacy: Communication and Adaptation in Antiquity.* Leiden: 56–76.

— 2017. 'Homeric Fate, Homeric Poetics', in Tsagalis and Markantonatos 2017 (eds.), 74–93.

Scully, S. 2015. *Hesiod's Theogony: from Near Eastern Creation Myths to Paradise Lost.* Oxford.

Scurlock, J., and Andersen, B. R. 2005 (eds.). *Diagnoses in Assyrian and Babylonian Medicine. Ancient Sources, Translations, and Modern Medical Analyses.* Urbana and Chicago, IL.

Scurlock, J., and Beal, R. H. 2013 (eds.). *Creation and Chaos. A Reconsideration of Hermann Gunkel's Chaoskampf Hypothesis.* Winona Lake, IN.

Seeher, J. 2011. *Gods Carved in Stone. The Hittite Rock Sanctuary of Yazilikaya.* Istanbul.

Sefati, Y. 1998. *Love Songs in Sumerian Literature*, Ramat Gan.

Sergent, B. 1997. *Genèse de l'Inde.* Paris.

Seri, A. 2017. 'Some Notes on *Enūma Eliš*', *JAOS* 137: 833–8.

van Seters, J. 1988. 'The Primeval Histories of Greece and Israel Compared', *ZATW* 100: 1–22.

Shai, I. 2011. 'Philistia and the Philistines in the Iron Age IIA', *ZPalV (1953–)* 127.2: 119–34.

Shaw, J. W. 1989. 'Phoenicians in Southern Crete', *AJA* 93: 165–83.
  1998. 'Kommos in Southern Crete: An Aegean Barometer for East–West Interconnections', in Karageorghis and Stampolidis 1998 (eds.), 13–27.
Shehata, D. 2001. *Annotierte Bibliographie zum altbabylonischen* Atramhasis *Mythos* Inuma ilu awilum. Göttingen.
Siegelova, J. 1971. *Appu-Märchen und Hedammu-Mythus*. Studien zu den Boğazköy-Texten 14. Wiesbaden.
Singer, I. 1999. 'A Political History of Ugarit', in Watson and Wyatt 1999 (eds.), 603–33.
  2002a. *Hittite Prayers*. Writings from the Ancient World 11. Atlanta, GA.
  2002b. 'Kantuzili the Priest and the Birth of Hittite Personal Prayer', in Taracha 2002 (ed.), 301–13.
Sjöberg, Å. W. 2002. 'In the Beginning', in Abusch, T. (ed.), *Riches Hidden in Secret Places. Ancient Near Eastern Studies in Memory of Thorkild Jacobsen*. Winona Lake, IN: 229–39.
Skempis, M., and Ziogas, I. 2013 (eds.). *Geography, Topography, Landscape: Configurations of Space in Greek and Roman Epic*. Berlin.
Sluiter, I. 2017. 'Anchoring Innovation: A Classical Research Agenda', *European Review* 25: 1–19.
Smith, J. Z. 1990. *Drudgery Divine. On the Comparison of Early Christianities and the Religions of Late Antiquity*. Chicago, IL and London.
Smith, M. J. 1984. 'Sonnenauge, Demotischer Mythus von', in Lexikon der Ägyptologie *V*. Wiesbaden: 1082–7.
Smith, M. S. 1994. *The Ugaritic Baal Cycle. Introduction with Text, Translation and Commentary of KTU 1.1–1.2. Vol. 1*. Leiden.
  1997. 'The Baal Cycle', in Parker 1997 (ed.), 82–176.
  2001. *The Origins of Biblical Monotheism: Israel's Polytheistic Background and the Ugaritic Texts*. New York, NY.
  2010. *The Priestly Vision of Genesis 1*. Minneapolis, MN.
  2016. *Where the Gods Are: Spatial Dimensions of Anthropomorphism in the Biblical World*. New Haven.
Smith M. S., and Parker, S. B. 1997. *Ugaritic Narrative Poetry*. Atlanta, GA.
Snider, G. L. 1973. 'Two Folktale Parallels to Hesiod's Prometheus–Pandora Myth', *CEA* 2: 131–3.
Soggin, J. A. 1996. 'Sons of God(s), Heroes, and Nephilim: Remarks on *Genesis* 6: 1–4', in Fox et al. 1996 (eds.), 135–6.
Sollberger, E. 1956. *Corpus des inscriptions 'royales' présargoniques de Lagaš*. Geneva.
Sonik, K. 2009. 'Gender Matters in the *Enuma Elish*', in Beal, R. H., Holloway, S. W., and Scurlock, J. 2009 (eds.). *In the Wake of Tikva Frymer-Kensky*. Piscatawy, NJ: 85–101.
Sourvinou-Inwood, C. 1997. 'The Hesiodic Myth of the Five Races and the Tolerance of Plurality in Greek Mythology', in O. Palagia 1997 (ed.), *Greek Offerings: Essays on Greek Art in Honour of John Boardman*. Oxford: 1–21.
Speiser, E. A. 1942. 'An Intrusive Hurro-Hittite Myth', *JAOS* 62: 98–102.

Spelman, H. 2018. *Pindar and the Poetics of Permanence*. Oxford.
Spronk, K. 1986. *Beatific Afterlife in Ancient Israel and in the Ancient Near East*. Klevelaer.
Stadelmann, R. 1967. *Syrisch-palästinensische Gottheiten in Ägypten*. Leiden.
Stamatopoulou, M., and Yeroulanou, Y. 2002 (eds.). *Excavating Classical Culture: Recent Archaeological Discoveries in Greece*. BAR International Series 1031. Oxford.
Stampolidis, N. C. 1990. 'A Funerary Cippus at Eleutherna: Evidence of Phoenician Presence?', *BICS* 37: 99–106.
— 2002. 'From the Geometric and Archaic Necropolis at Eleutherna', in Stamatopoulou and Yeroulanou 2002 (eds.), 327–32.
— 2004 (ed.), Eleutherna: Polis; Acropolis: Necropolis/ΕΛΕΥΘΕΡΝΑ. Πόλη - Ακρόπολη – Νεκρόπολη. Exhibition catalogue, Museum of Cycladic Art. Athens.
— 2016. 'Eleutherna on Crete: The Wider Horizon', in Aruz and Seymour 2016 (eds.), 283–95.
Stampolidis, N. C., and A. Kotsonas 2006. 'Phoenicians in Crete', in Deger-Jalkotzy and Lemos 2006 (eds.), 337–60.
Stavrianopoulou, E. 2013 (ed.). *Shifting Social Imaginaries in the Hellenistic Period*. Leiden.
Stehle, E. 2016. 'Larichos in the Brothers Poem: Sappho Speaks Truth to the Wine-Pourer', in Bierl and Lardinois 2016 (eds.), 266–92.
Steiner, D. T. 2001. *Images in Mind: Statues in Archaic Greek Literature and Thought*. Princeton, NJ.
Steinert, U. 2012. *Aspekte des Menschseins im Alten Mesopotamien. Eine Studie zu Person und Identität im 2. und 1. Jt. v. Chr*. Leiden and Boston, MA.
— 2014. 'Synthetische Körperauffassungen in akkadischen Keilschrifttexten und mesopotamische Götterkonzepte', in Müller and Wagner 2014 (eds.), 73–106.
Steinkeller, P. 2010. 'More on the Archaic Writing of the Name Enlil/Nippur', in Kleinerman, A., and Sasson, J. M. (eds.), *Why Should Someone Who Knows Something Conceal It? Cuneiform Studies in Honor of David. I. Owen*, Bethesda, MD: 239–43.
— 2013. 'An Archaic "Prisoner Plaque" from Kiš', *Revue d'assyriologie* 107: 131–57.
— 2017a. 'Luck, Fortune, and Destiny in Ancient Mesopotamia – Or How the Sumerians and Babylonians Thought of Their Place in the Flow of Things', in Drewnowska and Sandowicz 2005 (eds.), 5–24.
— 2017b. *History, Texts and Art in Early Babylonia: Three Essays*. Boston, MA and Berlin.
Stenger, J. 2014. 'Körper, Kognition, Kultur. Körperteilbezeichnungen im Griechischen', in Müller and Wagner 2014 (eds.), 163–83.
Stevens, K. 2019. *Between Greece and Babylonia: Hellenistic Intellectual History in Cross-Cultural Perspective*. Cambridge.

Steymans, H. U. 2010 (ed.). *Gilgamesh: Ikonographie eines Helden. Gilgamesh: Epic and Iconography*. Fribourg and Göttingen.

Stivala, G. 2016. 'Hattische Gesänge im Kontext der hethitischen Festrituale', in Müller 2016 (ed.), 133–44.

Stocker, S. S., and Davis, J. L. 2017. 'The Combat Agate from the Grave of the Griffin Warrior at Pylos', *Hesperia* 86: 583–605.

Stockhammer, P. 2017. 'How Aegean Is Philistine Pottery? The Use of Aegean-Type Pottery in the Early 12th Century BCE Southern Levant', in Fischer and Bürge 2017 (eds.), 379–87.

Stol, M. 2016. *Women in the Ancient Near East* (translated by Richardson, H. and Richardson, M.). Leiden.

Stoneman, R. 1992. 'Oriental Motifs in the Alexander Romance', *Antichthon* 26: 95–113.

Strauss Clay, J., and Gilan, A. 2014. 'The Hittite "Song of Emergence" and the *Theogony*', *Philologus* 58: 1–9.

Streck, M. P. 2004. 'Dattelpalme und Tamariske in Mesopotamien nach dem akkadischen Streitgespräch', *Zeitschrift für Assyriologie und Vorderasiatische Archäologie* 94: 250–90.

Strootman, R. 2013. 'Babylonian, Macedonian, King of the World: The Antiochus Cylinder from Borsippa and Seleukid Imperial Integration', in Stavrianopoulou 2013 (ed.), 67–97.

Süel, A. 2017. 'The Anatolian-Syrian Relationship in the Light of the Ortaköy-Šapinuwa Tablets', in Maner, Ç., Horowitz, M.T., and Gilbert, A. S. 2017 (eds.), *Overturning Certainties in Near Eastern Archaeology: A Festschrift in Honor of K. Aslıhan Yener*. Culture and History of the Ancient Near East 90. Leiden and Boston, MA: 634–44.

Swift, L. 2019. *Archilochus: The Poems. Introduction, Text, Translation, and Commentary*. Oxford.

Tafażżolī, A. 1995. 'Draxtī āsūrīg', in *Encyclopedia Iranica Vol. 7*: 547–9.

Talon, P. 2001. '*Enūma eliš* and the Transmission of Babylonian Cosmology to the West', in Whiting, R. M. 2001 (ed.), *Mythology and Mythologies*. Helsinki: 265–77.

2005. *The Standard Babylonian Creation Myth*. Helsinki.

Tanret, M. 2002. *Per Aspera ad Astra. L'Apprentissage du cunéiforme à Sippar-Amnānum pendant la Période Paléobabylonienne Tardive*. Mesopotamian History and Environment, Series III, Texts. Volume 1: Sippar-Amnānum: The Ur-Utu Archive, Tome 2. Ghent.

2004. 'The Works and the Days: On Scribal Activity in Sippar Amnanum', *Revue d'Assyriologie* 98: 33–62.

Taracha, P. 2002 (ed.). *Silva Anatolica: Anatolian Studies Presented to Maciej Popko on the Occasion of His 65th Birthday*. Warsaw.

Tatu, S. 2006. 'Jotham's Fable and the Crux Interpretum in Judges IX', *VT* 56: 105–124.

Teixidor, J. 1977. *The Pagan God: Popular Religion in the Greco-Roman Near East*. Princeton, NJ.

Tenney, J. S. 2016. 'The Elevation of Marduk Revisited: Festivals and Sacrifices at Nippur during the High Kassite Period', *Journal of Cuneiform Studies* 68: 153–80.
Thalmann, G. 1984. *Conventions of Form and Thought in Early Greek Epic Poetry*. Baltimore, MD.
Thiel, H.-J., and Wegner, I. 1984. 'Eine Anrufung an den Gott Teššub von Ḫalap in hurritischer Sprache', *SMEA* 24: 187–213.
Thomas, R. F. 1986. 'Virgil's Georgics and the Art of Reference', *HSPh* 90: 171–98.
Thompson, S. 1955–8. *A Motif-Index of Folk-Literature*. Bloomington, IN.
Tigay, J. H. 1982. *The Evolution of the Gilgamesh Epic*. Philadelphia, PA.
Tinney, S. J. 1999. 'On the Curricular Setting of Sumerian Literature' *Iraq* 59: 159–72.
Töyräänvuori, J. 2016. *'I Will Set His Hand on the Sea, and His Right Hand on the River': North West Semitic Kingship and the Sea of Combat Myth: A Survey of Hebrew Poetry in Light of Ancient Near Eastern Evidence*. Doctoral Thesis, University of Helsinki.
Töyräänvuori, 2018. *Sea and the Combat Myth: North West Semitic Political Mythology in the Hebrew Bible*. Münster.
van der Toorn, K. 1985. *Sin and Sanction in Israel and Mesopotamia*. Assen.
Torri, G. 2008. 'The Scribes of the House on the Slope', in Archi, A., and Francia, R. 2008 (eds.), *VI Congresso Internazionale di Ittitologia, Roma 5–9 settembre 2005 (SMEA 50)*. Rome: 771–82.
2011. 'The Phrase *ṬUPPU* ^{URU}*Ḫatti* in Colphons from Ḫattuša and the Work of the Scribe Ḫanikkuili', *Altorientalische Forschungen* 38: 134–44.
2015. 'Hereditary Transmission of Specialized Knowledge in Hittite Anatolia: The Case of Scribal Families of the Empire Period', in Archi, A., and Bramanti, A. 2015 (eds.), *Tradition and Innovation in the Ancient Near East*. Winona Lake, IN: 577–86.
Trautmann, T. R. 2015. *Elephants and Kings: An Environmental History*. Chicago, IL and London.
Treister, M. Y. 2001. *Hammering Techniques in Greek and Roman Jewellery and Toreutics*. ed. by J. Hargrave. Leiden.
Trencsényi-Waldapfel, I. 1959. 'Eine aesopische Fabel und ihre orientalischen Parallelen', *Acta Antiqua Academiae Scientiarum Hungaricae* 7: 317–27.
1966. *Untersuchungen zur Religionsgeschichte*. Amsterdam.
Trypanis, C. A. 1958. *Callimachus: Aetia, Iambi, Lyric Poems, Etc.* Cambridge, MA.
Tsagalis, C. 2011. 'Towards an Oral, Intertextual Neoanalysis', *Trends in Classics* 3.2: 209–44.
2017. *Early Greek Epic Fragments. Volume 1: Antiquarian and Genealogical Epic*. Berlin.
Tsagalis C., and Markantonatos, A. 2017 (eds.). *The Winnowing Oar – New Perspectives in Homeric Studies: Studies in Honour of Antonios Rengakos*. Berlin and Boston, MA.

Tsetskhladze, G., and de Angelis, F. 1994 (eds.). *The Archaeology of Greek Colonisation. Essays Dedicated to Sir John Boardman*. Oxford.

Tsomis, G. 2004. 'μένος in der frühgriechischen Dichtung und ἀμενηνός im homerischen Aphrodite-Hymnos (5,188)', *WS* 117: 15–29.

Tubach, F. C. 1969. *Index Exemplorum: A Handbook of Medieval Religious Studies*. Helsinki.

Tugendhaft, A. 2012. 'Unsettling Sovereignty: Politics and Poetics in the Baal Cycle', *JAOS* 132: 367–84.

  2017. *Baal and the Politics of Poetry*. London.

Ulf, C. 2009. 'Rethinking Cultural Contacts', *Ancient West and East* 8: 81–132.

Uther, H.-J. 2004. *The Types of International Folktales: A Classification and Bibliography*. Helsinki.

Vanderhooft, D., and Winitzer, A. 2013 (eds.). *Literature as Politics, Politics as Literature: Essays on the Ancient Near East in Honor of Peter Machinist*. Winona Lake, IN.

Vanstiphout, H. L. J. 1991. 'Lore, Learning and Levity in the Sumerian Disputations: A Matter of Form or Substance?', in Reinink and Vanstiphout 1991 (eds.), 23–46.

  1992. 'The Banquet Scene in the Mesopotamian Debate Poems', in Gyselen 1992 (ed.), 9–21.

  1997. 'School Dialogues', in Hallo, W. W., and Younger, K. L. (eds.). *The Context of Scripture Vol. 1*. Leiden and Boston, MA: 589–90.

de Vaux, R. 1959. 'Les combats singuliers dans l' Ancien Testament', *Biblica* 40: 495–508.

Veldhuis, N. 1997. *Elementary Education at Nippur: The Lists of Trees and Wooden Objects*. PhD Thesis, University of Groningen.

  2000. 'Sumerian Proverbs in Their Curricular Context' [review of Alster, B. *Proverbs of Ancient Sumer: The World's Earliest Proverb Collections*] *JAOS* 120.3: 383–99.

  2004. *Religion, Literature and Scholarship: The Sumerian Composition Nanše and the Birds, With a Catalogue of Bird Names*. Cuneiform Monographs 22. Leiden.

  2014. *History of the Cuneiform Lexical Tradition*. Guides to the Mesopotamian Textual Record 6. Münster.

Verbrugghe, G. P., and Wickersham, J. M. 2001. *Berossos and Manetho, Introduced and Translated: Native Traditions in Ancient Mesopotamia and Egypt*. Ann Arbor, MI.

Vernant, J.-P. 1965. 'Le mythe hésiodique des races: essai d'analyse structurale', in *Mythe et pensée chez les Grecs*. Paris: 13–41 [= 'Hesiod's Myth of the Races: An Essay in Structural Analysis', in Vernant, J.-P. 1983. *Myth and Thought among the Greeks* (transl. by Fort, F. and Lloyd, J.). London: 3–32].

Verreth, H. 2006. 'Kasion, Kasiotes and Kasiotikos', *ZPE* 158: 235–9.

Versnel, H. S. 1993. 'Kronos and the Kronia', in *Inconsistencies in Greek and Roman Religion. Vol. 2*. Leiden: 89–135.

Volk, K. 1996. 'Methoden altbabylonischer Erziehung nach Quellen der altbabylonischen Zeit' *Saeculum* 1996/II: 178–216.
    2000. 'Edubba'a und Edubba'a-Literatur: Rätsel und Lösungen' *Zeitschrift für Assyriologie* 90: 1–30.
    2015 (ed.). *Erzählungen aus dem Land Sumer*. Wiesbaden.
Waal, W. J. I. 2015. *Hittite Diplomatics: Studies in Ancient Document Format and Record Management*. Studien zu den Boğazköy-Texten 57. Wiesbaden.
    2019. 'Fate Strikes Back: New Evidence for the Identification of the Hittite Fate Deities and Its Implications for Hieroglyphic Writing in Anatolia', *Journal of Cuneiform Studies* 71: 121–32.
Wachsmann, S. 1998. *Seagoing Ships and Seamanship in the Bronze Age Levant*. College Station, TX and London.
Waetzoldt, H., and H. Hauptmann 1997 (eds.). *Assyrien im Wandel der Zeiten. XXXIXe Rencontre Assyriologique Internationale Heidelberg 6.–10. Juli 1992*. Heidelberg.
Wagensonner, K. 2009. 'What is the Matter with the Numun-Plant? BM 120011 Reconsidered', *Wiener Zeitschrift für die Kunde des Morgenlandes*, 99: 355–76.
Wakker, G. 1990. 'Die Ankündigung des Weltaltermythos (Hes. *Op*. 106–108)', *Glotta* 68: 86–90.
Walcot, P. 1962. 'Hesiod and the Didactic Literature of the Near East', *REG* 75: 13–36.
    1966. *Hesiod and the Near East*. Cardiff.
Warren, J. 2013. 'Gods and Men in Xenophanes', in Harte and Lane 2013 (eds.), 294–312.
Wasserman, N. 2008. 'On Leeches, Dogs and Gods in Old Babylonian Medical Incantations', *Revue d'Assyriologie* 102: 71–88.
Waters, M. 2017. *Ctesias' Persica and Its Near Eastern Context*. Madison, WI.
Watkins, C. 1995. *How to Kill a Dragon. Aspects of Indo-European Poetics*. Oxford.
    2001. 'An Indo-European Linguistic Area and Its Characteristics: Ancient Anatolia. Areal Diffusion as a Challenge to the Comparative Method?', in Aikhenvald and Dixon 2001 (eds.), 44–63.
    2007. 'The Golden Bowl: Thoughts on the New Sappho and Its Asianic Background', *ClAnt* 26: 305–24.
Watson, J. S. 1853. *Justin, Cornelius Nepos, and Eutropius*. London (repr. 2008).
Watson, W. G. E., and Wyatt, N. 1999 (eds.). *The Handbook of Ugaritic Studies*. Leiden.
Way, M., and Way, C. 2018. *Wild, Wild Country*. Netflix documentary.
Weeden, M. 2011. *Hittite Logograms and Hittite Scholarship*. Studien zu den Boğazköy-Texten 54. Wiesbaden.
    2013. 'After the Hittites: The Kingdoms of Karkamish and Palistin in Northern Syria', *BICS* 56.2: 1–20.
    2018. 'The Good God, the Wine-god and the Storm-god of the Vineyard', *WO* 48: 330–56.

Wellhausen, J. 1899. *Prolegomena zur Geschichte Israels.* 5th ed. Berlin.
West, M. L. 1966. *Hesiod: Theogony.* Oxford.
  1969. 'Near Eastern Material in Hellenistic and Roman Literature', *HSPh* 73: 113–34.
  1978. *Hesiod: Works and Days.* Oxford.
  1983. *The Orphic Poems.* Oxford.
  1985. *The Hesiodic Catalogue of Women, Its Nature, Structure, and Origin.* Oxford.
  1994. 'Some Oriental Motifs in Archilochus', *ZPE* 102: 1–5.
  1997. *The East Face of Helicon. West Asiatic Elements in Greek Poetry and Myth,* Oxford.
  2000. 'Fable and Disputation', in Aro and Whiting 2000 (eds.), 93–7.
  2002. "Eumelos": A Corinthian Epic Cycle?', *JHS* 122: 109–13.
  2003. *Homeric Hymns, Homeric Apocrypha, Lives of Homer.* Cambridge, MA.
  2007. *Indo-European Poetry and Myth.* Oxford.
  2011. *The Making of the Iliad.* Oxford.
  2013. *The Epic Cycle. A Commentary on the Lost Troy Epics.* Oxford.
  2018. 'Gilgāmeš and Homer: The Missing Link?', in Audley-Miller and Dignas 2018 (eds.), 265–80.
West, S. R. 1994. 'Prometheus Orientalized', *MH* 51: 129–49.
  2013. 'Divine Anger Management', in Whitmarsh, T. and Thomson, S. 2013 (eds.), *The Romance between Greece and the East.* Cambridge: 79–90.
Westenholz, A. 1999. 'The Old Akkadian Period: History and Culture', in Sallaberger and Westenholz 1999 (eds.), 17–117.
Westenholz, J. 2010. 'Heaven and Earth: Asexual Monad and Bisexual Dyad', in Stackert, J., Porter, B. N., and Wright, D. P. (eds.), *Gazing on the Deep: Ancient Near Eastern and Other Studies in Honor of Tzvi Abusch.* Bethesda, MD: 293–326.
Westermann, C. 1974. *Genesis. 1. Teilband: Genesis 1–11.* Neukirchen-Vluyn.
Whitley, J. (2001) *The Archaeology of Ancient Greece.* Cambridge.
Whitmarsh, T. 2015. *Battling the Gods: Atheism in the Ancient World.* New York, NY.
Wiesehöfer, J., Rollinger, R., and Lanfranchi, G. 2011 (eds.). *Ktesias' Welt/Ctesias' World.* Wiesbaden.
Wiggermann, F. 1992. 'Mythical Foundations of Nature', in Meier, D. J. W. (ed.), *Natural Phenomena: Their Meaning, Depiction and Description in the Ancient Near East.* Amsterdam: 279–306.
Wikander, S. 1952. 'Histoire des Ouranides', *Cahiers du Sud* 36: 9–17.
Wilcke, C. 1989. 'Sîn-abū-šu, ein Jugendfreund König Ibbi-Sîns', *Nouvelles assyriologiques brèves et utilitaires* 1989.4: 4–5.
  1990. 'Die Emar-Version von "Dattelpalme und Tamariske" – ein Rekonstruktionsversuch', *Zeitschrift für Assyriologie und Vorderasiatische Archäologie* 79: 161–90.

2007. 'Vom altorientalischen Blick zurück auf die Anfänge', in Angehrn, E. (ed.), *Anfang und Ursprung. Die Frage nach dem Ersten in Philosophie und Kulturwissenschaft*. Berlin: 3–59.

Wilhelm, G. 1997a. 'Die Könige von Ebla nach der hurritisch-hethitischen Serie "Freilassung"', *Altorientalische Forschungen* 24: 277–93.

1997b (ed.). *Die Orientalische Stadt: Kontinuität, Wandel, Bruch. 1. Internationales Colloquium der Deutschen Orient-Gesellschaft 9.–10. Mai 1996 in Halle/Saale*. Saarbrücken.

2001 (ed.). *Akten des IV. Internationalen Kongresses für Hethitologie Würzburg, 4.–8. Oktober 1999*. Studien zu den Bogazköy-Texten 45. Wiesbaden.

2008 (ed.). *Ḫattuša-Boğazköy: Das Hethiterreich im Spannungsfeld des Alten Orients. 6. Internationales Colloquium der Deutschen Orient-Gesellschaft*. Wiesbaden.

2009. 'Die Götter der Unterwelt als Ahnengeister des Wettergottes', in Hartenstein and Rösel 2009 (eds.), 59–75.

2010a. 'Pataḫuli – Die Tochter des Priesters?' in Cohen, Y., Gilan, A., and Miller, J. L. 2010 (eds.), *Pax Hethitica: Studies on the Hittites and Their Neighbours in Honour of Itamar Singer*. Studien zu den Boğazköy-Texten 51. Wiesbaden: 378–84.

2010b. 'Die Lesung des Namens der Göttin IŠTAR-li', in Klinger, J., Rieken, E., and Rüster, Ch. (eds.), *Investigationes Anatolicae – Gedenkschrift für Erich Neu*. Studien zu den Boğazköy-Texten 52. Wiesbaden: 337–44.

2012 (ed.). *Organization, Representation, and Symbols of Power in the Ancient Near East: Proceedings of the 54th Rencontre Assyriologique Internationale*. Winona Lake, IN.

2015. 'Zu verlorengegangenen Tafelsammlungen in der Oberstadt von Ḫattuša', in Müller-Karpe, A., Rieken, E., and Sommerfeld, W. 2015 (eds.), *Saeculum: Gedenkschrift für Heinrich Otten anlässlich seines 100. Geburtstags*. Studien zu den Boğazköy-Texten 58. Wiesbaden: 307–16.

Williams, R. J. 1956. 'The Literary History of a Mesopotamian Fable', *Phoenix* 10: 70–7.

Winiarczyk, M. 1991. *Euhemerus Messenius reliquiae (Bibliotheca Teubneriana)*. Stuttgart and Leipzig.

2002. *Euhemeros von Messene: Leben, Werk und Nachwirkung*. Munich and Leipzig.

2013. *The Sacred History of Euhemerus of Messene*. Munich and Leipzig.

Winitzer, A. 2013. 'Etana in Eden: New Light on the Mesopotamian and Biblical Tales in Their Semitic Context', *JAOS* 133: 441–65.

Winkelmann, S. 2003. 'Berliner Schlangenbecken, Trichterbecher und Cincinnati-Mann: verkannte Schlüsselobjekte der altorientalischen Archäologie?', in Dittman, R., Eder, C., and Jacobs, B. 2003 (eds.). *Altertumswissenschaften im Dialog: Festschrift für Wolfram Nagel zur Vollendung seines 80. Lebensjahres*. Münster: 567–678.

Winter, I. 1989. 'The "Hasanlu Gold Bowl": Thirty Years Later', *Expedition* 31: 87–106.
Wisnom, L. S. 2014. *Intertextuality in Babylonian Narrative Poetry: Anzû, Enūma Eliš and Erra and Ishum*. DPhil. Thesis, Oriental Institute, University of Oxford.
  2019. *Weapons of Words: Intertextual Competition in Babylonian Poetry. A Study of Anzû, Enūma Eliš and Erra and Išum*. Leiden and Boston, MA.
Witzel, E. J. M. 2012. *The Origins of the World's Mythologies*. New York, NY.
Wöhrle, J. 2018. '"Als die Götter Mensch waren": Zum Beginn des Atramhasis-Epos', in Kleber et al 2018 (eds.), 797–813.
Wolf, F. A. 1795. *Prolegomena ad Homerum sive De operum Homericorum prisca et genuina forma variisque mutationibus et probabili ratione emendandi*. Halle.
Woodard, R. D. 2007. 'Hesiod and Greek Myth', in Woodard 2007 (ed.), 83–165.
  2007 (ed.). *The Cambridge Companion to Greek Mythology*. Cambridge.
Wright, M. E. 2012. *The Comedian as Critic: Greek Old Comedy and Poetics*. London.
Wyatt, N. 2010. *The Archaeology of Myth: Papers on Old Testament Tradition*. London.
Yadin, A. 2004. 'Goliath's Armor and the Israelite Collective Memory', *VT* 54: 373–95.
Yakubovich, I. 2018. Review of Metcalf 2015, *JNES* 77: 128–31.
Yardley, J. C., and Heckel, W. 1997. *Justin: Epitome of the Philippic History of Pompeius Trogus 1: Books 11–12: Alexander the Great*. Oxford.
Yasumura, N. 2013. *Challenges to the Power of Zeus in Early Greek Poetry*. Bristol.
Yingling, E.O. 2011. 'Give Me Back My Idol: Investigating the Dating of *Enuma Elish*', *Studia Antiqua: A Student Journal for the Study of the Ancient World* 9: 33–8.
Zgoll, A. 2006. 'Königslauf und Götterrat: Struktur und Deutung des babylonischen Neujahrsfestes', in Blum and Lux 2006 (eds.), 11–80.
Ziegler, N. 2007. *Les Musiciens et la musique d'après les archives de Mari*. Paris.
  2016. 'Aqba-hammu et le début du mythe d'Atram-hasis', *Revue d'assyriologie et d'archéologie orientale* 110: 107–26.
Ziskowski, A. 2016. 'Networks of Influence: Reconsidering Braudel in Archaic Corinth', in Concannon, C., and Mazurek, L. A. 2016 (eds.). *Across the Corrupting Sea: Post-Braudelian Approaches to the Ancient Eastern Mediterranean*. Abingdon: 91–110.
Zogg, F. 2014. *Lust am Lesen: Literarische Anspielungen im Frieden des Aristophanes*. Munich.
Zorn, J. 2010. 'Reconsidering Goliath: An Iron Age 1 Philistine Chariot Warrior', *BASOR* 360: 1–22.
Zuntz, G. 1951. 'On the Etymology of the Name Sappho', *MH* 8: 12–35.

Index

Aesopica 3 Perry, 134–5
Aesopica 374 Perry, 151–3
Alalu, 25, 28–32, 154–8, 167–8
Antu, 195
Anu, 25–6, 62, 82, 154–6, 195, 256–8
Anunnaki, 217, 256
Anzu, 248–50
Aphrodite, 82, 180–1, 265–7, 284
Archilochus, 127–44
Aristophanes, 135–7
Athene, 82, 152, 253–4, 259–61, 283
Atrahasis, 215–18, 255–8
Avesta, 111

Baal, 41–2, 44, 49, 205, 207–9, 213–14
Babylonian Tree, 147–51
Book of Daniel, 111

Callimachus, 84, 142, 151–3
Catullus, 84
Crete, 45–9
Ctesias, 163–5
Cypria, 178–9
Cyrus the Great, 162–6

Date Palm and Tamarisk, 146–53
Dumuzi, 96–7

Enlil, 69, 192–3, 196–7, 216, 244–7, 249, 255–8
Enmešarra's Defeat, 59, 76–8
Enūma eliš, 59–78, 188–9, 195–8, 280–91
Epic of Gilgameš, 20, 80–106, 271–2
Esagil, 58–79
Etana, 126–44

fable, 137–41, 145–53

Genesis 2
 1–3, 218–20
Genesis 2–3, 262–4

Genesis 6
 1–4, 169–84

Hattusili I, 158
Hazzi, Mount, 33–6, 41–3, 203–6, see also Kas(s)ios, Mount
Hera, 225–7, 253–5, 259–60, 283–4
Heracles, 49–51, 175, 180, 225
Herodotus, 52, 165–6
Hesiod, 109–25, 167–8, 173–8, 206–7, 221–3, 262–75, 277–91
Homer, 80–3, 220–7, 233–42, 250–5

Igigi, 249, 255–6
Illuyanka, 41, see also *Song of Illuyanka*
Inan(n)a, 85, 96, 100–1, 244–8, 270–1 see also Ištar
Inana's Descent to the Netherworld, 245, 270
Indo-European
 phraseology, 231–3
 poetry, 13, 112, 173, 278–9
Ištar, 81–2, 270–2, see also Inan(n)a
Ištar's Descent to the Netherworld, 246, 270

Kantuzili, 35
Kas(s)ios, Mount, 41, 207–8, see also Hazzi, Mount
Kingship in Heaven Cycle (KIHC). See *Song of Emergence*
Kumarbi, 19–36, 154–6, 203–4, 206–7, 280, 286

Marduk, 58–79, 187–9, 218, 286–7
Mursili I, 160–2, 167

Nebuchadnezzar I, 61–2, 69–72, 248
Ninurta, 68–72, 246, 248–50, 288

Pandora, 122, 262–70, 274–5
Philistines, 182–4
Philon of Byblos, 26, 40, 54–6, 281
Phoenicians, 41–56, 208
purification ritual, Hittite, 30–2

Ramesses II, 205

Šamaš, 127–9, 131
Saphon, Mount, 41–4
Sappho, 119, 208
Sargon of Akkad, 157–62
Sennacherib, 68–9, 248
Song of Emergence, 19–36, 154–7, 277–91
Song of Illuyanka, 168, 173
Song of Kumarbi. See *Song of Emergence*
Song of Kurunta, 203–4
Song of Release, 21–2
Song of the (manly deeds of the) Sea, 22–3, 34–5, 204–6
Song of the Invocation of the Primeval Deities, 35–6
Song of Ullikummi, 22, 204
Storm God, 22, 26, 31–4, 36, 41–4, 49–51, 155, 173, 205–6, 213–14

Tessub/Teššub, 203, 207, 280, 286
The Song of Ullikummi, 195
Theogony of Dunnu, 161–2, 280–91
Tiamat/Ti'amat, 58–79, 286–7
Tudhaliya I/II, 162
Tudhaliya III, 203
Tudhaliya IV, 209, 213
Typhoeus/Typhon, 41–5, 207–8

Ullikummi, 41–2, 203, 206, 211, *see also Song of Ullikummi*

Virgil, 54, 56, 84

Xenophon, 165

Zeus, 41, 44–9, 53–6, 82–3, 117, 119, 121–2, 177–81, 207–8, 211–12, 243, 251–5, 258–61, 266, 282–4

CPSIA information can be obtained
at www.ICGtesting.com
Printed in the USA
LVHW011048030821
694401LV00005B/346